WAR IN
INTERNATIONAL
SOCIETY

WAR IN INTERNATIONAL SOCIETY

A Study in International Sociology

EVAN LUARD

YALE UNIVERSITY PRESS
New Haven and London

First published in Great Britain 1986
by I. B. Tauris & Co. Ltd.
Published in the United States 1987
by Yale University Press.

Printed in the United States of America.

Library of Congress Cataloging-in-Publication Data

Luard, Evan, 1926-
  War in international society.

  Includes index.
  1. War and society. 2. International relations.
I. Title.
HM36.5. L8   1987   303.6'6   87-8175
ISBN 0–300–04016–4

The paper in this book meets the guidelines for
permanence and durability of the Committee on
Production Guidelines for Book Longevity of the
Council on Library Resources.

10   9   8   7   6   5   4   3   2   1

CONTENTS

Introduction

This book is the third in a trilogy which I have sub-titled "Studies in International Sociology". Each volume is concerned with particular aspects of international society: the first, *Types of International Society* (New York, 1976), with the differing characteristics, structure, institutions and "ideology" of a succession of historical societies of states; the second, *Economic Relationships among States* (London, 1984), with economic relationships among the members of a number of such societies; this third one with armed conflict within those societies. I have described them as studies in international sociology because they seek to apply to international society the analysis and the concepts associated with the study of smaller-scale societies.

What are the essential features of this approach?

The first is that it is unashamedly empirical in method: based, that is, on a systematic survey of the available factual evidence concerning the behaviour of states. It is one of the oddities of recent controversy among students of international relations that the adjective "empirical" has come to be used almost as a term of abuse: it is identified by certain writers with an approach that is old-fashioned and unimaginative. Oddest of all, it is contrasted with the superior virtues of the so-called "scientific method", so that empirical methods become labelled as unscientific. But the fact is that science has always been above all empirical in method. And if international relations is indeed to be regarded as a science (which is by no means self-evident), it becomes all the more important that its conclusions be based on careful and systematic examination of the evidence: in a word, empirical.

On the basis of this survey an attempt is made to consider what conclusions can properly be drawn about national behaviour in international society. That does not mean that the aim is, as some political scientists demand, to present proofs that can be demonstrated and used as a basis for prediction, in the same way as the inductive "proofs" that can be presented in the physical sciences. Given that, in the field of international relations, controlled experiment under controlled conditions, such as takes place in the physical sciences, is impossible, scientific proof of this kind is not normally obtainable (see pp. 7-12). The method applied in these studies consists rather in

1

a relatively systematic review of the available evidence — evidence concerning the behaviour of states in international society — followed by an attempt to consider what significant conclusions may be drawn as a result.

The second feature of this approach is that it is one based mainly on the evidence of history. This follows from the fact that almost the only evidence available to us in international relations is the evidence of history (even if it is only last week's history): the evidence concerning the behaviour of states in past periods. There is no other raw material we can use. Any worthwhile generalisations about the actions or behaviour of states must be based on that evidence. It is, too, only the evidence of history that enables us to undertake a comparative approach. It is that evidence which makes it possible, in other words, to compare the societies of states that have existed at different times in the past, each exhibiting differing features — for example, different motivations among states, different distributions of power, different norms of behaviour and different international institutions; and to assess the reasons for the resulting differences in the *actions* of states.

The third special feature of the approach of "international sociology" is that, as the name implies, it seeks to apply to international society some of the methods and concepts applied by sociology to domestic societies. The society of states is obviously a very different type of association from any that exists among individuals. The bonds between its members are weaker and the social constraints less powerful. Yet it is not altogether different in kind. For states, like individuals, enjoy a social existence of a kind: they establish among themselves traditional patterns of interaction, differing types of domination or dependence, varying systems of status, accepted norms of conduct, even recognised institutions to resolve disputes or consider common problems. And many of the ideas used in examining smaller societies — roles, motivations, elites, stratification, authority and ideology — can therefore be usefully applied to that society too.

For, while it is arguable that there exists no such thing as an international "community" (since there do not exist among states the *common* expectations, traditions and values which are the essential condition of a community), or that there is nothing that can properly be called an international "system" (since the behaviour of states is too arbitrary, wayward and unpredictable to be accommodated by the mechanistic image which that concept implies), what cannot reasonably be denied is that there does exist an international *society* of a kind. States have constant intercourse with one another; they communicate with one another through diplomatic exchanges, in international forums, or through the speeches of statesmen; they reach agreements and understandings with each other; they engage in conflict and competition; they form groups and alliances which are ranged against other groups and alliances; there is even a kind of class structure — separating powerful and weak, rich and poor, great and small. In all these ways, many of the features of social existence among individuals are reproduced among states. And, though there are undoubtedly important differences between the two types of society — differences that must always be borne in mind — these differences are not such as to invalidate the attempt to examine the behaviour of states on a sociological model.

Within the general area of international sociology, the study of conflict among states obviously plays a central role. Just as the study of conflict within domestic society, as expressed for example in class conflict, in competition among interest-groups, organisations and individuals, even in crime and delinquency, represents a central area of sociological research, so the examination of the causes and nature of conflict among states must play a key role in any study of international societies.

For the study of international conflict the sociological approach has perhaps a special value. *Within* domestic societies, many observers believe, conflict between classes or between generations, within families or within cities, is best studied as a function of the society in which it occurs. It cannot properly be examined without examining the social factors that promote it: the particular organisation of society, the economic relationships, the social conventions and habits of thought from which it springs. It is logical to follow a similar pattern when studying conflict between states, and to examine this as a function of the international society within which it occurs.

For war, too, is socially derived: not in the sense that it results from the social situation *within* each country (though this also may be true, most obviously in the case of civil war), but in the sense that it is determined by the *international* society within which it takes place. It is international society which instils the ambitions and rivalries that are sometimes expressed in warlike action. It is international society which tells individual states when war is permissible, desirable or even obligatory. It is international society which creates the antagonisms and resentments that often end in violent conflict. Above all, it is the ideology of international society — the set of assumptions and expectations which are established there — which will determine the thinking of individual decision-makers, and so the way they will respond when faced with a particular threat, indignity or affront.

This means that the subject needs to be approached on a comparative basis. If conflict is socially derived, how has it differed from one international society to another? How far have the issues about which wars have mainly been fought differed from one society to another and why have these differences arisen? How far do these variations reflect differences in the underlying motives of states, and those who have exercised power in them, in different ages? How far have changes in the structure of power within states affected the way decisions for war have been reached at different times and the kinds of decision that were made? What are the different kinds of gains states have hoped to procure from war in different societies, and how have these been measured against the costs of securing them? What kinds of procedures and institutions for resolving conflicts has each international society established and how successful have they proved in achieving that aim? Finally, and perhaps most important of all, what have been the different ideas and attitudes concerning war prevailing in different societies and what has been the effect of these on the incidence of war among states or within them?

It is these questions which we seek to examine in the study that follows.

1 The Study of War

What is a war?

In undertaking a study of war the first task is to define the subject-matter.

Organised violence may take many forms: skirmishes among disorganised groups, whether of the same or different states; sporadic incidents along a border over a prolonged period, each relatively limited in scale; a single raid or naval bombardment against the territory of another state; an invasion by large-scale forces that is unresisted; a rapid *coup d'état*, involving substantial loss of life but rapidly accomplished; intermittent terrorist activity between or within states, directed at specific targets; as well as large-scale warfare undertaken by the regular forces of national states. Not all of these, even if they lead to substantial loss of life, would normally be classified as "wars".

What criteria, therefore, should be used? Those who have written on this subject in the past have adopted widely varying definitions. Quincy Wright, in his classic *Study of War* (Chicago, 1942), decided to confine his study, and the lists of wars he provided, to "wars of modern civilisation", which he defined as the Christian civilisation of Europe beginning in the fifteenth century: he therefore omitted a large number of wars involving the peoples and nations of Asia and Africa (though he included some "wars of defence or conquest" by recognised European states against Moslem or extra-European communities). Wright's list is also confined to conflicts "involving members of the family of nations . . . which were recognised as states of war in the legal sense or which involved over 50,000 troops". The wars of China, Japan, Turkey, Persia, Siam and Ethiopia were only included in the period after they "were recognised as members of the family of nations". This definition meant that the great majority of colonial wars were not included in his survey. In addition he omits altogether some important wars, especially in Latin America, but includes others that would not normally be defined as "war". Sorokin's *Social and Cultural Dynamics* (New York, 1977) purported to cover the main wars of each period; but though it covered a much longer time-span than most other studies (nearly 2,000 years) his list of wars, being confined only to particular countries, was in fact highly selective. L. F. Richardson's *Statistics of Deadly Quarrels* (Pittsburgh, 1960) includes perhaps the most comprehensive list of wars of any so far published for the period after 1815; but the study includes a wide range of small-scale encounters and riots, as well as one-sided massacres (such as the massacres of Armenians and Jews in Turkey and Russia), that would not normally be described as wars (his title makes clear that his book was not intended to be confined to these); yet he still omits one or two conflicts that would normally be so described and are listed as such in the present study. Finally, the most recent compilation, undertaken for the "Correlates of War" study of the University of Michigan by David Singer and Melvyn Small, is deliberately more selective than any of these. By adopting very restrictive criteria it confines itself to 93 international wars occurring between 1816 and 1965 (by comparison, Richardson lists 289 armed clashes between 1819 and 1949, Wright 133 wars between 1815 and 1964, and Sorokin 97 between 1819 and 1925).

Assessments of what represents a "war", or what kinds of conflict are worth studying (which is not necessarily the same thing), are inevitably to some extent subjective and must vary from one observer to another. Every list of wars compiled can be criticised from one point of view or another. No list can cover every use of armed force both between and within states without becoming unmanageably long as well as so diverse as to sacrifice comparability. If every use of violence were to be listed, every exchange of shots at a border between states, or every small-scale riot within states, a list many times as long as any of those mentioned here would be required. Nor, in many cases, would sufficient information be available to make analysis and comparison reliable. Somewhere a line must be drawn: a definition made of those conflicts thought significant.

The principle followed in this study is a relatively simple one. First, for a conflict to qualify here as a war, there must be a substantial measure of *organisation* on both sides. Riots and insurrections undertaken by unorganised mobs, even if prolonged, are excluded. This principle especially affects civil wars. Where armed action is undertaken within states by a totally disorganised rabble or a collection of bands, without any clear line of command, it represents "civil conflict" rather than "civil war". In international wars, the degree of organisation required is nearly always present on both sides, so that almost all sustained armed actions between states are included in our lists. The threshold at which a conflict becomes a "war" is thus rather greater for civil than for international wars. Secondly, there must be a significant degree of fighting for an act of force to qualify as a "war". Thus an action in which an army marches across a border unopposed is not here listed as a war. Thirdly, the engagement must be sustained over a significant period. For this reason a *coup d'état* which is completed in a night, even though it might involve considerable loss of life, is not counted as a war; nor are isolated engagements which are not persistent or sustained.

Put at its simplest, therefore, the principle applied is that only those encounters are included that would in normal parlance be regarded as a "war", international or civil. For this reason, wars are not omitted from our list (as they have been by some other writers) because of the low level of casualties involved. There are a number of reasons for this. First, the casualties which occurred in many conflicts of the past cannot be established with sufficient accuracy to make such a distinction possible or meaningful. Secondly, the international significance of war does not depend on the precise level of casualties which occurred. Thirdly, an exclusion of that kind does not correspond with normal usage: to most people the description of a conflict as a "war" does not depend on the number of people killed or injured in it. Even though it will be necessary, therefore, to take account of the wide range in the scale of the conflicts considered, we shall include within our examination all which fall within the general definition given above; all encounters, that is, which have involved substantial, organised fighting over a significant period.

The phenomena we shall be examining are listed in the appendices. It must be made clear that these lists have been compiled for illustrative purposes only: to assist the reader by recalling the essential subject-matter of our study. They are intended to provide the basis for informed judgement; not to provide the material for statistical conclusions, which will be kept to a minimum (they will be confined almost entirely to the next chapter). For reasons that will be explained shortly, there is reason to doubt the validity or value of numerical comparisons of this kind. The purpose of the lists provided is rather to give a reasonably full and fair picture of the nature and scale of warfare in each age. Long as they are, even these lists are not totally comprehensive (since they omit the lowest range of domestic conflicts, disturbances as against wars, as well as international fighting of a sporadic and unorganised character). They are, even so, more complete than most of those which have been compiled in the past; more accurate, I believe, than many; and therefore reasonably satisfactory for the purposes of this study.

Can war be studied scientifically?

Having established the subject-matter we are concerned with, how should it be studied?

Innumerable tomes have been produced over the years on the subject of war in general and wars in particular. In recent years particularly, the subject of war has been studied more intensively and more systematically than ever before. Many such studies have been concerned to build up a body of knowledge, and if possible a corpus of agreed conclusions, which could be said to represent reliable knowledge about war and its causes, and could even be a source of guidance to statesmen seeking, so their authors optimistically hope, to direct the affairs of their states in such a way as to minimise the risk of war.

Most people would agree that the study of war and its causes can best be pursued through the careful examination of the records of war in the past. Though the past is rarely an accurate guide to the future (nor necessarily to the present), greater knowledge of the factors that have most often precipitated armed conflict between states in previous periods may help us to draw some general conclusions about the conditions which are liable to create war: conclusions relevant to the conduct of international relations today, and even perhaps tomorrow.

Can these questions be studied "scientifically"? There are some engaged in the study of international relations today who have sought to elevate it to the status of an exact science. The only conclusions concerning relations among states that are ultimately persuasive, they have argued, are those that can be clearly demonstrated, or "proved", on the basis of carefully examined evidence, in the same way as the propositions demonstrated in the physical sciences; and they have favoured in particular for that purpose the use of quantitative techniques, regression analysis and other statistical methods, to provide the basis for those demonstrations. This method has been fairly extensively applied to the study of war. Rejecting a good deal of past writing on the subject, on the grounds that this has consisted frequently of somewhat discursive essays, and sweeping generalisations, often supported by little factual evidence, or surveys conducted without any systematic basis, they have, with some reason, demanded a much more rigorous examination of the evidence of history, with a view to arriving at firm and unchallengeable conclusions.

The most consistent effort to apply this method to the study of war has been that of the University of Michigan's "Correlates of War" study under the leadership of Professor David Singer. A large number of articles and several volumes have resulted from this project, reporting conclusions of a number of kinds.[1] Studies of this type undoubtedly represent a significant advance in the study of war. Far more systematically than ever before, they have examined some of the evidence available to us about the principal wars of recent times and sought to draw empirically reliable conclusions.

There are, however, considerable difficulties about efforts of this kind, difficulties which need to be examined before considering how our own study should be organised. The problems concern both the method itself and the way that method is applied.

The first and most obvious problem concerns the initial selection of facts. For a study to be in the proper sense scientific there must be no doubt about the data on which it is based. The phenomena it is examining must be unambiguously defined; and, if the conclusions are to be valid, evidence concerning all phenomena of a similar type must be examined. This is particularly important in examining such a subject as war over recent times: since the total number of wars that have occurred in any one period is limited, the exclusion of even a small number could seriously distort the conclusions reached. It is not clear that the attempt at a scientific approach to the study of war has always overcome this difficulty. The criteria adopted in the University of Michigan study, for example, had the effect of excluding from consideration a substantial proportion even of the international wars of the period: most colonial wars; all wars of countries with a population of less than 500,000, or (before 1919), of countries where either Britain or France had no diplomatic mission; and all wars in which total "battle-deaths" were less than 1,000 for all participants. The result was that the list contained less than a third of the conflicts included in the Richardson study, and little more than a third of those included in the present work for the same period. The wars omitted were not all small and insignificant (they included the two principal wars between European powers and China in the nineteenth century — the Anglo-Chinese war of 1839-41 and the war of Britain and France against China of 1856-60 — and some of the chief wars of Latin American history, for example, the war between Argentina and Uruguay of 1825-8, the three wars between Chile, Peru and Bolivia in the 1830s, and the long war between Uruguay and Argentina of 1839-52). Yet some of these wars are quite as significant as those that were included (for example the battle of Navarino, a single isolated engagement, is included as a "war" in its own right). Though there will always be problems, as we have seen, in the definition and selection of wars, the omission of such a substantial number of important conflicts must have a distorting effect on the conclusions finally reached; and these distortions are particularly damaging for studies which primarily rely on statistical comparisons.

There is a second, related difficulty. Quite apart from the questions of selection, there are problems concerning accurate knowledge of the facts. The evidence that we have about the wars of the past rarely provides a basis for accurate comparison or statistical conclusions. Many studies of the past have been particularly concerned, for example, about the level of casualties in different wars or periods (in the University of Michigan study not only are comparisons made of the levels of casualties in different wars and different periods of history; the number of casualties is also an important qualifying criterion for inclusion in the survey). But for most wars, until very recent times, no reliable figure can be given for the number of deaths that occurred.[2] Even for recent times casualty rates can probably not be known with sufficient accuracy to make such comparisons an important feature of the analysis.

A third difficulty facing a quantitative approach to war concerns the way the data are collated. If emphasis is placed on numbers, it is important not only how wars are selected, but also how they are counted. If one is comparing the number of wars in particular periods or regions, the principle of selection inevitably becomes important. For example, should the Napoleonic wars be considered as one war or several? Was there one war between Austria and Piedmont in 1848-9 or two? Were there two Balkan wars in 1912-13 or, as some historians prefer, three? At what threshold of violence should an armed conflict be counted as a war? If importance is attached to numbers, such questions become vital. The root of the difficulty is that the raw material we are here concerned with does not necessarily fall into clearly recognisable (and so easily measurable) units, such as a scientific, and especially a quantitative, approach demands. Essentially arbitrary decisions concerning the way the units are identified and counted can considerably affect the results arrived at.

A fourth difficulty relates to the *interpretation* of the facts, even if they could be easily agreed. In the social sciences, unlike the physical sciences, the events studied do not take place in carefully controlled experimental conditions, eliminating all haphazard influences. The factors influencing the course of events in history are so numerous and so complex that it is rarely possible to establish unquestionable correlations, giving a clear indication of cause and effect. Attempts to establish such correlations often depend on initial assumptions which are themselves arbitrary and questionable. Some studies, for example, seek to distinguish between the states which "initiate" war and those which are their victims (the Michigan study, for example, includes a table listing the powers responsible for "initiating" a given set of conflicts). But judgements concerning which states were mainly responsible for "initiating" particular conflicts are inevitably arbitrary and controversial. It is not always the case that one country can clearly and unquestionably be identified as the "initiator" or "aggressor". Even the country which declares war is not necessarily the nation that is responsible for it. Bismarck, for example, was a past master at manoeuvring other states into situations in which they were obliged to choose between fighting and suffering acute national humiliation: in this way he was able, for example, both in 1866 and 1870 to cause his opponents to make the first move even though he himself had in each case created a situation which made that move almost unavoidable. Britain and France declared war on Germany in 1939, but it would not be plausible to say that they initiated that war. In every case where one state issues an ultimatum to another which is rejected, it is not easy to say which country is the more responsible for war. And in many other cases where a situation of gathering tensions between two states exists over a considerable period, it may be hard to allocate responsibility.

A similar difficulty occurs over assessments of the power balance between states or groups of states, a question to which much effort has been devoted in "scientific" studies. There are great problems in arriving at accurate estimates of relative power which take account not only of the size of forces (the main factor normally discussed) but also of morale, experience, training, battle-readiness, geographical and other strategic advantages, the likely behaviour of allies and so on; still less is it possible to be sure how the power balance was *perceived* by the main parties at a given moment in considering, for example, the significance the balance had in causing or deterring war. And perhaps the clearest indication of the difficulty in reaching an agreed interpretation of the facts is the totally different, and sometimes opposite, conclusions reached by scholars on the basis of those assessments.[3]

This leads to the final, and probably the most important, of all the difficulties that arise in applying the scientific method to the study of war. The use of this approach has inevitably focused the attention of researchers in particular directions: on those factors that can most easily be measured and to which it is therefore easiest to apply a quantitative approach. Studies of that kind have thus focused especially on the numbers of wars and of casualties in particular periods, the amounts of war involving particular powers and types of power, the ranking of wars by "severity" and "intensity", the months and seasons in which wars most frequently began, the comparative length of wars, and so on.[4] This inevitably encourages the assumption that these are the subjects most *worth* studying — of most relevance to the study of war. Yet there are many other factors, of at least equal significance, which cannot be subjected to quantitative analysis: for example, the particular issues over which wars have been fought; the foreign-policy aims which most frequently lead states into conflict; the way in which decisions for war are taken and the influences that affect them; the assessments which are made about the likely costs and benefits of war; the effect, if any, of influences from outside the state, including those of allies and international organisations, on the relevant decisions; and finally (perhaps the most important factor of all but also the hardest to assess) the general climate of opinion and belief concerning war, both in the individual states where the decisions have been reached and in the international community as a whole. All of these are matters which require attention in any attempt to increase understanding of how and why wars occur. Yet they cannot easily be analysed by the so-called "scientific" method.

Thus the attempt to be strictly scientific in the study of war, in the sense that the conclusions presented will be accepted as incontrovertibly "proved" by outside observers, may not only turn out in the end impossible to achieve. It runs the risk of focusing our attention exclusively on particular factors which are not necessarily the most significant, and so to distract us from some that are more important.

This study, therefore, does not seek to be "scientific" in that sense. The aim here is a more modest one. The approach adopted is certainly, as explained in the Introduction, empirical: that is to say, it is based on a detailed examination of the evidence of the past. That evidence will be examined, if not scientifically, at least in as systematic a way as possible. The analysis is essentially comparative, applying similar methods to the study of a number of different periods, asking similar questions about them, and seeking to consider the reasons for the differences discovered. The aim, therefore, is not necessarily to *prove* any particular set of hypotheses — an aim which in our view the nature of the evidence does not normally allow. It is rather, by examining some of the essential facts, and where possible uncovering new correlations between them, to increase *understanding* of the factors which have been most significant in affecting the occurrence of war, between and within states, over recent times.

Conflict and society

The study of war, like the study of international relations generally, can be undertaken at two quite distinct levels. We can begin with the assumption that wars are made by individual states, and so direct our attention to the actions of states, the way in which decisions are reached within them, the influences that affect those decisions, the conceptions of national interest that are held and the foreign-policy objectives that result, including those that lead to war; or we can consider the wider international society — the interrelationships of states, the balance of power among rival blocs and alliances, the influences between one state and another, the rules and conventions of international conduct which arise, and the international institutions which are established — and consider the outcome of all these in permitting or preventing war.*

*In some views there exists a third alternative: the study of the aggressive attitudes of individuals. In the author's view, however, this is to remove the focus of study too far from the phenomenon we are concerned with here. Individual aggression can be expressed in so many alternative forms that its study belongs rather to the field of psychology than of international relations or the study of war. For a comparison of the three approaches, see K. N. Waltz, *Man, the State and War* (New York, 1959).

In practice the choice is not a stark one. As social scientists have often pointed out, it is not possible to study individual human beings except within their social context: all become human only in society. Nor, conversely, is it possible to study societies without regard to the individual psychology of those who are its members. Similarly among states. It is not possible to consider the behaviour of states without regard to the social context, the international environment, within which they exist; nor to consider a society of states without regard to the motivations and behaviour which characterise the individual states which are its members.

Thus to some extent any study of war must be concerned both with states and with societies of states. Certainly no such study can ignore the character of the entities which undertake war: the states and the groups within states that become involved in armed conflict. It must consider, for example, how they reach decisions to become engaged in war: are these conscious and deliberate choices of war, or are they rather decisions to undertake actions of a certain kind which may run the *risk* of war? Are the decisions affected by the social, political or constitutional systems prevailing in particular states, or by the procedures for decision-making that operate there? Are some states, or some types of state, more inclined to become involved in war than others? If so, is the greater propensity to war of some states related to their relative power, their geographical situation, their historical experience, their national character, or the psychology of their leaders?

All of these are relevant questions that arise in any study of war. And they are questions that relate especially to the nature of the state rather than to that of international society. A study on these lines carries the implication that there may be a substantial variation in the propensity of states to war: that not all will necessarily react in the same way to similar threats or challenges. Such a study, concentrating on the differences among states in their propensity to war, could cast doubts on the confident generalisations with which many textbooks of international relations abound: to the effect that "states" seek to do this or that — whether it be to "maximise" power, to "change the international system through territorial, political and economic expansion", to "win economic domination" in other states, or achieve some other specific objective. For, if different states have different characteristics, motivations and foreign-policy objectives, general statements about the policies of states are as meaningless as statements that people are "by nature" self-seeking, altruistic, greedy, generous, far-sighted, peace-loving or aggressive. In short, in each case "natures" can differ.

This hypothesis seems to correspond with the evidence of history. That evidence suggests that states have varied widely in the degree to which they have become involved in war. The variation has depended partly on geographical situation and available power. But it has depended also on the extent to which nations have had specific grievances or objectives which, they believed, could only be satisfied through war. Nations, even of a similar power, have varied greatly in their willingness to make war, or even to prepare for war, according to their level of satisfaction with the *status quo*: as seen for example in the 1930s in the difference between Britain and France on the one hand, content with the *status quo* and anxious to avoid war at almost any price, and dissatisfied Germany, Italy and Japan, each willing to take steps to redress believed wrongs, or to expand their own power, by means which they knew must carry the probability, or even the certainty, of war. The *same* state may vary greatly in its propensity to war in different periods: compare, for instance, Switzerland before and after 1516; Sweden in the seventeenth and eighteenth centuries and in the period after 1815; Spain in the sixteenth and seventeenth centuries and in the last century or two; the United States in the nineteenth century and in the twentieth. As these examples show, propensity to war has depended partly on the degree to which a nation has, at any one moment, been outward-turned, expansive in general orientation, as well as how far it has seen expansion as a goal to be achieved by military force. The United States since 1900, though powerful throughout, has fluctuated between periods when she has seemed disinclined to become actively involved in any area outside the Western hemisphere, and periods when she has become deeply involved in events in many other parts of the world. Even the same state in the same period can show variations in this respect. For example, Britain between 1815 and 1914, despite a considerable measure of armed power, was only once engaged in major war in Europe, less than any of its rivals, yet outside Europe was more often engaged in war than any other state.

If it were accepted that states may vary greatly in their motives and behaviour, and therefore in their propensity to war, one element in the study of war would be an examination of the reasons for these differences. Are they connected with the type of government in power? Are there, for example, reasons for thinking that, where military governments exercise authority, they may be more inclined to react in a warlike way to particular situations or provocations than civilian governments? Again, is it the case that the countries which are controlled by a single ruler exercising almost unchallenged authority — whether a dictator, a president for life or even a powerful statesman (such as Bismarck) — are, as has sometimes been suggested, more inclined to become engaged in war than constitutional and democratic states where power is more widely diffused? Or are differences in this respect related rather to the historical experience of states: is the state that has once made war successfully, the leader who has won glory by victory in conflict, more inclined to seek to add new triumphs by further victories? Or, conversely, are countries that have *not* had success, that have suffered defeat or humiliation and even territorial losses, more inclined to seek war as a means of avenging their defeat and making good their losses? Is it the case, as some evidence suggests (p. 63), that new states, having recently achieved unification or independence, or those with revolutionary regimes may be more inclined to war than long-established states; or that the most powerful states in each era are the most inclined to war (pp. 35, 45 and 53).

All of these are questions that are relevant in the study of war and that will arise, in one form or another, in the pages that follow. But within any society the character of conflict is not determined only, and perhaps not mainly, by the nature of the individuals who undertake it. It is determined partly by the character of the society as a whole. In the study of domestic societies this truism is taken for granted; and there have been many studies of the different forms which competition and conflict may take according to the goals and values which have been established within particular societies.[5] It seems reasonable to suppose that, in exactly the same way, competition and conflict among states is to a large extent determined by the aspirations and values, the conceptions of status and the measures of success, which are established within particular international societies. Thus, in studying war, even more important than a consideration of differences among nations in any one age may be a study of the differences between different international societies in different periods of history: to see how differences between these have altered the character, frequency or objectives of war among its members.

At any one period, though states may vary in their particular interests and motives, in their political and social structure and in the characteristics of their leaders, all will be to some extent influenced by the aims and aspirations which are instilled by the society as a whole. No state is an island (whatever its geographical situation). All states at all times have had regular contact with some other states. Usually they have diplomatic relations with a few, sometimes with many, of them. Almost always they have commercial relations with other nations. Their peoples are involved in innumerable personal contacts. In other words they take part in a constant interaction that exposes them to the wishes and demands of other states. These contacts influence their own wishes and demands and the way in which they react to situations of competition or conflict.

The main way in which this environment influences the behaviour of states is in creating expectations concerning the kinds of conduct that are normal among states in particular situations. Conventions are established defining the way states should react to other states. These conventions do not necessarily demand peaceful conduct. In many international societies, indeed the majority, war has been seen as a *normal* feature of national behaviour. It has been a tolerated, even if a sometimes unwelcome, phenomenon. But social pressures will still influence nations' behaviour and their liability to conflict. They may determine the kind of situations in which war is seen as an acceptable, or even a necessary, course of action: for example, if "national honour" is violated, territorial integrity threatened, the national flag dishonoured, and so on. Conventions may govern the ways in which war should be conducted. They may even determine the kinds of issues over which they should be fought.

This international environment is not a static or unchanging feature. It evolves all the time in imperceptible ways. Over the years, one type of international society may eventually be altogether transformed and replaced by another. The conventions that prevailed in one, the influences that were dominant, the ideas of national status which were widely held, the norms of conduct which were established, may disappear altogether in another. The entire social structure, the system of stratification among states, the kinds of elite that wield power within them, the alliance structures formed, the type of international institutions established and the prevailing norms of international conduct, may differ radically from one age to another.[6] These changes will affect the character of war, just as they affect every other aspect of national conduct. The kinds of war that occur, the issues over which they are fought, the motives that inspire them, the advantages that are sought or won by war, the costs that are incurred, the beliefs that prevail about the legitimacy or otherwise of war — all these vary widely from one age to another. In consequence the nature of war in different periods may itself vary so much that it would hardly be an exaggeration to say that there exists no single phenomenon of "war" (any more than there is a single phenomenon of "conflict" in all domestic societies at all times). War, in other words, may be a different kind of institution, and perform a different social function, in different international societies.

What this means is that, in any study of war, it is necessary to take careful account of the changing international environment within which it occurs. It is necessary to be cautious about comprehensive or general conclusions about the character of war, or of the national conduct which leads to it, regardless of the differing character of different ages. If there are wide variations between different periods (and so in the kinds of war that occur in them) it may be sensible to look separately at each age and its wars, so that we can isolate what they have in common and what distinguishes them and affects the changing nature of war in each.

This consideration guides the approach adopted in this study. If not only the types of conflict, but also the motivations among states which lead to conflict, are affected by the wider international environment within which those states live, it seems sensible to make separate analyses of different periods of history and then to make comparisons between them.

This study therefore distinguishes five main periods of recent history. The dividing-line between periods of history is never, of course, abrupt or precise. Some features of one period will be retained at least for the first part of the next; and some features of the following period may be anticipated in the latter part of that which went before. The dates that have been taken as the dividing-line between periods here are all dates of recognised importance in international history, and each age does, in the author's view, have recognisable characteristics which distinguish it from other ages.[7] While we should not discount altogether the effects of differences between states within the same age, we should also recognise the more important way in which the behaviour of states generally has varied from one period to another. And, in examining each of the different factors which appear to be important influences on the incidence and character of war, we shall need to take account of the changing character of this wider international environment.

The key factors

So far in this chapter we have considered some of the special problems that arise in the study of war; we have sought to show the difficulties that surround any attempt to undertake that study on the basis of a strictly scientific approach; and we have argued that the most fruitful type of study will be one that takes account of the changing character of the international environment in different periods of history, affecting the nature of national aspirations and expectations and so the kinds of conflict which take place in each. What, then, are the aspects of this vast and complex subject on which we should focus?

The first point we shall wish to consider — though surprisingly often omitted in many studies of this kind — is the elementary question: what do nations fight about? What are the *issues* that lead to war between states? How do these vary in the different international societies that we shall examine? There are certainly difficulties in seeking to answer this question. It is not always simple to determine beyond challenge what are the issues about which a war has been mainly fought. The issue that seems most important to one participant is not necessarily always the most important to another (in the Second World War, for example, Britain and France would probably have declared the central issue to be Germany's aggression against Poland or German expansionism generally, while Hitler might have declared it to be the rights of German nationals living in Poland, the need of Germany for living-space, or the injustices of the treaty of Versailles). Again, even if there appears to be one issue of central significance to many or all participants — perhaps even the recognised *casus belli* — it may not have been the most important *underlying* source of conflict: often there have been long-standing rivalries or resentments which, in some views, have been more important causes than the immediate issues over which war broke out.

These are both real difficulties, but they are not insuperable. It is usually possible to identify one or more issues which were believed at the time to be the most important questions in dispute; and there is a real significance in which questions or types of questions appeared of such importance that they became the justification for war. The most common issues disputed have varied significantly over time: from questions of dynastic rights in the late Middle Ages, to questions of religion in the late sixteenth and early seventeenth centuries, questions of political and commercial rivalry in the period 1648-1789, questions of national unification and national independence between 1789 and 1917, and questions of ideological competition in the most recent period. But there have been many other variations in the saliency of particular questions in different ages. It is thus worth considering why some issues have been important in certain periods and not in others. And it may be possible in this way to consider how far this reflects changes in the underlying conditions that lead to war.

A second, related question, of a more fundamental kind, relates to the *motives* of nations going to war. Particular issues become important to particular countries, and become the cause of war because of the nature of perceived wants. If what is desired by one country or its government is incompatible with what is desired by another — and if the differences cannot be resolved by other means — war may occur. What, then, is the nature of the wants which are most intensely felt by different countries at different times and which may lead them into war with each other? Are there general wants — relating to power or status or prosperity — which are held by *all* states and yet are incompatible, or is it only the particular wants of *particular* states that lead them into war? Are the same wants felt at all times, or do they vary from one age to another? Are there persistent desires of states — for status, wealth or territory — which must inevitably lead them not only into conflict but into war? If some motives, such as the desire for territory, for power, for absolute security are more likely to lead states into war than others — the desire for prosperity, commercial success and tranquillity, for example — is it a change in motives alone that will produce peace; or would a change in the means of obtaining satisfaction be sufficient? A society in which territorial criteria are dominant will clearly be different from one in which economic, or ideological, goals prevail. Though oversimplified, such examples are sufficient to show the importance of the motives of states in any study of war.

This in turn leads to a third question of importance: the way in which decisions to make war are reached. The outbreak of a war depends not only on the motives of states but on their actions: on the specific decisions their governments reach at a certain moment to achieve their ends through war. A threat may be perceived, a challenge resented, a desire held for a long time unrealised: whether they finally result in war depends on the particular decisions reached by particular people in particular situations. In the study of war the way decisions are reached may thus be almost as important as the motives that underlie those decisions. Are particular procedures for decision-making more or less likely to eventuate in a decision for war than others? Does the number of people involved in decision-making affect the kinds of decisions reached? Is a country ruled by a single autocrat more likely to take a decision for war — because decisions can more easily and quickly be reached there — than one ruled by a cabinet, council, parliament or other collective body, where more people are involved and take longer to deliberate? (This seems to have been the assumption behind the constitutional provision in the United States that a decision for war requires Congressional consent.) Are decisions in favour of war influenced by the nature of the information available, by the way it is presented, or by whom it is presented (by civilian officials or military officers, for example)? Another important aspect of decision-making concerns the *time* at which the significant decision for war is made: whether it is immediately before the declaration of war, or long in advance — in other words, whether war has been *planned,* or (as popular usage suggests) simply "breaks out" at the last moment in response to an immediate crisis situation.

Among the factors influencing these decisions are the beliefs held about the likely success and consequence of armed action. What are the precise benefits which those reaching decisions in favour of war have sought to acquire, and how far have they succeeded? This question too is a complex one. Do governments necessarily have a precise idea of the gains they hope to achieve at the time they initiate a war, or when they undertake actions which they know risk bringing about a war? Do they in some cases only have vague objectives — the righting of a wrong, the humbling of a rival, an expansion of national power of an unspecified sort — and only later, even during the course of war, formulate more precise "war aims"? Even if governments do have more precise intentions, have the final benefits and costs in fact resembled those first expected? Our concern is not only with what governments (or groups engaged in civil war) may originally have hoped to achieve at the time the war began, but,even more, with what they have in fact achieved. For the most significant point is whether or not war is generally *perceived* as a profitable undertaking, an activity that is attractive and worthy of imitation; and this will depend on final outcomes rather than original intentions. Against the perceived benefits of victory, if any, we need to set the costs, the losses in men and material, as well as the more intangible losses in goodwill and reputation, that have been incurred by nations in securing victory. In other words, we are concerned with the cost–benefit, or *profitability,* of war in each of the ages we examine: not because of a belief that each nation carefully calculates, before becoming involved, whether it will make a profit or a loss, but because there is a likelihood that, over the long term, the degree to which war proves to be profitable or unprofitable may influence the inclination of governments to adopt that course of action.

Decisions that lead to war, however, are not reached by individual countries in isolation. They are taken within a social context and are affected by the wider social environment within which each nation exists. They will be influenced by many intangible factors deriving from that environment: social pressures of which the decision-makers may be scarcely aware at all. It is therefore necessary to consider how far decisions for war have been influenced by the procedures and institutions established within the prevailing society to limit or influence the conduct of war. These have varied from the relatively primitive institutions of early international societies — the messenger, the envoy and the diplomatic conference, which have existed almost everywhere — to the comprehensive international organisations of the present day. In different international societies arrangements have been made to establish diplomatic contacts, truces, armistices, mutual guarantees, conferences at different levels, whether sporadic or regular, international organisations, regional or comprehensive, as means of preserving the peace. In some ages reliance has been placed on the balance of power as the principal instrument for maintaining stability and preventing undue dominance by any particular nation. In others multilateral arrangements, whether among a few governments, as in the Concert of Europe, or among many, as in more comprehensive international organisations of recent times, have been established which have sought, through discussion and deliberation, even by the organisation of appropriate enforcement action, to resolve conflicts among states. The form these procedures take will vary, according to the nature of the society concerned. How far any has been able to influence the behaviour of states and the incidence of war, and if so in what way, is another of the matters into which we shall need to inquire.

But the social environment within which wars occur includes not only institutions of this kind, but still more intangible factors affecting the decision of states. Decisions for war will always be affected by the *beliefs* about war which prevail within the society in question and the effects these have on national behaviour. These beliefs have varied greatly from one age to another. In some, war has been seen as glorious and honourable, in some as wicked; in some as cheap and in some as expensive. A widespread belief that war is a normal and inevitable feature of international life must affect the behaviour of all states (if only because every one must be in a position to counter the expected onslaughts of others). In other words, it is not only beliefs that exist within particular states that will affect their propensity to war, but also the beliefs that they know to exist elsewhere within their society. All are affected by the expectations and assumptions of the international community as a whole. If the social environment is one in which it is regarded as normal to go to war to prosecute dynastic claims, then each ruler is likely to regard that course of action as normal too. If it is generally seen as normal to make war to defend one religion or to persecute another, or to win commercial advantage at the expense of rivals, or to win national independence for one's own nation or for others, or to promote or defend an ideology, or an ideological partner, which seems threatened, then we can expect each state to find it normal likewise. Thus how far war is seen within each state as glorious and honourable, or wicked and wasteful, will depend as much or more on the views prevailing internationally as it will on the views held in each individual nation. In other words, states, like individuals, are essentially social creatures. They have their being within a wider society, and they borrow not only their opinions and ideas, but to some extent even their motives and feelings, from that society too.

Thus for each of the factors we have identified, we shall be concerned not only with the influences within each state that affect its willingness to make war, but also with the effect of the wider international society to which it belongs. Just as it may be impossible to say of individuals how far their decisions are determined by nature and how far by nurture, how far by inward disposition and how far by external influence, so among states it may be impossible to say precisely how far the propensity to war derives from factors within the state and how far from those derived from the world outside. But because a substantial influence, at least, derives from this wider environment, one of our tasks must be to distinguish between different international societies, different periods and places of history, so that we can compare the factors influencing war in each.

In the pages that follow, therefore, we shall seek to examine how each of these factors has influenced the character of war in a succession of international societies. After looking briefly at our basic raw material — the record of warfare over recent centuries — and the more obvious conclusions that can be drawn from it, we shall consider the issues about which wars have mainly been fought; the motives of states that have brought them into war; the way decisions about war have been reached; the costs and benefits of war in each age; the procedures established to influence or limit war; and the beliefs about war that have been generally held and the extent to which these have influenced warfare among states. On the basis of our findings, we shall seek, finally, to consider what more general conclusions may be drawn about the role of war in international society.

2 The Conflicts

In this chapter we shall present the basic raw material on which the rest of our study is based: the principal wars that have occurred in each of the periods under discussion.

The definition of the wars examined follows that described in the last chapter. Two points should be made. First, we are concerned here only with wars involving at least one sovereign state. There is no attempt to include armed conflicts between entities not generally recognised as states, or between tribes and other groups not under the control of states (as in Africa or Asia, for example, during the earlier parts of the period covered). This follows partly from the definition we have adopted: that a conflict, whether civil or international, requires a considerable measure of organisation to be classified as a war; and partly from the fact that information about conflicts of that kind is in any case inadequate to provide a proper record or basis for comparison. For this reason — and because we are concerned with six centuries when European states were generally dominant — much of our discussion will be (for the first three periods at least) about wars within Europe, or by European states in other parts of the world: these are the wars of which we have most knowledge in this period.

Secondly, we have, as already indicated, adopted a somewhat higher minimum level of scale and duration for civil conflicts than we have for international wars. This follows the usage of normal speech: even a very brief and almost bloodless armed conflict between states (such as the so-called "football war" between El Salvador and Honduras in 1969 or the brief frontier conflict between Algeria and Morocco in 1962) would normally be classified as a war; while a domestic conflict of similar duration and intensity would often not be accorded that title (being described, perhaps more often than not, as a revolt, riot or disturbance).

In this chapter we shall be concerned not only with listing the wars but with noting some of the most striking features revealed about warfare in each period. We shall be concerned, first, with the type of wars mainly fought in each period and how far this has changed over time: for example, the main subject-matter of wars, the proportion of civil and international wars, the proportion of limited or more general wars, and the amount and types of colonial warfare. Second, we shall consider the frequency of wars in each period; how this has

23

varied from one age to another; whether war has become more or less frequent over the years; and what other general conclusions can be drawn in that respect. Third, we shall examine their distribution over time: a number of earlier writers have suggested that there is a periodicity in the outbreak of wars, or at least of major wars,[1] and we shall wish to consider how far such theories are justified. Fourth, we shall be concerned (for more recent periods) with the regional distribution of wars; with any differences that may be apparent in the character of wars in different regions of the world; and the relationship between the wars fought in different regions (how far, for example, wars fought in other parts of the world have sometimes been extensions of conflicts originating in Europe). Fifth, we shall wish to note at least the more important changes in military technology in each period with their effects on the character, intensity and duration of wars. Sixth, we shall look at participation in the wars of each period: the average number of countries involved in each conflict, and differences in the degree of participation of individual countries. Finally, we shall consider the general level of casualties in the wars of each period and how far these have reflected changes in the nature and purposes of warfare or simply changes in military technology in each age.

Each of these questions will be discussed at this stage extremely briefly. In general the aim here is merely to set the scene for the more detailed examination of particular aspects of warfare among states which will be undertaken in the chapters that follow.

The age of dynasties (1400-1559)

The principal wars of our first period are listed in Appendix 1. Even though the list omits many of the lesser uses of armed force that were common at this time — riots, revolts and disturbances not amounting to civil war, isolated raids and other clashes — the list is a long one. It includes 229 wars in Europe in a period of 159 years: in other words an average of over 1.4 listed wars a year. However, the total number of wars a year is not a good measure of the incidence of war (even if all problems of definition, which are particularly acute for this period, are left on one side): it is obviously affected, for example, by the number of states in existence in each period. A better measure for purposes of comparison with other ages is the degree to which *individual* states were involved in war, both foreign and domestic. During this period France was involved in significant international wars in 78 years out of 159 (48 per cent) and in serious domestic wars in about 26 (16 per cent), while for England the corresponding figures are 69 years (44 per cent) and 36 (23 per cent). During the same period, the empire was engaged in 114 years of international war (72 per cent),

Venice in 76 (47 per cent), Poland–Lithuania in 79 (49 per cent), and the Turks in 114 (72 per cent). (These are the figures for the calendar years during which each state was involved in a significant war — not of the precise number of months each was at war, a figure that, especially for earlier periods, would be almost impossible to provide. A year in which a country was at war is counted only once, regardless of the number of conflicts in which it was engaged.)

Because of the omission of many lesser forms of warfare — for example, sporadic raids, peasant disturbances (especially common in this period) — these figures understate the amount to which armed conflict affected the lives of ordinary people. Even on this basis, however, they indicate that warfare of one kind or another was extremely prevalent. The years of war were much greater for most states than in each subsequent period. Though probably a rather smaller proportion of the population was directly involved in warfare than in most later times (because armies were small — about 10,000-15,000 men at first, rising to 30,000-40,000 in major wars at the end of the period), its indirect effects — in terms of demands for taxation, demands for services of various kinds, not to speak of the occasional ravages of invading armies, the siege and sacking of towns and the general economic consequences of war — were substantial for all sections of the population.

As always the pattern of warfare reflected the character of the international society as a whole; and especially its dominant *ideology:* that is, the pattern of values and beliefs which prevailed among its ruling groups. This was above all a dynastic society, in which the dominant concern was with dynastic competition. The groups who wielded power — not only the rulers themselves but also their principal supporters and even their main opponents — shared a belief in the overriding importance of extending the power, and above all the territories, of their own families: by marriage and inheritance if possible, by war if necessary. This international ideology reflected — in this as in other ages — that of the domestic society. Just as, within states, the great magnates and even lesser nobles and squires were concerned to win advancement for their own houses by the acquisition of titles to great estates, whether by marriage, patronage or seizure, so among states the rulers sought, by skilful matrimony, by ingenious claims, or if necessary by conquest, to add to the territories and titles of the royal house. The wars of the age reflected these aspirations: a substantial proportion of those in our list, both international and domestic, resulted directly from the attempts to prosecute claims to crowns elsewhere (see Table 1 below).

This universal urge gave ample opportunity for conflict. Rules of inheritance were often not clear (pp. 86-7) and there was often widespread scope for rival claims. Because marriage had long been the main means for securing territory, most of the ruling families had become closely interbred and could often find some plausible grounds for claiming a vacant throne. Edward III, whose mother was the daughter of Philip the Fair and the sister of the last three French kings, and who came from a country which recognised succession through the female line, could believe himself to have as good a claim to the French throne as his rival, Philip of Valois, who was descended from the same king's younger brother yet under French rules of inheritance better qualified. The Angevins could base their claim to rule in Naples on the offer of the throne by the childless Joanna I in 1380 to Louis of Anjou, while the House of Aragon could base it on the offer by the equally childless Joanna II in 1421 to Alfonso of Aragon (Joanna subsequently changed her mind, but not before the basis for the Aragon claim had been established). Francis I could trace his claim to Milan through an inheritance from a Visconti great-grandmother, while Charles V could claim it as a lapsed imperial fiefdom. So, on the basis of such rival claims, the dynastic struggle was fought out all over Europe. The typical wars of the period, those that recurred most frequently and most engaged the energies of rulers, were fought over that question: the long war between the French and English kings for title in France, lasting, with intervals, for nearly 120 years; the successive conflicts between the Angevin and Aragon families for Naples (seven wars in 80 years, including Charles VIII's invasion of 1494 based on the Aragon claim and the wars of 1495 and 1502); the repeated wars fought by the Danish kings to establish their title in Sweden (seven wars in 90 years); the continual dynastic struggle, with much mutual intervention, in Portugal, Castile and Aragon during the late fifteenth century (three wars in 30 years); the bitter contest between Valois and Hapsburg rulers for territory in Italy and elsewhere between 1494 and 1599 (11 wars in 65 years*).

Even the domestic struggles of the age were typically between families competing for power and territory: between Bourbon and Berry, Burgundy and Orleans in France; between Beaufort and Gloucester, York and Lancaster in England; between Luxemburg and Hapsburg, Wittelsbach and Hohenzollern in Germany; between Borgia and Colonna in Rome, Medici and Pazzi in Florence, Visconti and Sforza in Milan. Both between states and within them, the wars of this age were wars between families rather than between states — still less between peoples.

---

* i.e. the wars of 1495-6, 1499-1501, 1502-4, 1510-13, 1515-16, 1521-5, 1526-9, 1536-8, 1542-4, 1552-5 and 1556-9; the war of 1515-16 involved the Emperor Maximilian, though not — directly — Ferdinand of Aragon or Charles of Burgundy.

TABLE 1   PRINCIPAL DYNASTIC WARS IN EUROPE, 1400–1559

| Date | Throne | Claimants | |
		Foreign	Local
[1337]–1453	France	English kings	[French kings]
1401–2	Milan	Rupert, elector ("emperor")	Gian Galeazzo Visconti
1407–12	Naples	Dukes of Anjou	[Ladislas, duke of Naples (first Anjou line)]
1420–4	Naples	King of Aragon	
1435–42	Naples	Duke of Anjou	
1425–40	Muscovy	–	[Grand Duke Vasilii] Prince Yuri (the grand duke's uncle) and sons
1438–9	Bohemia	Albert of Austria Casimir of Poland	
1440–2	Bohemia and Hungary	Ladislas of Poland	Elizabeth on behalf of her son Ladislas
1447–50	Milan	Charles of Orleans	Francesco Sforza
1449–52	Saxony		[Frederick II] William (Frederick's brother)
1455, 1495–65, 1470–1	England		Duke of York [Henry VI]
1467–74	Castile		Joanna (the king's daughter) Alfonso (the king's half-brother) Isabella (the king's half-sister)
1468–78	Bohemia	Matthias Corvinus of Hungary	[George Podiebrad of Bohemia]
1475–9	Castile	Alfonso II of Portugal (betrothed to Joanna)	Isabella
1485	Naples	René of Lorraine	[Alfonso II of Naples]
1491–2	Brittany	Charles VIII of France	[Anne of Brittany]
1494–5	Naples	Charles VIII of France	[Alfonso II]

Date	Throne	Claimants	
		Foreign	*Local*
1499–1501	Naples	Louis XIII of France	[Federigo]
1502–4	Naples	Ferdinand of Spain Louis XII of France	
1511–13, 1515, 1521–5, 1536–8	Milan	Louis XII and Francis I of France	Francesco Sforza
1542–4		Emperor Charles V (from 1535)	
1527–38	Hungary	Ferdinand, brother of emperor	John Zapolya
1531–2	Denmark		[Christian II]
1534–6			Frederick I (uncle to Christian) Christian III (son of Frederick)
1546–7	Saxony (electorate and lands)		[Elector John Frederick Maurice of Saxony (Albertine line)
1553	England		Northumberland (on behalf of Lady Jane Grey) [Mary]

Incumbents, or locally accepted successors, appear in square brackets.

The character of war was affected by another feature of this society. It was, compared with the others we shall examine, a highly disorganised, almost inchoate association of states. The total number of political units capable of making war was very large. They varied hugely not only in size but in character: from the innumerable petty states of Germany and Italy to the vast and loosely organised kingdoms of Eastern Europe, such as Poland–Lithuania, Hungary and Muscovy; from the many small self-governing cities, internally cohesive but militarily weak, to semi-nomadic hordes, such as the Tartars, or the military colonies of the Cossacks; from associations of trading cities, such as the Hanseatic League, to the priest-led crusading orders, such as the Knights of St John, the Knights of the Sword and the Teutonic Order; from the amorphous Holy Roman Empire, without forces of its own (despite the forlorn pleas of Maximilian I) and now only intermittently responsive to the will of its emperor, to the disciplined military machine wielded by the Turks; from the declining power of the Papacy, military as well as spiritual, to the increasingly threatening pirate communities of North Africa. In other words this was not a society of states, each roughly homogeneous, all organised in a roughly similar way and sharing similar assumptions, such as was to appear a century or two later. In this age organisation, ambitions and beliefs all varied widely among these diverse entities. There were few recognised rules of intercourse. There was not even any clear conception of sovereignty; acknowledgement of the unfettered authority of each state within its own borders. In most cases power was divided horizontally as well as vertically: that is, in any one geographical area it was shared between authorities at different levels. The dominion that could be wielded by a ruler depended as much on personal loyalties as on military power; and a king who authorised a war could have little clear knowledge, at the time he authorised it, of how far his followers, the great magnates and their knights, who controlled armed force, would follow the call, or of whether his estates would vote the money required. Only so far as they could command the loyalty of their followers, therefore, could the rulers pursue their ambitions successfully in war against rivals elsewhere.

The disorganised character of each individual state and the lack of any all-powerful central authority had another effect on warfare in Europe. A substantial proportion was of the type then called "private wars": that is, they were undertaken not by rulers or recognised governments but by independent forces — nobles, knights, cities, or simply the companies of disbanded troops who roamed many of the lands. Almost everywhere rulers lacked the military power, the financial independence and the system of communications which might enable them to maintain their authority throughout the territories they claimed to rule. Everywhere great magnates, controlling their own independent armed forces, rebellious cities and regions, marauding knights or peasants in revolt, were able to challenge their authority. At the time our period opens this situation was to be seen in almost every state in Europe. In France, even though it was the richest and probably the best organised state of the continent, not only was a large part of the territory occupied by a foreign power, but huge fiefdoms were controlled by nobles from the great families, two of which were then engaged, totally oblivious of the king's authority, in a murderous civil war against each other. In England a usurping regime, the House of Lancaster, had seized the throne, yet was still not confident of its hold on power, already faced a rebellion in Wales, and within 60 years was to be challenged and finally overthrown in a bloody conflict which wiped out or attainted a large part of the country's nobility. In Germany a hotchpotch of states, cities and bishoprics were in constant contention with each other, and the nominal authority of the emperor counted for little outside his own domains. In Italy a multiplicity of states were engaged in interminable struggles for territory, as well as consumed by frequent civil conflicts. There were two popes and two emperors (and for brief moments three of each) in bitter conflict with each other. In Eastern Europe the power of the great magnates was still greater and the central control of the rulers still more limited.

In such conditions it is not surprising that civil, or "private", warfare was endemic. Table 2 shows the extent and the character of these domestic wars. They included nine which resulted from revolts by nobles against royal authority; 13 which were peasant revolts of various kinds (this number would be much greater if small-scale revolts were included in the list); and 38 which were local or regional revolts against central authority — including repeated uprisings by the citizens of Liège against their bishop, and by Ghent against the dukes of Burgundy; and major struggles by Wales (1402-09), Ireland (1493-6 and 1534-6); Catalonia (1461-72), and the Moors of southern Spain (1499-1500 and 1509-11). In Germany there were a number of wars between cities and the rulers of surrounding areas: as between the Hohenzollerns and the Brandenburg towns, including Berlin, in 1440-2; between the archbishop of Cologne and Goest and other cities a few years later: between the dukes of Mecklenburg and Rostock and other cities in 1486; and so on.

There is little evidence of any clear cyclical pattern. Wars were perhaps somewhat more frequent in the early part of the period than in the latter, reflecting the still more disorganised character of international society in that period. Gradually, as the power of the rulers in most states increased — a development more visible in the west of the continent than in the east — domestic conflict, especially in its smaller forms, declined. For international wars there was a period of somewhat lesser intensity from around the middle of the fifteenth

TABLE 2   PRINCIPAL PRIVATE WARS IN EUROPE 1400–1559

(a) Revolts of Nobles

Date	Country	Leaders of revolt
1404–8	England	Earl of Northumberland
1411–18	France	Dukes of Bourbon and Alençon
1441–5	Castile	Alvaro de Luna
1465	France	Dukes of Bourbon
1485	France	Louis of Orleans
1485	Naples	
1485–7	England	Henry of Richmond
1522–3	German states	Sickingen, imperial knights
1554	England	Sir Thomas Wyatt

Wars of succession are not included: see Table 1.

(b) Revolts of Peasants

Date	Country	Region
1409–13	Catalonia	[Widespread]
1432–7	France	Normandy
1434–5	Denmark	Sweden and Norway
1437	Hungary	Transylvania
1450	England	Kent
1464	Denmark	Sweden
1478	Austria	Carinthia
1497	England	Cornwall
1514	Hungary	South Hungary
1515	Austria	Styria
1524–5	Germany	Mainly south Germany
1525	Austria	Tyrol
1549	England	Norfolk

Only major rebellions are listed: local peasant revolts were endemic in all countries.

(c) Revolts of Regions

Date	Country	Region
1400–9	England	Wales
1432–7	France	Normandy
1448–51	Denmark	Sweden
1461–72	Aragon	Catalonia
1467, 1470–1	Denmark	Sweden
1485–6	England	Ireland
1488	Burgundy	Flanders
1492	France	Brittany
1493–6	England	Ireland
1494	Burgundy	Gelderland
1496–7	Denmark	Sweden
1499–1500	Spain	Moors
1505	Spain (Burgundy)	Gelderland
1509–11	Spain	Moors
1510–12	Denmark	Sweden
1515–17	Spain (Burgundy)	Gelderland
1516–17	Spain	Sicily
1520–3	Denmark	Sweden
1522–3	Spain (Netherlands)	Gelderland
1528	Spain (Netherlands)	Gelderland
1534	England	Ireland
1549–50	England	Cornwall and East Anglia

(d) Revolts of Cities

Date	Country	City in revolt
1408	Bishopric of Liège	Liège
1409	France	Genoa
1430	Bishopric of Liège	Liège
1436–40	Burgundy	Ghent, Bruges
1448–53	Burgundy	Ghent
1465–8	Bishopric of Liège	Liège
1467–8	Burgundy	Ghent
1483–5	Burgundy	Utrecht, Ghent
1489–93	Burgundy	Ghent, Bruges, Cleves
1507	France	Genoa
1519–21	Spain	Valencia
1520–2	Spain	Cities in Castile
1528	Spain (Netherlands)	Brussels
1532	Spain (Netherlands)	Brussels
1538–40	Spain (Netherlands)	Ghent

century. France and England, their long duel at last come to an end, became for a period preoccupied with domestic conflicts. From about the same time, the Italian states, after the peace of Lodi of 1454, enjoyed a short respite, though it was not long before their struggles were to resume. But there was no reduction in warfare in the east, where a succession of Turkish onslaughts, beginning with the final conquest of Byzantium in 1453, involved most of the states of the region in continual defensive warfare. And from 1494 for 65 years Western Europe was once again taken up with a long series of conflicts between the rulers of the two leading states, in which many of the other rulers frequently joined on one side or the other.

The duration of wars varied widely. Military technology and the state of communications were not such as to make quick victories or the continued control of large areas easy to achieve. Some wars were very long. The so-called Hundred Years War, though punctuated by substantial periods of peace, did represent a continuous series of conflicts all fought over a single issue (the English king's claim to the French crown). Similarly the succession of wars fought between the Valois and Hapsburg rulers in the last 65 years of our period can be seen as a continuous series of operations devoted to a single objective: control of Italy, especially Naples and Milan, and (to a lesser extent) Burgundy and the border areas of France. The struggle for Naples between the Angevins and the Aragon kings was carried on intermittently over a period of over 80 years. Poland and the Teutonic Order fought over more than a century (from 1391 to 1522) for authority in Prussia and Livonia. Against this a few wars were relatively short. Rupert, the elector Palatine, abandoned his attempted invasion of Italy (1401) within a year, as did Ladislas of Naples his expedition to win the crown of Hungary in the following year. Poland fought two brief campaigns against the Teutonic Order in 1422 and 1466; and Edward IV abandoned his invasion of France within a few months in 1475 (when the necessary support from Burgundy failed to materialise). But such brief encounters were relatively rare. Most wars, slowed by poor communications and increasingly effective fortification, went on for at least five years, many for ten, often divided between a series of campaigns, which, even if successful, were often not conclusive.

Casualties were not generally high, at least in comparison with those of later ages. Though the proportion of those killed or captured in a battle could be very great — for example among the French at Agincourt or among the Burgundians at the battle of Morat (in which two-thirds of Charles the Bold's forces are believed to have been killed) — the number who took part in each battle rarely reached 40,000 and in most cases was much less. The rapidly changing technology of war affected the nature of the losses. In the earlier part of the period, mounted and armoured knights, mainly from the noble and upper classes, were often the most vulnerable (for example the imperial knights felled by Swiss pikemen and the French horsemen falling to English archers), and it was they who suffered the greatest losses. But, as the key weapons became the pike, the halberd and the arquebus, it was the infantry who became the key arm, and it was among them that the losses were usually heaviest. As the period progressed, war was increasingly undertaken by professionals, often mercenary armies skilled in the art of war. Mercenary commanders, usually controlling their own companies of professional soldiers, sold themselves to the rulers and governments that desired their services and were able to pay for them. Royal armies, such as the force established by the French kings from 1439, or the "black army" set up by Matthias Corvinus in the 1470s (largely of victorious Hussites), the Spanish national force set up to fight in Italy at the end of that century, and the tercios created by Charles V in 1534, were professional forces of another kind, and they too became increasingly proficient and effective against the less seasoned levies they fought. The capacity to pay for such forces, and to pay them regularly (they frequently rebelled if left unpaid for long periods), became one of the most important conditions for successful warfare. Only more important was the morale and commitment of those who fought, possibly the most decisive factor of all; as was demonstrated by the armies of the Hussites (never defeated except by other Hussites), by the Turkish janissaries, and by the Swiss fighting to defend their homeland against foreign threats.

The wars of this age were not mainly fought by large alliances. Because they were essentially the conflicts of rival rulers and families, the typical wars were single duels (France-England, Denmark-

Sweden, Milan-Venice, Poland-Teutonic Order). Sometimes allies could be bought by suitable offers: Edward III had literally bought allies for cash at the beginning of the Hundred Years War. Almost as important was the buying of neutrality, as when Charles VIII made huge gifts, in territory or cash, to England, Spain and the emperor Maximilian to buy their *non*-involvement in his Italian adventure. Most alliances were opportunistic and short-lived: so successive popes switched between France and Spain during their great struggle, while in the same period England and Denmark also changed sides from war to war. Only in the last 60 years of the period were larger groupings put together, often for balance-of-power reasons: against Venice in 1508, against France in 1511, 1515 and 1521, against the emperor in 1526 and 1542 (p. 282 below). Differences in ideology did not deter such arrangements: France had no compunction in calling on the aid of the Turks in 1526 and again in 1536, nor in making herself champion of the protestants in Germany. For these reasons, the average number of participants in a war grew as the period went on: by the end of the period a number of the wars involved eight or more states. Even these larger alliances, however, were formed only for the purpose of a single war: there were no long-term groupings affecting the willingness or capacity of each state to make war.

The list, then, reveals an age of constant, if low-level, warfare. Casualties were not enormous as a percentage of population and there were few continental struggles, such as were shortly to become common. But the dynastic competition led to continual conflict. Title and territory were everywhere in great demand, and were both in short supply. Within states the aim of the rulers to increase their authority, together with the determination of the great magnates, regions and cities to resist that process, also stimulated frequent warfare. Eventually a slow growth in the power of the rulers led to an increasing concentration of power at the centre and so to some decline in private war. Internationally too, power began to be increasingly concentrated among a few great rulers, especially those of Spain and France. The settlement reached between those two powers in 1559 symbolised the end of an era of dynastic struggle. In that settlement Spain gave up her pretensions to Burgundy, France hers to Italy, England hers to Calais and the rest of France. In this way the ambitions of rulers to rule in distant lands began to be more modest. The shadowy outline of national states, with more clearly defined territorial boundaries, started to be discernible.

In other words, there was a change in the character of the units which wielded armed power and the motives which inspired them. A different pattern of warfare began to be revealed.

The age of religions (1559-1648)

As can be seen from the list in Appendix 2, war in this age remained endemic. Though long, the list once again understates the total amount of armed conflict. Over and above the wars listed, there were a very large number of lesser uses of armed force, not coming within the definition of "war" employed here. These included, for example, regular large-scale raids by the Crimean and other Tartars into southern Russia (in 1571-2 they reached and sacked Moscow), which caused heavy loss of life; the corresponding raids by Cossacks from Poland-Lithuania into Turkish-controlled territory; constant clashes on the border between the Holy Roman and Ottoman empires, especially in Hungary, Bosnia and Croatia (the so-called *Kleinkrieg*); naval warfare between the Turks and the Portuguese in the Red Sea and Indian Ocean; constant piratical attacks on shipping (and sometimes on land — in southern Italy, France, Spain and once or twice in England) by corsairs from North Africa, and corresponding attacks on east Mediterranean shipping from Malta; action by English, Dutch and French privateers against Spanish shipping in the Caribbean and elsewhere; sporadic warfare between Spain and Indians in South and Central America; as well as frequent riots and disturbances among peasants and occasionally urban populations all over Europe.

Though marginally less frequent, the wars of this age were more intense and more costly than in the previous age. In Europe alone there were 112 wars in 89 years; an average of 1.25 a year. Of these 53 were international (0.59 a year) and 59 domestic (0.66 a year). In every year of the period there was at least one substantial war going on somewhere in the continent: in most years two; and in many three. But, as we saw before, the overall total is a misleading measure. For comparative purposes the proportion of years each state was at war is the best indicator. This varied widely according to the circumstances of each state. Out of the 89 years of the period, Spain was engaged in war, foreign or domestic, in 83; Sweden in 74; the Hapsburg emperor in 63; France in 59; Turkey in 79 (48 in Europe). Thus, as in other ages, it was the most powerful states, and especially the most powerful of all, that were most frequently at war. Conversely, it was those powers that were more detached from the European scene, geographically or politically, such as England, Denmark and Russia, that were rather less frequently involved.

As always, the wars of the age reflect the dominant preoccupation. This was above all an age of religious concern and religious dissent. Overwhelmingly, therefore, religion was the most important single subject of war. This is especially true of civil wars, which, as our list shows, were very frequent.

Many of these religious wars concerned the right of minorities to practise their own faith. Almost everywhere there was a belief in the need for uniformity of creed in any one territory (pp. 93-4 below). That belief inevitably implied intolerance. It also therefore implied the necessity for revolt by religious minorities if they were to be able to practise their own creed. So the eight successive civil wars of religion in France between 1562 and 1593, the 80-year rebellion of the Netherlands, the conflicts in Scotland and Ireland, the revolt of the Moriscos in Spain, the civil wars in various German states (for example, Cologne, Donauwörth and Cleves-Jülich), and above all the rebellion in Bohemia and neighbouring Hapsburg provinces which ushered in the last great war of the period, were all partly or wholly about the right of religious minorities to practise their faith. Of the 59 civil wars of the period, about 26, or 44 per cent, were concerned mainly with religion (see Table 3).

TABLE 3   RELIGIOUS WARS (CIVIL) IN EUROPE 1559–1648

Years	Country	Community in Revolt	Intervening States
1559–60	Scotland	Calvinist	England (for protestant lords), France (for Catholic regent)
1560–1	Savoy	Vaudois (Calvinists)	
1562–3	France	Huguenots	England
1565[b]	Scotland	Calvinists	
1567–8	France	Huguenots	
1568–70	Spain	Moriscos (converted Moslems)	
1568–70	France	Huguenots	
1569	England	Catholics	
1572–1611	Netherlands	Calvinists	England (from 1585)
1572–3	France	Huguenots	
1575–6	France	Huguenots	
1576–7	France	Huguenots	
1579–80	Ireland	Catholics	Pope, Spain
1580	France	Huguenots	

Years	Country	Community in Revolt	Intervening States
1583–9	Cologne	Catholics	Spain, Palatinate
1585–94	France	Huguenots	Spain (from 1589)
1594	Scotland	Catholic lords	
1594–1603	Ireland	Catholics	Spain
1559–1603	Transylvania	Protestants	Emperor (for Catholics) Turks (against Catholics)
1604–6	Hungary (Hapsburg)	Catholic	Transylvania, Turkey
1607	Donauwörth	Protestants	Bavaria (against protestants)
1618–20	Bohemia, Austria, Moravia, Lusatia	Protestants	Palatinate (for protestants), Bavaria (for Catholics)
1620–3	Valtellina	Catholics	Spain (for Catholics), France (for protestants)
1626	Austria	Protestants	
1632–3[b]	Upper Austria	Protestants	
1641–3	Ireland	Catholics	

[a] Only intervention with armed force included. Intervention for minority in revolt unless otherwise indicated.
[b] These wars were only partly about religion.

But international wars too (see Table 4) were at least in part concerned with the same question. The long war between Sweden and Poland from 1600 to 1629, though primarily concerned with the dynastic question, was fuelled and intensified by religious differences (Catholic countries all over Europe supported the Polish king because they believed his success would mean that Sweden would be made a Catholic country once more). The successive interventions by national governments in the internal religious conflicts of others — by France and England in Scotland (1559-60), by England in France (1562-3) and the Netherlands (1585-1604), by Spain in Ireland (1579-80), England (1588) and France (1589-94), by Poland in Russia (1608-12), by the Hapsburg rulers in Poland (1588), by Denmark (1625-9) and Sweden (1630-48) in Germany, for example — were largely motivated by religious concerns. The wars between the Ottomans and the Christian powers were still seen on both sides mainly as struggles to defend the true faith against unbelievers. Even the wars between Ottomans and Persians were partly fuelled by religious antagonism between Persian Shias and Turkish and Uzbek Sunnis. Of the international wars listed perhaps 25, or 49 per cent, were concerned mainly or largely with religion (see Table 4).

This universal concern with religion had an important effect on the character of war. Many of the wars of this age (like those of the next great ideological age, 300 years later) were no longer international but transnational; no longer between states, and the entire populations within them, each owing allegiance to a particular ruler, but between groups, scattered among different lands, each owing allegiance to a particular faith. So minorities in one state would look to outside powers of the same faith for support and protection (as the Huguenots of France looked to England, the Catholics of Cologne and France to Spain, the Catholics of Donauwörth to Bavaria, the protestants of Bohemia to the Palatinate and those of Germany to Denmark and Sweden, the Moriscos of Spain to North Africa and the Ottoman Turks). Conversely, major powers could hope to find fifth columns of their own faith elsewhere: as Spain could among Catholics in England and Ireland, or among members of the League in France; as England could among the protestant rebels in France and the Netherlands; as France could among Catholics in Scotland (though France made use not only of Catholic minorities but of any that could assist her against Spain: protestants in the Netherlands, Moriscos in the south of Spain, Catalan bandits in the north). Religious faith, in other words, was now sometimes as powerful a source of allegiance as loyalty to the ruler or state, and as important as a stimulus to war. This transnational character of war affected the methods that were employed. "War underhand", the secret despatch of assistance to minorities in another state — a practice rarely known in the preceding age (nor in the age of sovereignty to come) — became in this age among the most important strategies of war (as it was to be again in the next great period of transnational politics 300-400 years later).

This preoccupation with religious conflict at home meant that for some states international war declined (compare column 1 in Appendix 2 with the corresponding column in Appendix 1). For much of the period most states had little mind or strength for wars abroad. France, for example, prostrated by internal conflict for nearly 30 years, could during that time play no effective role elsewhere and for 60 or 70 years even suspended (except in self-defence) her long duel with the Hapsburg rulers. Similarly English governments under Elizabeth and James I, primarily concerned with domestic problems and apprehensive of foreign-inspired threats, adopted a policy of minimum involvement in the struggles of the continent (the only marginal exception was Elizabeth's intervention in the Netherlands from 1585, but even this was cautious and half-hearted[2]). The Austrian Haps-

TABLE 4   INTERNATIONAL WARS CONCERNED PARTLY WITH RELIGION, 1559–1648

Date	Contestants	Religious issue
1551–62	Turkey – emperor	Moslem – Christian
1559–64	Spain, Venice – Turkey, Tripoli	Moslem – Christian
1564–6	Emperor – Transylvania	Religion in Transylvania
1565	Turkey – Malta	Moslem – Christian (Knights of St John)
1566–8	Turkey – emperor	Moslem – Christian
1570–8	Turkey, Barbary states – Venice, pope, Spain (Holy League)	Moslem – Christian (Religion in Cyprus)
1585–1604	Spain – England	Religion in England and Netherlands
1588–9, 1602–3	Savoy – Geneva	Catholic – Calvinist
1593–1606	Turkey, Tartars – emperor, pope	Moslem – Christian
1594–8	Spain – France	Religion in France
1600–29	Poland – Sweden	Religion in Sweden
1601–4	Emperor – Transylvania	Religion in Transylvania
1604–6	Transylvania – emperor	Religion in Transylvania and Hapsburg Hungary
1607	Bavaria – Donauwörth	Religion in Donauwörth (protestants expelled)
1609–10	Emperor – Jülich (aided by Brandenburg)	Religion in Cleves–Jülich
1611–13	Emperor – Transylvania	Religion in Transylvania and Hapsburg Hungary
1616–17	Poland – Turkey	Christian – Moslem
1618–22	Emperor, Bavaria – Bohemia, Lusatia, elector Palatine, etc.	Religion in Bohemia, Lusatia, etc.
1619–20	Poland, emperor – Transylvania, Tartars, Turks	Catholic – protestant, Moslem
1624–6	France, Savoy, Venice – Spain, emperor, Genoa	Religion in Valtellina

Date	Contestants	Religious issue
1624–30	England – Spain	Protestant–Catholic
1625–9	Denmark, Brunswick, etc. – emperor, Bavaria, etc.	Religion in Germany
1630–48	Sweden, Saxe-Weimar, etc. – emperor, Bavaria, etc.	Religion in Germany
1635–48	France, Savoy – Spain, emperor, Bavaria, etc.	Religion in Germany
1644–49	Turkey – Venice	Moslem–Christian
1644–5	Transylvania – emperor	Religion in Transylvania and Hapsburg Hungary

burg rulers, beset with religious controversy throughout most of their domains, as well as by periodic threats from the east, steered clear of West European adventure for nearly 60 years from 1559. Even Spain, the great power of the continent, though scarcely cautious, was so distracted and weakened by protracted warfare in her own colony of the Netherlands, and later by the series of rebellions that began in 1640, that she had difficulty in making her power effective elsewhere. Domestic controversy limited the capacity or desire for foreign adventure. Only as, within each state, the religious conflict began to subside, and the dominance of one faith came to be unmistakably established, could the major powers, in the last 20 years of the period, afford to resume once more the ancient struggle for dominance, in Germany and in Western Europe as a whole.

The importance of religion also affected the type of alignments established. Alliances were now often determined mainly by religious belief. It was in general the case (though France was, as before, a glaring exception) that protestant states would look to other protestant states for allies, and Catholic to Catholic. Even if state interests demanded it, alliance across the religious divide could prove difficult. So James I, who for a time sought an alliance with Spain and a dynastic marriage to accompany it, was obliged to abandon the project largely because of religious differences; and, conversely, was later constrained, for all his hesitations, to take up briefly the cause of the protestants (and his own son-in-law) in Germany. The German states were increasingly aligned in groupings — the Evangelical Union and the Catholic League — which corresponded to religious beliefs, rather than political interests; just as the provinces of the Netherlands formed leagues — the League of Arras and the Union of Utrecht — in accordance with religious sympathies. The ability of a ruler to succeed to a throne could also now be dependent on his religious faith; so the Neuberg family had to become Catholics, and the ruler of Brandenburg Calvinist, to secure the inheritance each claimed in Cleves-Jülich; James I in England could not have succeeded if he had followed his mother's religion; nor Henry IV in France if he had not abandoned his. Conversely, a ruler of the wrong faith could be disowned: so Sigismund of Poland was unacceptable as a ruler of Sweden, despite his strong dynastic claim, in part because of his Catholic faith (while his son was unacceptable to Russia for the same reason).

Religious affinities were, of course, not the only factor affecting alliances. It was still possible for states of the same faith to make war against each other. Traditional enmities could cause protestant Sweden to fight protestant Denmark, or Catholic France to fight Catholic Spain. National interests could cause Catholic Venice and Catholic Savoy to combine with the protestant United Provinces against Catholic Spain. But in general, in this age as in no other, the religious complexion of a state became a major factor in determining the allies which it chose.

No substantial fluctuation in the incidence of war can be discerned from Appendix 2. Frequency did not vary significantly in the course of the period. The only variation visible is that in the first half of the period there was a rather greater preoccupation with internal problems, primarily — but not exclusively — religious; while in the second half problems that were originally internal, and mainly religious in origin, increasingly became internationalised and subsumed in a wider struggle for power among states: the conflicts of Cleves-Jülich, the succession in Mantua, the Bohemian revolt, the Netherlands revolution, the war in Valtellina, all originally domestic conflicts, were each internationalised in this way. It was not only that, as the internal conflicts were increasingly resolved, the larger powers were better able to turn their attention outwards. As the forces of each side became better organised, they were more concerned to do so. In becoming internationalised most of the wars became larger in scale and scope, and heavier in cost. This was especially so after several conflicts were merged in the continental struggle of the Thirty Years War.

In the East too there was a change over the period. The Ottoman Empire, which in the early part of the period was engaged in successive confrontations with the Christian powers, on land and at sea, after 1606 was at peace with them for 40 years, being increasingly preoccupied with a long and bitter struggle with Persia in the East. This in turn left the Hapsburg emperors freer to take part in the protracted war for Germany, a war important to them for political as much as religious reasons. So conflict moved from the periphery —

from the struggle for dominance in the Mediterranean, on the Danube and in the Baltic — towards the centre, where it became a struggle for power in the heart of the continent, in Germany and along the Rhine, between the two major powers of Europe — a struggle in which the advantage now began to turn from Spain to France.

For this reason there was an increase in the scale of war. Because religious sympathies spread across borders, wars spread outwards: from the Netherlands to the Palatinate, France and England; from France to England and Spain; from Germany to the whole continent. More important, because of religious passion war became more ferocious. Thus casualties were far higher, both in absolute and in relative terms, than in the preceding age (p. 246-7 below). Even purely military casualties were higher, if only because armies were larger and the numbers engaged in major battles — such as Breitenfeld and Lützen — were far greater than even before. While the army of Charles V when he invaded France in the 1530s had been about 50,000 strong (already double the size of the armies of earlier wars), by the 1570s Philip II had nearly 90,000 men in the Netherlands alone, and 50 years later, at the beginning of the Thirty Years War, the Spanish army had a total strength of about 300,000. Huge mercenary armies could now be raised (assisted by high unemployment and a low standard of living) in a matter of months: so Wallenstein could recruit 50,000 men for the emperor in two or three months in 1625, and another 40,000 in about the same time at the beginning of 1632.

The military technology of the age also made war more lethal. The armed horseman, the broadsword, the crossbow and the arquebus were now increasingly replaced by musket, pike and artillery having a far greater destructive power. In the major battles of the day — the battles of Breitenfeld (1631), Lützen (1632) and Nordlingen (1634) — between 10,000 and 20,000 are believed to have been killed — far bigger totals than occurred in the age before. Though the new fire-power was to some extent counterbalanced by the development of the art of fortification, first perfected in Italy and rapidly spread across the continent, this did not prevent many sieges ultimately proving successful, often to be followed by large-scale slaughter, of civilians as much as of military: over 20,000 lost their lives in a few days at the end of the siege of Magdeburg in 1631. Sea battles occasionally involved still higher casualties: 30,000, mainly Turks, were killed at the battle of Lepanto.

It was above all the extension of warfare to civilians, who (especially if they worshipped the wrong god) were frequently regarded as expendable, which now increased the brutality of war and the level of casualties. Appalling bloodshed could be attributed to divine wrath.

The duke of Alva had the entire male population of Naarden killed after its capture (1572), regarding this as a judgement of God for their hard-necked obstinacy in resisting; just as Cromwell later, having allowed his troops to sack Drogheda with appalling bloodshed (1649), declared that this was a "righteous judgement of God". Thus by a cruel paradox those who fought in the name of their faith were often less likely than any to show humanity to their opponents in war. And this was reflected in the appalling loss of life, from starvation and the destruction of crops as much as from warfare, which occurred in the areas most ravaged by religious conflict in this age: Württemburg, Bavaria, Bohemia, for example (p. 247 below).

The duration of wars varied widely. A few campaigns ended quickly in rapid conquest or defeat: for example, Turkey's unsuccessful assault on Malta in 1565, Portugal's abortive attack on Morocco in 1578, and Spain's rapid conquest of Portugal in 1580. These were the rare exceptions, however. Religious fervour often brought tenacity as well as ferocity. So the religious struggle in France, maintained through eight separate wars, each ended by treaty, in effect consisted of 30 years of almost continuous confessional struggle. The religious contest in Germany also went on for 30 years (the only part of that complex struggle to which such a duration can properly be applied*). The war in the Netherlands, though a national struggle even more than a religious one, lasted, with only one short interval of a dozen years, for 80 years altogether. Wars that were not mainly religious could last almost as long; like the 30-year struggle between Sweden and Poland from 1600 to 1629 (only finally concluded, after another bout of fighting, in 1660). Turkey was involved in 40 years of war with Persia interspersed with 20-odd years of peace, between 1578 and 1639. The average length of the wars among major powers was over ten years; and it was the length of wars in this age, as much as their bitterness, that made them sometimes so costly.

Though there was not yet the explicit commitment to a "balance of power", such as was to have such a dominant influence on politics and warfare in the following age, there was none the less, as in the previous period (p. 282), an automatic process by which, in practice, excessive power was balanced. Great powers were feared and ultimately challenged. The dominance of Spain aroused antagonism almost everywhere, as that of France was to do in the age to follow, and, as in that case, led to the creation of alliances against her. This overrode religious sympathies, so that even Catholic states such as Venice, Savoy and the Papacy (not to speak of France) were willing

---

* For this reason the different component parts of this war, each having different origins and motivations, are listed separately in our tables.

to contribute to the coalition that finally destroyed Spanish power.

Moreover, in this, as in later ages, a position of dominant power, and especially territorial power, often brought in its train over-commitment and over-extension of forces, which finally weakened once more. It was not only Spain which was cut down to size in this way. Poland, having acquired vast territories, subject to constant attacks from Turks and Tartars from the south-east while at the same time engaged in long and costly engagements with Sweden to the north and Russia to the east, found her hold on her outlying territor-ies gradually weakened: a process that was to reach its climax at the beginning of the following period. The Hapsburg emperors, by assuming leadership of the Catholic cause in Germany, took on a burden they were unable to sustain and eventually, by arousing the opposition of the German rulers, saw their authority there drastically weakened. The Turks, who had expanded almost without cease for centuries, now found themselves met with increasing resistance, to west and east alike. Thus any excessive accretion of power by any state of the system automatically created a balancing reaction; and a number of wars of the period were fought, at least in part, to make that opposition effective.

The wars of this age, therefore, had a character of their own. Fuelled by the fire of religious controversy, they were frequent and very costly. Many were fought, directly and explicitly, to assert the right to practise a particular religion in particular areas, or by exter-nal powers to defend that right. Others that were fought, as in the previous age, about questions of succession or territorial control, were now intensified by religious antipathies. Succession could now matter more than ever precisely because it could determine the religion that would be practised in a particular place: as in England (1558-87), Scotland (1567-9), France (1589-94), Cleves-Jülich (1608) and Sweden (1600-29). Territorial issues became more important for the same reasons: as in the struggles for Alsace and Bohemia in the later years of the Thirty Years War. Civil wars were especially often concerned with religious issues. The universal concern over religion affected above all the *intensity* of warfare: no wars, in recent times at least, have been fought with such brutality as those of this age.

So, as in other periods, the dominant preoccupations of the age gave its warfare a special character, a character which differentiated it from that of other times.

The age of sovereignty (1648-1789)

Once again the list of wars in this period (Appendix 3) shows that warfare, though somewhat less prevalent than in the age before, remained extremely common. In Europe alone there were 41 international wars (including two wars which began in the earlier period and two which ended in the next, or roughly 0.29 wars a year (compared with a rate of 0.59 a year in the preceding period). Though a few of these were small in scale and of little international significance, the great majority (27) were substantial wars, involving a number of nations and lasting for several years each. Civil war was less common than in the previous age, but on occasion remained very destructive.

But once again, it is more relevant to consider the amount individual countries were involved in war. Some European countries were engaged in war almost as much as in the age of religions. For example, France, the most powerful country in Europe for much of the period, was involved in international wars in 80 of the 141 years in the period, Russia in 77, Austria in 77, Britain in 63 and Brandenburg-Prussia in 56: only a little less than the proportions common in the previous period. Other states — Spain, the United Provinces, Sweden, Poland and most German states — were involved in war far less. All, however, experienced a much larger proportion of war years than in any subsequent age.

As always, the wars reflected the character of the age and the motivations that prevailed at the time. This was above all an age of state-building. Many of the wars of the age resulted directly from the widely shared ambition to extend or consolidate the national territory. Each major state had reasons for making war to achieve that end. France persistently sought to expand her borders, especially to the north-east, to end Spanish encirclement and humble her rivals, in turn arousing other countries of the continent to resist her pretensions. The result was four major wars and several lesser uses of force (against Alsace, Luxemburg and Genoa, for example, all in the 1680s) between 1668 and 1714. Russia, as a rapidly rising power (it became the strongest in the continent by the end of the period), was determined to expand to the Baltic in the west and the Black Sea in the south, yet constantly came into conflict with the declining powers of Sweden and Turkey barring her way: she accordingly fought four wars against the first and six against the second. Austria, as a major power of both Eastern and Western Europe, with territories stretching from the Balkans to Belgium, from Bohemia to Italy, could not escape involvement in the main conflicts of Western Europe (six wars in the course of the period), yet became embroiled too in successive confrontations with the Turks to the east (five wars in the same time). Britain's growing commercial and colonial interests, challenging those of the United Provinces and France, and her concern to resist threats to the Low Countries and to defend her territory in Hanover brought her into regular conflict with other powers of the continent (eleven European wars in the course of the period). Prussia's position as a rapidly rising power in Germany, determined to challenge Au-

strian dominance and to unite her scattered territories, led her too
into frequent wars (seven wars from 1700 to 1789 alone, including
two separate interventions in the War of the Austrian Succession).
Even lesser nations — the United Provinces, Savoy, Denmark, not to
speak of Sweden and Poland (neither of them lesser powers when the
age began) — had reasons, political, strategic and economic, to be
involved in frequent conflict. Of all the countries of Europe, only
those that were relatively isolated geographically — Portugal, once
she had regained her independence in 1668, Switzerland and some of
the smaller German and Italian states — managed to keep themselves
somewhat less involved in warfare.

There is no discernible periodicity in the wars of the age. Sometimes two major wars involving the same powers followed each other
with only small intervals between (for example, the Nine Years War
and the War of the Spanish Succession, the War of the Austrian
Succession and the Seven Years War); sometimes there was a relatively long period of peace following a period of frequent war (as in
south-eastern Europe for 30 years after 1739; in the Baltic for about
the same period after 1743; and in Western Europe for 30 years after
1763). Sometimes the same two countries fought each other several
times in swift succession, as did England and the United Provinces
between 1652 and 1672 (three wars), Sweden and Denmark between
1657 and 1700 (three), and Spain and France between 1648 and 1697
(five), following which they were at peace for a long period. Sometimes two rivals were involved in a series of conflicts at fairly regular
intervals throughout the period: for example, Sweden and Russia
(four wars), Russia and Turkey (six). Sometimes a country experienced a period of repeated wars, followed by a relatively long period
of peace: England was engaged in major wars for much of the period
between 1689 and 1713 and then fought no serious engagements until
1739 (she was involved only in two minor wars with Spain, in 1718-20
and 1727-8); the United Provinces was still more heavily engaged
from 1653 to 1713 and was then almost entirely at peace until 1780
(France declared war against her in the last year of the War of the
Austrian Succession but she was involved much against her will and
experienced little of the fighting). This evidence indicates, in other
words, that there is no more reason in this period than in earlier days
to postulate any regular cycle in the incidence of war among states.

The wars that were fought were of a very different character from
those of the preceding age. In that period, as we saw, a large proportion of wars, whether international or civil, were concerned in one
way or another with religion: with what faith should be practised in
particular territories. In this period there is scarcely a single war that
was concerned primarily with that issue; and very few, even among
civil wars, in which it was an important factor (see pp. 100-108

below). The wars in this age resulted overwhelmingly from another cause: the competition among the monarchs and their chief ministers to build up the power and prestige of their own states. Both power and prestige were still seen often in territorial terms. Most of the significant wars, both in Western and in Eastern Europe, resulted from attempts by particular states to extend their borders at the expense of their neighbours, or from efforts by others to prevent it: France's War of Devolution (1667-8), her war against the United Provinces of 1672-8, the Nine Years War, the two Northern wars (1655-60 and 1700-21), the Spanish wars of 1718-20 and 1727-8, the War of the Austrian Succession, the Seven Years War and the wars involving Turkey — in other words all the principal wars of the period — resulted directly from attempts at expansion of this kind (see pp. 154-5 below).

But expansion by some created resistance by others. As in the previous age an accretion of power by one state immediately caused others to join against it. This affected the many disputes over succession. The so-called wars of succession — which included not only the four wars bearing that name but several others in which questions of succession were at issue (see Table 5) were, in almost every case, as we shall see, concerned not so much, as before, with the rights of particular *dynasties,* but with the balance of power among *states* (p. 156 below). It was above all this balance of power (as the speeches of statesmen, which so frequently referred to it, attested) that was now the most important single subject of conflict.

Wars were substantially shorter than in the preceding age. But they were still extremely long as compared with most of those that occurred in later ages. There were few that lasted less than two years, and most lasted more than six. Some of the longest involved only two states: such as the 50-year struggle between the United Provinces and Portugal, mainly in colonial territories (1625-63), the 28-year struggle between Spain and Portugal (1640-68), the 25-year war between Venice and Turkey (1644-69) and the 24-year war between France and Spain (1635-59). A few wars between two states were extremely short; but this was almost always when there was substantial disparity of power between the states concerned: for example, the wars between Sweden and Bremen (1652 and 1666), France and Genoa (1684), Denmark and Hamburg (1687-7), Sweden and Saxony (1700). The majority of wars involved more than two countries; and they lasted for at least four years. One or two of these multi-national wars were very long indeed: such as the Great War of the North, which lasted 21 years. And all the other important wars of the period — the First Northern War, the War of 1672, the Nine Years War, the War of the Spanish Succession, the War of the Austrian Succession and the Seven Years War — lasted for five to ten years.

TABLE 5   EUROPEAN WARS MAINLY OR PARTLY CONCERNED
WITH SUCCESSION, 1648–1789

Date	Participants	Issue	Outcome
1667–8	France–Spain	Succession of French queen (Spanish princess) in Spanish Netherlands	Claim withdrawn
1689–97	France–England	Succession of William and Mary in England[a]	Succession accepted by France
1702–14	England, Austria, United Provinces, etc. – France, Spain	Succession of Bourbons in Spain	Succession accepted if French throne renounced
1704–7	Saxony–Sweden	Right of Saxon elector to Polish throne	Augustus compelled to renounce Polish crown
1718–20	Spain – Austria, Britain, etc.	Right of Spanish royal family in Sardinia and Sicily, and of Austrian emperor in Spain	Most of these claims renounced.
1733–5	France, Spain, Poland – Austria, Russia, Saxoy	Succession in Poland, Lorraine, etc.	Succession in Poland for Russian candidate; Lorraine to pass to France
1740–8	Prussia, France – Austria, Britain	Succession of Maria Theresa in Austria[b]	Maria Theresa succeeds but loses Silesia
1741–3	Sweden–Russia	Succession in Sweden	Sweden accepts heir demanded by Russia
1778–9	Prussia, Saxony – Austria	Proposed transfer of part of Bavaria to Austria	Transfer prevented

[a] This also partly concerned succession in the Palatinate and Cologne.
[b] This also partly concerned succession to the Empire (to which Charles Albert of Bavaria was elected after Austrian setbacks in 1742, to be succeeded by Francis, husband of Maria Theresa, in 1745).

There were a number of reasons for the relatively long duration of wars. It resulted partly from the military technology of the age: the low level of mobility, the importance attached to fortification and siege warfare, the cautious and economical methods of campaigning. There was normally little fighting in the winter, so that the period of active engagement was only half the length of the wars themselves. But it also resulted partly from the character of international politics in this period. Most wars had a number of participants on either side, each with varying aims, their operations only loosely connected, still less closely co-ordinated. Few were willing to subordinate national objectives wholeheartedly to the common aim of defeating their enemy. Some would change sides when new opportunities presented themselves (Brandenburg changed sides in the First Northern War — so winning recognition of her rights in East Prussia from each new ally; Portugal changed sides in the War of the Spanish Succession, Saxony in the War of the Austrian Succession; while Savoy changed to the side of France in the course of the Nine Years War and back again early in the war that followed). More often, individual countries would conclude a separate peace. Separate negotiations were frequently carried on for many years among different participants, even while fighting continued. During the Nine Years War and the War of the Spanish Succession, France was negotiating with her opponents, singly or together, but mainly singly, almost continuously from an early stage (1691 and 1705 respectively). In the War of the Austrian Succession, Prussia and Austria twice concluded separate peaces with each other, with little consideration for, or consultation with, allies. All this made many wars protracted affairs.

Many of the wars of this period consisted in fact of a number of separate conflicts, only tenuously connected. The wars of coalition against Louis XIV consisted to a considerable extent of separate struggles: by the maritime countries to prevent France securing power in the southern Netherlands, and by Austria to prevent her securing it in Germany and Italy. The two Northern wars (though both concerned with the struggle to reduce Sweden's power) consisted of separate Danish, Polish (or Polish-Saxon) and Russian conflicts with Sweden, only loosely related to each other. The War of the Polish Succession consisted in part of a northern struggle related to succession in Poland and the future of Lorraine, and in part of a Spanish effort to win territory in Italy. The War of the Austrian Succession was made up of at least five separate conflicts: the war between Britain and Spain over trade to South America, the two wars between Prussia and Austria for Silesia, the war between Bavaria and Austria for the imperial succession, the war between France and the maritime powers for the Netherlands, and the war between Spain and Austria for Italy. The Seven Years War was sharply divided between a Western struggle between France and Britain, carried out largely in colonial territories overseas and in Western Europe, and a separate struggle between Prussia and her neighbours in Germany and Eastern Europe. Given these separate encounters and the great distance between them, it is perhaps not surprising that the participants were so often tempted to seek separate settlements whenever this was seen to be in the national interest. Britain, as a non-continental power with distinct interests of her own, was perhaps the most inclined to take this course: she deserted her allies to secure a separate peace in almost all the wars she fought between 1672 and 1763. (The only exception is the Nine Years War, and even in that case she had been involved in negotiations with France long before the war came to an end. In 1748 there was no separate peace, but by entering first into negotiations with France, Britain ensured that the main losses were suffered by Austria.) But the difference was only one of degree, not of kind. The United Provinces made a separate settlement with France in 1678; Frederick the Great deserted his ally France three times in five years in the War of the Austrian Succession; Russia abruptly deserted hers in 1762; while Austria deserted Venice in 1720-1 and Russia in 1738 and 1791 (with disastrous consequences for her allies in each case).

This tendency reflected the underlying concern of all countries to maintain the balance of power. This meant that it might be almost as important to ensure that an ally should not succeed too well as that the enemy should not. One effect was that in a number of wars some allies did much better than others. Britain did quite well out of the War of the Spanish Succession, while her ally the United Provinces got little, and Austria far less than she was aiming for. Britain won handsomely from the War of the Austrian Succession, while her ally Austria lost heavily. Britain won substantial gains in the Seven Years War, her ally Prussia none.

The other consequence was that many of the wars of this age had only inconclusive results. More than in any other age, the wars of the period usually ended in a kind of draw. Spain and France settled for such a draw in 1659, with a virtually equal exchange of the main territories. Two of the three Anglo-Dutch wars were inconclusive: the settlement of the last explicitly provided for the restoration of the *status quo*. At the end of the First Northern war in 1660, Sweden and her enemies agreed to settle on the basis that Sweden returned new conquests (for example, in Denmark) but retained the territories she had held before. The Nine Years war ended with no clear victory for either side. On the central issue of the War of the Spanish Succession a compromise was reached: a French prince succeeded in Spain but was not allowed to inherit both kingdoms (and the attempt of the coalition in 1709-10 to win a total victory — by securing an undertaking by Louis that he would expel his grandson from Spain — was defeated). In the War of the Austrian Succession, most of the settlement, both overseas and in Europe (except on Silesia), involved a return to the position before the war. At the end of the Seven Years War, there was an explicit agreement among the participants to restore the *status quo ante bellum* in Central and Eastern Europe.

The nature of the military power available made total victory often extremely costly; and, because the final defeat of an enemy could leave the balance even more unequal than before, outright victory was not often universally desired in any case. Thus, in the War of the

Spanish Succession, Britain and the United Provinces became as concerned (after the succession of Charles VI) that their ally Austria should not win the whole Spanish legacy as they were that France should not. As a result of these conflicting motives a power that seemed on the verge of total annihilation might miraculously survive, as a result of a change of heart among one or more of its opponents: as did the United Provinces in 1673-4 (when England, increasingly concerned about her ally's ambitions, deserted France), France in 1710-11 (when Britain, for the same reason, deserted Austria and the United Provinces), and Prussia in 1762, with the succession of a new pro-Prussian ruler in Russia (though it was not so much Peter III's sudden change of sides, based on personal sympathies that reflected the balancing motive as Catherine's confirmation of it after his death).

The cost of war was somewhat less than in the age before. Certainly there were no conflicts as devastating as the Thirty Years War in loss of life. The most expensive to any single nation was probably the Seven Years War, in which Prussia faced the combined might of Austria, Russia, France, Sweden and the south German states, for much of the time with little assistance from elsewhere: according to Frederick the Great's own estimate she lost 500,000 lives, or a ninth of her population, in the war. For the most part the form of warfare that was now generally practised, involving long sieges, elaborate manoeuvres and often the deliberate avoidance of large-scale battles, brought about smaller casualties than had often been known in earlier times. When large set battles did take place (as at Steenbeck in 1692, at Zenta in 1697, Malplaquet in 1709, Zorndorf in 1758 and Kunersdorf in 1759) the toll could be very heavy, with deaths of 10,000-12,000 or even higher. But battles on that scale were exceptional. Some of the heaviest loss of life took place at sieges: for example, the siege of Barcelona (1714), the sieges of Landau and above all the siege of Ochakov (1788), which is said to have cost 30,000 lives.[3]

In any case casualties were now confined mainly to servicemen. The large-scale slaughter of civilians, such as had occurred during the Thirty Years War, was now rare (though huge suffering was sometimes caused by the systematic razing of inhabited areas, as in the two French devastations of the Palatinate in 1674 and 1689, the Russian destruction of Memel, and similar actions elsewhere). Civilians might also be affected by the financial consequences of war, which was, with the amount spent on raising and equipping forces, on paying for auxiliaries and providing subsidies to foreign allies, often huge: it was largely the economic consequences of war, rather than the cost in lives, which caused Louis XIV to sue for peace in 1696 and 1709 — as it was for Sweden in 1719-20, for Britain in 1747-8, and almost compelled Prussia to do so in 1761-2. Thus, though relatively few civilians lost their lives as the direct result of war, they were, owing to these economic effects, by no means insulated from the consequences.

The character of war in this age was thus in many ways different from what it had been in the period before. It was fought about different issues. Religion, the main source of contention in the previous age, featured relatively little in the struggles of this one. Wars were fought overwhelmingly to determine the balance of power between states. Territory remained an important objective, since it could influence that balance; but it was now mainly the territories required by the interest of states (p. 154-5 below), rather than those important to the prestige of dynasties or demanded by religious zeal, that were desired. There were few long-term alliances or groupings of states. Alliances were formed to suit immediate interests, on a short-term basis, and could change rapidly to suit the needs of the moment. Objectives were often relatively limited; and many wars in any case ended in a draw, from which no country secured its maximum aims. Many wars were lengthy, but the method of fighting was often deliberately restrained and casualties were less heavy than in either the preceding age or subsequent ages.

It was, in other words, an age in which *raison d'état* became the main motive for state action: wars were fought to promote state interests, as these were seen by the monarchs and chief ministers who now controlled the destinies of states.

The age of nationalism (1789-1917)

The list of wars of this age in Appendix 4 reveals a number of features.

First, it is not the case, as is sometimes suggested, that this was, even in Europe, a peaceful age. Wars were frequent. In Europe alone there were 74 conflicts of consequence in this period (for the sake of comparability the French revolutionary wars are reckoned as three, the Napoleonic wars as seven and the Latin American wars of independence as six: see footnotes to Appendix 4). In the world as a whole there were at least 244 wars or about 1.9 a year on average.

This overall total, and the number of wars a year, cannot of course be compared with the totals for earlier periods, both because there were now a larger number of significant sovereign states (with the independence of Latin American colonies), and because in earlier periods there were many conflicts outside Europe not involving recognised states and so not recorded in our lists. But for Europe alone a reasonable comparison with earlier periods can be made. The 74 conflicts that took place in Europe represent an average of 0.57 a year, which compares with an average for the two preceding periods of 1.26 and 0.63: a significant further decline. For international wars alone the decline is very much greater: to 28 only in 128 years, 0.22 a year. For the period after 1815 the decline in such wars is even more dramatic: to 14 in 102 years, or only 0.14 wars a year.

But once again the best comparison is the degree to which individual states were involved in war. This too shows a big reduction for almost every state. Even if the 22 years of the Napoleonic wars (as well as the first three years of the First World War) are included, France was involved in international war in Europe in only 32 years out of 128, Britain in 29, Russia in 23, Austria in 19 and Prussia in 13. For the years between 1815 and 1914 the decline is even more dramatic. Prussia, though involved in more wars than any other power (four), was at war in Europe in only five years out of 99. For Russia (in three wars) the corresponding total is eight years; for France, five; for Austria, four; and, for Britain, three (these figures exclude interventions short of full-scale war, as by Britain and France in Greece and Holland or by Austria in Italian states). If wars outside Europe, including colonial wars, are included, however, the number of war years rises dramatically for the chief colonial powers: for Britain, for example, it becomes 91 (in 46 wars — again, the most powerful state is the most involved in war); for France, 71; for Russia, 56; for Italy, 11.* It might almost appear as if war-making energies were, for such powers, redirected to other areas of the world. Whatever the reason, Europe itself became substantially more peaceful than in any previous time.

The decline was especially significant for international wars. There were now substantial periods (1815-54 and 1871-1914) when major powers did not fight each other at all; in the previous age there were no such intervals longer than seven years (1720-7). The wars they did fight were brief: while in the previous age the longest had lasted over 20 years and the average was seven to eight, no such war between 1815 and 1914 lasted more than three years. Though some of the powers were heavily engaged in warfare in other parts of the world, this did not apply to all of them. Such wars were, anyway, totally different in kind, in that the European powers faced opponents who, though often brave and tenacious, disposed of a military power and technology that was far inferior to their own.

---

* As before, these are for years of war, irrespective of the number of wars taking place in each year. The figures do not of course include every military involvement by each power in their colonial territories, but only those which are here classified as "wars".

Matching this decline in international war, however, was a revival of civil war. Though nearly all the major powers suffered from serious civil conflict in the early years of the previous period, it became insignificant for most of them after 1690, apart from the Hungarian war in Austria (1703-11) and the Pugachev revolution in Russia (1773-4) (see column 2 in Appendix 3). Now, however, it became more common than international war in Europe. Altogether there were 47 civil wars in the course of this period, against 28 international wars; and even of the latter a significant number resulted directly from civil conflicts which had already broken out (for example, the wars of 1828-9, 1848-9 and 1877-8). Thus, little more than a third of the European wars were fully international (the 28 cases in column 1 of Appendix 4, together with the Polish war of 1794-5 — a war that was partly a civil conflict within occupied Poland, and partly international, between an independent Poland and the

TABLE 6   WARS OF NATIONAL INDEPENDENCE IN EUROPE, 1789–1914

Date	Country	Minority People	External Supporter[a]	Outcome
1794–5	Russia, Austria Prussia	Poles	None	Suppressed
1798	Britain	Irish	None	Suppressed
1804–12, 1815	Turkey	Serbians	None	Autonomy granted
1821–4	Turkey	Moldavians, Wallachians	None	Russian occupation (1828)
1821–4	Turkey	Cretans	None	Suppressed
1821–9	Turkey	Greeks	Russia, France, Britain	Independence granted
1830–1	Turkey	Albanians	None	Suppressed
1830–3	Netherlands	Belgians	France, Britain	Independence granted
1831–7	Turkey	Bosnians	None	Suppressed
1831	Russia	Poles	None	Suppressed
1846	Austria	Poles	None	Suppressed
1848	Prussia	Poles	None	Suppressed

Date	Country	Minority People	External Supporter[a]	Outcome
1848	Turkey	Moldavians Wallachians	None	Suppressed
1848/1849	Austria, Papal States, Naples, etc.	Italians	Sardinia	Suppressed
1848–50	Denmark	Schleswig–Holsteiners	Prussia	Danish rule restored
1849	Austria	Hungarians	Russia	Suppressed
1852–3, 1858–9	Turkey	Montenegrins	None	Suppressed
1860–1	Austria, Naples, Papal States	Italians	None	Independence for central and southern Italy
1862	Turkey	Serbians	None	Turkish troops withdrawn
1862	Turkey	Bosnians	None	Suppressed
1863–4	Russia	Poles	None	Suppressed
1866	Turkey	Cretans	None	Suppressed
1867	Papal States	Italians	None	Suppressed
1875–8	Turkey	Bosnians, Bulgarians	Montenegro, Serbia, Russia	Autonomy granted to Bulgaria
1878	Austria–Hungary[b]	Bosnians, Herzegovinians	None	Suppressed
1878	Turkey	Cretans	Greece	Suppressed
1896–8	Turkey	Cretans	Greece	Crete placed under Greek governor, with international force
1903	Turkey	Macedonians	None[c]	Suppressed
1905	(Turkey)[d]	Cretans	None	Suppressed
1912	Turkey	Albanians	None	Albania becomes independent in 1913

[a] Only armed support is included.
[b] Administrators (recognising Turkish suzerainty).
[c] Bulgaria mobilised but her troops were not involved.
[d] Crete was at this time under international control.

occupying powers). Conversely, of the 47 domestic conflicts only 23 involved a single government, in conflict with peoples within its own territory (the conflict in Bosnia-Herzegovina in 1878 is included here though Austria-Hungary did not claim sovereignty in that territory at that time; so is the Polish revolt of 1863-4, because Prussian intervention in that case was only marginal). In about half, therefore, at least one outside power became involved.

A typical war of this age, therefore, was both internal and international at the same time. External intervention could be both for and against the government concerned (see Table 7). In 7 cases outside intervention was on the side of the rebel forces (Greece 1821-9; the Principalities 1821-4; Belgium 1830-3; Schleswig-Holstein 1848-50; the Balkans 1875-8; Crete 1878 and 1896-8). In ten it was in support of the government against rebels (Austria in Naples in 1820-1; France in Spain in 1820-3; Austria in Piedmont in 1821; Austria in Palma and other cities in 1831; Britain in Spain in 1833-40; Spain and Britain in Portugal in 1846-8; Austria and France in Italy in 1848; Russia in the Principalities in 1848; Russia in Hungary in 1848-9; Prussia in other German states in 1849). There is only one case of intervention on both sides in a civil war (as was to be so common in the age to follow): in Portugal in 1828-34, when Britain and Spain intervened on opposite sides, both claiming to support the lawful government.

TABLE 7   EXTERNAL INTERVENTIONS IN CIVIL WAR IN EUROPE, 1815–1914

Date	Country of Civil War	Intervening States	Outcome
1820–1	Naples	Austria (a)	Liberal revolution suppressed
1820–3	Spain	France (a)	Liberal revolution suppressed
1821	Piedmont	Austria (a)	Liberal revolution suppressed
1821–9	Turkey (Greece)	Russia, France, Britain (f)	Independence for Greece
1828–34	Portugal	Britain (f), Spain (a)	Conservative revolution defeated
1830–3	Netherlands (Belgium)	France, Britain (f)	Independence for Belgium
1831	Palma and other cities	Austria (a)	Liberal revolts suppressed

Date	Country of Civil War	Intervening States	Outcome
1833–9	Spain	Britain (a)	Carlist revolution defeated
1846–7	Portugal	Britain and Spain (a)	Liberal (Septembrist) revolution defeated
1848	Turkey (Principalities)	Russia (f)	Russian occupation takes place
1848	Italy	Sardinia (f); Austria, France (a)	Revolutions defeated
1848	Denmark (Schleswig–Holstein)	Prussia (f)	Treaty of London maintains *status quo*
1849	German states	Prussia (a)	Revolution suppressed
1860–1	Italy	Sardinia (f)	Revolution succeeds in central and southern Italy
1863–4	Poland[a]	Russia (supported by Prussia) (a)	Revolution suppressed
1876–8	Turkey (Bosnia and Bulgaria)	Montenegro, Serbia, Russia (f)	Autonomy for Bulgaria; Austrian occupation of Bosnia–Herzegovina
1878	Turkey (Crete)	Greece (f)	Revolution suppressed
1896–8	Turkey (Crete)	Greece (f)	International force sent to Crete, which joins Greece in 1913

(a) = against the revolutionaries;
(f) = for the revolutionaries. Only interventions involving the use of armed force are included.

[a] This case is included because Russian forces, not normally stationed in Poland, were sent for the purpose of defeating the revolution and were given support by Prussia.

There is another significant change in the character of war. This was above all an age of nationalism, and wars were now fought overwhelmingly for nationalist ends. The French revolutionary wars both expressed the emergent national spirit of France and aroused the national spirit of those she conquered. The international wars of the following age were fought either to bring about national unification (the three Prussian wars of 1864, 1866 and 1870-1), or to assist national struggles (the French war of 1859 in Italy and the Russian war in Bulgaria and Bosnia in 1876-8). The three Balkan wars at the end of the period expressed the competitive nationalism of the age. Most of the civil conflicts in Europe also resulted from revolution among national minorities, fighting for recognition of their national identity: this was the main reason for the renewed prevalence of civil wars. Out of the 43 civil wars in Europe after 1815, 26 represented national uprisings of this kind: demands for national independence among subject peoples, or for national unification among those divided among several states. Outside Europe, nationalism was at least a significant factor in most of the wars that were fought. The 74 wars of colonisation were inspired to some extent by nationalist competition among the European powers. More obviously, the 33 wars of decolonisation that were fought expressed the embryonic national feelings of colonised peoples. Both within Europe and outside it, therefore, quite a new pattern of warfare now emerged, having different objectives and different outcomes from wars in the previous age.

Another major change from the previous period is that no wars were fought overseas between the major powers of Europe. Though they still competed for overseas territories, they did not fight each other for them. But France, Britain and Spain each fought wars with the United States; Russia fought one with Japan. The only Asian powers engaged in war with each other during this period were China and Japan in their war of 1894. Almost all other wars outside Latin America were wars between European powers and local peoples, rather than wars among local nations and peoples (though in Africa this is partly because there were only two, very weak, sovereign states in the area).

The periodicity of conflict was relatively constant, both in Europe and elsewhere. If the wars of 1793-1815 are counted separately, those two decades were especially warlike. But after 1815 there were about two international wars per decade in Europe, about 1.3 per decade in Latin America, and about 1.9 per decade elsewhere (including 17 colonial conflicts where the power colonised was a recognised state) with no significant variation in frequency overall. However, if wars involving the great powers alone are considered, a considerable bunching becomes visible. During the century from 1815 to 1914 the only wars in Europe in which the great powers were significantly involved all occurred in the relatively short period between 1853 and 1878. The only ones in which they were involved against each other took place between 1854 and 1871. In other words, for nearly 40 years between 1815 and 1854, and just over 40 years between 1871 and 1914, all these countries were at peace with each other, both in Europe and outside, despite many disputes and much competition for territory in both periods. This represented a dramatic change from the pattern of war in the preceding age, when the major powers were in recurrent warfare against each other.

There was no obvious change in the overall balance of power in Europe to account for this difference between 1854-71 and the peaceful decades that preceded and followed it. As in the previous era there was a roughly even balance of power between the five or six major members of the system throughout the period, with one or two marginally declining as the period proceeded (France and Russia) and one rising (Prussia-Germany). While this even distribution of power was associated, as we saw, with very frequent conflicts in the preceding era, in this age it coincided with two prolonged periods of relative peace (yet was still unable, despite precisely matched alliances, to maintain the peace in 1914). The difference between the three periods 1815-54, 1854-71 and 1871-1914 may partly have been that peace-making procedures, highly developed in this age, worked less effectively in the middle period (p. 308-9 below). But the crucial difference was rather that the nature of the issues was then more difficult. They related at that time to fundamental problems affecting the balance of power in Europe: the degree of influence Russia was to be allowed to enjoy in the Ottoman Empire; whether or not Austrian power was to be allowed to prevail over national demands for unity and independence in Italy; the balance of power between Prussia and Austria in Germany; and the balance of power between Prussia and France in Europe. These were not issues that could easily be resolved through the processes of international discussion and bargaining that were able successfully to resolve the lesser disputes that occurred in the other periods. They could only be settled, some at least felt, by armed force.

Outside Europe there was a different pattern. In Latin America the main trend is that the conflicts became less frequent as the period developed and substantially less frequent after the early 1880s. After that time almost the only international wars that took place were in Central America and were relatively brief and inexpensive conflicts (the almost bloodless conflict between Brazil and Bolivia over a small border region in 1902 was the only exception). Until that time they were fairly frequent and sometimes lengthy and bloody. They were almost entirely between immediate neighbours. Some neighbouring countries, such as Peru and Bolivia, Argentina, Uruguay and Brazil, were relatively frequently involved in conflict; others rarely (Venezuela not at all, Colombia and Ecuador only once each). For most of the countries of the region internal violence played a much larger part in their affairs than external wars.

In Asia and Africa most of the wars were for or against colonisation. Although the acquisition of colonies took place mainly in a relatively brief period in the last two or three decades of the nineteenth century, principally in Africa and the Pacific, the wars associated with colonialism took place at fairly regular intervals throughout the period. A number of these were not connected with the original acquisition of such colonies, but resulted from challenges to authority from within at a later stage, or attempts to defend the colony from threats from without by the extension of power to other areas. In many cases colonies had been established originally in relatively small coastal areas for the purposes of trade, the protection of which later necessitated conquests further inland, where new wars sometimes took place. In other cases expansion occurred because colonial powers sought to forestall the efforts of rivals to acquire power in a particular area. In a few cases commercial interests engaged in the area encouraged their own governments to intervene so as to provide greater security for their activities.[4] Colonising wars were far more frequent in this age than in any other in history. The imbalance of power between the colonising powers and the peoples being colonised was so great that it made conquest appear simple and inexpensive. And the belief that there was no recognised sovereignty in such areas made it appear — at least to the colonisers — justifiable.

Thus the number of wars of colonisation and decolonisation (119) was almost as great as the total for all other wars combined. Of the 195 conflicts outside Europe almost two-thirds consisted either of wars of colonisation (83) or wars of resistance to colonial powers after colonisation (36) (these two categories are not always easy to distinguish: in general, conflicts *initiated* by people already colonised are listed as wars of "decolonisation"). Of the wars of colonisation 29 were undertaken by Britain; 21 by France, 12 by Russia, four by Holland, four by Italy (including the war of 1911-12 against Turkey for Libya), and the rest by assorted powers. The four US occupations in Central America and the Caribbean (of Nicaragua and Honduras in 1912, of Haiti in 1915 and Dominican Republic in 1916) were almost in this category, but no formal colonisation took place. In addition, most of the colonial powers were involved in frequent "law and order" operations not large enough to be included in our list of the wars of decolonisation; a few occurred during the dissolution of old empires (Turkey and Spain), but most in areas relatively recently colonised (India and Indonesia in the early part of the period, Tanganyika, the Philippines, Morocco and Libya at its end). In general, once the colonial powers had firmly established their hold, revolts occurred less frequently.

Wars were on average very much shorter than in earlier periods, especially in Europe. This reflected changes in military technology and communications: the use of railways to transport mass armies, strategies based on high mobility and the concentration of large forces, and the hugely increased fire-power of artillery, which made it possible to secure overwhelming victories in a very short space of time. A number of important wars were decided in a few weeks, sometimes as a result of only one or two major battles: the war of 1866 between Austria and Prussia was decided, after one main battle, within three weeks and was finished in seven; that between Prussia and France in 1870-1 was decided, mainly on the basis of a single engagement, within six weeks and completed in six months; the war between Serbia and Bulgaria in 1885 was decided in a fortnight; both the First and Second Balkan wars were effectively over in three weeks. Wars as short as this were unknown in previous ages. Their brevity was important because it created the belief that future wars were likely to be short also, and that their results would depend on rapid mobilisation and efficient transport. Germany's Schlieffen plan before the First World War assumed that France would be defeated in six weeks, after which the German army would be freed for war against Russia; and many on both sides believed the First World War would be over in three or four months.

Wars outside Europe, on the other hand, were rarely short: there the communications problems were often greater and the available forces smaller. Even in Europe wars were longer where several nations were involved. And it was the greatest conflicts of the day, at the beginning and end of the period, each of which involved many powers, that were the longest of all (though this results partly from conceiving them as single conflicts — Austria's four wars against France between 1799 and 1814 lasted on average two and a half years each, Prussia's two wars in that period scarcely more).

Changes in the technology of war had contradictory effects on the level of casualties. The possibility of quick victory sometimes reduced them. Where a victory could be achieved in one or two battles, the cost in lives was sometimes small. Outside Europe especially, European powers were able, through superior military technology, to secure victories over less advanced peoples at small cost to themselves. But at the same time the use of mass armies and the development of very powerful artillery meant that the casualties in a single battle could be heavier than at any earlier time: the number of casualties in the battle of Leipzig (1813) — alone probably 125,000, including at least 30,000 dead — was greater than in many entire wars in the previous age. As a result the scale of casualties varied widely from one war to another. In many of the wars on our list the total deaths were under a thousand. But the Crimean War cost several hundred thousand lives (estimates vary from 250,000 to more than double that figure), the Balkan war of 1877-8 300,000, and the Franco-Prussian War about 200,000. By far the most expensive of the international wars in this period was the First World War, in which the number of dead was probably at least 12 million. Some of the most expensive wars were civil conflicts: the American Civil War (300,000-400,000), the Moslem revolution in China (250,000) and the Taiping rebellion in the same country (probably over 2 million). The most costly of the colonial conflicts was the Cuban revolt in 1868-78, in which at least 200,000 are believed to have been killed. The casualties in other colonial conflicts were often relatively small, though sometimes very one-sided (at the battle of Omdurman in 1898 11,000 Sudanese were killed against only 400 British and Egyptians). The most costly war in terms of its effect on a single nation was undoubtedly Paraguay's war with its neighbours in 1864-70, in which the greater part of the adult male population of Paraguay was destroyed: probably the greatest loss ever encountered by one nation in war.

Another major feature of the wars of this age concerned the number of participants. A substantial number of the wars of the previous era were continental conflicts involving at least four of the major powers of Europe. In this age, apart from the global conflicts at its beginning and end (in some ways untypical of the age), none involved four major powers. Only two (the Crimean War and the Austro-Prussian — if Italy is included as a major power) involved even three of them. In Latin America about half the wars involved only two countries, and none more than four Latin American states. Inevitably, almost all the colonial and anti-colonial struggles of the age were fought on a one-to-one basis. This development too may have partly reflected changes in military technology. Because victories could be won more quickly and easily, sometimes on the basis of only one or two major battles, individual nations could more easily rely on their own efforts alone and do without the assistance of unreliable allies, to whom concessions might need to be offered. Equally important, the aims of the wars were different (pp. 163-9 below): because they were often for specific national ends — national independence, national unity — having little impact on other countries, they were less likely to draw in many participants than the conflicts of the previous age, which often concerned the balance of power and distribution of territory in Europe as a whole.

There was a bigger variation than in previous times in the degree to which individual countries were involved. In the previous age, because several of the wars involved all or most of the major powers, all were involved in war to a roughly similar extent. In this age some were involved relatively little, some a great deal. Some of the smaller countries of Europe were now, for the first time, almost free from involvement in war. Holland and Sweden, both heavily engaged in warfare in the previous two centuries, were now (apart from Holland's brief resistance to Belgian independence in 1830-2) at peace throughout the period from 1815; and both escaped participation in the First World War. Portugal and Spain, once frequent participants in wars in Europe, were now, though deeply involved in internal conflict, not engaged in any of the wars of Europe after 1815 (excepting only Portugal's hesitant participation in the First World War). Switzerland, Belgium and Luxemburg secured an internationally recognised neutral status, though this did not spare the last two from involvement in the war of 1914. For the first time in European history, therefore, in this age it began to be possible for some nations to be altogether free from war for long periods.

Even among the major powers there was a substantial variation. If the major conflicts at the beginning and end of the period are excluded, Turkey was involved in eight of the international wars of Europe; Russia in five, Prussia in four, Austria in four, France in three, and Britain only in one. The level of participation is not, of course, a measure of aggressiveness. Turkey was in several cases the victim rather than the instigator of war. Austria, though she was responsible for declaring war in almost every case, was herself the power under challenge, and was almost invariably defeated*.

Newly emerging and rising powers, assuming the ambitions that international society instilled, were most often the instigators of war. So the rising powers of Prussia and Russia were largely responsible for precipitating war four times each (in 1864, 1866, 1870 and 1914; and in 1805, 1808, 1828-9 and 1877-8), while the new nation of Italy was involved in three wars in Europe between 1866 and 1915. Outside Europe too, rising or newly emerging countries seemed to be most prone to war. The United States was involved in three foreign wars in the course of the period (excluding her wars against the Barbary pirates), in addition to four armed expeditions leading to the prolonged occupation or domination of countries in Central America and the Caribbean. Japan, within 50 years of emerging from seclusion, became engaged in two major conflicts, during which she acquired substantial overseas territories (themselves only the first stage in a career of expansion). The new states of Latin America became involved in frequent conflicts during the first 50 years of their history: though sometimes short and painless, one or two of these were long and exceptionally bitter. As in Europe, some countries remained at peace for long periods. The only two independent countries of Africa, Liberia and Ethiopia, engaged in no foreign adventures, although Ethiopia defended herself effectively against encroachments from European powers, especially Italy. Similarly Siam, the only indepen-

---

* The only exception was when she defeated Sardinia, in 1848-9: she also overcame Italy in 1866 but lost the war because of her defeat by Prussia.

dent country of Asia, managed to retain her independence without war throughout the period (though she too was challenged and compelled to relinquish her protectorate over Cambodia to France).

The general character of war in this age was thus different from in the preceding age. The rise of nationalist sentiment — that is, increasing consciousness of nationhood among groups sharing a similar language, culture and history — bred wars of a new kind. Within states, such groups, feeling themselves possessed of a common identity, sought to free themselves from rule by governments increasingly regarded as alien. Between states, national sentiment fostered and intensified rivalry and competition: competition that in some cases, it was felt, could be resolved only by war. Within Europe international wars became less frequent: for the first time that continent experienced periods lasting decades without war among the major powers, while a few smaller countries enjoyed a century or more of peace. When it did occur, however, war was more intense, and far more costly in human lives, than in any earlier age; and in the last conflagration of all, in 1914, its destructiveness reached a scale never previously even imagined. Outside Europe the great majority of conflicts were wars of colonisation by European powers seeking to win control of territories not ruled by any other such power; a smaller number were wars of decolonisation, designed to win independence from distant colonial masters. In other words, most of the wars of the age were of a kind infrequent in earlier times: wars of national independence in Europe, and wars of colonisation and decolonisation outside.

The underlying motives which led to war, therefore, had changed significantly. What had not changed was the conviction that war remained an inevitable feature of human existence, and was the principal available means by which the balance of status and advantage among nations could be from time to time adjusted.

The age of ideology (1917-   )

The list of wars of our final period (Appendix 5) once again reveals a change in the character of the wars mainly fought; and once again that character reflects the dominant preoccupation of the age.

This was above all an age of ideological competition. Even the First World War, which brought it to birth, had been seen by many as an ideological struggle, fought by governments committed to liberal and democratic systems against reactionary and authoritarian regimes: a war "to make the world safe for democracy". From that war's end, with the arrival of the first communist power, ideological competition intensified. For a time it became a three-sided contest between the otalitarian creeds proclaimed in Germany, Italy and Japan; Marxist ideas, as preached by the Soviet Union and her supporters in other states; and the libertarian, democratic beliefs of the Western powers. After the defeat of Germany and her allies in 1945 the world increasingly became divided into two camps, communist and non-communist, East and West. A substantial proportion of the wars of the age were fought out between adherents of these rival forces, each often receiving support, direct or indirect, from their patrons elsewhere (see Table 8). The wars in which the super-powers themselves became engaged were in every case contests on behalf of their own political clients elsewhere against ideological opponents (Table 9).

TABLE 8   IDEOLOGICAL CIVIL WARS, 1917–84

Date	Country	Revolutionaries	Intervening powers
1918–21	Soviet Union	Anti-Bolsheviks	Britain, France, USA, Japan Czechoslovakia
1918	Finland		Soviet Union
1918–19	Ukraine	Various	Soviet Union
1919	Hungary	Anti-communists	Romania, Czechoslovakia
1926–36	China	Communists, warlords	None[a]
1936–9	Spain	Nationalists	German, Italy (for rebels); Soviet Union (for government)
1945–55	Philippines	Huks	None
1946–50	China	Communists	None
1946–54	Indo–China	Left-wing nationalist forces	None
1948–	Burma	Red-flag and white-flag communists	None
1952	Bolivia	Left-wing forces	None
1954	Guatemala	Right-wing rebels based in Honduras	USA (CIA) Honduras
1954–8	China (off-shore islands)	Nationalists	None

Date	Country	Revolutionaries	Intervening powers
1956–9	Cuba	Left-wing forces	None
1958	Lebanon	Left-wing Moslems and nationalists nationalists	Syria (for rebels), USA (for government)
1959–62	Laos	Communist and nationalist forces	None
1959–75	South Vietnam	Vietcong	North Vietnam (for rebels); USA and others (for government)
1960–79	Nicaragua	Sandinistas	None
1961	Cuba	Anti-Castro forces	USA
1962–7	Yemen	Traditional tribesmen	Saudi Arabia (for rebels), Egypt (for government)
1965–	Colombia	Various left-wing forces	None
1965	Dominican Republic	Various	USA (for rebels)
1965–6	Indonesia	Left-wing forces	None
1968–75	Oman	Dhofari Liberation Front	South Yemen (for rebels); Britain, Iran (for government)
1970–5	Cambodia	Khmers Rouges	USA (for government)
1975–9	Argentina	Various left-wing groups	None
1975–	Philippines	Communists (New People's Army)	None
1976–	Angola	Right-wing forces (Savimbi)	South Africa
1976–	Guatemala	Left-wing groups	None
1978–	Afghanistan	Assorted opponents	Soviet Union (for government)
1979–	El Salvador	Left-wing groups	USA (for government)

Date	Country	Revolutionaries	Intervening powers
1980–	Cambodia	Khmers Rouges and other forces	China
1980–	Mozambique	Right-wing forces	South Africa
1980–	Peru	Sendero Luminoso (Maoists)	None
1983–	Nicaragua	Right-wing forces	USA

Revolutionary wars were primarily anti-colonial or secessionist rather than ideological are not included.

Interventions listed in the right-hand column are in support of revolutionaries unless otherwise stated. Only large-scale interventions (going beyond the supply of arms) are mentioned.

[a] Japan intervened in China during this period but the intervention was not mainly concerned with the Civil War.

Later new ideologies — Islamic fundamentalism, revolutionary Maoism, Castroism or Qadafism — became the source of conflicts of various kinds. The cause for which peoples and governments alike were prepared to give their lives was no longer that of dynastic supremacy, religious freedom, state power or national aspirations: increasingly it was the defence of an ideological system and of the governments, all over the world, that supported it.

The overall frequency of war was not very different from that in the previous age. Altogether there were approximately 161 significant conflicts over a period of 67 years, or approximately 2.4 a year. This is a rather higher frequency per year than in the preceding period, but since there is now a much larger number of states the comparison has little meaning. The average amount of war per state, the more significant measure, is now somewhat lower if the comparison is made with the entire period 1789-1914. But if the comparison is made with 1815-1914 alone there is little decline. Most European states were at war for about five to ten years out of the 67 (depending on the number of years of participation in the Second World War) and often participated in two wars only — an even lower frequency of war than in the previous period. There is, however, a major difference between the periods 1917-45 and the period after 1945. Before 1945 war in Europe, domestic or international, remained frequent: there were 12 wars altogether in 20 years. Since 1945 there has been only one significant war in Europe (the Greek Civil War) and none at all since 1956. A few European countries have been involved in wars elsewhere — for example, the Korean War. And the colonial powers almost all faced decolonisation conflicts of one kind or another. But Europe itself has enjoyed a period of peace longer than it has ever known before. Most European powers have not been involved in war at all, domestic or foreign, within Europe or elsewhere, for 40 years, a luxury most of them have never previously enjoyed.

This decline in war in Europe resulted partly from greater stability within states. Civil wars, which were the most common source of conflict there in the previous century, and which in turn sparked off a number of international wars, now almost ceased. Whereas in the period 1789-1917 there were 47 civil wars in Europe, since 1945 the only such conflict has been the Greek Civil War (the conflict in Hungary in 1956 is classified here as an international conflict, since what domestic fighting there was *resulted* from the Soviet invasion). North America, Australia and much of the Pacific were also entirely free of domestic conflicts during this time.

Most wars of the period thus now took place in developing continents: of those since 1945, 98 per cent occurred in Asia, Africa or Latin America. Of these Latin America has been the least subject to war, though even there there have been 30 wars since 1917. Most of these have been civil conflicts. The international wars in the region have — with the exception of the Chaco War between Bolivia and Paraguay in 1932-5 — been short and relatively inexpensive (the three small border incidents of 1932, 1942 and 1981, and the brief skirmishes between Nicaragua and Honduras, and El Salvador and Honduras, of 1957 and 1969). Far more costly in casualties have been the prolonged civil conflicts, especially the *violencia* in Colombia, in which casualties are believed to have reached 250,000 over a period of ten years, and the guerrilla wars in Guatemala, Nicaragua, El Salvador and other countries.

In Africa there have been a number of anti-colonial wars (Algeria, Zimbabwe, the three Portuguese territories, Namibia); a number of civil conflicts occurring soon after independence (Congo, Nigeria, Sudan and Chad); and a number of frontier disputes most of which emerged fairly soon after independence (Algeria-Morocco, Somalia-Kenya, Somalia-Ethiopia). But war has been most widespread in Asia (55 throughout the period). Here too there have been several anti-colonial wars (Malaysia, Philippines, Indo-China, Indonesia); several frontier disputes resulting from independence (Kashmir, 1948-9 and 1965; China-India, 1962; Bangladesh, 1971; Malaysia, 1962-5; West Irian, 1971- ; East Timor, 1974-) and political conflicts following independence (Korea, Burma, Indo-China, Philippines). Warfare has been especially intense in the Middle East: there were six separate conflicts related to the Arab-Israel dispute alone between 1948 and 1982. Altogether this represents a major change in the geographical distribution of war.

Because this has been above all an age of ideological concern, most of the wars have concerned the political system to be established in particular states. This applied to several conflicts in the immediate aftermath of the First World War: in Finland, the Ukraine and Hungary, for example. Even the wars of Italy, Germany and Japan before 1945 were inspired partly by the political creeds they professed. Since 1945, wars have overwhelmingly been civil wars, fought between the adherents of different political philosophies. Already in the previous period, as we have seen, civil wars (43 after 1815) were substantially greater in number than international wars in Europe (15 in the same period); and even the international wars of that age in many cases resulted from domestic conflicts which had already broken out (p. 56 above). That trend becomes much more pronounced in the present age, especially since 1945; and it is now even more true outside Europe than within it. Of the 144 conflicts since 1945, only 29 have been international wars (in which at least two sovereign states were in direct conflict). The rest have been either colonial wars (16 — see Table 10) or civil wars (66). And even the international wars have often arisen, as in the previous period, from the intervention of one or more outside powers in the internal struggles of particular states, and have usually been fought out entirely within a single state, as in the case of the wars in Hungary, Yemen, Vietnam, Somalia-Ethiopia, Afghanistan and Grenada, for example. This predominance of internal war is similar to the situation seen in the previous age of ideological conflict (pp. 38-9 above).

TABLE 9   CONFLICTS INVOLVING DIRECT USE OF FORCE BY SUPER-POWERS, 1945–84

Date	Conflict	Super-power Concerned
1956	Hungary	Soviet Union
1961	Cuba	USA[a]
1965	Dominican Republic	USA
1965–73	Vietnam, Cambodia	USA
1968	Czechoslovakia	Soviet Union[b]
1979–	Afghanistan	Soviet Union
1983	Grenada	USA

(US participation in the Korean War is excluded as a UN operation.)
[a] Training of forces, logistical support, transport and air cover only.
[b] Since this invasion did not meet organised resistance it does not appear in the list of wars in Appendix 5.

But even when no outside power has been directly involved in domestic conflicts (in the sense that its forces have been engaged there), such powers have become increasingly engaged indirectly: in the supply of arms, the sending of "advisers", the despatch of "volunteers" or political support of various kinds. This strategy too — "war underhand" — was typical of an earlier age of ideological conflict (p. 38 above). On the one hand, political differences within states have been extremely acute; often they have concerned not merely which political party should rule but the entire character of the system, economic as well as political. On the other, ideological alliances, and especially the leaders of each alliance, have had a deep interest — strategic as well as ideological — in the result of such struggles; and therefore have felt it necessary to intervene, more or less directly, to determine the outcome. Above all, technological changes, especially increased mobility, have now made such intervention everywhere practicable. So in Greece, in Indo-China, in Angola, in Afghanistan, in Central America and in many other places one super-power or other, occasionally both, have become heavily involved, intensifying both the scale and the bitterness of domestic conflicts (p. 177 below).

TABLE 10   PRINCIPAL WARS OF DECOLONISATION 1917–84

Dates	*People Seeking Independence – Colonial Power*
1917–18	Dominican Republicans
1919–22	Irish – Britain
1919–26	Moroccans – France
1920–30	Libyans – Italy
1921–2	Indians (Moplahs) – Britain
1921–6	Moroccans – Spain
1925–7	Syrians – France
1926–7	Javanese – Netherlands
1930–1	Vietnamese – France
1945–54	Indo-Chinese–France
1947	Malagasy – France
1947–56	Malayans – Britain
1952–4	Tunisia – France
1952–7	Kenyans – Britain[a]
1953–6	Moroccans – France
1954–62	Algerians – France
1955–9	Cypriots – Britain
1955–60	Camerounians – France
1957–8	Western Saharans – Spain, France
1961–74	Angolans – Portugal
1963–74	Bissau Guineans – Portugal
1963–7	South Arabians – Britain
1965–74	Mozambicans – Portugal
1966–	Namibians – South Africa
1973–80	Zimbabweans – Britain

[a] In these cases war took place between the peoples of the colonial territory as well as against the colonial power.

Even the international wars of the age have often resulted, more or less directly, from the great ideological divide. So the two fiercest and most expensive conflicts since 1945 have been those in Korea and Vietnam, both countries divided along an ideological frontier, in which the two halves became engaged against each other. Several others (seven between 1956 and 1984) have resulted from direct intervention by one or other super-power in political struggles in neighbouring states (see Table 9). Thus, however they may have begun, many of the wars that have broken out have in time become part and parcel of a single world-wide ideological struggle.

As in other periods, the character of war has been affected by changes in military technology. The most obvious and dramatic change has been the development of nuclear armaments: weapons of a power previously unimaginable. This has brought an apparently unbridgeable disparity between nuclear and non-nuclear nations in the power available to them. The difference those weapons have made, however, is more apparent than real. Nuclear weapons have been used only in one conflict and have since been universally avoided. A very large number of wars continue to take place all over the world, uninfluenced by their existence. At best their importance has been negative, in making rather less likely the outbreak of war between nuclear powers. It has not seemed to affect the incidence of war between nuclear and non-nuclear powers (though one might have expected these to have been the most deterred). These conflicts remain relatively frequent; and in at least one of them (the Vietnam War) a non-nuclear power has prevailed over a nuclear one (the Vietnamese repulse of China's attack in 1979, and the Soviet Union's lack of success in Afghanistan could be quoted as similar examples). Even between nuclear powers, the increasing improbability that such weapons could ever be used has progressively reduced their deterrent power.

Far more significant, therefore, have been the other developments in military technology. Weapons of all kinds have now become more lethal, more sophisticated and much more expensive. One effect has been that military power has become even more closely related to economic power: victory has often gone to the country which could afford the most advanced equipment (as evidenced in Israel's repeated victories, and in the brief war between Britain and Argentina in 1982). Yet even these differences in equipment have counted for less, in many of the encounters of the day, than differences in morale and faith in a cause: as shown, for example, in the decisive victory of communist forces in China over far better equipped nationalist armies, in the success of inferior rebel forces in Nicaragua and Afghanistan against better-armed government forces, and in the victories secured by North Vietnam and the Vietcong over far better equipped but less committed opponents. Here is yet another parallel with the previous ideological age 350 years earlier: as the Hussites had demonstrated then, neither technological superiority nor overt military power are always decisive in the struggles of such an age.

As in earlier ages, there has been no significant variation in the frequency of war over time. Wars were perhaps became marginally more numerous in the immediate aftermath of major world conflicts. These left instabilities within states, as well as uncertainties about new frontiers, which provoked further small conflicts: thus there were eight wars in Europe in the first three years after the First World War and five in Asia in the first three years after the Second World War. Similarly there was a proliferation of decolonisation conflicts as that process reached its peak: about 12 in the period between 1952 and 1965. But neither of these fluctuations brought a large variation in the overall frequency of war: there has been a fairly steady average of just over 20 per decade throughout the period (compared with just under 20 in the previous period). The duration of wars has varied more widely in this age than perhaps in any other. When wars are fought by regular forces with conventional arms in open territory, they can be won and lost with incredible speed: as in the Six Days War between Israel and the Arab states of June 1967, the almost equally rapid war between Israel and Egypt of October 1973, the wars between India and Pakistan of 1965 and 1971, and the war over the Falklands in 1982. But other wars have been enormously long. Especially if fought by unofficial forces using a guerrilla strategy, they can extend over 15-20 years or more, as, for example, the protracted civil wars in Colombia, Vietnam, Eritrea, Sudan, Chad and the Philippines.

A substantial proportion of the wars, especially since 1945, have involved smaller, weaker and poorer states. Since 1945 no major power has ever been involved against another major power (Chinese forces were engaged against US forces in Korea, but China did not participate officially in that war). The super-powers have themselves been engaged in warfare on a number of occasions, but always in the territory of smaller powers; usually through involvement in civil conflicts there. These actions have almost invariably involved forcible intervention in areas near to their own borders, seen by them as essential to their security (see Table 9). So the Soviet Union has intervened by force in Hungary, Czechoslovakia and Afghanistan; the United States in the Dominican Republic and Grenada and (less directly) in Guatemala, Cuba, El Salvador and Nicaragua; China in Korea, the Indian border and Vietnam (1979). The only direct intervention in more distant regions has been the long and costly US involvement in Vietnam, and even this was an area declared by some US statesmen to be essential to her security. Except in the Soviet invasion of Hungary developed states have made war only in the territory of developing countries, where the wars have mainly started.

Casualties have varied hugely from one war to another. The period has seen by far the costliest war in world history, with total deaths reckoned by some at 40 million; and other wars that, even if sometimes important in their consequences, yet cost relatively few casualties (such as the Six Days War of 1967 or the 1965 war between India and Pakistan). In some cases it has been where technology is most advanced that casualties have been least (since such wars are likely to be short and sharp and mainly confined to military personnel); whereas protracted guerrilla warfare, involving large numbers of civilians, such as the wars in Spain, Algeria, Vietnam, Colombia and Guatemala, have been hugely expensive in human lives. Of the international wars the Korean and Vietnam wars, each reckoned to have cost some 2 million casualties, have been the most expensive since 1945. The main difference from the previous period is that war now brings a far higher proportion of civilian deaths. The development of air bombing has meant that even in conventional warfare (as in the Second World War) there are heavy civilian casualties; and nuclear weapons mean that the casualties from a single weapon could now amount to tens of thousands, primarily civilians (though conventional air raids on Dresden and Tokyo in 1945 each caused more deaths than were caused at Hiroshima).

There is a similar trend towards the extremes in the number of participants in each war. Our list includes one war, the Second World War, in which more different nations participated than in any earlier war in history; operating too in a greater number of separate theatres of war, which together spanned most of the world. For the most part, however, the list consists overwhelmingly of wars that have involved either only one sovereign state (more than three-quarters of the total); or two such states (over three-quarters of the international wars); and have been fought out entirely within the territory of a single state. Though there have been some closely knit alliances, especially in Europe, they have rarely become involved in war (perhaps helping to deter it). The relatively few international wars of the age have overwhelmingly been private quarrels, between immediate neighbours. The two main exceptions since 1945 are the Korean and Vietnamese wars, in each of which a number of ideological allies became involved on one side or both; and the series of Middle East wars, in most of which two or more Arab states have fought as allies (though with little co-ordination between them) against Israel. Most wars, however, have been civil wars, which have not affected the territory of more than one state, and in which usually only one government has been directly involved.

The wars of this age, therefore, again show a marked difference from those of earlier times. Before 1945 some were still expansionist wars by ultra-nationalist governments, a heritage from an earlier age (though even they were usually dignified by ideological justifications). Since 1945 some wars have, as in the previous age, been wars of national independence; but occurring now mainly in colonial territories overseas rather than in Europe. But the great majority have been civil wars. A few have been revolutions by ethnic minorities seeking independence or autonomy. But most have set ideological opponents against each other, each often drawing support of one kind or another from ideological patrons or partners elsewhere. In contrast to the previous age these wars now almost never take place in Europe or any of the developed countries of the world, where political structures, in East and West alike, are relatively firmly established and the forces of law and order powerful enough to make rebellion a hopeless enterprise. Overwhelmingly these civil wars now take place in the poorer regions of the world — and mainly the poorer countries within them. In those countries political structures are shaky, political traditions weak, institutions unstable and standards of living so low that many have little to lose by taking up arms against governments whose policies they detest and whose authority they reject. Where those struggles are believed to threaten the security interests of major powers they too may intervene to determine the outcome of such conflicts.

Conclusions

What are the main conclusions to be drawn about the varying patterns of warfare revealed in these different international societies? Are there any significant trends to be detected, or any marked differences between the different periods that are worth noting?

There are some obvious contrasts. A major distinction, affecting the kind of war conducted in each age, relates to the types of unit engaged in warfare in each society. There have, for example, been some ages in which war has been made as much by *unofficial* groups of various kinds as by governments. In the first of our societies a substantial proportion of the wars were waged by peasants, cities, knights, *écorcheurs* and other disaffected sections of the population. In the present period again they have been launched mainly by revolutionary groups, ethnic minorities and ideological factions (with or without the assistance of outside governments). In other ages the units engaging in war have been almost exclusively governments, engaged in war against other governments: this was true, for example, during the age of sovereignty, when civil war was relatively infrequent, and when commitment to sovereignty meant that there was little disposition among outside governments to assist such rebellions. (This reluctance was not absolute: France gave assistance to rebels in Catalonia, Ireland, Hungary, and other places; but, as the list of wars makes clear, such action was less common than in any other age.) The difference in the units engaging in war is one of degree rather than of kind, since in nearly all ages the most important wars have been those made by governments, and there have been no periods when there were no wars waged by unofficial factions. But this still represents a significant difference between the patterns of warfare undertaken in different ages.

But even within these categories there were major differences. The unofficial groups which used armed power against their governments in the age of dynasties — nobles and knights, cities and peasants — were very different from those that sought to do so in the age of religion — religious minorities — and different again from the political organisations which have mainly waged war in the age of ideology. There have been still more important differences between the kinds of government engaged in war in each of these different ages. In one society governments were dominated by autocratic rulers, concerned above all about personal power and dynastic rights, and undertaking war primarily to promote them; in another they have been dominated by groups of ministers concerned primarily with national ends, and undertaking wars to achieve those purposes. In one, in other words, the decisions have been primarily those of individuals, in another those of collective groups, reflecting the ambitions of those groups and the societies they served.

Again the difference is one of degree rather than of kind. There has been no age in which leaders have not been subject to some degree of influence from outside, and none in which more than a handful of individuals have taken part in decisions to make war. But in general it is true to say that in the first of our societies, single powerful individuals — primarily the dynasts themselves — played a more dominant role in determining such decisions than in more recent ages, when a wider range of influences at least, including those of parliaments, press and public opinion, have been brought to bear. In some ages the military have played a substantial part in influencing the actions of each unit; in others they have played far less. In some societies the attitude of the units towards each other has been highly competitive, and that competition has been seen largely in military terms, so that status has depended on military success (the age of dynasties and the age of sovereignty); while in others competition has been less intense, or at least has not been seen exclusively in terms of military power (the two most recent ages). In some international societies (especially in the age of sovereignty) the units have operated primarily in isolation, each seeking to promote its own interests against all others; while in others (especially the two ideological ages) they have been more inclined to group themselves into more or less stable alliances in competition with rival alliances. In some societies the only desired outcome has been total victory (again mainly the two ideological societies); in others there has been a willingness to consider more limited gains, secured through negotiated settlements (the age of sovereignty and, to a lesser extent, the age of nationalism). While some differences of this kind can be seen among different governments within the *same* society (some less influenced by public opinion, some more competitive, some more determined on total victory than others), there are even more clearly marked distinctions to be found between entire international societies, reflecting the different character of the units within each and of the conventions that govern their behaviour.

The most important distinction concerns the motives of the units in each age. Again fairly marked contrasts can be seen. In one age the main concern has been to secure territory or title for a ruling family; in another, to defend the right to practise a particular faith in a particular country or region, or to build up powerful states in competition with rivals, or to create states on the basis of the national principle, or to secure success for an ideological alliance. Each of these has determined a different form of competition, and therefore a different pattern of warfare. Where the concern has been primarily with the internal situation in other states (as during the two ages of ideology), warfare has more often taken the form of "war underhand", assistance to minority groups, attempts to overthrow governments, and intervention in civil wars. Where the objective has concerned the relative power or advantage of states (as in the ages of sovereignty and of nationalism), it has more often taken the form of large-scale inter-state warfare for territorial objectives. In other words, it is the motives of the units that control armed power that is the decisive factor. Different kinds of military action and different types of military capacity have been required to secure different types of ends. These differing motives of states in different periods will be examined in greater detail in Chapter 4. In this preliminary survey it is necessary only to note that it is this difference in motives more than any other factor which has determined the wide variations between ages in the kind of war occurring and its different outcomes (for example, territorial change in one age, political change in another).

Is there any correlation between the changes in the units wielding armed power in each age and the frequency of war? If there is a relationship, it is not easy to discern. We have noted the main trends in the frequency of war in each period (though also noting the pitfalls inherent in any such assessment). Overall it would seem that there has been a slight but steady reduction in frequency during the six centuries with which we have been concerned. The number of years in which an average country has been involved in war has declined fairly steadily over this time. Against this, however, must be set another trend: the hugely increasing scale and cost of wars, especially the largest of them, when they do occur. This has had the effect that the total casualties in the wars of this century are almost certainly several times higher than those of all the wars that took place in the five centuries before. It has been estimated that, over and above the 40 million or more lives lost in the Second World War, 20 million have been lost in war in the years since 1945. This would give a total approaching 80 million for the century as a whole. The increase in the destructiveness of weapons is particularly pronounced in the last few decades. And any future war in which presently available weapons were employed would (whether or not nuclear weapons were used) undoubtedly be far more costly still. Whatever satisfaction may be taken, therefore, from the small reduction that may have taken place in the frequency of war has to be set against the recognition that those wars which do occur are now far more lethal. With this huge increase in the capacity to kill, even one further war of the wrong sort could be more significant in its consequences than a hundred wars of lesser kinds in earlier periods.

In any case, the reduction in the overall propensity to war (which is not sufficiently marked to be very significant) conceals important variations among particular countries and groups. Among the most striking features of our survey is the huge variation it reveals in the geographical incidence of war. There has been, first, a considerable change over the past two centuries in the extent to which individual countries have become involved in war. For the first time in history a few states have been free from war altogether. Switzerland has known no external war for nearly two centuries, Sweden for almost as long. In Latin America, Venezuela and Costa Rica have known nearly a century virtually without foreign war (enabling the latter to dispense altogether with armed forces). Even more striking, however, have been the changes in the incidence of warfare among entire regions. For over a century there has been no war in North America north of the Rio Grande (and only one — the Mexican Civil War — in North America as a whole). For a similar period there has (except for the brief incursion by the Japanese in the Second World War) been almost no war in the South Pacific area (the only exceptions are the conflicts in West Irian and East Timor). Most startling of all has been the change that has come about in Europe, where there has been a virtual cessation of international warfare over the last 40 years and an end to any kind of warfare for nearly 30 years (from 1956). Given the scale and frequency of war during the preceding centuries in Europe, this is a change of spectacular proportions: perhaps the single most striking discontinuity that the history of warfare has anywhere provided. Though there are some obvious explanations which can be put forward to explain the change (pp. 295-9 below), it is one of such importance in the history of war that we shall need to return to it again when we consider our conclusions to this study.

Next, there is a significant variation in the distribution of power within the different international societies we have examined. Usually there have been one or two states enjoying a significantly greater level of power than other members of the society: in the age of dynasties the Ottoman Empire, and in its final stages Spain and France; in the following age Spain; in the age of sovereignty France, and later Russia and England; Britain and later Germany in the age of nationalism; the United States and the Soviet Union in the most recent period. In almost every society it has been these most powerful states which have become the most heavily engaged in war. This may have been partly because such states normally have the greatest prospect of success in war and therefore the greatest temptation to engage in it. But it seems to have had far more to do with the fact that power has frequently involved its holder in ever-increasing commitments, which have tended to expand faster than the power available to meet them. So, in the age of religion, Spain, despite the supremacy of her army, her access to the wealth of South America, and her huge assembly of taxable territories, found herself with responsibilities stretching from the Netherlands to Tunis, and Milan to Peru, responsibilities which she was eventually to find she was neither economically nor militarily capable of sustaining. So, in the succeeding period, France, though more powerful than any other state in the continent, found the conquests of Louis XIV, and still more those of Napoleon, more extensive than her armed strength was able to defend. So again Britain, though the ruler of the waves and of a vast overseas empire, found herself increasingly saddled with commitments all over the world which eventually (in and after the Second World War) it was beyond her capacity to maintain. Likewise Germany, with a power that far outbalanced any in the rest of Europe, yet deprived, in her eyes, of the status to go with it, twice found her ambitions greater than her power. And so equally today, the United States and the Soviet Union alike, each determined to be able to respond to developments in any part of the world, however remote, which they see as a potential threat to their security, and to match the armed power of the other, have undertaken responsibilities they find increasingly difficult to fulfil.

Against these most powerful states, often seen as the principal threat, medium and smaller states have been inclined to band together to maintain their independence and integrity. This process of combination against the powerful is a phenomenon visible in each of the societies we have examined (pp. 282-307 below). In most ages that process has finally succeeded in taming the excessive dominance of the major power: as French-led coalitions weakened and destroyed the power of Spain (in 1648 and 1678*); as English-led coalitions twice defeated France (in 1713 and 1815); as the coalitions of the United States, Russia, Britain and France defeated Germany (also twice, in 1918 and 1945). In other ages something more like a direct balance between two powers has been achieved; as with France and Spain in the early sixteenth century, or the United States and the Soviet Union today. Occasionally similar balances operate at the regional level: as between Sweden and Denmark in the age of sovereignty, Russia and Austria in the age of nationalism, Iraq and Iran in the contemporary world. Such balances, however, while often preventing domination by a single power, have not prevented war. On the contrary, war has usually been seen as the means of preserving the balance.

There have also been differences in the kind of alliance system employed in each of these societies. This too has affected the character of war in each. Sometimes alliances have been short term and opportunistic, created in the interest of immediate national advantage (as in the age of sovereignty, when they were reshuffled almost from year to year). In others, though constantly changed, they have been more deliberately established with a view to balancing the greatest threat to peace at the time (as at the end of the age of dynasties — see pp. 282-3 below). In others again they have been still more stable, being often based on ideological sympathies, and directed towards containing the threat a rival alliance is thought to pose (as between 1904 and 1914, or after 1949). Each of these types of alliance system reflects, and in turn influences, the structure of the society concerned and the kind of wars conducted within it.

There is no clear trend affecting the length of wars in each age. In all the societies examined here there have been some short wars (a year or less) and some long ones (ten years or more). Very short wars (two months and less) have been virtually confined to the last century or so, since it is only in this period that mobility has been sufficient to allow the type of lightning military campaign required. The average length of international wars has, for this reason, probably declined somewhat. But the variations between the longest and the shortest remain so large that no clear-cut trend can be established.

Similarly, there is no evidence in our survey that there is any periodicity affecting the outbreak of major wars. It is indeed difficult to see why it should ever have been believed that any such regularity

---

* The earlier war continued until 1659, but Spain's power was effectively broken when she made peace with the United Provinces and other states in 1648.

might exist.* There seems no good reason to predict it, nor is it visible in the pattern of history. Wars in the age of sovereignty, though very frequent, occurred according to no discernible pattern. In the age of nationalism, the international wars involving the major powers were bunched together in the short space of 25 years (1853-78), flanked by two long periods of relative peace. And in recent times the 20-year gap between the two greatest wars has not been repeated in any other period, either before or since. Whatever does determine the outbreak of wars, therefore, it does not seem to be influenced, in some semi-automatic fashion, as sometimes suggested, by the clock of history.

Finally, the technology of war too does not seem to have a decisive impact on the number or character of the wars which occur. A consistent increase in the destructive power of weapons has affected the way in which wars have been fought but not the occurrence of war itself. The replacement of bow and arrow and armoured horsemen by arquebus and infantry, or of the musket by the rifle, or of wooden sailing ships by iron-clad, had no discernible impact on the willingness of rulers to make war on each other. The same is true for the more dramatic technical advances of recent times. Horror at the

---

* Wright suggested that the 50-year cycle he believed he had discovered might be related to the longer (Kondratieff) economic cycle. "If the international system exerted a persistent pressure towards war and if the economic and technological period necessary to recover from a severe war and to prepare for another were identical with the psychological and political period necessary to efface the anti-war sentiment after such a war and to restore national morale", this could account for a 50-year cycle. With the progress of civilisation, the periods of economic and political recovery should tend to "become identical at some duration of less than two generations" (*A Study of War*, pp. 231-2). These arguments (formulated before the Second World War, which suggested to others a shorter, 20-year cycle) are not persuasive. While for a single nation some period of recovery is likely to be necessary after a war, it is unlikely (as a number of historical examples would indicate) that this is more than five years or so; and even this would not affect the frequency of wars involving other states. Singer and Small suggest that the periodicity they believed they found in wars in progress might result from "systematic changes in (a) the size of wartime partnerships, (b) the duration of wars and (c) the interval between war onsets. . . . Even if none of these factors shows any individual periodicity it is nevertheless possible that the frequency distributions of all three could account for the periodicity in the amount of war under way" (Singer and Small, *The Wages of War*, p. 156). It would however require a remarkable degree of chance for these to bring about a consistent periodicity; in general these factors seem even less plausible than those mentioned by Wright as an explanation of believed regularities in amounts of war.

Neither Sorokin, nor Richardson, both of whom examined the question carefully, found any evidence of periodicity.

consequences of the use of gas in the First World War ensured that it was not used in subsequent major wars; but it did not (any more than the development of bomber aircraft, more powerful bombs, or experiments with missiles and nuclear arms) deter the launching of the Second World War. The development and use of nuclear weapons in that war has likewise not prevented the frequent waging of war in subsequent years, even against nations equipped with such weapons. This suggests only the not surprising conclusion that governments make use of those weapons appropriate to the purposes they have in mind. Like duellists, they will always choose the weapons that will, they believe, cause the maximum damage to their opponents at the least possible risk to themselves: which are not necessarily the most dangerous. Though more powerful weapons may cause governments to behave somewhat more cautiously, especially in their dealings with other governments having similar capabilities, they certainly have not had the effect of banishing warfare by or against the nations that possess them. What they cause is the adoption of different strategies.

Thus, of the various factors we have considered, the one that appears to have the greatest impact on the character of war in different societies is the changing character of the units in each society; and above all the changing motives which inspire these. In each age different kinds of state or ruling elite seek different advantages and assets in their dealings with other states, and choose different types and methods of war to achieve them. Because of these changes in motives, the issues about which wars are fought also change radically from one age to another. And it is to the changing nature of these issues that we now turn.

3 Issues

What have wars been fought about? What, that is, have been the issues which nations have believed were important enough to be worth going to war for in each of our different periods? Have they been similar in all ages, or have they varied radically over time?

If the word were defined in sufficiently general terms, it would not be difficult to show that the "issues" about which wars have been fought have been the same throughout history: conflicts of national interest; mutually incompatible objectives; rivalry for power, status or influence. Conversely, the more specific the definition used, the more unique are the issues over which particular wars have been fought: for example, only one war has been fought about Jenkin's Ear (if that). There is probably little that can usefully be said about issues if interpreted in either of these extreme ways. Issues of the first type are so general and so interchangeable that almost all wars could be shown to be alike; issues of the second type so particular that almost no useful general conclusions can be drawn about them.

We shall be concerned therefore with issues at a middle level: specific enough to distinguish one war from another, but not so specific as to relate only to one or two conflicts each. Even then there are considerable difficulties about classifying wars in this way. First, few wars are fought about one specific issue: usually they are fought about a number, of varying degrees of immediacy and importance. Secondly, the issues over which a war is fought are not necessarily identical in the eyes of both or all the combatants: even allies on the same side may believe themselves to be fighting about dfferent things — still more so those fighting against each other. Thirdly, the issues may change over time: the issues that seem important at the end of a war may be quite different from those that were important at the beginning. Finally, the issues involved in different wars, even if they can be identified, may be so heterogeneous that they cannot easily be compared with each other: some short-term and some long-term; some political, some economic; some related to general principles (the restoration of the balance of power, resistance to aggression), and some to immediate interests (the recovery of a lost territory, the humiliation of a particular rival); some related to one enemy, some to all.

These are real difficulties (and they perhaps partly account for the surprising fact that so little of the extensive writing about war has been concerned with the issues about which wars have been fought). They are not, however, sufficiently serious to make a study of this question either impossible or valueless. For most wars there is usually a fair measure of consensus concerning what were the most important issues. It is not usually difficult to establish at least what the main contestants on either side believed the issues to be (and it is what nations *thought* they were fighting about which is most important for our purpose). Though there may have been changes in objectives and perceptions, it is the issues at the time war was declared that are most significant. And, though there are real difficulties in distinguishing between types of issue (immediate and underlying, short-term and long-term), so long as that difficulty is continually borne in mind it is not one that is insoluble: in general in this chapter we shall be concerned with the more immediate and short-term issues — as against the more long-term conflicts of objective and interest, which we shall be considering in the next chapter.

It should be made clear that in neither chapter is there any attempt to identify the "causes" of war: either of particular wars or of war in general. The search for "causes" is a highly ambitious quest, which the present study does not presume to undertake. The assumption that a war — still more, war in general — has identifiable causes itself begs a fair number of questions. It would be nice to believe that, with adequate research, diligence and insight, it might be possible to show, beyond possibility of doubt, that a particular war has been "caused" by particular actions, persons or groups of persons, by one nation rather than another; by aggressiveness, pride or insecurity; or by a particular set of circumstances which could have had no other outcome. But there seems no reason to believe that the causes of any war — let alone of war in general — can be neatly labelled in that way. The word "cause" itself can have a wide range of meanings, ranging from the most immediate and proximate origin (such as the declaration of war itself) to the most remote and indirectly related set of conditions which may ultimately have contributed to the emergence of conflict (such as the existence of a system of separate states, each disposing of armed power). Thus the total number of "causes" — that is, of factors which may have contributed, directly or indirectly, to the eventual precipitation of war, ranging from the most immediate to the most general — is almost infinite (as the many billions of words about the causes of the First World War — often arriving at totally different conclusions — would indicate).

The search for "causes", even of particular wars, therefore, would seem an unprofitable one: still more the search for the causes of war in general, such as some writers have sought to produce (whether they find the answer in the struggle for "power" among states, economic competition, territorial rivalry, class struggle, the psychology of individual rulers or ruling classes, the demand of armed forces for the chance to exercise their skills, pressures of population, desire for adventure or martial exhilaration, to mention only a few favourite solutions). The total number of separate factors which may contribute to the making of war — and which therefore could be classified as "causes" — are so numerous and so complex that it may well be as meaningless to talk of the "causes" of war as to talk about the "causes" of murder, quarrelling, or conflict in general.

Rather than pursuing any such will-o'-the-wisp therefore, the aim here is rather to help improve knowledge, and so possibly *understanding*, of the use of war by states. One small part of that endeavour is an examination of the issues about which wars have been fought.

The age of dynasties (1400-1559)

The issues which principally gave rise to war in the first of our international societies were inevitably the issues of concern to personal rulers in an age of dynastic competition. Some stemmed from the feudal or semi-feudal relationships which still persisted in that age. These relationships, resting on custom rather than power, were of a type which easily gave rise to conflict, both within states and between them.

One such issue concerned allegiance. During the Hundred Years War the rulers of England and France were concerned less with the direct control or administration of the territory for which they fought than with the theoretical right of overlordship: who owed allegiance to whom and for which territories? Thus in the negotiations of 1415 and again in 1435-6, the English negotiators were willing to accept effective French control of most of the areas in dispute so long as the French king was willing to do homage for them to the English ruler: a condition the French negotiators would not accept. Conversely, Henry V would have been willing in 1415 to abandon his claims to the French throne if he were accorded full sovereignty in some of the most valuable provinces of France — Normandy, Flanders, Maine, Anjou and Touraine (in addition to Guienne, of which he already had sovereignty). In the series of wars between Poland-Lithuania and the Teutonic Order the main point at issue for much of the time was the demand that the latter should do homage to the Polish king for the territory it controlled: thus on his defeat in 1466, the grand master of the Order was obliged to do homage to the king of Poland-Lithuania for East Prussia and to agree to sit on the left side of the Polish king in the Polish diet. One of the issues between the rulers of Burgundy and the French kings concerned the duty of the former to pay homage to the king of France for their territory (given to their ancestor by John II as an apanage). Allegiance was also an issue in the long duel between the houses of Hapsburg and Valois: Francis I provoked conflict by calling on Charles V, who owed him allegiance for Flanders and Artois, to join him in war against his own grandfather, Maximilian, in 1513 (Charles, aged 13, declined). Conversely, in the war of 1521-5, Charles wanted Francis to do homage for Milan. And in all the domestic wars between the rulers and the great magnates, so common in every state, allegiance — and what it implied — was the main issue at stake.

Somewhat similar were issues relating to personal honour. Just as a knight might challenge in a tournament another that had done him dishonour, so would one ruler challenge another for the same reason, or demand reparation for any act regarded as an affront. Charles V (himself skilled in the tournament) told the pope in 1536 that he would undertake single combat with the French king to demonstrate the justice of his cause; and a few months later war between the two was resumed. Henry VIII was said by Pope Clement VII to have joined the war against France in 1522 "to revenge himself for the slights he has received from the king of France and from the Scots, and to punish the king of France for his disparaging language".[1] And he made war against Scotland in 1542 on the grounds that James V, by refusing to meet him in York to discuss differences, had defied him and challenged the suzerain rights he claimed in Scotland. An injury to a king's envoy could be seen as especially insulting and so as requiring reparation. In 1541 Francis I made the murder of a French diplomat travelling in the Milanese (where he should have been under the emperor's protection) the occasion for the war he launched against the emperor later that year. In this spirit heralds were sent from one ruler to another to "bid defiance": as when the English herald Clarencieux was sent by Henry VIII to the Spanish court in Burgos to declare war on the emperor in January 1528.

Another issue stemming from the traditions and preoccupations of a dynastic age was royal succession. A number of the longest and most bitter conflicts of the era were, as we saw in the last chapter, fought over such questions: the 120-year war between the English and French kings over the right to the French throne; the repeated conflicts between the houses of Anjou and Aragon over Naples; the successive wars fought by the French king for Naples and Milan between 1494 and 1559; the struggle between the kings of Bohemia and Hungary for succession in Bohemia in 1468-78; the struggles for the throne of Castile in 1467-74 and 1475-9; the campaigns fought by the Danish royal house for Sweden; and the wars between the rival Ernestine and Albertine lines of the Wettin family in Saxony, or between Yorkists and Lancastrians in England. In an age in which the right to title and territory was so prized, wars on the question were almost inevitable. The immediate issues in dispute in such wars were of many kinds. Could succession pass through the female line (whether or not a woman could herself succeed)? This was the main difference between the English and French kings in the Hundred Years War. Could a brother inherit before a son or other descendants in the direct line? This was the issue in a number of the wars of the age. Could a mother inherit from a son, as Margaret of Denmark claimed to do in Denmark and Norway in 1387? Could a son born posthumously inherit, as a Hapsburg prince was allowed to do in Austria in 1440 but not allowed to do in Hungary at the same time? Should a bastard be excluded (leading to war against Ferrante of Naples in 1458, Joanna of Castile in 1467-9, and John, son of Matthias Corvinus in Hungary)? Could a fiefdom be inherited through the female line, or did it revert to its overlord? This was the issue between Francis I and Charles V in the case of Milan. Had the descendant of a former ruling family a better claim than the indirect descendant of the current one? This was the question at issue between Angevins and Aragon in Naples. Could the children of a second wife, married bigamously, inherit: the issue between Ladislaw, ruler of Bohemia-Hungary, and his rivals in the 1480s.*

These are only examples of the kinds of conflict over rules of succession which could easily arise in a dynastic age. There were no universally accepted answers to such questions. The rules were often subject to doubt even in a single state. For example, the Lancastrians in England sought to maintain that succession through the female line was impossible in England, and passed an act of parliament to establish the fact: one reason why Henry VIII was so anxious to have a male heir was that he feared that, on this ground, his daughter Mary's right of succession could be challenged. It is not surprising, then, that disputes about succession could often lead to war. Such disputes were not simply the justification for demands for territory desired on other grounds. Beliefs on either side were passionately held because they concerned the central issue of the day: the legitimate *right* to rule. The demand for territory, and the succeeding war, resulted from, rather than caused, the disputed claim.

The importance attached to succession had the effect that the marriage of heirs and heiresses could be another vitally important issue. Since marriage was the main means of acquiring possessions elsewhere, it was often itself the price demanded in war. So one of the issues between England and France before war was resumed in

---

* Ladislaw married the widow of Matthias Corvinus, whom he had conquered, while his first wife, Barbara (whom he had never seen) was still alive: the pope eventually released him from both marriages, enabling him to take yet another wife.

1415 was the demand that the French king should give his daughter, with a substantial dowry, in marriage to Henry V. Marriage in many cases was imposed by force. This might be done by the subjects of a ruler, as when the nobles of Hungary sought to compel Elizabeth, widow of Albert II, to marry Ladislas, king of Poland, against her will; or when the people of Burgundy compelled Mary, daughter of Charles the Bold, to marry Maximilian, son of Emperor Frederick III, after her father died. Alternatively, the marriage might be forced by a conquering power. Thus Henry V in 1420 secured by his victory the marriage he had been unable to secure through negotiation. Similarly, Louis XI made Maximilian I, under the treaty of Arras of 1482, agree to send his only daughter (aged three) to France as the intended bride of the *dauphin*. So too the *dauphin* himself, having become Charles VIII, after invading Brittany in 1492, compelled Anne of Brittany to marry him (even though she was already married — by proxy — to the Emperor Maximilian and even though he himself was betrothed to that emperor's daughter). Again, Francis I, after his victory at Marignano, imposed on Charles V his daughter Charlotte (aged one). So he himself, after his defeat and capture at Pavia in 1525, was obliged, as part of the peace settlement, to marry Charles V's sister Eleanore. Henry VIII sought, by his war against Scotland in 1544-7, to enforce the marriage of the infant Mary Stuart to his son Edward. But such imposed marriages could often only provoke further conflict and violence. Thus Elizabeth of Hungary launched a war to prevent the union of herself and her kingdom with Poland, which Hungarian nobles had tried to force on her in 1440; the people of Brittany rose up against the French the year after their duchess was forcibly married; and Francis I, though he duly married the Hapsburg princess who was imposed on him, continued to fight successive wars against her father, the emperor. War in other words, could produce a bride, but not necessarily an equally submissive territory. And this in turn produced new wars.

Wars on this question were not prevented by the fact that in large parts of Europe a ruler's succession was dependent on the consent of his estates or parliament. About half the kings of the continent were elected, sometimes or always. In Poland, Bohemia and Hungary the kings were for most of this period elected by estates or diet (even if the diet sometimes elected the son of a previous ruler). The masters of the Teutonic Order, controlling Prussia, and of the Livonian Order, controlling Livonia and Estonia, were both elected. In Denmark and Sweden succession was dependent on at least the approval of the diet (often given only in return for a limitation of the powers of the new monarch, especially in relation to the taxation of the nobility). In Portugal the kings were sometimes elected or chosen by the nobles (for example in 1383). In Aragon the states had sometimes to make a choice between potential claimants: in 1412 a committee representing the *cortes* of the three provinces was established and chose, among several contestants, Ferdinand Trastamar (despite the fact that his claim came through the female line). Finally, the popes and Holy Roman emperors, the most important potentates of the day, were always elected. But elections could become the subject of dispute as much as inheritance. Thus in 1410-11, three emperors, each claiming the support of different electors, competed for the throne. The election of Ladislas, son of Casimir of Poland, to the Bohemian throne in 1471 did not prevent Matthias Corvinus of Hungary from persisting in his war to secure the throne for himself. The decision of the Swedish diet to end the union with Denmark and to elect their own king (in 1448 and again in 1467) did not prevent successive Danish kings from continuing to make war to assert their claims by force. The elections of Polish kings frequently caused conflict and occasionally war (for example in 1588). In other words, even where it did not depend on rights or inheritance, succession could still be an issue about which wars were fought.

Succession to a foreign throne was especially likely to lead to conflict. Usually, in this age, when a ruler succeeded to a throne elsewhere it was a "union of the crowns" only that resulted. This meant there was no attempt to impose the laws, customs or institutions of one state upon another. Language, culture, laws and political institutions remained largely unaffected. Of this kind were, for example, the unions between Lithuania and Poland (1387); between Denmark, Sweden and Norway (1397); between Aragon and Catalonia (1150); between these two and Valencia (1238); between these three and Castile (1479); between England and Ireland (1155*); between England and Wales (1284); between the 17 duchies and counties assembled by the dukes of Burgundy; between the Hapsburg duchies of Austria, Styria, Carinthia, Carniola and Tyrol; and later between these and Hungary and Bohemia (themselves joined in 1490). The looseness of these unions may have made them for a time more acceptable to each party; but it also made them more subject to dissolution later. A number of wars in this period resulted when one party to such an artificial union attempted to break away from it: as Wales did from England in 1402-9; as France did from England from the time the union was created in 1422; as Sweden did from Denmark

---

* This is the date when the pope conferred the kingship of Ireland on Henry II. In 1171 Henry crossed to Ireland to assert his supremacy and receive the allegiance of the Irish lords. English law was extended to Ireland in 1495 and the Irish parliament accepted the English king's supremacy in 1541. It became an integral part of the UK only in 1800. Since the union was to be broken by war 120 years after that, this is a typical example of an enforced union that led ultimately to war.

in successive wars from 1448 onwards; as Catalonia did from Aragon in 1462-72; as Bohemia and Hungary did from Austria in 1457; and so on. The slow growth of national sentiment meant that dynastic unions often became increasingly unacceptable and so eventually only precipitated further conflict. In a dynastic age wars to unmake states created by unnatural accretion were almost as common as wars to make them by imposed succession.

Only rarely did territory become an issue for its own sake, and almost regardless of claims of succession. The territory that lay immediately between two states was especially liable to be coveted by both. So wars were fought between French and Spanish rulers over Navarre in 1512 and 1521 (eventually they partitioned it between them); over Cerdagne and Roussillon (passed backwards and forwards several times before finally passing to France in 1659); for Burgundy in 1479-82 and subsequent wars (lost by Spain in 1482 but not finally relinquished until 1559); and over Flanders and Artois in 1521-5 and later wars (to remain in dispute for another century). In the same way England and France fought over Calais, England's gateway to the continent, which she only finally abandoned in 1559. The five main Italian states fought for the control of the small states which lay between them: Venice and Milan for Verona and Padua; Venice, Florence and the pope for Ferrara; Venice and Naples for Brindisi and the ports of Apulia; Naples and the Papacy for the Romagna. Poland and the Teutonic Order fought in six wars (in 1409-11, 1413-22, 1434-5, 1454-66, 1512-14 and 1519-22) for ultimate control of Prussia; Poland and Muscovy in their wars of 1492-4, 1507-8, 1512-22 and 1534-7 for the Ukraine; Spain and the Turks for North Africa.

Territorial conflict of this kind was made more likely when there was genuine reason to doubt who possessed legitimate authority. This was so in many areas. The idea of absolute sovereignty barely existed at this time. In most places it was taken for granted that authority was shared, with day-to-day power enjoyed by a local lord in turn owing allegiance to an overlord, who had ultimate rights but little effective control. This meant that sovereignty was often ambiguous. Even within states this ambiguity could be the cause of war. Many of the civil wars of the age resulted from conflicts of authority between rulers and their subjects: as between the French kings and the dukes of Bourbon, Brittany and Burgundy; between the archbishop of Cologne and the cities in the surrounding areas; between the bishop of Liège and his city; between Lancastrian kings and Yorkist nobles; between Charles V and the Spanish *comuneros* who disputed the degree of authority he claimed within their towns. But the lack of clear-cut sovereignty was also the cause of war between states. Often there was genuine cause for disagreement and dispute. What was the right which Danish kings enjoyed in Sweden or Norway (the subject of wars in 1464, 1467, 1470-1, 1496-7 and 1517-23)? What degree of authority did the emperor enjoy in Switzerland and northern Italy, both formerly parts of the Empire (the subject of wars in 1401-2, 1404-8 and 1442-50)? What was the meaning of the "suzerainty" claimed by the Turks in Transylvania, Wallachia and Moldavia (this last the vassal sometimes to the king of Hungary, sometimes to that of Poland, sometimes to the Turkish sultan, and occasionally to all at once)? What kind of authority did the Teutonic Order enjoy in Prussia; the Knights of the Sword in Livonia; or the Knights of St John in Rhodes, Tripoli or Malta? What kind of authority did the popes enjoy, as they claimed, over these crusading orders; or in Naples, which they held to be a papal fief? What rights did the Crimean or Kazan Tartars enjoy in the places they temporarily occupied? All of these were the subject of conflict and often of war. Because the idea of a sovereignty that was clear-cut and exclusive had not yet emerged, the exact rights enjoyed by particular rulers in particular places was often uncertain. And, because they were thus the subject of legitimate dispute, they were inevitably a frequent cause of war.

Another issue that could be the cause of war was the question of religion. The traditional type of war on this subject, the crusades of Christians against the forces of Islam controlling the holy places, no longer took place. The last genuine crusade was that to Nicopolis, which took place just before the period began (1396). There continued to be many wars between Christians and Moslems, but they were not true wars of religion. The wars which took place between the Turks and the states they invaded or threatened, between the Catholic kings of Spain and the Moors in the south of their country, between the Emperor Charles V and the states of North Africa, or between his brother Ferdinand and the Ottoman possessions in the east, though often claimed as "crusades", were not primarily wars for and against a particular faith, but wars for territory. The Order of St John fought to defend its bases in Rhodes and Tripoli, not to drive the Turks away from the Holy Land. The campaigns of the Teutonic Order against the Lithuanians were not wars of conversion: the Lithuanians had already been converted. The true wars of religion were now those between Christian and Christian. So the crusades which were truly well supported were those mounted between 1420 and 1435 against the Hussites (Cardinal Beaufort, the uncle of the English king, even took time off from the Hundred Years War for the purpose, though, when a crisis arose in France, he prudently diverted the crusading troops to that campaign instead). That war genuinely did concern religious beliefs and practices; and its main result was that the Hussites secured for themselves, uniquely, the acknowledged right to take the communion in both kinds, a demand hitherto regarded as heretical. Another inter-Christian war was that waged by Matthias Corvinus of Hungary in 1468 against the Bohemian king, allegedly to oppose his support for heretical Hussite practices. Ivan the Great made war against the king of Poland-Lithuania in 1500 because of the support the latter had given to a union between the Greek orthodox and Russian churches and his alleged attempt to convert his Russian queen to the Roman faith. But it was above all from 1520 onwards, with the renewed demands for reform made by Luther, Melancthon, Zwingli and Calvin, and the contrary campaign to oppose them these provoked, that religious war in Europe — again between Christian and Christian — broke out in earnest. The conflicts of 1546-7 and 1552-5 in Germany foreshadowed the armed struggle between protestants and Catholics which was to dominate European politics for most of the following century. Differences in belief among Christians had now replaced differences between Christian and Moslem as the issue about which many wars were fought.

Economic issues too were sometimes a significant source of conflict. These were not often in this age the main questions in dispute among rulers. The war between the Hanse towns and Denmark in 1426-35 did mainly concern the demands of the king of Denmark for a new toll on ships passing through the Sound; and that between the same towns and England in 1468-74 resulted from a long dispute concerning the trading rights which each should enjoy in the territory of the other. The war between France and Spain in 1502-4 was sparked off by a dispute concerning the division of the economic spoils both had acquired in conquering Naples the year before. Lübeck and the Netherlands fought about trading rights in the Baltic in 1534-6. But more often economic factors were an additional issue, exacerbating a conflict that had occurred mainly about some other question. Thus the wars between Venice and the Turks were intensified by conflicts concerning Venice's trade through the Levant and the eastern Mediterranean; those between Poland-Lithuania and Muscovy by disputes concerning trade through the Baltic. For the most part, and for most states (though the Hanse towns were always an exception), economic contacts with other countries were not yet of sufficient importance to make them a major issue in most of the wars of the period.

The immediate disputes over which wars broke out in this age were thus in many cases typical of the concerns and preoccupations of a semi-feudal age. They included affronts to the honour of one ruler by another; rights to succession, whether by birth or election; disputes over royal marriages, projected or desired. Many other conflicts arose from the universal concern over dynastic rights. One effect was that territorial disputes at this time often concerned territories which were geographically and culturally remote, usually of little strategic or economic benefit to the rulers who claimed them but happened to become subject to a dynastic claim. Only towards the end of the period, as the kingdoms gradually acquired more of the character of organised states, did this begin to change. Some of the issues that led to war then came to be those related to the concerns and ambitions of states, as much as those of personal rulers: territories believed to be of special strategic value, attempts to round frontiers or join disconnected fragments of territories, or to secure commercial privileges elsewhere.

The issues that led to war, therefore, in this as in later times, directly reflected the social structure and prevalent ideology of the age. They were typical of a particular kind of international society and reflected its characteristic traditions and beliefs.

The age of religions (1559-1648)

In the age that followed there was a change in the issues about which wars were mainly fought. Overwhelmingly the most important single issue was now religion. Nearly half the international wars and over half the civil wars of the age were fought mainly or partly about that question (see Tables 3 and 4).

But wars occurred over particular aspects only. The detailed issues about which individuals mainly disputed were not usually the subject of wars, either within or between states. The questions about which contending churchmen showed such passionate concern — transsubstantiation; predestination; the relative importance of faith or works; the right of the laity to receive the communion in both kinds; indulgences, clerical fees and clerical immunity; plurality and non-residence; the veneration of the Virgin; the place of ritual, images, music and incense in worship; the role of the pope, of bishops and of the clergy as a whole — these were not the questions about which the wars of the period were contested (perhaps the only exception is the war in Cologne in 1583-9, which was fought, at least in the eyes of some, about the right of the clergy to marry).

By far the most important single issue on which wars were fought concerned whether, and if so where, a particular faith could be practised. In most places the prevailing ideology rejected toleration. The general belief was that in each state there could be only one religion: as French Catholics declared, "un roi, une loi, une foi". Minorities therefore, everywhere under threat, had to fight for the right to practise their own beliefs. So in France the Huguenots fought eight wars for the right to worship as they chose. In the Netherlands the Calvinists, a small minority when the period began, fought for nearly 80 years (1572-1648) to safeguard the same right (a right which, as soon as they had won the ascendancy, they denied equally fiercely to Catholics). Catholics fought for their faith in Scotland (1567), England (1569) and Ireland (1579-80), as protestants did in Bohemia and Austria (1618-26), and both in different parts of Germany. Since there could be no sharing of rights, the contest was a zero-sum game. Everywhere the central issue was: which faith should prevail? Of the principal civil wars of the age, 26 concerned religion (see Table 3).

But it was not only an issue in domestic conflicts. The rulers, often themselves passionate upholders of a particular faith, were deeply concerned about the outcome of religious struggles elsewhere and felt it their duty to seek to affect the outcome. Thus a number of the most important *international* wars were about the same question. Philip II intervened on behalf of the Catholics in France, and planned the conquest of England, at least in part for the same reason; Elizabeth intervened on behalf of protestants in France, Scotland and the Netherlands, as Christian IV of Denmark and Gustav Adolph of Sweden did on their behalf in Germany. Though often religion was not the only reason for intervention (p. 148-9 below), the desire to help fellow believers in other lands provided the initial inspiration and subsequent justification for war. Of the international wars in Europe, 25 were concerned mainly or partly with religious issues (see Table 4). Among Moslem states the same factor was important. Turkey's four wars with Persia were intensified by the conflict between the Sunni and Shia faiths; and, because of their Sunni persuasion, Persia found it difficult to win allies among the Central Asian states which she was contesting with the Ottomans.[2]

The conflict concerning religion promoted conflicts concerning territory: who should control a particular area. Since it was almost everywhere assumed that the ruler who governed a land could also control its religion (a principle explicitly endorsed in the peace of Augsburg at the end of the previous period, and similar to that enunciated even earlier at the diet of Speyer of 1526), the best way to assure the practice of a particular faith in any one area was to secure power for one's own side there. In Scotland, Catholics and protestants fought to win control of the throne to ensure that the land as a whole should be of their own faith. Frederick the elector Palatine, and Ferdinand of Austria fought for Bohemia and neighbouring territories to ensure that it was their own religion and not the other's that should be practised there. In the Netherlands the ultimate issue for both sides was how great would be the area which each should control and in which therefore their own faith would be practised. In Germany, both in the conflicts of particular states and in those of cities (such as those of Cologne, Donauwörth and Cleves-Jülich), and in the more general war of 1618-48, the fundamental issue concerned the boundaries that would be established between the protestant and Catholic parts of Germany. Religious and political aims were thus closely related: the contest to be king of the castle would also determine who would be ruler of the church. And a war to win political control (for example, by Spain in the Netherlands or by Sweden in Germany) could for that reason always be given a wider and nobler justification.

Because the ruler could normally control the religion that would be practised, the religious contest became intertwined with another traditional issue: the competition of dynasties. Philip II, intervening in France largely for religious reasons, put forward claims to the French throne for his daughter which made the issue partly a dynastic one. His concern for the Catholic religion in England made him a supporter of Mary Stuart's claim to its throne: a claim which she in turn, for the same reason, bequeathed to him. State interests sometimes indeed became a more pressing concern than those of religion. France, in her competition with her Hapsburg rivals, was willing to make herself a champion of the protestant cause in Germany. Sweden, in intervening in the Thirty Years War in support of the protestants, sought to promote Swedish interests in the Baltic in a way which aroused even protestant German states against her. Since often it was only by political means that the religious cause elsewhere could be promoted, it was inevitable that religious and political issues became in this way closely interconnected (p. 149-50 below).

Religious conflict could also raise a more mundane question: the control of property. In many places, and above all in Germany, religious wars were concerned as much as anything with the right to church property. The dispute on this question in Germany, and the apparent compromise reached in 1555, remained a major source of conflict for the next 75 years (the issue was not a purely material one: the transfer of secularised lands from one faith to another could also cause many to be reconverted at the same time). The war in Cologne in 1583-9 was concerned fundamentally with the right of an archbishop who had changed faith to retain his ecclesiastical state and property, a right the peace of Augsburg had denied (though the war was also important because, like that in Bohemia 35 years later, it could determine the balance in the electoral college). Denmark entered the Thirty Years War at least as much to seize secularised church property in Germany as to help spread the practice of the protestant faith. Brandenburg and Saxony, which had refused to lift a finger to assist the cause of the protestants in Bohemia, were finally willing to do so to resist the emperor's claim to re-acquire secularised property for the Catholic church. And, when negotiations for the end of the war began in 1642-3, the most bitterly contested point of all was the date to be chosen as the terminal point for recognised secularisation: a date that would determine the disposition of large quantities of church property and land.

But not all the issues about which wars were fought were related to religion. Territory remained an important source of conflict, even where no religious competition was involved. Wars were now not often fought, as they had been in the preceding age, to promote claims to relatively distant territories (like England's in France, that of Naples to Hungary, France's in Italy in that period). For the most part it was now territories that lay immediately adjoining two powers that were contested between them. So Spain and France, having concluded their long battle for Italy, began to struggle for the areas on their borders: Roussillon, Artois, Flanders and Alsace (in the wars of 1594-8 and 1635-59). So too Sweden, Russia and Poland competed for the Baltic territories that adjoined them: especially Livonia and Estonia (in the wars of 1558-81, 1563-70, 1600-29, 1632-5). Sweden and Denmark competed for the Baltic islands, for parts of Norway, for Alfsborg and Lapland (in the wars of 1563-70, 1611-13 and 1643-5). Sweden and Brandenburg competed for Pomerania (in 1635-41). Spain and Turkey fought to dominate the areas between them: North Africa, Malta and the western Mediterranean. Turkey and the Holy Roman Empire fought for control of Hungary; Turkey and Venice battled for Cyprus and Crete.

Territorial conflicts were inevitably, once again, most acute in areas where existing sovereignty was weakest or most ambiguous. The concept of sovereignty had still scarcely emerged, and in large parts of Europe the exact rights enjoyed by whom in which area remained questionable. The precise nature of the authority enjoyed by the Holy Roman emperor over those parts of Germany outside his patrimonial lands was one of the underlying issues in the Thirty Years War. The questionable authority enjoyed by the Teutonic Order in Livonia and Estonia, rapidly disintegrating at the beginning of this period, encouraged the long war between Sweden, Poland and Russia (1558-81), and for a time Brandenburg, to inherit the areas the Order had controlled. The semi-autonomous status of Transylvania, Moldavia and Wallachia led to war with their nominal overlord, the Ottoman sultan (for example in 1595); to wars between themselves (in 1599-1600); and wars between themselves and outside powers, such as the Hapsburg Empire and Poland (in 1618-25). "Suzerainty" was in Transylvania for a time even shared (between the Ottoman sultan and the Empire), leading to still greater ambiguity, and to six wars there between 1595 and 1645. The Cossacks, recognising no clear sovereignty and offering their allegiance at different times to the prince of Transylvania, the king of Sweden and even the sultan of Turkey, both initiated and invited military attacks. The Knights of St

John in Malta, accepting no authority but the pope's (and this only when it suited them so that, for example, they long resisted his efforts to get them to abandon piracy[3]), represented a tempting target for Turkey (1565). The tenuous suzerainty exercised by Turkey over the North African states led to conflict and uncertainty, allowing them effective freedom of action against Christian powers, while leaving uncertain the degree of support they would receive from their over-lords when they themselves were attacked. In an age when territorial competition remained intense, uncertainties of this kind often in-creased the risk of conflict.

Rights of succession remained another important source of con-flict. Such disputes were now often stimulated or exacerbated by the all-pervasive concern with religion: for example, in the case of Philip II's attempt to secure succession for himself in England (offering his hand to Elizabeth almost as soon as her sister — his previous wife — was dead) and for his daughter in France — claims put forward almost as much for the Catholic church as for himself; in the case of the Cleves-Jülich conflicts of 1609-14; and in that of the Polish king's fight to regain the Swedish crown (1600-29). Religion could harm as well as assist a claim: it helped prevent Mary Stuart from retaining the throne of Scotland, and the Polish king Sigismund from acquiring that of Russia (either for himself or his son) in 1608-12, and that of Sweden in 1600-29. In other cases succession conflicts were intensi-fied by the strategic interests of outside powers: as in the two wars of Mantuan succession, in which both France and Spain were concerned to prevent the throne from falling to any client of the other. Occa-sionally valid claims were resisted, as in the subsequent age, on balance-of-power grounds. But, because the dynastic principle re-mained so powerful, resistance in this age was still half-hearted and usually unsuccessful: so Philip II was allowed to add Portugal to his innumerable domains with only a feeble effort by France on behalf of his rival; there was no attempt to prevent Matthias and Ferdinand from reuniting the huge eastern Hapsburg territories; and it was Swedish action, not external intervention, which prevented Sigis-mund from holding Sweden in addition to the vast territories of Poland and Lithuania. The balance of power had not yet, in other words, become the major factor in determining succession that it was to be in the age to follow.

Affronts to national honour could still be important issues. The Scandinavian war of 1563-70 began when an embassy from the Swed-ish king to the ruler of Hesse (whose daughter he desired in marriage) was detained by the king of Denmark as it passed through his terri-tory. An important issue in the same war (as well as that of 1611-13) was the right of the Danish king to wear the colours of the three kingdoms Denmark once controlled (Denmark, Norway and

Sweden) in his coat of arms. The official reason for Henry IV's planned war against the emperor in 1609 was the refusal of the Spanish authorities to return to France the duke of Condé, who had fled from royal authority in France. The war between Sweden and Denmark of 1611-13 partly concerned the Swedish king's disputed claim to the title "King of the Lapps in Nordland". One of the issues in the war between the Holy Roman Empire and Turkey in 1593-1606 was the long-standing obligation of the emperor to pay tribute to the Ottoman sultan (an obligation that his success in the war brought to an end). Olivares told Philip IV that it was necessary to make war in Mantua to "mortify" the duke of Nevers and teach him to "respect, esteem and venerate the royal dignity of your Majesty". The immediate justification for France's entry into the Thirty Years War was the seizure by Spain of the elector of Trier, who was under French protection. It would be wrong to see these purely as pretexts for wars desired on other grounds: such questions were seen as important in their own right. Concern for national honour could not only stimulate wars but also frustrate efforts to end them. Negotiations between France and Spain in 1636-7 failed largely because Spain insisted that it should be France which publicly sued for peace (on the grounds that she had declared war), even though it was Spain herself which most needed peace and had made the first approaches for a settlement.

A contributory subject of dispute was the right to trade. One source of conflict between Spain and the other maritime powers was the attempt of the former to reserve to herself all trade to South America and the Caribbean territories, and even the right to sail to those areas. One of the main issues in the latter part of the war between Spain and the Dutch (for example, in the negotiations of 1609-10 and 1644-7) was the right of the United Provinces to trade to the East and West Indies. A major issue in the conflicts between Sweden and her neighbours in the Baltic was the right to trade to particular ports and areas: by her victory in 1613, for example, Denmark won an explicit acknowledgement of her right to trade to Livonia and Courland; conversely Sweden in 1643-5 won from Denmark exemption from the tolls through the Sound for shipping from all ports in her possession. In 1624 the same two countries almost went to war on the questions of trade and tolls. Competition for trade in the Caspian and across the Caucasus was one cause of the four wars between Turkey and Persia in this age.[4]

A related question concerned free navigation on the high seas and the control of piracy. The wars between Turkey and Venice of 1559-64 and of 1570-3 resulted from Turkey's dissatisfaction at Venetian failure to control Christian pirates based in Cyprus. The successive wars by the Christian powers against the chief North African states (Algiers, Tunis, Tripoli and Morocco) resulted mainly from the constant interference of the latter with shipping and their attempts to extort payment in return for passage. The war of the Uscocchi between Venice and the Hapsburg archduke Ferdinand (who then ruled Styria) resulted from the failure of the latter to control piracy against Venetian shipping from the Dalmatian coast (Turkey had complained about the failure of Venice to control the same pirates 70 years earlier). The marauding of the Christian corsairs, especially the Knights of St Stephen and the Knights of St John, in the eastern Mediterranean was one of the causes of Turkish naval warfare in the late sixteenth century; while similar action by North African corsairs in the west stimulated Spain's attacks on North African ports in that period. In the same way, the piratical raids of the Crimean Tartars into southern Russia to seize prisoners for sale into slavery (about 200,000 were taken and sold in this way in the first half of the seventeenth century) caused repeated retaliatory attacks by the Cossacks of Russia and Poland, as well as more organised campaigns, such as the war undertaken by Muscovy in 1591-8. In other words, in a lawless age, lawless action could be the spur to large-scale warfare to deter it.

Thus the immediate issues about which wars were fought in this age differed in many ways from those of the age before. In a large number of conflicts, both within states and between them, the most important issues were religious: most often the right of religious minorities to practise their faith, build churches or make converts. Sometimes the issue concerned the right to church lands or other property. Religious differences also often motivated, or at least exacerbated, disputes over other questions: for example royal succession and competition for territory. But there were many other issues, unrelated to religion, which could lead to war. Questions of national honour, especially the honour of the ruler, could still cause a declaration of war. So too could conflicts about rights of navigation or the right to trade in particular areas. States came into conflict over territory, especially territory adjacent to their borders: above all territories believed to be of strategic importance (p. 151-2 below). While a few of these issues looked back to the previous age (questions of honour and dynastic succession, for example) and one or two — conflict over trade — were to become more important in the age to come, others, especially those concerned with religion, were almost unique to this particular period. Religious differences had an importance in this age that they were to have at no other time. As always, it was the dominant concerns, and therefore the underlying ideology, of the international society that determined which were the issues that most often led to war.

The age of sovereignty (1648-1789)

In the following age the issue that had been most bitterly contested in the previous era — religion — was almost never the cause of war. The settlement of Westphalia (1648) had generally laid to rest the long struggle on that question. In partitioning Europe between the faiths according to the beliefs of the rulers, it epitomised the victory of the emerging state over the declining power of churches; of practical statesmen over doctrinaire zealots; above all of national sovereignty over individual conscience. However dubious the principle on which it was based, in a world where the rulers were supreme there was now (unlike after 1555) little disposition to challenge that settlement, in its religious aspects at least, especially since it was in most cases applied with some tolerance.

Of the 38 international wars that were fought in the following age, there is not a single one in which religion was a primary issue. It was rarely even a factor. The constantly changing alliances were now formed with little regard for religious allegiance. German princes could band together regardless of faith (as in the League of the Rhine, 1658); Catholic France would ally itself with protestant Sweden, with orthodox Russia and even Moslem Turk; protestant England with Catholic Portugal; Catholic Austria with protestant England and protestant United Provinces. Conversely, Lutheran Denmark fought Lutheran Sweden, while Catholic France fought Catholic Austria. Only in Eastern Europe did religion play a slightly larger role. It was a factor in the bitter wars for the Ukraine in 1648-67. And in forming a "Holy League" to resist the Turks in 1683-4, Austria, Poland and Venice revived a spark of the spirit of the crusades. But even in such conflicts the fundamental issue was usually the control of territory; desired in this age as a way not so much of saving souls as of defending states. Religion played a rather larger part, at least in the first half of the period, in the civil conflicts of the age (for example, in the two brief civil wars in Switzerland, resistance in Ireland to English rule, the Cossack rebellions in Poland and the Hungarian resistance to Austria between 1670 and 1710). But even in domestic struggles it was now far less important than it had been in the age before.

At first sight the most important issue of this age was the question of succession. Not only is this a period in which there were a number of wars specifically named as wars about that issue (the wars of Spanish, Polish, Austrian and Bavarian succession); but there were also a number of other conflicts which were fought largely on the same question: the First Northern War in 1655-60 (caused partly by Poland's continuing claim to the Swedish crown), Louis XIV's "War of Devolution" of 1667-8 (in which he put forward spurious claims on behalf of his wife to the Spanish Netherlands); the Nine Years War (sparked off by Louis's support for succession claims in Cologne and the Palatinate); the Great War of the North (partly about succession in Saxony); Spain's war of 1718-20 (which concerned claims in Italy and the Mediterranean put foward by the Spanish queen on behalf of her sons); Sweden's war against Russia in 1741-3 (which became a war of succession when Elizabeth of Russia demanded that Sweden accept a royal heir acceptable to her); and the Seven Years War (which concerned the dispute over Silesia, not finally resolved in the previous conflict). In addition, the first Anglo-Dutch war was partly about the rights of the House of Orange and its potential claims in England; the Nine Years War and the War of the Spanish Succession were about succession in England as well as in Spain; the War of the Polish Succession was about succession in Tuscany, Naples, Sicily and Parma as well as in Poland. Altogether, therefore, about a dozen, or perhaps a third, of the international wars of this period in Europe arose directly or indirectly out of claims to succession.

There was, however, a major difference between these struggles and those that took place over that question in the age of dynasties. In the earlier age the issue in dynastic conflicts genuinely concerned (however partisan the views of each contestant) which ruler had the better right to succeed in a particular territory; which law of inheritance was valid; who was the true king. In this age the question of dynastic rights was not the fundamental one. The real issue was not so much the right of the *ruler* to succeed, as the claims of the *state* to territory. In other words, while in the former age the desire for territory only resulted from a claim to succession, in this age the claim to succession in many cases resulted only from the demand for territory. It was because Louis XIV wished to acquire the Spanish Netherlands for France that he manufactured his tortuous devolution claims (based on a law of property inheritance accepted only in some parts of the Low Countries and never applied to royal succession). It was because Frederick the Great wished to acquire Silesia that he set his legal experts to dredge up ancient and long defunct dynastic claims to at least a part of it.* It was because Austria desired, largely for strategic reasons, to acquire Lower Bavaria that she persuaded its ruler to renounce it. And so on.

---

* Frederick, who was totally cynical about the claim, congratulated his foreign minister, Podewils, on his ingenuity in devising a claim ("Splendid, that's the work of an excellent charlatan"). His claim was anyway only to part of Silesia, the territories of the duke of Liegnitz, who had died in 1675; and even that claim had already been renounced by Prussia. He had a much better claim to the duchies of Berg and Jülich but declined to prosecute it for fear of arousing French hostility.

But because state interests were now the essential factor, even valid claims could not be allowed to succeed if that should be too disadvantageous to other states. The validity of the claim was less important than the effect on the balance of power. Thus many of the wars were now fought not to *assert* claims, as in the age of dynasties, but to *prevent* the claims of others from succeeding. And in almost every case it was the objectors, even when fighting against the application of normal rules of succession, who now prevailed. So the legitimate heir named by the king of Spain was prevented from inheriting that country unless he first renounced the throne of France; Poland was denied the Polish king its parliament had elected in favour of the Saxon king that Russia and Austria wished her to have; Silesia had to be ruled by Prussia, which had seized it, rather than by Maria Theresa, who had inherited it (under an arrangement which most of the rulers of Europe, including Frederick himself, had explicitly endorsed); the duchies of Italy were parcelled out among foreign rulers according to the convenience of Europe and regardless of dynastic rights (still less of the will of their peoples); and Austria was not to be allowed to acquire Lower Bavaria, even if the latter's ruler himself desired it, against the will of her powerful neighbours. In other words, the distribution of territory in this age was no longer necessarily determined by the laws of succession or by the wishes of individual rulers; it was determined by decisions of the powers seeking, often through war, to maintain a reasonable balance of advantage among them.*

The most important single issue in this age was thus the balance of power. This meant above all that no single state was to be allowed to acquire a preponderance of power which would enable it to dominate the continent. The country most liable to do this — Spain's dominance having been destroyed at the end of the previous period — was France. And for 50 years between 1665 and 1715 the major issue in all the principal wars of Western Europe was the conflict between France's aim to expand her power and the determination of most of her neighbours to prevent this. In the north Sweden's neighbours were equally concerned to limit and contain the excessive power she

* It was partly because of expected resistance by other powers to claims of succession that in this age claims were increasingly put forward on behalf of children rather than of rulers themselves. Already in the sixteenth century Charles V not only shared his own inheritance with his brother, but sought a settlement of his conflict with France about Milan and other territories by devising solutions which distributed them among children of each family. In 1608-12 both Polish and Swedish rulers put forward claims to Russia on behalf of their sons. And in the War of the Spanish Succession claims to Spain were made on behalf of French and Austrian princes rather than of ruling monarchs.

wielded there: the main issue in the wars of 1655-60 and 1700-21. In south-eastern Europe it was at first still Turkey's power (momentarily revived in the early 1680s, in 1710-12 and in 1739) that had to be gradually pushed back, by appropriate alliances, in the wars of 1663-4, 1683-99, 1714-18 and 1735-9. After that it was Russia's power that needed to be resisted in turn (for example, by the pacts of 1790-1). Thus the classic way to balance power was seen to lie in the creation of a coalition against the principal threat to the region: what Frederick the Great described as "that wise equilibrium by which the superior force of a single monarch is counterbalanced by the united powers of several princes".[5]

But wars could also be fought to determine the balance between particular powers in particular places. So Prussia and Austria began their century-long struggle for dominance in Germany; Sweden and Denmark fought for control of the Sound; Britain and France fought for dominance in the Low Countries, in the Mediterranean and above all in colonies overseas; and Russia and Austria began to balance each other in Eastern Europe. In each part of the continent, as well as in Europe as a whole, this constant effort to balance the power of others brought states into continual conflict.

Within that struggle the control of territory remained a vital issue. Most of the wars began with demands for territory, and they ended almost always with peace treaties providing for its transfer. But territory was now an issue mainly because of its effect on the balance of power. It was thus the territories which were believed essential to the strategic, commercial or other interests of states that became the subject of war. It was Louis XIV's acquisition of the great forts of Strasbourg (1681), Casale (1681), Luxemburg (1684) and Philippsburg (1688), above all his advance to the Rhine, that was the immediate stimulus to the creation of the League of Augsburg and to the outbreak of the Nine Years War in 1688. It was because of its strategic importance that the southern Netherlands was fought over during almost every war of the period. It was because of their strategic importance that Belgrade, the Banat and Bukovina were fought over by Austria and Turkey; Ochakov, Azov and the Crimea, by Russia and Turkey; Stettin and Stralsund on the Baltic, by Sweden and Prussia; Ingria, Livonia and the Aaland islands, by Sweden and Russia. Holstein was of vital strategic importance for Denmark since it could threaten her rear, especially if controlled, as it was for a long time, by Sweden and was thus the main issue in their wars of 1675-9 and 1700-21. Bremen was similarly vital to both Sweden and Britain-Hanover, bringing wars in 1652 and 1666.

But territories that were strategically important to one state could become a strategic threat to another and therefore the subject of war. The "gates" to France on the Pyrenees, the Alps and the Rhine, which Louis XIV coveted and in many cases acquired, were also the gates that let France menace other countries. The so-called Burgundian Circle, which had linked Spain's Italian territories to the Spanish Netherlands, could represent a threat to France in the hands of Spain; but in the hands of France it represented a threat to the United Provinces. The Rhine fortresses, which France so ardently desired for her own security, in her control were a threat to Germany and Austria. Gibraltar and Minorca, desired by Britain for strategic reasons, in her hands represented a threat to France, Spain and other Mediterranean countries.

Another type of territory that became the subject of war was that which had special importance for trade: trading posts, and above all colonies. This is almost the only age of history in which wars occurred between European powers for the possession of colonies. In later times, though the search for colonies caused frequent conflict between colonisers and colonised, it did not occur between the colonisers themselves. In this age alone European powers fought each other for such territories. In some cases these began as local conflicts between traders and trading companies, often without causing full-scale war between their countries. So the Portuguese and Dutch fought each other in the Far East, Africa and Latin America for 50 years from 1621 without overt warfare in Europe; England and the United Provinces fought in West Africa and North America in 1664-5; and Britain and France in North America and India in 1754-6, without being formally at war with each other. Often (as in all these cases) the colonial struggle led in time to war among the home states. But Britain and Spain fought for two years in the West Indies in 1655-7 without precipitating full-scale war between them. All these were wars that had colonial causes. But in other cases major wars were fought primarily because of their colonial *consequences:* Britain's wars against France in 1740 and 1756, and that of France against Britain in 1776-83, were fought largely to promote conflicting claims to huge colonial territories overseas.

A related issue that was almost unique to this age as a cause of war was trade. Though there have been disputes about trade between states in every age, this is the only one in which they regularly went to war about them. Both the first two Anglo-Dutch wars were primarily about rights to trade and fishing (even the other issues in those wars — rights in the North Sea and piracy — were closely related). France's war against the United Provinces in 1672 (though influenced by Louis's resentment at Dutch conduct in the previous war) was seen largely as a means to conquer Dutch trade, especially in the East Indies.[6] And war between the same two countries in 1688 was brought closer by the tariff wars in which they had become engaged against each other. Though the War of the Spanish Succession was not fought primarily about trade, it was preceded by stringent French measures against English trade, which intensified anti-French feeling in England, and trade featured prominently in the peace settlement at its end. The war of 1739 between Britain and Spain was caused mainly by friction concerning trade to South America; and the war between Britain and the United Provinces in 1780-2 concerned Dutch trade with Britain's enemies and the rights of neutrals to maintain such trade. Similar disputes about the rights of neutrals to trade with belligerent powers caused conflicts between Britain and other countries, especially in the Seven Years War and the War of American Independence, and eventually led to the creation of the Armed Neutrality among powers hostile to British policy.

Another subject of conflict, also somewhat peculiar to this age, was competition for prestige and precedence. There is no other period in which such questions have been so passionately debated and disputed. At peace conferences and international congresses long hours were spent in arguing on the relative status to be enjoyed by different states and rulers — the titles each could claim and the courtesies that should be accorded to them: the whole of the first year of the peace conference at Nijmegen was taken up by such conflicts (it is true such disputes had been equally important in the negotiations for the peace of Westphalia, but that anticipated this age by only a few years.) Competition for prestige could also be a contributory factor in causing war. A major issue in two of the Anglo-Dutch wars was whether or not Dutch ships should dip their flags to English ships in the North Sea and the Channel, a matter that had been disputed between them for years. French fleets fought armed engagements with Spanish vessels in 1685, and with Dutch in 1687, to compel them to salute the French colours. Louis XIV almost went to war with Spain over a dispute concerning the precedence to be accorded to their ambassadors in London; and he later occupied the papal territory of Avignon over a similar dispute with the Vatican. Louis made no secret of the fact that a main reason for war with the United Provinces in 1772 was to humiliate her for having defied France five years earlier; and it was on these grounds that he devised peace terms designed to maximise humiliation (under which the Dutch would be obliged to send a deputation to France every year to present him with a gold medal and offer him their heartfelt thanks for having graciously allowed them to retain their independence). The declared reason for Russia's declaration of war against Sweden in 1700 was that insufficient honour had been paid to Peter the Great by the Swedish authorities when he passed through Riga three years earlier (despite the fact that he had been travelling incognito at the time). Such conflicts could even affect the way a war was conducted. During the war for Crete in 1645-69, the commander of the papal fleet and the general of the Knights of

Malta, who was supposed to be helping Venice, each withdrew their ships and returned home because they were not allowed the place of honour at the right of the line of battle.[7]

Another matter that could lead to conflict in this as in earlier ages was the situation of ambiguous sovereignty existing in a number of areas. The Holy Roman Empire, for example (even after a further degree of sovereignty was transferred to the states in 1648), continually created such ambiguities. The emperor's periodic claims to "lapsed" imperial fiefs, for example, clashed with the claims of other states: Austria's grounds for invading the Milanese in 1701 were that, with the death of the Spanish king, it had become such a lapsed fief; and this was one of the grounds given for her claim to parts of Bavaria in 1778. There could be conflict between imperial authorities and individual states; as when imperial forces intervened in Mecklenburg over a constitutional issue in 1715. The degree of independence that free cities could claim was a cause of wars: for example, those between Sweden and Bremen in 1666, and between Denmark and Hamburg in 1686-7. The status of the imperial city of Luxemburg caused war between Spain and France in 1683: and that of Strasbourg and Alsace (its status left even more ambiguous than before by the 1648 peace of Westphalia which, in order to satisfy the conflicting claims of France and Austria, contained contradictory provisions on Alsace) was an important issue between Austria and France in 1688-97 and even in 1742-8 (see p. 155). The status of Lorraine, in theory subject to its own duke, in practice occupied by France, yet still generally accepted as a part of the Empire, gave rise to constant conflict and was a major issue in the War of the Polish Succession. The precise rights enjoyed by the king of Denmark and the duke of Holstein-Gottorp in the latter's territories were the source of a long-running dispute and were the main cause of wars in 1675-9 and 1700-21. The status of the Dutch barriers, erected for Dutch defence but in the territory of another state (the Austrian Netherlands), was the cause of dispute for well over a century, and almost caused war when Austria sought to assert sovereign rights in 1782-3. In the East there were other uncertainties. Doubt about the type of "suzerainty" enjoyed by the Ottoman sultan in Transylvania, the Principalities and the Crimea led to constant friction in those areas, both with local people and with rival protectors, such as Russia, and was a main cause of war in 1735-9 and 1768-74. Conflict over the precise nature of the rights enjoyed by Austria in Hungary, still seen by many as a separate kingdom, exacerbated the wars of 1678-82 and 1703-11. The ambiguous status of Cossacks and Tartars, who claimed no precise sovereignty and had no formal diplomatic relations, led to disputes with Russia, Poland and other countries.

Quite often the issue which fuelled war was a situation of unrest in a neighbouring state. So it was the rebellion of the Cossacks against Poland in 1648 and their request five years later for Russian assistance that led eventually to a 13-year war between Russia and Poland. It was a similar revolt against the Poles in 1672 that led Turkey to launch a war to exploit it. France and Spain took advantage of the revolt of the American colonies to settle their own private scores with Britain. In other cases outside powers, without declaring war, gave assistance to rebel forces in another state: France aided Portuguese rebels against Spain in 1659-68 (even after her own war with Spain was finished), assisted Catalan rebels in 1688-9, stirred up rebellion in Ireland in 1689-90, and subsidised Hungarian rebels fighting Austria in 1705-10; Sweden and Spain both assisted the first Stuart rebellion in Britain in 1715-19. Conversely, a subject people could take advantage of an international war to pursue its own struggle: as when Mazeppa, the Cossack leader, made use of Swedish help against Turkey in 1711-12. In other cases outside powers profited from a rebellion without directly assisting it. Turkey was encouraged by the Hungarian revolt in 1678-82 to launch her own war against Austria in the following year, just as Austria had taken advantage of the Transylvanian revolution against Turkey 25 years earlier. Sometimes those who planned war would deliberately incite rebellion in a hostile state, as when the anti-Swedish coalition in 1700 plotted with a disaffected Livonian nobleman to start a rebellion in that territory. In general, however, this was not a common stimulus to war during this period. In an age of legitimacy most rulers had little sympathy for rebellion elsewhere. Wars were not, as in the age which followed, waged primarily to give assistance to revolutionary movements; such assistance was rather a strategy sometimes used to win advantage in wars engaged in for other reasons.

So a significant change took place in this age in the questions over which wars occurred. Religious disputes, the most important cause of war in the age before, were now rarely an issue. Though wars frequently occurred over the question of succession, they were usually concerned far less with dynastic claims as such than with the balance of power which would result if particular claims were admitted. Wars still frequently concerned territory; but territory was desired now not because it would add to the titles and domains of a particular ruler, nor because it would extend the area in which a particular faith was practised, but because it could strengthen the power of a particular state. Territories of strategic value, therefore, or those, such as colonies overseas, affording commercial benefits were those which especially often stimulated conflict. Disputes arose over precedence and prestige, and these too could occasionally lead to armed conflict. Finally, conflicts on trade questions and on colonies were important issues in a number of wars.

Once again, therefore, the issues about which wars were fought reflected the prevailing ideology. It was now a different set of issues which mainly provoked conflict. They were issues which reflected the dominant concerns of the sovereigns and their powerful ministers who ruled within the major states — concern above all with the power and prestige of their own states.

The age of nationalism (1789-1917)

In the period that followed, the issues that led to conflict arose often from domestic affairs within particular states. All the civil wars and all wars of national liberation, which between them represented more than half the wars fought in Europe in this age (46 out of 74), arose from this cause. But some of these wars led also to international conflict: that is, to the involvement of one or more outside powers seeking to influence the outcome.

This external intervention could be for different reasons. Especially in the early years, it was often designed to help a traditional, conservative government against "liberal" forces threatening it (the four interventions by Austria in Italy in areas outside her direct control, French intervention in Spain in 1823, intervention by Prussia in various German states affected by revolutions in 1848-9, intervention by Russia in support of Austria in Hungary in 1849, and Prussian support for Russia in Poland in 1863). In a few cases it was designed to help an established liberal government against conservative forces that were threatening it (the intervention by Britain against conservative forces in Spain in 1833-40 and by Britain and Spain in Portugal in 1846-8). But increasingly intervention was designed to help rebellious forces against the government of the day: most often nationalist movements, which frequently secured substantial sympathy elsewhere. Of this sort were the successful interventions by Britain, France and Russia in support of the Greek rebellion against Turkey in 1827-9; by Britain and France in support of the Belgian revolt against Holland in 1830-3; by Prussia and Austria in support of Schleswig-Holstein against Denmark in 1864; by Russia and other countries in support of revolts in Bosnia and Bulgaria in 1877-8. Unsuccessful interventions of this kind were those by Piedmont in support of Italian independence from Austria in 1848-9, and Greek support for revolution in Crete in 1896-8 (although the powers ensured that autonomy was granted to Crete, Greece was defeated). Some threatened interventions were never launched: in 1903 the Bulgarian army mobilised in support of the Macedonian revolt but never crossed the frontiers. Partially successful was French and Piedmontese support for Italian revolution in 1859. Much more rare was intervention in support of conservative rebels against a liberal government (perhaps because liberal governments were themselves rare): Russian intervention in Poland in 1792 was purportedly for this purpose. Altogether, of the 48 European wars between 1815 and 1914, 35 were entirely domestic conflicts or originated as such (all of those in columns 2 and 3 of Appendix 4a); while, in addition, of the 13 international conflicts at least six (those of 1828-9, 1848-9, 1864, 1877-8, 1898 and 1912) resulted, directly or indirectly, from civil conflicts elsewhere and the intervention of outside powers in them. In other words, 41 out of 48, or five-sixths, of the conflicts in the period between 1815 and 1914 arose from domestic conflicts within states.

It was particularly national revolutions that led to wider international involvement and so to war. Whether or not a national revolution led to international conflict depended on a number of factors. Clearly such support was most likely to come if there were individual powers of the same nationality as the people in revolt. So Italian rebels could look for support from Piedmont, those in Schleswig-Holstein could look to Prussia and Austria, and those in Crete to Greece. The national movements of Eastern Europe could look for support to the Russians, who, if not of the same language or culture, were fellow Slavs and mostly shared the same religion. The national movement of Poland, on the other hand, could look to no other nation of the same language and religion for help. In addition Poland was under the control of more powerful masters than the other peoples mentioned: three major powers of Europe shared an interest in suppressing Polish aspirations, while none of the other powers had sufficient interest in defying them. It was for this reason that, despite the considerable sympathy in many parts of Europe for the Polish national movement, five successive Polish revolutions did not stimulate armed action in their support by any outside power.

The prevalence of wars of this kind reflected an age of nationalism. The demand among particular groups, sharing a common language, culture or history, for national identity and independence had caused virtually no wars in the preceding period, even though there were many such groups deprived of a national existence (the two wars of Hungarian rebels against Austria are the main exception). In this age, out of 67 wars in Europe, 23, or over a third, were wars of national liberation, resulting directly from the demand for independence; five of the civil conflicts broke out partly for that reason (the revolutions in Naples, Piedmont and the Italian cities, the German risings of 1849 and the Italian war of 1860-1); and six of the international wars broke out because of external support for such movements: the wars between Russia and Turkey in 1828-9, those between Piedmont and Austria of 1848-9 and 1859, the war over Schleswig-Holstein in 1864, the war of Russia against Turkey in 1877-8 and the Greek war against Turkey in 1898. To this might be added the Italian part in the war of 1866, fought for Venetia. Nationalist sentiment played a significant part in the Napoleonic wars: first in France and in countries aroused by France (for example, Italy and Belgium); later in stimulating the movement against her (for example, in Spain, Germany and Russia). Finally, sympathy for nationalist movements elsewhere played a major part in the outbreak of the first Balkan war and the First World War.

The issue causing war in these cases was at root the conflict between national sentiment and traditional sovereignty. The whole history of the period can be seen as a remaking of the map of Europe, usually through armed force, to make it conform more closely to the "national principle". The settlement at Vienna in 1815 was in many ways a typical settlement of the preceding period: one devised largely for reasons of state, to suit the political convenience of the major powers and to establish a reasonable balance of power between them, with territorial "compensation" to each in return for losses else-where. So territories were shuffled around from one state to another: Norway taken from Denmark and given to Sweden, in recompense for Sweden's loss of Finland in favour of Russia; Belgium transferred from Austria to Holland; Poland allocated mainly to Russia, in return for the grant of a large part of Saxony to Prussia. Much of the political and military history of the next century was devoted to redrawing the boundaries so created — as well as those of the Ottoman Empire, which were unchanged by the Vienna treaty — so that they paid greater regard to the national sentiments of peoples. A large proportion of the conflicts in Europe between 1815 and 1914 arose from that cause (the 14 wars of national liberation; the three wars fought to bring about the unification of Germany; the two and a half fought to bring about the reunification of Italy — counting her unsuccessful participation in the war of 1866 as a half; the war of 1877-8, from which Serbia, Montenegro and Romania won final independence and Bulgaria provisional independence; the first Bal-kan war and several of the civil conflicts). This process led to the creation of nine new European states in the century before 1914 (Greece, Belgium, Italy, Germany, Romania, Serbia, Montenegro, Norway and Albania), and to six more in 1918-19 (Finland, Czecho-slovakia, Hungary, Lithuania, Latvia and Estonia). It is therefore not too much to say that the issue about which wars were fought during this period in Europe was, above all others, the national principle: the principle of creating states on the basis of national language, culture or sentiment.

Thus revolution, and especially national revolution, rarely the source of international wars in the previous age, was in this era its most common single cause. Conversely, territory, the most important single issue in the age before, was now rarely a significant cause, at

least in Europe. It played only a minor part in the French revolutionary and Napoleonic wars: it was resentment at the disproportionate
power acquired by France in general, and by Napoleon in particular,
which caused war against him to be continually renewed, rather than
the changes in frontiers that he imposed, which (if disliked at all)
intensified rather than created that resistance. After 1815 none of the
major powers, with the temporary exception of France, was disposed
to challenge the territorial disposition laid down at Vienna. It is
difficult to point to a single war involving a major power that was
primarily caused by territorial ambitions, as were most of the significant wars in the previous period. France's desire for Savoy and Nice
was a factor in motivating her participation in the war of 1859, but
alone would not have been sufficient to bring about that war. Prussia's aims in her three wars were concerned with German unity and
Prussian glory, not territorial gains for Prussia herself.* Italy's territorial claims against Austria-Hungary were the main reason for her
participation in the war of 1866 and in the First World War, but
played no significant part in bringing those wars about. Russia's
acquisition of Bessarabia in 1878, together with other territorial
changes made at that time, were the result, not the cause, of the
preceding conflict. The only wars of the period that can be said to
have been waged primarily for territorial reasons were the three
Balkan wars of 1885, 1912 and 1913: Serbia's desire for compensation
for Bulgaria's acquisition of eastern Rumelia was the immediate
cause of the war of 1885; the designs of the Balkan Alliance countries
on Macedonia were the main cause of the first Balkan war; and the
resentment of Bulgaria at the territorial acquisitions of her former
allies were the main cause of the second Balkan war. For the rest,
territorial demands were the *result* of wars rather than their cause.

More significant than competition for territory, as an issue leading
to war in Europe, was competition for influence. Thus the war
between Russia and Turkey in 1806-12 was caused by competition for
influence in the Principalities. The most important single issue underlying the Crimean War was the amount and type of influence Russia

---

* Bismarck later claimed that in negotiating on Schleswig-Holstein "from
the beginning I kept annexation steadily before my eyes"; but this aspiration
was for Germany rather than for Prussia. Similarly, though Prussia annexed
Hanover, Cassel, Nassau and Frankfurt in 1866, she took no Austrian
territory, and her aims were rather to unify Germany under her leadership
than to expand Prussia's own frontiers. The annexation of Alsace-Lorraine
was a result of the Franco-Prussian War; that territory was in no sense a
cause, and its transfer was almost an afterthought of Bismarck's to please his
high command, which wished to acquire Metz for strategic — and sen-
timental — reasons.

should be allowed to enjoy in the Ottoman Empire. The main issue between France and Austria in 1859 was the degree of influence each should enjoy in Italy. The primary issue between Prussia and Austria in 1866 was the influence each should wield in Germany. The war between France and Prussia in 1870 (though at root more about status than about influence) directly resulted from France's demand to exclude Prussia from a dynastic connection with Spain thought likely to bring her influence there. The various wars in which external help was given to a national revolution in part concerned the desire of the intervening power to acquire influence in the new-born state. And the main immediate issue underlying the First World War was the relative degree of influence which Austria-Hungary and Russia should enjoy in the Balkans: in particular whether Serbia should fall under Austria-Hungary's domination.

The same issue caused war elsewhere. The main point in dispute in the war between Japan and China in 1894-5 was the influence each should enjoy in Korea; and the issue in the war between Japan and Russia ten years later was specifically the influence each should enjoy in Korea and Manchuria (Russia had not agreed to recognise dominant Japanese influence in Korea in return for the offer of dominant influence in Manchuria). French resentment at British influence in Egypt almost led to war between the two countries in 1898, just as German resentment at French influence in Morocco twice almost led to war in 1905 and 1911. Even colonial wars were occasionally fought on this issue: the second Afghan war in 1878 was brought about by the competition between Britain and Russia for influence in Afghanistan. In Latin America, too, the contest for influence was frequently the most important issue precipitating war. The first significant war after independence, that between Argentina and Brazil in 1825-8, concerned the degree of influence that each should have in Uruguay; the long war of 1839-52 between Argentina and her neighbours concerned the degree of domination Argentina should have in the same area; and the bitterest war in Latin American history, that between Paraguay and her neighbours in 1864-70, was largely caused by Paraguay's resentment at Brazil's influence in Uruguay. Similarly, in the north, the wars between Peru and Gran Colombia in 1827 concerned the influence the latter should enjoy in Bolivia, and those between Bolivia and Peru in 1835 and between Chile and Bolivia in 1836-8 concerned the influence Bolivia should enjoy in Peru.

Conflicts over influence were intensified by the ambiguous status that still surrounded certain territories in this age. Though some of the amorphous, semi-sovereign entities of the previous era had ceased to exist — the Holy Roman Empire (after 1806), the Tartars and Cossacks, the mini-states of Germany and Italy — other anomalies remained which often gave rise to dispute. The immediate cause of the two wars over Schleswig-Holstein arose from differences of interpretation concerning those duchies' immensely complex status (mainly inhabited by Germans, ruled by a Danish king but not as part of Denmark, one a member of the German Bund but not the other). The status of Luxemburg (ruled by the Dutch king but belonging to the German Bund) caused similar problems, giving rise to a French claim which almost led to war in 1867. Sometimes such ambiguity of status was deliberately created. The concept of "autonomy", for territories held to be still under the "suzerainty" of another ruler, was deliberately devised, largely to ease the process of decolonisation, especially in the Ottoman Empire. The effect was to acknowledge the reality of power enjoyed by local governments while leaving the figment of authority to the traditional overlords — in other words, to attempt to reconcile the principles of nationalism and sovereignty. Serbia, Montenegro, the principalities of Moldavia and Wallachia, Bulgaria and Crete were each in turn formally accorded the status of "autonomy"; and only after a considerable period finally graduated to full independence. Similarly, under the treaty of London in 1852 Schleswig-Holstein was accorded "autonomy" under Danish over-lordship, so reconciling the claims of Danish legitimacy with those of German nationalism; but this led to dispute and war in 1864. The "autonomy" attributed to Tibet for similar reasons (to allow effective decolonisation while assuaging Chinese pride) allowed a British invasion in 1904, and eventually led to civil war when full sovereignty was imposed by China in 1950 and 1959.

Thus the status of "autonomy" left the degree of power which the "autonomous" state and "suzerain" power could expect to enjoy in continual doubt and was the cause of a number of disputes, some of which led to war. One of the causes of the Crimean War was the granting to Russia in 1774 of the right to protect the Orthodox population; another the Russian occupation of the Principalities, which Russia had also won the right to "protect" in 1774, and had thereafter regularly occupied when it suited her convenience, even though they remained under Turkish "suzerainty". The autonomous status accorded to eastern Rumelia in 1878 (to prevent Russia enjoying the benefit of the greater Bulgaria she then sought) led to war between Serbia and Bulgaria in 1885 when the territory none the less opted to join with Bulgaria. The tenuous nature of Turkey's rights in Serbia at the beginning of the nineteenth century, and in Montenegro in the 1850s, helped provoke the conflicts which broke out there at those times, while the equally ambiguous nature of Turkey's rights in Bulgaria and Bosnia made it easier for Russia to intervene there in 1877-8. The even more anomalous status accorded to Bosnia-Herze-govina in 1878 — still formally under Turkish rule, yet both adminis-tered and garrisoned by Austria-Hungary — led not only to armed conflict within that territory when the Austrians first entered in 1878, but also to acrimonious dispute and almost war when they proceeded to undertake a formal "annexation" in 1908. The "veiled protectorate" which Britain enjoyed in Egypt, according her absolute control even while she vaguely acknowledged Ottoman suzerainty, led to continuous friction with France and almost resulted in war in 1898. Britain's attempt to secure a fictional "suzerainty", including control over foreign affairs, in the Transvaal in 1881 was one factor contributing to conflict and eventually to war nearly 20 years later.

Somewhat similar uncertainties occurred in other parts of the world. The "protectorates" which were so widely declared during this period (almost all the territories made dependent from the middle of the nineteenth century onwards were named as protectorates rather than colonies) provided an indeterminate degree of authority to the protecting power. The term implied that the metropolitan power would offer only guidance and advice to existing authorities within the territories; yet in practice, as time went on, control became absolute, and they were scarcely distinguishable from full colonies. That situation could lead to acute conflicts between local rulers and metropolitan governments, and occasionally to war: for example, in South-west Africa in 1903-8 and Tanganyika in 1905-6. A slight variation was the "protected state", where the independence of the local government was nominally somewhat greater (and misunderstandings therefore still more likely). Still more nebulous was the concept of "paramountcy", which implied the right of a particular power to dominant influence (but which gave no indication how much influence either the local government or other powers were to be allowed): Britain's claim that she should be allowed to despatch observers to Afghanistan, where she believed herself to enjoy paramountcy (a claim unrecognised by the Afghan ruler) was the cause of the second Afghan war in 1878. Most ambiguous of all, perhaps, was the situation in substantial parts of the world where, until almost the end of the nineteenth century, administration was undertaken by chartered companies* rather than by metropolitan governments (in Portuguese East Africa there existed the still stranger situation in which local administration was undertaken by British companies though the territory remained Portuguese): this too could give rise to conflict. And other types of dispute over jurisdiction could lead to war: both the Anglo-Chinese wars of 1839 and 1856-60 were caused

---

* For example, the three German companies that administered South-West Africa, East Africa and New Guinea, the Royal Niger Company in Nigeria, the British South Africa Company in Rhodesia, the African Lakes Company in Nyasaland, the Imperial British East Africa Company in Kenya and Uganda, and the North Borneo Company in Borneo.

by disputes over jurisdiction when China sought the prosecution of criminals in or off her own territory.

Against this, rights of succession, frequently a cause of war in previous ages, were now rarely the occasion for conflict. Though the Franco-Prussian War of 1870 arose indirectly from a dispute about the succession to the Spanish throne, that question was in no way a cause of the war (the German Kaiser had already acceded to French wishes on the matter before the conflict broke out). The quarrel over the future of Schleswig-Holstein, which led twice to war (in 1848 and 1864), was in appearance about succession; but in reality about whether the two duchies should be Danish or German — a national question. A dispute about the future succession to Spain, especially whether this could go to a relative of the French royal family — the very question that had caused a major war in the age before — caused serious dispute between France and Britain in the 1840s, but there was never any disposition to go to war on the matter. The decline in the importance attached to the question is shown by the fact that at the end of the Napoleonic wars the victorious powers were willing to allow a Napoleonic general (who had abandoned his master only two years earlier) to retain the throne of Sweden: an extraordinary abdication of the principle of legitimacy. And decisions concerning new royal families for Greece, Romania and Bulgaria were all settled relatively amicably among the major powers. With the decline in royal power, which occurred in almost all European countries, questions of succession were now no longer usually seen as worth a war.

Against this, challenges to national honour were still often a source of conflict. Such challenges were sometimes seen as requiring a forcible response, if national self-respect was to be retained. An insult to the flag, or to the crown or its representatives, was frequently seen as demanding armed action in response. So in 1857, at the opening of the second Anglo-Chinese war, Palmerston, in a note to the Chinese government, demanded satisfaction for a Chinese action taken "in utter disregard of the respect due to an officer of the British Crown" and proceeded to despatch the armed force "necessary in order to vindicate the honour and dignity of the British Crown". An insult to a country's armed forces was especially inflammatory in effect (at least when inflicted by a less powerful state). So in 1845, in retaliation for the arrest of two British sailors by Brazilian police for being drunk and disorderly, Britain seized three Brazilian ships; and in 1863 she bombarded a Japanese town, with the loss of 1400 lives, because the Japanese government had failed to apologise when two British sailors were killed by Japanese police. Likewise in 1914, in retaliation for the arrest, for a few hours, of US sailors who had docked a gunboat in Mexican territory in violation of martial law there, the United States demanded a 21-gun salute by Mexico as apology, and proceeded to bombard Vera Cruz, causing the loss of 150 lives, when no such act of contrition was forthcoming. The murder of a national in another country could be made a *casus belli* (if it took place outside Europe, that is, and if the effort to find the culprit was regarded as inadequate). So in 1856 the French government declared war against China because of the murder of a French missionary there; the murder of an Italian explorer was made the justification for the Italian expedition against Massawa in 1885; and the murder of two German missionaries was the reason given for the German seizure of Kiaochow in 1897. It was the murder of a French doctor in Morocco in 1907 which was used by France as justification for extending her occupation of that country (just as the murder of a German national had been claimed by Germany to justify the extension of Germany's presence in the country in 1904-5). So well established was this principle as a justification for armed retaliation that Japan prepared a plan for the murder of a Japanese national in Korea, with his own consent, to provide a justification for intervention there in 1873.[8] The murder of a representative of the crown brought an especially powerful response. The murder of the German minister in Peking brought the despatch of a joint European force to defeat the Boxer rebels in 1900; and the murder of the Austrian archduke in Bosnia in 1914 was seen in Austria-Hungary as a threat to national honour as much as to national security.

Even if there was no loss of life the treatment of nationals could be made the reason for war. The treatment of British residents in the Orange Free State was the overt cause of the Boer War of 1899. The treatment of Italians in Libya was the reason put forward for the Italian invasion of that territory in 1911. Even attacks on property could be made the justification for war. So the threat to British property caused by riots in Egypt brought about the British occupation of that country in 1882, which continued in one form or another for more than 70 years. Mysterious explosions aboard a US ship in a Cuban harbour were the reason given for the US declaration of war on Spain in 1898. All of these issues, of a kind that in the age to follow might cause angry remonstrance but certainly no more, in this age provoked war.

Another issue that led several times to war in this age was the threat to freedom of navigation. The danger to navigation represented by the Barbary pirates was the cause of three major naval actions against them, two by the United States (in 1801-5 and 1815) and one by an Anglo-Dutch force with the authorisation of the "powers" (in 1817). Interference with US shipping by Britain to enforce her blockade against France was the main reason for the War of 1812 between Britain and the United States. Indeed Britain, though constantly affirming her belief in the freedom of the seas, was regarded by most other nations of the age as the principal threat to it; and her interference with shipping was no more acceptable to them when undertaken (as it increasingly was after 1815) to stamp out the slave trade than it had been when used to enforce British war aims in the age before. And it was to eliminate, or at least reduce, the disputes on this subject, which had been the cause of conflict among states for so many years, that new rules governing maritime warfare were concluded, as part of the peace of Paris, in 1856.

Finally, in an age of much lending from strong countries to weak, force was now sometimes used to enforce financial claims. Palmerston described the thinking behind this in justifying the use of force against Greece in 1848, to demand redress for loss of property by a British subject:

It is . . . essential for the preservation of that commerce to which we attach so much importance that it should be known and well understood by every nation on the face of the earth that we are not disposed to submit to wrong and that the maintenance of peace on our part is subject to the indispensable condition that all countries shall respect our honour and dignity and shall not inflict any injury upon our interests.

This was a sentiment widely shared among more powerful states. So the failure by Mexico to honour its debts was the justification given for the French expedition designed to place a foreign ruler on its throne in 1863. Britain, Germany and Italy bombarded Venezuela to enforce debt repayment in 1902; and the United States occupied Honduras, Nicaragua and Haiti between 1911 and 1915 mainly for the same reason.

Outside Europe the immediate issues which led to war were often different. Territorial disputes, which in Europe played a relatively small role, were elsewhere still an important issue. In Latin America a significant proportion of the wars were partially or mainly concerned with territory. Of the two most important wars of the period, the War of the Pacific of 1879-83 between Chile and Peru almost entirely concerned territory (an area on the border believed to contain minerals), while the war between Paraguay and her neighbours in 1864-70 was at least partly concerned with a disputed border. In most of the wars in the early part of the period — that between Argentina and Brazil in 1823-6, the successive wars between Peru and Bolivia and between Chile and Bolivia — control of territory was a major issue. It was of less importance in the struggles of Central America, where issues mainly concerned the internal political situation in particular states, and where frontiers remained largely unchallenged from 1839 onwards. In the Far East, Japan's desire for territorial expansion was an important issue in her wars with China in 1894 (in which she acquired Taiwan and the Pescadores, and would have acquired more but for the intervention of outside powers) and with Russia ten years later (in which she acquired the Liaotung peninsula and southern Sakhalin, as well as a protectorate in Korea, soon afterwards annexed). Similarly, the United States acquired vast territories from her war with Mexico in 1846 (an objective her President had declared when first elected) and substantial territory from her war with Spain in 1898 (Puerto Rico, Guam, the Philippines and effective control of Cuba).

Territory was clearly a major issue in most of the colonial wars of the period. These were not, however, disputes about boundaries, of the kind that occurred in Latin America. Many colonial boundaries were determined peacefully, through agreements among the European powers or treaties with local rulers. Territories, whether in Africa or Asia, that were not effectively occupied by any recognised government (which to Europeans normally meant a European government), were regarded as without sovereignty and so subject to occupation. But that occupation was, not surprisingly, resisted by local rulers and peoples. This was the cause of the series of wars fought by Russia during her penetration of Asia, of the wars by which Britain, France and Italy extended their power into different parts of Africa, and of a number of the colonial wars in Asia. In other cases the initial European impact created a "proto-nationalist" reaction which in turn made necessary the application of still more power by the colonising nations.[9] Sometimes, as in Europe, domestic violence stimulated intervention, usually by a European power: examples are the interventions by Britain in Egypt in 1882, and by France in Tunis the same year, and the two British wars in Sudan. Thus, whatever the long-term motives of the colonising powers (pp. 170-1 below), the *immediate* issues that caused war were often local and unplanned.

Similarly, most of the wars of decolonisation arose from the immediate response of local people to an extension of authority by a colonising power. In a small number of cases there was an organised movement aiming at total independence: for example, in the wars of independence in Latin America, the war of Mexico against Spain, and of Texas against Mexico (though this was planned and fought mainly by citizens of the United States rather than native Texans), the two wars of Cuba against Spain, and the war of the Transvaal against Britain in 1879-81. Most of the rest took the form of confused resistance to alien rulers, with little or no clear political objective: as, for example, in the revolts in Achin and Java; the Indian Mutiny; and the resistance of the Ashanti and the Somalis to Britain, of the peoples of South-west Africa and Tanganyika to Germany, of the Moors to France, and of the Senussi to Italy. And it was perhaps because they were rarely planned or carefully organised that most of the wars of decolonisation in this age were finally defeated.

So the issues that mainly caused war in this age were quite different from those of the age before. Territory and succession, previously the two most important issues, now counted for little. This was above all an era of nationalism and the dominant issues were related to that widely shared concern. These included not only nationalist rivalry among existing states, but, more importantly, strong nationalist movements within states. So, in Europe, five-sixths of the wars derived from domestic conflicts, beginning as civil wars and often as wars of national independence. Even other issues that led to war — competition for status or influence, challenges to national honour — derived in part from the same nationalist sentiment. Outside Europe, the large number of wars fought by European powers to acquire or extend colonies can also be seen as an expression of European nationalism; while a substantial number fought by colonial peoples to resist colonisation expressed nationalism of another kind. As in previous ages, changes in the issues over which wars were fought reflected changes of a more profound kind: changes in the ideology of the society as a whole.

The age of ideology (1917-   )

The issues about which wars were fought changed again after 1917. Some of the issues which had been important in earlier ages faded still further in importance. Dynastic disputes — questions of royal succession, which had already become of minor importance in the previous age — now disappeared altogether. Wars of colonisation, designed to create colonies, ended — succeeded for a time by wars of decolonisation, designed to end them. Wars over areas of ambiguous sovereignty* became, with the extension of more clear-cut juridical

---

* Before 1945 ambiguous sovereignty was still a factor in stimulating some disputes. The Japanese incursions into China in 1931-7 were made easier by the fact that at that time, under the Boxer protocol of 1901, Japan had armed forces stationed both in Peking and in the area between Tientsin and Peking; while in addition substantial parts of northern China were controlled by warlords who were under the influence of Japanese advisers (on these grounds the Japanese government held that the Chinese government's jurisdiction did not extend to Peking). After 1945 the nearest equivalents were the disputes over Berlin (in 1948-9 and 1959-61), which resulted from conflicts over juridical rights there but did not lead to war; conflicts over waterways subject to international agreements, such as the Suez and Panama canals; and disputes concerning rights to Antarctica, the sea-bed and outer space, where no clear-cut sovereignty exists.*

rights all over the world, almost extinct. Economic disputes, though more important than ever as a political issue, were now almost never the cause of war between states.

In their place issues of a new kind began to arise. Many were issues characteristic of an age of conflicting ideologies. The First World War, which ushered in the era, was seen by many, especially after 1917, as a war between Western parliamentary democracies and the autocratic governments of the central powers. The Second World War was equally presented as a struggle between the forces of totalitarian dictatorship and democratic or socialist regimes. Many of the lesser wars of the age even more clearly concerned what kind of government should rule in a particular state. These conflicts were mainly domestic, at least in origin, and, as might be expected, have almost all occurred in non-democratic countries where there was reason to question the legitimacy of the established government; there were virtually no civil wars in democratic countries. Since 1945 such conflicts have taken place primarily in developing countries characterised by widespread poverty, fragile political systems, deep social divisions and embryonic administrations. The underlying issue in all these cases has been which group had the right to rule, either in a particular area (where, for example, a minority group was seeking independence, or autonomy); or, more often, in the country as a whole (where groups of conflicting ideology were struggling for power).

A significant proportion of these conflicts have concerned the more specific issue: should the country concerned be ruled by a communist (or at least left-wing) or non-communist (or right-wing) government? The series of wars on this question began with the Russian Civil War in 1917-21; and continued with the civil war in Finland in 1918; the conflict in Hungary in 1919; the civil war in Spain in 1936-9; the Greek Civil War in 1944-9; the civil war in China in 1946-9; the wars in the Philippines, Burma and Malaysia in the years after the Second World War; the war in Guatemala in 1954; the civil wars in Cuba (1957-9), Lebanon (1958), Laos (1960-3, 1970-5), Vietnam (1959-75), the Dominican Republic (1965), Indonesia (1965-6), South Yemen (1967), Cambodia (1970-5), Angola (1975-) and Mozambique (1976-); and a number of wars in Latin America from the early seventies onwards (see Table 8). Because each individual conflict was seen as part of a world-wide struggle between the two ideological alliances, there was frequently external assistance to one side or both. Often this was given by one of the two super-powers leading each ideological alliance. The ideological divide thus became the most important issue of international as well as civil wars. A substantial proportion of international wars, and all of those involving the super-powers (Table 9), have resulted from such conflicts. The two most serious international wars since 1945, those in Korea and Vietnam, both resulted from political conflicts between the two halves of what had once been single states, now divided on ideological lines.

Ideological struggles have not always been between communist and anti-communist forces, however. There have been other types of ideology which have inspired other types of domestic conflict. The war in Yemen (1962-7) was a contest between Nasserist (modernising Arab nationalists) and anti-Nasserist (traditional tribal) factions, assisted by Egypt and Saudi Arabia respectively. In Chad the conflict (though complicated by personal factors) has largely been between radical Moslem forces assisted by Libya and Christian conservative forces assisted by Sudan, Nigeria, France and other countries. In Iran and elsewhere the struggle has been between fundamentalist Islamic forces and more Westernised political philosophies of left and right alike. In some cases civil conflict was partly ideological but had other causes as well: the civil war in the Congo was largely regional and tribal, but had ideological overtones, as had the war of Moslem forces in the southern Philippines after 1969.

A closely related issue concerned the security fears of major powers. The super-powers in particular were deeply concerned about political developments in neighbouring areas believed vital to their security. Any change in the situation there which threatened to bring these under hostile control was seen by them as a threat to their own security and so might stimulate armed action. Such countries acted on the assumption that only countries under governments of a similar political viewpoint to their own would not represent such a threat. In effect they demanded buffer states that could be relied on to remain well disposed to them; and they regarded the political complexion of their governments as the test of reliability. It was on these grounds that the Soviet Union occupied eastern Poland in 1939, the Baltic states in 1940, most of Eastern Europe at the end of the Second World War, reoccupied Hungary in 1956 and Czechoslovakia in 1968, and intervened in Afghanistan in 1979 (as well as supporting a military takeover in Poland in 1981); and in so doing determined the political character of their governments. It was for similar reasons that the United States intervened (sometimes by proxy) in response to political developments in Guatemala in 1954, in Cuba in 1961, in the Dominican Republic in 1965, in Grenada in 1983 and in Nicaragua from the same year, and gave support to the existing government against left-wing threats in El Salvador in 1981-4. It was for the same reason that China intervened in Korea in 1950, in Vietnam in 1979, and in Cambodia from 1980. Lesser powers have taken action in neighbouring states for similar reasons: thus Israel intervened in Sinai in 1956 and in Lebanon (twice); Egypt intervened in Yemen; India in Bhutan, Sikkim and Bangladesh; Vietnam in Cambodia and

Laos; and South Africa, partly through proxies and partly through her own forces, in Angola, Mozambique, Lesotho and other states of the area. Thus a substantial proportion of the relatively few international conflicts of this era have arisen from this concern of stronger states to safeguard their security through intervention in weaker states in their own immediate vicinity.

Another substantial group of wars occurred over colonies (see Table 10). These were now almost entirely wars of independence. While in the previous age wars of colonisation were two or three times more numerous than wars of decolonisation (69 against 29), in this age the former were almost extinct: the Italian conquest of Ethiopia is perhaps the only true example. Anti-colonial wars on the other hand have been frequent. There were several between the wars: in Afghanistan, in Ireland, in Morocco, in Libya, in Java and in Indo-China. The Second World War itself, both by demonstrating that an Asian country could win military successes against important colonial powers, and by detaching a number of important territories from their former rulers, was another war that furthered that process. In consequence the attempt to restore colonial rule itself provoked conflicts: for example in Indo-China and in Indonesia. From this point the determination of the colonial powers to hold their colonies progressively weakened, while that of the colonial peoples to secure their independence grew stronger. Where the colonial powers committed themselves, with a reasonable timetable, to decolonisation, the transition was usually completed relatively peacefully (though conflict could still arise over the speed at which it was to occur or what form it should take, and to whom independence should be given, as in Cameroun, Tunisia and South Arabia). But it was above all where the colonial power refused to accept even the principle of decolonisation that wars occurred; as in Algeria, declared to be for ever a part of France; Cyprus, where independence was at one time "never" to be contemplated; the Portuguese African territories, where no programme for decolonisation was proposed; Rhodesia, where power was seized by an unrepresentative minority denying majority rule for the foreseeable future; and the Falklands, apparently destined for indefinite colonial rule. Sometimes conflict occurred as much between different local groups, each concerned to win control for themselves before independence arrived, as between the colonised and the colonisers as a whole: for example in Cyprus in 1955-9, and in South Arabia in 1963-7. Finally, in a few cases, colonialism has been ended through the warlike actions of a neighbouring power already independent, seeking not only to liberate the peoples still colonised but itself to absorb their territory: as in the case of the Indian invasion of Goa and the Indonesian annexation of West Irian and East Timor. Altogether there were 25 wars of decolonisation in the period: 16 per cent of the total number of wars (see Table 10).

In addition to these wars associated with the achievement of independence another group of wars occurred in the immediate aftermath of independence. Here once more the issue was: who should rule? Often the political structure of newly independent states was fragile, there was no tradition of peaceful political change and a number of groups competed for political power. In such circumstances civil war could easily break out. Of this kind were the communist uprising in the Philippines and other countries of Asia in the 1940s; the interminable conflicts of Burma, involving two communist and several other groups; the inter-communal fighting in India and Pakistan immediately after independence; the bitter and complex war in the Congo which immediately succeeded independence there; and the prolonged struggles, aggravated by extensive intervention from outside, in Angola and Mozambique after 1974. The wars in Korea and Vietnam, each of which followed within five years the independence of bisected countries, can be seen as examples of an opposite type of war in the aftermath of independence, designed not to create separate states but to join two held to be artifically divided (though they were equally widely seen as attempts by one ideological camp to acquire territory previously belonging to another).

A number of civil conflicts resulted from the demands of minorities for independence or autonomy. These too occurred especially often in newly independent states (see Table 11). The widespread acceptance of the principle of self-determination as the basis for creating states, proclaimed at the opening of the period by Woodrow Wilson and in the terms of the treaty of Versailles, and especially powerfully endorsed by a majority at the United Nations after the Second World War, gave every substantial minority group grounds for a claim to independence or at least autonomy. The struggles of the Kurds of Iraq and Iran over many years, of the Karens, Kachins and Shans in Burma, of the Eritreans, Tigreans and Somalis in Ethiopia over almost as long, of Turkish Cypriots in Cyprus, of the Nagas and Mizos in India, of the Somalis in Kenya, and of the Ibos in Nigeria in their brief bid to create their own state, are all examples of struggles of this kind. Sometimes the people who felt oppressed were a majority rather than a minority of the whole population: such as the Hutus in Burundi or the Indians in Guatemala, resisting oppression or assimilation by a minority who dominated them. Sometimes the conflict was between entire regions, representing totally different cultures and religions: as in the long war between Christian north and Moslem south in the Philippines and between mainly Moslem north and mainly Christian south in Chad and Sudan. Sometimes the aims of such struggles were merely a vague aspiration among the peoples

TABLE 11   PRINCIPAL WARS CONCERNING MINORITIES, 1918–84

Dates	*States and minorities*
1918–19	Soviet Union (Ukrainians)
1918–19	Serbia (Montenegrins)
1946	Iran (southern tribesmen)
1947–8	India (Moslems), Pakistan (Hindus)
1948–	Burma (Karens, Kachins, Shans)
1955–72, 1983–	Sudan (southerners)
1955–69	India (Nagas)
1959	Ruanda (Tutsis)
1959	China (Tibetans)
1960–5	Congo (Katangans and others)
1961–	Ethiopia (Eritreans)
1961–75, 1979	Iraq (Kurds)
1963–4	Cyprus (Turks)
1966–8	India (Mizos)
1967–70	Nigeria (Ibos)
1968–76	Oman (Dhofaris)
1969–78	Philippines (southern Moslems)
1971	Pakistan (Bangladeshis)
1972	Burundi (Hutus)
1972–	Indonesia (West Irian)
1974–	Morocco (West Saharans)
1974–	Indonesia (East Timoreans)
1975–	Ethiopia (Tigreans)
1979–	Iran (Kurds, Azerbaijanis, Turcomans)
1979–81	Vietnam, Laos (minority tribesmen)
1983–	Sri Lanka (Tamils)

In addition minorities have undertaken substantial campaigns of violence short of war: as by Basques in Spain, Corsicans in France, republicans in Northern Ireland and Sikhs in India.

concerned to be allowed to maintain their own traditional way of life: as in the struggles of the tribespeople of Vietnam and Laos against successive governments, and those of the Mezquito and other Indian peoples in South America. Sometimes wars occurred in opposition to an attempt by an external power to take over control in succession to a colonial power: for example, the resistance of the peoples of East Timor to Indonesian rule, or those of the Western Sahara to Moroccan annexation. Finally, there have been a large number of other cases, not recorded in our lists, of struggles by minorities which have erupted in sporadic violence short of war: for example, the struggles of Basques in Spain, of Corsicans in France, of Catholic republicans in Northern Ireland; or the corresponding cases of violent oppression of minority peoples by ruling governments, as of the Bahais in Iran or of some Indian tribes by settlers in Brazil and Paraguay. Altogether there have been 24 wars about minority rights since 1945: 19 per cent of the total.

TABLE 12   PRINCIPAL FRONTIER WARS, 1918–84

Dates	Combatants
1918–19	Poland–Ukraine
1920	Lithuania–Poland (over Vilna)
1932	Peru–Colombia
1932–5	Bolivia–Paraguay
1939–40	Soviet Union–Finland
1941–2	Peru–Ecuador
1947–9	India–Pakistan (over Kashmir)
1957	Nicaragua–Honduras
1962	Algeria–Morocco
1962	India–China
1963–6	Indonesia–Malaysia
1964	Somalia–Ethiopia
1965	Pakistan – India (over Kashmir)
1965–7	Somalia–Kenya
1972	South Yemen–Yemen
1977–8	Somalia–Ethiopia
1978–9	Uganda–Tanzania
1980–	Iraq–Iran
1981	Peru-Ecuador

This list only includes conflicts about the precise position of frontiers: it omits wars concerning entire territories (the Baltic states, Israel, West Irian, East Timor, Western Sahara, the Falkland Islands). A substantial number of cases where armed force has been used to assert a frontier claim but where no significant fighting has occurred are also not listed.

The issue in another considerable group of conflicts concerns differences about frontiers (see Table 12). These differ from the territorial conflicts of earlier times in that they have not resulted from attempts at large-scale expansion. Most of them have not concerned large areas of territory but have arisen from genuine differences of view concerning the precise location of frontiers. In many cases they have occurred in the immediate aftermath of independence, when a newly emerging government has first had the opportunity to challenge boundaries which may have been acceptable to colonial masters but are less acceptable to indigenous governments or peoples. So the two wars between India and Pakistan for Kashmir, the skirmishes of 1959-62 between India and China, the brief frontier conflict between Morocco and Algeria in 1962, the successive challenges raised by Indonesia to parts of Malaysia, to West Irian and finally to East Timor, Somalia's attempt to acquire territories occupied by Somalis in Ethiopia and Kenya, the complex struggle between Morocco, Mauretania, Algeria and the Saharan peoples about the Western Sahara, among others, have all been struggles concerning frontiers in the years immediately following independence. Sometimes more long-standing frontier disputes have erupted into armed conflict mainly because the area was believed to contain valuable raw materials: this has been the case in several of the Latin American conflicts (the wars between Peru and Colombia in 1932, between Bolivia and Paraguay in 1932-5, and between Peru and Ecuador in 1942 and 1981). Sometimes the claims have been based on ethnic grounds, as Somalia's claim against her neighbours has been. Sometimes they have been based on historical claims and the interpretation of treaties: like the conflicts between China and India, Indonesia and Malaysia, the Philippines and Malaysia, and most of the Latin American disputes. Sometimes they have concerned territories to which both parties can lay claims on different criteria, as in the conflict between India and Pakistan over Kashmir (the Indian claim being based on the principle of accession by rulers — the principle accepted at independence; the Pakistani claim on self-determination). Whatever the basis of the claims, they have frequently aroused passions on both sides quite disproportionate to the value of the areas in question, which were often of very small intrinsic value. The conflict between the Soviet Union and China in 1969 and between Iraq and Iran (1980-) concerned the precise location of river boundaries; yet the latter has caused (and the former almost caused) one of the most bitter and costly conflicts of the age. Altogether 18 of the wars listed for this period have concerned frontier questions of this kind: about 11 per cent of the total.

The issues over which war occurred in this age, therefore, have been distinctive in many respects. There has, at least since 1945, been little concern for territory, little overt expansionism, and very few wars of conquest (the main exceptions have been Uganda's war against Tanzania in 1978-9 and Iraq's war against Iran from 1980). In many cases the issues over which war has occurred have related to events within countries: the balance of political power within them, the rights of minorities, revolution and counter-revolution. Sometimes such conflicts have led to considerable intervention from without and so to wider wars. The armed conflicts in which the super-powers have become involved — the ones that have, therefore, been potentially the most dangerous for the peace of the world — have never arisen from issues occurring directly between them (the balance of military power, border frictions, territorial demands or even the situation in directly contested areas such as Berlin) but have been precipitated by events in third territories, usually adjoining one or other of them, which they believed important for their own security but were unable to control: in Eastern Europe, in Afghanistan, in Korea, in Vietnam, in Central America and the Caribbean. In such cases the super-powers have nearly always been responding to events elsewhere. Neither the super-powers, nor even the blocs to which they belong, have created these conflicts: it cannot be said that the crises in Vietnam, the Dominican Republic or El Salvador were caused by US intervention or those in Poland and Afghanistan by Soviet intervention (though in each case they may have been made worse by it). In other words, the issues that have ultimately led to war, especially to war involving a super-power, have often been highly localised: they have become significant because, in a rapidly shrinking world, the leaders of each ideological bloc believe that even wholly domestic events in neighbouring areas could be of vital concern to them. Any major political change in areas close to their own borders, they held, could represent a threat to their security or to that of the bloc they led. Security and politics, in other words, are now closely intertwined. And the issues over which wars are now most often fought are issues of domestic politics — what kind of government should rule in this place or that — issues that are increasingly believed to be of direct and legitimate concern to the governments of other states.

Conclusions

What conclusion can be drawn from this examination of the issues about which wars have been mainly fought in different ages?

Our survey shows that states have been willing to go to war at different times over a wide range of different issues. Though there has been a substantial variation in the kinds of dispute which have led to war in the same age, far more striking is the wide difference between the issues thought worthy of war in different international societies.

Thus claims to succession in another state, the issue that most often caused war in the age of dynasties, was progressively less often an issue in each succeeding period, and ceased altogether to be a cause of war in the last two international societies we have examined. Disputes concerning the religious rights to be accorded to particular faiths, the most common cause of war between 1559 and 1648, was rarely an issue in the following period, and never in the two ages after that. War over commercial rights, not uncommon in the first three societies we have considered, never takes place today (and almost never did so in the age of nationalism). Disputes concerning the ideological persuasion of the government of another state, probably the most common cause of war in the contemporary society, was rarely an issue in the wars of any earlier age. And so on.

These are striking differences, which indicate how widely the immediate stimulus to war has varied from one age to another. It is true that these immediate issues have not necessarily been the only reasons why war has occurred. There have often been more general rivalries, inherited resentments, domestic pressures for war, or other factors stimulating conflict. But it is not self-evident that the latter have been more important than the former in bringing war about. On the contrary, in the minds of those most closely involved, the kinds of issue that we have been concerned with in this chapter have often appeared the most important questions in dispute. Without that stimulus war in many cases would not have occurred. The diversity of these issues suggests that the fact of warfare cannot be put down, as is sometimes suggested, to a single overriding passion — whether nationalism, economic interest, the competition for power, or political concern — which continually causes nations or peoples to engage in war against each other. War is rather an instrument which can be utilised in pursuit of many quite different aims, if it is seen, in particular circumstances, as the best means available for promoting that cause: whether to win a crown, to defend a faith, to enhance the glory of a state, to promote national revolution, or to further the interests of an ideological alliance.

Whether or not an issue becomes the cause of war does not necessarily depend on its intrinsic importance. Often the issue can stimulate war only because it is *seen* to be of importance, perhaps for symbolic reasons. Whether Dutch ships dipped their flags to English (or vice versa), whether the Chinese responsible for the death of an English sailor was adequately punished, whether the German Kaiser had been discourteous to the French ambassador or not were of very little material importance to the rulers of the countries that made them a *casus belli*, still less to the mass of their people. They were thought worth war by those who wielded power because they were symbolic: they became questions of national pride, and were believed to have important implications for the relative status of the two powers concerned. For similar reasons governments in all ages have been prepared to go to war for the possession of small and largely valueless territories, irrespective of their intrinsic worth: because disputes of that kind, it was generally accepted, were to be settled by war. Against this, matters of far greater material consequence to governments and peoples have *not* been thought to be issues about which war could or should be undertaken. Questions concerning the price to be paid for particular raw materials, concerning monopolies established for trade in particular products or particular areas, concerning the levels of tariffs or other barriers imposed against trade, concerning aid policies, the rescheduling of debts or the level of interest rates — these matters, which really do have a substantial impact on the welfare and standards of living of millions of people, are not seen as issues suitable for resolution by force. Nor are certain kinds of political dispute, however important they may be to both parties: those concerning, for example, the powers and functions of international organisations of various kinds, the nationalisation of foreign companies, the protection of human rights in another country, or the way in which other governments conduct their economic or other policies generally — these too are not seen, and never have so far been seen, as issues for which war can legitimately be made.

In other words, there is a strong conventional element determining which issues are, and which are not, thought suitable to be resolved through war. It is naturally issues where there is direct competition between two states that have been most generally resolved through war: the struggle for territory, trade or colonies for example. But in many other areas where there is competition (such as trade or investment today) no wars take place. Competition alone, even competition for status, is not sufficient to create war. There must be an issue of a particular kind on which a battle of wills occurs.

Such issues arise above all where there is a conflict of expectations between two or more countries. It is where each believes it has a legitimate claim to particular kinds of trading right (as between Britain and China in 1839), or to control of a particular waterway (as between Britain and Egypt in 1956), or to a piece of territory (as between Britain and Argentina in 1982), that war is most likely to erupt: all typical cases, where each party had good reasons, based on different preconceptions, to believe itself in the right. Such conflicts are especially common where there exists a situation of ambiguity or uncertainty, an ambiguity which is often interpreted by both parties in contradictory ways. Thus we have several times noticed above, for example, how in almost every age conflicts have arisen in places where there existed a situation of ambiguous sovereignty. Here the conflict of expectations has existed in classic form. What was the right enjoyed by whom in feudal duchies such as Brittany, or cities such as Liège, where control was shared between fief-holder and overlord? Or in areas where no clear sovereignty existed, as in Prussia, disputed between Teutonic Knights and Poland? Or in the places emerging from Ottoman control, where local people were held to enjoy the right of "autonomy" under Turkish "suzerainty"? Or in places where sovereignty had been deliberately circumscribed, as in the Rhineland and Danzig between the two world wars, or in Berlin and the Suez and Panama Canals afterwards? Because there existed genuine and legitimate differences of view about these points — which could not occur where sovereignty was firmly established — war was especially liable to take place over them. A similar conflict of expectations arose over other types of issue: over rights of free navigation in the age of sovereignty, over treaty rights (in Schleswig-Holstein or the Ottoman Empire) in the age of nationalism, over the right of intervention in civil wars in the age of ideology. It has been above all over questions of this kind, where there has existed no consensus about the rights and obligations of states, that a clash of expectations has been most likely to lead to all-out war.

Another wide category of issues which in every one of our societies has been a potential cause of war is that comprising threats to security, especially to the security of larger powers. In different ages security has inevitably been conceived in different ways. In one society it was seen to demand control of territory required for purposes of communication: such as that demanded by Spain in the Valtellina and Alsace. In others it was seen to demand control of the "gates" of a country, controlling access to its borders: such as that demanded by France, in the days of Louis XIV, in Roussillon, Savoy, Alsace, Flanders and Artois. In yet another age it could be seen as demanding control of sea routes or naval stations protecting access to overseas territory, such as that demanded by Britain in Gibraltar, Malta, Egypt, Aden, the Seychelles and Singapore. In others again, it has been held to demand control of major political developments in neighbouring states: such as that demanded by the Soviet Union in Eastern Europe and the United States in Central America today. But whatever form the demands for security have taken, it is where it is seen to be threatened that a major power is especially likely to resort to force: as when threats to Catholic power in the Valtellina in 1620 stimulated Spanish intervention there; as when Louis XIV's intervention in Alsace, Luxemburg, Genoa and the Palatinate in the 1680s seemed to threaten France's neighbours; as when Serbia seemed to threaten Austria's position in the Balkans in 1914; or when radical political change in neighbouring states was seen as a threat to the security of the Soviet Union in 1956, 1968 and 1979, or to that of the United States in 1954, 1961, 1965 and 1983.

Another range of issues that has arisen in most, though not all, of the societies we have examined are those that relate to economic concerns. Again our survey shows that these have taken totally different forms in different ages, according to the character of economic interests in each age. Most common have been conflicts concerning the economic rights one state can enjoy in the territory of another, especially trading rights: conflicts such as the wars between the Hanseatic cities, on the one hand, and Denmark, England and the Netherlands, on the other, in the age of dynasties, or those between the United Provinces and England, and the United Provinces and France, in the age of sovereignty. Some have concerned access to trading *routes:* such as the conflicts between Russia and Poland, and Russia and Sweden, in the sixteenth and seventeenth centuries, and between Britain and Spain in the same period. Others have concerned the right to tax trade in particular areas: that of the Danes to *tax* trade through the Sound, or of Britain to tax trade in the American colonies. In recent times, however, as we have seen, no wars have been fought on economic issues. Here too conventions have changed. Although economic issues are now probably more important in relations between states than in any earlier time — both among rich countries themselves (disputes over investment, interest rates, protectionism, subsidies and unfair competition of various kinds) and between rich countries and poor (the whole range of North-South issues) — war to resolve such disputes is no longer regarded as acceptable.

In other words there is no consistency in the issues which have been seen as worthy of war in different ages. Questions that seem of vital national importance in one age, and a justifiable cause of war, in another are matters of indifference. Questions that are resolved exclusively by diplomatic means in one age are settled by brute force in another. But whether an issue seems important enough for war in a particular age is not only a matter of convention. It depends, as we have seen for each of the periods examined, on the ideology which rules in each international society. That in turn is determined by the concerns which nations have most at heart in each age: in other words, their underlying motives.

4 Motives

The preceding chapter has shown us that the immediate issues about which war has occurred have varied widely from one age to another. Those that stimulated many wars in one period caused none in another. Succession to a throne, about which many wars were fought in one age, never aroused conflict in others. Religious questions about which a large proportion of wars were concerned in one age were a matter of indifference in others. Whether or not a particular type of issue is thought worth a war or not, therefore, does not depend on the intrinsic character of the issue but on other and ulterior factors: the concerns, preoccupations and aspirations of states in each age — in other words, their motives.

In talking about the motives of states we are, of course, using a figure of speech. In looking at the actions of nations over a period, it is natural to attribute to them motives that may account for those actions. In doing so we are to some extent talking about the real motives of individuals, those individuals that exercise decision-making power within a nation or group. But even here we are speaking of motives of a special kind: the motives they feel and express as representatives of a nation or group, not their personal motives. An individual may be unassuming and pacific in personal conduct, yet may lead his nation into aggressive action in his collective role; may be personally pugnacious and intolerant, yet as the leader of a nation conciliatory and peace-loving. Usually, in any case, the actions of states reflect the feelings and attitudes not of individuals only but of substantial ruling groups or even of large sections of the population. And here, still more, it is group feelings and aspirations that are decisive. We are concerned, in other words, with *collective* motives; the motives of organised states as expressed in their actions.[1]

Understood in this way, it is not unreasonable to speak of nations (or groups within nations) as having motives. If they act consistently to attack their neighbours, one can reasonably speak of their motives as being "aggressive". If they act consistently to seek territory from surrounding areas, it is reasonable to describe them as having "territorial" or "expansive" objectives. At first sight the motives of states are less firmly rooted, and can change more quickly, than those of individuals: for while the character of an individual is likely to show considerable consistency throughout his or her natural life, that of a nation may change radically whenever there is a change of government. But though this can happen — it occurred, for example, for France when Louis Napoleon became ruler, or for Libya after the revolution of 1969 — normally, when governments fall, the goals of states change much less than might be expected. For usually those motives reflect the fundamental interests of the state, rather than personal concerns: traditional beliefs and aspirations as well as the attitudes of the current rulers. And for that reason they are not usually quickly altered even when changes in leadership occur.

The motives of states — or, put more simply, their foreign-policy aims — are clearly of crucial importance in the study of wars. If we assume that war is in most cases an intentional activity, then we must, in studying it, be concerned about the nature of the intentions that bring it about. Even if we assume that in some cases it is not intentional — that some times actions are undertaken which, though they clearly risk war, were not necessarily intended to cause it — we must still wish to know what were the intentions which had that consequence. In either case, therefore, in examining war it is important for us to consider carefully what are the motives of nations and groups which in practice lead them into war against each other.

The motives of states (like those of individuals) can be defined in general or specific terms. As we found in the case of issues, if we define them in a sufficiently general way — the desire to "promote national interests", for example, or to "win power" — they can be shown to have been shared by all states in all ages (just as all individuals can be shown to pursue "desire" or "self-interest" if these are defined as "what humans seek") and to be attainable as much by peaceful as by warlike activities. Conversely, if we define motives in too specific terms (the desire to "recover Alsace-Lorraine", or to "crush Serbia") they may not apply to more than a single state at a single moment. Thus, as with issues, we shall be concerned with motives at a middle level, of a kind that have applied to some states in some ages but not to all in every age; and we shall be concerned not with all motives but with those particular motives which have the effect of leading states into war against each other.

Clearly conflict, whether among nations or individuals, occurs especially where goals are incompatible: where what one party badly wants — whether money, power, territory or trading rights — can be secured only at the expense of another. If the parties have motives that are by their nature competitive, can only be satisfied by frustrating the goals of others, conflict is likely to be frequent between them. If it were the case, for example, that all states in all ages desired territory, and desired it so much that they were willing to make war to acquire it; if other nations prized it so much that they would not give it up willingly; and if there existed no unoccupied territory — then warfare between states must automatically occur. Conversely, if they have wishes that are mutually compatible — if they most wish for higher economic growth or better social services or a rich cultural life (which all can have together), if all are content with the territory, wealth, security or power they already have, or at least are not so discontented that they will make war to make good the deficiency — a situation of peace between them is likely to be maintained. Though over-simplified, such examples show the importance which the motives of states must have in determining whether or not war is likely to occur.

It is thus of some importance in studying war to examine what have been the main motives of states which have brought them into conflict, how far these are constant goals of all states at all times and how far they have changed over the years; and, if motives have changed, how far this has affected their propensity to war in different periods of history. It is to these questions that we address ourselves in this chapter.

The age of dynasties (1400-1559)

The motives that are of concern to us in this age are primarily those of the rulers themselves. In most states it was they who decided, subject only to the influence of their immediate advisers, whether or not a war should take place. And it was their concerns and ambitions which were therefore the decisive factors in determining policy.

The most intense desire of most rulers was to increase the possessions, and so the prestige, of their own houses. As Machiavelli put it, "the desire to acquire possessions is a very natural and ordinary thing, and when those men do it who can do so successfully, they are always praised and not blamed".[2] This is certainly what most rulers themselves believed; and it was an ambition that must inevitably lead them into frequent warfare, both at home and abroad.

The aim was not one of simple conquest (Machiavelli also made clear the difficulty of holding down a disaffected population[3]). The best way to acquire possessions, was, as we have seen, to prove a right of succession to a throne elsewhere. That ambition was not limited by considerations of geography, race, language or culture: any territory, however distant, could be claimed; and was worth fighting for if a basis of claim could be found. The importance of this objective in the consideration of rulers is shown by the sacrifices they were willing to pay in order to promote it. Alfonso V of Aragon was willing to spend most of his life in distant Naples, a substantial part of it engaged in war, for the sake of maintaining his claim to that city and its possessions. Danish kings were willing to imperil their throne by huge concessions to the nobility, and in many hazardous campaigns, for the sake of pursuing their claim to rule in Sweden. Charles VIII of France was willing to give up assets of huge value — Roussillon and Cerdagne in the south and claims to Flanders and Artois (the "gates" of France to which Louis XIV was to attach such value) to Spain, as well as pay huge sums of money to England — to buy off potential enemies for the sake of asserting claims in Italy. English kings were willing to fight for 120 years for the right to wear the crown of France; the houses of Anjou and Aragon contested for almost as long the right to rule in Naples and Milan; members of the Jagellon family fought to add the crowns of Hungary and Bohemia to those of Poland and Lithuania which they already wore. Few begrudged the expenditure, in blood and treasure, that those struggles made necessary. Such dynastic ambitions were even directed at the offices of emperor and pope. The imperial title, though officially elective still, in practice had become, from before our period began, the prerogative of two or three great clans — the Wittelsbachs, Luxemburgs and Hapsburgs — and from the mid- fifteenth century became to all intents and purposes a hereditary office, held by a single family almost without break for over 300 years. Popes too, though nominally elected, were increasingly chosen from the great families of Italy — Borgia, Medici and Farnese (Lorenzo the Magnificent had his son appointed a cardinal at the age of 17, as a first step to becoming eventually Pope Leo X). And once installed they devoted themselves above all else, like other dynasts, to promoting the interests of their own families, appointing their nephews and other relatives (even sons) to every possible position of influence within and outside the church. Pope Paul II appointed five nephews and great-nephews as cardinals and married three others to the most eligible families of Italy, while Paul III devoted most of his period of office to promoting the interests of the Farnese family. Moreover, church offices themselves were often hereditary: thus for 200 years the office of archbishop of Cologne was held continually by the younger sons of the Bavarian Wittelsbach family. Everywhere, in other words, the dynastic ambition prevailed.

This was the underlying motive behind many of the wars of this age. The goal of the rulers was not usually direct control, nor even taxable revenues. It was theoretical overlordship. During their negotiations with the French in 1435 the English negotiators were prepared to hand vast territories back to the control of France if only the French king would pay homage to the English monarch. Geography was no limit to such ambitions. None thought it strange that English kings should wish to rule in France, Danish in Sweden and Norway, Aragonese in Sardinia, Sicily and Naples, Hungarian in Bohemia and Polish in Hungary. No family demonstrated so clearly the scale of this ambition to rule in distant, and quite disparate, territories as the

Hapsburgs, who, through ingenious matrimony, brought together most of the more prosperous territories of the continent, as well as of the known world beyond the seas, irrespective of ethnic or geographical considerations. Even then they were not content: so Charles V, obsessed by the dynastic imperative, proceeded to marry his son to the queen of England, his four sisters to the kings of France, Portugal, Hungary and Denmark, his brother to the princess of Hungary, his nieces to the king of Poland, the duke of Milan, the duke of Lorraine and the elector Palatine, and his natural daughter to the pope's grandson, Ottavio Farnese, thus tying almost every royal family in the continent to his own. But matrimonial policy alone was not always enough. The pursuit of dynastic ambitions might finally require war. For it was a motive which was by its nature competitive. The number of available crowns and territories was limited; the number of possible claimants large. Claims were never difficult to manufacture, because, as we have seen, a large number of alternative bases for claims could be put forward (pp. 86-7). The desire to succeed to foreign thrones, therefore, could not fail to bring the rulers into conflict with each other. Here was a motive that inevitably, therefore, carried within itself the seeds of war.

The desire for territory was another goal that was widely shared and also by nature competitive. In a feudal age one of the most universal desires, among monarchs as among their subjects, was to become the possessor of new lands elsewhere.

> Ruling dynasties laid province to province, as the more successful landlords among their subjects laid field to field, by purchase and exchange and foreclosure, but chiefly by marriage and inheritance. Force was employed not to advance a rational interest, but to support a legal claim . . . . In consequence the leading thread in the diplomacy of all this period was dynastic interest. . . .[4]

Underlying the desire for thrones, therefore, was a more fundamental desire for the lands which the thrones brought with them. Rulers prided themselves on the long list of titles to such land which they could attach to their names. Kings of England continued to style themselves as kings of France and lords of Guienne and other provinces long after the last English soldiers had left French soil. Kings of France would declare themselves dukes of Naples and Milan, whether or not they happened to be in control of those duchies at the time. Charles V could of course boast the longest list of titles of all, including duke of Burgundy (though his family had long ceased to hold the duchy itself), king of Castile and Léon, king of Aragon, count of Barcelona, duke of Naples, ruler of Peru and Mexico, holder of innumerable other duchies and counties and assorted titles, even including "King of Jerusalem" and "Lord of Asia and Africa". None could match this vast assemblage of territories, but all agreed that, the greater the territory to which a monarch could claim a title, the greater and more glorious he must be. And most were therefore willing to fight another war to win the title to another land.

As the period progressed, the dynastic and territorial objectives of the rulers began to be rather more sharply focussed. Though they were still ready to acquire lands in any part of the continent, they became especially concerned to win control of territory which they hoped would be of special value to their own state. Strategic positions were specially desired. So they fought especially for fortresses (Pinerolo and Casale), ports (Alfsborg and Reval), islands (Cyprus, Ösel). Spain and France fought so fiercely for Milan not only because of its wealth but also because of its strategic position at the head of the peninsula. Don Diego Mendoza, Charles V's ambassador to Venice, implored Charles, when he was thinking of conceding the city to France on dynastic grounds, to hang on to it on the grounds that "Milan is the gateway to Italy. Let it but fall into the hands of the French and all your friends in the peninsula will desert you."[5] Such wars demonstrated that territory was no longer coveted by rulers exclusively to maintain dynastic rights: increasingly such claims were likely to be directed at territory that was especially valued for geographical, strategic, economic or other reasons.

The power of the dynastic principle in this age is, however, nowhere better illustrated than it is by the concern of the rulers, having conquered by force, to prove their *rights* of succession. Even after he had won unchallenged power in England, Henry VII thought it necessary to marry the Yorkist contender who had the strongest claim to the throne. Even after he had already succeeded to the French throne, Francis I found it prudent to marry the daughter of his predecessor to place his crown beyond challenge. Years after the absorption of Brittany by France, Louis XII found it necessary to divorce his wife to marry the current duchess of Brittany to validate the annexation. Long after Spanish Navarre was unmistakably conquered by Spain in 1512, Spanish rulers sought to justify the conquest, *post hoc*, by the proposed marriage between the emperor's son and Jeanne d'Albret in 1539, "so that these claims . . . may be settled at last", as Charles V put it. Even after he had already acquired Montferrat in 1533, the duke of Mantua felt it necessary to divorce his wife to marry the sister of the last marquis and so prove his right to it. Long after he had himself won firm control of Milan, Charles V contemplated prejudicing Spain's entire position in Italy by an arrangement to pass that city to a French prince and a Spanish princess (or even for the two countries to share it alternatively) to satisfy French dynastic claims which he felt he could not altogether deny. In other words, conquest alone was not enough: dynastic rights were never totally disregarded in cases of territorial conflict in this age.

The consolidation of territories that were scattered or divided became an important objective, and the frequent cause of war. The dukes of Burgundy, having accumulated by marriage two great blocks of separate territory, made war to acquire the intervening or adjoining lands: annexing Luxemburg in 1443, intervening in Alsace in 1469, conquering Gelderland in 1473, attacking Cologne in 1474 and Lorraine in 1475. Louis XI fought successive campaigns in France to win back fiefdoms for the crown: so he seized Burgundy, Artois and Picardy (the latter two temporarily) in 1477, Anjou in 1480, Maine and Provence in 1481 and Brittany in 1491. The Hapsburg rulers sought to acquire or regain territories that would link their patrimonial lands in Germany: Alsace, acquired from their kinsman Sigismund in 1491, and Württemberg, purchased in 1522 (but conquered from them again in 1534). Ivan the Great subdued the independent enclaves of Russia — Novgorod (1478), Pskov (1510), and Vyatka (1489), for example — and won new territories in the Ukraine and eastern Lithuania. Conversely, rulers were now more willing to abandon designs on distant lands that were less central to the interests of their state. By the end of the period French kings were willing (in the treaty of Cateau-Cambrésis) to relinquish their claims to territory in Italy in exchange for full recognition of their rights in Burgundy. Spain became willing to forget about French Navarre across the Pyrenees, so long as she won recognition of her rights in Spanish Navarre on her own side. Denmark eventually abandoned her claims in Sweden, as England did hers in France (even, at the very end of the period, her hold on Calais). In Italy the same process was visible. Genoa abandoned distant Trebizond and Cyprus, and concentrated on Corsica and mainland Italy. Venice, now largely deprived of her empire in the East, built up a body of territories in mainland Italy. Milan absorbed more and more small city states to her south. The Papacy recovered the Romagna and consolidated further areas to the north under its own control. Florence assimilated Pisa. And so on.

Another important objective of the rulers was to win status for themselves and their own house. This did not always require war. Renown could be won by the creation of a lavish court (as undertaken by the dukes of Burgundy); or by conspicuous display (as exhibited by Francis I and Henry VIII at the Field of the Cloth of Gold); or by the patronage of great artists (as displayed by Pope Leo X and the dukes of Bavaria). But in many cases the simplest and surest way to secure glory was through war. For the knights, for the nobles, and above all for the kings, war was the means of winning renown and advancement. Honoré Bonet, writing just before our period begins, believed that the truly strong and valiant man "finds all his pleasure and all his delight in being in armes".[6] Machiavelli wrote, "Nothing causes a prince to be so much esteemed as great enterprises and giving proof of prowess"; and he quoted the example of Ferdinand of Aragon, who had acquired both reputation and power among the nobles of his country by his successful campaign against Granada.[7] Again this was an exhortation that was scarcely needed. Henry V, in renewing the campaign in France; Charles VIII, in launching his country on the Italian campaigns; Charles V, in assaulting Tunis and Algiers — all saw these as an opportunity to win glory, for their country and their royal house almost as much as for themselves.

The converse of the desire to win glory for one's own house was to bring about the downfall of another. Much of the diplomacy of the age, and many of the wars, were aimed primarily at causing discomfiture to some foreign ruler. An important means of doing this was to give assistance to rebels in another state. So Francis I gave his help to rebels in Navarre, Gelderland and Sedan against Charles V, as assiduously as the latter assisted the duke of Bourbon against Francis. Louis XI stirred up rebellion in Liège and Ghent, just as Charles the Bold assisted the dukes of Berry and Bourbon against Louis, and as Maximilian I and Henry VII assisted Brittany against his successor. A simple way of causing difficulties to a foreign ruler was to support pretenders in his state: so England supported pretenders in Brittany and Artois in the early part of the Hundred Years War, while later France, Burgundy and Scotland all gave their support to Perkin Warbeck in England.

These efforts directly challenged another widely shared aim of the princes, as important to them as any ambitions they might harbour abroad. This was their concern to establish unchallenged royal power at home. Confronted as they were by threats to their authority — from the great magnates, from regional uprisings, from rebellious cities and discontented peasantry — they were determined to assert their authority by war if necessary. A substantial proportion of the wars of this age resulted from that endeavour. Some were general conflicts between a ruler and a number of magnates in league against him: such as the wars of the French kings against the Praguerie in 1440 and the League of the Common Weal in 1465; the *Guerre Folle* of 1485; the Wars of the Roses in England; and the efforts of successive kings of Denmark, Poland and Hungary to tame the nobles there. Sometimes they took the form of more limited duels between a ruler and particular nobles: for example, the successive wars of Louis XI against the dukes of Bourbon, Berry and Brittany, the rebellions of the dukes of Northumberland and Warwick in

England; the challenge of the Zapolyas to the Hapsburg rulers of Hungary; and the clashes between successive Turkish sultans and brothers challenging for their throne. The leaders of these revolts, often close relatives — uncles, brothers or even sons — of the ruler, could frequently call on substantial military resources: the decentralisation of power in most states encouraged rebellion. In Germany the division of the family lands on the death of a ruler among several sons often prompted conflict among the rival heirs: it led, for example, to centuries of conflict between the Albertine and Ernestine branches of the Wettin family (just as similar family wars had resulted from the division of Charles IV's Bohemian lands in 1378 and those of the Viscontis in 1354). Because of such problems the practice was increasingly abandoned in Germany from the end of the fifteenth century. But even at the end of this period there were still two dukes of Saxony (in frequent conflict with each other), two dukes of Brunswick, two dukes of Bavaria, a Brandenburg-Kustrin and a Brandenburg-Kulmbach, and so on.

But domestic war did not always result from challenges from the great magnates. Conflict arose often from the demands of discontented peasantry, rebellious cities or entire regions. Peasant revolts were endemic throughout this period (only the most serious are included in our list). Cities, especially the most industrialised, frequently arose against aristocratic or ecclesiastical rulers: as in the successive risings of Ghent against its duke, of Liège against its bishop, of Florence against its Medici leaders, and of Valencia and other cities against Charles V in 1520-2. Perhaps most common of all were the uprisings of entire regions, resentful of neglect or foreign rule in general: as by Wales in 1401-9, Catalonia in 1461-72, Brittany in 1492-4, Ireland in 1493-6, and Gelderland over almost a century before 1543 (see Table 2). Though by the end of the period the rulers, at least in Western Europe, had generally been able to impose their rule throughout most of their territories, this was achieved only at the cost of constant warfare; and often it was the very attempt to achieve centralised control that led to conflict. Cities fought for customary liberties and traditions (as in the Netherlands and Spain); regions for the right of self-rule (as in Wales and Catalonia). Here too were incompatible motives. At a time before national loyalties had been created, the desire of many cities and regions for independence, conflicting with that of their rulers to establish unfettered authority throughout their lands, inevitably bred continual warfare.

Another objective that could lead to war was the concern of many rulers to maintain the "true" religion (whatever it might be). Charles V declared that, "since God had called him to the highest honour in the world . . . he would set his own life and all he had on the preservation of the Christian faith".[8] Though true crusades — expeditions to reclaim the Holy Land from heathen occupation — were no longer undertaken (p. 91 above), the term was still employed to dignify almost any military campaign that could be claimed to have a religious purpose. So Urban VI's campaign against the Avignon pope, the assault of the Catholic kings in Granada in 1483-91, naval action against the pirates of North Africa, the League of Cambrai's war against Venice in 1508-10, and even the second French invasion of Italy in 1499, were all dubbed "crusades" (just as John of Gaunt had adopted the same title for his dynastic war in Castile in the previous century). The Spanish advance into North Africa after the conquest of Granada in 1491 was explicitly accepted as a crusade by the pope, so allowing the use of the *cruzada,* a crusade tax, to pay for it. The war of the League of Cambrai against Venice in 1508-10 was also declared a crusade by Pope Julian II in a papal bull. Yet real crusades, such as the efforts which popes still occasionally made to mobilise Christian rulers against the Turkish threat, in practice now normally secured only a lukewarm response: thus when Pius II declared a new holy war against the Turks in 1464, and even offered to lead it himself, there was virtually no response from the rulers of the day. Nothing showed more clearly the decline in crusading fervour. At the end of the century the ruler of Naples was even willing to call in the Turks to defend his territory; while in the next century his Most Christian Majesty, the king of France himself, would openly align himself with the Turkish sultan.

Increasingly, in any case, this motive — to spread Christianity — was displaced by another, equally likely to result in war: the desire to maintain the true faith among Christians. In an age of new questioning about traditional belief and practice, it was disputes between Christians themselves which now aroused most passion. Dissent among Christians had been anticipated, at the very beginning of the period, in the bitter conflict among rival popes and their supporters in 1400-15, as well as in that between successive popes and reforming councils of 1425-45. It was seen still more clearly in the fierce wars against the Hussites in 1420-35. But it was shown above all after the reformation writings began to appear so profusely, from 1520 onwards, in the bitter confrontations between the reformers and their opponents. It was increasingly accepted that the differences which divided them might eventually only be resolved through war. The English Catholic bishop William Allen wrote that "There is no warre in the world so just or honourable . . . as that which is waged for religion, we say for the true, ancient Catholique, Roman religion."[9] And the puritan divine William Gouge stated that wars "made by expresse charge from God . . . had the best warrant that could be, God's command", and that, "for a soldier to die in the field in a good cause, it is as for a preacher to die in a pulpit".[10] In 1530 Luther declared, after the publication of the imperial recess of that year: "proceed then joyfully, come what may, be it war or revolt, as the wrath of God shall decide". Calvin and his followers explicitly justified rebellion in the cause of religion. Charles V, though genuinely looking for compromise, increasingly resigned himself to the ultimate necessity of war, even preventive war, to determine the issues. He formally proposed this to the imperial electors in January 1531; and, when he finally declared war against the protestants in 1545, he wrote to his sister Mary on 9 June, that the heretics were anyway

> determined to rise in revolt . . . Thus we have determined . . . that force alone would drive them to accept reasonable terms. The time is opportune for they have been weakened by their recent wars. . . Unless we take immediate action all the estates of Germany may lose their faith and the Netherlands may follow. . . .[11]

War was encouraged by the fact that it was taken for granted that the ruler could determine the religion of his subjects. Thus on his defeat by Charles V in 1543 the duke of Cleves had to agree to return to the Catholic religion (just as King Christian of Denmark had been obliged to promise to return to the Catholic faith in order to win the assistance of his brother-in-law the emperor a few years earlier). Here then were two motives that were totally irreconcilable: the desire to suppress a new faith and the desire to maintain it. That conflict was expressed at its clearest in the two wars on the issue in Germany in 1546-7 and in 1552-5, when the aim of Charles V was to compel the rulers to accept the formula for Christian belief which he believed was the furthest that could be reconciled with the traditional faith, while that of his opponents was to allow each ruler to determine freely the faith of his own people (so long, at least, as he did not choose Calvinism).

For some rulers and some states economic objectives began to be important. Economic motives had some part to play in almost every war. Often war was profitable: both for the rulers who declared war and for the nobles and knights who fought it (pp. 239-40 below). Rulers could acquire indemnities and other assets; commanders, and even common soldiers, plunder, ransom and loot.[12] But for most rulers in this age wars were not undertaken primarily for economic motives. Only states that depended totally on foreign trade undertook war as a means of securing economic objectives. The cities of the Hanseatic League did, as we have seen, make war to enforce trading conditions favourable to their merchants: as in the war against Denmark in 1426-35, or that against England in 1468-74, for example. In the same way in 1534-6 Lübeck and the Netherlands, though appearing to support rival contenders for the Danish throne, in reality fought to promote their competing economic objectives in the area; and as a result the merchants of the Netherlands won the right to free trade and free passage in the Baltic. But for most rulers economic gains were not a major consideration in decisions for war. And in some cases economic interests could be a reason for *avoiding* war. Where there were close economic relations between two countries, war could damage the interests of important sections of their population and could thus be extremely unpopular. On these grounds England and Burgundy, between which there was a flourishing trade, normally sought to avoid war with each other (even Henry VIII and Charles V, despite contrary national interests, were constrained, mainly for this reason, to avoid war, apart from one brief engagement, against the other.)[13]

So there were a number of policy objectives in this age that were likely to lead states into conflict. A number were competitive goals, the objects of which could not easily be shared. Chief of these was the aim to secure possession of a throne elsewhere: whether contested by a rival claimant or by the local people, such claims must often lead to war. The demand for territory, especially strategically valuable territory, whether or not by way of a dynastic claim, was another that most usually met resistance and so bred conflict. The desire to secure a well-endowed bride was equally likely to be widely shared, and so could cause contention. The aim to establish royal control throughout a kingdom often, for different reasons (since there were many who had good reason to resist it), had the same effect.

These were not the inevitable drives of every state in every age. They were objectives which, if not peculiar to this age, were all to become less significant in subsequent periods. Against this, other aims of the day were to become more important later. The desire to protect or promote a religious faith, or to eliminate a heresy, would, with rising religious passions, be still more powerful in the age which followed. The attempt to promote economic interests, for example by winning access to trade in particular areas, which was not a common reason for war in this age, was to become more significant in the years to come.

This reflected a more general change, already being felt as this period came to a close. As time went by, the personal interests of the rulers, in promoting the power and glory of their own royal house, was gradually supplemented and replaced by another objective: the desire to promote the interests and power of the state with which that house was identified. In the period that followed the latter aim was to become still more important. And it was the one which, in the following two centuries, was most often to bring states into conflict with each other.

The age of religions (1559-1648)

In the age that followed the motive which most frequently led states into war against each other was concern about the doctrine and practice of religion. It was a concern that was shared by most of those who controlled policy: that is, the rulers and their ministers. And it was reflected in the decisions they reached on questions of peace and war.

A primary aim, among rulers as among peoples, was to secure the widest possible acceptance of their own faith. Catholics and protestants alike sought to spread their own gospels, and if possible to eliminate the practice of other beliefs: at least in their own territory and sometimes further afield. Given the general belief that only one faith could be tolerated (p. 93 above), here was another motive which must lead to conflict. It did not necessarily imply war. Preachers and pamphleteers could be sent out to win converts and save foreign lands from error: such as the Calvinist preachers who flooded from Switzerland and Germany to the Netherlands to spread their faith there; or the Jesuit crusaders who were sent by the Emperor Ferdinand to convert, sometimes by ruthless means, the misguided peoples of Bohemia and neighbouring areas; or the Orthodox teachers sent to reclaim the people of the Ukraine from the errors of the Uniates. Since rulers could often determine the religious practice of an entire people, the conversion of a ruler might be another peaceful means of establishing a faith throughout his land: as when the Calvinists, having already twice converted electors Palatine to their faith, won the elector of Brandenburg and the ruler of Hesse at the beginning of the seventeenth century; or when Pope Clement VIII sought to woo back James I of England and Henry IV of France to Catholicism in the same period. The same effect could be achieved by a ruler's replacement: hence the attempt by the Lutheran mother of the elector of Brandenburg to dethrone her Calvinist son in 1619; and Saxony's threat to invade Brandenburg for the same purpose the following year.[14] Finally, dynastic marriage could be another pacific means to the same end: as when Philip II, immediately following the death of his first wife, the Catholic queen of England, proposed marriage to her protestant successor to preserve the true faith in that country; or when, later, other Catholic suitors (such as the Archduke Charles of Austria) were encouraged by the pope to woo the same queen for the same reason.

But in the final resort war might be seen as the only available means of saving another land for the "true" religion. Military action of this sort was generally felt to be defensive in purpose. There was widespread fear of the opposing religion and its chief supporters (p. 339 below), and in general intervention in this age was designed (as in the age of ideology 300 years later) to *protect* a religion under threat, whether Catholic or protestant, rather than to spread it to new territories. England intervened to defend protestants in France in 1562; Spain to defend the Catholic faith against a protestant king in the same country in 1589-94; Sweden to preserve the protestant faith in Germany against victorious Catholics in 1630. Sometimes only joint action for that purpose was thought sufficient: Philip II and Henry II of France were believed to have planned such a campaign against the protestant heresy in 1559*; and the meeting between the duke of Alva and Catherine de Medici at Bayonne in 1565 was generally taken by protestants in France to have had the same objective (the march of Alva's forces from Italy to crush a partly protestant revolt in the Netherlands two years later seemed to confirm this fear). Sometimes a wider coalition still was formed for that purpose: such as the "holy leagues" set up against the Turks in 1570 and 1593, and the coalition put together between England, Denmark, the United Provinces and Sweden to defend the protestant cause in Germany in 1625. Normally the motive in such cases was not to defend the rights of protestants generally but of particular protestant creeds. It was only Calvinist German rulers who were willing to intervene in the wars of the Netherlands and France in the 1570s and 1580s. Lutherans refused, because the archbishop of Cologne had become a Calvinist, to participate in the Cologne war of 1583-9. The Lutheran elector of Saxony refused to help the protestants of Bohemia in 1618-21 partly because their leader, the elector Palatine, was a Calvinist.

The degree to which military action was felt to be necessary, either by local believers to assert their rights, or by external supporters to assist them, depended on the degree of toleration enjoyed in the territory concerned. At the beginning of this period there still existed in large parts of Europe a substantial degree of toleration. Only in Spain and England was an almost total uniformity demanded, and active persecution undertaken against non-conformists. In Transylvania equal religious rights for Catholics, Lutherans, Calvinists and Unitarians were established in 1571. In Poland four or five types of protestants as well as Catholics practised their faith freely (a right the

---

* William of Orange, who was present, later stated that the two rulers agreed on this during the negotiations for the treaty of Cateau-Cambrésis. This threat aroused his own defensive motives, as shown in the letter he wrote to his brother in 1574: "If this country should one day be lost and brought back under the yoke and the tyranny of the Spaniards, the true religion will be gravely endangered in all other countries and may even, humanly speaking, be uprooted for ever, leaving not the least vestige" — quoted in *Texts Concerning the Revolt in the Netherlands,* ed. E. H. Kossman and A. F. Mellink (Cambridge, 1974), p. 113.

Confederation of Warsaw of 1573 proclaimed). In France conflicts centred on the precise rights to be granted to protestants — where and how they could practise their faith and defend themselves — rather than on the right to practise it at all. Even the Emperor Ferdinand I pleaded, at the resumed council of Trent, for a relatively liberal approach to dogmatic differences (he was prepared to concede clerical marriage and even communion in both kinds). In at least some of the Hapsburg domains different faiths were allowed at different times to coexist reasonably amicably: in Bohemia Lutherans, Calvinists and Utraquists were in a majority, and even the strongly Catholic Rudolf II accepted the rights of the reformed churches in his Letter of Majesty of 1609. The supposedly fanatical Ottomans set the best example of all, not only tolerating the Orthodox faith in large parts of their possessions but also permitting Jesuit and Capuchin missions to set up Catholic churches in Istanbul and other places, and allowing to Jews the freedom of worship they were denied in almost all Christian countries.

Where toleration existed, armed intervention was not necessary. Increasingly, however, as the period progressed, the willingness to allow rival faiths declined. Within the same state a rival creed was felt to be a threat to stability. As a Spanish priest put it,

> never has a republic been well governed or peaceful where division and diversity of faiths prevailed, nor indeed can it be. The reason for this is that . . . everyone considers his own god to be the only true god, and everyone else blind and deluded. . . . . And where there is such rancour and inner power, there cannot be good fellowship or lasting peace.[15]

Protestants were no more tolerant: Luther himself had written in 1524, "if we can possibly avoid it we must not tolerate contrary doctrines in the same state: to avoid so great an evil those who do not accept a faith must be made to attend sermons and to conform at least in appearance". A heterodox faith came to be regarded as a threat not only to the established religion but to the state itself. It was because Catholics were seen as a threat to the throne, as well as to the protestant faith, that they were persecuted so ruthlessly in England (usually for "treason"). It was because the Moriscos and the Moslem-influenced form of Christianity they practised was believed to be a threat to the Spanish state that they were first uprooted and dispersed, and finally expelled from the country altogether. More and more the same attitude affected other countries. In France the Huguenots came to be seen by Richelieu as a threat to the integrity of the state, and the rights accorded to them in 1598 (for example, to retain their own fortified places) were gradually withdrawn or whittled away. In the Netherlands minorities were increasingly distrusted, so that in the north Catholics, who had once been among the main leaders of the revolt (Egmont, Hoorn and Montigny were all Catholics, as William of Orange had once been) and who remained in the majority until the late 1570s, were finally forbidden to practise their religion; while, conversely, in the south, where the reformed religion first took hold, protestants were eventually, in 1609, expelled altogether. In Germany likewise, tolerance declined and tension between the faiths increased — as seen in the break-up of imperial institutions in 1601-8: the protestants ceased to accept the decisions of the ecclesiastical courts in 1601; they demanded equal representation in the diet and the *Reichskammergericht* in 1603; and most of them left the diet altogether in 1608 (the diet was finally suspended in 1613 and did not meet again for 25 years). The total elimination of minority faiths was increasingly demanded. Maximilian of Bavaria made his entire population go to mass (at Easter they had to obtain a certificate to show they had been to confession); and after he invaded Donauwörth in 1607 the protestants, though they had been a majority, were expelled altogether (they had already been expelled from Cologne, Aachen, Strasbourg and Münster, which were controlled, directly or indirectly, by Bavaria). In the Hapsburg domains toleration ceased from the time Ferdinand II became emperor in 1619 (he had already rooted out heresy in his own archduchy, Styria): the Letter of Majesty was abrogated and after the reconquest of Bohemia and other provinces in 1621 protestant practices were systematically extirpated. As tolerance was everywhere abandoned, war came to be seen as the only means for protecting a faith that was under threat. The religious destiny of a country was at stake. The survival of a faith could now depend on the relative success of the different factions at arms, or of rival interventions in civil wars.

Religious motives, however, were not always overriding. Political aims were almost as important. Sometimes political and religious objectives mutually reinforced each other. Spain's "enterprise of England" was designed not only to restore the Catholic faith in that country (which is why the pope offered a million ducats to support it) but to secure Spain's sea route to the Netherlands and remove threats to the Spanish monopoly in South America. Her intervention in the French wars of religion could not only help the cause of militant Catholics in France but also win another round for Spain in the ancient conflict between the two monarchies — even, it was hoped, win the throne for a Spanish princess. Her war against the Turks in North Africa and the Mediterranean would not only help the crusade against the heretics but also safeguard Spanish communications throughout the Mediterranean, especially to her possessions in Italy. Her war in the Valtellina in 1620-6 would not only assist Catholic believers against protestant oppressors but also protect the vital communications link between Spanish Italy and the Spanish Netherlands. It was in recognition of these aims that Pope Sixtus V said that "the preservation of the Catholic religion, which is the principal aim of the pope, is only a pretext for His Majesty [the Spanish king], whose principal aim is the security and aggrandisement of his domains". In the same way France's support for Catholics in Scotland could help her political as well as her religious aims there. England's intervention to help the protestant cause in France might not only help coreligionists in that country but win Le Havre (promised to Elizabeth by the protestants) and even restore Calais to her; while her intervention in the Netherlands could not only help the protestant cause but also weaken the power that was the main threat to her independence. Sweden's intervention in the Thirty Years War could not only assist the protestant cause in Germany but also win important territorial and strategic gains for Sweden. And so on. Sometimes there was a corresponding identity of religious and political interests among the opposing forces: thus in the Netherlands resistance to Spanish rule was motivated as much by national as by religious sentiments, as was Irish resistance to English domination, and Bohemian resistance to Hapsburg rule in that country. In the same way the protestant faith was adopted by the nobility in many countries as a means of asserting their independence of the rulers.

But religious and national interests did not always coincide. Sometimes a choice needed to be made. In deciding to intervene in the Netherlands, even at the time when her own religious wars were raging, on behalf of protestant rebels against a Catholic king, France placed her political objectives above her religious ones; just as later she had equally little compunction in intervening in the Thirty Years War in a way that prevented a Catholic victory in Germany. Catholic Savoy assisted protestant Bohemia at the start of the Thirty Years War because her interests against Spain demanded it; just as Catholic Venice and the protestant United Provinces mutually supported each other for the same reason. Catholic France, Venice and Savoy were willing to take up arms in support of the protestant rulers of the Valtellina against the Catholic population because the latter were supported by Spain. Conversely, Philip II felt unable to give support to the Catholic cause in Scotland because this might drive England into the arms of France. Even the antipathy between Christians and Moslems could be bridged if state interests were sufficiently compelling: so United Provinces entered into alliance with Algiers, Morocco and Turkey between 1608 and 1612, seeing their hostility to Spain as more important than the perversity of their religion. Domestic political aims would also sometimes overcome traditional religious loyalty. Henry of Navarre (who had once declared that he would not give up his beliefs to gain a crown "or even thirty crowns") later thought Paris worth a mass; while Count Wolfgang of Neuburg, previously a devoted Lutheran, was willing to become a Catholic to help him become ruler of Jülich.

Religious minorities sometimes had to make the same choice. They too could cross the religious divide if their interests made it necessary. So Netherlands protestants accepted the help of French Catholics (and even offered the Dutch crown to a Catholic ruler); the protestants of Bohemia accepted help from Catholic Savoy (which provided their main military force and commander); and protestants in Hungary accepted the championship of Moslem Turks. In all these cases immediate necessities outweighed religious ties. In the last case the Hungarian leader, István Bocskay, defended his alliance on the grounds that it was "not to abandon political or religious freedom but to preserve it". But pragmatism could not always be carried so far. Sometimes political interests were sacrificed because of the strength of religious feeling. So Spain and England could not agree on a dynastic marriage in 1615-23, as James I had hoped, largely because of religious antipathies; Spain and the United Provinces were unable to make peace in 1628-31 for the same reason (mainly because Calvinists in the United Provinces refused to allow toleration for Catholics, as Spain demanded). Minorities were even willing to sacrifice the interests of their states for the sake of their religious cause: French protestants were prepared to give away Le Havre to England to win her support (just as German protestants had given away the imperial cities of Metz, Toul and Verdun to secure French assistance a few years earlier); French Catholics promised French Navarre, Cambrai and other towns to Spain in return for her help. Quite often, therefore, in this age (and almost alone in this age), for some at least religious motives prevailed over national objectives.

But rulers had other goals that had nothing to do with religion. They were still often concerned to claim succession in other states, even when there was no religious consideration. At the beginning of the age some highly ambitious claims were maintained. English rulers still styled themselves as kings of France (as they continued to do on their coins till 1802) and harboured serious claims to Calais; France still claimed the Milanese, Naples and Sicily, and declared the wife of their *dauphin*, later briefly their queen (Mary Stuart), the true queen of England; the Danish king still claimed Sweden (as well as Norway, which he held); the Polish king claimed both Sweden and Russia for his family at different times; Savoy claimed large parts of southern France. This dynastic motivation was now, however, less powerful than before. Not all such claims were altogether serious, if only because they could not be pursued except at excessive cost. It was naturally when a ruler died without obvious successor that rival claims were most likely to lead to war (for example, over Cleves-Jülich in 1608 and Mantua in 1613-17 and 1628-31). But wars to claim succession did not necessarily require the death of a ruler. Mary Queen of Scots bequeathed her claim to the English throne (a claim undeniable to any Catholic) to Philip II, who launched the armada partly to promote it. The duke of Savoy invaded Provence when civil war in France made enforcement of his claim appear more practicable. Sigismund of Poland fought for the Swedish throne because it had been, in his eyes, stolen from him by his uncle.

Whether or not there was a dynastic claim, territory remained a widely shared objective. But, as we saw earlier, territorial aims were now more specific than in the previous age. It was no longer the case that any territory, however remote, to which a dynastic claim could be found would be claimed. The territory that was desired was mainly territory that was contiguous or otherwise valuable. In this age, unlike the last, expansion was usually at the expense of near neighbours. So France, surrounded by Spanish territories, sought to expand her borders, mainly at Spain's expense, to escape that embrace (in the wars of 1623-6, 1628-31 and 1635-48). Sweden, equally enclosed by Danish territory, aspired to the lands across the Baltic which would give her access to trade which Denmark blocked in the west (in the wars of 1558-82, 1600-29, 1630-48 and 1643-5). Russia, recovering from an era of weakness, fought to regain ground to the west: against Poland for Smolensk and the Ukraine (1578-82, 1613-18, 1632-5), and against Sweden and Poland for Livonia and Ingria (1558-81, 1590-5, 1623-5). Savoy, frustrated in her attempts to win territory from France in the west, began her long attempt to nibble at Italian territories to the south (1613-16, 1628-31, 1635-48). Poland, with more territory than she could easily control already, fought long wars for the lands to the north-est (1559-82, 1600-29). Saxony coveted neighbouring Lusatia, and twice abandoned the protestant cause in the Thirty Years War to acquire it. But it was symptomatic that in this religious age even purely territorial ambitions often needed a religious justification. So Sweden took Pomerania in the name of defending protestantism; Poland aspired to the Swedish throne in the name of Catholicism; and Spain demanded the French throne in the same cause.

Often there were strategic motives behind these territorial aims. In a number of wars of the age Spain and France competed for control of the gateway to Italy: France took Saluzzo in 1600, Casale in 1632 and Pinerolo in 1637; Spain, concerned to defend her route from Italy to the Netherlands, absorbed small states or cities in northern Italy (Parma, Modena, Mirandola, Finale and Monaco), took over control of Alsace from her Hapsburg partner in 1617, intervened to secure Catholic control of the Valtellina in 1620-6, occupied the Palatinate in 1620, and tried to keep Montferrat in friendly hands in 1628-31. France was equally concerned to control the crossings of the Rhine: she secured Philippsburg (by treaty with the elector of Mainz in 1632); conquered Alsace during the Thirty Years War; and won Breisach at its end. Seaports could be of special value since they gave economic benefits (the capacity to tax trade) as well as strategic. Thus Sweden, through her successive wars in the Baltic, eventually controlled all the ports on its southern shore except Danzig. Denmark's wars against Sweden were designed partly to regain control of the Sound and of the Atlantic route to northern Norway; while her intervention in the Thirty Years War was partly aimed at control of the Weser and the Elbe. Turkey fought Spain for control of Tunis, Malta and the Mediterranean generally; Venice for control of Cyprus (1569-73) and Crete (1644-69); the Holy Roman Empire for Kanisza and Gran (1593-1606); and Persia (four times) for Iraq and Erevan.

Another important motive which sometimes led to war was the desire to win trade or access to trade routes. A number of wars in this period can be attributed wholly or partly to this aim. Sweden's wars for the Baltic coast resulted partly from her desire to control and tax the important trade routes — from Russia and Southern Europe — which passed through Narva, Reval and other ports. Russia's wars for Livonia were aimed at controlling and taxing the same trade. Denmark's wars against Sweden were aimed at retaining Danish control of both sides of the Sound, and so her capacity to levy tolls on the shipping that passed through. The raids of the English and Dutch fleets against Spanish shipping in the Caribbean were designed to secure access, legal or illegal, to the South American trade. The Dutch expeditions that displaced the Portuguese from parts of the East Indies, Ceylon, West Africa and Brazil were aimed at securing control of the valuable trade from these areas. In some wars an objective was to prevent the trade of others which might compete: a major aim for the United Provinces in the war against Spain of 1621-48 was to keep the Scheldt closed and so prevent competition from Antwerp to her own trade (she managed to keep her neighbour's chief river closed for the next two centuries). So, though to win trade was rarely the only objective of an act of war, and was certainly not as important a motive as in the following age, it could sometimes be one significant motive for war against another state.

The underlying motives for war became therefore somewhat different in this age. With the universal concern now felt about religious questions, the most widespread concern was to influence what religion was practised in a particular country: to defend the right to maintain the reformed worship, or to uphold the supremacy of the Catholic church. For the most part this was seen as a defensive aim: to protect the Roman church from the threat of heresy, or to safeguard the rights of protestants against persecution. Each might seem to opponents, however, as hostile threats, attempts to eliminate all who supported the reformed religion, or to spread a heretical doctrine seen as dangerous. The claim to know the "true" word and the "true" religion implied a refusal to tolerate falsehood; and so a threat to all who upheld a different truth. As the only possible path to peace, toleration, was refused, by Catholic and protestant alike, war to decide which faith should prevail was the only alternative. These religious aims did not totally displace others of a traditional, and quite secular, kind: for territory — especially now territory of strategic value; for succession; for trade or other economic benefits. But even these were sometimes affected by the pervasive concern with religion. So succession was desired the more if it could spread a faith (as might be achieved, it was hoped, by Philip's claim to England and France, or by Sigismund's to Sweden, or by Mary Stuart's succession in Scotland and claim to England); and economic gains were desired the more if they could be claimed to benefit one church or harm another (as with Christian IV's rape of bishoprics or Ferdinand's edict of restitution). In this age religious considerations were rarely lost from sight. So new types of motives inspired new types of war for a different set of objectives.

The age of sovereignty (1648-1789)

After the peace of Westphalia change in the social and political structure of states produced a new set of motives among states. Power no longer rested exclusively in the hands of the rulers and their immediate advisers. It was shared increasingly with chief ministers who exercised day-to-day authority on their behalf: such men as Mazarin and Colbert in France, Walpole and Pitt in Britain, de Witt and Heinsius in United Provinces, Haugwitz and Kaunitz in Austria. Since these often had more control over the details of policy than the royal rulers they served, their conceptions of state purposes began to have as much influence as those of their masters.

Monarchs and ministers alike held a new conception of the objects of national policy. They were concerned above all now not with the future of the royal house, nor with the fate of a particular religion, but with the interests of the state they both served. Frederick the Great described himself as the "first servant of the state". And Louis XIV, in declaring himself to *be* the state, emphasised not so much his own personal power (which nobody ever doubted) but, on the contrary, the subordination of that power to the interests of the state he ruled. To win glory was the prime objective. "The first thought of kings", Louis XIV told his son in his *Mémoires,* "is that all their counsels must be for what may or may not win the acclaim of the public. Kings, who are born to possess everything, must not be ashamed to accede to renown".[16] But the principal way of winning glory was now the building of a powerful and prestigious state. The great ministers adopted these aims as much as the monarchs they served. As Mazarin told Louis XIV, "I am interested in your *gloire* and the conservation of your state more than anything else in the world."[17] For rulers and ministers alike the supreme end of policy, therefore, justifying whatever means might be found necessary, was *raison d'état*. "State interest", as Frederick declared, "is the only motive which should govern the councils of princes."[18] The uses of war reflected these dominant motives. It was now above all a means — not the only means but a vital one — by which the power and prestige of the state could be extended.

One of the main objectives of states was to promote the security of their territory. This might require the conquest of further territory. Both Louis XIV and Frederick the Great publicly asserted that the acquisition of territory could be essential to state interests (see pp. 346-7 below). But more than ever it was not any territory that was desired — on the grounds that a reasonable claim could be made to it — but particular territories believed to be necessary for promoting state interests and state power. Often this was territory immediately adjacent to the borders, especially if strategically important. In his two political testaments Frederick the Great explicitly described and named (see p. 351 below) the territories it was desirable for Prussia to acquire. Louis XIV equally declared his determination to secure the "gates" to France; and his successive wars (in 1667-8, 1672-9, 1683-4, 1688-97) were largely designed to secure strategically valuable territory, especially on France's north-eastern borders (Flanders, Franche-Comté, Alsace, Strasbourg, Luxemburg, Philippsburg). Russia, under Peter the Great and later rulers, fought to extend Russia's borders to win access to the Black Sea. Britain fought for strategically important assets in Gibraltar, Minorca, Bremen, St Lucia, Louisburg, and other places. Sweden and Denmark struggled for Zealand and Wismar controlling the Sound; and for Holstein and Scania, where each could threaten the other. Since the territories that strengthened one state would often threaten another, and could be desired by more than one state for that reason, this was a motive that was almost certain to lead to armed conflict.

Another major aim was the *consolidation* of territory, often scattered through the hazards of inheritance or conquest. So Prussia fought to win territories, in Pomerania, Silesia and Saxony, that would join together its divided lands (and on these grounds sought to exchange distant east Frisia for northern Bohemia). So Austria abandoned territories in the south of Italy for parts of the north; and would readily have exchanged distant possessions in the southern

Netherlands for closer and more defensible lands in Bavaria (an exchange on these lines was considered by Austrian governments several times between 1714 and 1789). Denmark sought to absorb the Holstein-Gottorp territories that were intermingled with her own. France absorbed Franche Comté, Alsace and Lorraine; eventually substituting a *pré carré*, or straight dividing line, for the higgledy-piggledy south Netherlands border of 1659. Adjoining territories, however ethnically or culturally diverse, were increasingly assimilated and absorbed: as Hungary was by Austria, Scotland by England, Finland by Sweden and Russia; and as unhappy Poland was progressively swallowed up by her three more powerful neighbours. Territories that were geographically isolated, on the other hand, were both more difficult to hold and less worth holding. So Sweden's possessions to the south of the Baltic, Denmark's to the north, Spain's in the Netherlands and Italy, Turkey's in North Africa, were during this period gradually detached: either becoming independent or becoming subject to other powers.

A special concern in this age, on both strategic and commercial grounds, was to secure access to the sea. A major aim of Russian policy was to win a foothold on the Baltic coast (an aim she achieved in the Great Northern War in 1721) and on the Black Sea (which she secured by successive wars against the Turks, and finally by the conquest of the Crimea in 1781-2). An important aim for Brandenburg-Prussia in her wars against Sweden was to establish adequate port facilities in the Baltic: at Stettin, Stralsund and Wismar. Savoy, in her war of 1672-4, sought to acquire Genoa for the same reason. Saxony made war against Sweden to acquire Livonia. One reason for France's ambitions in the Netherlands was to win access to ports on the North Sea and the lucrative trade that went with them.

Just as important as the acquisition of territory was its *recovery* after it had been lost. In a substantial number of wars a major motive was the desire of nations that had lost territory in one war to recover it in another. So one of Austria's prime objectives in the Nine Years War was to recover Alsace, lost to the Empire over the previous 40 years.* In successive wars (1718-20, 1727-8, 1733-5, 1740-8) Spain sought to recover the Mediterranean territories which she had lost in 1713-14. Venice made war against Turkey in 1714 to recover Dalmatia and Morea, lost 15 years earlier. The Seven Years War was carefully planned by Austria with the explicit purpose of recovering Silesia, lost to Prussia a decade earlier. Sweden launched two wars, in

---

* The official document relating to the election of the emperor continued for years to refer explicitly to his duty to recover Alsace, until the provision was removed during the reign of the non-Hapsburg, French-supported, Charles VII in 1742. See W. L. Dorn, *Competition for Empire, 1740-1763* (New York, 1940), p. 144.

1741 and 1788, to recover territories lost to Russia in the preceding war. The Turkish war against Russia in 1787 was designed to recover the Crimea, lost 15 years before. As it turned out, in every case these efforts proved unsuccessful: in other words, a losing power usually went on losing. Even if it had no clear-cut intention of recovering a particular territory, a country that had lost a war might be inspired by a desire for revenge: this motive was a factor, for example, in the successive conflicts between Denmark and Sweden between 1641 and 1721, in France's attack on the Netherlands in 1672, and in the war of France and Spain against Britain in 1778-83.

States were still deeply concerned about questions of succession, if only because these could affect the balance of power between states (p. 102 above). There was, however, a new approach to the question. It was recognised that such matters must now in many cases be decided by multilateral agreement, not unilateral enforcement. So Louis XIV was willing, from 1668 onwards, to accept that the succession to Spain should be regulated by international agreement, even though this might bring less territory to France (and though his own claims were good), since he knew other rulers would never tolerate the accession to France's power that would otherwise occur: he thus accepted from the beginning that either Spain's territories would be divided or they would not go to the ruler of France.* Similarly, Louis XV was willing to abandon the excellent claims to Poland of his father-in-law in return for advantages to himself (including the absorption of Lorraine) which would secure international consent. Charles VI knew that he could never bring about his daughter's succession in Austria without obtaining the explicit assent of other European monarchs, which he laboured over 25 years to secure. It was equally by international agreement that the Farnese princes, to satisfy their mother's ceaseless ambition on their behalf, were eventually found duchies in Italy. In other words it was increasingly the convenience of states, collectively agreed, rather than the rights of rulers (still less the desires of populations) which now determined questions of succession.

To suit the convenience of states, territories were swapped around in unscrupulous dealing. Sicily was handed over from Spain to Savoy in 1714, exchanged in 1720 for Sardinia, and 20 years later joined with Naples and awarded to a foreign prince. Parma and Piacenza were awarded to the same prince in 1732, transferred to Austria in 1739, and transferred yet again to his brother in 1748. Tuscany was

---

* Louis was careful never totally to rule out a union of the crowns but he never regarded it as a practical possibility: he fought in the War of the Spanish Succession for French domination in Spain (through his grandson), not rule by the French king.

handed to the duke of Lorraine in 1739, while the unsuccessful contender for the Polish throne was compensated with Lorraine, and Poland handed to the elector of Saxony. Such transfers to alien rulers were imposed not only regardless of the wishes of the inhabitants (which was nothing new), but often quite regardless of any normal rules of inheritance (which was).* Everywhere the desire was now to win reasonably favourable settlements that were acceptable to other major powers rather than to win succession at any cost.

An important aim, therefore (whether or not normal rules of inheritance had been followed), was to secure international acknowledgement of any new regime. Disputed succession could lead to international tension and an acute sense of insecurity in the states concerned. One of the principal war aims of England in the Nine Years War and the War of the Spanish Succession was to secure explicit acknowledgement of the succession of William and Mary in England and repudiation of the Stuarts. The main aim of Charles VI's Pragmatic Sanctions was to secure international recognition of a controversial succession. In 1714-15, even after a settlement of the preceding war, the succession was under challenge in three of the most important states of Europe: in France (which it was feared could be claimed by Spain), in Spain (still claimed by Austria), and in Britain (where the succession was still challenged by some in France and Spain). The main aim of each power was to remove those threats: an aim which in 1720, at the end of yet another war, they all secured by solemn pledges of mutual recognition.

But governments were concerned not only to extend their own power but also to limit the power of other states which could threaten theirs. One of the main reasons, as we saw earlier (pp. 102-3), why governments entered into alliances and finally took part in war was to limit the pretensions of any other nation that threatened to become over-powerful.

There was also a more general desire to weaken other powers

---

* The primacy acquired by the convenience of states (or *raison d'état*) is demonstrated by the indifference now shown to normal rules of inheritance. It is striking how frequently throughout this age rules of inheritance were bent to suit the convenience of states and the known necessities of the balance of power. So both Louis XIV and the emperor Leopold were willing to renounce their own claims to the Spanish inheritance in favour of younger relatives. In other cases the rules were bent to suit personal convenience. Charles VI had no scruples in adjusting the succession established by his father in favour of his own line. In Russia the rules concerning succession were thrown aside by Peter the Great in favour of his wife, with little protest (leading to three more women rulers in the next four reigns and the accession of another widow 40 years later). The convenience of states in other words, now increasingly superseded traditional dynastic principles.

elsewhere. In a system of ruthless competition no state could neglect an opportunity to cause damage to another. Thus sometimes a nation went to war to exploit the difficulties that others were experiencing. A major motive for Sweden in her war with Poland in 1655 was the desire to destroy a potential claimant to the Swedish throne at a time when the Poles were already embroiled in conflict elsewhere (the Cossack revolt and the war with Russia). Turkey sought to exploit internal problems in Poland in 1672 (during the Cossack revolt), and in Austria in 1683 (when Austria was also challenged by France and a Hungarian revolt) by making war against them. It was partly the weakness, disunity and chronic civil war of Poland that encouraged her neighbours to seize more and more of her territory in the last 30 years of the eighteenth century. Finally, in declaring war against Britain in 1776, France and Spain sought to take advantage of her problem with her American colonies to settle old scores with her.

The search for national power also promoted the desire for trade and other economic advantages. In this age more than any other war was seen as the means of promoting that objective. Louis XIV never concealed the fact that one of his main purposes in going to war against the United Provinces in 1672 was to destroy her commercial pre-eminence and win it for France; Colbert, his chief minister, had clearly declared that aim:

> As we have crushed Spain on land, so we must crush Holland at sea. The Dutch have no right to usurp all commerce . . . knowing that so long as they are the masters of trade their naval force will continue to grow and to render them so powerful they will be able to assume the role of arbiters of peace and war in Europe. . .[19]

In England there were many who favoured war against the Dutch for commercial reasons: Pepys records the talk among English merchants that "the trade of the world is too little for us two, therefore one must down", and that in consequence all the court were "mad for a Dutch war".[20] Both the English and the French wars against the Dutch in the second half of the seventeenth century were motivated largely by concern for trade. The importance of this as a motive is demonstrated by the fact that provisions relating to trade represented such an important part of many peace treaties in the period. So the Dutch won trading concessions as a result of their success in 1678, and Britain and United Provinces, victors in the War of the Spanish Succession, negotiated favourable trade agreements as part of the settlement with Spain. Access to fisheries was another important objective: the right to fishing in the North Sea was settled by the Anglo-Dutch wars, as was the division of the Newfoundland fish stocks and the right to fur-trapping in the Hudson's Bay area in successive peace treaties between England and France. The right to exemption from tolls in the Sound was a principal concern in wars between Sweden and Denmark.

Another important objective, springing partly from the same commercial ambitions, was the desire for colonies or trading posts. These were seen by many statesmen as a source of trade, raw materials, strategic positions and even employment.[21] Often there was competition for the same colonies. The United Provinces and Portugal fought in 1657-61 for colonies in Africa and South America; the United Provinces and Britain in 1665-7 for positions in the Caribbean and South Africa; Britain and Spain in 1739 for the Caribbean and trade to South America; and Britain and France for Canada and India in 1756. Again the settlements reached at the end of wars clearly demonstrate the importance of this objective. According to the fortunes of war, Caribbean islands were shunted back and forth from one nation to another; Louisiana and Florida were pushed from one master to another; and the most valuable places in West Africa, Canada and India continually changed hands. Only where a colony could provide exports that would compete with those from existing colonies was their acquisition, even after conquest, declined: as when the valuable sugar islands of Martinique and Guadeloupe were abruptly returned to France by Britain in 1763. Though, therefore, states rarely announced that they were going to war to acquire colonies, they were often aware that colonial acquisitions could be the consequence of war.

Religious motives, as we have seen, played little part in this age. Though religious opinions were still strongly held, there was less inclination to fight wars on behalf of religious minorities elsewhere. Austria's persecution of protestants in Hungary and the ending of protestant rights in France in 1685 might arouse indignation elsewhere, but they did not provoke interventions on behalf of those oppressed, as they might well have done in the previous era. While religious minorities were helped (for example, when the protestants of the Cevennes were aided in the War of the Spanish Succession) it was usually for national, not religious, reasons. There was less of a sense of duty to assist coreligionists elsewhere than before; greater willingness to respect the constraints of sovereignty.

Ideological motives were equally insignificant. There were no wars that can be said to have been fought in support of a particular political system, or against another. Most Englishmen probably felt themselves to have more in common with the constitutional arrangements in the United Provinces than with the absolute monarchies of other states of Europe; but England none the less fought three wars against her between 1652 and 1674 (the first at a time when both states were anti-monarchical), and later it was common interest against France, and their common ruling family, rather than their parliamentary systems, which brought them so frequently together. Absolute monarchies were still less deterred from war against each other by the similarity of their political systems. Where a government pursued a constitutional goal in another state it was from motives of national interest, not ideological zeal: so absolutist Russia consistently sought to maintain a non-absolute system in Sweden because this was thought more favourable to Russia; just as Prussia imposed on United Provinces in 1787 the non-monarchical constitution that suited her interests. The absolute Hapsburg monarchy found no difficulty in allying itself with the republics of United Provinces and Venice; nor in fighting regularly against other absolute monarchies in France and Prussia. The *ancien régime* monarchies of France and Spain had no compunction in allying themselves with the revolutionary, republican and semi-democratic American colonies when it suited their national interests to do so. Thus, in general, neither religion nor political ideology had any significant influence in determining friendship or hostility during this period. And perhaps the most striking feature of the age is the ease with which alliances were continually made and unmade, with little regard for the beliefs and sympathies of other powers, or for anything other than immediate national self-interest.

A more important influence on state actions was traditional rivalry between two states. Occasionally this still reflected that of royal families. The centuries-old conflict between France and Austria, Bourbon and Hapsburg, exacerbated conflicts in which the two countries became involved and made it the more likely that these would end in war. Conversely, traditional friendships made war less likely. So Spain would usually find herself on the same side as Austria so long as both had Hapsburg monarchs (though Austria gave Spain little help in the latter's wars against France in the first 50 years of this period); and after she acquired a French royal family she was (after some frictions in the first decade or so) almost always on the side of France. The same periodic "family compact" which had formerly joined the two Hapsburg monarchies now cemented friendship between the Bourbon powers (in 1733, 1743 and 1761). But these old dynastic relationships were now increasingly replaced by those of states, competing with each other for power. Thus the dynastic competition between Austria and France was increasingly replaced (long before the diplomatic revolution of 1756) by new rivalries that were more potent: between Austria and Prussia, struggling for power and influence in Germany, and between Britain and France, competing equally bitterly for colonies in Canada, India and the Caribbean, as well as for power in the Low Countries. Nothing more clearly proves that these had become more fundamental than the old dynastic feud between Hapsburg and Bourbon than the fact that these contests alone remained unchanged by the switch in alliances of 1756. At the local level similar rivalries — between Sweden and Denmark in Scandinavia, between Sweden and Russia in the Baltic, between Poland and Russia in Eastern Europe — also led to frequent wars between them. Other rivalries were commercial (as between Britain and the United Provinces); or colonial (as between the United Provinces and Portugal in the seventeenth century, and between Britain and France in the eighteenth). Whatever its original source, the sense of rivalry could provide an additional motivation for war when any immediate issue aroused hostility between the two countries concerned.

The most important single aim, therefore, in the eyes of both monarchs and ministers in this age, was the promotion of state interests. Many of the leading rulers of the day explicitly declared that the primary aim of their policy was to promote the glory and the power of their own state. Often they recognised that this might require war. War might be necessary to win territory, especially territory believed essential to the security of the state; to consolidate into a defensible whole lands that were scattered; to recover those that had been lost in previous encounters; and to revenge past humiliations. It could be required to win trading advantages, often at the expense of other states; or to win colonies abroad, mainly for commercial reasons, too. But an almost equally important aim was to prevent the growth in the power of other states; and that also might be a reason for war in some circumstances. In short, the motive that was now most important, for monarchs and ministers alike, was to increase the power and prestige of their own states in relation to other states. It was an aim, it was widely believed, that often could be achieved only through warfare.

The age of nationalism (1789-1917)

The French Revolution gave birth to a new era. From that point war was increasingly seen as the means of promoting the interests of nations, rather than of states. And increasingly it was the motives of nations rather than of states that were decisive. In the age of state-building the essential actors had been *governments*, mainly monarchical and aristocratic, each seeking to maximise the advantage of their own state against others, whether through accommodation or conflict; and that aim had generally been pursued without regard to the sentiments of peoples, either in their own or in other states. In this age, the essential actors began to be *nations*; that is, whole peoples (especially their now middle-class leadership) that felt themselves, on grounds of language, culture, race or geography, to share a common destiny. The dialogue was no longer only between state and state, but often between states and nations; between governments and peoples. A significant proportion of wars now began in the actions of non-official groups rather than governments. The old motive of state-building, the desire to extend the power of the state through territorial and economic gains, was thus increasingly re-placed by that of *nation*-building, the creation of states based on nations sharing a substantial ethnic, cultural or linguistic identity. This change affected international relations in a fundamental way.

The motives of states themselves were changed. For they too were affected by the new faith in the national principle. The change took place gradually over the course of the century. It can be measured in the contrast between Lord John Russell's declaration in 1849 (in relation to the proposal to divide Schleswig-Holstein on the national boundary) that "the Great Powers had not the habit of consulting populations when questions affecting the Balance of Power had to be settled", and that of Gladstone, his then colleague, only 20 years later (in the wake of the Franco-Prussian War), that it was a "crime against the conscience of Europe" that Alsace and Lorraine should be transferred without consulting the wishes of their inhabitants. As the period progressed the latter view was increasingly to prevail over the former. Plebiscites came to be widely held to justify a change of sovereignty: for example, in the Principalities in 1856-7, in Naples and Sicily in 1861, and elsewhere (a plebiscite was due to occur in Schleswig-Holstein but was prevented by the Prussian king). This change of attitude — the growing belief that claims to sovereignty should be based on the loyalties of populations — was seen even more dramatically in the contrast between the principles on which the treaty of Vienna was based, when territories were transferred accord-ing to the convenience of states and without regard to the wishes of peoples (p. 110 above), and those applied, just over a century later, in the treaty of Versailles, under which territories were explicitly distributed on the basis of the principle of "self-determination": that is, at least in theory, in accordance with the wishes of populations (even if that principle was somewhat selectively applied).

The dominant motive therefore, among both governments and peoples, was that of nationalism, which now acquired both a new strength and a new legitimacy. This altered the character of the wars that were fought. In the previous age nationalist aspirations, even where they existed, were not usually expressed in armed revolt: the revolutionary movement in Hungary is perhaps the only major excep-tion. In this age the importance of the new motivation is shown by the fact that of the wars in this period 26 were wars designed to create states on the national principle (column 2 in Appendix 4), while several other civil conflicts (column 3) resulted at least in part from the same aspirations. Those ambitions were expressed in two ways. On the one hand minorities within existing states (Greeks, Serbs, Romanians, Bulgarians and others) struggled to achieve national independence; on the other, peoples who were divided among several states (the Germans and Italians) or subject to different foreign rulers (such as the Poles) fought to achieve unification in a single state. Of the wars on our lists five resulted from the former cause (the independence wars of Greece, Belgium, Montenegro, Bulgaria and Bosnia) and thirteen from the latter (the four Polish revolts, the four Prussian wars and the five Italian wars of 1848-9, 1859, 1860, 1866 and 1867).

The new sentiments affected not only the states and peoples most directly involved. Other states, sometimes already established on the national principle, were influenced by sympathy for the aspirations of the people in revolt. That is the main reason why, in a substantial proportion of the wars of national independence, outside governments became involved on the side of the revolution. This was widely seen as a justifiable motive for war: as Mazzini pleaded in England, "It is not enough to preach . . . non-intervention, and leave Force unchallenged ruler over three-fourths of Europe. . . . ?"[22] Such motives were especially likely to affect countries and governments of liberal tradition: for example, in Britain and France, where there were influential sections of opinion who supported such struggles elsewhere, and who sometimes succeeded in stimulating their governments to support them too. So these two countries were prepared to use armed force to help the Greek revolutionaries to secure independence in 1827-8; compelled Holland to grant independence to Belgium in 1831-2; supported the demands of Italy for freedom from Austria (and in France's case went to war for that purpose). Even governments with little ideological sympathy for nationalism would, when national interest demanded it, support such struggles (as when Russia supported the revolution in Greece in 1828-9 and that in Bulgaria and Bosnia in 1877-8). This had a major effect on the character of war. In at least eight of the relatively small number of international wars of this period, the main motive for participation by one or more nations was the desire to assist national minorities to secure or maintain independence, or to unify states on the basis of the national principle (the wars of 1828-9, 1848-9 [Sardinia], 1859, 1864, 1877-8, 1896-8, 1912 and 1914).

Motives were affected by nationalist sentiment in another way. The strength of national feelings was increased, and competition between states as a result intensified. Nationalism sharpened the struggle for status and influence among nations. The power of patriotic feeling was perhaps especially pronounced in the new states that had themselves been created on the national principle, and sometimes felt that they had unfinished national business. So Serbia was involved in four wars between 1885 and 1914; Greece in five between 1898 and 1920; Bulgaria in three within three years after 1912. Italy, having been involved in five wars in under 20 years during the course of her creation (in 1848, 1859, 1860-1, 1866 and 1867) became involved in two more in the first two decades of the next century, over and above a series of colonial adventures. Germany, besides being involved in four wars in 22 years during her creation, became, 20 or 30 years later, perhaps the most ambitious and bellicose power in Europe. But nationalist sentiment was by no means confined to such countries. It was diffused among the nations of Europe as a whole, and it sharpened the competition between them to still higher levels of intensity.

One result was that another motive, already powerful in the previous age, was now intensified. This was the desire for status. That motive was expressed now in new ways. It encouraged the arms race, especially in the building of warships: Britain's two-power standard partly expressed the desire for status, as did Germany's desire to challenge it. It fed the demand for colonies, especially among rising powers without colonies, such as Italy and Germany: though this in itself did not produce war among the powers, nor, always, wars in acquiring them (Germany fought no wars in acquiring her substantial colonial empire, though she had to fight substantial wars to put down subsequent revolts there), it intensified feelings of rivalry and the resentment of those dissatisfied, above all Germany. In other cases rivalry for status undoubtedly did stimulate war. So the war between Prussia and Austria of 1866 resulted essentially from competition for dominance in Germany: Bismarck already foresaw this ten years earlier, before his rise to power, when he declared that "in the not too distant future we shall have to fight for our existence against Austria. . . . The course of events in Germany has no other solution." Similarly the competition for dominance between Prussia and France was largely responsible for their war of 1870, at a time when there were no substantial issues, other than mutual jealousy, between them. Rivalry between Serbia and Bulgaria was the major cause of wars between them in 1885, 1913 and 1915. Finally, and most important of all, it was Germany's demand for status, a status — measured in terms of colonies, naval strength and, above all, influence in world affairs (*Weltmacht*) — corresponding to the power which she felt she had by then attained, that was probably the most important single cause of the First World War.*

* Germany was not alone in her concern for status. Each of the powers shared that preoccupation. One of Austria's main reasons for seeking to crush Serbia in 1914 was that she believed that her status as a great power would be prejudiced if she failed to respond with sufficient vigour to her archduke's assassination: Conrad, the Austrian chief-of-staff, said that "it

Another motive which continued sometimes to lead to conflict was the demand for strategically advantageous positions. For some powers at least that demand became among the most persistent and strongest aims of foreign policy. So for Britain the defence of India (and therefore of the Suez Canal, which led there) and the preservation of the Low Countries from potentially hostile influences were perhaps the most vital objectives of foreign policy, objectives which sometimes brought war with other powers. The Indian connection was responsible for wars with Persia (1856-7) and with Afghanistan (1838-42 and 1878-81), the occupation of Egypt (1882), the two expeditions against Sudan (1882-5 and 1897-9), the occupation of Uganda, and the expedition to Tibet in 1904, in addition to near-wars with Russia (in 1882 and on several other occasions) and with France (in 1898). Concern about developments in the Low Countries was responsible for action against Holland (and France) in 1831 and Britain's entry into the First World War. For Russia, the desire to control the Straits, and ideally to win Constantinople, were important factors in stimulating war in 1828, in 1853 (in her renewed occupation of the Principalities: it was Turkish action to end this that precipitated war) and in 1877-8 (one reason why Russia and Britain were so persistently in conflict during this period was that — over and above their ideological antagonism, which alone would not have been decisive — their strategic aims, both in Asia and in the Straits, were nearly always mutually opposed, so that a strong strategic position for

---

was not a question of a knightly duel with poor little Serbia . . . nor of punishment for the assassination; it was much more the highly practical importance of the prestige of a Great Power" — quoted in S. B. Fay., *The Origins of the World War* (New York, 1940) Vol II, 185. An Austrian foreign-office official told the British ambassador in Vienna that Austria-Hungary was determined to take action against Serbia, whatever action Russia might take, because she "would lose the position of a Great Power if she stood any more nonsense from Serbia" (*ibid.*, p. 247). For Russia the same consideration was almost equally important: at the meeting of the Russian council of ministers immediately after the assassination, Sazonov, the Russian foreign minister, declared that "if Russia now abandoned under threat her historic mission [to protect the interests of the Slav peoples] she would be considered a decadent state and would have had to take second place among the powers" (quoted in D. C. B. Lieven, *Russia and the Origins of the First World War* (London, 1983), pp. 141-2). Nor was Britain any less touchy about her status: in his famous Mansion House speech, of 21 July 1911, threatening war with Germany, Lloyd George declared that it was "essential in the highest interests, not merely of this country but of the world, that Britain should at all hazards maintain her prestige amongst the Great Powers", for if she allowed herself to be treated "as if she were of no account in the cabinet of nations", the peace so obtained "would be a humiliation intolerable for a great country like ours to endure".

Russia in the Straits or in Central Asia was seen by Britain as a danger, and vice versa.) For France, the desire to establish the Rhine frontier and the wish to acquire Savoy — controlling her border with Italy — were objectives that helped motivate two wars: the first was a motive for many in 1870 (members of the French chamber shouted "to the Rhine" when the declaration of war was announced) and the latter in 1859 (Cavour was persuaded to make over Savoy as the price of French assistance against Austria). For Prussia, control of the Rhine was equally important, so that the recovery of the Rhineland was an essential prize at the end of the Napoleonic wars; while one reason for winning Schleswig-Holstein for Germany was to reduce Denmark's power to control entry to the Baltic. For Austria, the desire to block Serbia from the Adriatic was the motive for winning control of Bosnia-Herzegovina in 1878, for formally annexing it in 1908, and for sponsoring the creation of Albania in 1913. As in other ages, this strategic motive, though conceived as defensive in nature, could often stimulate war. Positions seen as defensive by one power were regarded as a threat by another; and a strategic objective first seen as a means became ultimately an end in itself, which could lead directly to conflict with other states. So Russia's desire for security at the Straits was seen as a threat by Britain and other countries; Britain's desire for a two-power standard conflicted with Germany's desire for naval equality; Austria's desire for security against Slav nationalism conflicted with the desire of Serbia to promote Slav interests (and precipitated a war which ultimately destroyed her empire). The search for "security", when pursued by all simultaneously, was to prove the main threat to the security of all.

Some motives that had been important in former times now became less powerful. Territorial aims diminished. In the previous age the demand for territory, though already less powerful than in the age of dynasties, had remained a significant factor influencing national behaviour. Nations had desired territory on historical, strategic or geographical grounds, irrespective of ethnic character; as Austria had sought territory in Belgium and Bavaria, Sweden in Pomerania, France in the Rhineland, Russia in Courland and the Crimea. At the end of every war victors demanded a wholesale disposition of land which took no account of popular wishes. After 1815 European nations no longer looked for significant territorial gains. In the few cases where claims were put forward and pressed through war, it was for relatively marginal areas; and they were areas to which, usually, reasonable claims might be put forward on ethnic or geographical grounds. So France had reasonable grounds in 1859 for demanding French-speaking Savoy and Nice. Prussia fought her four wars almost entirely for German-speaking territory (apart from the northernmost parts of Schleswig, which were Danish-speaking, and Lorraine, which she had never seriously coveted but was part of the old German empire). Greece made war (five times) for Greek-speaking territories. And Italy entered the First World War, against her allies, mainly for Italian-speaking lands in Istria (though she did not mind taking the German-speaking south Tyrol or Greek-speaking Dodecanese as well). Where no such grounds existed, demands for territory were (after 1815) modest. Britain and France won no territories for themselves at the end of the Crimean War; Prussia took none from Austria in 1866. Of the 67 wars in Europe during this period there were only a handful in which the demand for territory was a significant motive, and then usually only for marginal areas (pp. 110-1 above). Here too the "national principle" had modified the motives that generally prevailed among nations.

Another change was that economic motives, though a significant influence on foreign policy, were now hardly ever a factor which led to war. Even if trade was not quite the force for peace which Bright and Cobden (and even Gladstone) had hoped, it was also seldom, as it had been in the previous era, a cause of war. This is demonstrated by the fact that economic conditions now rarely featured in the terms of peace imposed at the end of wars. Wars were not fought between European states to win better trading terms, reductions of tariffs, or even access to the colonies of others (perhaps the most contentious economic issues among states at the time). Only in Latin America did economic motives play a small part in some wars of the age: especially in the War of the Pacific of 1879-83, and in one or two minor conflicts (such as that between Brazil and Bolivia in 1902). The United States secured economic advantages for herself in the places she took, such as the Philippines, Hawaii and Cuba, but this was not a motive for war. Nor was it a prime motive in colonial conquests.

Ideological motives too, later so important, were rarely a cause of war in this period. The French revolutionary war can be seen as partly ideological in its beginnings — a war for liberty, fraternity and equality, or, perhaps more, for the right of revolution and republicanism, against monarchical legitimacy and conservative autocracy. But it quickly became much more a trial of strength between France, with her new territorial acquisitions, on the one hand, and her traditional rivals on the other: in other words, a war about the balance of power in Europe. During the 1820s and 1830s there were important ideological differences among the powers: between the more conservative powers of the east, concerned to preserve legitimacy and oppose revolution (even, if necessary, by intervention), and Britain and (later) France in the West, more sympathetic to liberal, constitutional and national movements, and hostile to attempts to maintain the old order by interference from without. But this antagonism was never consistent: Russia, the most conservative power of Europe, was willing to support revolution in Greece when national interests dictated it; Britain, the opponent of collective counter-revolution, was willing to support Austrian intervention to maintain the old order in Italy; Prussia opposed national revolution for the Poles in Russia, but demanded it for Germans in Schleswig-Holstein; France supported the Italian and Polish revolutions in theory but abandoned them when national interests made that support inconvenient. Though alliances constantly shifted, the most frequent combinations for most of the time were between arch-conservative Russia and liberal France, and between parliamentary Britain and autocratic Austria: scarcely ideological partnerships. In any case, such ideological differences as existed rarely inclined the powers to make war against each other. When formal alliances were established, apparently on ideological principles, in the mid 1830s, the first major crisis that arose, over Egypt, was settled, contrary to those alliances, with Britain siding with Russia against France. There is no war in the entire period that can be said to reflect an ideological conflict of principle. In the Crimean War the liberal powers of Britain and France were allied with Turkey, the most reactionary and illiberal power of Europe; and in the First World War (sometimes claimed to be an ideological struggle) the conservative powers of Central Europe were opposed by a combination of the most autocratic state of the continent, Russia, and parliamentary democracies, (Britain was in fact more parliamentary than democratic: universal male suffrage, which had existed in Germany since the state's foundation, was introduced in Britain only after the First World War). While ideological sentiments sometimes dictated sympathies, they were never the cause for which wars were fought or allies chosen.

A more important conflict of motives, in this as in other ages, was between those countries which favoured the maintenance of the *status quo,* or something like it, and those "revisionist" powers which wanted a total change in the existing order. For much of the period the chief revisionist power was France. During the French Revolution and the Napoleonic wars this revisionist sentiment took the form of a drive to establish a totally new order in Europe. After those wars the aim became to overturn the settlement imposed at Vienna and the imagined humiliation this represented for France (even though, apart from the reparation payments, those terms had been notably mild). So Lamartine, the French foreign minister, immediately after the 1848 revolution, denounced the treaties of 1815, which, he said, "have no legal existence in the eyes of the French republic" (though he prudently added immediately afterwards that "nevertheless the territorial provisions of these treaties are a fact, which the republic admits as bases and starting points in its relations with other nations"). Louis Napoleon constantly declared his desire to wipe out the humiliations of Vienna and re-establish France's former glory.

After her defeat in the Crimean War, Russia in turn became a revisionist power (even ready to contemplate alliance with the upstart emperor of France), concerned above all to revise the main disability imposed on her in 1856, the neutralisation of the Black Sea: an aim which she secured eventually, under the cover of the Franco-Prussian War, in 1870). Greece, from the date of her creation, was consistently a revisionist power, seeking to win for Greece all the Greek-speaking territories remaining under Turkish rule. Most of the Balkan states were to some extent revisionist in their aims in the last 30 years of this period, seeking to further the dissolution of the crumbling Turkish and Austro-Hungarian empires. And in Asia Japan, borrowing the motives of the international society into which she emerged, was equally and publicly determined to change the map of that region.[23]

Other states had a contrary interest. All governments of conservative inclination, and especially those of the multinational empires, Turkey, Austria-Hungary and Russia, which had most to fear from national revolutions, naturally favoured the *status quo*. They feared internal as much as external change. The Holy Alliance was established explicitly to resist political change wherever it might occur. Such powers would help each other to prevent changes in appropriate cases: so France and Austria intervened against revolution in Spain and Italy in the 1820s; Russia helped Austria against Hungary in 1849; and Prussia helped Russia against Poland in 1863. Movements for unification could also be seen as a threat by other states. So Austria did everything possible to prevent the unification of Italy; and de Lhouys, Napoleon III's foreign minister, committed himself to opposing German reunification, on the logical ground that "everything that promotes the division of the great powers is useful to us". Intervention to preserve the *status quo* thus became almost as important a cause of war as intervention to overturn it. In general, however, as the age progressed intervention against national revolutions became less common (the civil war in Spain in 1868-9, despite the fact that it was explicitly republican in aim, and actually established a republic for several years, aroused far less concern elsewhere than the civil wars of 1820-3 and 1833-40 and stimulated no demand, as then, for external intervention). The successive international congresses of the age became increasingly conferences to *manage* change rather than to prevent it altogether.

In Latin America the most powerful motives leading to war were patriotic sentiment and national rivalry. In that continent the roots of nationalism did not lie in ethnic, linguistic or cultural rivalry. The ruling classes in all the states shared a common ethnic, linguistic and historical background, yet found little difficulty in engaging in warfare with each other. Sometimes these contests resulted from the ambitions of individual rulers (Paraguay's war of 1864 and Nicaragua's of 1906). In other cases, the economic interests of nations were involved (the War of the Pacific of 1879, for example). Ideological factors, far more than in Europe, played a part in these conflicts, spilling over from the political struggles within states: so in 1863 the Liberal government of Colombia made war against Ecuador to overthrow the clerical autocracy prevailing there; and in Central America both civil and international wars were mainly concerned with rival political beliefs (for example, the war of 1855-7). More often the underlying motive was a desire of one power for influence or domination over another: Argentina seeking dominant influence in Uruguay (1825-8 and 1838-52), Bolivia in Peru (1834), and so on. In Central America the desire for the unity of the region conflicted with the desire of individual states for independence: this was the issue in the long struggle which took place there from 1828 to 1839 and in the war of 1885, when Guatemala sought to re-establish a united Central America. Civil wars were concerned frequently with the power which one region or city should enjoy in relation to others: as in the conflicts produced by the rivalry between Buenos Aires and the rest of Argentina (the cause of at least three civil wars); between inland Quito and coastal Guayaquil in Ecuador; between liberal León and conservative Granada in Nicaragua (causing Managua to be made capital as compromise); between the mountainous north and agricultural south in Bolivia (causing La Paz and Sucre to be made joint capitals as compromise).

Finally, a different set of motives underlay colonial wars. Colonial expansion was not a universally shared desire in Europe. Most of the smaller countries of Europe showed no inclination to acquire possessions in other parts of the world. Nor did major powers if they had no maritime tradition. Austria-Hungary, though at least as concerned with national status as others, never looked for colonies overseas (perhaps feeling she had subject peoples enough at home). Russia, though certainly not without the imperial mentality, contented herself with expansion in areas contiguous to her own borders, which she saw as part of her own territory rather than as colonies. Even those powers which did secure substantial territories overseas did so haphazardly and sometimes reluctantly, rather than as a carefully established policy; often to compete with rivals which might threaten their own position, or in response to the demands of nationals abroad who sought protection. Only in a few cases was there a deliberate policy of conquest. Jules Ferry of France had no hesitation in proclaiming the desirability for France* of securing further colonies, to create mar-

---

* And for the people of the country colonised. "Is it possible to deny", he asked, "that it is good fortune for the unhappy populations of equatorial

kets for the surplus goods and capital of Europe, though many in the French chamber opposed that view. Bismarck, though he once declared that he was "never a man for colonies", had no compunction in the mid-eighties in appropriating substantial territories in Africa and the Pacific. Disraeli, who had seen all colonies "as nothing but a millstone around the neck" of colonial powers, came to rejoice in the glory of an empire on which the sun never set. Such sentiments were widely spread among the populations of colonising powers. Associations glorying in colonisation were established in several of them: in Germany there were the Society for German Colonisation and the Colonial Association; in Britain the Primrose League, the Imperial Federation League and Chamberlain's Tariff Reform League all ardent supporters of the imperial role; in France the Société de Géographie Commerciale, dedicated to expanding French trade in outlying parts of the world. This sense that colonial empires were a source of glory as well as of profit came to be a dominant motive, among governments as well as peoples. It was a motive that frequently brought armed conflict with the peoples colonised (83 wars altogether), though never, in this age, with rival colonial powers.

So a new set of motives brought new kinds of wars in pursuit of different types of interest. Concern over succession in other states became less significant. The desire for territory declined in importance, especially in Europe. Against this, the desire for territory beyond the seas, for strategic or economic reasons, for some nations at least increased. The desire for prestige and for influence (p. 111-2), especially in immediately surrounding areas, was a widely shared objective. But everywhere the most powerful aim and the most common cause of war was the desire for strong national states based on national sentiment. That aim stimulated wars by minorities within states, seeking independence or unity, and wars between states seeking status or domination.

The age of ideology (1917-   )

After the First World War some of the motives which had influenced state behaviour in the previous age now counted for less. The demand for status declined in importance at least as a factor in causing war. In the previous century, as we saw, it was a significant factor: precipitating wars, for example, in 1866, 1870 and 1914. It remained a major factor in stimulating the Italian, German and Japanese search for power in the 1930s. After 1945 it became far less significant. Rivalry between the super-powers was undoubtedly in part a com-

---

Africa to fall under the protectorate of the French nation or the English nation?" (speech in the chamber of deputies, 31 October 1883).

petition for status. Both for them and even more for lesser powers, it probably helped motivate the desire for nuclear weapons and other advanced military technology. It intensified the competition for economic growth, for cultural achievement and sporting victories. Yet it is difficult to find examples of wars since 1945 in which the demand for status has been the major stimulus (a possible exception is Uganda's abortive invasion of Tanzania in 1978). Occasionally it could be a reason for not abandoning a war already begun on other grounds (making it more difficult for the United States to withdraw from Vietnam or the Soviet Union from Afghanistan). It may have played a part in intensifying wars in some cases: as between China and India in 1962, between India and Pakistan in 1965, and between El Salvador and Honduras in 1969. But it is now rarely a significant factor in the starting of wars: certainly far less than in earlier generations.

The desire for territorial expansion is now also insignificant. Governments are still less inclined to assess status or success in terms of the amount of territory controlled. This has been seen especially in a decline in the desire to colonise distant parts of the world: that aim, the most frequent single cause of war in the previous age, is now almost extinct. For the most part nations have sought now to end imperial responsibilities rather than to extend them. Expansionary drives of other kinds have also been less powerful, especially since 1945. Until that time territorial aims remained significant among a few highly nationalistic governments. The ultimate causes of the Second World War, both in the Far East and in Europe, were the demands of such states for expansion into the territories that surrounded them: as seen in Japan's successive attacks — on Manchuria in 1931, on parts of North China in 1933 and 1935, on China itself in 1937, and on the United States and most of East Asia in 1941; in Germany's successive efforts from 1936 onwards to win control of the Rhineland, Austria, Czechoslovakia, Poland and finally most of the rest of Europe; and in Italy's attacks on Albania and Greece. Such efforts were in a sense a hangover from the age before. In the inter-war period these three states remained (as they had been in the last 50 years of the previous period) revisionist powers, concerned to change the *status quo* in their favour, by force if necessary.

Since 1945 there have been — apart from the wars of reunification — virtually no attempts at large-scale expansion of that kind. Newly independent powers — India, Indonesia, Somalia — have sought to expand into limited neighbouring territories to which they believed they had a historical claim. Other new states have sought to win control of small amounts of territory disputed with another power: as shown in a number of frontier wars (see Table 12). But the aim in such disputes has not been large-scale expansion, an increase in the power or territory of one at the expense of another; rather it has been to maintain (or regain) control of something each state held to be rightfully its own. This applies not only to the 18 frontier conflicts but also to some other wars as well. So the successive wars in the Middle East have all been ultimately rooted in conflicting territorial claims in Palestine which are mutually irreconcilable (which side is seen as the aggressor depends on what situation is seen as the *status quo*). In some cases the aim has been pre-emption, to seize disputed territory at a favourable moment: as in Pakistan's two attacks on Kashmir in 1949 and 1965, and Algeria's occupation of disputed territory in the Sahara in 1962. In others the objective has been not so much to win control of the entire area in dispute, as to jockey for position, to lay down a claim to issue a challenge (for example, in Peru's actions against Ecuador in 1941 and 1981,* India's against China in 1959 and 1962, China's against the Soviet Union in 1969-72, or the occasional skirmishes between Chile and Argentina over the Beagle Channel).

In some cases the purpose of armed action has simply been to *coerce* an opponent. One of the objects of Britain, France and Israel in attacking Egypt in 1956 was to secure the overthrow of its president, Nasser; a second was to win control of the Suez Canal, whose future was in dispute; and a third (in Israel's case) to prevent Egyptian irregulars from carrying out raids on Israeli territory. In other cases the motivation for war has been *retaliatory*. The objective of El Salvador in attacking Honduras in 1969 was to retaliate for attacks on her own citizens in Honduras, which had themselves been stimulated by attacks on the large Honduran colony in El Salvador; the objective of China in attacking Vietnam in 1979 was to teach Vietnam a "lesson" for her intervention in Cambodia (just as Vietnam had conquered Cambodia the year before to retaliate against prolonged incursions into Vietnamese territory); while Tanzania, at about the same time, conquered Uganda in response to an incursion against her by Ugandan forces and a declared claim to Tanzanian territory. Whether the motive has been coercion or retaliation, the attacking country has felt itself justified in using force to prevent a neighbour from acting in a way that it believes threatens itself (and, since the attacking country has nearly always been the more powerful, there has not necessarily been any proportionality between the scale of the initial provocation and that of the counter-action taken).

But a substantial proportion of the wars of this age have resulted from none of these traditional motives: attempts at large-scale expan-

* Peru was concerned to maintain her hold on disputed territory, potentially oil-rich, Ecuador to assert her right to navigate the Amazon. This is only one of the several Latin American disputes which concerned rights of access to the sea. The Beagle Channel dispute between Argentina and Chile at root concerned Chile's rights in the Atlantic. Bolivia's century-long dispute with Chile concerned Bolivia's access to the Pacific.

sion, or to assert rights over marginal border areas, or to coerce opponents. Many wars have developed from the concern of major nations with internal developments in other states. In this, however, there has been a major divergence from the previous era. In the preceding age the aim was, overwhelmingly, to give support to movements for national independence (p. 163 above). In the present age, perhaps surprisingly, this has rarely been a reason for intervening. Though there have been a large number of wars of independence within colonies, and almost as many wars undertaken by minorities seeking independence or autonomy, and though there has been widespread sympathy for these struggles elsewhere, there have been relatively few cases of direct intervention in struggles of either kind. Arms might occasionally be supplied (for example, to the Nagas in India, or to the Ibos in Nigeria); training and other assistance offered, or political support provided (as was given by the United Arab Republic to independence movements in Algeria, Tunisia and South Arabia, or by the Soviet Union and China to freedom-fighters in Southern Africa). But only occasionally has more active support been given: decisively in the form of the despatch of forces by India for Bangladesh in 1971 and by Turkey for the Turkish-speaking minority in Cyprus; more cautiously by South Yemen for the Dhofaris of Oman, by Algeria for the Polisario Front in the Western Sahara, or by Iran and Iraq for Kurds in the territory of their opponents. But the first two of these are virtually the only cases of active intervention by regular forces in independence struggles, comparable to the successful help given to national rebellions in the previous century (for example, in Greece, Belgium, Bulgaria, Crete and other places). In general, outside powers, including the super-powers, have refrained from becoming too openly involved in wars of both these types. The conventions now developed increasingly restrain neighbouring countries, whatever sympathies they might feel for a rebellious people, from becoming directly involved in such wars, still less from actively planning wars aimed at national liberation (such as France had planned with Piedmont in 1859). Even where the grossest violations of human rights occurred, as in Cambodia under Pol Pot, Uganda under Amin, and Equatorial Guinea under Nguema, external intervention (which might have been justified under traditional international law as "humanitarian intervention") was avoided on similar grounds. In general, external assistance to secessionist movements has been seen not as help to the wave of the future, as in the previous century, but as quixotic and fruitless meddling, which would antagonise the government of the country concerned without giving effective assistance to the minority people in rebellion. Perhaps the most striking example of this is that even assistance to rebel forces in South Africa, where power has been monopolised by an unrepresentative minority, was generally relatively half-hearted, being widely seen as a laudable but ultimately quixotic venture.

This hesitation about the propriety of intervention in colonial or minority wars has, however, rarely been felt in the case of *political* struggles between rival factions in another country: especially those that are broadly communist and anti-communist, or at least left-wing and right-wing. For the motive that now dominates all others is the desire to promote the cause of a particular ideology, or rather (which is not quite the same thing) of a particular ideological alliance. This type of intervention was seen even in the early years of the period: in the large-scale intervention by Britain, France, the United States, Japan and others in the Russian Civil War; in the Romanian action against the communist government of Hungary in 1919; in the intervention by Germany and Italy in support of rebels in the civil war in Spain in 1936-9. But it has been far more visible since 1945: for example, in the support given by Yugoslavia, Albania and Bulgaria to communist forces in Greece in 1946-9; in the interventions to overthrow the left-wing governments of Guatemala in 1954, of Cuba in 1961, and of the Dominican Republic in 1965; in the intervention of North Vietnamese forces in South Vietnam in 1959-75; in the assistance given by Cuba and other countries to rebel forces in different parts of Central America in the late seventies, by the United States to Nicaraguan, Afghan and Angolan rebels in the early eighties, and by China and others to dissident forces in Cambodia and Afghanistan at about the same time. All of these are examples of assistance given to rebel forces in struggles between communist and anti-communist factions. But assistance has sometimes been given in civil struggles of other kinds: as in the Syrian intervention in Lebanon in 1958 and from 1975 onwards; Saudi intervention in Yemen in 1961-9; Libyan intervention in Chad during the late seventies and early eighties; Israeli intervention in Lebanon in 1978 and 1982; and large-scale South African support for rebels in Angola, Mozambique and other countries at about the same period. Everywhere, as in the previous ideological age, intervention to support a cause elsewhere (now a political cause rather than a religious one) has become a major aim and a major factor intensifying war.

One effect of the universal concern about politics has been that the overthrow of government leaders has become a widespread objective, abroad as much as at home: something which had almost never been a war aim during the previous two periods (the Napoleonic wars are perhaps the only exception). So "hang the Kaiser" became a slogan among the victorious allies in the First World War; Britain and France saw the overthrow of Nasser as a major war aim in 1956; the United States organised the invasion of Guatemala in 1954 to overthrow the government there and the Soviet Union undertook that of

Hungary in 1956 for the same reason; the overthrow of Castro was the main objective of the Bay of Pigs operation, just as the overthrow of Amin was a major aim of Tanzania in invading Uganda in 1979; and the overthrow of the leaders of the opposing state was the main aim of Iraq and Iran in their war of 1980. These are only a few examples. Even assassination has once more become (as in the age of religions) a means adopted by governments for that purpose: for example, in attempts on the life of Castro, Diem and other personalities; as shown in the attempts by Libya, Bulgaria and other governments to kill political opponents abroad; and in the advice on the assassination of opponents given by the US Central Intelligence Agency to the faction it was assisting in Nicaragua.

But the one side's concern to support rebels has usually been matched by the other's concern to support an existing government. Interventions on behalf of rebel forces have thus usually been met by at least equivalent intervention in support of the government under threat. The latter indeed has usually been even greater in scale (partly because it is held by most to be more permissible but mainly because there is even greater concern to maintain positions already held than to win new ones from the opponent). It is perhaps for this reason that in the great majority of these factional struggles it is government forces which have finally prevailed, and the rebellions which have been defeated. This is the opposite of the outcome in most cases of intervention in the previous century, when, as we have seen, in most cases national rebellions finally prevailed (see Table 6).

The success of government forces in most of these struggles reflects the fact that the underlying motive of the major powers has in most cases been defensive rather than offensive. The paranoia of the age of religions has been reproduced in an intense fear of an opponent believed to be spreading its tentacles across the globe. Outside powers, especially the super-powers, have therefore, as in the previous era of ideological conflict (pp. 145-6), been mainly concerned to prevent an opponent from securing gains in some area as a result of political developments, rather than themselves to acquire power in regions not previously controlled. Each has been determined to maintain domination within its own sphere of influence; but was willing to show considerable restraint in the sphere claimed by its opponents. This defensive motive is a powerful one and has often brought about decisive action. So the super-powers have intervened to prevent a change of regime in Eastern Europe (Hungary and Czechoslovakia), or in Central America (Cuba, Dominican Republic and Nicaragua), or in Asia (Korea) of a kind that could be unfavourable to themselves. Where changes in strategically sensitive areas have taken place, temporarily or permanently, it has been the result of *internal* events, not action by the opposing super-power: for example, in Guatemala in 1953, in Hungary in 1956, in Cuba in 1958-9, in the Dominican Republic in 1965, in Czechoslovakia in 1968, in Nicaragua in 1976-9, and in Afghanistan in 1978. Such internal changes have often not been easy to reverse. Even so, in all of these cases they stimulated defensive action by the neighbouring super-power to restore the previous *status quo* (action that was successful in four out of the seven cases — failing only in Cuba, Nicaragua and, so far, in Afghanistan).

Such actions reflect the primary motive of the super-powers — the desire to preserve their strategic interests and those of the alliance which each leads. That motive is sometimes more powerful than the desire for ideological victory itself. The latter is often desired only as the means of assuring security interests (though, conversely, the security gains are demanded partly for genuine ideological reasons that is, in the interests of the ideological alliance). The United States desires non-communist governments in Central America partly because she desires the victory of democracy everywhere, but *mainly* because she believes victory for left-wing forces to pose a threat to US security. The Soviet Union requires communist governments in Eastern Europe partly because she wishes to see communist governments everywhere, but *mainly* because in that area they are seen as essential to her security. Even in areas further from the super-powers' borders, this defensive motivation is often paramount. The United States sought victory in Vietnam partly as a matter of principle — no government should be overturned through armed action instigated from outside its borders — but mainly because she believed a communist Vietnam (leading possibly, it was claimed, to a communist South-east Asia) could be a threat to her security (just as some had said 20 years earlier that a communist China would be a threat to essential US security interests). The Soviet Union assisted left-wing governments and factions in Africa partly because she wanted to see the victory of such forces everywhere, but mainly because such a victory would promote the interests, strategic as well as political, of the Soviet Union herself. This security interest has also been the major motivation in causing intervention by other powers: for example, by China in Korea and Vietnam; by Israel in Lebanon; by India in Bangladesh, Sikkim and Bhutan; and by South Africa in neighbouring states. Every government wants above all to prevent hostile forces from establishing themselves in areas close to its own borders.

The fact that intervention now takes place, at least by major powers, mainly for defensive purposes has created a strongly conservative bias in the system. Most countries, particularly the more powerful states, prefer the existing situation, especially in neighbouring areas, to any alternative that is likely to come about, and are willing to intervene powerfully to maintain it or restore it. This reflects a major change in motivations in this age. During the previous period — and even until 1945 — there still existed powerful members of the international community which were concerned to bring about fundamental changes in the international *status quo*: to alter international boundaries or at least the prevailing balance of power and influence among states. In the nineteenth century this revisionist role was undertaken in turn by France, by Russia, and finally, above all, by Germany. Each was resisted in that age by the other powers; each was militarily defeated at one time or another; and none finally succeeded in its ambitions. But their aims were none the less the main cause of instability during that period. During the inter-war period powerful pressures in favour of radical change were still exerted by Germany, Italy and Japan, each of which was willing to make use of force if necessary to bring about the changes it desired. They too were resisted by others powers and they too finally failed in their attempt. But again it was their pressure for change that was the main cause of war throughout that period. Since 1945 no major power has sought to change the *status quo* in a radical way, and certainly not by force. The Soviet Union and other communist powers have proclaimed a theoretical belief that capitalism would be "buried" and socialism triumph throughout the world; while some in the West have expressed a similar faith that communism would be "rolled back" and the Western democratic system finally prevail everywhere. But each has only half believed it; and neither has been willing to risk the unimaginable dangers of a major war to achieve those ends. Both have been cautious even about limited actions for that purpose: they will both, for example, tolerate without response the use of force by the other to preserve the *status quo* in the areas adjoining its own borders, rather than risk a conflagration. Among the major powers, none had a sufficient interest in major change to seek to bring it about by acts of war. And their own acts of intervention were always to defend or restore the *status quo,* not to change it.

This tolerance (which requires the sacrifice of political independence by a number of small states) has in a sense been the mechanism by which peace between the super-powers themselves has been maintained. Given the demand of each super-power to control political events in its own neighbourhood, attempts by the opposing super-power to influence developments there (even its support of a small state's independence) could lead to confrontation between them and eventually to war. This can be seen by reference to the outbreak of the First World War. At that time Austria-Hungary believed, in much the same way as super-powers often do today, that political events in neighbouring Serbia represented a threat to her own security. She responded by making demands on Serbia that were incompatible not only with Serbia's own sovereign rights but with the commitments made to Serbia's independence by Russia. In that situation Austria-Hungary was able to protect her own security interests (according to her own subjective judgement) only in a way that must lead to all-out conflict with Russia, and so to world war. Peace in the modern world has been maintained only because of reluctance by both super-powers to make commitments to their rivals' neighbours comparable to that made by Russia to Serbia. And an increase in the independence of neighbouring small powers may, paradoxically, occur only with increased assurance that such commitments will not be made by distant patrons: in that way political independence for small states may once more be willingly granted without prejudice to super-power security.

Lesser powers have sometimes had a more direct interest in challenging the *status quo*; and faced less powerful deterrents in seeking to change it. Thus both Israel and the Arab states have, in diametrically opposite ways, been hostile to the *status quo* in the Middle East; and both have been willing on occasions to initiate the use of force to adjust it — the Arabs in 1948 and 1973, Israel in 1956, 1978 and 1982 (the 1967 case is ambiguous: Egypt disrupted the *status quo*; Israel initiated the use of armed force). In South-east Asia, North Vietnam challenged the *status quo* that followed the Geneva settlement of 1954; a challenge which the forces favouring the *status quo*, even including powerful outside forces, were not finally able to overcome. In Southern Africa black African states have been hostile to the *status quo* in the white-ruled states of that area and have contributed marginally to the changes that destroyed white rule in Angola, Mozambique and Rhodesia and have modified it even in South Africa itself (though these changes have resulted in each case mainly from domestic events). The *status quo* that has been of concern has usually been the political *status quo* within particular countries; and outside states, however much they might desire change, will not normally challenge it by overt armed intervention — only by discreet assistance to the local forces challenging the existing order. When they have attempted to bring about major political change by force, they have often failed. Israel's invasion of Lebanon in 1982 is one of the few cases since 1945 where one state has occupied much of a neighbouring state, including its capital. But neither her forces, nor these of the United States that followed, were able to influence the political situation there in their favour. Nor could far greater US forces in Vietnam, or Soviet forces in Afghanistan. External efforts to determine political events elsewhere, therefore, have rarely proved effective exercises of military power (and this failure of conventional uses of armed power may partly account for the increasing resort to terrorism rather than war, as the means of promoting change or at least attracting attention to a cause or imagined wrong).

For the most part, the forces seeking to promote political change have been domestic. In many countries especially where authoritarian governments held power, revolutionary movements emerged to challenge them. Sometimes these looked to external powers. In ideological conflicts the two super-powers have often been seen as the most likely patrons and sources of aid. But there have been other states — especially those which had themselves recently experienced revolution — which have also been willing to encourage or assist such movements: Cuba since 1959 in Latin America, Libya since 1969 in Africa, Iran since 1979 in the Middle East, and Nicaragua since 1979 in Central America. Even these, however, have rarely been willing to send their own armed forces to help revolutionary movements in other countries. Throughout the world revolutionary forces can expect sympathy and moral support from other states; but rarely the full-scale armed assistance which was given in similar situations during the nineteenth century. If armed assistance is given at all it is mainly to the governments fighting *against* such movements.

Economic objectives have declined still further in importance. They played some part in motivating Japanese attacks in the Pacific in 1941. But it is difficult to point to any other war in which they have had any significant role. There is no evidence that pressure on resources, for example, though of acute importance to many states, especially in the case of oil, has played any part in stimulating war. The conflict between rich countries and poor all over the world, though of increasing importance in international relations generally, has not led to war between them. This may have been partly because of the disparity of power between such states. But it is mainly because economic grievances have not been seen in this age as justifying the use of force: even rich and powerful states have not used force to settle such disputes (for example, over debt problems, as they did in the age before). Poverty may have made war within some countries more likely to occur; but even there it has not of itself been a sufficient condition of war (many of the poorest countries of all have experienced no civil conflicts): it is inequality and injustice, political as well as economic, rather than poverty alone which has sometimes become the cause of war. And in those cases the motive for revolution has usually been to bring a change in the entire political system, rather than to win a redistribution of income, land reform, the ejection of multinationals or the satisfaction of other purely economic objectives.

Once again, therefore, dominant motives changed in this age. The most widespread concern was not, as in earlier periods, territorial ambition, nor even national power, but political change within states, the success of an ideology, or an ideological bloc. This has changed the aspirations of states. Among the major powers territorial claims are now of minimal importance. Most have no such claims: and where they do have them (as Japan has against the Soviet Union, or West Germany in desiring the reunification of Germany) they are content to pursue them by peaceful means only. Among lesser powers such claims have existed, and have led to minor frontier wars; but these have mainly been limited encounters confined to the border areas in dispute (Iraq's prolonged and costly war against Iran is an exception). More significant than concern about territory is now concern about the internal system of government in other countries. Declining distance and the universal ideological struggle have made this more important than ever. It has led to attempts to intervene in various ways to influence political developments in other states. Especially where the security apprehensions of major powers have become aroused, this concern has brought about forcible intervention. Though these interventions have often been swift and decisive (Hungary, Czechoslovakia, Dominican Republic, Grenada), sometimes they have led to prolonged entanglements from which the powers concerned have found it difficult to extricate themselves (as in Vietnam and Afghanistan).

In developing countries too there has been increasing concern with the spread of political doctrines and systems in neighbouring states. But even those states that have proclaimed doctrines of revolution — as did Nasser's Egypt, Castro's Cuba, Qadafy's Libya and Khomeini's Iran — have mainly been relatively cautious in applying these doctrines in practice. Most wars now begin within states. And the motives that have been most significant in building them into major conflicts of the age — in Korea, Vietnam, Afghanistan, for example — have been the desire of outside states to ensure, by whatever means are seen as appropriate, that the outcome of such conflicts should not threaten the security of neighbouring powers, still less that of an entire ideological alliance.

Conclusions

During this survey we have considered a wide range of motives which, in different periods, have brought nations and other groups into conflict with each other.

Motives are never themselves the cause of war. However much a country desires territory, or power, or victory for its own religion or ideology, these will only bring about war if it determines that it can secure those objectives by no other means. Governments have not normally, in any of the periods we have considered, desired war for its own sake. Warfare has been employed only when it has appeared that a desired objective can be secured in no other way.

War is, in other words, always a means and not an end. And because of its high cost it will only be considered as a means of achieving objectives that are very highly prized. We have seen in the course of this survey that over the years a number of different ends have been so prized, and have accordingly appeared to governments to be worth that cost.

The ends believed to justify war, however, have varied greatly from age to age. The aim that most often brought rulers into war with each other in the age of dynasties, the acquisition of a throne elsewhere, was far less often a stimulus to war in the next two ages, and has ceased altogether to be one in more recent times. The desire to protect a religious faith or to impose it on another land, which often led to war in the second of the ages we have examined, has rarely brought armed conflict in any of the subsequent periods that we have considered. The aim of promoting state power by the acquisition of territories seen as being strategically, commercially or otherwise valuable, a major source of war in the age of sovereignty, has been much less often such a cause in the last two of our societies. The demand for national independence or national integration, common as the source of war in Europe in the last century, has ceased to be such a cause in recent times in Europe, though it has remained one — until recently at least — in other parts of the world. Finally, the desire to see governments of a particular political persuasion in power in neighbouring countries, very rarely the cause of war in previous times, has become the most frequent single incentive for warlike action in the age in which we now live.

In other words, the questions about which national leaders feel most strongly have changed significantly over time; and so therefore have the issues about which they are willing to go to war. Of course, the change in motives is not equal for every nation, still less for every individual within each nation. Often there will be some that retain the attitudes and desires that are typical of the age before. So, for example, in the late seventeenth century Louis XIV retained dynastic ambitions for the Bourbon family at the same time as he acquired national ambitions for France; so in the 1930s the leaders of Germany, Italy and Japan continued to be inspired by a strong nationalist sentiment that was more typical of the age before (however much they sought to cloak their nationalist ambitions in ideological rhetoric). Individuals in the age of sovereignty remained affected by religious fanaticism, even if this was rarely reflected in state policy; just as some individuals in the modern age remain infected with ardent nationalism. But these were the exceptions, not typical of their age, and they did not stamp their motives on their nations' policies or on the international society in which they lived. To a considerable extent national leaders and decision-makers, and peoples generally, have borrowed their emotions and wishes from the society to which they belong. Just as individuals within a domestic society learn the values, aspirations and desires that their society teaches them to have, so in the wider international society nations learn their values, aspirations and desires from the wider society in which their nation lives: so they learn to fight for the victory of a dynasty in one age, of a particular religious creed in another, of the state they serve in one, of the national entity to which they belong in another, and of a particular political cause in still another. Though there is never an identity of motives among the states in each society, there is at least a general resemblance; and it is these widely shared motives which determine which issues are thought worth making war about and how often war is made.

Clearly motives are most likely to lead to conflict if they can be achieved only at the expense of other states: if they are by nature competitive. During the whole period that we have surveyed some of the goals that were most competitive and so most likely to cause war have been abandoned. The demand for royal succession in another state, a highly competitive motive and the most common cause of war in our first period, does not now influence governments at all. The demand for territory, equally competitive, no longer motivates the most developed and highly armed countries of the world, and is no longer an important factor for most other countries. The demand for status, though it still exists, is for the most part no longer felt to require military victory for its attainment. Some of the objectives that are most widely held among states today — for economic growth, commercial success, good relations with neighbours, international good name, even for peace itself — are aims whose attainment does not demand serious conflict and certainly need not require war. Probably the motives among states today which are most likely to lead them into conflict are the demand for security — a demand which (since security is interpreted in subjective terms) may often appear incompatible with the security of other states; and the demand to secure victory for a particular ideological creed. Both of these are, or can be, mutually exclusive goals. The steps one state believes necessary to safeguard its security may seem to threaten that of another. The victory of one ideological faction may involve the defeat of another. The risk of serious conflict from that source may be reduced only by some modification of goals so that security is conceived in mutually compatible ways, or ideological coexistence tolerated. Such changes in motivation are likely to occur only slowly.

Even these motives cannot in themselves, however, be the cause of war. Whether they result in war depends on how they are put into effect. And how far governments seek to secure their ends by means likely to result in war depends on a number of factors. These include their beliefs about the cost of war, their willingness to accept war as a legitimate policy alternative, their ability to prevail in war, their belief about the reactions of other states, and many other things. But it depends too partly on who reaches the decisions about whether or not war should be made and the way in which those decisions are reached. It is thus to the question of decision-making that we turn in the next chapter.

5   Decisions

If we wish to study war we must be particularly concerned to examine the way in which those who have chosen to embark on it have arrived at that decision.

A knowledge of the way such decisions have been reached is the best evidence available to us about the factors that lead nations into war. What have been the considerations that have mainly influenced governments when they have finally decided to resort to armed force to secure their ends. Have the decisions been based on a careful and rational consideration of the options available, of the balance of power between the parties on either side, of the precise outcome to be expected? Or have they been based only on an immediate and emotional response to a challenge, an insult or a threat, largely devoid of rational calculation?

The first aspect to be considered in such a study must be who made the decision to go to war? Was it a single individual, exercising unlimited authority; a cabinet; or a still wider assembly? Was it made by civilians, concerned with political interests at home and abroad, but possibly unversed in judgements of relative military capability; by military leaders, well aware of the relative power available on either side yct perhaps inspired by an inflated conception of the skill or bravery of their own forces; or by some combination of the two? Was advice sought — military, political or diplomatic — in reaching the decision? How far was popular feeling, whether expressed in parliament, press or other channels, a decisive factor in determining the response made?

Secondly, *when* was the decision reached? Was it made on the spur of the moment, in response to a sudden crisis, to a hostile move made by another power, an unanticipated threat or an unexpected opportunity? Or was war planned for months or years in advance, and the occasion only manufactured at the appropriate time, to provide the necessary justification when the attack needed to be launched? In other words, was the decision for war a short-term or a long-term one? That question is important, since the conclusion may determine the answer to some of the other problems traditionally associated with war. If decisions have been mainly short-term and emotional responses to particular challenges, the best way of reducing the

185

likelihood of war may lie in seeking to minimise sudden movements, mobilisations, threats and other wrong signals which might provoke such a response, and in seeking to develop better techniques of crisis-management and communication so as to reduce misunderstandings and allay fears, rather than in attempting to secure a long-term balance of power, which, at a time when emotions are high, may have little influence on decision-making. On the other hand, if wars are usually planned long in advance, measures to improve crisis-management and communication will have little effect in influencing leaders who have already made a decision in principle; and attempts to deter such decisions by mobilising an appropriate balance of power or other forms of deterrence will be a more effective means of preventing war.

Thirdly, what were the factors which mainly influenced the decisions made? Were those decisions, whether short-term or long-term, based on a careful consideration of the likely chances of success; of the balance of advantage between pursuing the desired objective by military victory and doing so by further negotiations; of the estimated economic costs of war of varying durations; of the loss of life likely to be incurred; or of the precise gains to be demanded in case of victory? Or did they result rather from a far less rational consideration of the options, a crude determination to secure revenge for past humiliation, or to exploit a favourable opportunity for the humbling of a rival? Was there any careful calculation of the balance of military power on either side? Was the participation of outside powers, on one side or the other, carefully or accurately anticipated in advance, or merely left to chance and the outcome of rival diplomatic endeavours? And even if such assessments were attempted, perhaps in the calm back-rooms of foreign offices or war departments, during the days of peace, did they actually have much influence on the thinking of the leaders who finally, when the crisis came, had to make the decision? Or did the mood of anger, of righteous indignation, or blind self-confidence, make all such calculations appear in the heat of the moment largely irrelevant? Finally, was there any *intention* of war at all; or did it simply "break out", undesired by any party to the conflict, as a result of misunderstandings or miscalculations on one side or on both?

On many of these questions it will not be possible to provide certain answers. On the one hand, our knowledge about the way many decisions for war were taken is inadequate, so that our assessment of the thinking of those who made them must be based largely on conjecture. On the other, the answer to many of the questions will, anyway, not be uniform: we may find that in some cases wars were planned for years in advance, while in others they were the result of skilful opportunism or chance reaction to an unexpected event; that in some cases there was careful calculation of the balance of military power and political advantage, while in others there was only an emotional response with little calculation at all.

This does not mean that no conclusions at all can be reached. But a comprehensive examination of all the various factors which have affected all the decisions to make war over the past few centuries would require a lifetime of research and many volumes of conclusions. All that can be attempted here is a brief survey of some of the evidence in a number of cases of which we have knowledge in the different periods we are concerned with. From this we may get some idea of the kind of considerations which have been in the minds of decision-makers in each of these periods, and of any changes over time that may have taken place in the way those decisions have been reached. We can then go on to see how far the decisions finally reached have proved justified by events: how far, that is, nations, or their leaders, in embarking on war, have in practice secured from that enterprise the advantages they had hoped to acquire.

The age of dynasties (1400-1559)

How were decisions to embark on war generally reached in the first of our international societies?

In an age of kingly power it was largely the rulers themselves who reached those decisions. It was Henry V personally who decided in 1415 on the resumption of England's war with France at a time of maximum French weakness. It was Charles the Bold who decided, regardless of contrary advice, on his successive aggressions against his neighbours in 1458-75; just as it was Louis XI who, equally following his own counsel, determined the action to be taken against Charles. It was Charles VIII personally who decided to launch his country on war in Italy in 1494, a venture that was to occupy his country at intervals for the next 65 years. It was Francis I who determined to make war against his enemies five times between 1515 and 1542. It was Charles V who decided to make war for Tunis in 1535 and for Algiers (disastrously) in 1541; who decided to embark on a trial of strength with the protestants of Germany in 1546 and (again disastrously) in 1552.* Yet the power of rulers was not absolute, even in this age. It depended crucially on the loyalty of their supporters and

---

* It is true that it was France and the protestant states, led by Maurice of Saxony, which took the initiative in the use of force in this war; but by his refusal to compromise — especially to consider releasing the landgrave of Hesse — it was Charles who made war inevitable: certainly the decision for peace or war was entirely in his hands.

War in International Society

subjects. They were dependent for finance on the votes of estates and parliaments. They were dependent for military power on the support of the great magnates (the first royal army of consequence was that created by Charles VII in France in 1439-45). And any decisions on warlike action had to be taken in the knowledge of these constraints.

That knowledge, however, was not usually inhibiting. The assumption in most cases was that, once the decision for war had been taken, the necessary funds would be voted, the necessary soldiers supplied. Thus there was not usually an elaborate process of consultation, whether with estates or magnates, before a declaration of war was made. If adequate support for the decision was lacking, it normally became visible only after war had already begun. The great magnates could decide that a war was no longer worth pursuing and leave their ruler in the lurch: both Polish and Hungarian kings were occasionally compelled to abandon military enterprises when the chief nobles, who supplied virtually all their soldiers, refused to support the exercise (it was on these grounds that Matthias Corvinus established his own "black army", including former rebel soldiers, as a more reliable military machine). Parliaments or estates might fail to vote the funds required: the Emperor Maximilian twice had to abandon wars (in 1490 and 1516) because the Bundesrat would not vote the money required to pay his army; while Henry VIII, having embarked on war with France in 1522, had great difficulty in securing the necessary supplies from parliament and gave up the war two years later with little profit.[1] The financial cost of war was considerable and the failure to secure funds from parliaments or estates was therefore crucial. Armies that were unpaid could pass out of the control of their commanders, as did the army of Charles V which sacked Rome in 1527; it was on these grounds that Gattinara had warned Charles that "a hundred well paid soldiers are worth two hundred without pay".

Rulers therefore continually had to bear in mind the degree of support they were likely to enjoy. But it was none the less they who made the initial decision for war, influenced, if at all, only by their closest personal advisers. Nearly always they at least discussed proposed military actions with these close advisers. That advice was not always taken. De Commynes recommended caution to his master, Charles the Bold, when the latter planned war in 1477, but was ignored. Henry VIII's counsellors favoured a policy of peace in 1512-13 (the Venetian ambassador reported that they believed "peace suited England better than war"[2]) but the young king none the less chose war. In other cases the advisers were at least as anxious for war as their rulers. In 1521 it was Wolsey who negotiated the alliance with the emperor for a war with France (though the plan of the negotiations "was determined by the king and cardinal in consultation and every important detail in that and in the subsequent preparations for war was submitted to Henry"[3]); and it was Wolsey who, against Henry's advice, allowed the seizure of English ships at Bordeaux which finally precipitated war. In 1528 it was Wolsey who favoured a declaration of war against Charles V, which ultimately came about directly against Henry's will.[4]

This meant that the character and views of a ruler's chief advisers could have a vital influence on the likelihood of war. The replacement of the pacific de Chièvres by Gattinara as his chief minister helped to spur the young Charles V to a more warlike posture towards France in 1520-1. In the summer of 1521, not long after his appointment, Gattinara submitted a long memorandum to Charles setting out the arguments for and against war with Francis I. Though he advanced seven reasons against war at that time (uncertainty of outcome, lack of financial resources, unreliability of Swiss mercenaries, failure of French support for rebels, and so on), he was careful to find ten even stronger arguments in favour (the need to support the pope, who would otherwise desert Charles for Francis; the fact that the army was already mobilised, so that there would be loss of face if it were stood down; the emperor's need to win honour and glory; the fact that the occasion was ripe; because "God was on Charles's side", and so forth). In such cases the character of the adviser might make all the difference to the decision reached. While de Chièvres would have found the financial arguments for peace to be overriding, Gattinara now saw the need for the emperor to win honour and glory, and to begin to establish the universal empire in which he so strongly believed, to be the supreme aim. Similarly, whereas Cardinal Tavera, archbishop of Toledo and the most trusted of Charles's ministers after Gattinara's death, opposed the emperor's plan for military action in Tunis and Italy in 1535 and was hostile to the concept of universal empire, Charles's confessor, Pedro de Soto, in 1545 urged Charles to make war in alliance with the pope against the protestants.[5]

But rulers were subject to influence not only from individual ministers and advisers but from the chief nobles of their realm. Often the king's relatives, brothers and uncles were especially powerful figures sometimes having as much influence as the monarch himself: men such as Gloucester, Beaufort and Bedford in England during Henry VI's reign; Orleans, Berry and Bourbon in the time of Charles VI of France; Ludovico the Moor in Milan (uncle of the ruler, Gian Galleazzo, but the chief decider of policy and largely responsible for Charles VIII's invasion). Whether or not related to the king, great nobles exercised substantial power. Their influence was often favourable to war: "The nobility had been educated for war and in peace was at a loss. Land was no longer so profitable and the tourney was no adequate compensation for actual combat. For financial and emotional reasons the knight longed for war and foreign adventure and the wars of Italy were encouraged and prolonged by a nobility whose functions at court had been taken over by a professional administrator and whose estates were often incapable of supporting a large family. For the non-mercantile classes war offered the main chance of getting rich quickly, by loot and ransom. And, once war had started, the same motives led to its continuing."[6] Inclination and interest alike, therefore, often caused the nobility to use the influence they enjoyed in favour of war.

A principal channel for the influence of the nobles and other great magnates was the royal council. This had almost everywhere the specific function of advising the ruler on all questions, including the making of war. Its actual influence varied widely from state to state. In some countries such councils had great power. In Denmark and Sweden they were the instruments by which the great nobles exercised strict restraint on the rulers (for example, the Danish council deposed King Eric in 1439 and chose his nephew as his successor, while the Swedish council chose their own king in 1448, 1467 and 1503); occasionally removing them altogether and often restricting the right to tax and therefore to make war. In France the *grand conseil* discussed the conduct of the war with England during the Hundred Years War and took over much of the control of taxation from the estates-general. The system of councils was perhaps most highly developed in Spain, especially after the unification of the kingdom there. Even in the days of Ferdinand and Isabella there were eleven separate councils, including the council of state, the council of the Indies, the council for Castile, and so on. By the time of Charles V that system was further extended.[7] Though there were separate governments for Spain, the Netherlands and the Empire, each had councils (the *Bundesrat* in the case of the Empire) which were consulted on questions of peace and war. Though often susceptible to royal influence, such councils, if united, undoubtedly carried weight. Because the great magnates who often favoured war were heavily represented in them, however, it is unlikely they were usually a major influence for peace.

In time such councils, especially in Spain, Burgundy and in England under the Tudors, brought forward "new men", lawyers and professional administrators who brought a different approach to the question of peace and war. Some among them, such as Thomas Cromwell in England and de los Cobos in Spain, secured a power that was rarely acquired by the non-noble class in earlier times. Such people acquired a commitment to the state as well as the ruler. They became more concerned about the financial costs of war and less about the glory and honour of the prince, more concerned with national interests and less with those of the dynasty, than either the nobles or the rulers themselves. (Thomas Cromwell, for example, argued strongly in parliament against a continental war at the time when Henry VIII and Wolsey had already embarked on war with France in 1522.[8]) They were, however, usually more concerned with the conduct of a war that had already been declared than they were with the initial decision to make war. And in any case the influence of such cautious bureaucrats was often less than that of the nobles within the councils. "A king's councillors, especially the professional bureaucrats among them, might urge caution, but in the immediate circle of advisers to the crown nobles were in the majority, men who as leaders of the second estate had been educated for war."[9]

Another influence on policy came from the estates. In many places the theory remained that the ruler held power only on sufferance from his people. His legitimacy therefore rested on the assent of the estates. Many monarchs were obliged at their coronation to undertake to abide by the customs of the land, to grant traditional liberties, to exempt particular groups from taxation, to appoint only local people to offices of state, to speak the national language and so forth. The *joyeuse entrée*, which the dukes of Brabant were obliged to swear at their coronation, explicitly demanded that the prince was not to undertake war without the consent of the three estates. While the powers of the estates over questions of peace and war were not always as explicitly laid down as this, they enjoyed almost everywhere a large degree of financial power, which meant that wars could not be sustained without their consent. In most places a ruler could not raise taxation, certainly not direct taxation, without their assent (only in France from the days of Charles VII could the king raise substantial revenues — the direct *taille* as well as the indirect *aides* — without such authority). In Saxony the electors could raise no money at all without the consent of the estates. In Burgundy the Flemish estates categorically refused to pay the money which Charles the Bold demanded to fight his last and ultimately disastrous war; and after his defeat it was explicitly laid down that declarations of war required the consent of the estates. In Aragon all declarations of war and all peace treaties were supposed to be submitted to the *cortes*. Charles V, who was nearly always in financial difficulties, spent a considerable amount of time travelling to speak to his estates in Castile, Valencia, Aragon and other parts of his lands to persuade them to vote the money he needed for his wars (though his grandfather Ferdinand had secured new sources of income, such as the *alcabala*, or sales tax, which were independent of the *cortes*, these alone were quite insufficient to defray the costs of war). The German *Bundesrat* rebuffed the efforts of the German emperors, especially Maximilian I, to win a more secure supply of funds for their wars (they point-blank refused funds to enable him to join the war against Venice in 1509, which had the result that Maximilian was unable to play any significant part in that war); and it was largely because of their reluctance to yield this power of the purse that Maximilian's attempts at that time to establish a permanent imperial force (and those of Charles V in 1548-9) never bore fruit. Only in France did the power of the estates-general decline (it did not meet between 1488 and 1560), its authority, including its power to vote the *taille*, passing to the more amenable royal council; and this partly accounts for the freedom with which Francis I was able, despite constant defeats, continually to renew war against his enemies (he launched five major wars between 1515 and 1542, mainly for Milan, and lost all except the first).

The financial leverage the estates exercised in this way was, however, essentially negative. It does not mean that they normally had any influence on the initial decisions for war. Their power was indirect. Aware of the possible difficulties they might have in raising finance to undertake their wars, rulers might in consequence be made somewhat more cautious. But they certainly did not invite the estates to share in the decision for war itself.

Still less did the mass of the people expect to influence decisions of this kind. "Everyone knows," wrote Honoré Bonet at the end of the fourteenth century, "that in the matter of deciding on war, of declaring it, or of undertaking it, poor men are not concerned at all. . . . " The assumption was that if the ruler decided for war his people would follow. "No case had to be laid before a country to woo it to arms, and as increasing reliance was placed in professional soldiery the bulk of the population was ignored. War was waged at the discretion of the king."[10] Even if the mass of the population had been consulted, they would not necessarily always have been unfavourable to war. Enthusiasm for the dynastic cause, knowledge of the profits to be made from war, even an emergent nationalist sentiment in some cases, all meant that ordinary people were sometimes by no means averse to a decision in favour of foreign adventure. Though it is doubtful if many rulers were much concerned about the attitude of the mass of their population, therefore, they probably normally assumed that, once a decision had been reached, their subjects' consent, even their goodwill, could usually be secured. In their eyes the only important condition was not whether they could win the support of the people for any particular venture, but whether they could be sure of victory. As Gattinara told Charles V (and as most of the rulers anyway believed), "defeat is the only crime".[11]

If this is how the decisions were reached, when did they occur? Were wars planned long in advance, or did they "break out" almost unheralded?

Certainly there was always a substantial degree of intention on one side or the other (often on both). Henry V had almost certainly determined to make war on France long before negotiations broke down on 6 July 1415 and even longer before he led his army across the Channel in the following month. Charles VIII planned his descent into Italy at least two years before his invasion took place, having already begun his diplomatic preparations (making substantial concessions to potential enemies) in 1492. Pope Alexander VI carefully planned his war to eject Charles from Italy in 1495, writing to all the chief rulers of Europe for their support; just as Pope Julius II planned his war against Venice in 1508 and against France once more in 1510. In 1520-1 Charles V and Henry VIII (or Wolsey on his behalf) planned in detail the war against Francis I which was only fully launched in 1522 (for example, preparing jointly for simultaneous invasions of France and assistance to a planned rebellion by the duke of Bourbon). Five years later Francis I, in recruiting allies from all over Europe, planned in advance the war by which he sought to reverse the humiliation he had suffered at Pavia. Charles V and Pope Paul III planned war against the protestants of Germany for a year before their attack was launched in 1546, even agreeing by treaty the forces each would provide (which did not prevent the pope deserting within a few months).[12] There were few if any wars that broke out totally unexpectedly. And for the most part one side at least, anticipating conflict, plotted with some care the attack it would launch against the other at the appropriate moment.

Despite this considerable measure of intention, it does not seem that there was ever in this age any serious attempt to calculate in advance the balance of power available on either side, and so the chance of success. In 1415 Henry V took to France a force of only 9,000 or so men; and he committed less than 6,000 to the battle of Agincourt against a vastly superior force. The forces available to Charles the Bold were far inferior to those of the countries he challenged in his final war. In Italy, small cities, such as Pisa, would challenge great ones, such as Florence, sometimes with considerable success. Even if the desire to make a calculation had been present, it would not have been an easy one to make, since the numbers that would be available could never be calculated easily in advance. It could not be accurately forecast how many soldiers would be provided from feudal levies on either side, still less how much money parliament or estates would vote to buy forces from elsewhere. Even if the relative numbers could have been known, this would not necessarily have given an indication of the outcome. Often it was believed that a brave king (most of the rulers of the day led their men in battle), a brilliant commander (such as a Gonzalo, a Leyva, or a Maurice of Saxony), a new armament or a new fortification, might make all the difference between victory and defeat. For the most part bravado, confidence in divine benevolence (having "God on your side" — Charles V's confessor, Pedro de Soto, precisely echoed Gattinara's words in exhorting him to join the pope in war against the protestants in 1545), the justice of the cause, the valour of native armies and the glory of national destiny were all thought far more important than any exact calculation of available forces in determining the outcome of war.

So generally decisions for war in this age were made by individual rulers, each making a judgement about how he (or she*) could best promote the fortunes of his family or kingdom. They were influenced by conceptions of honour derived from the chivalric tradition, by the love of war that influenced many of their closest supporters, by the martial spirit of the age, in other words by the conventions of the

---

* Often it was women who took such decisions. Though this is sometimes thought of as an age of subjection for women, they have probably never at any other time enjoyed such power. Even in countries where succession to the throne was denied them, they frequently had a dominant influence: thus in France effective power was exercised by, among others, Isabel, the wife of Charles VI; Anne of Beaujeu, daughter of Louis XI and regent for a number of years; Louise of Savoy, mother of Francis I; as well as the mistresses of Charles VII and Henry II. (Catherine de Medici, another queen-mother, was similarly influential in the following age.) In England, Mary and later Elizabeth succeeded to the throne, and dominant consorts such as Margaret of Anjou and Elizabeth Woodville enjoyed a powerful influence. In Spain, Isabella of Castile was at least as commanding a ruler as her husband, Ferdinand of Aragon; while royal princesses could have considerable influence and even serve as their country's ambassador in a foreign state (as did Catherine of Aragon). For most of the seventeenth century the Netherlands, the most prosperous and strategically important part of the Spanish empire, was ruled by a succession of supremely able and intelligent women (Margaret of Burgundy, Charles V's aunt; Mary of Hungary, his sister; and Margaret of Parma, his natural daughter — a tradition carried on by his granddaughter, Isabella, at the beginning of the next century). Other examples of powerful female rulers are Margaret of Denmark, the two Joannas of Naples, Yolande of Savoy and Jeanne d'Albret of Navarre. There is no evidence that women rulers were any less inclined to war than their male counterparts. Isabel of France was determined on war against her successive enemies there (as well as against the English), just as Margaret of Anjou was the most implacable fighter for her husband's cause in England; Margaret of Denmark not only created a Scandinavian empire but led her country into a war against Hol-

international society, as much as by calculation of advantage for themselves and their dynasties. In so far as they sought advice it was often from others who loved war as much as they did. They were constrained, if at all, by lack of money or supporters, rather than by fear of failure or any precise calculation of the odds. It was in peace-time that the rulers sought to strengthen their forces — through the creation of the *tercios* by Charles V in Spain, through the building of the navy by Henry VIII in England, through the fortification undertaken by Italian cities. It was assumed that when war came these would be enough to secure the victory; if not, it was hoped that any deficiency in numbers or armaments might still be made good by purchasing mercenaries or allies after the war had already begun. Thus, whether war was planned well in advance — as it often was — or on the spur of the moment, calculations of balance had little influence. The decision for war was made, in response to a particular challenge or a particular opportunity, in hope and in faith, rather than as a result of rational calculation.

The age of religion (1559-1648)

In the following age the monarchs retained almost everywhere the main power of decision. In most places their authority was now more absolute than ever. Except in one or two places — Switzerland and the United Provinces, where there were no kings, and Poland, where the magnates still had ultimate power — they had been able increasingly to centralise authority in their own hands. The power of

---

stein which was to last for 30 years; while Yolande of Savoy made war against her own brother (Louis XI) on behalf of her adopted country. Joanna I led a war against her enemy Charles of Durazzo, while Joanna II, by naming, in turn, two different successors, sparked off a dynastic war which was to continue for nearly a century. Mary, regent of Burgundy, though, like other rulers of that country, averse to war with England, and urging caution against precipitate war in Germany, proved an indomitable war-leader against France in 1543-4. Mary of England, in the course of a brief reign, took her country into yet another continental war, just as she launched a war against protestants at home. Elizabeth of England was even fiercer against Catholics than her sister had been against protestants, and, though she showed a cautious spirit abroad, this was more because of the dangers she faced at home than because of any lack of warlike spirit. Maria Theresa and Catherine of Russia are examples from a later age of women rulers who showed no aversion to war and no lack of the qualities of leadership which it required. In other words the cultural pressures for war in each age were far more important than gender in determining a ruler's conduct. And the hope that, if women ruled the world, war would be abolished would therefore appear to be a rash one.

the nobles and the great landholders in most countries was diminishing; that of the estates was weak or even extinct (they did not meet in France after 1614, they were soon to be abolished in Prussia, while in the two great Hapsburg empires, though still powerful, they exercised only regional rather than national authority). Whether or not a state should make war, therefore, depended now neither on the views of the nobles, still less on those of parliaments. It was decided normally by the rulers themselves, in consultation with their closest ministers and advisers.

Thus it was Philip II, who, after consultation with those he chose to consult (including his close religious advisers), decided on war for Portugal in 1580; on the "enterprise of England" in 1587-8; on intervention in France in 1590-1. It was the Emperor Rudolf who, after a series of frontier clashes, decided on war against Turkey in 1593; the Emperor Ferdinand who decided on war to recover Bohemia in 1618; and they consulted the imperial institutions and the estates of their hereditary territories only after the event, to secure the finances and forces necessary to implement the decision. In Sweden, though the diet was theoretically to be consulted on such questions (Gustav Adolph had to swear an oath to this effect when he took the throne), in practice it was the Vasa kings, having now made themselves hereditary rulers, who decided on the series of wars in which Sweden became engaged: for Estonia, Livonia, the Baltic coast and ultimately northern Germany. In Denmark it was Christian IV who, directly against the will of his parliament, declared war in 1625. In England, though parliament possessed important financial sanctions and was not unwilling to express its views about military engagements elsewhere, it was in practice Elizabeth and her close advisers who decided on intervention in France in 1562 and (after many hesitations) in the Netherlands in 1585; James I, urged on by Charles and his favourite, Buckingham, who decided on war against Spain in 1624.[13] Even in Poland-Lithuania, where the power of the nobles remained greatest and where the kings remained dependent on election,* the kings, foreign though they were, were still able to lead the country into a succession of interminable wars, often for their own non-Polish interests — to liberate Transylvania in 1577-82, to secure the Swedish crown in 1600-29 and to win that of Russia in 1609-17.

Because the monarchs exercised the decisive power over such questions, much could depend on the personalities and beliefs of each. It was Philip II's personal commitment to secure victory for the

---

* In theory the kings of Bohemia and Hungary were also still elected at this time, but the system was abolished in Bohemia in 1627 and was no longer genuinely free in the small part of Hungary which the Hapsburgs still controlled.

Catholic faith which projected Spain into wars against most of her neighbours in Western Europe (in addition to his wars against the Moors in North Africa and the Turks in the Mediterranean); while the more easy-going temperament of his son allowed Spain a brief period of relative peace between 1609 and 1618. It was the martial spirit of the Vasa family that caused Sweden to be engaged in constant wars against all her neighbours for nearly a century; and which, allied with commitment to the protestant cause, led Gustav Adolph to add an 18-year war in Germany to the protracted war in Poland in which Sweden had been engaged for the previous 30 years, as well as the intermittent duel with Denmark. Conversely, it was the cautious personalities of Elizabeth and James that kept England from almost all official participation in land wars in Europe for nearly a century (support for the protestants in the Netherlands and the brief and inglorious intervention in the Thirty Years War are the only exceptions). The coming to the throne of a new ruler could thus materially affect or reduce the likelihood of war. While the conciliatory Maximilian II kept the Empire out of war in the West throughout the early years of this period, and, while even the more fervent Matthias and his minister Khlesl would have been willing to negotiate with the protestants of Bohemia, the coming to the throne of the doctrinaire Ferdinand soon brought the immediate removal of the peace-loving Khlesl and a determination to subdue Bohemia and extirpate protestantism from the Hapsburg domains. On the protestant side, equally, while the impulsive and quixotic Frederick, believing himself to have a "divine calling which I must not disobey" to accept the crown of Bohemia (against all the advice of his own court and most of the protestants in Germany [14]), plunged his electorate into a disastrous defeat, the cautious and undogmatic protestant rulers of Saxony and Brandenburg were able to keep their states free of war for another 12 years (and even then were dragged into it largely against their will).

But, though the rulers dominated decision-making, they were always, in this as in other ages, subject to influence from elsewhere. Since they were themselves often passionate upholders of one or other religious faith, it was sometimes their religious advisers who had the greatest influence on them. Philip II consulted his confessor and other religious authorities about his wars in the Netherlands and against Portugal. He was strongly urged by religious advisers to take action against the Moriscos in 1568.[15] He was influenced by the despatches of the fanatical Augustine friar Vilavicencio into taking stronger action in the Netherlands than his political and military advisers proposed.[16] He consulted the pope (and secured a substantial subsidy) before his expedition against England. His son Philip III was strongly influenced by his confessor in refusing peace in the

Netherlands in 1607; and it was only when another of his confessors, the Dominican friar Father Brizuela, who had been sent to strengthen the will of the Netherlands negotiators, was himself convinced of the necessity for peace that he was finally persuaded to relent. In the same way, the Emperor Ferdinand was encouraged by his confessor, the Jesuit Lamornaini,[17] to crush the protestant revolt in Bohemia and assert Catholic supremacy throughout Germany. Philip IV consulted a special committee of theologians and jurists in deciding whether he should make war over the succession in Mantua in 1628. Richelieu was himself a cardinal of the church and concerned to promote its ends: in his political testament he declared that "there is no sovereign in the world who is not under an obligation to bring about the conversion of those under his rule who have erred from the path of salvation"[18]. He raised the Capuchin father Joseph into a position of power and influence on foreign affairs, sending him on important diplomatic missions (for example, to negotiate the peace which ended the War of the Mantuan Succession in 1630-1); and the latter showed his commitment to his faith in agreeing with the representative of the emperor at Regensburg (contrary to Richelieu's instructions) that France would give no aid to the emperor's protestant enemies (for the same reason the dévots, a powerful group of Catholics in France, publicly opposed Richelieu's two interventions against Spain, in the Valtellina and in Mantua, on the grounds that they distracted from the war against the protestants). In England the bishop of Salisbury urged Elizabeth to action against Spain on the grounds that "it pleased God that she should scourge the Spaniards"; and 50 years later the archbishop of Canterbury, George Abbot, strongly urged that England should intervene on the protestant side in the Thirty Years War, to "comfort the Bohemians . . . strengthen the [Evangelical] Union . . . and stir up the king of Denmark".[19] All over Europe the Jesuits powerfully swayed the climate of opinion in favour of the crusade against the protestants (on those grounds they were the first to be expelled from Bohemia after the protestant revolution there and the first to return when it was reconquered by the emperor). On the protestant side, the Calvinist preachers who poured from Geneva "like wolves sending their books before them, full of pestilent doctrines, blasphemy and heresy to infect the people", as the Catholic bishop of Winchester declaimed,[20] often urged on the cautious rulers of protestant states a more militant policy against the scarlet woman of Rome.

At least as important in their influence on decisions on peace and war were the rulers' closest political advisers. Every monarch, whatever the precise constitutional position, had favourites, advisers or ministers whose views carried weight when such matters were discussed. This was true even in states regarded as highly autocratic, such as Spain. Philip II, though he alone finally decided, was influenced by his private secretaries (Gonzalo and Antonio Perez, de Leyas) and close advisers (Ruy Gómez, Espinosa, Escobedo). The decisions of Philip III and IV were strongly influenced by the *privados,* or royal favourites, such as Lerma and Olivares. At the beginning of the War of the Mantuan Succession, when Philip IV was considering whether or not Spain should become involved, Olivares submitted a long memorandum setting out the arguments for and against Spanish involvement; and his conclusion — that war would be justifiable given the importance to Spanish security of Montferrat (a Mantuan territory) — was ultimately accepted by the king.[21] In England, the views of Cecil and Walsingham on policy to Spain and other countries carried some weight with Elizabeth; and it was the advice of Buckingham (and his son Charles) that persuaded James I, half against his will, to declare war on Spain in 1624. In the Empire the advice of the pro-Spanish and anti-protestant minister von Eggenburg had great influence on Ferdinand II at the opening of the Thirty Years War (so much so that Ferdinand visited him in his bedroom to discuss affairs of state when he was ill [22]). Ambassadors abroad, corresponding directly with their sovereigns, also had influence. The question of whether or not Spain's war with the Netherlands should be resumed was discussed among top officials for two years before the expiry of the 12-year truce in 1621; and the views of the ambassadors and pro-consuls abroad — men such as Gondomar, the ambassador in London, the governors of Milan and Cambrai, de Zuniga, former ambassador to the emperor, and Bedmar, former ambassador to Venice (nearly all convinced that Spain's greatness could only be restored by a resumption of the war) were listened to with care and ultimately prevailed.[23]

The rulers were sometimes subject to influence from a wider body of opinion. In most countries there were channels through which these could make themselves heard. Nearly always there was a royal council which offered advice on most questions of foreign policy, and especially on matters of peace and war. In Spain there was a council of state, which had the main responsibility for advising on questions of this kind, as well as innumerable more specialised councils. Philip III is said to have "endorsed virtually without comment nine-tenths of the recommendations made in the field of foreign affairs".[24] But the great majority of these were undoubtedly fairly uncontroversial recommendations; on the more vital questions the king would be obliged to make up his own mind and the views of the council were only one factor to be considered. During the early years of the Netherlands revolt there was considerable debate between the hawkish faction, headed by the duke of Alva, and the group favouring more conciliatory policies, led by the duke of Eboli and the king's powerful secretary, Antonio Perez. Philip II would reach a final decision only after he had heard the outcome of such deliberations. (In addition to his 14 councils Philip also had smaller committees, or *juntas*, of three or four people to consider the most important and urgent questions; for example, the campaign in the Mediterranean in 1570-8 and the "enterprise of England" — the Armada — ten years later.) When Philip III and his ministers were considering whether or not to resume the war with the Netherlands in 1618-21, the different councils took different views (just as different ministries might do today): the council of finance was opposed to a war that might increase public spending, while the council of state, supported by the councils of Portugal and the Indies, believed war was necessary to frustrate the actions being taken by the Dutch against Spanish interests in South America, the Caribbean, Italy and elsewhere.[25] In Denmark, the council of state had considerable power: when the Danish king planned a war against Sweden from 1603 onwards, he was for years unable to win the consent of the council (they agreed only when their appeal to their Swedish opposite numbers to get the Swedish king to abandon his expansionist policies had failed). Similarly, in 1625 the council of state refused to give their support to Christian IV's intervention in the Thirty Years War, though they were unable to prevent it. In other cases a powerful king or a powerful minister could sway such bodies in the direction they favoured: thus the French council of state was easily persuaded to endorse Richelieu's strong recommendation for war against Spain in 1635.

In some countries parliament and estates, representing a wider body of opinion, had at least a theoretical influence over questions of peace or war. In Sweden the king had to swear a solemn oath at his inauguration that he recognised that both the starting and the ending of a war required the consent of the diet; and in 1628 a select committee of the diet met at the request of Gustav Adolph to consider, and eventually endorse, his proposal for war in Germany. In Poland, where the kings were dependent on the diet for election, it was still more powerful: after 1570, the consent of the diet was declared necessary for any declaration of war and, armed with these powers, it successfully prevented Stefan Bathory from resuming his war with Russia after the death of Ivan the Terrible in 1584; nearly 40 years later it refused to let Sigismund III assist his brother-in-law the emperor (except in an insignificant way) at the opening of the Thirty Years War. Elsewhere the influence of such bodies was more marginal. In England, as we have seen, parliament was discouraged from discussing foreign affairs. In France the estates-general rarely met in the second half of the sixteenth century and not at all after 1614. In Germany, the *Reichstag* was increasingly disabled by religious disputes and broke up altogether in 1613. Only rarely, because of the financial power they often still enjoyed could such bodies sometimes still have some influence.

Even those outside parliament could, in some countries at least, have a marginal influence on the decisions reached. Power began to spread to a new class of upper gentry: small landowners or wealthy merchants. In the United Provinces ultimate power rested for much of the time in the hands of the "regents", representing mainly the better off merchant interests, especially those of the province of Holland: these were in general more peace-loving (as well as more tolerant in questions of religion) than the House of Orange and its supporters and much more so than the Calvinists. In England the influence of the new commercial classes was one of the factors which motivated the cautious continental policy of the rulers at this time. In Poland, the so-called "gentry", mainly owners of small estates throughout the country, numbered 40,000-50,000 and wielded substantial power which could not be ignored by the monarchs: often they resented the preoccupation of their foreign kings with essentially non-Polish goals — Bathory's desire to free his homeland, Transylvania; Sigismund's to regain his Swedish crown — and sought to redirect their attention to dangers nearer home (such as the depredations of Cossacks and Tartars in the south).

There is little evidence that rulers in this age took much account of military advice in reaching decisions of this kind. Few had regular commanders-in-chief; indeed except in France and Spain no regular armies at all. Such military leaders as there were could often expect to benefit from wars and certainly could not be expected to urge restraint. Mercenary generals, such as Mansfeld, Wallenstein and Bernard of Saxe-Weimar, had a direct pecuniary interest in war (p. 246 below); feudal lords had the opportunity of acquiring new lands and titles or at least of placing the ruler in their debt; the commanders of royal or imperial forces had the chance of glory and promotion. So it is not surprising that what influence they had was often in favour of making, or resuming, war. In the East that influence was greater. An important factor in the decisions of the Ottoman sultan in favour of war with Persia in 1578, and with the Holy Roman Empire in 1593, was the advice given by the successful general Koja Sinan, who wanted the chance to acquire glory in the wars: he is said to have been influenced by jealousy of a younger rival (Ferhad Pasha) and by his desire to "add a more spectacular victory to his title 'Victor of Yemen and Tunis'". When the sultan called together a council of chief dignitaries, opinion was divided; some were against war on the grounds that the army and state finances were exhausted, but Koja Sinan "made a passionate plea for war, stating that he would bring the Hapsburg 'king' to the Sultan's threshold".[26]

Yet military leaders were, paradoxically, by no means always hawkish in their advice. On the one hand, they were (usually) less influenced by religious zeal than their royal masters, as is demonstrated by their readiness to abandon the cause they were fighting for: von Arnim (possibly the best commander of the day), Albrecht, Kritz and Götz all changed sides during the Thirty Years War, while both Mansfeld and Wallenstein were generally thought willing to do so. Bernard of Saxe-Weimar and his successor Erlach, without changing sides, abandoned protestant Sweden for Catholic France. It is noteworthy, too, that Wallenstein, the principal leader of the Catholics in the Thirty Years War was born a protestant, whilst Mansfeld, one the main generals of the protestants, was born a Catholic. On the other hand, military leaders were more conscious of the costs of war. Thus it was the most successful Spanish commanders in the Netherlands, Requesens, Farnese and Spinola, who most clearly recognised the need for a settlement with the rebels there (just as Mondejar had in relation to the Moriscos); and Wallenstein, who had acquired huge honours and vast territories through success in war, was against the provocative Edict of Restitution, and favoured for the whole of Germany the same toleration he accorded in his own territories.

If these were the main influences on them what kind of decisions were arrived at? How far were wars carefully planned in advance; how far did they "break out" from isolated incidents or through miscalculation?

Overwhelmingly, it seems, they were deliberately planned. In Spain the "enterprise of England" was planned and widely known for two years before it was launched in 1588; intervention in France in 1590-1 was deliberately decided on as the best means of promoting Spanish interests; the resumption of war against the Dutch in 1621 was, as we have seen, widely debated, and the pros and cons carefully analysed for at least two years before; while the advantages and disadvantages of intervention in Mantua in 1628 were carefully weighed before the decision for war was finally taken (p. 204 below). The enemies of Spain were equally deliberate. The Orange-dominated states-general in the United Provinces, having overcome the peace party and executed their leader, were planning war against Spain for two years before the truce expired in 1621. Frederick, the elector Palatine, in deciding whether to accept the crown of Bohemia and so initiate war against the Hapsburgs, consulted for months with all his closest advisers before eventually deciding (contrary to most of that advice) that religious duty compelled him to do so. Sigismund III of Poland took a deliberate decision to fight to regain his Swedish crown (though he may not have realised he would go on fighting for 30 years). Gustav Adolph discussed with a secret committee of parliament plans for intervening in Germany two years before he finally landed there; while his chancellor, Oxenstierna, effective ruler in the years after his death, secretly planned war against Denmark for three years before suddenly launching it (without declaration of war) in 1643. In the East likewise, Turkey planned war against Persia in 1578 because she was concerned about the development of Persian influence in the Caucasus and her trade across the Caspian, and deliberately chose a moment when Persia was especially weak because of the death of the former shah (having been advised by a close observer of the Persian court that this was the right "time for gaining revenge for ancient grievances and taking booty from the enemy"[27]). Though some of these wars undoubtedly proved far longer and more costly than had originally been anticipated, it is hard to point to any throughout the period that was not, at its inception, deliberately intended by one side or the other (occasionally by both).

Was there any serious calculation of relative strength on either side when such decisions were taken? It certainly seems doubtful if such calculations (if they were made at all) had much influence. When the French council of state decided on war against Spain in 1635, France's forces were much weaker than those of Spain and it "could only guess at the strength of the different French enemies".[28] When Gustav Adolph decided on Swedish intervention in the Thirty Years War in 1629-30, Swedish forces were only a fraction of the size of the imperial armies opposing him: it was his concern at the approach of those forces to the Baltic, his commitment to the protestant cause, his faith in the previous successes of the Swedish army, rather than any clear calculation of power, which influenced his decision. Even if there had been any disposition to make such a calculation of forces, it would have been almost impossible to work out. Armed forces in most cases were bought from elsewhere: nine-tenths of the Swedish forces in the Thirty Years War were foreign, mainly German and Scottish; Frederick's forces consisted mostly of the polyglot Mansfeld mercenaries bought from Savoy; while the Empire's equally polyglot forces had to be borrowed from the duke of Bavaria and the Catholic League, or raised from scratch by Wallenstein. So the strength each ruler could bring to bear could never be clearly known in advance. In the long run it depended mainly on financial strength. Thus it was Denmark's financial strength (derived from the tolls on traffic in the Sound) that made her relatively strong (capable of defeating Sweden in 1611-13, for example); just as it was Spain's financial exhaustion (and the rebellions that resulted) rather than military weakness (until 1643 her *tercios* were never defeated) which ultimately caused her downfall.

Though calculations might still have been made of the relative capacity to raise and equip armed power, at best they could have been only rough and ready estimates. Wars could last many years and it would have been rash to claim to forecast taxable capacity several years ahead. It was generally assumed that new revenues could be found from somewhere; in Spain there were continual debates about the relative merits of different taxes for raising revenues — the *alcabala* (a sales tax), the *servicios* (the traditional tax from which many were exempt), and the newly invented *millones* (an excise tax on food and wine). Even if these were inadequate it was usually possible to borrow abroad. In most cases commitment to the right-eousness of the cause (national or religious), or faith in the bravery and skill of native soldiers, was sufficient to convince monarchs and statesmen alike that victory could be secured, and that its benefits outweighed its costs. So, in his memorandum about the merits of intervention in Mantua, Olivares concluded that the advantages out-weighed (just) the disadvantages, but only as long as the war could be kept short (which it was not); and in his many memoranda about the war in the Netherlands he concluded likewise (except for a brief moment in the late 1620s) that, for all the huge problems it was causing to Spain, at home as much as abroad, Spain's long-term interests dictated that the war must be sustained. In both cases the estimates were wrong. As in other periods, therefore, over-optimism distorted judgements: faith in the national destiny, or in God's be-nevolence, or in the righteousness of the cause, brought persistence in wars which in the end brought ruin to the country.

Decisions concerning war in this age, therefore, were still mainly those of the rulers themselves. They had no shortage of advice: from their chief ministers, their councils of state, their religious advisers, their military leaders, even sometimes from parliaments. Occasional-ly no doubt, because of their power, they were given only the advice it was believed they wished to hear. (In Spain in Philip II's day, for example, it is said that in the council of state "the councillors knew that their opinions were reported to the king by the president or secretary of the councils. They knew that Philip might pretend to accept their advice, yet take a contrary decision. Thus they tried to conform their views to the yet unknown wishes of the king. Their advice became conservative, their statements of opinion half-hearted and qualified."[29]) What decisions were ultimately reached depended therefore largely on the character and views of the rulers themselves: on the degree of their commitment to a religious cause, to dynastic power or to national aggrandisement. A cautious ruler, or peace-loving ministers, could avoid foreign adventures and the heavy costs involved; as the rulers of England, for example, did for much of this period. A crusading ruler, such as Philip II and Ferdinand II, or one determined on national expansion, such as Sigismund III or Gustav Adolph, could lead his country into frequent wars. Ultimately the main reason why a decision in favour of war was so often made was simply the prevailing conventions and attitudes of the age. War was still everywhere seen as a normal means for attaining goals that were widely held, including the defence of a beleaguered faith. It was thus a course of action which, whatever the odds, was frequently decided on.

The age of sovereignty (1648-1789)

Even in the following age decisions relating to war were still made primarily by the monarchs themselves. Though now more subject to influence and advice than in earlier ages, it was they who ultimately determined whether or not war should occur.

It was, for example, Louis XIV personally who in 1668 determined to attack the Spanish Netherlands in pursuit of his wife's dubious succession claim; who, shortly after the conclusion of that conflict, decided on the preparation of a future war against United Provinces; who gave the order for forcible intervention in Cologne and the Palatinate in 1688; and who, by unilaterally accepting Charles II's will in violation of an earlier agreement, and treating Spain thereafter as a French satellite, made war inevitable in 1701. It was Charles X of Sweden who decided, on the basis of his own expansionist instincts, rather than of official advice, to make war against Poland in 1655. It was Peter the Great and Augustus of Saxony who together decided, in the summer of 1698, on the joint war against Sweden which was launched two years later. It was Elizabeth Farnese, the Spanish queen, determined to find kingdoms for her two sons, who goaded her husband and his ministers to war in 1718-20 and 1727-8. It was Frederick the Great who reached the decision to seize Silesia, and so plunge his country into war, in 1740 (regardless of the contrary advice put to him by his advisers).

The decisions of the rulers on such questions were not reached in isolation. They were in constant contact with ministers and officials who were in a position to influence their judgements. Even Louis XIV, though seen as the most "absolute" of the rulers of the age (and indeed priding himself on the absolute nature of his rule, which he was convinced promoted the interests of his people better than the parliamentary systems prevailing in Britain and United Provinces) was in constant communication with ministers. He would often spend several hours a day in discussion with them, especially the minister of foreign affairs: the ministers had daily, often twice daily, conversations with Louis and this was the source of much of their influence.[30] He studied carefully the despatches of his ambassadors and other official advice, as well as discussing the most important questions in the *conseil d'en haut*. But it was he himself, on the basis of his own strongly held views and in the light of the "maxims" (or guiding principles) which he believed should determine the policy of every state, who reached the final judgement.[31] Advice to him was given in the knowledge of his own views (and in the knowledge that, if the advisers lost favour, as did the dovish Pomponne at the end of the Dutch war, they might lose influence for many years). William III took more account of the view of Dutch ministers, such as Heinsius, with whom he was in constant communication, than English (even keeping secret from them some of his correspondence with Heinsius[32]); but it was his own strong opinions, rather than those of advisers, which prevailed when there was any difference of views.[33] Maria Theresa heard and respected the views of those who were expert in foreign affairs, such as Kaunitz; but on the main outlines of policy she made up her own mind (and on the necessity of a further war with Prussia to recover Silesia there was no difference between them). Least inclined, possibly, to listen to advisers on questions of peace and war, were the rulers who were also accomplished military leaders, such as Frederick the Great and Charles XII: Frederick the Great undertook the invasion of Silesia in 1740 "against all advice",[34] while the decision of Sweden to send troops to Holstein-Gottorp in 1699, the immediate stimulus to the Great Northern War (though not its cause — the war would have occurred anyway), was the "king's personal one . . . quite unknown to either College or Council".[35] Even those who listened regularly, who took part in a regular system of consultation and advice, therefore, were influenced only in so far as they wished to be. In general it can be said that in this age it was still the case in most countries that war did not occur unless the monarch wished it; if he did wish it, it happened.

This does not mean that rulers were never affected by outside advice. Major foreign policy questions were discussed not only in direct conversation between rulers and ministers, but also in various bodies established for the purpose. These institutions varied from state to state. In France policy questions were discussed in the *conseil d'en haut*. Until 1700 this usually included only three or four secretaries of state but it was later enlarged to take in members of the royal family, marshals of France and other important figures. Opposing viewpoints were put forward: for example during the War of the

Spanish Succession there was a clearly defined peace party (including the king's son) and a more hawkish faction, and the two disagreed at many points on policy concerning the war and the peace negotiations.[36] But, having heard their views, it was the king himself who finally reached the decisions which counted: "Louis XIV was particularly jealous of his powers as the director of foreign policy and kept his diplomatic officials in strict subordination. Even the minister who assisted him in this field, the secretary of state for foreign affairs, was hardly more than an executive officer".[37] In Spain there still existed a council of state which dealt with all international issues, and a council of war to which members of the council of state belonged; but both were advisory bodies, consisting of members of noble families without official experience and their advice carried no great weight.[38] In the final resort it was the king (or queen in the time of Elizabeth Farnese) that made the important decisions, sometimes helped by confidential advisers such as Nithard, Valenzuela and Alberoni. In Austria the question of whether or when war against Prussia should be renewed was discussed over several years in meetings of the privy council (*Geheimrat*): Kaunitz first made his name in that body, as advocate of a new war in alliance with France. In Sweden there were, on the one hand, periods of absolutism (for example, between 1680 and 1720 and again after 1772), when all decisions rested in the hands of the monarch and a few trusted advisers: Charles XI, for example, "established a system whereby the Council and the high officials of the Chancellery debated and prepared foreign policy issues, while he read, listened and discussed, reserving the ultimate decision for himself after consultation with individuals that he trusted";[39] and Charles XII "was the originator of policy along broad lines, usually arrived at after consultation with his trusted advisers".[40] On the other hand, there were periods in which the council exercised a power at least equal to that of the king. Either could reach decisions for war: the Swedish war against Russia of 1741 was determined by parliamentary leaders (resulting directly from the coming to power of the anti-Russian Hat party, committed to revenge), while that of 1788, launched with identical aims (the recovery of territory lost in the preceding war), resulted directly from the decisions of Gustav III during a period of absolutism.

Parliamentary opinion was significant only in Britain and the United Provinces, and then only as a barometer of public feeling generally. It was in any case rarely an influence for peace. The British parliament was full of fury against the Dutch in the 1650s and 1660s; against the French in the 1680s and 1690s; and against Spain in 1739. It was an influence for peace only when the country as a whole was already weary of war: as in 1710-13 and at the end of the War of the

Austrian Succession. Parliament forced the abandonment of war against the Dutch in 1674, but this was only because it felt even more hostile to the French. In the United Provinces the regents were for war if it was believed this would bring commercial benefit (as in 1688) and against if it was believed that trade would be damaged by war (as during the War of the Austrian Succession). Sweden pursued at least as aggressive a policy during the periods when parliament was powerful as during the periods of absolutism. In most other countries, though estates existed in most places, they were almost always without influence, except (sometimes) on questions of taxation. In general, therefore, parliaments, where they existed at all, had little direct influence on decisions concerning peace and war and were certainly no strong influence for peace.

When was the decision for war reached? Wars in this age were frequently planned over a long period. Decisions were sometimes made many months, and even years, before war was declared. Charles X planned war against Poland for a year before it was launched in 1655 and considered various different pretexts for making it. Louis XIV decided to make war on the Dutch at least three years before it was finally launched in 1772 (a year after his original target date); and he supervised minutely the preparations for the conflict in the intervening period, taking great pride in this careful preparation; "It is a good thing that I have prepared as I have for so long. . . . I am in a position to instil fear in my adversaries, to cause astonishment to my neighbours and despair to my enemies."[41] The coalition of Russia, Saxony-Poland and Denmark which declared war on Sweden in 1700 had been discussing, through diplomatic contacts and personal meetings of their sovereigns, the precise way of launching that war and the justifications that would be used for it two years beforehand.[42] Austria, and in particular her military commander, Prince Eugene, deliberately planned a war of conquest against Turkey in 1716.[43] Elizabeth Farnese and her chief minister, Alberoni, had been plotting war to recover Mediterranean territories for Spain from Austria (and were generally known to be doing so) for years before Sardinia and Sicily were seized in 1718.[44] Austria planned for nearly ten years her war to recover Silesia (the alliance between Austria and Russia of 1746 explicitly referred to this goal). Russia's leaders had decided in principle in favour of a new war to win territory round the Black Sea from Turkey for four or five years before war was initiated in 1735.[45]

So war did not "break out", as though by spontaneous combustion. It was deliberately made, often prepared long in advance. The degree of deliberation and the period of preparation varied. Sometimes a declaration of war was, at least in part, a response to events elsewhere. This was true, for example, of all the wars of succession (including the War of Devolution), which usually followed the death of a ruler. Yet even in these cases there was sometimes a fairly long period of calculation before the decision was made to launch a war. Over a year passed between Louis's acceptance of the will of Charles II and the declaration of war by the Grand Alliance created against him (though Austria took action in Italy against France before the Alliance declared war.) Six months passed between the death of Augustus II of Poland-Saxony in February 1733 and France's declaration of war against Austria over the succession in October. There was an interval of six months between the cession of Lower Bavaria to Austria in January 1778 and the Prussian declaration of war on Austria in July of that year. It is true there were only two months between the death of Charles VI and Frederick the Great's seizure of Silesia in 1740, but Frederick himself claimed that the action had been planned well in advance (in a letter to Algarotti he said that it is "only a question of executing designs I have long had in mind"[46]): it certainly fulfilled a long-standing ambition to acquire the province, and it was carefully designed to exploit the known weakness of Austria's army and finances, as well as the succession of a young and inexperienced queen.

As in other ages, there were frequent miscalculations in such decisions for war, deliberate though they were. An act of force that was intended to be swift and conclusive could prove to precipitate an unexpected war. In 1688, for example, Louis XIV had hoped to strike a quick blow that would determine the succession in the Palatinate and Cologne at a time when Austria was preoccupied by war in the East, and was unprepared for the long war against numerous opponents which finally resulted.[47] In seizing Sardinia and Sicily in 1718-19, Spain expected to present Austria with a *fait accompli* she could not reverse; and did not expect the united front among the major powers which eventually compelled her to disgorge her conquests. In seizing Silesia in 1740 Frederick the Great hoped for a rapid victory, or even no war at all;[48] and certainly quite miscalculated the temper of the Austrian queen.

These errors usually resulted from a miscalculation of the response of other powers. For this and other reasons wars in very many cases had a result quite contrary to that forecast. Louis's war against the Dutch of 1672, despite long and careful preparation, had a totally different consequence from that which he had calculated and most had supposed (no victory over the Dutch but important gains from Spain). The war launched by Russia and Austria against Turkey in 1735, instead of winning for them the territory each coveted (Russia hoped for lands around the Black Sea, Austria for gains in the

Balkans), in fact brought serious defeat for Austria and only marginal gains for Russia. The war launched by Maria Theresa to regain Silesia in 1756, despite apparently overwhelming odds on her side (Prussia was for long fighting, virtually single-handed, against Austria, Russia, France, Sweden, Saxony and other German states) ended in a humiliating failure that left Prussia's hold on Silesia more impregnable than ever. Both Sweden's wars to recover territories from Russia in 1741 and 1788 proved unsuccessful, hopes of success being based on memories of Sweden's former greatness rather than any realistic calculation of the balance of forces on either side. Even when a war was ultimately successful, its course could be quite different from what had been anticipated: Denmark and Saxony-Poland, in planning war against Sweden in 1699-1700, did not anticipate that each would be defeated within a year or so, and that final victory would take them 20 years: still less that they would merely succeed in replacing Sweden's hegemony in the Baltic with that of Russia.

Such miscalculations resulted from the inherent difficulty of forecasting either the pattern of alliances or the effectiveness of forces on either side. Nor is there much evidence that there was ever any careful and conscious calculation of the balance of power (an exception was the careful assessment of relative Austrian and Prussian strength made by Maria Theresa in urging her son to abandon the War of the Bavarian Succession in 1778[49]). In so far as any such assessment was made it was usually crude and instinctive rather than deliberate or scientific. Certainly a state that planned to make war would seek to mobilise allies on its own side (and to reduce the likelihood that its enemies could do so.) Thus Louis XIV, before embarking on his war against the Dutch in 1672, took the precaution of purchasing (literally) the alliance or neutrality of England, Sweden (the recent allies of his enemy) and a number of German states, especially Cologne and Münster, whose territories adjoined those he planned to attack. Denmark secured the alliance of Saxony-Poland and Russia before resuming her war against Sweden for the Holstein-Gottorp lands in 1700. Austria made sure of the alliance of France and Russia before renewing the struggle with Prussia for Silesia in 1756. Prussia won the support of the other German states in going to war with Austria over the question of Bavarian succession in 1778. Such balances, however, were always precarious. Allies could desert (as when England deserted France in 1674 and Prussia France in 1741, 1742 and 1745). The death of a ruler could transform the balance: as when Elizabeth of Russia was replaced by the Germanophile Peter III in 1761. Conversely the enemy might win fresh allies that had not been foreseen: so Poland found new friends to help her against Sweden in 1655 (including two of her former enemies); Spain found unexpected supporters against France in 1668 (the Triple Alliance), as the Dutch did five years later; Venice won the support of Austria against Turkey in 1716; just as Austria in turn was powerfully supported against Spain in 1718-20.

Even the strength of a single power's forces could not be measured accurately. The number of regular forces was not an accurate guide; if its own forces were weak a country might be able to purchase others elsewhere. Britain (which had herself been in receipt of subsidies in the 1670s and 1680s) was able, as her financial situation strengthened, to buy forces — from the United Provinces, Germany and even Russia in the next century (she purchased a large Russian force in the War of the Austrian Succession and seriously considered doing so in the War of American Independence). Though Austria's own forces were weak in 1740, she was able to supplement them with auxiliaries from other German states. Economic strength was for this reason almost as decisive as military and could less easily be forecast: French rulers knew the size of France's huge armed forces, but were less able to anticipate her ability to withstand the financial and social strains which prolonged war could bring (in 1696-7 and 1709-10). Above all, wishful thinking often played a major part: thus Frederick the Great, facing three of the strongest powers in Europe in 1756 (the total population of his enemies was 20 times that of Prussia) asserted that "Prussian officers who have been through the wars with me know that neither numbers nor difficulties can rob us of victory", a rash forecast which only sheer luck prevented from being confounded.

Thus, whether or not serious attempts were made to calculate the balance in advance, there were many reasons why such calculations went astray. And it is therefore not surprising that in so many cases the outcome of war was totally different from what those who launched them had anticipated. So, at the end of his war against the Dutch, Louis XIV was to find that he had by no means crushed that country, nor acquired the Spanish Netherlands; on the other hand he had acquired the valuable Franche-Comté, defeated the Spanish yet again, humbled Brandenburg and won the gratitude of Sweden, all eventualities he had at no time anticipated at the beginning of the war. So, at the end of the War of the Spanish Succession, Austria found that she had not evicted the Bourbons from Spain, still less won the whole Spanish inheritance for the Hapsburgs, as she and her allies had demanded, but on the other hand had won valuable territory in Italy and the Netherlands. So, at the end of the War of the Polish Succession, France had failed to place her candidate on the throne of Poland (if that was ever her real aim), but had acquired Lorraine and secured a complex exchange of territories in Italy. So, at the end of the Seven Years War, Prussia had not acquired Saxony, nor Austria Silesia. So too in many other cases hopeful assailants had to be satisfied with far less than they had planned. However carefully planned the war, therefore, its outcome could never be foreseen with any confidence.

Decisions in this age thus continued to lie mainly in the hands of a very small group of people, primarily the monarchs themselves, together with a small number of advisers. Their main purpose, as we saw in the last chapter, was to promote the prestige, power and territory of their own states; and they continued to decide, fairly frequently, in favour of war, or at least of acts which they knew could well lead to war, for that purpose. Usually there was a large element of deliberation in these choices. Often wars were planned for several years in advance. If the interests of the state seemed to demand it — to win territory, to secure trading advantages, to promote strategic interests, or to counter the pretensions of other states — such decisions often appeared rational ones to make. But their rationality depended on calculations of relative armed strength, forecasts of alliances and so on, assumptions which in very many cases proved misplaced. The final outcome was thus usually quite different from what had been expected (often by both sides). The factors which affected that outcome — the effectiveness of particular armies, the skill of generals, the loyalty of allies, the strength of economies, the steadfastness of populations, the course of negotiations — were so complex and unpredictable that (even if any serious assessment was made) the calculation could always go astray. Often decisions were based as much on wishful thinking, vainglory and over-confidence as on prudent calculation. And they were strongly influenced by the ideology which governed international society as a whole — the ideology of sovereignty; that is, belief in a perpetual contest, for power and pre-eminence, among competing sovereign states in which war was seen as the main means of securing supremacy.

The age of nationalism (1789-1917)

As we saw, the following period was above all an age of nationalism. Many of the wars in Europe in this period were wars of national independence, in which the original decision to take up arms was undertaken, not by governments, but by unofficial groups within the territory of a sovereign state. Such groups at a certain point decided that, unable to secure independence or other national ends by other means, they would attempt to secure what they sought by armed force. Sometimes such a decision followed the refusal of demands first put forward by peaceful means: for example, the revolution in

Crete in 1866 followed the rejection by the Turkish rulers of a petition asking for liberty of conscience and equal rights for Christians in the island. Sometimes it was triggered by a particular act of repression by the government concerned: the 1863 revolution in Poland followed the attempt by the government to conscript young Poles for the Russian army. Sometimes it resulted, by infection, from a revolution elsewhere: the Belgian revolt in 1830 and the Polish revolution of 1830-1 were sparked off by the July revolution in France; the 1848-9 revolutions in Italy, Germany, Austria and Hungary were inspired by the successful revolution which had overthrown the monarchy in France. Sometimes a revolution resulted from actions by outside powers designed to assist its aims: the revolution in Italy in 1860-1 was set in motion by the war launched to promote it by France and Piedmont in the previous year. In such cases the decision to resort to force was rarely influenced by the size of the forces available, or the balance of power. The glory of the cause, the commitment of the fighters, the oppressiveness of the government — these were the decisive factors which, it was believed, would allow even a small and ill-armed force to prevail in the end. So Garibaldi, with only a thousand men, was not deterred from challenging the massed regiments of Austria; nor a small number of Greek or Cuban freedom-fighters from launching struggles against vastly superior forces.

The situation was similar in the case of the other civil wars of the age. Here too a particular movement or group, having failed to change the political system by peaceful means, at some point took the decision to seek change by force. This too was a deliberate and calculated choice. Not surprisingly it was a choice reached almost entirely within political systems where there was little prospect of securing change by peaceful means. All took place in the relatively autocratic states of Southern and Eastern Europe; or at least in states of limited franchise (such as France in 1848). In the parliamentary states of Northern Europe there were no civil wars during this period. The only exception was in Switzerland in 1847: but there the chief issue was not a demand for more liberal or democratic institutions but the relationship of the cantons to the federal government, together with certain religious issues. Whether armed conflict was initiated by "liberal" forces demanding a "constitution", more representative institutions, or similar reforms (as in the revolutions in France, Austria and Germany in 1848-9, the French Commune of 1871, and in the four Italian cases — though there they were associated with the demand for Italian reunification); or, as in the two civil wars in Portugal and those in Spain in 1833-4 and 1872-6, were initiated by conservative forces against a (relatively speaking) "liberal" government,* the decision to resort to arms in all cases was deliberate. In such situations there seemed usually little hope of securing change by other means. The use of revolution in such situations had been sanctified, indeed glorified, by the French revolution. Here too the balance of forces was rarely an important consideration. Enthusiasm or despair might be sufficient to trigger action. Such decisions, apparently hazardous or irrational, might or might not be justified by results: revolutionary wars succeeded in less than a quarter of the cases where they were attempted (four out of 18: the successful cases were Spain in 1808-12, Portugal in 1828-34, France in 1848 and Spain in 1868-9). Whether the aim was national independence or political reform, such movements most often secured success, total or partial, in states that were loosely integrated or poorly organised, such as Turkey, Spain and Italy; they failed in those having powerful central governments, such as Russia, Austria or Prussia (see Table 7).

The decisions by governments to make war were clearly wholly different. Such decisions were now less often those of personal rulers, deciding almost alone (as could Louis XIV, Frederick the Great or Catherine the Great) whether or not to go to war. Power was usually at least shared, with chief ministers or whole cabinets. Thus decisions for war were likely to be more deliberate than those of monarchs in earlier times, and much more so than those of revolutionary groups in the same age. They were now considered acts of judgement by a number of statesmen meeting together to decide where national interests lay.

What effect did this collective decision-making have on the making of war? For example, how far were wars deliberately planned? Some were certainly still carefully planned long in advance. The war of 1859 was deliberately plotted months before it broke out, by Louis Napoleon and Cavour at their meeting in Plombières, where they agreed on a common enterprise against Austria, and even searched the map together to find a suitable issue to start the war. Cavour himself later described the occasion:

> The Emperor began by saying that he had decided to support Sardinia with all his forces in a war against Austria, provided the war shall be undertaken for a non-revolutionary cause and could be justified in the eyes of diplomacy, and even more in the eyes of public opinion in France and Europe. The search for this cause presented the principal difficulty. . . . We put our heads together and went through the whole map of Italy looking for the cause of

---

* In one case, the civil war in Spain in 1868-9, the revolution was directed primarily against the monarchy but was supported by conservative and liberal forces alike.

war which was so difficult to find. After having traversed the whole peninsula without success we arrived almost with certitude at Massa and Carrara and found what we sought with such ardour.[50]

The first Balkan war was equally carefully planned in advance by Serbia, Bulgaria and Greece, determined to take advantage of Turkey's weakness to secure territorial acquisitions for themselves. Prussia's three wars of 1864-70 were only a little less deliberate. Bismarck subsequently prided himself on having carefully planned all three; and even surprised Disraeli by blandly announcing his precise intentions years before they began. Neither story proves categorically that the three conflicts were caused by this intention alone. The reality is rather that Bismarck seized suitable opportunities as they arose to impose his will on all three adversaries, well aware that this involved the probability of war: in the last two cases he deliberately adopted courses of action that made it impossible for his rivals to avoid going to war without abject humiliation. In all three cases his opponents were little less ready for war than he himself; and all eventually obligingly took the steps which finally made war inevitable: Denmark declared the annexation of the duchies; Austria demanded a federal execution, that is, war, against Prussia for her actions in Holstein; and France, not content with the Kaiser's assurance that a Hohenzollern claimant would not accept the Spanish throne, demanded a humiliating promise that such a claim would never be renewed, and exploded in anger at the way this was refused. Thus there was a strong element of deliberate intention in each case.

Even where there was no long-term preparation for a war, war was often still deliberately intended at the time it began. The wars in the Balkans of 1885 and 1913 were not planned — both were the immediate reaction to events which had been previously unforeseen — but both were equally deliberate. Each was the exact mirror image of the other. In 1885 Serbia attacked Bulgaria in anger at her enlargement (through the decision of eastern Rumelia to join her) without compensation to Serbia; while Bulgaria attacked Serbia in 1913 because the latter had been enlarged unduly by the outcome of the first Balkan war at the expense of the gains hoped for by Bulgaria. Against this, the first Balkan war of 1912 was quite deliberately planned: the signatories of the Balkan League committed themselves to make war together against Turkey. The three Balkan wars were therefore all equally intentional; but in one case the decision reflected a long-term intention, in the other two cases short-term responses to believed humiliations. In these cases, however (unlike that of the Prussian wars just considered), the intention was entirely on one side: one or more nations made the decision to attack another. The country attacked had originally no desire for war; but in two out of three cases none the less finally came out successful. This could be taken to show a greater rationality in long-term than short-term decisions: the long-term decision (by the Balkan League to attack Turkey in 1912) was successful; both the short-term decisions, resulting from emotional reaction to disappointment (Serbia's attack on Bulgaria in 1885, and Bulgaria's on Serbia in 1913) failed. If more time had been taken in calculating the likely outcome, both attacks might not have been undertaken at all.

The most ambiguous cases, so far as the nature of intentions are concerned, are the Crimean War and the First World War. In the former case the war was not intended in advance by any of the parties, still less deliberately planned. Initially Russia had made demands on Turkey — in particular, reasserted the right to protect the Orthodox population of the Ottoman Empire, a right which had been accorded her by treaty but which would have given her a dominant influence there — but, in the face of opposition from Britain and France, acting in support of Turkey, had largely retreated from that claim before war began (while still remaining in occupation of the Principalities). Her retreat indicates that Russia did not want a war if it were to involve those two countries as well as Turkey. Conversely, Britain and France did not plan or seek war with Russia for its own sake: they wished to reduce Russia's claims on Turkey, and hoped that their support for Turkey would be sufficient to achieve this without war. The only country which had an interest in war was Turkey, the weakest of the four, since she could be fairly confident that she would fight the war (unlike her previous encounters with Russia) with the support of two powerful allies, and that the effect would be to reduce Russian pressure more permanently than any settlement reached among the powers. It was thus Turkey, the weakest of the four states, which finally precipitated the war (and still might not have succeeded if she had not been so disastrously defeated in the initial battle). In this case, therefore, while there was between the main antagonists a conflict of interests and an underlying hostility, there was no deliberate intention of war; and it was the nature of the relationships — the danger to the Western powers of a Russian defeat of Turkey — which made it possible for the weakest party to bring about a war, in her own interests, at a time when most of the issues in dispute had already been resolved.

In the case of the First World War it was again one of the weaker parties, Austria-Hungary, which finally precipitated the war: through her determination to crush Serbia in response to an incident for which Serbia had no proved responsibility. And again it was the nature of commitments previously made by other powers which caused this decision inevitably to lead to a wider European conflict. Russia was committed to support Serbia, France to support Russia, and Germany to support Austria-Hungary. The commitment in each case was moral and political rather than by the terms of treaties, which created no absolute obligation: Russia had no obligation to come to the aid of Serbia (but had been so humiliated by her failure to act in 1908 that she could not have failed to do so without disastrous loss of face); France was committed to support Russia only if the latter was attacked; Germany had no obligation to support Austria-Hungary in an offensive war; Britain had no treaty obligation in Europe at all. This discredits the thesis, put forward by Wilson and others after the war, that the war resulted from alliances and "secret treaties". Each of the powers was likely, for good reasons of national interest, to have responded in identical fashion to an Austrian attack on Serbia, even if it had had no treaty obligations at all. The difference from the Crimean case is that here there was ample time for the weaker power with an interest in war (Austria-Hungary) to be restrained if her ally had had any wish to exercise restraint. That wish did not exist. Many in Germany at the time, including her chief of general staff (who played an active role throughout the crisis), actively wished for a major European war at this point. No doubt if Serbia could have been destroyed, and so a major victory won for the Central Powers, without a European war, the latter would have been willing to accept that triumph without the cost of paying for it. But both Germany and Austria-Hungary were well aware that Russia, France and possibly Britain were unlikely to allow any such major change in the international *status quo* to be made without resistance. So, while no power may have actively planned war before 28 June 1914, two powers, Austria-Hungary and Germany, were willing to take steps after that date which they knew involved the strong probability of war with at least two, and possibly three, of the major powers of Europe.

In all these cases, therefore, there was a substantial measure of intention, either short-term or long-term, by at least one of the powers involved, that war should occur. Actions were taken which involved at the very least a high risk of producing war. This does not mean that they were based on any deliberate calculation of the balance of power and the probability of success. It is clear that in a substantial proportion of cases there was no clear assessment of the balance of forces on either side. As we have seen, this is particularly true of most of the civil conflicts and wars of national revolution, in which relatively small groups, with inadequate armaments, took on national forces almost invariably far more powerful than themselves. In some cases there may have been vague hopes of winning an increased number of adherents at home, and even assistance from overseas. But it is doubtful if in most cases there was any clear assessment of relative strengths at all: only blind faith in the justice of the cause. Even in the wars made by national governments such calculations seem often to have been lacking. Sardinia declared war against a far more powerful Austria in 1848 and revived it in 1849, though any objective calculation of strength must have shown that her cause had little hope. Bulgaria made war on two countries, each at least as powerful as herself in 1913, and soon found herself at war with four. Denmark in 1863-4 invited conflict with Prussia and other German states despite their vastly superior power. Greece declared war on Turkey, against hopeless odds, in 1897.

Even where the balance of military power was more even, it is doubtful if any very careful calculation was made.[51] Usually there were arguments that seemed far more decisive than the precise balance of military power: the justice of the cause, the enormity of the enemy's offence, national destiny, the special qualities of native troops or weapons, the believed moral or military weaknesses of the opponent. It is probably on these grounds that miscalculations of the probability of victory were so frequently made. So it was Austria that declared war in 1866, yet within three weeks was totally defeated. France provoked conflict with Prussia in 1870, her chamber clamoured for war and her government declared it (even if Prussia desired it at least as much as she) yet was rapidly and decisively defeated. In other cases governments took rash steps which they knew must increase the odds against them: so Germany, expecting a rapid victory, persisted in invading Belgium in 1914, though she was aware this must bring Britain into the war against her; and intensified submarine warfare in 1917 though she knew this was likely to bring in the United States. All of these examples suggest that a calculation of the balance of military power, if made at all, rarely played a decisive part in deterring a decision for war if other arguments were sufficiently powerful.

Even if such calculations were attempted, there were many uncertainties which rendered them fallible. One of these concerned the participation of outside powers. In 1859, though the war had been carefully planned, France had still failed to anticipate the attitude of Prussia to the conflict, and was eventually obliged to abandon the enterprise half finished when Prussia refused to commit herself to remain obligingly neutral. In 1914 none of the four main participants knew accurately in advance the attitude to be taken by Italy, Bulgaria, Romania, Turkey, or even (for certain) Britain (the first three of these all finally entered the war on the opposite side to that which most people had anticipated). Even the conduct of allies could not be clearly foreseen: in 1859 and 1912, though formal alliances had been established with the firm intention of war, in both cases they quickly broke up as a result of the conduct of the war itself. Given such uncertainties, it was not possible to make any plausible calculation of the probable balance of power.

The fact is that in an era of nationalism decisions in favour of war were often as much emotional as rational, so that calculations of precise military strength or the likely conduct of allies played little part. A wave of national feeling in many cases was aroused by particular events which seemed to provide no alternative to a response by armed force. The passionate response of the French Assembly and the French public to the Ems telegram in 1870 left Napoleon III little choice but to commit his troops.* In 1866 Bismarck was careful to frame his challenge to Austria's role in Germany in such a way that her national honour was put at stake: she could not avoid war whatever the balance of power, without humiliation. In 1885 the anger among Serbia's rulers against the enlargement of Bulgaria without compensation for herself was such that it overrode any calculation of relative military capacity on either side. In 1914, though the balance was almost perfect, the sense that national commitments (and therefore national honour) were at stake — Russia's to Serbia, France's to Russia, Germany's to Austria, Britain's to Belgium — blurred any calculations, such as they were, of the military strength ranged on either side. Given this fact, the balance of power, though it might marginally reduce the risk of war, could not be decisive in preventing it.[52]

Decisions were also influenced by long-term factors: age-old resentments and traditional rivalries. Resentment at the humiliation suffered in 1815 influenced French foreign policy for the next 50

---

* The Empress Eugénie later described these pressures:

You cannot imagine what an outburst of patriotism carried all France away at that moment. Even Paris, hitherto so hostile to the Empire, showed wonderful enthusiasm, confidence and resolution. Frantic crowds in the boulevards cried incessantly, À Berlin! À Berlin! I can assure you, it was beyond human power to prevent war any longer. (Quoted from J. M. Thompson, *Louis Napoleon and the Second Empire* (Oxford, 1954), p. 297.

The Empress, more French than the French, added her own powerful support to this pressure; she insisted on attending the council meeting where the declaration of war was discussed, and there declared that the honour of France demanded war.

years, and partly motivated France's decisions for war in 1859 and 1870. Resentment at the loss of Alsace-Lorraine fuelled warlike feeling in France after 1870, as it was to do in Germany after 1918. Traditional enmity of this kind could tip decisions in favour of war, even in disregard of considerations of balance. So the traditional hostility between Turkey and Russia made it more likely that Russian anger against Turkey in 1806 and Turkish anger against Russia in 1853 would result in war. Traditional hostility between Serbia and Bulgaria and between Romania and Hungary, based partly on rivalry for territory and national minorities, influenced their decisions to make war against the other in 1913 and the First World War respectively.

These pressures for war were intensified by the fact that parliaments, press and public opinion began to have a greater influence on decisions. All of them were far more often favourable to war than against it. In many countries there were nationalist demagogues who inflamed warlike sentiment: Boulanger and Gambetta in France, Garibaldi and Mazzini in Italy, Katkov and Skonelov in Russia, Schliemann and Keim, among many others, in Germany. Often there was also a jingoist press which had a similar influence (p. 360 below). In a crisis situation parliaments were more often a force in favour of war than a restraining influence: as was the French chamber of deputies, which almost compelled Louis Napoleon to make war in 1870; the British parliament, much of which was baying for war with Russia in 1853-4; the Italian parliament, which acclaimed the aggressive actions of its government in Ethiopia and Tripoli.[53] Still more striking is the example of the Bavarian parliament in 1870, which, inspired by nationalist sentiment, forced Bavaria into the Prussian war against France directly against the wishes and advice of their own government. In Britain in 1857, Palmerston won an election which he had fought mainly to justify his war with China (and the following year lost one because he was thought to be too conciliatory to France).

In other parts of the world decisions for war were influenced by similar factors. A precise calculation of relative power rarely played a major part if other reasons for war were sufficient. In Latin America, because in many cases major decisions rested in the hands of caudillos — personal rulers of great power — they were less likely to be based on careful assessments of national interest and more on emotional factors, sometimes rooted in ambition. So it was that Francisco Lopez, having been made commander-in-chief of Paraguay's armed forces before he was 30, soon afterwards inheriting total power over the state, and having built up the strongest army of the region, could commit his country to war against the two most powerful countries of the sub-continent and refuse all negotiation till most of the male population of his nation were dead. So Santa Cruz, the dictator of Bolivia, could deliberately make war to conquer Peru in 1835 (and so, indirectly, brought about the war to overthrow him which followed). So in 1879 a local Bolivian *caudillo* could, by raising the tax on nitrate production in southern Bolivia, precipitate the War of the Pacific. So, in the early years of this century, the dictators of Guatemala and Nicaragua, Cabrera and Zelaya, could each launch wars against their neighbours because, they declared, they were sheltering enemies of their regimes. Even less than in Europe was there a precise calculation of armed strength; even more than there, emotional decisions and a reliance on native valour and national destiny to determine the outcome were in themselves a sufficient incentive to war.

Elsewhere most of the wars were colonial wars of one kind or another. Here the decisions were decisions to extend European power into some area previously uncontrolled: in South-east Asia, in the outer parts of India or the inner parts of Africa. Such decisions were the deliberate decisions of governments, often concerned to protect the security of areas already ruled, to exclude hostile European powers, and occasionally to win trade. Considerations of military balance played still less part than in Europe. It was normally taken for granted (not always correctly) that European arms would prevail over local peoples. The calculation was thus whether the expenditure of lives, effort and cash was proportionate to the objectives to be attained. Sometimes the calculations proved wrong: none anticipated the total destruction of the British force which took part in the first Afghan war; or the defeat of the Italian forces at Adowa; or the difficulty of defeating the Boers in 1899-1902; or the 30-year campaign the Dutch would have to fight to defeat the Achinese at the end of the century. Usually, however, the decisions eventually proved justified (in military terms): finally the European powers came out successful, even if sometimes at greater cost than they had anticipated.

In other cases the decision for war was taken by those who had been colonised: to resist the authority that was being imposed from elsewhere, or some new manifestation of that authority which they particularly resented. Here there was still less calculation of cost. As in the case of European civil wars, resort to arms seemed the only possible means of resistance, however hopeless the odds. Once or twice such struggles were successful: for example, the two long struggles of Cuba which (with some external help) finally secured independence. Occasionally, resistance, though unsuccessful, would be continually renewed: as by the tribesmen of the north-west frontier of

India or by the Berbers in Morocco. More often such wars of resistance were ultimately defeated.

It is no more possible in this age than in the previous one, therefore, to find examples of wars that arose by accident or by miscalculation. In many cases wars were deliberately planned (though not all of them succeeded as intended — for example in 1859 and 1912). In other cases they were not planned in advance, but were none the less intended: the deliberate response to a threat, challenge, or initiative by others (1864, 1866, 1870). In some cases action was taken which while it did not inevitably imply war, clearly involved a substantial risk of it: the actions of Prussia's opponents in 1864, 1866 and 1870; Russia's actions in 1852-3. In yet others, action was taken by one power which almost inevitably would bring war not only for itself but for others too (1853, 1914). War was part of the normal language of international relationships. In certain situations, in response to certain provocations or challenges, the decision to initiate or at least threaten it might still seem the only proper, the only reasonable, the only honourable decision to take.

The age of ideology (1917-   )

In the age that followed the power to take decisions about war remained concentrated in all states. Nowhere did it extend beyond a small group of ministers in a cabinet or council. Often it was more concentrated still. In Europe between the wars, and in most other continents after 1945, supreme power was often effectively in the hands of a single individual, subject to little restraint by colleagues or subordinate officials, still less by the pressure of public opinion, domestic or foreign.

A significant proportion of the decisions made for war have been reached by autocratic rulers of this kind. The main conflicts of the inter-war period — the successive aggressions of the thirties — were launched by Germany and Italy, where single dictators wielded almost unlimited personal power, and by Japan, where ultimate power was held by the emperor but at a lower level was wielded often by the military or those under their influence (the main aggressions of Japan before 1941 were originally launched by commanders in the field without authority, or only limited authority, from Tokyo: the occupation of Manchuria in 1931 was planned and organised by a small group of officers of the Kwantung army, mostly relatively junior; the encroachments in Inner Mongolia and northern China in 1933 and 1935 were planned by the army and undertaken by them without government approval; and even the decision to engineer and exploit the Marco Polo bridge incident in 1937 to launch full-scale war against China was mainly that of the military (and the emperor) rather than that of the government as a whole. Since 1945 there have continued to exist, outside Western Europe and North America, large numbers of governments effectively controlled by single dictators (often military rulers), by presidents holding unchallenged authority, or by small factions wielding almost permanent power. Many of the decisions for war have been reached by such governments: the assault by North Korea in 1950; the Soviet Union's military interventions in Hungary, Czechoslovakia and Afghanistan; the attacks of Indonesia against Malaysia and West Irian, of Pakistan against India (1965), of Vietnam against Cambodia (1978), of Uganda against Tanzania (1979), of Iraq against Iran (1980), and of Argentina against the Falklands (1982), among others. Decisions for large-scale intervention in civil conflicts elsewhere have also often been reached by similar figures: for example, those of Nasser's Egypt in Yemen, of Somalia in Ethiopia, of South Yemen in Yemen and Oman.

Decisions in favour of war are probably marginally harder to reach in more democratic societies, where the assent of a larger group of people is usually necessary. Even so, such decisions have been made almost as frequently. The United States has been as often involved in intervention among neighbouring countries as the Soviet Union (though sometimes less directly). Britain, France and Israel, under fully democratic governments, were able to collude in a blatant act of aggression in 1956. India, perhaps the most democratic government of the Third World, has engaged in successive interventions in her sub-continent (in Hyderabad, in Goa, on the Chinese border, and in Bangladesh). Indonesia under a semi-democratic government was as determined to conquer East Timor as she had been, under a dictator, to conquer West Irian. Given the smaller proportion of democratic governments in the world, warlike acts have probably been undertaken as frequently by them as by authoritarian governments.

Whether or not a country is "democratic" is unlikely to affect its propensity to war because in decisions concerning war no country acts democratically. Neither parliament nor public opinion normally have any opportunity to influence such decisions. The decisions of Britain and France to participate in the Suez adventure were reached by the governments in each case, and press and parliament were informed only after the attack had been launched. The US decision to participate in a major way in Vietnam in 1965 was reached by the administration; and Congress not only was not consulted in advance but was given deliberately misleading information (for example, at the time of the Bay of Tonkin resolution) to win their support. In practice, therefore, even in "democratic" societies the numbers involved in decisions to make war are always tiny. Even if public and parliamentary opinion were more genuinely consulted, it is doubtful if war would be less likely. For in many cases such opinion has proved more warlike than governments themselves have been. Opinion polls in Britain, at the time of the Suez and Falklands operations, and in the United States in the early years of the Vietnam War, showed the majority of the population in favour of strong military action, even while a vocal minority protested. At the very least public opinion can nearly always be led into support for military operations once they have already been launched. The most that can be said about differences between systems, therefore, is that decisions for war are likely to be more widely challenged and more effectively scrutinised in democratic societies than in others: not that such decisions are less likely to be reached. In authoritarian states opposition to warlike actions cannot normally even be voiced; in democratic countries it is widely expressed and reported, and occasionally even has some influence on government actions (for example, US involvement in Central America, and perhaps in Africa, has probably been somewhat inhibited by congressional pressures since 1975).

The number of those who could *influence* decisions for war in most countries became greater than in earlier times. Governments themselves are now larger and more complex machines. Bureaucracies have come to play a larger part in influencing the thinking of ministers. Military staffs have increased in size and influence. Parliaments are more vocal and better informed. The "military-industrial establishment", which has a direct interest in a continual increase of military spending, has found innumerable means (as even President Eisenhower, who had once belonged to it, complained at the time of his retirement) for influencing policy-making. All of these restrict the scope for idiosyncratic decisions. But in each case they represent only new or more powerful sources of influence. None has altered the fundamental reality that the number of people involved in the final decision for war remains only a handful.

It is thus the attitudes of this small group that are decisive. Those who do share in the decisions — who held office in governments, that is — are of a different type and background from their predecessors in the preceding age. They come now mainly from a far humbler background: middle and lower class rather than from the aristocratic and semi-aristocratic class who wielded power in that age. More important, their background is in almost every case, in communist states as much as in democratic countries, political. This affects their attitude to foreign relations. Their concern as politicians with winning and holding power means that they are more closely in touch with and concerned about public opinion than were most of their predecessors. Their whole way of thinking is dominated by political — that is, ideological — questions. As a result in many cases nothing has seemed more important to them than the defeat of political creeds of which they disapproved. In the international sphere this has meant that nothing has mattered more for a communist statesman than the defeat of "Western imperialists" or the "capitalist system"; or, for a Western statesman than the defeat of the communist creed and those who upheld it. Where civil war has broken out in another state, and especially when there has seemed a danger that a hostile faction might come to power there, leaders have been more inclined therefore to reach decisions that could involve the use of force, or assistance in its use, to influence the political outcome.

Because wars are thus often a response to political developments elsewhere, they have perhaps been somewhat less often than before carefully and deliberately planned in advance: in the way, for example, that the 1859 war was carefully planned by France and Piedmont, or that of 1912 planned by the Balkan Alliance (or as Bismarck planned to make war against Austria and France when suitable opportunities arose). In a few cases, where a country has believed it had a justified grievance, it would suddenly launch a war against an unsuspecting neighbour, an attack which must have been planned at least some weeks in advance: for example, the Indian attack on Goa (1962), the Pakistani attack on Kashmir (1965), the Somali invasion of Ethiopia (1977), the Iraqi war against Iran (1980) and the Argentine invasion of the Falklands (1982). In other cases, an act of force has been prepared, sometimes over a shorter period, in response to some development that was seen as a threat. So Britain, France and Israel plotted over three or four months the seizure of Sinai and the Suez Canal in response to the nationalisation of the canal; the Soviet Union planned and executed invasions of Hungary and Czechoslovakia in response to political developments there; and the United States planned and executed military action in Guatemala, Cuba (unsuccessfully), the Dominican Republic, Grenada and Nicaragua in response to the growth of left-wing power in each of those countries. In the Middle East, where the situation was continually unstable and the *status quo* contested by both sides, such attacks were planned by each side in turn: by the Arab countries in 1948, by Israel in 1956, by Egypt in 1973, and by Israel in 1978 and 1982. Sometimes such operations may have been devised originally as "contingency plans", to be put into operation only if certain conditions were fulfilled (in the way that the Japanese government decided in September 1941 to declare war on the United States if she did not withdraw her oil embargo within two months) but they were none the less carefully planned in advance.

All these are cases of the initiation of armed force by a particular country. More frequent, however, especially among the major powers, have been situations in which they have responded to the use of force elsewhere: often becoming increasingly involved in a conflict that was already taking place. So, for example, with each successive step, from the despatch of "advisers" in 1961, to the decision to send US forces on a large scale in 1965, to the decision to undertake bombing raids against the North two years later, the United States gradually became ever more deeply entangled in Vietnam. The Soviet Union progressed from providing military assistance to the revolutionary government of Afghanistan in May 1978 to the decision to send in her own troops at the end of the following year, and has had steadily to reinforce those troops in subsequent years. This process of gradual embroilment may be experienced equally by lesser powers: so Egypt became progressively ever more deeply involved in Yemen, as Indonesia has in East Timor, Vietnam in Cambodia, and Israel in Lebanon. A similar process of gradually increasing commitment took place in a number of colonial wars: for example, the French wars in Indo-China and Algeria, the Dutch in Indonesia and the British in South Arabia, where extrication became increasingly difficult as time went by. In all these cases, rather than a single decision in favour of war, there was a series of decisions in favour of ever greater involvement. Involvement cannot be said to have been carefully planned in advance. On the contrary, the degree of involvement that eventually occurred was nearly always unforeseen and unplanned; and so contrary to the initial intention. Even so, in each such case the decision to intervene was a conscious and deliberate one, and not the effect of confusion or "accident". What occurred, in these and other cases, was that, although intervention was deliberate, the cost of success eventually proved considerably greater than had originally been estimated; yet a decision to withdraw, which would have involved considerable loss of face, was rarely contemplated, even though as a result the overall cost finally far exceeded the benefits to be gained. Whether or not the original decision had seemed "rational" (in the sense that the expected gain to be secured — usually the denial of victory to a hostile faction — appeared proportional to the likely cost), the ultimate (and unforeseen) cost proved excessive in relation to the gains secured. This was the case in Vietnam, for example, and seems likely to be the outcome in Afghanistan.

Even in these cases, therefore, though acts of war may not have been planned long in advance, they were none the less decided on, consciously and deliberately. There is no more evidence in this age than in earlier ones of wars that have occurred "accidentally". In every case there has been a substantial measure of intention, on one side or another, sometimes both. Even where a conflict might appear to have "broken out", to have erupted almost unintentionally from a series of small-scale incidents — for example, the Korean War, the Vietnamese conquest of Cambodia, the Ugandan attack on Tanzania (all of which succeeded a series of frontier incidents) - in practice there has always come a moment when a deliberate decision has been taken to exploit such incidents with the aim of securing a clear-cut and unmistakable victory. Whether or not that aim was successfully achieved, the intention for war was none the less present at the moment the decision was taken.*

As in previous ages, the balance of power seems usually to have had little influence in influencing such decisions. As before, belief in the justice of the cause, or in the superiority of the native troops, or of better organisation or better weapons, or in the advantage of surprise attack, have frequently counted for more than any calculation of the balance of manpower or hardware. So North Vietnam was willing to challenge the embattled might of the United States, Iraq to confront the forces of the larger and wealthier Iran, Argentina to take on those of Britain, Pakistan those of India, Somalia those of Ethiopia, irrespective of the apparent balance of power. Still less have estimates of the balance affected the willingness to engage in guerrilla conflicts, fought by unconventional strategies, since here differences in fighting fitness or morale are normally much more significant than the balance of armaments. A large proportion of the wars of the age have been civil wars, minority rebellions and anticolonial wars, undertaken within a single territory, in which the original decision to resort to arms had been taken not by governments but by groups of people who had despaired of securing their ends by other means. In such cases decisions for war could be reached even though the odds against success seem overwhelming. The hope has been that in time even inferior forces might wear down their enemy and win sufficient support among the population at large to make the struggle worthwhile: an aspiration which successful struggles in Cuba and Nicaragua, in Angola and Mozambique, in Vietnam above all, showed were not wholly unrealistic.

* Possibly the only case where it can be said that an unplanned international conflict emerged almost wholly unintended by either side was that of the "football war" between Honduras and El Salvador in 1969. In that case events moved so swiftly that the two governments found themselves involved in substantial hostilities that probably neither desired or planned. Usually in such situations — as in that case — peace is re-established within a few days. Only where one side or both intends conflict on a larger scale will warlike action continue.

The essential difference between this age and previous ones in the decisions reached, therefore, derives from the new types of objectives that are held. In many cases the aim is now political: to win hearts and minds rather than territory or trade. Those who hold these aims and reach the decisions that count are not only governments themselves, now composed of party politicians or others with strong ideological beliefs and willing to go to war to defeat a hostile ideology, but unofficial groups of many kinds (minority peoples, political factions, movements for colonial freedom) seeking to secure political change within their own states. Whichever kind of group was responsible, a decision to use armed force is for them only one alternative among a range of available weapons for securing political change. Armed force is often employed in the first place only on a limited scale, but is then gradually increased as support builds up, or resistance mounts. On either side it remains usually only a very small group which is responsible for reaching decisions. But because those groups are concerned above all with the nature of the political system to be established within a particular territory, rather than with the flag to be flown over it, they are influenced even less than in earlier times by the exact balance of forces on either side. Decisions are determined by political rather than military considerations: the decision-makers' assessment of the final effect of their actions on the political situation within their own or other states.

Only at the highest level of all, in the decisions reached within the two super-powers and their immediate allies — decisions now probably influenced by a rather wider group than before — have considerations of precise balance played a larger role. Here rationality did begin to have an influence, especially in thinking about the major war that nobody wanted and has never taken place. The exact measure of power available to each side, the precise balance of missiles or kilotons, whether to deter or defend — these have become matters of acute importance, which now, more than ever before, are the subject of minute calculations. In thinking about the lesser wars that have occurred, now fought mainly by unconventional means — with "volunteers", agents, military advice or the supply of weapons — quite different kinds of consideration have applied. Here overall balance has been largely irrelevant. Decisions on action of this kind depend on a calculation of political effectiveness, the reaction of world opinion, the probability of success. In such a society as the present, it is the political, rather than the military, balance therefore which is the crucial factor affecting decisions.

Conclusions

What general conclusions can be reached about the way decisions for war have been reached in the different international societies we have been considering?

We have observed some major differences between the way decisions have been taken. First, the numbers involved in reaching them have varied greatly. In general, during the earlier periods single individuals played a more decisive role, and were less subject to restraint, advice and influence from elsewhere. In later periods, when power became somewhat more widely dispersed, decisions have more often been reached by a group within a cabinet or government, who have been more subject to influences from outside, including parliament, press and public opinion. This is of course not only a difference between one age and another: it is equally a distinction that divides different governments in the same period.

It is perhaps a smaller distinction than might appear at first sight. There have been virtually no decisions for war in any period which have been taken solely and exclusively by one person, unaffected by advice or warnings from without: even those who appeared to wield almost total power — Henry V, Charles the Bold, Charles V, Louis XIV, Napoleon, Hitler or Sukarno — were all subject to some external influences in reaching decisions to make war. Conversely, there are few if any recorded instances where the final decision for war was made by any number larger than a cabinet of 20 or 30 ministers; and in the great majority of cases effective decisions have been taken by a much smaller number, a handful of leaders, who have then expected to be able to explain and justify their decisions to far greater numbers after the event. Thus it seems probable that the number involved in decisions is a less significant factor than the number with the opportunity to *influence* them. Even this is less important than the kinds of influences that are brought to bear: civilian or military, from foreign office or defence department, parliament or church, bureaucrats or party activists. It is the balance among these influences, rather than the number of people who participate in the ultimate decision, authorise the final declaration of war, that has most significance in determining the kind of decision which is eventually reached.

The time of decision too has varied greatly. In almost every age there have been some decisions for war that were reached long in advance of war being declared: where, in other words, war was carefully planned and prepared for months and even years before it was finally launched. For example, Charles VIII of France planned for war in Italy for two years before 1494, Oxenstierna of Sweden planned for war with Denmark for three years before 1643, Louis XIV for war with the United Provinces for about three years before 1672, Peter the Great and his allies for war with Sweden for two years before 1700, Louis Napoleon and Cavour for war with Austria for nearly a year before 1859. Such long-term plans have perhaps been somewhat less common in recent times (though the difference may only be that our knowledge in those cases is more limited: who can know precisely when Iraq began to prepare the war she launched against Iran in 1980?). But there have been other cases where a decision has been reached not so much to make war at a certain time in the future, but to be prepared for a war that was believed desirable if the right occasion presented itself: thus, when subsequently an issue arose that was thought to provide a reasonable justification, that was made the *casus belli* which caused the plan to be put into effect. That was the case with the three wars engineered by Bismarck and, to some extent at least, with the First World War, when the assassination of Franz Ferdinand was used, by some in Germany and perhaps elsewhere too, as the justification for a war desired on other grounds. We might distinguish these two categories by saying that in the former case war is both prepared and decided in advance; in the latter, it is prepared for in advance, but decided on only at a later stage. In each case war is equally intentional; it is only the timing of the decision that is different.

Is the distinction important if the outcome is the same? Can it be said that the wars in the second category were in any case certain to take place sooner or later, so that the difference is only in the uncertainty of the timing; or was there a more fundamental difference in intention? Does a willingness for war lead as certainly to war as an intention of war? The situation in the early part of 1914 might suggest this is the case. At that time, it would be generally agreed, the attitude everywhere was closer to willingness than to intention: no government (certainly before 28 June) had made a definite decision that it wished for a war. Almost all were prepared for war if the necessity should arise; some in each country positively desired it (pp. 356-7). Was it possible, therefore, for no war to have occurred at all? Could the situation which prevailed in the early part of the year have persisted for many years, failing the unforeseen crisis arising from the assassination, which alone and of itself precipitated war? Might relations have improved in time, to such an extent that military preparations were relaxed and the long years of peace continued almost indefinitely? Speculation about the might-have-beens of history is always uncertain. But it cannot be said that the chances of peace being preserved in that way were good. Though some problems were solved (the Baghdad railway, the von Sanders affair, the disposal of

Portugal's African colonies), the widespread speculation, even expectation, that war would occur; the sentiments of mutual distrust and hostility being expressed (pp. 358-9); the military calculation that, if it was to occur at all, war should occur soon; the pressures for rapid mobilisation and surprise attack — all of these make it likely that, even if there had been no assassination, sooner or later some incident would have occurred in some part of the continent or beyond — in the Balkans, on the Rhine, in Morocco — that would have become the spark to set the tinder-box alight: which would have brought about a conviction within one power or another — most probably Germany — that the hour had come when the trial of strength, so long expected, must be embarked on. In other words, although there may not have existed anywhere a positive intention of war, sufficient to inspire a totally unprovoked attack, there was sufficient readiness for war to make it almost inevitable that the occasion would soon occur when it would be seen as more prudent to exploit the opportunity provided than to let it pass by unused.

Thus in practice the existence of willingness for war is often little different (especially if it exists among a number of powers, or even if it is merely believed to exist among other powers) from an active desire for war. The danger is, of course, especially great if, as in 1914, there is thought to be an overwhelming military advantage for the power that launches its attack first (there would thus be a greater danger today if it was thought possible, by launching a first strike to secure with nuclear weapons an even more decisive advantage). But even without that additional factor, a willingness for war, though confined to only a single government, may make war almost as inevitable, sooner or later, as a definite intention of war among a number of powers. Against this, if there exists a general unwillingness for war, then precisely the opposite is the case. The same crisis that would otherwise have been exploited by one power or another to justify war will be met in a wholly different way: with prudence, caution and a general concern to avoid provocation. Even an unexpected assassination will be met with sober deliberation; outside powers will use their influence to restrain; every opportunity for compromise will be promoted. In that situation a conciliatory Serbian reply will be carefully explored, rather than dismissed out of hand; a threatening Austrian response will be avoided at all costs, by Austria's ally as much as by herself. There is, in other words, a spectrum of attitudes to war that governments may take, ranging from deliberate intention to faint desire, to weak acquiescence, to faint reluctance, to determined refusal. Where the attitude of any government is in the upper ranges of the spectrum, sooner or later, whatever the particular incidents and crises that arise, a war is likely to take place.

Where the initial attitudes of governments is in the lower, and especially in the bottom, part of the spectrum, that outcome becomes
much less likely.

Can war none the less occur accidentally? The evidence of history
certainly provides no indication that this is likely. Throughout the
whole of the period we have been surveying it is impossible to
identify a single case in which it can be said that a war started
accidentally: in which it was not, at the time when war broke out, the
deliberate intention of at least one party that war should take place.
Though accident through mechanical fault is apparently a greater
danger in the modern world — because of the increased power of a
single weapon and the impossibility of recall — these very dangers
have induced greater caution and the use of elaborate fail-safe
mechanisms to eliminate human or mechanical error. Whether a
decision to make war results from active desire or more passive
willingness, therefore, it remains the case that the decision, when it
occurs, is deliberate and intentional.

This does not mean that there cannot be miscalculation. Miscalculations can be of a number of kinds. Whenever a war is lost by the
initiator, there is miscalculation. It was started only because it was
thought that it would be won. Again, there may be miscalculation of
the intentions of another party. War may be initiated by one state
because it believes that another is planning it (when in fact it is not).
But even here there must exist a substantial willingness for war, if
such a suspicion alone is felt to justify an act of war. Thirdly, miscalculation may occur because it is believed that a certain action will be
tolerated by another state or states, when in fact it will not: a canal
may be nationalised, missiles may be placed in a threatening manner,
a UN peace-keeping force may be removed, assistance may be given
to rebels in another state; and these actions, while seen as legitimate
by one party, may be regarded by the other as a threat to vital
national interests. But here too a substantial willingness for war must
exist, either on the part of the country that risks provocative action or
of the one that is prepared to make war over such an issue.

In other words, as we have seen before, war is regarded by states as
an instrument which it may be in their interests to use, in certain
circumstances, to promote or defend their interests. But it remains an
instrument that is used deliberately and intentionally and not by
accident or oversight. A calculation has been made: should I suffer
peaceably the humiliation, the threat, the challenge which a particular action represents, or do I prefer war? In the past war has often
been chosen in that situation as the less undesirable alternative. As
the possible costs of war increase, the situations in which that choice
is likely to be made may become fewer. It becomes more likely that

leaders may sometimes conclude, like Khrushchev in 1962, that it is more prudent to suffer some sacrifice of interest, some loss of face, some political setback, than to accept the incalculable risks of all-out confrontation, whether conventional or nuclear. The gambler's attitude to war, so widespread in the past, may become less frequent.

Decisions for war have therefore been, in each of our societies, intentional acts, intended to promote particular interests and objectives. States and groups, each having a wide range of objectives which can be secured in a variety of ways, have sometimes decided that war is the best or the only means by which they can secure them. Such a decision has implied that, whatever the costs involved in making war, they are worth incurring for the sake of the overall benefits likely to be acquired. Whether that decision has proved justified or not has depended on whether the ends desired have in fact been obtained and what the costs of obtaining them have finally proved to be. Thus, only an assessment of the profits that have in fact resulted, and the losses which have been incurred, can determine whether those decisions have proved to be rational ones. It is to a consideration of that question that we must now turn.

6 Profitability

How far have decisions for war proved to be justified by events?

Whenever a decision to make war has been made, that course has been chosen as one that offered the hope of a favourable outcome to the leaders or governments that made it. Has that decision proved to be a sound one? In other words, has war brought to those who made it the gain — in this world if not the next — that they expected when they first opted for war?

Of course, every leader or government, in making such a decision, has known that there would be costs. Some of these have been certain: costs in human lives, in human suffering, in financial burdens, in equipment and property destroyed, sometimes in loss of reputation or goodwill. Other costs have been problematical, depending on the degree of success to be obtained: heavier than expected expenditure of blood and treasure, loss of popular support, defection of allies, trade foregone, social upheaval; in the final resort, the humiliation, personal and national, of defeat. These losses, certain and potential, have had to be weighed against the potential gains from victory. The possible *material* gains have included the acquisition of a foreign crown, the conquest of territory, the winning of trade, colonies, indemnities, reparations and other economic rewards. The *intangible* gains, which have probably always been more important, have included the glory of victory, national and personal, the enhancement of national status, the humiliation of a rival, justification for a cause or creed, and popular acclaim.

In other words, we are concerned with a balance of costs and benefits, profit and loss. This does not mean that we are assuming that any conscious calculation of this sort is normally made, either before a war is launched or after it is concluded. We saw in the last chapter that there has often been very little deliberate assessment of the chances of success before a war is begun. But it is probably the case that some *unconscious* calculation of this sort must take place in any decision to make war. It is always implicitly assumed that the benefits to be gained will exceed the losses to be borne. What we are concerned with in this chapter is whether that assumption has been justified: whether in practice war has proved a profitable undertaking. Has it brought benefits that at least the decision-makers themselves have believed were worth the cost involved? Or has it in some

235

cases been concluded after the event (even of a successful war) that the loss of lives and property, of wealth and welfare, was disproportionate to the gains (if any) that were acquired?

The question is obviously important since the answer must indicate the degree to which war can be expected to remain a feature of international society. The knowledge, conscious or unconscious, that war has proved, whether for one's own nation or for others, a successful means of securing important national ends (or religious ends or ideological ends) must colour general beliefs about its usefulness as an act of policy. If war had always proved an unmitigated disaster to all those that engaged in it, it is likely to have been abandoned as a policy option years ago. Even if one believes that acts of war are partly irrational, that governments have been little affected by precise calculations of advantages and costs in their response to particular threats or opportunities, their propensity to war is still likely to be affected by unconscious beliefs concerning the success of warlike endeavours in the past.

There are two quite separate aspects of this question. One is the relatively straightforward question: have those responsible for bringing war about in fact proved victorious in the war that followed. Where they have not, it can be fairly confidently stated that the launching of war, or of actions which carried a strong risk of war, has eventually proved unprofitable. The second is the more difficult, but also the more important, question: where a country has finally proved victorious, have the gains which it has made eventually proved, or generally been held to be, worth the costs involved in making the war?

Such questions are even more difficult to answer than those posed in the last chapter. Subjective judgements are clearly involved. Some would no doubt argue that, however spectacular the apparent gains made in a war, however large the territories acquired or the economic benefits that have been won, they could never justify the loss of life — or loss of reputation — incurred in gaining them. That, however, has not necessarily been the judgement of most of those involved at the time when the war took place. There can be little doubt that in most ages a successful war has been widely held to be worth the costs it involved. There would probably have been few in Prussia who would have maintained that Frederick the Great's seizure of Silesia in 1740-1 was not worth the loss of life (some would have argued the loss of good name as well) which its acquisition made necessary. Against this, few probably would with hindsight maintain that Austria's counter-attack in 1756, which ultimately failed to recover that province as intended, was worth the loss of blood and treasure which the attempt incurred. Most cases fall somewhere in between. Were the losses suffered by Britain and France in the Crimean War worth the success in marginally reducing Russia's influence in the area of the Ottoman Empire (some of which she regained in any case within less than fifteen years)? Was the benefit of preventing Austria from imposing her will on Serbia in 1914 (and depriving Germany of some undeserved accretion of national prestige) worth the loss of 12 million lives which occurred in the ensuing struggle? Not all would find it easy to answer those questions with confidence.

It is not the purpose in the pages that follow to seek definitive answers to questions of that sort. Each would require a volume in itself if all the imponderables involved were to be given their due weight (it would require, for example, in the last case an assessment of the likely effect on the future power balance and the climate of international relations generally if Austria-Hungary had been enabled to undertake a successful act of aggression against Serbia unchallenged from elsewhere). There can be no clear or sure answers to such problems. An act of war that in one view would be regarded as well worth the costs entailed, in another would be seen as a lamentable squandering of lives and livelihoods. The price of victory which one observer would reckon as exorbitant, by another would be held cheap in relation to the benefits that were won. All we shall attempt to do here, therefore, is to examine briefly the record of success of acts of war in each of the periods we have been examining; and to consider how far, in different ages, war has appeared, in the eyes of statesmen or the general public, to have proved in consequence a worthwhile activity.

The age of dynasties (1400-1559)

Many of the wars of our first period were, as we have seen, aimed at the acquisition of foreign crowns or other titles. A few such ventures proved successful: Alfonso V of Aragon eventually secured the duchy of Naples for himself and his descendants; the Viscontis and Sforzas in turn won Milan for their families by armed force. But most of the wars fought for that purpose eventually failed. The English kings ended 120 years of war in France with much less territory than they had begun (Calais against Guienne); the Angevins fought over three generations to win Naples for their family without success; Matthias Corvinus failed in his attempt to add the throne of Bohemia to that of Hungary (though they were later joined, it was under the rule of his enemy, Ladislas); the French kings fought ten wars in Italy for Naples and Milan but ended without either of them (though she did secure some gains in these wars, acquiring Turin, Pinerolo and Saluzzo in Italy, and Metz, Toul and Verdun in Germany); the Danish kings, despite repeated campaigns, were finally defeated in their effort to hold Sweden. The strategic problems of holding distant possessions, the financial cost involved, particularist sentiment among the local inhabitants, the competition of rival claimants — all these had the effect that campaigns to win crowns elsewhere, frequent as they were, often ended without success. Only because the potential gains were so high, perhaps, were such enterprises continually renewed.

Wars to secure marriage had an equally mixed record. Immediately after a victory a desired marriage could often be imposed. Henry V could get himself married to Katherine of France at the height of England's successes there; Charles V could be made to accept Francis I's infant daughter immediately after Marignano; Francis himself could be made to accept Charles's sister in the aftermath of Pavia (and reaffirm his acceptance at the end of the following war). But such efforts often ultimately failed, whatever was agreed at the time of victory. Charles V never married the bride apportioned to him in the Treaty of Noyon; Henry VIII did not win the hand of Mary Stuart for his son, despite his victory over the Scots at Pinkie; the duke of Orleans married neither of the sisters ordained for him under the treaty of Crépi (if only because he died before he could be apportioned either*). Unless the marriage was undertaken immediately, virtually at gunpoint (as with that of Katherine of France to Henry V) there were too many hazards that could intervene to prevent the match from going forward in the way the victors planned. For that purpose too, war often failed in its objective.

In other cases the hoped-for prize of a war was territory, for its own sake, as much as for any dynastic rights that might be claimed (although, as noted above (p. 138), there was virtually no war for territory throughout this period that was not at least justified on dynastic grounds). This was the traditional booty of wars. Sometimes success in this age could provide huge territorial gains, at least over the short term. Perhaps the most consistently successful in acquiring territory through war were the Turks, who, in the century or so before 1530, extended their hold over the whole of South-eastern Europe, and at one time threatened Vienna and even south Germany. Muscovy during the same time established control over large areas of central and southern Russia, stretching from the Urals in the east to Smolensk in the Ukraine. Spain, mainly through success in war, won for herself Naples and Milan, as well as much of Central and South America; just as Portugal by the same means won colonies from China to Southern Africa, from India to Brazil. Who could doubt that wars which had brought such spectacular prizes could be worthwhile?

A still more important fruit of war was the extension of the power of the rulers over territories adjoining their own domains, and so

---

* The choice was not to be his but Charles V's.

creating a viable state. Ferdinand and Isabella in that way finally extended their control over the whole of the Iberian peninsula except for Portugal; as the English kings did theirs over Wales and to a limited extent Ireland; and as Louis XI and his successors did theirs in and around their own domains. Above all such conquests secured royal supremacy over over-mighty subjects. Whatever its value in securing territories or titles elsewhere, therefore, war undoubtedly enabled rulers to establish unfettered control within their own lands, and in so doing to begin to build up viable states. No ruler doubted that the achievement of that goal more than justified the blood and tears it cost.

War could also be the means of acquiring substantial economic gains Trading rights could be secured. The Hanseatic towns had fought a series of successful wars in the fourteenth century for such rights in Scandinavia and the Baltic area, and they continued now to fight for similar gains: for example, against Denmark in 1404-35, against England in 1468-74 and against Denmark again in 1532-6. A successful war could win control of trade routes (one result of Portuguese conquests overseas and of Poland's in the Baltic); or special trading privileges (as the Hanse won from England in 1474); or access to rivers, ports and sea-coasts (as the Netherlands won in the Baltic in 1536). But there could be economic costs as well as gains. Economic costs could result from the deliberate action of another state. Prosperous Burgundy suffered severely in its war with France when Louis XI blockaded the country, organised a boycott of Burgundian fairs, got the Hanse towns to abandon Bruges as their chief staple, encouraged privateering against the Burgundian fleet, and persuaded the Swiss to reduce their trade. And we saw earlier (p. 144 above) that fear of the economic consequences could in some cases be a significant factor in deterring war. Charles V's regents in the Netherlands, his aunt Margaret and his sister Mary, consistently advised against war with England on these grounds.[1] (Mary was equally concerned about the cost of any war in Germany against the protestants: "Your majesty is the greatest prince in Christendom," she wrote, "but you cannot undertake a war in the name of all Christendom until such time as you have the means to carry it through to certain victory.")[2]

Financial gains and losses therefore had to be weighed. War could bring direct financial benefits for those who undertook it. Victorious powers, for example, would regularly extort large financial payments from the defeated. So England (having already obtained a substantial indemnity from France after her first victory in 1360) demanded and got a payment of 75,000 and a yearly pension of 50,000 in return for abandoning her invasion in 1475; and under the treaty of Étaples in 1482, after her next war, obtained a promise of 125,000 of arrears.

The Swiss Confederation secured an indemnity of 10,000 gulden from Sigismund of the Tyrol at the end of their war with him in 1468 (failing which he was to forfeit Waldshut and part of the Black Forest). Matthias Corvinus secured the promise of a huge indemnity from the Emperor Frederick III in 1485 and held eastern Austria in pledge until he should be paid. Or states could sell back territory captured in a previous war. So England secured an indemnity in exchange for the return of Tournai, captured five years earlier, in 1518; and still another in exchange for returning Bologne in 1549. Under the treaty of Noyon in 1516, impoverished Maximilian I secured a price from wealthy Venice for returning to her Brescia and Verona, captured seven years earlier.

Ransoms provided another important source of financial gain not only for kings but for military commanders and anybody who could obtain an important prisoner. The needy Charles V obtained 2 million crowns from Francis I as the price of returning his two sons under the treaty of Barcelona in 1529. Individual magnates and knights could extract for themselves rewards almost as handsome from the plunder and booty which they obtained. Even humble soldiers had something to gain from war: thus the duke of Gloucester urged on the English king a resumption of the war with France, on the grounds that this was necessary for the sake of "poor knights and squires and archers, whose comforts and station in society depend upon war".

The various gains that could be won by war had to be measured against the costs of securing them. There was, first, a heavy cost in lives. There are no accurate records of total casualties in war. Even the estimates for individual battles are little more than guesses. Casualties in some wars (for example, the French wars in Italy) were probably relatively low; those in others (such as the wars against the Turks) much higher. Sometimes civil wars were the most costly of all: so the Peasants' Revolt in Germany, for example, is believed to have cost 500,000 lives, far more than any of the international wars of the age. Even when casualties were high, however, there is little evidence that they weighed heavily with rulers or military commanders. They were seen, for the most part, as the inevitable price of war, which in itself was honourable and glorious.

Of more concern to most of the rulers was probably the heavy financial costs of wars. Most rulers recognised that *nervus belli est pecunia*. Robert de Balsac, in a handbook advising princes how to succeed in war, printed in 1502, concluded that, "most important of all, success in war depends on having enough money to provide whatever the enterprise needs".[3] None of the rulers, as we have seen, was financially independent (the kings of France were perhaps closest to being so) and all had difficulties in raising the money needed to fight their wars abroad. Armies grew substantially during the course of this period: from 12,000-15,000 men in the first half of the fifteenth century to 25,000 in the second half and 50,000 or more in the last 60 years of this period (the English rarely had armies of more than 12,000 in France during the Hundred Years War and the standing army established by Charles VII to withstand them in 1445 was of 12,000; Edward IV took an army of 13,000 to France in 1475; the Swiss sent 20,000 men to raise the siege of Nancy in 1477; Charles VIII took an army of 30,000 to Italy in 1494; Suffolk's army in France in 1523 was 25,000; and Charles V had an army of 35,000 in Germany towards the end of the period). The costs of paying such armies could be a severe strain on limited revenues. Artillery became an increasingly important arm, as did fortification to resist it; and both cost money. As levies declined in their military capabilities, professional mercenaries increasingly needed to be bought. Money was needed to pay allies and to provide pensions for military commanders and nobles. For all these purposes (and whether a national army was used or foreign mercenaries) large amounts of money needed to be found. "The costs of war, already crippling in the fourteenth century, had risen again so steeply with changes in the equipment and composition of armies that no power was always in possession of, for instance, sufficient artillery or the ready cash to pay the mercenaries."[4] An army that was not paid could go on the rampage (like the imperial army that sacked Rome in 1527) or even desert to the enemy. Worse still, without money an army might not be raised at all: as we have seen, Maximilian I had to abandon two wars (in 1490 and 1516) because he had no money to pay for his troops.

So some means had to be found for raising the money required. Much would be borrowed: as the English kings borrowed from Italian bankers and English wool merchants; as Charles V borrowed from the Fuggers of Frankfurt and the bankers of Antwerp; as Francis I did from the citizens of Toulouse, and Henry II from the bankers of Lyons. Occasionally extraordinary measures would be adopted: Francis I sold most of his own silver plate and persuaded noble families to do likewise to finance one of his wars against Charles V; and Charles V himself admitted that one reason for pressing his marriage to the infanta of Portugal was that the dowry which she brought with her could help defray the large expenses in which his wars had involved him.[5] But in the long run most of the money would have to be raised through taxation. The estates and parliament that voted the taxation, however, did not necessarily see the same value in a foreign war as the ruler and his advisers, and frequently made difficulty: as we saw earlier, the estates of Flanders and other parts of Burgundy refused point-blank to provide the taxation which Charles the Bold demanded of them; Maximilian I could never secure anything approaching the amount he needed to fight his wars; Charles V had to spend much time going from one *cortes* to another to beg the money he needed; the English parliament were reluctant to provide the money Henry VIII asked for to fight his war with France in 1523-5 (though they paid up quite happily in 1544-5).[6] Even together, all these measures were often not enough to meet the exorbitant costs of war: both France and Spain went officially bankrupt in 1557 at the climax of their long duel. What all this meant was that there were not only financial but also political costs of war to be met, the risk of substantial unpopularity at home; and this was a further factor that had to be put into the balance in weighing costs and benefits.

If there was a price to be paid for any war as well as profits to be won, was there ever any attempt to balance the two? Did rulers calculate whether the possible gains to be won were worth the price that would have to be paid for winning them? It is difficult to believe that there was no awareness at all, even if only subconscious, of the balance between profit and loss, costs and benefits. But, if any such assessment was made, it was only of the crudest kind, and it had to be taken in the context of the general assumption that war was a source of honour and glory, and indeed a way of life (p. 331 below). At the same time, as we saw in the last chapter, such judgements were frequently distorted by blind optimism, faith in the cause, or belief in personal and national destiny. Sometimes an initial success — for example, the victory of Charles the Bold in Gelderland or that of Francis I at Marignano — might breed ambitions that were misguided and unrealistic. On all these grounds a military adventure could seem to the prince that contemplated it a far more attractive proposition than it would appear to the less partial eyes of outsider observers. Certainly in practice few were deterred by such judgements from the enterprises which appealed to their imaginations. The English kings went on with their forlorn search for the crown of France for 15 years after it was apparent to most that victory was unattainable. Danish kings went on trying to impose their rule on Sweden, the Hungarian king went on trying to subjugate Bohemia, for years after it should have been apparent that their efforts were doomed to failure. Francis I persisted over and over again in his ambitions in Italy, despite persistent failure and the huge cost to his country.

It is difficult to avoid the conclusion that, at the end of the day, calculations of possible profit and loss played little part. For the most part, war was an adventure, like the tournament; and, as in the tournament, it was the challenge to honour and ambition, the desire for display and glory, which were the stimulus to warlike action, rather than any cold-blooded calculation of possible gain against potential loss.

The age of religion (1559-1648)

In the age that followed the gains that were hoped for from war were different.

Military intervention now took place quite often, as we saw, to influence what religion was practised in some other country or region. The record of success in these cases was mixed. Spain's three military campaigns, in the late sixteenth century, in the Netherlands, against England and in France, were uniformly unsuccessful. In every case she was defeated, wholly or partly; in the end protestantism prevailed in England and the United Provinces, and was tolerated in France. Spain was more successful 40 years later in her campaign to restore Catholic control in the Valtellina (though the primary concern in this case was with strategic interest rather than the fate of the church). The Hapsburg rulers of Austria were successful in establishing the supremacy of the Catholic faith in their own domains (even in provinces, such as Bohemia, Moravia and Austria, where the protestants had formerly been in a majority). But in Germany as a whole 30 years of military effort were eventually, after brief moments of apparent success in the late 1620s and late 1630s, unsuccessful: the religious map of Germany at the end of the period was, outside the Hapsburg lands, little different from what it had been at the beginning. French intervention in Scotland did not succeed in furthering the Catholic cause there, any more than English intervention to assist protestants in France succeeding in the 1560s and the 1620s. Poland did not bring the Catholic faith to Sweden or Russia; any more than Sweden brought the protestant faith to southern Germany.

This record of failure was not so much because the faiths were so strongly held as because the military actions were eventually unsuccessful. The balance of religion depended finally on the balance of military force. It was the relatively even balance of power between protestant and Catholic forces in Europe, rather than steadfastness of conscience, that preserved a diversity of religious beliefs in Europe. Where military superiority was sufficient, as Ferdinand II's power was in the Hapsburg domains, as Bavarian power was in Donauwörth, as Catholic power ultimately proved to be in France, it had little difficulty, through the conversion of some and the expulsion of others, in imposing one faith and eliminating another. Military success could therefore, in this age, successfully establish a particular faith in a particular land (just as 400 years later a predominance of military power was able to impose a particular *political* faith in particular regions, even while a balance was preserved within the world as a whole).

For minority faiths war might be the means of successfully *defend-*

ing a religion (as it had been for the Hussites of Bohemia in the previous period). The Huguenots of France, after 30 years of struggle (assisted by the accident of succession and the manifest self-interestedness of Spanish actions), did finally manage to secure for themselves nearly 100 years of toleration. The Calvinists in the Netherlands, by dogged and ferocious resistance to Spanish power, were able finally to establish an independent protestant state in that country. The Calvinists of Scotland (as in the Netherlands, a small minority at first) were able to make their faith (or a version of it) the national church of Scotland. The protestant rulers of Transylvania, by maintaining their independence from Ottoman and Hapsburg empires alike — usually by playing one off against the other — succeeded in maintaining their religion throughout this period (Catholic conquest was for them still to come). Military success, in other words, could be the means of defending a faith as well as of imposing it. So long as toleration, the peaceful coexistence of religions, was not acceptable, military force was the only means available for determining which faith should prevail, and for that cause was everywhere seen as worth the cost.

But in many wars different kinds of gains were sought. As in the previous age, the objective in some cases was to win the throne of another country (or to prevent others from winning it). Sometimes such ventures succeeded. This depended partly on the merits of the claim. Philip II was able, with a brief war and little expense, to make good his claim to Portugal, which was reasonably well founded. He had little success with claims to England and France, which were less so (as well as much more difficult to enforce). But such claims were everywhere harder to prosecute. With the embryonic growth of national feeling, populations became less willing meekly to acknowledge foreign rulers. Thus Philip II would have found it hard to hold France or England under Spanish rule however successful his military action; even contiguous Portugal, where he carefully refrained from interfering with national traditions and institutions, he could only hold for 60 years. Sigismund of Poland, whose claim to the Swedish throne could not have been better (he had been its lawful occupant), was unable, appearing as he did more Polish than Swedish, to enforce it in more than 30 years of fighting, still less to promote his own or his son's claim to succeed in Russia. Because of this emerging national sentiment such wars were now less likely to reap rewards. They might be prevented from succeeding too, in this religious age, by religious factors. Sigismund was unacceptable to Sweden for religious as much as for national reasons, as his son was to Russia. On these grounds the Neuburg family had to become Catholic to inherit Jülich; the elector of Brandenburg had to become Calvinist to acquire Cleves. James I could not have succeeded to the English throne as a protestant, any more than his mother (whatever the nature of her private life) could expect to hold Scotland as a Catholic. Attempts to conquer lands of totally alien culture or faith, as in Portugal's attempt to seize Morocco, Spain's to seize Tunis, Turkey's to seize Malta, were especially hard to sustain, since resistance there was often fiercer. Finally, success in such wars began to be affected by another factor. Claims, however well founded, were now sometimes contested on balance-of-power grounds alone. The two wars of Mantuan succession, for example (which related to territory of vital strategic importance), as well as the abortive war for Cleves-Jülich, foreshadowed the succession wars of the succeeding age: that is, they were fought mainly by external powers, each concerned to prevent others from acquiring advantage by the succession to valuable territory. For all these reasons, wars to claim succession were now even less often profitable than before.

Wars were more frequently worthwhile when the objective was to acquire territory. Sweden's successive victories enabled her to acquire control of most of the coast of the Baltic including all its southern ports except Danzig, control of its most important rivers and even a foothold in Germany. France, through her success in the Thirty Years War, began the steady expansion of her frontiers, which was to continue in a more spectacular way in the age that followed. Russia, once her time of troubles was past, began to compensate herself for the loss of Baltic territory by securing huge areas of the Ukraine, the southern steppes and even Siberia. The most spectacular territorial gains of all were found beyond the seas, often at the cost of little fighting. Here it was above all the new state in the Netherlands which, with its powerful shipping and strong commercial interests, was able to make the most impressive gains, acquiring mainly at the expense of Portugal, large territories in South America, the Caribbean, Africa, Ceylon and the Far East. Territorial gains of this kind represented the most obvious and spectacular prize to be had from war in this age: a prize that was certainly believed to be well worth the cost involved.

Trade and the control of trade was another asset that could be won. Denmark, already controlling the lucrative tolls in the Sound, won, through her war of 1611-13, the right to trade in Livonia and Courland, which Sweden had hitherto barred to her. Sweden, by her victories over Russia and Poland, won control of the trade up the rivers that issue into the Baltic and so the capacity to tax it. Russia fought both Sweden and Poland for control of trade to the Baltic. The United Provinces, in settling her account with Spain, was careful to secure, in the interim settlement of 1609, the right to trade with Spanish colonies abroad and the closing of the Scheldt, which preserved her from the competition of Antwerp's previous prosperous commerce.

There were also more immediate financial returns to be won by war. Not many rulers were as brutally mercenary as the Crimean khan, who extorted from his victims protection money — promises to provide annual subsidies and "gifts" in return for immunity from attack. But most exacted a price for their support. Bethlen Gábor of Transylvania sold his to Frederick of Bohemia in return for a "perpetual stream of titles, subsidies and rewards, which were necessary to keep him even superficially loyal".[7] Even in apparently religious wars payments of this kind were widely demanded. Gustav Adolph of Sweden, for all his protestant fervour, insisted not only on territories but also on direct financial compensation in return for his support to the protestant cause in Germany. Christian IV of Denmark, while claiming his devotion to the same cause, was still more determined to acquire, as a price for intervention, rich bishoprics in that country. The duke of Bavaria, for all his commitment to the Catholic interest, was careful to secure the promise of both the territories and the electoral chair of the Palatinate in return for providing troops and finance to the emperor. Rulers would even happily abandon their co-religionists for the sake of reward. So the protestant elector of Saxony sold his support to the emperor in return for the promise of Lusatia; while the Catholic duke of Savoy provided an army to the protestant cause in the hope of acquiring at least the crown of Bohemia, and possibly that of the empire itself. None were more insistent than the military commanders in extracting a heavy price for their services. So Mansfeld expected to secure a "modest but independent principality" as the price of continuing his support for Frederick after the White Mountain disaster.[8] Bernard of Saxe-Weimar, having failed to get Franconia as undertaken by Sweden, demanded and got from the French the promise of Alsace (together with 150,000 livres) as the price of his services in 1635; while Wallenstein secured, in addition to huge estates in Bohemia, the large and wealthy north German state of Mecklenburg, and was believed to be negotiating for Bohemia, and even for an electorate, in the last months of his life. The Swedish General Baner entered into secret negotiations with his enemies in the hope of acquiring from them substantial estates in Silesia as a price for defection.[9] So, in this religious age more than at almost any other time, war was expected to produce direct material benefits in this world, in addition to more intangible rewards in the next.

But any of these various kinds of return, even if they could be successfully secured — even, that is, if victory was achieved — had to be measured against the cost of acquiring them. First, there was the cost in human lives, which could be enormous. A large proportion of the casualties in this age were of civilians, dying of starvation (which was common), disease (plague was rampant), fire (when cities were sacked) or simply indiscriminate slaughter by conquering armies. Devastation of the countryside, often a deliberate policy to deprive an enemy of food, in many cases deprived local populations of the sole means of existence. About 2.5 million lives are reckoned to have been lost in Russia during the time of troubles at the beginning of the seventeenth century. During the Thirty Years War 40 per cent of the German population in the countryside and the towns may have perished. The population of the state of Württemberg fell from 450,000 in 1620 to under 100,000 in 1639.[10] In the siege of Magdeburg in 1631, three-quarters of the inhabitants are believed to have lost their lives and many of the buildings were destroyed. Much of the suffering fell on civilians. But there were substantial losses even among the armies. The appearance of the musket in place of the bow, the use of the pike in close-formation fighting, the emergence of more mobile and accurate artillery, the use of much larger armies in set-piece confrontations, all these produced new levels of death and injury which were only partially counteracted by the development of the art of fortification. Siege warfare was not necessarily cheap in human life (see p. 42), though much depended on how a surrendering garrison was treated. Armies suffered from disease (including plague), as much or more that they did from battle wounds. Entire armies were sometimes decimated by death, disease and desertion (as was Mansfeld's army in 1626-7). During the period of continuous warfare in which Spain was engaged between 1618 and 1659, about 300,000 men of Castile out of a population of six million — that is, about 5 per cent — are believed to have lost their lives. In Sweden, including Finland, out of a population of little more than a million about 100,000 were enlisted between 1621 and 1639, and of these about half — again, nearly 5 per cent of the population — were either killed or wounded. In considering the advisability of making or continuing a war, these huge losses of life (in relation to the size of population) could scarcely have been left out of account altogether. But there is little evidence that it was ever a major consideration in the minds of those who reached the decisions.

More important probably, in the eyes of most rulers, was the financial cost of war. Even for Spain, by far the wealthiest country, this was a continual constraint. All the riches of South America, which reached a new peak in the 1580s, together with the considerable tax revenues available, from Italy and the Netherlands as well as from Spain, still could not match the scale of her ever-growing commitments. She was thus continually in a state of financial exhaustion, experiencing successive bankruptcies (in 1557, 1575, 1596, 1607 and 1627) and piling new tax on new tax; bleeding the peasantry of Castile and Sicily and the southern Netherlands to find new resources. Philip II continually despaired of being able to hold the Netherlands because of the financial (not the human) cost of the war.[11] The Emperor Ferdinand II (like his predecessors in the previous age) had constant difficulty in paying for his armies, and in the Thirty Years War was humiliatingly dependent on the wealthier duke of Bavaria. Even the vast Ottoman Empire could not escape this problem: when war against Persia was proposed in 1578, the grand vizier warned that the result would be that the "peasant would be oppressed by taxes and the incursions of the army; and even if Persia is conquered its peasantry will not accept becoming subjected to our rule. . . .The revenues we have from the provinces will not be sufficient."[12]

Conversely, a state that was financially viable was also militarily strong. Denmark, with its large revenues from the Sound tolls, was able to build a strong navy and to hire good foreign mercenaries. Sweden, though relatively poor, had revenues from copper and iron which helped not only to equip a powerful Swedish army but (with plentiful French assistance) to hire nearly 120,000 mercenaries. Spain's wealth enabled her to increase the size of her armies (which had numbered only about 20,000 in the 1490s) to 150,000 in the 1550s, 200,000 in the 1590s and 300,000 at the height of the Thirty Years War.[13] That is why Richelieu declared that "gold and money are among the chief and most necessary sources of the state's power" and that "a poor prince would not be able to undertake glorious action".[14] In most countries a substantial part of government revenues came to be spent on armed forces. Even in peace-time this proportion was usually 25 per cent or so, and in war-time (which was most of the time for a number of countries) the figure increased to 50 and even 80 per cent.[15] These heavy financial costs brought corresponding political costs: the danger of discontent in town and country. During the Thirty Years War there were frequent tax riots in France, and the rebellions Spain confronted in Catalonia, Sicily and Portugal were all intensified by the ever-increasing financial burden which the war imposed on the populations. In assessing the profitability of war, these heavy financial and social costs too had to be placed in the balance.

It is not clear, however, that any conscious calculation of profits against loss was ever made. Certainly every statesman was from time to time obliged to consider whether or not a war was worth embarking on or worth continuing. In the more highly organised states, such as Spain, this was a continuing process: the constant memoranda which Olivares sent to Philip IV about the course of the war, the financial consequences, and the state of the Spanish empire did in effect seek to balance costs against gains, but often reached no clear conclusions. Few openly confronted the question of whether the possible gains were worth the cost. Before a war began it might sometimes be possible to make a general assessment of likely costs and benefits: as in the memorandum Olivares sent about the War of the Mantuan Succession (p. 98 above) and the report put by Richelieu to the French council of state in 1635. But the action take on such reports, and even the conclusions of the reports themselves, were often reached on emotional as much as on rational grounds: the concern with national prestige, to score a point against an opponent, to take advantage of a strategic opportunity, to avenge a past humiliation, usually outweighed or totally submerged thought of the price likely to be paid. In most cases it was taken for granted that war, once begun, must be seen through to the conclusion. No statesman could have been more closely aware of the hideous costs, social and political as well as financial, of the wars in which Spain was engaged, than Olivares; and he did indeed enter into discussions of peace terms at various moments with various enemies (with the United Provinces in 1628-9 and with France in 1636-7). But both the potential gains from victory and the potential costs of losing — in terms of national prestige, the honour of the dynasty, the viability of the Spanish empire — all these would have been hard to quantify, even if he had been disposed to make such a calculation.

In the end the decision whether or not to make war (or whether to continue it) was not seen as one for calculation; nor, even if it was, was the equation sufficiently clear-cut to allow any accurate calculation to be made. Rulers and ministers alike were more likely to reach an instinctive judgement as to where the interest of the ruler (or his nation, or his religion) lay. Subconsciously there must have been some vague conception of the possible costs to be weighed against the benefits. But these were not evenly distributed. The costs fell for the most part not on the rulers and ministers themselves but on their populations — above all on those who fought the wars. Against this, the benefits — in terms of personal glory or national aggrandisement — were enjoyed more by the decision-makers. It is perhaps partly for this reason that war so often appeared to the rulers and their ministers in this age, whatever its cost, to be a worthwhile undertaking.

The age of sovereignty (1648-1789)

Did the wars of the age that followed procure greater gains for those who waged them?

To gain advantage from a war, the first essential is to win the contest. Even that condition was not met in most of the conflicts of this age. In well over half the wars of this period the countries that were mainly responsible for starting the war were finally unsuccessful. Either they were clearly defeated or they did not achieve their primary objectives. Many other wars were inconclusive in their results (p. 50) and in most of these cases too the outcome can scarcely have seemed to the initiators to have been worth the cost. Frederick the Great himself recognised that this tendency was reducing the value of war in his age. In his *History of my Time* he wrote: "Since the establishment of a certain equilibrium between sovereigns the largest enterprises rarely produced the expected results, as a result of the equality of forces and the alternative of losses and gains, the antagonists find themselves at the close of a most desperate war much where they were before it began."[16]

There were many reasons why wars often proved unsuccessful. As we saw in the last chapter, it was often difficult to foresee the line-up of contestants, still less to guess their relative success at arms. In an age so deeply concerned about the balance of power, acts of force frequently stimulated the creation of a coalition against the aggressor, a coalition which successfully prevented that country from securing the fruits of victory. Sweden's war against Poland of 1655, for example, brought such a coalition into being against her which deprived her of success. The four wars provoked by Louis XIV, each met by a similar alliance, ended either in failure (the wars of 1688 and 1702) or in only limited success (the wars of 1667 and 1672). Turkey's wars of 1663 and 1682, each of which brought about the creation of a league of Christian states against her, failed for the same reason. Spain's wars of 1718 and 1727 were unsuccessful because of a similar collective response.

Or it might be that the initiating power was over-confident and underestimated its opponent. A state under attack might put up an unexpected resistance and so avoid defeat: as did the United Provinces in 1672-3 and Turkey in 1735-9. Or the attacker might find it harder than expected to carry the fight into the enemy's homeland: so Denmark's wars of 1675 and 1700 against Sweden brought defeat for her; as did Sweden's wars against Russia of 1741 and 1788. United Provinces' war against England in 1652 was as unsuccessful as that of England against the United Provinces in 1665. Turkey's attacks on Russia in 1768 and 1787 ended in disaster for her. The most decisive victories were, on the contrary, sometimes those of the defenders. the most spectacular victory of the age was possibly that of Austria against the Turks in 1699, the result of an expansionary move by Turkey herself. Sweden (at first) overwhelmed her attackers in 1700-5. Turkey, against all expectations, largely defeated hers in 1735-9.

In many cases, therefore, war did not pay. It remained tempting because, as we have seen, leaders were over-optimistic; and because where it was successful it could bring substantial prizes. The most important booty and still, perhaps, the most coveted, was territory. Louis XIV's successive acts of force, for all his defeats and half defeats, brought a significant expansion of France's borders to the south, east and above all the north-east. Russia won enormous territories to the west and south from her successive wars; though more from the defensive wars (ending in 1681, 1699, 1774 and 1792) than from the offensive ones (ending in 1739 and 1782). Brandenburg was able to add to the poor territories it had acquired through inheritance (for example, in East Prussia) the rich provinces it won by conquest in Pomerania and Silesia. England and United Provinces made big colonial acquisitions across the seas. Strategically important territories were especially valuable fruits of war. So France was able to acquire the "gates" to the country in the Pyrenees, the Alps and the Rhineland; Britain won valuable naval facilities in Gibraltar, Minorca, Bermuda and other places; United Provinces won her barrier in the southern Netherlands; Russia won Azov, Ochakov and the Crimea. Most of the rulers of the period certainly regarded such acquisitions as well worth the costs involved.

Commercial benefits were often as important as territorial gains. The United Provinces won tariff concessions from France in 1678, 1697 and again in 1713. England won commercial concessions from United Provinces in 1654, as the latter did from her in 1667. Both Britain and the Dutch won important commercial privileges from Spain in 1713 (though Britain did far better). Other economic benefits gained by victorious powers included access to fisheries (contested between Britain and France in Newfoundland); rights to fur-trapping (contested between the same two powers in Canada); exemption from tolls (won by Sweden in the Sound); and rights to participate in trade in particular products (for example, slaves, a right won by Britain in 1713) or in particular areas (for example, South America, won by Britain at the same time). In mercantile countries such as Britain, United Provinces and Denmark, commercial benefits could often seem the most important profit of war and helped to make its costs seems more acceptable. In United Provinces the regents — as against the House of Orange — saw war primarily as an opportunity for winning such advantages. The Tory administration which came to power in Britain in 1710, though more ready to abandon allies for the sake of peace than its predecessor, was even more determined than they to secure essential commercial gains from war; and at a later stage Whig administrations were equally concerned about such goals.[17]

If these were the profits of war, what were the costs which had to be set against them? This is sometimes said to have been an age in which war was fought with limited means for limited ends, so that its costs were light. It is true that there were no wars in this age that involved the murderous loss of life, for civilians as well as soldiers, or the barbarous cruelty of some wars in the previous age. Many, especially in the early part of the period, consisted of long campaigns of manoeuvre, in which large-scale battles were sometimes deliberately avoided. Further improvements in the art of fortification encouraged a defensive strategy, so that some campaigns consisted of a series of sieges of fortified towns (after which the besieged forces were frequently allowed to leave with colours flying). Mobility was limited by bad roads, long baggage trains, many camp followers, and above all the need to remain close to magazines. Surrenders and desertions led to the taking of many prisoners. Somewhat better discipline prevented the grossest of atrocities. And this, together with primitive rules concerning warfare, including the treatment of prisoners and civilians (p. 353 below), probably somewhat reduced the loss of life.[18]

Against this, however, there were other trends that had a contrary effect: new weapons — the flintlock musket and eventually the rifle, quicker firing and more mobile artillery, the bayonet (replacing the pike); new formations — the column to supplement the line, mobile light infantry, increased fire-power and especially the concentration of fire power. A new generation of generals — Charles XII, Marlborough, Eugene and Frederick the Great — brought a new mobility to armies and increased the size of armies and battles. Battles involving 150,000 and 200,000 men and death tolls of 20,000-30,000 were now not uncommon. 500,000 are believed to have fought at the battle of Beresteszka in 1651, where the Cossacks alone had an army of 300,000. The total numbers engaged in warfare also increased as the age went on. Most of the nations of Europe began to keep standing armies, whose size progressively grew. Though the use of mercenaries (non-national contingents under their own commander, hired for fighting) declined, this was balanced by the increasing use of auxiliaries (that is, troops borrowed or hired from a friendly state). The armies engaged in war, though smaller than those of the age that followed, thus now became very large. Prussia's army grew from 8,000 men in 1648 to 40,000 in 1713, to 80,000 when Frederick the Great came to the throne, 165,000 at the beginning of the Seven Years War, and 190,000 in 1786. France had an army of 250,000 in the last decades of the seventeenth century, and during the War of the Spanish Succession this rose to 400,000 (with another 100,000 men in the navy). Russia's army grew rapidly: it was already nearly 150,000 in the middle of the eighteenth century and rose to over 400,000 at the end of this period. Austria had an army of 80,000-100,000, but could call on many more from German and other friendly states. Britain had a regular army of only about about 25,000, but, with the use of auxiliaries, could put an army of about 150,000 into the field if necessary. Though "voluntary" enlistment remained the basis of most armies, with the effect that many soldiers came from the poorest and most desperate sections of the population (including many criminals), from the end of the seventeenth century there was increasing use of forms of conscription. Louis XIV established a militia, originally intended for home defence, but increasingly incorporated into the fighting forces. Russia and Sweden, during the Great Northern War, and Prussia shortly before the War of Austrian Succession, introduced systems by which particular districts, parishes or groups of households, were required to provide so many recruits for national service.[19] Austria and Spain introduced conscription after the Seven Years War. Though there were many exceptions, the effect was that an increasing proportion of the ordinary population was involved in warfare. Losses in war would thus be more widely felt. Moreover, armies could still behave with great brutality to civilians. They would still sometimes live off the country, and would almost always demand heavy "contributions" from the local population to help pay the cost of war. Sometimes both towns and countryside were brutally ravaged to prevent enemies from making use of these assets. So, during the Dutch war, French troops caused huge hardship in Flanders and the Palatinate; the latter territory was again devastated, still more brutally, in 1688; Bavaria suffered heavily from the effects of occupation by troops of the Grand Alliance in 1704; and Silesia and Saxony were ravaged by Frederick the Great to pay for the wars during which they were occupied.

Quite apart from this loss of life, the financial costs of war in this age could be very great. The cost of paying large armies, of equipping and supplying them, of building and equipping warships and of meeting all the other expenses of war, grew rapidly. In the middle of the eighteenth century four-fifths of the revenues of Prussia were used for military expenditure. 95 per cent of Russia's budget during the Great Northern War is supposed to have been devoted to warfare. Auxiliary forces, so widely used in this period, cost substantial sums*. General subsidies for allies were similarly costly. France in the time of Louis XIV gave subsidies to England, Sweden and many German states to procure alliance or at least neutrality. In the next century, Britain, now herself financially stronger, paid substantial amounts for that purpose: during the Seven Years War she provided subsidies for Hanover, Hesse and Brunswick in addition to a very large one (£670,000) to Frederick the Great. Russia financed Poland during the war against the Turks in the 1680s and later financed most of her allies against Sweden in the Great Northern War. All these

* Troops from Switzerland, from Ireland and from a number of German states were widely used; the United Provinces hired troops from Britain and Britain from the United Provinces; Russian troops were hired by Austria during the War of the Polish Succession and used by Britain and United Provinces 12 years later to defend the Netherlands against France.

costs fell ultimately on the ordinary population. But there was a limit to their capacity to bear such burdens. France during the War of the Spanish Succession (in 1708-10) and Prussia during the Seven Years War (in 1760-1) were both on the point of financial collapse. One of the main reasons for the relative success of Britain in the wars of this period was the superiority of the financial system in raising revenues, often through extensive government borrowing, without excessive hardship for the population.[20] Other countries managed much less successfully. Because of its inefficient, unfair and burdensome tax system, France, despite its size, wealth and population, suffered far greater financial difficulties than its enemies during the Nine Years War and the War of the Spanish Succession. The importance of administrative and financial strength to success in war was recognised. Frederick the Great was encouraged to make war on Austria in 1740 because of the latter's known administrative and financial weakness; conversely, Maria Theresa, determined to wrest Silesia back, made her first task the reform of the financial and administrative system of her country. For this reason the financially powerful countries could obtain a strong hold on those in a different situation. The United Provinces lent, either officially or through its finance houses, to Sweden, Denmark, the emperor and the German states. Marlborough's armies were financed by Dutch as well as domestic loans. Later, continental powers, in addition to securing official subsidies from Britain, borrowed on the London market.

The final cost of war, both in lives and treasure, probably proved in most cases to be far higher than had been anticipated. But it does not seem that in any case there was any careful weighing of the likely cost against probable benefits. It was one of the assumptions of the age that states made war against each other and that war was a normal means for increasing the glory and power of the state (pp. 348-52). Once it had been concluded that war was necessary — to acquire coveted territory, to right a wrong, to humble a rival, to maintain the balance of power — it was assumed that the necessary resources must be found to secure the victory. If the resources appeared at first sight inadequate, there was little inclination to call off the war; more likely there would be new efforts to win allies, to buy auxiliaries, to amend the strategy or wean away opponents. Only as the costs of war, and the difficulty of securing the gains anticipated, became more apparent, did war-weariness set in (as in France in 1710, Britain in 1746 and Prussia in 1760, for example). In many cases, as we have seen, the original ambition proved unattainable; and those who had launched the war had thus in practice to recognises that they could win less, and would have to pay far more, than they had hoped.

It was at that point, during the protracted and complex negotiations which so often went on as the war proceeded, that ambitions had to be moderated and, for the first time, the gains that were attainable had to be adjusted to the balance of military advantage. Because in so many cases the aggressors were unsuccessful, most wars could scarcely in the end be assessed as profitable. Even an apparently victorious ruler could doubt the long-term benefit of a war to his people: as when Frederick the Great in his *History of My Time,* felt of his second Silesian war that "reputation in arms . . . was all we got and it aroused envy"; or when Louis XIV, on his death-bed, warned his great-grandson against war, admitting that he himself had "loved war too much". Not many rulers were so honest. Most still felt that war could be a profitable undertaking. Certainly they were rarely deterred by the heavy costs (to their populations rather than to themselves) of undertaking it.

The age of nationalism (1789-1917)

In the age that was ushered in by the French revolution wars were undertaken to procure different gains. A large proportion of the wars in this age were, as we have seen, wars of national independence: revolutions designed to create states based on the national principle, to win national independence for those subjected or national unity for those divided. In general, war for that purpose proved highly successful for those who undertook it. In Europe, national independence was achieved by that means for Greece, Belgium, Serbia, Montenegro, Romania and Bulgaria in turn. Often success was achieved only with the assistance of outside forces; where such assistance was lacking the efforts often failed (as did the successive revolutions in Poland and the revolts in Bosnia-Herzegovinia and Macedonia). National unity for divided people was secured by the same means: for Germany after four wars and for Italy after five. Armed struggle was also sometimes a successful means of winning independence outside Europe if the colonial power concerned was sufficiently weak. It won independence for the people of South and Central America, and much later (with help from a powerful neighbour) for Cuba. In Africa and Asia, on the other hand, where the subject peoples were everywhere inferior in military technology and organisation to their rulers, such struggles, though attempted — for example in Tanganyika and South-west Africa — had a low record of success.

Such wars could also be profitable for those who assisted them. External powers supporting an independence movement could hope to win a powerful influence in the new state so created. Russia hoped for such influence in assisting the independence wars of Greece and Bulgaria; as did France to a lesser extent in helping to win independence for Italy. Prussia gained from her four wars between 1848 and

1870 by being accorded unquestioned leadership in a united Germany. But in practice an extension of influence was rarely the only, nor always the chief, objective of such powers. Over and above the satisfaction of bringing to birth a new nation, which might be expected to show suitable gratitude, they could expect other gains. Russia won territorial and other concessions as a result of her war to help Greece; France won Savoy and Nice through her war for Italy; Prussia Alsace-Lorraine in 1871; Russia Kars in 1878. All won in addition the self-satisfaction and the status which victory in war could always secure. These were not insignificant gains. Few among the population of the victorious nations reproached their governments on the grounds that the benefits secured did not match the costs involved. In such cases the decision for war appeared to have, to those involved at least, been justified by the results obtained.

There were, however, wars, including some of the most important of the period, that proved highly unprofitable. Napoleon's adventures across Europe, for all their brilliant and temporary successes, finally left France with (over and above the stupendous casualties which she had suffered) her overseas territory diminished, a heavy indemnity and an army of occupation on her soil, not to speak of the humiliation that rankled with French governments for 50 years or more. Russia (which, through her pressure on Turkey and her refusal to evacuate the Principalities, must take the major responsibility for bringing about the Crimean War) finished it far worse off than before, with some loss of territory, the Black Sea neutralised, and her position in the Near East greatly weakened. Austria and France failed in their challenges to Prussia in 1866 and 1870. Finally and most decisively of all, Austria-Hungary and Germany, the two powers most responsible for the First World War, found themselves, at its end, defeated, bankrupted and humiliated: the former split into fragments; the latter deprived of all its overseas possessions, its European territory bisected, its most strategic land demilitarised, its armed forces limited, and saddled with huge financial obligations which crippled its economy and could have taken decades to liquidate.

One reason for the heavy costs of defeat was a major change in the results of war in this age. In this period virtually every European war (that of 1859 is the only true exception) had a clear-cut outcome: there was always one state or alliance that was unmistakably the victor and one that was unmistakably the vanquished. Sometimes, as we have seen, an all-out victory could be secured without excessive cost through one or two decisive battles (as in 1866 and 1885); so that for the victor the triumph seemed easily worth the cost involved. But in other cases the determination on each side to secure total victory, and to fight to the bitter end to achieve it — a determination that was usually as strong in the country being defeated as in that which believed it had victory in its grasp — added hugely to the cost and to the scale of total casualties. So, in the Napoleonic wars, in the Franco-Prussian War, and above all in the First World War, both sides were equally determined to fight to the bitter end and were willing to undergo huge casualties and unimagined privations for the sake of winning a clear-cut victory. So the accommodations and the compromises which had often (though not invariably) helped to reduce the cost of war in the previous age were now scorned. The passionate commitment to the national cause meant that the possibility of discussing terms before defeat could not now even be contemplated. This inevitably meant that the costs of war were often extremely heavy. Increasingly too they were shared, almost equally, by both sides. In the most severe conflicts even the victorious powers, as some had correctly forecast (p. 260 below), lost far more, in lives, resources and expended energies, than they gained, through the provisions of the final peace treaties. For perhaps the first time in history, even victory in war could bring losses rather than gains.

Overseas the benefits to be secured by war were less problematical. There the European powers normally had little cause to fear defeat. Apart from the failure of Spain's half-hearted attempts to regain her former colonies, the only clear-cut exception was the defeat of the Italians by Ethiopia in 1896 (Britain was temporarily defeated by Afghanistan in 1840, but quickly re-established her supremacy the following year). In general, European nations could be confident that armed force would assure them of control of vast territories, often at relatively low cost. Britain won the right to trade with China on reasonable terms, as well as control of Hong Kong, for only a few hundred lives in 1839-42. France won control of Indo-China with relatively little military effort, European powers won control of most of Africa for insignificant losses in men and material. In only a few cases were such conflicts long and costly. The Dutch war to win full control of Achin in Sumatra, which lasted for 30 years, is reckoned to have cost over 20,000 lives altogether on both sides. Spain's struggle to keep control of Cuba cost her two protracted struggles, lasting almost 20 years altogether and involving the loss of nearly 100,000 Spanish lives, and even so was finally unsuccessful. In most cases however, though individual battles could be fierce and costly, the final outcome of such wars was rarely in doubt. They aroused little controversy in the countries that undertook them (even during France's colonial adventures in the 1880s, and Britain's involvement in the Boer War, home opposition, though vocal, was confined to relatively small groups of middle-class radicals). It was generally taken for granted that the costs involved in acquiring such territories were far outweighed by the benefits (to the conquered as well as the conquerors) they would bring in their train.

So there were often substantial gains to be had from war, both within Europe and elsewhere, so long as victory could be secured. But against this had to be set the costs of acquiring them. Casualties, at least in major wars, were heavy: far heavier than in earlier ages. Even single battles, fought with huge armies and powerful artillery, could cost hundreds of thousands of lives. 500,000 are believed to have fought at the battle of Leipzig, the most decisive encounter of the Napoleonic wars and of these a quarter were killed or wounded. 90,000 were killed or wounded at Borodino, 40,000 at Waterloo. France lost nearly 600,000 men (not all French) in the Russian campaign alone: about half were killed or died of disease and cold; the rest were wounded, captured or deserted. The Crimean War is estimated to have cost half a million dead, the Franco-Prussian War 200,000. Some of the more expensive wars were civil wars: the American Civil War cost perhaps 400,000 lives (though estimates differ widely), the Taiping rebellion in China at least 2 million (some estimates are far higher). Casualties in the First World War, generally reckoned at at least 12 million lives, dwarfed all these. Conscription, used ruthlessly by Napoleon to replace his casualties with younger and younger age-groups, was widely adopted to provide the manpower for these battles: most of the major powers apart from Britain adopted it, in one form or another, so as to create a permanently available reserve of trained manpower. Not many of these governments would boast, as Napoleon did, that "soldiers were made to be killed" and that he could afford to expend 30,000 men a month; but many, in the knowledge that they had large forces of trained men who could be expected to give their lives if necessary, felt more willing to take decisions that could lead to war. The general sentiment among most statesmen was probably that armies were created for fighting; and that if the national interest, national honour or national glory, demanded it, they must be expected to make the final sacrifice for the sake of their country.

But the human cost was not the only sacrifice war involved. Statesmen had also to be aware (though it is doubtful if they often were) of the material costs as well. The financial costs of war rose steadily during this age. Every type of armament became more complex and more expensive to produce. The simple guns of the eighteenth century were replaced by the more powerful and rapid-loading guns of the nineteenth. The simple, smooth-bored musket was replaced by the fast-loading rifled weapon. Wooden sailing boats were replaced as men of war by steel-hulled, steam-propelled cruisers, battleships and finally dreadnoughts, of ever-growing size. Military budgets, as a result, rose astronomically. Russia and Austria were consistently near bankruptcy largely because of the size of their military budget (since other government expenditures were low, a substantial part of national budgets in this age was taken by spending on armed forces). If wars were short enough, and many were, the costs of undertaking them did not necessarily add much to these regular military budgets: thus the *additional* expense to Prussia of the wars of 1864 and 1866 was negligible.

The main financial cost of war, therefore, was the cost of being ready to make it: of maintaining armed forces large and well equipped enough to defeat most likely opponents. Most governments were prepared to budget to this end rather than risk the possibility of humiliating defeat. It was only when a war was bitter and prolonged, as were the Napoleonic wars (which cost Britain £830 million and added £620 million to the national debt) and the First World War (which involved the mobilisation of an entire nation's resources), that these costs rose higher still. But, because that escalation of costs was rarely clearly anticipated in advance, it is doubtful whether it acted as any significant deterrent on statesmen against taking action which might lead to war.

Did statesmen make any kind of calculation of the probable total cost of war, in lives and money, to be set against the likely fruits of victory? There is little evidence of any conscious calculation. There are no signs that Louis Napoleon and Cavour, when they made together their deliberate decision to go to war with Austria in 1859, made any careful assessment of the probable cost to each of their countries in blood and treasure. Bismarck, in consulting with von Moltke before the war against Austria in 1866, was concerned to know the likelihood of victory, not the cost of achieving it. When the French chamber clamoured for war against Prussia in 1870, it made no attempt to estimate the number of lives that the decision would cost, still less the monetary expenditure involved. Statesmen normally simply assumed that, if war was found necessary to promote national interests, the resources would be found: whatever the cost, it had to be paid and would be justified by victory.

Such a calculation appeared less necessary because of the growing assumption that wars would be short. The overheads had already been borne in preceding years. If there was any calculation of cost, it was made in time of peace: in the decisions on the level of expenditure then thought necessary. In those decisions statesmen normally merely looked at the level of armaments held by their rivals and determined that, whatever the cost, they must be able to match them. The human cost, however much it might be regretted, was seen as the sad but necessary consequence which war brought in its train: a cost that must be borne if national honour, national self-respect and essential national interests were to be preserved. Of course, statesmen differed in their weighing of costs against profits. There were a few who believed that the costs should be avoided if at all possible. Aberdeen in Britain, Giers in Russia, Delcassé in France, even to some extent Bethmann-Hollweg in Germany were more conscious of the costs than the benefits; Louis Napoleon and Bismarck were more aware of the benefits than the costs. But these were emotional attitudes to war, not calculations. Considering what was at stake, it is incredible that there was so little careful calculation (see pp. 356-7). Most statesmen took it for granted that in certain circumstances war might be necessary and damn the cost.

Immediately before the First World War, in his much-read book *The Great Illusion,* Sir Norman Angell tried to introduce a more rational approach: to bring about a conscious effort to relate the probable gains of war to the probable costs. He concluded that, given the scale of casualties to be expected in modern warfare, and above all the economic consequences, all alike must be losers. He found supporters, not only in Britain but elsewhere. War, these felt, was no longer a rational act of policy, since the cost would always be greater than the gains, for victors and for vanquished alike. But this was not the view that prevailed in the world as a whole. When attempts were made, halfway through the mass slaughter in the following years, to arrange an armistice, there were few on either side who believed it would be better to call a halt to that slaughter if it meant renouncing the chance of victory. The general consensus was not that the costs of war might outweigh the fruit of victory (not to speak of the agonies of defeat); it was that, if war was necessary to defeat an enemy, to fulfil national aims, to arrive at "final victory", the means to fight it must be found, whatever the material and human costs might prove to be.

The age of ideology (1917-   )

Calculations of the probable costs and benefits of war in the following age changed radically.

For all-out international war, the likely costs rose disproportionately to the likely benefits. In the previous era it was still possible for a Bismarck or a Napoleon III to believe that the benefits his country might win through successful war would far outweigh the costs, human and material, likely to be incurred. The unprecedented toll of the First World War for the first time created a sense, both among the public and their leaders, that all-out war could bring no gains commensurate with the suffering entailed. Sir Norman Angell, it seemed, had been proved right: there were no winners, only losers. Even the victors could win back only a fraction of what they lost. However much they might try to recoup something of the cost — through large-scale reparations, by territorial compensation (France receiving Alsace-Lorraine, Italy winning territory in the Adriatic and the Aegean, Britain the dubious honour of administering mandated territories overseas), these offered poor consolation for the millions of lives that had been given up. As for the countries mainly responsible for bringing the war about — Germany and Austria-Hungary — the balance was for them even more unfavourable. Both countries were shattered, economically and politically: Germany losing all her overseas territory as well as some in Europe, Austria-Hungary suffering total disintegration. There could hardly be a clearer demonstration that war no longer paid.

Yet even that demonstration was, for a time, not enough. For a while, a few continued to believe that even total war, if sufficiently swift and successful, could bring its rewards. Within defeated or dissatisfied states — Germany, Japan and Italy — some were able to persuade themselves that this time, if they could conquer speedily and successfully, the winnings would outweigh the cost. Rapid blitzkrieg campaigns might be less expensive than the previous war, yet bring bigger prizes. So it needed a second Armageddon before the message finally went home. The total cost, this time, was even heavier than before; and again it was the countries mainly responsible for bringing about the war that suffered the heaviest losses. More than ever, it now seemed inconceivable that war between major powers could bring profits that were in anyway comparable to the costs.

After 1945, moreover, the potential costs continued to multiply. The emergence of nuclear weapons, already briefly christened in the previous conflict, most obviously demonstrated the new dangers war could entail. On these grounds Churchill in 1953 was already proclaiming the "balance of terror" as the guarantor of peace in the years to come. But nuclear weapons were, in fact, only one in the new range of armaments than modern technology had procured, capable of wreaking destruction on an unprecedented scale: an arsenal including chemical and biological weapons, faster, more accurate and far more powerful artillery, much larger and more destructive bombs, missiles of almost unlimted range and accurcy, guidance devices of every kind, electro-magnetic launchers, directed energy lasers and particle beams. Even if it could be assumed that some of these, especially nuclear weapons themselves, might be too powerful to be used, the cost of war would still be horrendous. "Conventional" weapons alone, with much more powerful warheads, new guidance systems, improved means of delivery, greater penetration and accuracy, promised a destructive power far greater than any in earlier times. Any war among the major powers therefore, however fought, must bring unprecedented costs. The launching of such a war could no longer anywhere be seen, as it was by some at least before 1914, as a rational act of state: the continuation of policy by other means. External wars between major powers, it was generally concluded, must now be altogether avoided, or at the least clearly limited in scope.

Ways were found of reducing costs to a more acceptable level. So long as a confrontation of the most serious kind — especially between the super-powers themselves — could be avoided, the expense of war, many believed, could still be made manageable. "Limited war" could be made: against or within smaller and weaker states; confined to particular geographical areas; or restricted to a particular range of weapons. The super-powers were therefore careful to avoid direct confrontation with each other. Neither sought to challenge the actions of the other in areas of most interest to it, while their own territory was in each case totally inviolate. They became involved against each other only indirectly. War was undertaken in the territory of other states: in Korea and Vietnam, Hungary and Cuba, Czechoslovakia and the Dominican Republic, Afghanistan and Nicaragua. By confining such wars to conventional weapons they have tried to contain costs (though these have often been, as in Vietnam and Afghanistan, for example, far higher than originally contemplated). Yet the gains expected could be significant: usually increased security in strategically important areas. If operations could be limited in this way, therefore, the benefits secured, even if the forces of the super-powers themselves became involved, could still be seen as outweighing the anticipated costs.

In many cases, however, costs could be reduced still further. Major powers were able to avoid the involvement of their own forces altogether. In such cases operations have been undertaken in a masked form. They could be performed through surrogates: the North Koreans in Korea, Hondurans and Nicaraguans in Guatemala, Cubans in Angola, local rebels in Southern Africa, Central America and Cambodia. "Advisers" could be sent rather than operational units (as in Vietnam and Nicaragua). "Volunteers" could be sent, but not regular forces (as by China in Korea). Assistance could be given to local factions; arms supplied; diplomatic support provided; propaganda undertaken. In other words, rather than fight their own wars, major powers could help others to fight them on their behalf. In these ways the expense of war could be minimised, their own territory immunised and the cost-benefit ratio vastly improved.

The use of force by major powers, even in these limited ways, has anyway been the exception rather than the rule. Even among the international wars of the period a majority have been undertaken by lesser nations. These too have avoided the unacceptable costs of advanced technological warfare. The wars have in almost all cases been undertaken against other powers of the same rank, and of limited military technology, so that the risks undergone have been similar to those of the previous age rather than to those of the advanced warfare of the modern age. Though the costs of such wars — between Israel and Egypt, India and Pakistan, Iraq and Iran, Somalia and Ethiopia — could still be heavy, they have been heavy in the conventional way. They mainly had little impact on civilian populations. The bombardment of cities, whether by air, sea or land, has generally been avoided (the only significant exception is the Gulf War and even here civilian casualties have been a tiny fraction of those of the Second World War). The calculations to be made have therefore been not unlike those of European countries in the nineteenth century, in which the prizes to be had by winning — the acquisition of small pieces of disputed territory, the removal of a threat or the humiliation of a rival — could be measured against the cost in service lives or expected financial burdens. Such wars have frequently been fought for limited ends in limited areas and for the most part have been relatively brief: except for the Iraq-Iran war, the long wars of the period have all been civil wars (p. 72).

Even so, it may be doubted whether, at the end of the day, the assets won have been thought worth the costs incurred. A number of such wars have been fought to promote a territorial claim in contiguous territory. Only in rare cases has such a claim been successfully enforced by these means. In a few cases the results have been inconclusive (Peru-Colombia, India-Pakistan in 1948-9, Algeria-Morocco, Nicaragua-Honduras). But over two-thirds of such attempts have been unquestionably defeated (Lithuania-Poland, Bolivia-Paraguay, Somalia-Ethiopia (twice), Somalia-Kenya, India-China, Indonesia-Malaysia, Pakistan-India (1965), South Yemen-Yemen, Uganda-Tanzania, Iraq-Iran, Argentina-Britain). Where the attacker has been large and powerful enough, and the victim weak, such assaults have sometimes been successful (as was the Soviet Union in seizing the Baltic States, and China in seizing Tibet). In some cases such external wars have been designed to win a dependent territory or part of it, before or soon after independence. Here too several attempts failed (Indonesia-Malaysia, South Yemen-Oman, Somalia-Ethiopia), while a few, against very weak states, have been successful (as when India conquered Hyderabad and Goa, and Indonesia East Timor). The six conflicts between Israel and her neighbours, though undoubtedly partly concerned with territory (who was to control Palestine, Sinai or the West Bank), perhaps more fundamentally concerned the security, even the survival, of Israel: here, of the two wars launched by the Arab states, one (1948) failed in its objective, while the other (1973) had only partial success; the four launched by Israel (1956, 1967, 1978 and 1982) were all wholly or partially successful in an immediate military sense (though at their end Israel's security had not been finally assured in consequence). Of the other two international wars of the period, China's attack on Vietnam in 1979 to "teach her a lesson" cannot be said to have succeeded (the Vietnamese remained in Cambodia); while the so-called "football war" between El Salvador and Honduras in 1969, with no clear motive on either side other than mutual anger, was inconclusive in its result. In other words, a substantial proportion of the external wars of the age have failed to secure their objectives.

The majority of the conflicts of this age have, however, not been international conflicts at all: they have taken place entirely within the territory of a single state. About 20 have been colonial wars (Table 10). On a crude assessment, it could be said that resort to force produced results in virtually all these cases, in the sense that the conflicts were followed, sooner or later, by the granting of independence. In a good many cases the use of force probably did play a significant part in securing concessions: sometimes a willingness to grant independence which had previously been refused (Cyprus, Algeria, Portuguese territories); sometimes independence on more favourable terms (Indonesia, Palestine); sometimes independence rather earlier than had been originally proposed (Indo-China, Cyprus, South Arabia). In other cases the effect is more doubtful: in the case of the Mau Mau rebellion in Kenya (which was defeated long before independence was granted) or the revolt in Cameroun, for example, it cannot be said that resort to violence produced any clear return. Yet even in these cases there may have been indirect consequences. All these wars took place at a time when the willingness of colonial powers to retain their colonies was sharply declining, and the fighting, even if contained, often increased the desire among the governments and people of colonial countries to be rid of such problems altogether.

More common have been revolutionary wars designed to overthrow a particular government. Here it is still harder to equate the results achieved to the amount of force applied. The fact that a government fell during a civil war does not necessarily prove it fell as a result of that war, nor that the same result might not have been achieved by other means. Conversely, the fact that a rebellion against a tyrannical regime failed to overturn it, does not necessarily mean that the attempt was altogether without effect. In a few cases revolts proved successful, even against all the odds: as in Spain, China, Cuba, South Vietnam and Nicaragua, for example. In a much larger number of cases similar movements have been defeated, as in Greece, Lebanon (1958), Colombia, Indonesia (1965-6) and several Latin American countries (such as the Dominican Republic, Guatemala and — so far — El Salvador). In other cases the result has been inconclusive as in Laos (1961-4), Yemen, Ethiopia, Sudan and Chad.

In general, the chances of rebel forces succeeding against entrenched governments has declined with time. The extension of administration into more remote areas (where previously rebel control could have been easily established), the increasing military power available to governments, higher standards of living (reducing the willingness to fight for change), as well as the assistance now widely given by outside powers to a government under threat, have had the effect that in most places it has become gradually harder for such movements to succeed.

But their capacity to do so has depended on other factors than comparative armed strength: morale, the social structure, the honesty and efficiency of administration, degrees of external support and so on. If injustice was great enough, it was often still possible for a rebel force to prevail, however much the initial balance appeared to be weighted against it (as in China, Cuba and Nicaragua, for example). And, even where a prolonged armed struggle produced no immediate or visible result (as was the case in Colombia, Guatemala or Afghanistan), it is not certain that it had no consequence at all.

Intervention by outside powers in such struggles has also had a mixed record of success. As we have seen earlier (p. 176), intervention, whether by super-powers or others, has usually been designed to ensure that, in areas believed essential to security, power would be held only by politically congenial governments. In most cases super-power intervention succeeded in that aim: for example, in Guatemala (1954), in Hungary (1956), in the Dominican Republic (1965), in Czechoslovakia (1968) and in Grenada (1983). So, often, has intervention by lesser powers: by South Africa and India in neighbouring territories, or by France in African states. But not all such attempts have been successful. Among super-power interventions, large-scale operations in Vietnam and Afghanistan failed to secure their objectives even after many years of heavy military commitment; while at the other extreme the tiny Bay of Pigs operation (involving fewer than 2,000 men, with minimum US support) within a day showed itself a disaster, and interventions by Israel (1978 and 1982-5) and the United States (1982-3) in Lebanon were also ultimately unsuccessful. Among the operations of lesser powers, that by Indonesia in Malaysia failed to secure its objective, while her intervention in West Irian and East Timor faced prolonged difficulties. Operations of this kind continued to be undertaken because the possible benefits to be won — in terms of increased military security or political prestige — were great. But they still sometimes proved unsuccessful because the hazards, both military and political, of direct intervention, were not only great but often quite unpredictable.

The likelihood that a revolutionary movement would succeed has been substantially less in the case of revolutions among minority peoples. Of the 25 wars launched by such movements (see Table 11) only two can be said to have succeeded, and then only after massive external intervention. Turkish-speaking Cypriots, through Turkey's intervention, won autonomy, though their state secured practically no recognition; Bangladesh, with substantial assistance from India, won full independence in 1971, the only case where this was achieved by a minority. In other cases minorities have achieved at best a limited form of autonomy (as did the southern Sudanese, and the Kurds of Iraq). Often they have received little sympathy from other sections of the population. Usually they have had little assistance from outside. Even where the minority has secured substantial external support, moral or material, in its struggle (for example, the Ibos in Nigeria, the Eritreans and Somalis in Ethiopia, the West Saharans in Morocco), they were rarely ultimately successful. In many cases those actively engaged in the revolt have been only a minority among what was in any case only a minority people. More often they have continued, sometimes over very long periods (like the various peoples in revolt in Burma, the Kurds of Iraq and Iran, the Nagas in India, the Moslems of the Southern Philippines, the Eritreans of Ethiopia), in bitter and apparently hopeless struggles. On any rational assessment the costs of these struggles bore little relation to the benefits likely to be gained. But in question of national or group survival rational calculations inevitably have played little part. The potential gains of victory — independence or at least autonomy — were so great as to make continued struggle, even against hopeless odds, seem worthwhile.

Assessments of possible costs and benefits have often been distorted by mistaken beliefs about the chances of victory. Just as, in the previous century, Austria and France embarked on war with Prussia, falsely confident of their prospects of success, so in this age similar miscalculations have been made. In a few cases the power balance has been so disproportionate that success was assured from the outset: the Soviet Union could be confident of quick victory in Hungary and Czechoslovakia, the United States in the Dominican Republic, India in Goa and East Pakistan, Vietnam in Cambodia. In other cases initial confidence, even if apparently justified, has proved misfounded. This has been true even of decisions by the superpowers: the US decision to cross the 38th parallel in Korea in 1950 and to extend its commitment in Vietnam in 1965, the Soviet decision to intervene in Afghanistan in 1979, the Chinese decision to "teach Vietnam a lesson" — all led to engagements far more difficult and costly than had been anticipated. Among lesser powers similar miscalculations have been made. Egypt's decision to intervene in Yemen, Uganda's decision to invade Tanzania in 1979, Iraq's decision to invade Iran in 1980, Argentina's decision to invade the Falklands in

198?, were all taken in the hope that a quick and easy victory could be secured, with few uncomfortable after-effects; yet all proved costly and disastrous failures. Judgements were sometimes distorted by personal ambition. The fact that these latter decisions were all reached by dictators or military rulers may indicate that such leaders, having a strong personal stake in successful foreign adventure, are more prone to miscalculation of that kind. But, though this may have been a factor in some cases, miscalculation did not always arise from that cause. The faulty assessments made by Britain and France over Suez, by the United States over the Bay of Pigs and Vietnam, by Israel over its second Lebanon invasion of 1982 (among other examples) show that fully democratic governments are equally prone to miscalculation of that type on occasion. The benefits to be had from an act of war are often over estimated by governments of all kinds.

So, though in this age there was almost nobody who believed that a major confrontation among advanced military nations could promote national interests, more limited uses of force were still sometimes seen as advantageous. So long as the scale could be confined and costs reduced, resort to force was still sometimes a tempting course of action. In practice a large proportion of these attempts failed in their objectives — frontiers were not altered, governments were not overthrown, minorities were not given the independence they demanded. The most common use of force was in civil conflicts; by revolutionary groups seeking to overthrow their governments and by outside powers seeking to support them. In an age of conflicting ideologies, the overriding aim, both in civil and international conflicts, was to win power for those favouring a particular political viewpoint. For that purpose, certain types of military action still often appeared profitable. But here too the effort often failed. But the fact that successes were sometimes achieved by such means meant that, when no alternative seemed possible, when the victory of political opponents could be prevented in no other way, war still sometimes seemed the course of action most likely to produce the desired end. Where the pressures, political and emotional, for such a use of force were sufficiently strong, the knowledge that similar attempts in the past had failed was not usually a decisive influence.

Conclusions

What conclusions is it possible to draw about the profitability of war in the different periods we have examined?

Any calculation of the gains that have been had from war must be subjective and arbitrary, since it depends on placing a value on human lives, to be set against an equally arbitrary valuation to be placed on the acquisition of territory, the vindication of national "honour", or the promotion of a religious or ideological cause,, The relative value placed on each of these has differed from one society to another. For that reason the judgements that might be made about the profitability of particular wars have also varied greatly from one age to another. In general the value placed on human life today is probably higher, and that placed on national prestige (or "honour") probably lower, than in earlier times. Thus the calculation of the gains to be had from a war to win national prestige would probably be different today from a century ago. Against this, there might now be a greater toleration of the financial costs (since the capacity to sustain these costs is much greater); and a higher value would be placed on the benefit gained by successfully promoting an ideological cause or overcoming an ideological opponent. Changes in valuation of this kind will alter judgements about the cost-benefit ratio in many cases: wars which in one age would have been thought eminently worthwhile, in another may be seen as costly or irresponsible.

But, even making allowances for such variations in judgement, a significant proportion of the wars of each age would probably have been regarded as worthwhile, at least by those who launched them, and often by a majority of the population generally, at the time they were undertaken. This is scarcely surprising. It is unlikely that war would have been engaged in so frequently over so many years if it were not thought that it brought a reasonable chance of acquiring net gains as a result.

There are, however, considerable qualifications that must be made to this judgement. First, an essential condition of a profitable outcome is to secure victory. This is not a logical condition: it is logically possible to conceive of an unsuccessful war that was none the less reckoned to have brought long-term gains, whether material or immaterial, to the country which engaged in it (for example, Sardinia's unsuccessful war against Austria in 1848-9 could still have been seen as worth its cost in establishing her as the unchallenged leader and inspiration of the Italian *risorgimento*). But in general it is true to say that to procure the gains anticipated from a particular war it is necessary first to win it. In fact, in all our periods, and especially in the last three of them, a substantial proportion of the wars that have been fought have not been won by those who initiated them (where such a country can reasonably be identified). To take some of the more obvious examples, selected almost at random, Louis XIV lost the Nine Years War and the War of the Spanish Succession; Spain the wars of 1718-20 and 1728; Austria the Seven Years War (at least, she did not win it); France the Napoleonic wars; Russia the Crimean War; Austria the war of 1866; France the war of 1870-1; Bulgaria the second Balkan war; Germany the two world wars; the Arabs the war of 1948; Britain and France their Suez venture; Pakistan the war of

1965; Argentina the Falklands War; Iraq her war against Iran (or at least she did not win it in the way intended); and so on. For all the dangers of generalisation, it can probably be said that, if colonial wars are excepted, the initiating powers, despite all the advantages available to them, have more often lost wars than they have won them. The reason is not far to see: the power that initiates a war is often seen by others as a serious threat to the peace and in this way may bring about a substantial coalition committed to its defeat, and in any case, will stimulate passionate resistance in the country attacked. In addition to these cases where those waging war have lost it, there are a substantial number of other cases, especially in the age of sovereignty, where the outcome has been indecisive (p. 50 above): here too it cannot be said that the victorious power has secured worthwhile gains from war — certainly not gains proportionate to the cost. In other words the first condition for securing gains — victory — has not often been achieved.

There are of course a large number of exceptions. In general, wars involving only two powers have more often produced favourable results for those that began them. This of course applies especially to wars in which large powers have been engaged against weaker ones. Thus in the age of sovereignty France could defeat Genoa, Sweden Bremen and Russia Sweden; in the nineteenth century Prussia could defeat Denmark, Britain and France could defeat their numerous colonial enemies, and the United States could defeat Mexico and Spain; in the current age the Soviet Union could subdue Hungary and may finally subdue Afghanistan, just as the United States could impose her will on Guatemala, the Dominican Republic and Grenada. In other words, war is, unsurprisingly, more likely to produce some return for the powerful than for other states. And this no doubt partly accounts for the fact, noted earlier, that in almost every age it is the powerful who are most frequently engaged in war.

But, if, for most states at least, war is so frequently unsuccessful, why has it been resorted to? Should states not have learnt, however late — whatever value, great or small, they may place on human lives — that it frequently does not pay? Some of the reasons why this has not happened have been indicated in the preceding pages. As we have many times seen, it does not appear that there has been, in most periods, any serious attempt to balance possible gains against likely costs, or even accurately to assess the likelihood of victory. Governments that resort to war are not usually in a mood for calculations of this kind. They are often filled with passion, indignation, vengefulness of greed; inspired by patriotic estimates of the quality of native fighting men, weapons and strategies; and so inflated with over-optimistic conceptions of the prospects of success. These factors, as we have seen, have made governments sometimes ready to initiate war, against hopeless odds, against enemies far more powerful than they. Calculations of costs and benefits, if made at all, have been totally distorted by such subjective judgements.

There is another factor which affects calculations of this kind. Any assessment of costs and benefits must depend upon who pays the costs and who secures the benefits. In most ages the highest costs of war have been paid by common soldiers and their families, and to some extent by the armed forces generally (though among them officers and commanders have at least enjoyed a better chance of winning glory and promotion). Conversely, those who authorised wars, even unsuccessful wars, have paid little. Francis I lost four wars against Charles V, with no consequence to his throne and little to his reputation. Louis XIV lost little credit from his last two long and unsuccessful wars. Napoleon is still regarded by many with veneration, for all the death and destruction resulting from his wars, and despite their having ended in his total defeat. Against this the benefits of victory have gone mainly to those in positions of authority, often those responsible for launching the wars. Louis XIV won, as he himself often boasted, substantial "glory" from his wars, for all the sufferings they caused his people. It was Napoleon, not the people of France, who secured the greatest benefit, in power and reputation, from his victories; Frederick the Great, not the people of Prussia, who gained most glory from his. One thing differentiating the modern age from all previous ones is that those responsible for launching wars now bear risks - in the case of major wars at least — that are almost equivalent to those of the men who fight them. And it seems possible that this may affect the assessment by political leaders today of the likely costs and benefits to be had from war.

Another factor which can distort calculations of this kind is uncertainty: of costs as much as of victory. Even if a serious attempt is made to do so, it is not easy to calculate in advance how long a war is likely to last, how many allies will join on one side or the other, what will be the willingness of the enemy to reach a settlement, what a final peace treaty may provide, and what the eventual cost will therefore prove to be in blood and treasure: in other words, what will be the final price to be paid. In a substantial number of cases the costs which a particular war has involved have finally proved to be far higher than was ever imagined at the time that war began. It is unlikely the leaders in 1914 had any conception of the total level of casualties that would eventually result from the actions they then took. Nor is it surprising that they should have calculated as they did. The most recent wars between major powers, in 1866 and 1870, had been brief and relatively cheap. The general expectation was that any new war would also be quickly finished. If Germany's battle plan had succeeded, the war could well have been over by Christmas, as many had forecast. Would the cost then have been disproportionate to the gains acquired by the victorious powers? It is by no means certain that they would have thought so. As it turns out, Sir Norman Angell was proved right and his conclusions justified. But he could well have proved totally wrong: the costs incurred might have then been seen (at least by the victorious)) as entirely reasonable in proportion to the gains.

In other words, the assessment of benefits against costs can be affected not only by overestimates of the benefits but also by underestimates of the costs. In most times in the past even the maximum conceivable cost of defeat was not altogether unbearable. In the age of dynasties, even the most disastrous defeat was to some extent survivable. Only two years after total humiliation at Pavia, Francis I was again free and in a position to launch yet another war against his enemy. In subsequent ages the maximum costs have steadily increased. Even Louis XIV found the sufferings of 1709-10 far beyond what he had imagined possible, as did Frederick the Great those of 1760-1. The cost to France — and especially Paris — of defeat in 1871 was much greater than any had foreseen. The consequences to Germany of defeat in 1918 and 1945 were still greater, and far above what even her foolhardy leaders can have envisaged. Today the possible costs of war for a major power, if it were fought with all the weapons available, are still further beyond what any leader could believe proportionate to the gains which victory could procure.

It is the secular increase in the possible costs of war which has caused governments in recent years to go to such lengths to limit, in scale and intensity, the kind of wars which they fight. It is not only that the use of nuclear weapons is avoided by nuclear powers, even in adversity (as in Vietnam). They avoid all the more lethal types of weapons; avoid equipping their allies with the most advanced weapons; and even refrain from large-scale bombing of cities. To match this limitation of costs there is often a corresponding limitation of potential gains. Warfare is confined entirely within a single state or a limited geographical region. Demands for major concessions — large-scale territorial changes or major economic concessions — are generally avoided. Force is used in limited ways, in limited areas, and for limited ends.

Thus the gains to be had from war have varied considerably from one period to another. And the gains that have actually been acquired have often been quite different from those expected before war began. If calculations have been made of potential benefits, to be measured against possible costs, they have in many cases proved fallacious, not only because in a large number of cases wars have been lost by those who initiated them, but also because even wars that have been won have had quite different consequences from those expected. Over the years the maximum possible costs of defeat have sharply risen. Yet the gains likely to be acquired have not increased proportionately.

It would none the less be rash to assume that for these reasons war is less likely to be chosen as a course of action in future years. As we have seen, there is little evidence that in the past any careful calculation of the balance between the two has ever been made. Though most governments are more prudent today, non-rational considerations may continue to be powerful among some. The highest level of war will certainly continue to be avoided — since potential gains can never, in that case, even in victory, match the potential cost. But lesser uses of force may continue to be chosen when those who wield power within states believe they can secure advantage, for themselves or their countries, as a result.

It is because governments have continued to make war where they have seen potential advantage from doing so that, over the centuries, attempts have been made to devise procedures for resolving conflicts among states. It is to the different forms that these procedures have taken in different international societies and their relative success in containing warfare among states, that we must turn in the chapter that follows.

7 Procedures

Whether or not warfare has produced profit for the victors, it has always produced serious costs for the losers. In addition it has produced disruption and insecurity for international society generally. For this reason almost every society of states that has been known has sought to develop procedures for reducing the effect of armed conflict among its members.

These procedures have been of a number of kinds. Almost everywhere facilities have been developed for *communication*. Though communication in itself cannot ensure that a peaceful settlement will be reached, without it disputes cannot be discussed at all. So, from the earliest times, messengers have been sent from one state to another, to propose a parley or suggest terms for an understanding; and almost the first rules developed have been those surrounding the treatment of messengers and provision for their safe conduct. As the need for contact has grown, the system of communication has been extended. Envoys have been sent more frequently and more regularly; resident embassies have been established; finally, foreign offices have been organised to control the conduct of foreign affairs.

But arrangements for communication have not in themselves been enough to secure peace. They can as easily be used to issue threats as to negotiate agreements. Secondly, therefore, arrangements designed to secure settlements have been devised. In almost every society of states of which we have knowledge the help of *third parties* in promoting agreements has been invoked. Procedures for mediation, arbitration and good offices have been established to resolve disputes and bring an end to conflicts.

Without effective sanctions for imposing settlements, however, these too may fail to promote peace. One or other of the parties — especially the stronger — might reject all the proposals made and seek to resolve the conflict by armed force alone. Thirdly, therefore, other arrangements, based on the assumption that in the long run peace will only be maintained by force, have been established. Under these, all members of the community have been expected to conduct their policies, and choose their partners, in such a way as was most likely to deter action to disrupt the peace by other members. In other words, policies have been pursued and alliances formed designed to mobilise concerted power against the principal threat to the peace:

273

that is, to maintain the *balance of power* that would best deter resort to force by any state.

In time these three methods have been supplemented by a fourth, designed to mobilise greater and better organised pressures against aggressive action: the creation of multilateral arrangements through which *collective action* to keep the peace might be undertaken. On the one hand, these might examine disputes and seek appropriate means for resolving them; on the other, they could organise the joint use of force to contain or deter aggressive actions.

All of these four principal types of procedure for maintaining peace have been used to some extent in all of the different international societies we have been examining. The form that each has taken, however, and the choice made between them, has varied from one society to another, according to their principal preoccupations: that is, according to the international ideology of each. A dynastic society has required the type of procedure that would best resolve conflicts on the issues about which dynasts have mainly disputed. A society preoccupied by religious concerns has required the kind of procedure that would best resolve disputes on that question. A society concerned with sovereignty has required the procedures that would best overcome the differences among competing sovereign states, each asserting absolute power within its own borders and recognising no external authority. And so on. Each has thus, as we shall see, chosen a different combination among the various types of procedure that are available.

A number of questions thus need to be considered about the role of these procedures in containing war. First, which *kinds* of procedure or institution have been adopted in each age? Why have the ruling groups of different types in different international societies favoured one set of institutions rather than another? How have these been related to other features of each of the societies we have examined?

Secondly, what has been the aim of these institutions in each age? How have they reflected the general motivations of states within each age? Have they been intended simply to discuss war; to civilise it; to reduce it; or to abolish it altogether? Have they been well adapted to those purposes?

Thirdly, how well have any of these institutions succeeded in their aims? Have they in fact been able to modify the behaviour of states, to civilise their methods of conducting warfare, or even to reduce the incidence of war among any or all nations?

Finally, what are the reasons for their relative success or failure? Are there any particular kinds of institution that can generally be expected to prove more successful than others in influencing the way that nations behave and in lessening their propensity to war? What does the history of the various procedures established over the years demonstrate about the type of institution that can generally be expected to be most successful in regulating the conduct of war?

In this chapter we shall look at some of the evidence which may help to provide answers to these questions.

The age of dynasties (1400-1559)

The procedures developed in our first international society were inevitably those appropriate to an age of dynasts in a semi-feudal age.

In such an age the first requirement was direct communication between the rulers who controlled the destinies of each state. Since it was they who reached decisions concerning war and peace, it was contact between them that was mainly required.

Such communication was brought about mainly through the developing network of diplomacy. Well before this age began, envoys were being sent from one ruler to another — to present respects, to celebrate a marriage, or to negotiate an alliance on their master's behalf. At the beginning of our period, for the first time, ambassadors began to be sent to reside permanently in the other state concerned: the duke of Milan, for example, was sending such resident envoys before the end of the fourteenth century. They were sent not to seek peace but to promote the interests of their own state. As the Venetian Barbaro, who served his country as ambassador to the emperor and to the pope, put it, "The first duty of an ambassador is exactly the same as that of any other servant of government, that is, to do, say, advise and think whatever may best serve the preservation and aggrandisement of his own state."[1] For that purpose Ferdinand of Aragon sent ambassadors to the five courts which he hoped to recruit into his alliance against France; Venice sent them especially to the states of Italy which she hoped to mobilise against Milan;[2] and so on. Though their aim therefore was to promote friendship with one state, this was often done in order to make war more effectively against another. And, though they helped to promote communication between particular rulers, they did little to promote peace more generally.

Ambassadors were personal envoys of the rulers, and were thus accredited not to a state but to a court. They presented credentials, establishing them as the personal emissary (sometimes entrusted with "full powers") of their ruler. An ambassador's credentials might declare that he was sent to "extend the ancient friendship between our two kingdoms", or "because of the loyalty and affection with which my father and I have always held you".[3] Ambassadors were thus the intermediaries through which the dynasts themselves could negotiate with each other if they chose to do so. And the understandings they arrived at were thus highly personal agreements: undertakings made by one prince to another, to keep peace with each other or make war against another.

Just as ambassadors were personal envoys sent from one ruler to another, treaties were also in this age essentially personal arrangements between the rulers. It was the honour and good faith of each ruler personally that gave them force. Sometimes a treaty would consist of undertakings that were dependent on the fulfilment of corresponding pledges by another: the payment of a ransom (such as that which Francis I had to pay to redeem his two sons, whom he had given as hostages in his own place in 1526), or of an indemnity (such as Louis XI agreed — but failed — to pay to Edward IV in 1475). The failure of one party to fulfil his obligations would, it was generally held, release the other party from his. These material sanctions were reinforced by elaborate oaths, under which each ruler promised himself hideous penalties if he failed to fulfil his obligation (when James IV of Scotland made war against England in violation of an oath, he asked the pope for dispensation to relieve him of these penalties). Another way out was to take a contrary oath in private: Francis I, when a captive of Charles V, made a secret oath to his supporters to release him from his undertakings. In the same way the Council of Ten in Venice, after her defeat by the League of Cambrai in 1510, recorded a secret decision that, since the terms of the treaty had been extorted by armed force, they were not bound by them; and thus subsequently repudiated the treaty. Maximilian I broke the oath he made to the people of Bruges after he had been captured by them in 1488, on the grounds that it had been extorted under duress, and claimed imperial warrant (he was the emperor's son) for doing so. The procedures for securing peace were arrangements between individual rulers, therefore, and were dependent on the good faith each ruler was willing to demonstrate.

In the same way truces reached during the wars in this age were personal arrangements between the rulers concerned. They too were undertakings between princes, not between states. If one of the parties to such an agreement died, the truce too expired, unless it were renewed again with his successor: thus when Richard II was deposed in England, the truce he had made with France, on marrying a French princess, lapsed and had to be renewed with his successor. Sometimes truces were agreed for a year at a time; sometimes for longer periods, and they could continue for decades (the truce agreed between the Swiss Confederation and the Hapsburgs in 1512 was for 50 years). However, they were frequently broken long before the date of their expiry. The truce between England and France which was renewed for 28 years in 1396 was broken by Henry V in 1415; the truce of Nice between Charles V and Francis I of 1538, which was supposed to be for ten years, was interrupted by a renewal of the war only four years later. In 1526, Pope Clement VII broke the truce he had agreed with the emperor, Charles V, only two years earlier. And so on. Because they depended on good faith alone, such truces were a fragile instrument for sustaining peace in an age when good faith was not always to be relied on.

Royal marriage was another form of peace-making typical of this dynastic age. Marriages were frequently arranged between the royal families of the contending sides at the end of a war as a symbol of future peaceful intentions. So, on his conquest of France in 1420, Henry V himself married the daughter of the king he had just defeated in order that (as he put it in Shakespeare's play) "the contending kingdoms... May cease their hatred, and this dear conjunction / Plant neighbourhood and Christian-like accord / In their sweet bosoms". So too, under the treaty of Noyon in 1516, as a pledge of peace, Charles V had to undertake to marry the daughter of his successful enemy, Francis I. Conversely, after his defeat and capture at Pavia nine years later, Francis I was made to agree, as part of the peace terms, to marry the sister of the emperor as a pledge of future peaceful intentions. Charles V recommended to his son Philip in 1548 a marriage to the French king's daughter as a "living guarantee of peace and the treaties between them".[4] It cannot be said however that dynastic marriage was particularly successful in promoting peace (see p. 286 for a similar failure in the following age). Francis I, having agreed to marry Charles V's sister in 1525, immediately made war on his future brother-in-law, and was to make war twice more within 15 years of the marriage. James IV of Scotland, having married the daughter of the English king, proceeded to make war on his father-in-law a few years later. Charles V was continually at war with France despite the fact that his sister was queen of France and he himself was affianced at different times* not only to the daughter of Francis I but to both the sister and daughter of Louis XII (generations were rarely important in this age if the diplomatic need was great enough: Catherine of Aragon was seen as a possible wife for Henry VII between her marriages to his two sons;

---

* Charles V was affianced first (when he was two years old) to Claude, daughter of Louis XII, who eventually married Francis I instead; to Henry VIII's sister Mary (who eventually married Louis XII instead); to Louise, the daughter of Francis I (aged one); to Mary, the daughter of Henry VIII (subsequently his daughter-in-law); and finally to Isabella of Portugal. He was also nearly betrothed to the second daughter of Francis I (aged two) and to Anne of Hungary (who eventually married his brother). None of these ties, any more than the marriages of his sisters and nieces to almost every ruling family in Europe (see p. 137), managed to save him from constant war. Even blood relationships could not ensure peace: as we saw, Yolande, the regent of Savoy, joined an alliance against her own brother, Louis XI.

Charles V was betrothed at different times to both Henry VIII's sister and his daughter; Mary Tudor was betrothed both to Charles V and to his son; while Anne of Hungary was seen as an equally suitable bride either for Maximilian I or for his grandson Ferdinand).

Another procedure frequently used in this age was mediation. Again it was typical of an age of dynasts: an offer by one ruler to intercede between two of his fellow rulers who were in conflict. So, for example, Ferdinand of Aragon travelled to Edinburgh in 1489 to mediate between the kings of England and Scotland; while in 1533 Francis I mediated peace between Henry VIII and his nephew James of Scotland. Archduke Philip of the Netherlands, son of the Emperor Maximilian, tried to mediate between his parents-in-law, Ferdinand and Isabella, and Louis XII of France over Naples in 1501-2. Occasionally the Emperor was thought especially well suited to perform the function: the emperor Sigismund travelled to France and England to mediate between those two countries when war was imminent in 1415 (but somewhat prejudiced his impartiality when he decided instead to ally himself with England). The pope was often seen as a still more acceptable mediator, possessing an authority it was difficult to question. Several popes attempted to mediate between England and France in the Hundred Years War, and one brought about the congress of Arras in 1435, where the papal legate and the cardinal of Cyprus acted as presidents and mediators. Mediation, however, was rarely used (and was rarely seen in this age) as a means of preventing war from occurring in the first place. It was a procedure used almost entirely to secure a peace between countries that were already at war.

In some cases a more formal procedure was used. A conflict was submitted to arbitration which was binding. For example, under the treaty of Vienna in 1515, the king of Poland and the master of the Teutonic Order agreed to submit the dispute between them (about the allegiance which the former demanded from the latter) to arbitration by the emperor and the king of Hungary. In 1524 Lubeck arbitrated between Denmark and Sweden over their dispute concerning the rights of the king of Denmark in Sweden. Wolsey set himself up as arbitrator between Charles V and Francis I when he met both of them in Calais in 1521 (though in fact he used the occasion to negotiate an alliance for war with the emperor against the latter). Again the pope was a widely used authority for this purpose. Ferdinand of Aragon, for example, proposed that the pope should arbitrate between England and France in 1513, while Henry VIII wanted him to arbitrate between Ferdinand and Venice in 1508-9. But the pope was no longer seen as invariably impartial in disputes that came before him. It was generally believed that Spain appealed to the pope for judgement concerning the division of the Americas in 1493 because a Spanish pope (Alexander VI) was likely to be favourable to her claim (he was). For this reason, although "theoretically the papacy was an international arbiter ... no one believed in this practice, and only a power which had reason to believe that the pope would arbitrate in its favour was prepared to submit to his decision."[5] (The pope's unreliability as an arbiter is indicated by the fact that Julius II, having been asked to mediate between Henry VIII and Ferdinand of Aragon in 1513, assured Ferdinand privately that he would make no award that had not been cleared with him in advance.)

Peace might be secured for a particular state by establishing its neutrality. A ruler or city which wished to avoid becoming implicated in a particular conflict could insulate itself in this way. Under the peace of Donchery of 1492, for example, the city of Liège won a recognition of its neutrality after years of conflict. During the war of the Holy League of 1512-13, Margaret, the regent of Burgundy, declared the neutrality of that territory in the war her father, the Emperor Maximilian, was fighting with France. Occasionally neutrality was adopted on a more permanent basis. In the "Eternal Peace" of Fribourg in 1516, the Swiss, having been badly defeated by the French at Marignano, adopted the policy of neutrality which they were to preserve ever afterwards, though this was not formally acknowledged by other states until 300 years later, and Swiss soldiers continued to fight in many of the wars of other states, occasionally, as in 1520, on both sides (their ubiquity could cause embarrassment for those they fought for; in 1500 Swiss mercenaries deserted Lodovico of Milan to avoid fighting against their compatriots fighting for the Confederation).

Another procedure typical of an age of dynasts was summit meetings between the rulers themselves. The hope was that, as Charles V once wrote to Wolsey, the rulers might "be able to do more in a day's personal conversation than their ambassadors in months".[6] The difficulty of travel and the obvious risks entailed did not make such encounters easy. John the Fearless of Burgundy, attempting such a meeting with the French king at Montereau in 1419, was brutally assassinated. Louis XI, travelling to Péronne for negotiations with his enemy, Charles the Bold in 1468, found himself for a time held prisoner there. On the whole, rulers were not much deterred by the risks. Lorenzo the Magnificent was widely admired for his courage in setting out, despite these dangers, to negotiate peace with his enemy the duke of Naples in 1479. Louis XI and Edward IV met personally at Péquigny in 1475 to negotiate peace between them after the latter's invasion in that year. In the next century such meetings became still more common. Louis XII met his rival and enemy Ferdinand of Spain at Savona in 1507 to discuss a settlement in Italy. The high point of the summit meeting came in the years around 1520, when Europe was again threatened by a renewal of continental war. The successive meetings between Charles V and Henry VIII in May 1520, between Henry and Francis I in the following month (at the Field of the Cloth of Gold) and between Henry and Charles immediately afterwards, followed by the conference called at Calais by Wolsey in the following year and yet another meeting between Charles and Henry in May-June 1522, represented the most intensive high-level diplomacy seen until that time. But such meetings did not necessarily produce peace. The meetings of 1520-2 were followed almost immediately by a major war (partly planned during their course). The meeting between Charles and Francis at Aigues Mortes in 1438 was used largely to discuss joint action against common enemies (the Turks, the Lutherans and Henry VIII): but it could not overcome their own deep-seated rivalries — within four years they were themselves once again at war.

Occasionally wider meetings were called: to bring together representatives of a large number of the rulers of the age. Such "congresses" were called mainly to conclude peace at the end of a war. But occasionally a meeting could take place while a war still continued. During the Hundred Years War the pope and the council of Basle helped convene the congress of Arras in 1435, which was intended to discuss peace between England and France (but which eventually only produced peace between France and Burgundy). Seven years later, in 1443, Filippo Maria Visconti called a congress of all the major Italian powers to consider what action they should take against Francesco Sforza, at that time conducting a war against the pope. In 1454 Pope Nicholas V called a congress of Italian powers to discuss a settlement of the war that had engulfed almost the whole of Italy two years earlier: a meeting which resulted in the establishment of a new collective security system in Italy (see below). A few years later Pope Pius II convoked a congress at Mantua, designed to discuss a new crusade against the Turks. Wolsey's conference in Calais in 1521 was intended to bring about the restoration of the peace of Europe by reconciling Charles V and Francis I.

Sometimes such meetings resulted in the establishment of more formal international arrangements for maintaining the peace. There had for many years been proposals for the establishment of some general league among Christian states. Already in the fourteenth century Father Dubois has proposed the creation of a "common council" of Christian sovereigns, who would forswear war with each other and agree to settle their disputes by arbitration, with the pope as final arbiter. However, peace was not the primary aim, since the purpose of the council was to organise more effectively war against the Turks, and it was made clear that Dubois's own country, France, was to be the council's acknowledged leader.* In 1455 the treaty of Venice, to which all the states of Italy acceded, established a kind of collective security system; they agreed to consult together immediately about any threat to the peace, to defend each other's territories, to take joint action against any aggressor, and to join no treaty or alliance that was not in accordance with these arrangements, while any member states which attacked another would be immediately expelled from the league. In 1495 the pope established a "holy league", designed in theory to promote peace and to repel the Turks, but in practice intended mainly to clear Italy of its French invaders. Pope Julius II established another "holy league" in 1511, which again had as its main purpose the expulsion of the French from Italy, while Pope Clement VII helped form a similar one to eject Charles V in 1526-7. In the treaty of London in 1518, perhaps the most ambitious of all these schemes, Wolsey established a collective security league designed to preserve the peace of Europe. Though agreed in the first place between England and France, the emperor, Spain and the pope soon joined, and the league was opened to Portugal, Denmark, Hungary, Scotland and the Swiss Confederation. In theory it was eventually to include all the nations of Europe and it contained provisions for joint consultation in case of war, for the arbitration of disputes, and for joint sanctions against an aggressor.[8] Finally a new Italian league was set up by Pope Clement VII and Charles V in 1532. All the member states agreed to defend the existing territorial settlement and to protect each other against attack; joint forces were established under a single commander-in-chief (Leyva) and each state was to pay a set contribution to maintain the force.

None of these various arrangements, however admirable in theory, proved very successful in maintaining the peace of the continent. The treaty of Venice, though it preserved peace in Italy for a decade or so, was rapidly forgotten as soon as the old disputes re-emerged. The popes' successive holy leagues were intended for war rather than for peace. The treaty of London maintained the peace of Europe for only a year or two before war was resumed between France and her enemies: none of the undertakings the treaty contained for consultation and peaceful settlement was implemented, let alone able to preserve the peace. The Italian league of the 1530s was never proper-

---

* A substantial measure of self-interest is evident also in other such proposals. George Podiebrad of Bohemia in 1458 proposed a perpetual union of Christian princes against the Turks with a federal parliament of princes and a combined army; but his main purpose was to resist the pretensions of his enemies, the emperor and the pope. In the same way, Sully's Grand Design, to be published in 1638 but written 30 years earlier, proposing a federal council to settle disputes and organise war against the Turks, was explicitly designed to bring about a reduction in the Hapsburg power and territories.[7]

ly put into effect, and Clement's successor, Paul III, was soon himself engaged in a war of aggression against Castro.

None of these various procedures, therefore, did much to reduce the incidence of warfare in this age. In consequence some states began to look to a new strategy for protection against threats from the more powerful. This was to combine with neighbours to fight the greatest apparent threat to the peace. From almost the beginning of this period the chief Italian states had adopted this policy. Florence, a middle state both in power and geographical situation, was often able to play the part of balancer: during the first half of the century she joined (three times) with Venice to resist the expansion of Milan; from 1551, when Venice itself appeared the greater threat, she joined with Milan and others to resist her. In the second half of the century the five main states of the peninsula (Venice, Milan, Florence, the Papacy and Naples) continually joined in different combinations to prevent any other from securing domination. As Francesco Gucciardini, writing in the early sixteenth century, put it, "it was the aim of each of the five major powers to preserve its own territory and to defend its own interests by carefully making sure that none of them became strong enough to enslave the others".[9] In a similar way, to counter the aggressions of Charles the Bold in the 1470s, Burgundy's neighbours — the Swiss Confederation, Lorraine, the Tyrol and the Swabian League — joined a coalition to contain and overcome her. By the end of the century the principle was being increasingly applied to the wider international scene. The Papacy, a weak state especially vulnerable to domination by the powerful, played a prominent part in bringing such combinations about. Pope Alexander VI mobilised the most powerful states of Europe (the emperor, Spain, Venice and Milan) to join in ejecting Charles VIII from Italy after his conquest of Naples in 1494; Julius II organised the League of Cambrai to drive Venice from northern Italy in 1508; the same pope created the Holy League to drive France from Milan in 1511-12; while the treaty of Mechlin created a still larger alliance against the French in 1513. From that point on, during the great duel between the Hapsburgs and the Valois, such powers as England, Venice, Genoa, and the Papacy shifted alliance regularly to create leagues against the main threat to peace: joining Charles against Francis in 1520 after the latter had conquered Milan; and joining Francis against Charles (in the League of Cognac) after the latter's triumph at Pavia (Henry VIII made war against France in 1512-13; joined with France in planning war against the Hapsburgs in 1515; made war against France once more in 1522-4; joined with France against the emperor in 1526-8; and again switched to the emperor against France in 1544). Even the Turks and the Scandinavian powers were occasionally brought in to maintain the balance: the former were invited by Naples to help her against

France in 1500, and by France to undertake "parallel action" against Charles in 1526 and 1537; while Sweden and Denmark were induced to join Francis I against Charles when others held aloof in 1542. Though not yet as systematic as it was to be made in later years, therefore, the creation of coalitions to restore the balance of power was already in this age regularly used as a means of containing major threats to the stability of the system.

So even at this time tentative steps were being taken to reduce the instabilities of international society and to create a less warlike world. In an age of personal rulers, depending on personal allegiance, many of these procedures depended on personal agreements among them. Thus they created diplomatic contacts to facilitate communication; they entered into pledges of peaceful conduct in treaties and truces; they contracted dynastic marriages to foster amicable relations; they took part in personal summit meetings; they personally undertook mediation and arbitration; and occasionally they explicitly recognised the neutrality of particular states. Sometimes they would conduct their own alliance policy in such a way that, by the creation of coalitions against the major threat, aggressive warfare might be contained or at least resisted.

It cannot be said that, even together, these measures did much to reduce the incidence of warfare, which remained endemic. However, this was not, for the most part, their intention. Few believed, and not all hoped, that warfare could be abolished as a feature of human existence. Procedures themselves could do nothing to keep the peace where there was still such a widespread will to war. The procedures established were designed mainly to facilitate contacts, to establish understandings, to discuss issues in dispute. But what they could not create was a desire for compromise. And by most it was still taken for granted that, if no agreement were forthcoming, the disputes that arose would have to be decided eventually by the final arbitrament of armed combat.

The age of religion (1559-1648)

With the emergence of a new type of international society, concerned above all about questions of religion, new kinds of procedures came to be needed. Many of the conflicts on that question began (like those concerning ideology 300-400 years later) within states. In the first place, therefore, it was procedures for resolving domestic conflicts of that kind that were required.

In a number of countries where religious controversies were acute, conferences were called, intended to seek some *modus vivendi* between contending faiths. Often the rulers themselves were responsible for calling these. In France Catherine de Medici, the queen mother, and her son Charles IX convened in September 1561 the colloquy of Poissy, which brought together spokesmen for the protestant faith (notably the Calvinist Theodore Beza, fresh from Geneva) and the leaders of the Catholic church in France, in an attempt to bring about reconciliation. In Germany the Emperor Maximilian II, equally concerned about the effect of religious conflict in weakening the fabric of the Empire, sought at the resumed Council of Trent to produce compromise solutions (p. 147 above). In Poland, Sigismund II convened the congress of Thorn in 1645 to promote debate between protestants and Catholics in that country.

Sometimes it was parliaments that took the initiative. In Poland the *sejm* itself at its convocation diet of 1573 discussed, and eventually determined, the principles that should govern relations between the faiths. In the Netherlands the states-general, in the pacification of Ghent of 1576, established for a time a system of mutual toleration between protestants and Catholics. Sometimes agreement was achieved directly between leaders of the different religions themselves. Thus in Poland the consensus of Sandomir of 1570 brought about agreement for mutual toleration among the various protestant denominations; and in 1596 the congress of Brest between the Orthodox and Catholic churches established the "Uniate" faith as a compromise between them.

Measures of this kind did sometimes succeed in establishing a basis of coexistence. Sometimes it was a royal decree that secured this. In France, the edict of Nantes laid down, more fully and more finally than earlier agreements, the precise rights that were to be enjoyed by the Huguenots, including their right to specified places of worship, to fortified towns for self-defence, to special legal protection and civil rights. In Bohemia, Rudolf's Letter of Majesty of 1609 guaranteed full religious freedom to the various reformed sects; while his brother Matthias, as king of Hungary, accorded a similar recognition to protestant churches there. In a number of cases national parliaments succeeded in establishing a system of toleration. The Transylvanian Diet in 1571 formally established equal religious rights in that country for Catholics, Lutherans, Calvinists and Unitarians. Two years later the Polish diet established the Confederation of Warsaw, under which it was agreed that, "in order to avoid sedition such as comes to other kingdoms ... all of us of differing religions will keep the peace between ourselves and shed no blood".

In some cases wholly new faiths were devised as a means of resolving the differences. So Anglicanism, as embodied in the 39 Articles of the Church of England, though more protestant than Catholic, was intended to have some appeal to members of both faiths. Arminianism in the Netherlands, in rejecting the Calvinist doctrine of predestination, represented a more moderate form of the reformed faith (and was attacked as crypto-Catholic by more extreme Calvinists in consequence). In Sweden, John III introduced a new form of Lutheran liturgy which was even more distrusted by many protestants as a surreptitious attempt to restore Catholic belief. In Germany in the decade before the Thirty Years War, so-called "syncretist" beliefs emerged, thought to combine the best features of Catholic and protestant doctrine. In Poland the Socinians, in a reaction to the doctrinal conflicts of the day, rejected all dogmatic theology and expounded a form of unitarian belief that had some appeal to Catholics and protestants alike. Since Calvinists and Lutherans distrusted each other almost as much as both distrusted Catholics, there were even new doctrines to bridge the gap between them too: for example, Philippism, a brand of the reformed religion which flourished for a time in Wittenberg, but was equally bitterly rejected by both parties. Rulers, concerned to reduce the conflicts dividing their subjects, sometimes gave endorsement to such compromise doctrines (as Elizabeth supported a modified protestant faith in England, James III a Catholicised one in Sweden, and as Oldenbarneveldt supported Arminianism in the Netherlands). Such doctrines were favoured too in many states by the *politiques,* the moderate people of the centre. But in the end nearly all these attempts foundered on the fanaticism of the age. The new doctrines, like the agreements for toleration so widely reached, were, almost everywhere, gradually swept away by the increasing intolerance of more simple and extreme faiths.

But religious conflict occurred not only within states but between them. In that case different types of understanding were required. Sometimes the answer was found in a form of partition: agreement on the practice of different faiths in different states. Since it was widely believed that to allow the practice of two faiths in the same state was a recipe for civil conflict, this seemed to many the only possible answer. Partition was in effect the principle underlying the peace of Augsburg, which had concluded the religious conflicts of Germany in 1555: Germany was to be divided between the Catholic and Lutheran faiths according to the wishes of each ruler (since there were no Calvinist rulers at that time there was no provision for that alternative, though in practice, as soon as Calvinist rulers appeared — for example in the Palatinate a few years later — that faith too had a share in the partition). That formula was formally reaffirmed, now on a tripartite basis, in the peace of Westphalia in 1648. In the Netherlands the pacification of Ghent in effect recognised a similar division between Catholic south and protestant north, though both agreed to co-operate for political purposes. In France the peace of Monsieur of 1576 recognised certain rights for the protestants outside Paris, including eight places of safety reserved to them, but reserved Paris for the Catholic religion. Partition of this sort was also sometimes the means of resolving international religious conflicts. So the Cleves-Jülich dispute of 1609-14 was ultimately resolved by letting one territory go to the protestant elector of Brandenburg and the other to a Catholic Neuburg (converted for the purpose).

Dynastic marriage was another device, formerly used to reduce differences between states, now adapted to help resolve conflicts between religions. In the very last year of the previous period it had been used for its traditional purpose, to bring some reconciliation between warring dynasties: the bitterly hostile Hapsburg and Valois dynasties had celebrated peace by intermarrying (as they were to do again exactly a century later, at the end of another long war, in 1659), though in neither case did the marriage produce much peace*. Now marriages were sometimes used to bridge the gap between religions. So Catherine de Medici deliberately married her Catholic daughter to the protestant Henry of Navarre in an effort to reconcile the warring faiths in France. In seeking to marry his protestant son to the Spanish infanta, James I of England was partly concerned to ease the division that religious conflict had created. But this was a measure which, as religious antagonisms increased, it became increasingly difficult to put into effect (the main reason why James I's plan finally foundered). Marriage with a royal family of another religion became increasingly taboo. After 1600 it was almost unknown. Increasingly dynastic marriages were used to strengthen solidarity between supporters of the same religion: so, for example, the devout Catholic Sigismund III of Poland demonstrated his faith by allying himself in two successive marriages to the equally ardent family of the Hapsburg emperor; the passionately protestant Orange family in the Netherlands married (twice) into the English royal family (though this did not prevent three successive wars between the two countries in the same period); the Vasas of Sweden sought only Lutheran consorts; the Hapsburgs of Spain and Austria only Catholic ones.

Summit meetings, another peace-making device formerly used to reach understandings between sovereigns, were also now used for religious purposes. Between states they became increasingly rare in this age: often made impossible by the religious chasm.

The era of personal interviews closed abruptly. Queen Elizabeth never left England. Once he got back from the Netherlands Philip II never left Spain. And Charles V was the last of the Hapsburg

---

* Though no royal families were so closely linked by marriage as these two, none made war on each other so frequently — of the three kings of Spain between 1556 and 1665, two had French queens; of the two kings of France between 1610 and 1715, both had Spanish queens: during that period the two countries went to war with each other six times.

emperors for a long time to cross the Alps or the Rhine. Catherine de Medici's attempt in 1564-5 to revive personal diplomacy . . . was fruitless and had no sequel.[10]

Between statesmen of the same faith, such meetings were still possible and often had a religious purpose. So the newly crowned Philip II of Spain could meet Henry II of France at Cateau-Cambrésis in 1559, and it was widely believed that they had used the occasion to plan a new crusade to recover Europe for the Catholic faith; just as the meeting between Catherine de Medici and the duke of Alva six years later at Bayonne was equally widely seen as designed to discuss the further stages of that campaign. On the protestant side, the meeting between Christian IV of Denmark and Gustav Adolph of Sweden in February 1629 was concerned with planning the protestant response to Catholic advances in Germany. Within the rival religious alliances such meetings had their uses. Between them — where they were most needed — they could scarcely take place at all; let alone secure a settlement.

The traditional procedures for resolving conflict were transformed in this new type of society. Diplomacy, the most long-established procedure for resolving disputes, was crippled by the religious divide. Diplomatic relations across that gulf were now often difficult or impossible.

As religious issues came to dominate political ones, any negotiations with the enemies of one state looked more and more like heresy and treason. The questions which divided Catholics from protestants had ceased to be negotiable. Consequently . . . diplomatic contacts diminished. Special embassies continued to go back and forth from time to time between powers in opposing ideological camps, but they were less frequent, and instead of expanding, the network of resident embassies actually contracted.[11]

Ambassadors from states regarded as heretical were often not given diplomatic status or were expelled (as was the Spanish Ambassador to London). Where they existed, they would often have close contact with the leaders of a religious minority, and with them undertake actions (as did the same ambassador) understandably regarded as seditious. There were acute conflicts about the right of such envoys to practise their own faith, even in the privacy of their own embassy chapels: England and Venice had no diplomatic relations for 40 years because of disputes on that question, and for a time no protestant power had a resident ambassador in Italy for the same reason.[12] As a result there was increasing recourse to less official channels: for example, to "agents" having only a quasi-diplomatic status. Even religious minorities would appoint such agents. They were, for example, able to negotiate "treaties", such as the treaty of Hampton Court negotiated between Elizabeth and the French Huguenots in 1562, and the treaty of Joinville negotiated between Philip II and the Catholic League in France in 1579. Meanwhile the traditional purpose of diplomacy, the negotiation of agreements between states, became, in an age of ideological conflict, increasingly difficult to perform. Even peace conferences could be split on religious lines: as at the Westphalia peace-making, when the Catholic powers congregated at Münster (where France was represented), while the protestant powers negotiated (together with Sweden) at Osnabrück.

The use of third-party settlement was also affected by the religious conflict. Though there was an increasing use during this age of mediation to resolve disputes, this too was limited by the religious divide. Mediation by the pope had, as we have seen, previously been the most commonly chosen. Among Catholic states this was sometimes still used. The pope mediated between Savoy and Spain over the first war of Mantuan succession in 1613-16; and he was one of the mediators, with Venice and Denmark, at the negotiation for the peace of Westphalia in 1644-8 (though ultimately disgusted at the outcome). A papal nuncio had a decisive effect in mediating between France and Spain when they negotiated the treaty of Vervins in 1598. When a protestant power was involved, however, an alternative mediator now had to be found. Increasingly this was a foreign ruler. The elector of Brandenburg mediated between Sweden and Denmark in 1644-5; the French king between Spain and the Netherlands in 1609 and between Sweden and Poland in 1629; the English king between Poland and the Turks in the 1590s and between Sweden and Denmark in 1612-13; the United Provinces between the same two powers in 1645. Even the emperor sometimes undertook the role: for example, he mediated between Spain and the Netherlands rebels in 1576-9. Sometimes more than one mediator was used: both the emperor and the king of France mediated between Sweden and her enemies in 1570; France, England and the United Provinces between Sweden and Poland in 1628-9. Occasionally the pope was now on the receiving end of mediation efforts: Henry IV of France mediated between the pope and Venice when they were in conflict over papal jurisdiction in 1606; and France mediated between Paul III and Parma over the former's attempts to acquire Castro by force in 1642.

Sometimes the more formal procedure of arbitration (under which a third party was asked to give a binding decision) was used. Among non-Catholic states a lay figure was now sometimes chosen for this too. In 1570 Sweden and Denmark agreed that the quarrel over the right to wear the three crowns (pp. 97-8) should be referred to arbitration by an imperial court. For Catholic states the pope was still frequently the authority referred to. So, under the treaty of Vervins in 1598, the pope was asked to arbitrate between France and Savoy about the future of Saluzzo; while his successor similarly arbitrated about the forts erected by Savoy in the Valtellina in 1626. But here too the religious divide caused problems. The Catholic lawyer Suarez claimed that the pope should have arbitral power over all Christian princes; the international lawyer Gentili, however, who was a protestant and lived mainly in England, refused to recognise the arbitral rule of the pope and recommended arbitration by "experienced judges".

The pope could take other action to promote peace. He could provide a (relatively) neutral peace-keeping force; as he did, at Spanish request, in the Valtellina in 1623.* The papal navy, together with that of the Knights of St. Stephen (which was also under ultimate papal authority), was used to control pirate activity off the Italian coast.[13] Finally, the pope could take international initiatives to promote peace: thus in 1634 Urban VIII proposed the convening of a great council of European rulers to agree on a system by which all disputes might be settled by arbitration. But the rejection of papal authority by all protestant and some Catholic powers (Spain, as well as France, was highly resistant to the authority of the pope during much of this period — Philip II, ardent Catholic though he was, would not even allow papal bulls to be published in Spain) sharply limited the effect which initiatives of this kind could have in promoting peace among European states.

The religious gulf even affected the effort to secure a balance of power, the third of our main categories of procedure. Here too the kind of balance that could be created was increasingly affected by religious loyalties. Alliances, which had previously been dictated by dynastic ties or by state interest, were now dependent largely on religious beliefs. Sometimes such leagues were formed originally as a form of self-defence. So the Evangelical Union in Germany was established in 1608 in direct response to the Catholic assault on Donauwörth in the preceding year; and it led immediately to the creation of the Catholic League in retaliation the year after. In the same way the creation of the Union of Arras in the southern Netherlands in 1579, to defend the Catholic provinces there from the infection of Calvinism, was quickly followed by the creation of the League of Utrecht by the protestant provinces of the north in the following

* Spain believed that France was planning an invasion but would not be willing to challenge papal authority. In fact France ejected the papal forces but later allowed them to return, so making it possible for Spain to retain the valley in friendly hands and safeguard the passage of her own forces.

year. Religion increasingly became the cement with which alliances were constructed. While alliances across the religious divide continued to be made — by Savoy and Venice, for example, and above all by France — the balance within the continent as a whole was increasingly one between religions. On the one hand stood the two great Hapsburg powers, united by religious ardour as much as by family ties: on the other, the protestant states of the North, all of which at one time or another supported (however feebly and hesitantly) the protestant cause in Germany. Thus the Hague convention of 1625 linked England, Denmark, the United Provinces and the Palatinate in resisting the threat posed by the alliance of Austria, Spain, Bavaria and the Catholic League, then threatening to overrun Germany. In other words, in this age the predominance of one religion needed to be matched by an alliance of the other, just as urgently as the predominance of one power might in other ages need to be so matched. Pope Sixtus V (himself a born balancer) recognised this need, saying, "Great Christian princes require a counterpoise; for if one prevailed the others run the risk of giving in over many things which he may ask for".[14]

Least affected by the religious division were the wider institutions. It was even possible to discern the beginnings of a system of multilateral diplomacy (the fourth of our categories of peace-making). Negotiations at the end of major wars could sometimes involve a large number of powers, including some that had taken no part in the preceding conflict. Spain, England and Scotland all took part in the conference at Stettin which brought the Scandinavian Seven Years War to an end in 1570, though they took no part in that war (mainly because their interests could be affected by the arrangements made concerning Baltic commerce). All the German states took part in the negotiations for the peace of Westphalia, whether or not they had been actively involved in the war; and altogether every significant power of Europe except England, Russia and Poland took part in that settlement. The idea began to emerge that only a major European congress of that sort could bring about major changes in the international system: for example, bring a state into existence and formally endorse its independence (as the peace of Westphalia did in the case of the Swiss Confederation and the United Provinces).

There even emerged a kind of embryonic system of collective security. Signatories of the peace of Westphalia all agreed to guarantee the settlement and, if necessary, to take up arms to defend it against any disturber (essentially the same principle on which the League of Nations was later to be based). At the same time a new constitution was established for the Empire. This was held by many to be part of the public law of Europe and was guaranteed not only by Sweden (now technically a German power, since she occupied German territory and was represented in the *Reichstag*) but also by non-German powers such as France. The idea that all European states, or at least all Christian states, belonged to a single system and were pledged to act together to defend it began slowly to emerge.

So, in a variety of ways, the institutions that were developed in this age reflected the character of a new international society. Because many of the most serious conflicts related to religion, some of the most important new procedures were those designed to resolve differences of that kind, both within states and between them. Conversely, a number of the older institutions were weakened by religious divisions. The importance of religion, paradoxically, reduced the role of religious authorities which were now often unable to resolve conflicts, as they had in the age before, because none was any longer universally recognised. As a result secular methods of mediation and arbitration, often by foreign rulers, became more common. The religious divide affected many other traditional devices: diplomacy, summit meetings, dynastic marriages, even the balance of power, each of which came to be employed in new ways. The division between warring sovereigns, which these institutions had originally been designed to bridge, was no longer the most important source of conflict. And for the division between religions, which increasingly replaced it, it was much harder to find the concessions and compromises on which peace-making must always ultimately depend.

The age of sovereignty (1648-1789)

The establishment of a new international system at the peace of Westphalia brought a new attempt to establish mutually accepted procedures for resolving conflicts. That settlement had asserted state power to replace the authority of dynasties and religions (even religious beliefs were to be decided on the basis of state authority). The new institutions now set up were thus those of sovereign states, and were designed to regulate the kinds of conflicts that occurred between such states.

Communication between states, the first type of arrangement we identified, was substantially improved. The congress of Westphalia established new rules concerning the way diplomatic relations should be conducted. Arrangements which had previously been spasmodic, and had been interrupted recently by religious differences, were now regularised. The grades of diplomatic envoy became standardised (ambassadors, extraordinary and ordinary envoys, ministers plenipotentiary, residents and diplomatic agents); rules concerning the treatment they were to be accorded won wider acknowledgement (though the precise privileges each government would grant still depended on bilateral rather than multilateral agreements); the immunity of diplomatic communications was more firmly established;* and it became generally accepted that the persons and households of all such representatives were inviolable and beyond the law of the host states. But there could still be conflicts concerning such matters; and these could sometimes be the cause of war. The dispute between Louis XIV and the pope concerning the right of embassies at the Vatican to harbour political refugees indirectly helped to cause the Nine Years War. Disputes concerning precedence and status several times caused armed conflict (p. 105 above). But at least there now emerged a regularised system for diplomatic communications, normally conducted through resident embassies rather than roving envoys, and controlled from the foreign ministries that came to be generally established.[15] That system became the principal instrument for negotiation on questions on peace and war.

For the more important negotiations there was a resumption of the use of *summit meetings:* direct meetings among heads of states. In most cases it was still the rulers who controlled foreign policy (p. 153 above). Often more absolute than ever in their power, they, and they alone, could fully commit their states. On these grounds Peter the Great (echoing the words of Charles V) told Augustus II of Saxony that the two of them could "achieve more in an hour than our ministers could accomplish in a month". Problems of protocol and of communication made such meetings still relatively rare; but this meant that, when they did occur, great importance was attached to them. Ambassadors were frequently known to be in the pay of other powers, and, even if they were not, their communications were frequently intercepted and decoded. Thus it was only in face-to-face meetings that total security could be expected. Such meetings were therefore often the most favourable occasions for planning wars. It was at a personal meeting at Rewi that Peter the Great and Augustus of Saxony planned the war against Sweden which was launched two years later. If a sovereign could not attend in person, close relatives could play a part. So Henrietta, sister of Charles II, was instrumental in concluding England's alliance with France for war against the Dutch in 1670; just as Marie Antoinette, daughter of Maria Theresa, sought to win France's support for her native country in the War of the Bavarian Succession.[16] Frederick the Great's brother, Prince Henry, agreed with Catherine the Great the first partition of Poland,

---

* Frederick the Great was generally considered to have committed a grave breach of international law when, after invading Saxony in 1756, he broke open the Saxon archives to prove that she had been planning war (though two centuries later such action was taken for granted at the end of the Second World War).

while his sister, queen of Sweden, sued for peace with her brother on behalf of her adopted country in 1763. Sometimes sovereigns sent their own personal envoys to other rulers to resolve conflicts between them: so Maria Theresa sent her own special ambassador (behind the back of her son, the emperor) to Frederick the Great to secure a settlement of the War of the Bavarian Succession. Both for starting and stopping wars, therefore, the old tradition of direct personal communication between sovereigns was still widely used.

Procedures for third-party settlement were also developed. Previously, as we have seen, *mediation* had often been undertaken by the pope or other ecclesiastical figures. In this age of sovereignty, that became far rarer. It was now undertaken more and more by the sovereigns themselves or by their representatives. In that form it became extremely common. So the English king was asked to mediate in the war between France and Spain in 1684; the maritime powers mediated between Sweden and Denmark in 1689; Sweden mediated between France and her enemies in 1694-7; the maritime powers between Russia and Turkey in 1711-13 (in rivalry with their current enemy, France); France mediated between Sweden and Russia in 1719-20, and between Austria and the Turks (most unfavourably to Austria) in 1739; Britain mediated between Prussia and Austria in 1741-2; France and Russia between the same two powers in 1778; and so on. These are only examples of a widespread phenomenon. Mediation, however, was still not generally seen as a way of preventing war. It rarely took place before a war broke out. In almost all these cases it occurred while a war was in progress; and it was designed to explore mutually acceptable terms for a settlement rather than as a means of avoiding fighting altogether.

Occasionally use was made of binding *arbitration*. The peace treaty which ended the first war between the United Provinces and England provided for arbitration by the Swiss cantons of any claims relating to commercial and colonial damage from 1611 onwards which the two countries were unable to resolve bilaterally. France proposed arbitration by England in her dispute with Spain over Luxemburg in 1682-3. It was, however, in this age, a relatively unusual proceeding. Most governments were reluctant to commit themselves in advance to a settlement which might be unwelcome to them. And there was no longer any universally recognised authority for performing the task. The pope was not only unacceptable to most protestant powers: Catholic countries too (notably France) would no longer necessarily accept his authority. There were other hazards. In an age in which sovereignty was so strongly asserted there was reluctance to allow important questions to be decided by outside parties. To accept arbitration could be taken to admit doubt about one's own case or sovereign rights: thus, when the French governor of Canada, in a dispute with the Iroquois Indians in 1683-4, sought arbitration from the British governor of New York, he was disgraced and dismissed for having cast doubt on French rights in this way.[17]

A new method used for containing war was the *neutralisation* of particular areas. In a period of continual warfare, it was understandable that some states should seek to insulate themselves by declaring their neutrality. So, during the Nine Years War the so-called "Third Party" of north German states declared their neutrality; and in the War of the Austrian Succession George II signed a convention (in total disregard of his obligations to his ally, Austria) providing for the neutrality of his electorate, Hanover. But a new development was that neutralisation was now frequently declared by outside powers. During the Nine Years War the neutralisation of the whole of Italy was agreed between France and Savoy (under the treaty of Turin, 1696) and was later recognised by the other belligerents. Similarly, in the Great Northern War, under the Hague convention of 1710, Britain, the United Provinces, Russia, Denmark, as well as the emperor and other German powers, agreed to the neutralisation of Germany. In 1756 Britain and Prussia, under the treaty of Westminster, jointly proclaimed (without consultation with other German states) the neutrality of the whole of Germany, and agreed to combine forces to prevent the passage of foreign troops through any part of it. Such agreements often favoured some external powers more than others. The neutralisation of Germany during the Great Northern War was directed in the first place against Sweden and later against Russia, each of which were feared to have designs on German territory. The neutralisation of Naples during the War of the Austrian Succession suited Britain (and was largely imposed by her) but was most unwelcome to her ally Austria, which at the time was planning to conquer the territory as compensation (or *dedommagement,* as Maria Theresa termed it) for the loss of Silesia.[18]

The most important change, at least in the eyes of most of the statesmen of the age, was a far more systematic use of our third system, the *balance of power*. This was now widely seen as the most efficient means of maintaining the peace. Frederick the Great described it as "the balance which is established in Europe by the alliance of many princes and states against the over-powerful and ambitious, a balance which is solely designed for maintaining the peace and security of mankind".[19] Walpole declared that "it is by leagues well concerted and strictly observed that the weak are defended against the strong. . . . By alliances . . . the equipoise of power is maintained." And the treaty of Utrecht stated explicitly in its preamble that it was designed to "confirm the peace and tranquillity of the Christian world through a just equilibrium of power (which is the best and most secure foundation of mutual friendship and lasting agreement in every quarter)". The system, however, was more successful in preventing undue dominance by any particular power than it was in securing peace. States had an obvious interest in combining for the former purpose. So, the year after the settlement of 1648, by which Sweden had become dominant in the Baltic, the United Provinces and Denmark entered into an alliance against her, an alliance joined by other powers when Sweden embarked on war in 1655. So, too, the League of the Rhine was established to resist imperial pretensions in Germany; successive coalitions were established against Louis XIV (in 1668, 1673-4, 1686-9 and 1701); and new coalitions were established against Russian domination of the Baltic in 1715-16; against a recently aggressive Prussia in 1756; and against Russia again (following her expansion in the Crimea) in 1789-90. But normally such coalitions were created only after conflict had already broken out. They were not usually effective, therefore (nor indeed designed), as a means of preventing wars. On the contrary, to put down the pretensions of the expansive power, war itself was usually required.

Nor was there much consistency about the way the system was used. There was no general tendency to combine against any country that attacked another. Some countries, for their own purposes, would ally themselves with the main threat to the peace rather than against it: as England and Sweden did with expansionist France in 1672, as Savoy did with the same country in 1696 and 1701; as France did with aggressive Prussia in 1740; and as Russia and France did with revanchist Austria in 1756. Traditional alliances, traditional enmities, above all the self-interest of the moment, induced a struggle of all against all rather than, as the collective security ideal demanded, one of joint action by all against any aggressor state.

More revolutionary was the development, in this age, of multilateral diplomacy. Over and above the system of bilateral diplomacy the custom grew up of convening from time to time — usually but not exclusively at the end of wars — general "congresses", which brought together the representatives of many states, sometimes including those not involved in the preceding conflict. The congress of Westphalia at the very beginning of the period had set the precedent for this: it had, as we have seen, been regarded as a collective undertaking to establish the peace of Europe. As a result it produced a settlement that governed the affairs of the continent for the next 150 years. It was widely quoted as the basis of European order. Even in 1778, a century and a half later, during the dispute over the Bavarian succession, both Austria and Prussia quoted France's obligations under the Westphalia settlement in seeking her assistance.[20]

In the age that followed there were a number of similar multilateral settlements. The terms of each had a collective authority. They represented legitimacy, the norm which was to be restored. In many cases the agreements were described, not as treaties, but as "peaces" — the "peace" of Westphalia, the "peace" of Nijmegen, Rijswijk or Utrecht or Paris, for example. The implication was that these were not merely temporary agreements but long-term settlements for a continental peace. In many cases they claimed to provide for "permanent" or even "perpetual" peace between the states concerned. Thus the Grand Alliance explicitly fought in the Nine Years War to reestablish the settlements of Westphalia and Nijmegen; and the treaty that brought that war to an end explicitly reaffirmed the terms of the peace of Nijmegen. The Quadruple Alliance of 1718 reaffirmed the provisions of the peace of Utrecht. Even powers seeking to change the *status quo* sought to justify their actions in terms of existing treaties. Thus the chambres de réunion, whose decisions awarded to France large parts of Alsace, used legalistic arguments said to be based on the relevant clauses of the peace of Westphalia (deliberately ambiguous) and the peace of Nijmegen.[21] Frederick the Great sought to justify his seizure of Silesia on the basis of agreements (relating only to four of its duchies) dating from the previous century. Spain and Britain, in fighting about trade to South America, both claimed to be demanding observance of the treaty of 1713 between them. The maxim, frequently quoted by international lawyers, *pacta sunt servanda,* provided one of the few bases that were recognised for regulating relations between states. And increasingly governments sought to show they were abiding by the terms of collective decisions to which they were parties.

General congresses of this kind sometimes took place even though war had not occurred. The so-called truce of Ratisbon of 1684 was not only a settlement of the brief conflict of 1683-4 between France and Spain but also a multilateral undertaking among other powers, not involved in that war, on quite unrelated questions (it formally recognised all French gains since 1678, but for 20 years only). The congress of Brunswick was called in 1712 to bring a settlement of the Great Northern War, even though the emperor, who called it, and other participants in the congress, had not taken part in that war. The congresses of Cambrai and Soissons (1724 and 1728-9) did not immediately follow major wars and were intended to resolve a number of outstanding problems facing the continent. In that sense such meetings foreshadowed the congress system as it developed in the following age (pp.299-305 below).

There even emerged, if briefly, a kind of elementary *collective security system.* The Quadruple Alliance of 1718, formed to counter Spanish aggression in that year, closely paralleled the Quadruple Alliance to be created almost exactly a century later. Both were originally intended to counter the main threat to the peace at that time (Spain and France respectively); and both were subsequently extended to include the very country against which they had been originally formed. Even the 1718 version applied the basic principle of a collective security arrangement. The three original signatories (it began as a Triple Alliance of Britain, France and Austria, but was subsequently joined by the United Provinces) agreed to create a "permanent union" between them and undertook to establish a defence pact to preserve that union, all determining "to attack whomsoever might contravene the treaties of Utrecht, Baden and London" (the treaties ending the War of the Spanish Succession), or might threaten the settlement to be reached at the subsequent congress ending Spain's war in Italy. Each signatory agreed to contribute 12,000 men to the arrangement, and to act jointly to "guarantee" the settlement established.

The use of *"guarantees"* of this kind, usually on a mutual basis, was another method that came to be widely used in the effort to maintain international security. The simplest kind of guarantee was the guarantee of territory. In their bilateral treaty of 1716, for example, Britain and France agreed to guarantee and defend each other's territories against hostile attack (a guarantee in which the United Provinces joined in the following year). Under the Bourbon family compacts of 1733 and 1743 France and Spain mutually guaranteed each other's territory, both within and without Europe. When Joseph I visited the Empress Catherine in 1780 they discussed a mutual guarantee of territories (which Catherine wanted extended to cover future conquests too[22]). These were bilateral undertakings. But such guarantees could be multilateral in character. The Quadruple Alliance contained mutual guarantees of this kind. And under the treaty of Aix-la-Chapelle in 1748 Frederick the Great secured a multilateral guarantee from all the signatories of his possession of Silesia (already acknowledged bilaterally by Austria in the treaty of Dresden three years earlier).

Somewhat similar in effect were guarantees of treaties. Often these were guarantees not by the parties to the treaty themselves but by some outside power. This, it was believed, could give greater strength and credibility to a settlement. So France was made a guarantor of the peace of Oliva between Sweden and Poland in 1660. The maritime powers, Britain and the United Provinces, became guarantors of the treaty of Altona between Sweden and Denmark of 1689 (under which Denmark restored the lands of the duke of Holstein-Gottorp); and both powers were accordingly called on by Sweden to enforce its terms when Denmark again invaded those lands in 1700. In some cases outside guarantees of treaties were made reciprocal: thus in this last case Britain and the United Provinces only agreed (provisionally) to implement their guarantee in return for a Swedish guarantee of the peace of Rijswijk (to which Sweden was not a party). Similarly, at the end of the War of the Spanish Succession, Sweden was only willing to guarantee the peaces of Baden and Westphalia in return for a renewed French guarantee of the peace of Oliva of 1660 (thus safeguarding Sweden's Baltic lands against Russia and Saxony-Poland). The provision of a guarantee by an outside power could of course give benefits to the guarantor as well as to the power guaranteed. By being made a guarantor of the provisions of the peace of Westphalia relating to Germany, for example, France acquired a position of influence in that area of which she was to take advantage for many years to come.

Another type of guarantee that had particular significance in this age was a guarantee of rights of succession. Given the frequency of conflicts over succession this too could be an important way of maintaining stability and avoiding war. Usually this was a guarantee of the right of an existing ruler. So, in the treaty of Utrecht, Louis XIV agreed not only to accept the rights of William and Mary in Britain but not to assist any action undertaken to overthrow them (a considerably stronger undertaking than he had made 15 years earlier in the peace of Rijswijk, in which he had merely recognised William III as king of Great Britain and Ireland but made no undertaking concerning his relations with the Stuart pretenders). Here too guarantees were often mutual: for example, in the Quadruple Alliance of 1718 all four signatories agreed to accept the succession in the others' states, previously the cause of bitter conflict in three cases (a commitment later joined by Spain). In 1728 Austria guaranteed Prussian succession in Berg against a Prussian guarantee of Maria Theresa's succession in Austria (pledges which each rapidly proceeded to violate). In some cases the guarantee was of *future* succession, in other words of a claim to be made against another state. For example, in 1768 Russia agreed to "guarantee" the succession of Prussia to Bayreuth and Ansbach when its ruler died. In the same way, under the family compact between France and Spain of 1733 France "guaranteed" the rights of Don Carlos (the son of the queen of Spain) in Palma, Piacenza and Tuscany, rights which that prince had yet to acquire.

Occasionally guarantees were even given not of a particular dynasty or ruler, but of a particular political system in another state. Thus Russia and Prussia in their treaty of 1764 agreed (without consultation with the countries concerned) to "guarantee" the constitutions of Sweden and Poland — constitutions they approved mainly because they were believed to weaken each of the countries concerned. Four years later in 1768, Russia again "guaranteed" the new constitution of Poland, also framed (mainly by herself) to suit her own advantage. In 1787 Prussia and Britain jointly "guaranteed" the constitution of the United Provinces (so strengthening the position of the *stadhouder*, William of Orange, to whom the royal families in both countries were related).

In other words, such guarantees, which might have been a source of stability, were used mainly not to promote peace but to promote the interests of the individual states that made them, in the universal contest among the powers. This was the underlying weakness of the procedures developed during this age. In appearance there was a great advance. For the first time widely recognised systems for conducting relations and resolving disputes emerged. Systematic contacts through permanent embassies in the major capitals; occasional meetings between sovereigns; multilateral conferences that examined the affairs of the continent; resort to mediation and even arbitration to resolve disputes — all these were now used more extensively than ever before and might in theory have made it more possible to resolve conflicts without resort to warfare. The emerging use of "guarantees" — whether of treaties, of territory, of succession, or even of a political system — could have had the same effect. So could the creation of a primitive collective security system, such as the Quadruple Alliance attempted. So, above all, might the systematic application of the widely proclaimed balance-of-power principle to deter aggression, as was sometimes urged. But in fact none could withstand the competitive struggle between states. Warfare remained endemic. As in every other age, institutions in themselves could achieve nothing without a corresponding determination to make them work: without, that is, an overriding desire for peace. That desire is precisely what was lacking. In many cases it was not even the intention that the new institutions should abolish war. Certainly it was not generally believed, whatever the theoretical intentions, that they could do so. The underlying assumption remained that the supreme object of national policy was to promote state interests; and that this would be done in peace if possible, but by war if necessary. So long as these assumptions were the dominant influence on policy, the new procedures and institutions, revolutionary though they were in some respects, were never likely to affect significantly the frequency of war.

The age of nationalism (1789-1917)

In the following age a still more spectacular development took place in the procedures used for containing conflicts between states.

In Europe especially, multilateral arrangements, of a kind barely seen before, began to emerge. It came to be generally accepted that conflict situations should be discussed not only by those countries immediately involved but by all the major powers of the continent. Statesmen began to talk seriously of the interests and needs not only of their own individual states but of the wider community ("Europe") to which all belonged.

These new arrangements began, as have most new international institutions at all times, from the experience of a major war. In 1814, at the conclusion of 20 years of conflict, the four main victors of the war against Napoleon pledged themselves, under the treaty of Chaumont, to take joint action together to prevent any breach by France of the settlement to be arrived at, each promising to supply a force of 60,000 men to keep the peace in this way. At the same time they agreed to meet together "at fixed intervals" (though the precise intervals were never fixed) "for the purpose of consulting upon their common interests, and for the examination of the measures which . . . should be considered most salutary for the repose and prosperity of the Nations and for the maintenance of the peace of Europe". In other words, the four powers set themselves up as the guardians of the peace of Europe. In practice the four quickly became five. Though the measures had been originally directed primarily against France, within three years France herself — the indemnity imposed on her having been paid and the occupation of her territories brought to an end — was invited to take part in the new arrangements.

It was originally envisaged that there should be a continuing series of "congresses", to be attended by heads of state, or at least by foreign ministers. In fact only three more meetings of that kind took place. Those meetings were devoted not to conflicts occurring between the participants, or between any of the states of Europe, but to political developments *within* states: especially revolutionary and nationalist movements in Naples and Spain (where the Austrian and French governments respectively were authorised to intervene to overthrow new governments proclaiming reformed constitutions there). The new institutions therefore became, instead of a means of peace-keeping, a system for maintaining the political *status quo* within the continent.

Since Britain was not prepared to take part in joint measures for this purpose, nor even to take part in collective decisions to that end, the congress system, as originally conceived, quickly came to an end.* After 1822 full-scale "congresses", attended by foreign ministers or above, took place only to consider settlements at the conclusion of wars: as at the congress of Paris in 1856 at the end of the Crimean War, and the congress of Berlin after the Balkan conflict in

---

* Britain did not disapprove of the principle of the intervention to overthrow revolutionary regimes — she endorsed actions by Austria for that purpose in Italy — but objected to such measures being the subject of collective decisions.

1875-8.* However, a system of intensive consultation among the five "powers" (the "Concert of Europe") about all important developments in the continent was still maintained.

For most of the period, apart from about twenty years after 1884, a series of *ad hoc* "conferences" took place, every two or three years or so on average, to consider particular conflict situations which had arisen and to devise mutually acceptable settlements. Normally these were attended by the foreign minister of the host state and the ambassadors of the other four powers (see Table 13 for a list of conferences).

In some respects the system so established was highly successful. Many of the main issues in dispute between the powers were consi-

TABLE 13   THE CONCERT OF EUROPE 1815–1914: PRINCIPAL CONFERENCES

Date	Place	Chief Subjects Discussed
1814–15	Vienna and Paris[a]	Peace Treaty, Quadruple Alliance
1818	Aix-la-Chapelle[a]	France, Quadruple Alliance
1820	Troppau[a]	Naples revolution
1821	Laibach[a]	Naples revolution
1822	Verona[a]	Italy, Spain, Eastern question
1830–2	London	Belgian independence
1831–2	Rome	Government of the Papal States
1838–9	London	Belgium (implementation of treaty of London)
1839	Vienna	Egyptian revolution
1840–1	London	Egypt and the Straits
1850–2	London	Schleswig-Holstein
1853	Vienna	Turkey
1855	Vienna	Settlement of Crimean War
1856	Paris[a]	Peace Treaty
1858	Paris	The Principalities (implementation of Paris treaty)
1860–1	Paris	Syrian revolution
1864	London	Schleswig-Holstein, the Ionian islands
1866	Paris	Navigation on the Danube
1867	London	Luxemburg
1869	Paris	Cretan revolution
1871	London	Black Sea
1876–7	Constantinople	Revolutions in Bosnia and Bulgaria
1878	Berlin[a]	Peace treaty
1880	Madrid	Morocco
1884–5	Berlin	African questions
1906	Algeciras	Morocco
1913	London	Settlement of Balkan Wars

[a] Congresses.

* Napoleon III more than once made proposals for "Congresses" which were not taken up. Russia proposed a congress in 1859 when war was imminent but Austria refused unless Sardinia disarmed first.

dered, and in almost every case a settlement of some kind was arrived at. The system provided mutually acceptable solutions first to a series of conflicts which emerged as a result of national revolutions (which in effect overturned the territorial settlement laid down at Vienna): those of Greece against Turkey (at the London conference in 1831); of Belgium against Holland (at the same conference); of Egypt against Turkey (at the London conference of 1840-1); of Schleswig-Holstein against Denmark (at the London conference of 1850-2); of Romania against Turkey and Russia (at the congress of Paris in 1856); of Bulgaria and Bosnia-Herzegovina against Turkey (at the congress of Berlin in 1878); and of Crete against Turkey (at meetings in London in 1897-8). In most of these cases the settlement provided for independence or at least "autonomy" for the territory in revolt, on terms which were acceptable to each of the major powers (including agreement on frontiers, and often on new royal families, or at least on the means by which these were to be chosen). Secondly, the system secured agreement on the *neutralisation* of particular states or areas (as the neutralisation of Switzerland had already been agreed in 1815): of Belgium in 1839, of the Black Sea and the Aaland Islands in 1856, of Luxemburg in 1867. Thirdly, it established new *rules* designed to reduce conflicts of particular kinds which had emerged over the years: for example, on maritime warfare and blockade (1856); on the treatment of prisoners and the wounded in war (1864); on the prohibition of certain kinds of weapons (1868); on the means of establishing colonial claims in Africa (1884); and on the conduct of war (in 1899 and 1907). Fourthly, new systems of *international administration* were set up; for particular areas — as for Tangier and Shanghai; or for particular waterways — as for the Rhine, the Elbe and the Suez Canal. Fifthly, *joint supervision* of the finances of particular states in debt was established: for Turkey, Egypt, Tunis, Greece and Bulgaria, among others (in some of these cases only two or three powers were involved in the arrangements). Sixthly, *collective measures* for implementing particular decisions were undertaken (usually by the despatch of joint missions): for guaranteeing the rights of the Orthodox church in the Ottoman empire after 1856; for supervising elections in the Principalities in 1857-8; for determining the future of Crete in 1897-8; and for putting into effect the settlement of the Balkan wars in 1912-13.

The system even provided for measures of international peace-keeping. In China in 1900 a joint international force was established to restore order in Peking when Western embassies had been attacked by Chinese rebels. More often one or more powers acted on behalf of the powers as a whole in undertaking such measures. So Britain and Holland undertook expeditions against the Barbary pirates, with the express authority of the powers, in 1817; Britain and France acted, with similar authority, to impose on Holland the decisions of the London conference of 1831; Britain and Austria intervened on behalf of the powers (acting with the authority of all except France) to secure the withdrawal of Mehemet Ali from Syria in 1840; Britain and France intervened to restore order in Greece in 1854;* France intervened in Syria, with the express consent of the powers, after civil conflict broke out there in 1860-1; Britain, on their behalf, sent a naval expedition to compel Albanian forces to withdraw from Montenegro in 1879, and, conversely, to compel Montenegro to withdraw from part of Albania in 1913; and Britain sent a naval force to compel Turkey to grant Crete autonomy in 1897. In 1885 a joint naval blockade was imposed on Bulgaria to prevent her pursuing her war with Serbia. In 1886 a four-power naval expedition was sent against Greece to prevent her pursuing territorial claims against Turkey in compensation for the enlargement of Bulgaria. And in 1898 a joint occupation force was sent to Crete which remained on that island for ten years.

This is a fairly impressive record of collective action. The major change which the system introduced was in establishing the principle of *multilateralism*. The powers as a whole had a responsibility for settling together, taking account of each other's interests, the problems of the continent. There was no longer any willingness to accept the unilateral use of force by any of them to determine issues in dispute. So Russia could not be permitted to determine unilaterally the nature of Greek independence in 1828-9, or of Bulgarian independence in 1878; France could not be permitted to determine unilaterally the nature of Belgium's independence in 1830-1; Prussia could not be allowed to determine unilateral the future of Schleswig-Holstein in 1848-50. In all these cases international conferences had to be called to ensure that settlements were reached acceptable to all the major powers. Similarly, Russia could not be allowed to determine unilaterally (even with Turkey's consent) the rule for navigation through the Straits in 1833: these had to be mutually agreed, by the powers as a whole, under the convention of 1841. Nor could she be allowed to undo unilaterally the neutralisation of the Black Sea which had been agreed multilaterally in 1856: so Britain insisted that another international conference should be held in 1871 to agree formally the end of neutralisation which had already been declared by Russia the previous year. So France could not unilaterally determine the future of Luxemburg in 1867 (even with the consent of the Dutch government, which controlled it) it was a matter affecting Europe generally and must be agreed among the "powers" as a whole at a conference for that purpose. Japan could not be allowed to

* In this case, they acted as guarantor powers of Greece (their then enemy Russia was the other) rather than on behalf of the "powers" as a whole.

decide unilaterally the settlement resulting from her victory over
China in 1894-5: she must agree with other powers arrangements that
gave them a share in the spoils. And Germany could not unilaterally
impose her will on France in Morocco in 1905 (whatever Morocco
might think): an international conference had to be called to determine the precise role which the two powers could be allowed to play
in that country. Even the annexation of Bosnia-Herzegovina by
Austria-Hungary in 1908, though not reversed or balanced by com-
pensations as Russia demanded, had to be legitimised by an exchange
of notes among the powers recognising this modification of the treaty
of Berlin. Since any of these developments, it was believed, might
affect the balance of power in Europe, or in the world as a whole,
each required joint consideration and joint decisions by the "powers"
as a whole.

Even the outcome of wars had (in some cases at least) to be
considered by the powers collectively, including some which had
taken no part in the preceding conflict. Austria, which had remained
neutral throughout the Crimean War, was allowed to play a prominent part in the congress of Paris at its end. Britain, France, Austria
and Prussia, which had not been involved in the Balkan conflict of
1875-8, insisted none the less in sharing in the decisions on its outcome (as well as in the spoils) at its conclusion. The six "powers"
(Italy by this time added to their number), which had played no part
at all in the Balkan wars in 1912-13, insisted on supervising the
settlement of those conflicts at the London conference. It was on this
principle that Louis Philippe had earlier pronounced the hope that
"no change, no alienation of territory would take place without the
concurrence of all the powers", and that in 1871 Russia demanded
the right to take part in the settlement of the Franco-Prussian war,
declaring that "it is impossible that the other great powers be excluded from the negotiations, even if they did not take part in the
war". What was necessary, it was believed, was an entente among the
powers as a whole for the solution of all great political questions. The
principle was set out by Palmerston in relation to the Egyptian crisis
of 1838-9:

> Europe would never endure that the matter should be settled by
> the independent and self-regulated interference of any one Power.
> . . . Therefore the only way in which [it could be resolved] without
> risking a disturbance of the peace would be by the establishment of
> . . . concert between the Five Powers. . . .[23]

There was therefore much more systematic and widespread discussion of conflict situations in this age than had ever occurred before.
Yet it cannot be said that the new system, however revolutionary,

was particularly successful in preventing wars. Though there were fewer international wars than before, this was not necessarily because of the working of the Concert. There were a number of deficiencies in the way the system operated.

First, the principle that every conflict required multilateral discussion was by no means universally applied. If the powers principally concerned resisted the idea strongly enough, international discussion could fairly easily be avoided: thus France and Austria, having reached their own peace settlement in 1859, resolutely refused participation by other powers except to endorse what they had already agreed. Again, where the conflict was between the great powers themselves, the multilateral system often broke down: so Prussia successfully resisted pressures for wider international conferences to consider the outcome of her wars with Austria and France (as proposed by France and Russia in the first case and by Russia in the second). Particular powers might be excluded for political reasons: so Prussia, though unquestionably one of the powers, was deliberately prevented from playing any part in the settlement of the Crimean War, as Austria did, in 1856. Most of the conflicts arising outside Europe were rarely considered at all on a multilateral basis: colonial disputes were resolved mainly by bilateral agreements between states (such as those between Germany and Britain in 1890, between Britain and France in 1904, and between Britain and Russia in 1907), rather than through the mechanism of the Concert (the conference of 1884 settled certain general principles, but was not concerned with resolving particular colonial conflicts of the time). The system, in other words, was at all times applied highly selectively.

Secondly, though the system provided for frequent consultation among the major powers, it afforded no representation for the smaller nations of the continent. Towards the end of the period Italy, and in theory, Turkey,* were admitted to the Concert, but their voices, even if heard, carried little weight. Other nations took part only by invitation, if they were immediately involved, and their voices counted for almost nothing. Sardinia, which took part in the Crimean War, played a much smaller role in the settlement than Austria, which had not. Representatives of Bulgaria, the future of which was principally at stake, played initially no role in the congress of Berlin (which decided to bisect her). The Balkan states played a smaller part in the settlement of their own wars in 1912-13 than did the great powers which had not been involved. It was, in other words, very much an *oligarchic* system, designed above all to protect the interests

* Under the treaty of Paris of 1856, Turkey was admitted to the "Public Law and Concert of Europe", but this did not mean that she was accepted as one of the "Powers" which took part in regular consultations on matters not affecting her.

of the ruling powers.

Thirdly, the system served usually only to resolve the less fundamental conflicts: immediate crises affecting parts of the continent where the interests of the powers were fairly marginal, or at least could be compromised. The underlying competition for status and influence between the major powers themselves could not be overcome by this mechanism. So the system could settle the details of Greek or Belgian independence but not whether Austria or Prussia should prevail in Germany. It could agree on the neutralisation of Luxemburg or the system of navigation in the Scheldt; not the degree of influence Russia should enjoy in Turkey, or Austria in the Balkans, the most crucial issues threatening the peace of the continent.

Fourthly, a substantial number of conflicts were in any case considered only after war had already occurred. The purpose of the discussions was to determine the nature of the settlement, not to prevent war occurring in the first place. Of the 25 or so conferences of the period (Table 13) over half were the outcome of a war or civil war, rather than efforts to prevent war from occurring. Other conferences discussed issues that were never likely to result in large-scale war (such as the government of the Papal States, the navigation of the Scheldt or the administration of the Principalities). Even where consultation did take place before armed conflict occurred — as in the discussions preceding the Crimean War in 1853, or the conference on Schleswig-Holstein in 1864 — they often did not succeed in averting war. Sometimes proposals for a conference were in that situation refused by one of the parties: Austria refused a conference before the war of 1859 unless Sardinia disarmed, and refused one before the war of 1866 if it was to consider territorial questions. In other words, where war was seen by a particular power as the best way of securing its ends, the fact that a conference of ambassadors might be proposed, or even called, to discuss the issues in dispute was rarely enough to prevent that war from occurring.

It is not easy, therefore, to say how far the system succeeded in reducing war. It is possible that some of the crises that were discussed — those over Belgian independence (1830-3), Egyptian affairs (1833 and 1839-40), Luxemburg (1867), the Balkans (1877-8) and Morocco (1906) — could have led to war (or more general war) if the system of great-power consultation had not existed. It is equally possible that war would have been averted in such cases without conferences, through the normal processes of diplomacy (as were the equally acute crises over Egypt and Bulgaria during the 1880s). Peace between the powers held up better between 1884 and 1906, when no large-scale conferences were held, than in the period between 1854 and 1871, when a succession of them took place. All that can be said is that the new system served to encourage a sense that international developments throughout Europe were matters of concern to all the major powers of the continent and needed to be discussed collectively if a balance of advantage among them was to be preserved and the dangers of conflict reduced.

Thus the conference system was designed to ensure that the interests of none of the powers should be forgotten. It was intended not to replace the balance of power, but to reinforce it. It was recognised when the system was first established that the purpose must be to sustain the balance of interests which, it was believed, the Vienna settlement had brought about. Though Castlereagh, somewhat intoxicated by the new system, declared it to be "a new discovery in European government, at once extinguishing the cobwebs with which diplomacy obscures the horizon . . . and giving the counsels of the Great Powers the efficiency and almost the simplicity of a single state",[24] he always recognised that it could only operate on the basis of a reasonable balance of power and interest among the powers that participated. And he himself continued, while resolutely defending the system, to seek an understanding with Austria with which to balance the combination which he believed Russia was establishing with the revived French monarchy; just as Palmerston later sought an understanding with France to match that of the three "northern courts" of Austria, Prussia and Russia.

The balance of power therefore, rather than the conference system, was still, in many people's minds, the main hope for preserving the peace of the continent. The first treaty of Paris (1814) declared that its purpose was to establish a system of "real and permanent Balance of Power in Europe". The purpose of the balance, as in the previous age, was not so much to maintain peace as to prevent undue domination by any single power and to protect each national interest with the minimum of conflict.* Thus when there was one generally agreed menance to the system, as in the years after 1815 (when France still seemed the main threat) the others could combine to resist it. Later, in the 1830s, a different kind of balance was established, based partly on ideology: the conservative powers of the East — Russia, Austria and Prussia — joined in the pact of Münchengratz (1833), were matched by the more liberal, or at least "constitutional", powers of the West — Britain, France, Spain and Portugal — brought together by Palmerston in the Quadruple Alliance (1834) to

---

* On these grounds many in Europe deeply distrusted balance-of-power politics. Not only radicals such as Cobden and Bright denounced them, as Wilson was later to do, as responsible for many of the conflicts of the period: even a conservative such as Disraeli, when in opposition, could declare that the balance of power "was founded on the obsolete traditions of an antiquated system" (believing, as he did, that Britain's essential interest lay overseas, where the balance was irrelevant).

represent, as he put it, a "counter-poise". But both of these situations were exceptional. For the most part there were only temporary and tactical alliances and understandings, usually related to particular issues or particular parts of the continent, and regardless of ideology. So liberal Britain would join with conservative Austria over Italy, and with conservative Russia over Greece and Egypt; revolutionary France would join with autocratic Russia over the Near East and with conservative Prussia over Egypt; Prussia joined with Russia over Poland, with Austria over the Balkans; and so on.

From the 1850s these tactical understandings came to be expressed in formal alliances. Since many of these arrangements were made for the purpose of fighting a war (or allowing one party to fight such a war while assured of the neutrality of the other), it cannot be said that they contributed much to the peace of the continent. Nor was there any attempt at this time (since many of the alliances were secret) to maintain a balance between alliances. In general their objective was to enable private wars between two of the major states — between France and Austria, Prussia and Austria, or Prussia and France — to be conducted with greater assurance of success: that is, with less danger of intervention by a third party — an objective in which they succeeded admirably. For example, in 1858 France allied with Piedmont to make war on Austria, and in 1859 engaged in a secret treaty with Russia providing for Russian neutrality in such a war, in return for French support for Russia's demand for revision of the treaty of Paris. In 1863 Prussia and Russia signed a convention providing for Prussian help to Russia over Poland, in return for Russian neutrality in a conflict between Prussia and Austria (which took place three years later). In 1864 Prussia and Austria entered into an alliance to maintain the London treaty of 1852 against Denmark, if necessary by war (which they proceeded to undertake later that year). In 1865 Prussia reached agreement with France that France would remain neutral in a war between Prussia and Austria, in return for an undertaking that, if Prussia won, Venetia would be ceded to Italy (France later secured a similar undertaking from Austria in return for offering the same neutrality); and in 1866 Prussia entered into an alliance with Italy for war against Austria within three months on the same understanding: and the war provided for in each arrangement swiftly followed. In the following year Prussia secured a promise from Russia to remain neutral in a war between France and Prussia if they fought alone, but to intervene against Austria if Austria took France's side. In other words, four successive wars, between 1859 and 1870, were fought under the protection of alliances of this kind.

From the 1870s a wider balance began to be visible. The tactical alliances were replaced by more long-term combinations, now of a more defensive character. These too at first created nothing approaching a balance. The alliance signed between Prussia and Austria in 1879, which remained a permanent feature of the international landscape until the First World War, was for more than a dozen years matched by no corresponding combination on the other side. On the contrary, since Russia and Italy were both loosely linked with that alliance, while Britain was almost totally isolated, largely as a result of her adventure in Egypt, the alignment of powers in Europe could scarcely have been less equal. Only when France and Russia, allowed to slip from Germany's embrace after Bismarck's fall, came into alliance in the early 1890s were the four continental powers arrayed in a roughly equal balance, with Britain floating uncertainly between. When Britain became more closely linked with France in 1904 and with Russia in 1907, and when Italy's links with the Central Powers began to loosen, the balance of Europe began to seem more equally poised than ever. Yet the danger of war became greater rather than less. While the peace of Europe was firmly maintained during the period of maximum imbalance, in 1878-93, it became increasingly precarious after 1907, when the alliances became more closely matched. There was no paradox in this, since the alliances were the effect of the tensions. It was the burgeoning conflicts between the powers which caused them to bind together, so producing a balance; but the balance was not in itself enough to prevent those conflicts from eventually erupting into war.

The balance, moreover, was never perfect. Of the alliances, that of Germany and Austria was more powerful than that of France and Russia alone. Britain's commitment to the latter was always ambiguous (to the last day of peace, and even after war had begun, the German Chancellor still hoped that Britain, which had no formal alliance with her partners, could be kept from joining them in war). The participation of smaller powers could never be accurately anticipated: Italy, Bulgaria, Romania and (in some views) Turkey all eventually joined the war on the opposite side to that which they had seemed likely to take (Italy and Romania were both formally allied with the Central Powers when the war began; Bulgaria had traditionally been the ally and protégé of Russia; Turkey had been consistently supported by Britain for more than a century and had sought a formal alliance with her as late as 1913). But, even if all partners had come in as planned, the balance could not be accurately measured. Superior strategy, superior weapons, superior fighting skills and men, might produce victory for either side, whatever the apparent balance. Or it might be possible to knock out each antagonist in turn: so in 1914 Germany hoped to conquer France within six weeks, before turning her attention first to Russia, and eventually to Britain. A blockade, revolution or defection could sap the enemy's strength (and might be encouraged by suitable strategies). As the generals continually had to warn the politicians, anything was possible in war.* But the politicians, however, confident in national destiny, or the justice of their own cause, habitually persuaded themselves of the certainty of final victory. Against such convictions an abstract and uncertain balance, even if it had been attained, could be of little influence. Indeed, nothing so clearly shows the irrelevance of balance than the fact that Germany promoted a war against Russia and France in 1914 while quite uncertain whether Britain would fight with them or not.

Procedures for "peaceful settlement", which were further developed at this time were no more effective as mechanisms for maintaining peace among nations. Over a number of territorial disputes overseas, foreign sovereigns still often acted as mutually accepted arbiters. So the king of the Netherlands arbitrated between Britain and the United States on the eastern frontier between Canada and the United States in 1831; Pope Leo XIII between Germany and Spain over the Caroline Islands in 1885; the Tsar of Russia between France and the Netherlands over the border of French and Dutch Guiana in 1891; the king of Italy between Britain and Brazil over the borders of British Guiana in 1904; and the king of Spain between Britain and Germany over Walvis Bay in 1909. A more novel procedure was the use of a collective body to arbitrate, with members appointed by either side (sometimes electing a neutral chairman): so Britain and the United States agreed in 1794 to appoint mixed commissions to determine disputed sections of the US-Canadian border. In other cases less binding procedures were preferred. So Britain used her "good offices" between Portugal and Brazil over the independence of the latter in 1825; France performed a similar service between Britain and Greece over the Don Pacifico case in 1849-50; Britain and France offered mediation between Austria and Sardinia when they fought in 1848; Austria in effect mediated between Britain and France and Russia before the Crimean War in 1853-4; France mediated between Greece and Turkey over Thessaly in 1880-1. There was now a widespread desire to promote the use of such procedures and so reduce the risk of war. Under a protocol of the treaty of Paris in 1856, the signatories declared their hope that states "shall before appealing to arms have recourse, so far as circumstances allow, to the good offices of a friendly power". There was a growing number of bilateral treaties providing for arbitration by mutual consent in particular types of disputes. In 1873 the Institute of International Law

---

* This was what the elder Moltke informed Bismarck before Prussia's wars against Austria and France. Before 1914 the younger Moltke was much more confident of German victory — so long as war came soon, before Russian re-armament had gone too far; and this was one of the major influences in favour of war in July 1914.

was established to promote and formulate the rules of international arbitration. In 1889 a tribunal of arbitration was established in Washington to decide disputes between the nations of the Americas. Finally, in 1899 at the first Hague conference, a "permanent court of arbitration" was established, a panel of judges who could be called on to settle disputes by arbitration if both sides agreed.

It cannot be said, however, that the new procedures did much to make war less likely. It was generally accepted that arbitration and mediation would be used mainly for conflicts of a less important kind. The Hague Convention of 1899 and 1907 recognised arbitration as the most effective way of settling only "questions of a legal nature, and especially . . . the interpretation and application of international conventions". Almost every nation, in agreeing in principle to make use of such methods where appropriate, made reservations excluding disputes involving "vital national interests", "national honour" or "national independence". Such questions of honour, they believed, like duellists, could only be settled by the arbitrament of armed struggle. But those were of course precisely the questions which were always most likely to lead to war.

As in previous ages, therefore, the so-called procedures for "peaceful settlement" had little effect in preserving peace. Nor, equally, did the measures taken for promoting communication between states. Diplomatic activity was now more intensive than at any earlier time. The diplomats themselves, coming from a generally similar aristocratic or semi-aristocratic background, acquired, through constant contact, a degree of understanding among each other.

All the ambassadors . . . moved in the same aristocratic society, their task to pick up the casual phrase and interpret it in terms of "great policy". . . . Many diplomatists were ambitious, some vain or stupid, but they had something like a common aim — to preserve the peace of Europe without endangering the interests or security of their country.[25]

Foreign ministers met more often, in the frequent conferences and congresses of the age. Summit meetings, bringing together heads of state or of government, were also now more often used to discuss the major crises of the day; so William I of Prussia met Alexander II at Breslau in 1859, Victoria at Coblenz in 1860, Napoleon III at Compiegne in 1861, and so on. Sometimes advantage was taken of holidays to bring about encounters of this kind: as when Napoleon III met Prince Albert and Palmerston at Osborne in 1857, when Bismarck went to see Napoleon III at Biarritz, and when Alexander II visited the Kaiser at Ems in 1879. Such meetings became even more frequent in the years before the First World War: Kaiser Wilhelm II met Tsar Nicholas at Bjorkoi (1905), Swinemünde (1907), Potsdam (1910) and Baltic Port (1912); and uncle and nephew corresponded frantically in the effort to halt war in July-August 1914. But none of these contacts did much in themselves to prevent war from occurring. If governments wanted war, they were not deterred by the fact that they had been able to discuss their differences with opponents. There was no problem of communication between Austria and Prussia in 1866, or between France and Prussia in 1870, or even during the frantic diplomacy of July 1914 (though in the early stages of the crisis the Kaiser was on holiday and Poincaré at sea, there is no evidence that this affected the outcome in any way). Louis Napoleon and the Prussian king were exchanging messages only days before the Franco-Prussian War broke out; the German and British governments were undertaking intensive discussions only hours before they went to war in 1914. It was not the availability of communications that counted but what was communicated. And this was not always pacific.

Thus at first sight there was a significant development in the procedures for resolving conflicts among states during this age. A system for regular multilateral consultation among the major powers was instituted and regularly used. It was successful in resolving a number of significant, though usually lesser, disputes. But it was rarely able to resolve the greater ones: those which arose between the "powers" themselves. The balance of power was more carefully maintained and protected, at least at the end of the period, than in any earlier age; but it could not keep the peace when a major threat to the peace emerged. Mediation and arbitration were perhaps more frequently employed than ever; but never over the conflicts that most mattered. Communication between governments was more intense than ever, but did not prevent them from deciding on war if necessary. All the powers were willing to make use of these procedures where appropriate. But few believed, and not all hoped, that they could be the means of abolishing war from the earth. Unfortunately the most fundamental feature of the international system was not affected: the long-standing belief in the availability, likelihood and legitimacy of war in the final resort. Thus the new institutions, revolutionary though they were, could do little to make war less frequent. They had neither the physical power, nor the moral authority, to deter states that believed they could secure their ends by force from fulfilling that intention.

The age of ideology (1917-)

The failure of the procedures established before 1914 to prevent the First World War created a determination to build new and more effective institutions.

The new system would overcome the weaknesses of the previous ones. They would provide for participation by all states in place of a few. Every dispute would be discussed and not only the least important. A more intensive effort would now be made to make law a substitute for war. During the next 25 years a whole set of new international bodies came into being, now almost universal in membership. Many of these were responsible for promoting international co-operation in a wide range of functional fields: labour, health, education, agriculture, communications, development and the international monetary system. But for preventing war the greatest hope was placed in the central international organisation — at first the League of Nations and later the United Nations — which was entrusted with the responsibility for maintaining international peace and security.

Both differed from the Concert of Europe in that their membership was much wider. The League was intended to include all the 60 or so sovereign states of that day, and for the first time brought Latin American, and even a handful of Asian and African, countries into discussion of the major international questions of the day. But it still remained incomplete. The United States never joined; and Germany, Italy, Japan and the Soviet Union did so only temporarily. Large parts of the world enjoyed no independent sovereignty and so took no part. Twenty years later, when the United Nations was founded, membership was again intended to be universal. And this time, though for a time limited by political disputes (which, for example, for long excluded mainland China and other divided countries), membership eventually included almost every state of the world, including many until recently under colonial rule. For the first time an international organisation of almost universal membership was created (by the mid 1980s, among significant states only Switzerland and the two Koreas remained outside).

This growth of membership, to 160 states by the mid 1980s, created a system entirely different from that which had existed in Europe in the century before. That system had been an oligarchy. Only five or six countries discussed the way disputes should be settled, and then imposed their will on the smaller states. The new organisation was more democratic. Small and weak states were members on equal terms, at least in theory, with the powerful.

In practice there was no strict equality. In the League, though every country in principle had a veto (since all decisions had to be unanimous), the more powerful states enjoyed permanent or semi-permanent membership of the Council, which exercised the main responsibility, and in practice dominated. In the United Nations which succeeded it in the corresponding Security Council the five permanent members were equipped with the power to veto any decisions of which they disapproved, and enjoyed almost permanent representation in other bodies. With that veto power they were able to prevent any decisions being reached that were totally unacceptable to them. This meant that in practice that it was often not easy to agree on anything other than pious calls for an end to hostilities or for a reconciliation of all differences. In the Assembly, the total membership was so large, and the number of voices likely to be heard so great, that even without a veto, it was almost as difficult to secure a consensus.

In other words, though more "democratic" than the old, the new system was — precisely for that reason — not well suited for effective decision-making. Even if large majorities could be secured, decisions did not necessarily appear authoritative to powerful states, which were often disinclined to listen to the passionate but importunate demands put forward by the small and weak in such bodies. As a result the new organisations were in practice even less successful than the Concert had been in containing war.

The most fundamental weakness concerned the difficulty of enforcing any decisions reached. Even if the Council could agree - that a war should cease, that an aggressor should withdraw, or that a particular settlement should be accepted — how could it bring this about? The Concert, because it brought together all the powerful states of Europe, could usually get its decisions to stick: Holland withdrew from Belgium, Turkey from Greece, Luxemburg accepted the neutrality imposed on it. Neither the League nor the United Nations has exercised any such authority. In its first few years, the League occasionally secured settlements of disputes affecting very small countries: for example, conflicts between Greece and Bulgaria, Finland and Sweden, Turkey and Iraq. But though it could "recommend" various measures, even including the use of armed force against an erring state, it had no power to impose these. Only once, against Italy, was there a feeble attempt to apply economic sanctions, and then they were only half-heartedly employed and rapidly abandoned. The United Nations had, in theory, much greater powers. Under its Charter (Article 25) it could *command* compliance with joint sanctions against an offender, including the use of force. But in practice it recognised that on most issues national views were so divided that an attempt to impose compliance by that means could split the organisation wide open. It has never reached a "decision" binding members to take to arms against an aggressor (the call for participation in UN action in Korea and the application of sanctions against China were recommendations, not "decisions"). And it has only once made a mandatory call for economic sanctions (against Rhodesia, after the illegal declaration of independence) which were then only patchily applied.

Only when there has already been a considerable degree of consensus, therefore, has successful international action been possible. The League organised a successful peace-keeping action to resolve the border conflict between Colombia and Peru concerning Leticia. The United Nations organised a series of similar actions, usually to maintain the peace after a conflict, or to speed a withdrawal: in Sinai (1956), in the Congo (1960), in Cyprus (1964), in Lebanon (1978) and elsewhere. But such peace-keeping forces by definition had no coercive power. Member states have not been prepared to send their troops to impose a solution by armed force. So such forces have only been able to operate when there has already been substantial agreement: that a cease-fire should be accepted, a border patrolled. Force has certainly not been available to stop a war in the way the UN Charter had anticipated.

The consensus required even for limited action has not been easy to achieve. In many conflict situations there were bitter disputes within the organisation: whether on East-West, North-South or other lines. The use of the veto, or the fear that it might be used, often prevented any effective UN response. A considerable proportion of the wars on our list were not even considered by the organisation: either because they were held to be civil conflicts and therefore outside its jurisdiction; or because it was believed that the organisation could do nothing effective (Vietnam, possibly the most serious war of the age, unquestionably involving outside powers, was for this reason never discussed); or simply because no member state decided to demand discussion. Even when a conflict was placed on the agenda in most cases nothing occurred other than the passage of resolutions; and these normally had little impact on the parties mainly concerned. Because the organisation gave an equal voice to states of quite unequal size and influence, because its debates were often strident and disordered, because its decisions were, or were held by some to be, politically partisan (though the fact that left and right, East and West alike believed this shows that it must have retained some impartiality), many states, and above all the largest and most powerful, were not disposed to take very seriously the exhortations it addressed to them.

The organisation did nonetheless develop some procedures to deal with conflict situations. These were an extension of the third-party procedures used for 500 years. In some cases it has appointed a mediator (or a representative of the secretary-general, whose function was similar) to help promote a settlement: this was done over Kashmir (1950-63), Cyprus (1964-), the Middle East (1967-71), Iraq-Iran (1980-) and Afghanistan (1980-). This may have served to lower the temperature in such situations. But in only one or two rare cases (for example, over Cambodia-Thailand in 1963-4) was a settlement achieved. Sometimes negotiations have been set up under the auspices of the Secretary-General himself: this was done over the first Berlin crisis in 1948-9 (successfully), over the Suez crisis in 1956 and over the Falklands in 1982 (in both cases unsuccessfully). Observers have been sent to obtain objective information about the situation on the spot: this procedure was used in Palestine, Lebanon, Kashmir and other places. Commissions of inquiry have been set up to investigate the causes of a dispute and make recommendations: this was done several times in the early years of the organisation — over Indonesia (1946), Greece (1947), Korea (1946) and Palestine (1947), for example — but only in the first of these cases did it make any contribution to securing a settlement. Sometimes a representative of the Secretary-General has been sent to establish contacts with one or both of the parties, or to assess the views of the population in a disputed area: the latter was used successfully in the case of Iran's claim to Bahrain. Occasionally a dispute could be referred to the International Court of Justice for a legal finding: this was done in the dispute between Britain and Albania over the mining of a British warship in the Corfu Channel, a territorial dispute between Thailand and Cambodia, and the conflict over the status of Namibia; but in two out of the three cases the judgement was rejected and flouted by the party most concerned.

These procedures may have marginally reduced the likelihood of war in one or two cases. They have certainly demonstrated international concern about situations of tension, and they have made it easier for international bodies to reach informed judgements about the nature of a dispute and the behaviour of the parties. But often they have been used for disputes that would not have led to war anyway. Or they have been invoked only after conflict had already broken out: when it was too late. Thus it is unlikely that in any case their use has directly prevented a war from taking place. Where a nation had already made a decision to use armed force to settle a conflict, the use of such procedures, or their availability, has had little effect in restraining it from doing so. The main effect of international organisations in such situations has been to expose countries engaged in conflict to the organised pressure of world opinion, and so marginally increase the costs — political and moral — of the actions taken. International organisations have made it less easy for a country to attack its neighbour, or occupy its territory, in privacy. All were compelled to justify their actions in a public body under the glare of the world spotlight. This has not been a major deterrent against armed action where the need for it was held sufficiently pressing; but it served perhaps, very slowly, to create some kind of international view, a new consensus concerning the types of international behaviour which were and were not acceptable. The hope was that little by little a new code of conduct would be established which, over the long term, could marginally deter resort to force.

There are a number of reasons why these procedures have done little to reduce the incidence of war. First, as we have seen, since 1945, the use of force has not occurred mainly in conflicts between states. In an age of ideological conflict (as between 1559 and 1648), armed force has been used primarily *within* states: to secure victory for a particular viewpoint or faction there. Yet that is precisely the type of conflict which it has been most difficult for the new international organisations to confront effectively. In theory all matters "essentially within the domestic jurisdiction" of a state are outside the jurisdiction of the United Nations. Governments themselves have not usually welcomed intervention by the organisation in such cases. And any member country, seeking to prevent discussion of such a situation, need only refer to the UN Charter to prevent the inscription of the relevant item on the agenda. As a result some of the most serious and protracted conflicts of the age — the 20-year wars in Colombia, Ethiopia, Chad and the Philippines, the long wars in Indo-China, and the Chinese, Nigerian, Angolan and Central American civil wars (among many others) — have not been debated in the organisation at all. In other words, the main international institution of the age has not proved well adapted to meet precisely the type of conflicts that have now become most prevalent.

Moreover, even where such disputes have been discussed, international organisations have often been unable to deal with them effectively. Because civil wars have been ideological conflicts, or at least acutely political, members of the organisation have often been deeply divided about the response that should be made. The super-powers, in particular, have almost invariably been committed to the success of opposite sides in the war under discussion, and so been unlikely to agree on the kind of measures required. One side might favour international action, the other oppose it. One might want one faction recognised, the other their opponents. So, over and over again — over Guatemala (1954), Hungary, the Dominican Republic, Yemen, Lebanon (1975-), Cambodia (1980-), Afghanistan, El Salvador, Nicaragua, and many more such cases — the organisation has been unable to take any effective action because of the divided views of the membership as a whole, and of the super-powers in particular.

A similar difficulty has prevented the development of international law from playing a major part in deterring or influencing resort to war. When the period opened the international lawyers had great hope of making "law a substitute for war". Within the League, semi-judicial procedures were established designed to establish which party to a "dispute" was in the wrong, and to secure a judgement about the appropriate redress. A new Permanent Court of International Justice was set up to dispense a supranational justice which would make it unnecessary for nations to go to war. Many governments were even induced to accept the "compulsory" settlement of disputes by the court (in cases involving other states which had also done so). But in practice the number of conflicts settled by legal means during the League period was small; and the disputes themselves were mainly of little significance. During the UN period the Court has been used still less to resolve bilateral disputes. There has been some development of international law through the adoption of new conventions setting out mutually accepted rules in areas formerly in dispute — such as diplomatic practice, consular protection, the law of treaties and the law of the sea; but none of these raised questions which were likely otherwise to have led to war. A new definition of "aggression" was arrived at; but it was in terms so general that most nations were able happily to adopt it in the belief that, in going to war, whatever they were committing it was not "aggression". In any case concerning the kinds of dispute which principally arose during this age, and above all the civil conflicts so characteristic of an age of ideologies, international law has either had nothing to say, or it has been disputed. On the legitimacy of giving assistance, whether to governments or non-government forces, in civil wars; the right of blockade; on the right to use force to protect nationals in other states; on intervention to protect human rights; on the preventive use of war — on all these vital questions concerning the ways armed force is most frequently used, international lawyers have remained themselves in bitter and continued dispute.

There have also been difficulties about the attempt to secure peace by reaching agreement on disarmament. Intensive discussions on that question began between the wars and have continued almost without cease since 1945. In both periods one or two limited agreements, temporary or permanent, have been reached: in the pre-war period, to restrict the naval strengths of a few powers (under the Washington treaty); and, since 1945, to refrain from testing particular weapons in particular ways, or from using bacteriological warfare, or from emplacing more than a limited number of anti-ballistic missiles, or from placing weapons of mass destruction on the sea-bed and in outer space, or from increasing the number of strategic missiles beyond a certain limit — and so on. All of these, however, have been agreements to restrict armaments, rather than to reduce them. None of them has reduced the overall capacity of the major powers to wreak destruction on each other — on the contrary, their total fire-power has continued to increase with relentless consistency. Above all, these agreements — and the entire disarmament effort — have been largely irrelevant to the kind of warfare which, in an ideological age, is most prevalent. Even if agreement had been reached on major reductions of nuclear forces (which has never appeared very likely), this would have had little, if any, impact on the kind of wars actually undertaken in this age: on the ability to conduct even the fiercest conventional wars, for example, still less on the desire or capacity of dissident groups to rebel against their governments, or of outside powers to assist them in doing so. Once again, the main peace efforts of the age were more relevant to the wars of the previous era than to those of the present day.

There was perhaps rather more encouragement to be had from the development of the first and most primitive of the types of procedure we have found in each of our societies. Communication between states at least improved. More intensive now than perhaps at any earlier time, this made each nation more aware of the intentions, apprehensions and concerns of other states. Regular contacts within a wide range of international organisations, better media coverage, continual meetings between heads of governments and many at lower levels — all these kept leaders better informed of the desires of other states and their likely reactions to the initiatives of others. Foreign ministers met regularly. "Summit meetings" took place from time to time. "Hot lines" linking heads of government were set up. In consequence, in times of crisis (such as the Cuban missile crisis) it was possible for communications to be exchanged which could sometimes affect the outcome and prevent wars.

There was thus perhaps a greater willingness, in framing policies, to take account of the apprehensions of other states and to avoid actions which might arouse a violent response. This may have marginally reduced the danger of all-out war among the major powers. But that, as we have seen, was not the main danger. No power had an interest in such a war. Intensive diplomacy did not prevent the use of force on a lesser scale, even by those powers themselves: for example, on the successive occasions in which they have intervened, without warning or apologies to their rivals, in neighbouring countries. Still less did diplomacy inhibit war between lesser powers: the fact that closer communication existed between Iraq and Iran, Uganda and Tanzania, China and Vietnam, Argentina and Britain, could not and did not prevent war between them from erupting when one party determined that this was the course it should adopt to promote its national interests. Least of all did diplomacy influence the type of war which was most widespread: civil war. In such conflicts one party at least lived altogether outside the world of diplomacy, and was largely unaffected by its communications. Whatever value, therefore, increased diplomatic, cultural and other contacts may have had in improving understanding, they have had little influence in reducing, either in number or in scale, the kind of wars which most closely reflected the aspirations of states and individuals, groups and governments, in an age of ideology: and the kind which therefore occurred most frequently.

Even the balance of power, the oldest and best tried of the devices used to reduce the risk of war, could not in this age do much to eliminate warfare from the system. Between the super-powers and their immediate allies that balance may have had some influence. In theory at least, in this age, and certainly after 1945, it was easier than ever before to maintain a balance between the powerful, since more than ever the world was divided between two great blocs of comparable strength, to one or other of which most of the advanced countries of the world belonged. Between those blocs, moreover, it was no longer necessary to seek a precise balance in military capability — a balance which it was never possible to establish with any accuracy and which, in any case, had never previously been successful in preventing war — since there existed between them at least the equality of fear which nuclear weapons created. The maintenance of such a balance depended only on maintaining the belief that each had a capacity to retaliate which could not be totally destroyed in one fell swoop, and that, in certain circumstances, nuclear weapons might actually be used. Though the latter belief has in time been gradually eroded, so long as nuclear war remained even a remote possibility it had (together with fear of the other almost equally terrible weapons now available) at least some influence in deterring war at the highest level.

But the balance of terror has not been able to prevent successive uses of force, even by those very powers, at a lower level of power, especially in the territory of third parties. Still less has it been able to deter wars among smaller countries (which have occurred with considerable regularity). The balance of conventional forces alone has had as little effect as in earlier ages in deterring war: a rough equality in power did not prevent wars between Algeria and Morocco, India and China, Iraq and Iran, Uganda and Tanzania. Even an inferiority in power did not deter an attack if there was sufficient motivation: as by Pakistan against India (twice), by Somalia against Ethiopia, or by Argentina against Britain, for example. Finally, for the type of war that was now commonest — those that occurred within states, whether colonial revolutions, ideological wars, civil conflicts or minority rebellions — a balance of power was irrelevant. Rebels fighting against an alien system did not calculate in advance the number of rifles available to themselves and to the government they opposed. They were willing to fight, and occasionally able to conquer, even though, on an objective reckoning, they fought against overwhelmingly superior power. And, even where external forces intervened, the balance did not always operate according to conventional expectations: as the examples of Vietnam, Afghanistan and

Central America clearly proved. Once more, therefore, for the kinds of warfare most widely pursued in an age of conflicting ideologies, the balance of power was not a system that could be expected to have much effect in deterring war.

Thus, in this age as in other ages, the various procedures available for securing peace have all been affected by the character of the international society. This was above all an ideological age. All the available institutions were weakened by ideological divisions. In such an age a large proportion of the conflicts were civil wars; but over these international organisations had no jurisdiction. International law was, partly because of ideological conflict, uncertain and disputed. Arms-control measures were, because of the same distrust, either unattainable or (where agreements were reached) irrelevant. Political conflict had the effect that the new institutions had little influence even over international wars. International bodies debated and discussed, passed resolutions, but rarely halted a war once started, still less prevented one from starting. Even the balance of power had no impact on the limited engagements now generally favoured. In an ideologically divided world, mutual suspicion has been such that none of the procedures used to promote peace secured general confidence or exercised unchallenged authority. Thus, while they might appear more advanced than any that existed before, the institutions of the new age had little greater effect than those of earlier times in reducing warfare among states.

Conclusions

Every society, large or small, needs to find ways of adjusting conflicts. Each will develop those that are appropriate for its own needs: methods that are both capable of resolving the kinds of conflict which arise most frequently, and are acceptable to the most powerful forces within the society, especially those most commonly engaged in conflict.

Of the international societies we have examined, each has made use of all four of the main categories of procedure for containing war we identified at the beginning of this chapter: those designed to improve communication between states; those relying on the mediation of outside parties; those depending on the attempt to mobilise armed force in a way that will balance power and so deter aggression; and those which involve the creation of multilateral institutions, more or less comprehensive in membership, whose task it is to consider disputes and, if possible, to find peaceful resolutions for them. But the balance between these four that has been chosen in each society has varied according to the needs and characteristics of each.

The type of procedure adopted has depended to some extent on the kinds of conflicts which have most frequently occurred. In the age of dynasties the conflicts that mattered were those between the dynasts themselves, competing for succession or territory; and it was therefore procedures that were acceptable to them and capable of resolving their personal rivalries that were most required. Among the four possible procedures, therefore, it was diplomacy, especially summit meetings, and to a lesser extent third-party settlement through mediation and arbitration, which proved to be most successful. In the age of religion, the conflicts were between different creeds and systems of belief. Often what was required was some framework for peaceful coexistence, either in the same state or in neighbouring states: here accommodation was achieved above all through conference, whether at a national or a multinational level, to lay down the principles on which the relations between the faiths would be based, as at a number of national conventions (p. 284 above), at the diets of Speyer and Nuremberg and at the congresses of Westphalia. In the age of sovereignty the conflicts were between states, struggling for status and power within a highly competitive system. The procedures most required, therefore, were those which would regulate that struggle and prevent any single member of the system from acquiring excessive dominance: here it was the balance-of-power system, *ad hoc* combinations and mutual guarantees which were mainly used to maintain some measure of stability within the system. In the age of nationalism, the most important potential conflicts were among a small group of five or six major powers, and the need was to maintain not only a reasonable balance of advantage among themselves but also some accommodation between the traditional claims of sovereignty and the challenge posed to it by the rising tide of nationalism: this was secured through a limited multilateral system, the regular conferences of the Concert of Europe. Finally, in the age of ideology, the principal struggle has been between rival ideological alliances under the leadership of competing super-powers, each bitterly suspicious of the believed aspirations of the other for world hegemony: here the main potential sources of conflict have been the super-powers themselves, who have sought to reach accommodation (when disposed to seek this) through bilateral negotiations, hot-line agreements, and super-power politics generally.

But there are other reasons why some procedures are more appropriate for one kind of society than for another. For example, the balance-of-power system in its true form depends on each state maintaining the capacity for independence of action, so that it can throw its weight into the balance in the most appropriate way as the situation demands, unaffected by ideological or traditional allegiances. That system, therefore, was appropriate to the age of sovereignty, where each state was uninfluenced by such allegiances and was determined to maintain its independence of action; but it has been difficult to operate in ages of ideology, such as the age of religion and the present age, where allegiances are strong and where most states are unwilling, because of those allegiances, to shift alliance in the way such a system demands. Ideological ages have therefore been best served by a system of bipolar alliances, where there is a need for strong mutual confidence within each alliance, but room for little between them. Conversely, in such ages procedures based on diplomacy and negotiation may be difficult to operate because of mutual mistrust (as in the age of religion); or multilateral institutions may be fatally divided as a result of ideological conflicts (as has been the case in the present period). Multilateral arrangements work best when there is a clearly recognised hierarchy among states, so that a relatively small number of powers can negotiate agreements which are readily accepted by smaller nations: as occurred during the nineteenth century. They work less well when, as today, there is a very large number of countries, each claiming "sovereign equality" and usually unwilling to concede to the powerful any special and privileged position. Procedures based on diplomacy and negotiation depend on a reasonable degree of mutual trust between those who engage in them. For that reason they operated reasonably well during the nineteenth century, when a considerable degree of mutual confidence among the major powers existed; but have worked much less well in ages (such as the age of sovereignty and the present age) when the necessary good faith and mutual confidence have been lacking. The use of third-party settlement depends crucially on the existence of powers or authorities that command the goodwill and trust of all those who come into dispute. This too is less likely to be the case in times of strong ideological dissent; and (though the system has been used to some extent in all periods) it has probably been least effective during the two periods when ideological concerns have been dominant.

What has been the relative success of the procedures used in each of these ages? Have some societies been more successful than others in finding the means to resolve disputes among their members? Have the methods used improved over the years and so been gradually perfected as instruments for securing peace among states? Clearly there have been changes over the years that may at first sight give the impression of a long-term development. Multilateral institutions are today more comprehensive in membership, and cover a wider range of activities, than those of earlier times. Diplomacy is more intense and more complex, and covers a broader range of national concerns, including commercial, cultural, scientific and many other fields. However, the only real test of the effectiveness of procedures is their relative success in resolving conflicts and preventing war. And there is little in the record that indicates that there has been any consistent advance in this respect. Wars still occur (as Appendix 5 attests) with obstinate regularity. And the procedures that are widely used today have little more success in preventing them from occurring than did those of earlier times.

Different conclusions could be drawn from this disappointing record. One might be that the deficiencies do not lie in the procedures themselves. It is simply that they have not been used sufficiently effectively. But, if this is the case, it may itself merely reflect the interests of powerful states within the system. These may prefer a system in which differences are resolved on the basis of power to one based on procedures for settlement which discount power. If this has been the case in the past, there is little reason to suppose that efforts to invent new procedures, or make existing ones work better will, without a change of heart on their part, produce different results.

Alternatively it could be concluded that, while the attempt to find appropriate procedures has been correct, those in fact adopted have not been the right ones; that there is a need, in other words, to search for totally different types of answer — for example, world government, universal disarmament, even a minimising of all contacts between states so that each can go its own way in greater isolation from the others. But, whatever the theoretical advantages which might result from any of these, there are clear practical difficulties in bringing about such a radical transition from one kind of world — that in which we live today — to another, quite different one such as these proposals presuppose: in other words, in persuading those who wield power in different states all over the world that their interests would best be served by adopting major departures from the types of relationship, and forms of organisation, with which they are at present most familiar — departures that might seem to threaten their existing power.

But there is a third and quite different conclusion which could be drawn. This is that the best way to seek a reduction in war may not be through the development of new and better procedures or institutions at all. The survey above has shown that, though a wide range of procedures and institutions have been used in different ages to resolve conflicts between states, none has succeeded in reducing the incidence of war significantly. Their failure to do so does not appear to have been significantly related to the different forms the procedures have taken in different ages; nor even to the ways in which they have been used. It has resulted rather from the attitudes and intentions — that is, the motives — of the member states, especially the most powerful member states of each society.

Diplomacy and the other methods designed to improve communication between states have obviously performed valuable functions. They have made possible confidential negotiations on a wide range of issues, and promoted a better understanding of the interests and motives of other members of the international community. But by themselves they have not been able to prevent war. Diplomacy can as easily be used as an instrument for preparing war as it can as one for making peace. We have seen how, in the age of dynasties, the first resident embassies were sent for the express purpose of concluding or cementing alliances against some other state. In the age of nationalism diplomacy was intense, and sometimes successful in securing agreement on lesser disputes; but diplomatic contacts were often closest between allies (Germany and Austria, France and Russia) and much less close between political opponents (for example, Germany and Russia, Austria and France). Even today diplomacy is sometimes used more effectively to link members within the same bloc — NATO and the Warsaw Pact, the EEC and Comecon — than in securing understanding between opponents. In itself, therefore, diplomacy is only a tool. Whether the tool's final product is peace or war depends on the intentions of those who use it.

Much the same is true of procedures for third-party settlement. Where two states actively desire an accommodation, these can be a useful way of producing the kind of compromise which is required. But, where one or other party has no wish for any such deal, the procedure will often not be adopted in the first place; or, if it is attempted, it will secure no results. A state engaged in an important dispute is often reluctant to allow others to determine its outcome. No state can be compelled to go to arbitration, or even to mediation, if it does not wish to do so. General commitments to make use of such procedures have usually been so heavily hedged by reservations that they have not significantly reduced each country's freedom of action. Governments, in accepting the jurisdiction of the International Court, have explicitly excluded disputes relating to the "honour", "security" or "vital interests" of their state; in taking such action they have explicitly declared that, on the most important questions, they reserve the right to make war if necessary. Though, therefore, such procedures have now been in widespread use for over six centuries, it is doubtful if they have often, if ever, resolved conflicts that otherwise would have led to war, or, therefore, had any significant effect on the incidence of war.

The balance of power too has, over the years, shown itself to be a highly unreliable mechanism for preserving peace. For much of the time that has not even been its aim. It has been seen as a means of limiting the power of others (often after war has already broken out) rather than of preserving the peace. Even where an almost exact symmetry between alliances has been established, as before the First World War, peace has not been preserved. And the numerous cases where nations have gone to war against overwhelming odds have demonstrated the limitation of the system as a means of maintaining the peace. In other cases, a balance in one area has only had the effect that potential enemies have been free to undertake adventures in another (as European powers did in the colonial territories before 1914, or as the United States and Soviet Union do outside Europe today). Or the balance may, because it does deter, also paralyse, and so allow each power freedom of action at least within its own sphere of interest: as the Soviet Union has in Eastern Europe, and the United States in Central America. Or the balance at one level may be irrelevant to that at another; so a balance of nuclear weapons may be undermined by an imbalance in conventional, or a balance in conventional may itself be irrelevant to a conflict fought by guerrilla methods. In other words, as in the earlier cases, where the will for war has persisted, a balance of power alone has usually been quite unable to deter it. Here too a procedure is of little value by and in itself if the fundamental motives of states remain unchanged. So long as governments continue to believe that they have the need, the right, the duty at critical moments to go to war, there is little evidence that they will be deterred from doing so by the balance of power existing between states.

Finally, multilateral institutions have suffered from the same difficulty. They have been able to secure conciliation, if at all, only where nations have been willing to be conciliated. None has ever exercised a coercive power equal even to that of even a minor state. Thus any country that has been determined to secure its aim by armed force has always been able to frustrate attempts made by such organisations to secure a peaceful resolution. The fact that the League of Nations established a commission of inquiry to examine the Manchurian situation could not prevent Japan (even while to all appearances co-operating with the inquiry) from imposing its will on that territory; any more than the League's pronouncements about Abyssinia and its half-hearted proposals for sanctions could influence Italy's determination to impose her will in that case. The fact that the Security Council and General Assembly of the United Nations denounced and deplored the Soviet invasion of Hungary could not prevent that invasion from none the less occurring. The fact that the UN secretary-general promoted negotiations about the future of the Suez Canal could not prevent Britain, France and Israel from taking the canal by force in October 1956. The fact that he appointed personal representatives to mediate between Iran and Iraq, or to seek a settlement of the situation in Afghanistan, could not secure peace in those cases if the parties themselves were determined to fight on — or if even only one was. International organisations can request and implore, pronounce and declare; but, so long as they possess no overriding armed power of their own, the member state which is determined on war is unlikely to be significantly deterred from undertaking it.

In a world where armed power remains decentralised, therefore, the final word rests always with individual states. Of the four types of procedure we have described only the balance of power relies on armed force to deter, but it has none the less consistently failed to deter. The other three, lacking armed force, have depended entirely on the goodwill of the parties involved in conflict. The only sanctions available to them have been intangible ones: the pressure of world opinion, the reluctance of states to incur criticism and condemnation, the influence of friends and allies. These are not totally worthless sanctions. They may marginally deter in particular cases. But in the final resort, where a state has believed that its vital interests were at stake, none of the various procedures and institutions available have significantly affected its actions. The likelihood of war has thus not significantly depended on the availability or otherwise of such procedures. It has depended on the intentions and attitudes of governments: on the beliefs they have held about war, its legitimacy, effectiveness and utility, in the light of the costs that it entails, and the profits it can procure. It is thus, finally, to these beliefs — the ideas held about war by governments in different ages and their influence on the extent to which war has been made — that we must now direct our discussion.

8 Beliefs

Wars are made by people — individuals within governments or other collective bodies — who decide at some point to try to secure their ends by armed force. Those decisions are determined ultimately by the beliefs they hold about war: about its usefulness, legitimacy or morality, about its value in enhancing national prestige, upholding national honour, or asserting national will; above all about its *normality* as a constant feature in the behaviour of states.

But the beliefs that are held in this respect are not those of individuals in isolation. They are moulded by those that are held in society as a whole: in this case international society. In studying the institution of war, therefore, one of the most important matters to be considered is the beliefs about war and its uses that are widely held within a given international society.

Beliefs are not of course uniform. Within international society they may vary from state to state; and within each state they will vary among groups and individuals. But the views of nearly all will be strongly influenced by the attitudes that prevail throughout the international society. Thus the beliefs held by different people and groups within each international society — that is, in any one period of history — will usually have much in common, yet may differ sharply from those generally held in another.

What is of concern to us is not so much the beliefs of moralists seeking to establish ethical standards, or of scholars claiming to lay down the international law; nor, again, is it the views that have been held among the great mass of the uninformed public, who have normally had little influence on the actual conduct of events. What is important for our purpose is the view that has prevailed among those who have in practice been responsible for the decisions that have been taken concerning peace and war: monarchs and statesmen, heads of government, foreign ministers and their advisers. It is the beliefs of these that have most influenced the character of war in each age, and it is with their ideas, therefore, that we shall be mainly concerned in this chapter.

There are a number of questions, more or less obvious, that are important in any study of the changing beliefs about war in international society. How far has war been seen as a legitimate or an illegitimate form of activity: as a source of honour and glory, or even of pleasant exhilaration, or as a delinquent act, undertaken only by international malefactors and social outcasts? How far has war been seen merely as the "continuation of policy by other means", or on the contrary as a last resort, forced on an unwilling government by the nature of the international situation in which it finds itself, or by the evil intentions of opponents? How far has it been seen as an activity engaged in only by *other* nations, against which adequate defences must be maintained, how far as a course of action that may at any time be legitimately adopted in pursuance of the national goals of the decision-makers themselves? Equally important, how far have the beliefs that have been generally held actually had influence when a crucial decision came to be made? A statesman may well hold in all sincerity that war is an unmitigated evil, to be avoided at all costs, yet at the moment of crisis none the less commit his country to armed action in the belief that this is a special case; that war has been forced on him against his will, or that it is not really a war at all, but only a "law and order operation", an "intervention", a "pacification", or an act of "anticipatory self-defence". So our concern is not so much with theoretical ideas but with the beliefs and attitudes that have been reflected in actual behaviour.

Finally, we shall, as always, be concerned with the way beliefs have changed over the years, with the differences in the beliefs concerning war held at different periods in history. What are the reasons for the changes that have occurred? How far do the beliefs held at any one time, theoretical or practical, reflect changes in the fundamental motives of states at that time? Is there a secular process of increasing abhorrence of war and the destruction that it entails, a gradual civilisation of human conduct? Or has there merely been a turning away from the more obviously suicidal forms of conflict or armament, with no real reduction in the willingness to countenance uses of force, at the appropriate level (preferably in somebody else's country), if the purposes to be achieved, national or ideological, are seen as sufficiently compelling?

These are some of the questions that we shall be concerned with in tracing the changing nature of beliefs about war in the different periods we are concerned with. On the basis of that examination we may be able to determine how far the character of the beliefs generally held on this question is a fundamental factor in influencing the propensity of states to make war.

The age of dynasties (1400-1559)

What then were the attitudes to warfare in the first of the societies we have been examining?

For many in this age war was seen as a glorious undertaking. The epic, the minstrel song, the tales in common circulation, all told of the military exploits of knights and kings who had won lasting renown through success on the battlefield and were held up as models of valour and virtue. The institutions of chivalry inculcated among the ruling circles a profound respect for martial qualities. Tournaments in which those qualities were displayed enjoyed the patronage and even the participation of kings (Charles V and Henry VIII were both expert at the joust and Henry II of France was killed taking part in such a tournament); and they demonstrated what virtues and skills were most valued by the leaders of society. For example, when Charles V first arrived in Spain from Burgundy in 1518 he organised jousting to "display to the Spaniards the great valour of the Burgundian lords". This chivalric tradition inevitably influenced the attitudes of rulers to wars abroad. The knightly challenge was mirrored in the challenge of ruler to ruler. So Francis I took the protests made by Charles V in 1521 about his actions against Gelderland and Navarre as a personal challenge to which he must in honour respond.[1] In a similar situation in 1528 Charles V challenged Francis I to hand-to-hand combat,[2] a challenge reciprocated by Francis in his reply.[3] In 1536, Charles told the pope that, though he desired peace with Francis with all his heart, he was not afraid to fight; and, to spare the blood of his subjects, he would be willing to engage in personal combat, either on land or sea, with his opponent, the prizes to be Burgundy for himself, if he should win, and Milan for the king of France if he should lose.[4] Declarations of war were influenced by the same tradition. In 1528 the English and French kings thought it necessary to send their senior heralds to Burgos formally to declare war on Charles V, while the return declaration by Charles was issued by his own herald before the assembled French courts.

But war was seen in this age not only as a glorious enterprise but as a reliable source of material reward. For kings it could be the means of winning crowns, territory and large indemnities, as well as renown. For the magnates it could procure ransoms and booty; for the common soldiers, plunder and other rewards (p. 240 above). For substantial and influential sections of the population it was the only road to advancement and success. Even for those who could expect little direct return from it and might fear the loss of a relative, increased taxation or crops burnt, it was seen as an essentially normal feature of human existence, a favourite pastime for princes and the great lords, which must affect all who lived under them.

War was a way of life, an ingrained habit of late feudal society. The landed aristocracy, who were almost everywhere the ruling class, had no other serious occupation, and indeed no other valid excuse for existence. Kings existed to lead them from one war to another and thus keep them from one another's throats.[5]

Warfare was endorsed in another way. It had a religious as well as a secular purpose, and so found the church among its patrons.

> The Church, by supporting the institutions of chivalry and the knightly orders, had blessed weapons that were not always to be used against the oppressor or the infidel, and by admitting that it was permissible to wage a just war, she had in effect sanctioned all wars. . . . The Church, too, needed war to support her authority and punish those who defied it. And she was partly responsible for the view that in great causes war was a divine judgement, an extension of the judicial duel, where two armies instead of two rival champions fought to decide who was in the right.[6]

For this reason, guns were sometimes named after the apostles; swords and halberds were engraved with religious scenes; and generals launched attacks in the name of their patron saint.[7] The Knights of St John and of St Stephen, the Teutonic Order, the Knights of the Sword, the three knightly orders in Spain — all these revered institutions demonstrated that religious devotion could sometimes be almost synonymous with military activity. Charles V, embattled against both Moslem and protestant heretics, could declare himself as "God's standard-bearer". With such purposes as this, war could not be an entirely evil undertaking.

It was seen, equally, as essential in some circumstances for secular purposes: especially for protecting the interests of rulers and their states. So Charles V's minister Gattinara, having set out the arguments for and against war with Francis I in 1521, had no difficulty in showing that, in the circumstances, war was the right course, essential for preserving the interests of Spain and the Empire and Charles's own reputation. Having set out some of the gains to be won, he concluded that (since God was on his side):

> to let the enemy escape would be to tempt providence. His own subjects, who had shown themselves so ready to make sacrifices, would be disappointed if he weakened now and would think less of him in future. Lastly, it was the emperor's duty to win honour and glory: now that Spain was quiet again, all the world was expectant. Italy was calling for his help, Germany feared and loved him, the Switzers were disinclined to oppose him and the enemy themselves were losing heart.[8]

The advisers of other monarchs reasoned in a similar way. The reputation of a ruler could depend on his showing that he was willing to make war to protect his interests. Besides, such wars could be useful in occupying the minds and energies of unruly elements at home. As the Italian writer Giovanni Botero argued, "Military enterprises are the most effective means of keeping a people occupied. . . . A wise prince can placate an enraged people by leading it to war against an external enemy."[9] This belief in the utility of war in occupying the minds of a dissatisfied people was one which was to continue to appeal to rulers for many years to come (p. 340 below).

Of course, the belief that war was the source of glory, or a useful way of promoting a ruler's interests, did not mean that all wars were believed to be equally justified. There was a sufficient awareness of its miseries and cruelties for many to prefer, most of the time at least, the manifest blessings of peace. Charles V, though he himself had spent much of his life at war, told the son who was to succeed him, in a memoir written in 1548, that "that which God most commends to princes is peace. . . . Preserve peace and avoid war, unless you are forced to it in your own defence, for war is a heavy burden. . . ." He himself was gratified when, on his visit to Sicily in 1535, he was hailed as the "peacemaker of all Italy": an indication that making peace was, to some at least, almost as glorious as making war. Most rulers paid lip-service at least to the duty of a ruler to provide peace for his people. Religious writers and preachers were especially inclined to denounce the iniquity of war, which they sometimes blamed on the wickedness of princes. So Erasmus blamed the rulers themselves for that "madness of war that has persisted so long and so disgracefully among Christians"; just as Sir Thomas More held that "the common folk do not go to war of their own accord, but are driven to it by the madness of kings".[10]

Even the rulers therefore had to find reasons to justify war. There was no shortage of justifications they could put forward for that cause. As Erasmus put it, "among such great and changing vicissitudes of human events, among so many treaties and agreements, which are now entered into, now rescinded, who can lack a pretext . . . for going to war?"[11] Even so, some attempt was made, among theologians and sometimes among statesmen, to distinguish between the occasions when war was, and when it was not, justified. The ancient doctrine of the "just war" sought to categorise those uses of force which were allowed and those that were not. It was, however, not always easy to distinguish between the two. According to medieval doctrine there were three just causes of war: to secure reparation for a wrong, to retake something unjustly taken, and to repel an injury or attack. This meant that in theory a war must be a response to some tangible harm done by the state attacked and must not result simply from hostility, rivalry or greed. This still left plentiful reasons why war could in practice almost always be justified by the attacker.[12]

Acts of "reprisal" for a wrong were widely held to be justified; but, since virtually any war could be held to be a reprisal for something, this afforded an almost universal justification. Preventive war — war designed to anticipate the planned war of another — was widely regarded as justifiable. Ferdinand of Aragon claimed that his war to seize southern Navarre in 1512 was necessary to "prevent" an invasion of Spain which he claimed was being planned by the kings of Navarre and France. In 1538-9, the protestant states of Germany, fearing an imminent attack by the emperor, contemplated the launching of a preventive war against him.[13] Conversely, Charles V himself in 1531 proposed to the imperial electors that, since his proposal for a council had failed and the protestants had rejected the compromise plan he had put foward at the diet, a preventive war might be necessary.[14] Wars in flagrant violation of treaties could be found permissible with sufficient ingenuity: Louis XI, having summoned prelates, nobles and officials to advise him on the matter in 1470, announced that he could "justly" disregard the treaties of Conflans and Péronne, which he had entered into only a few years earlier, and so resume his war against Burgundy. Even the pope in 1443 advised Hunyadi to violate a treaty with the Turks.

There was greater unanimity that "private war" was impermissible and unjust. As we have seen, a substantial proportion of the wars in this age resulted from attacks launched not by established rulers or states but by rebellious magnates, maurauding knights, free companies and *écorcheurs* (disbanded soldiers engaged in plundering). These created such disorder and suffering that there was widespread agreement (and not only among rulers, who had an obvious interest in the matter) that all such warfare was impermissible and outside the law. Thus in Catalonia, for example, where the nobles had been explicitly granted the right to make war by the kings of Aragon, that right had to be formally withdrawn from them. Thomas Aquinas, had held that, to be "just", a war had to be authorised by a prince. Most of the theologians of the day held a similar view. The diet of Worms of 1495, in declaring a "perpetual peace", formally banned all private war in Germany. And early in the next century the Spanish theologian Vitoria, one of the founders of international law, held that only a "perfect" state, in effect an independent state under a lawful sovereign, had the right to make war. This became one of the only generally accepted rules concerning warfare in this age.

In general, therefore, the rules, such as they were, were not particularly exacting in this age. It was usually not difficult for the rulers to show that the wars of their enemies were unjust but that their own were just. Because they were Christian rulers in a Christian age, they would often wish to show that their own actions fell within the guidelines which the theologians laid down. Charles V, for example, consulted Vitoria about the justifiability of certain of his actions (for example, before launching war against the Zambales in South America[15]). He asked the pope to judge between the justness of his own cause and that of Francis I during his personal meeting with him in 1536. His minister Granvelle was sufficiently concerned about good name to advise Charles to "show the utmost punctiliousness in fulfilling his own obligations to all states . . . so that peace could be maintained through all Italy", and to avoid giving his opponents any justification for accusations about his own conduct.[16] Such actions showed that there was at least among rulers some concern to demonstrate to the world that they abided by accepted rules, and that, if war occurred, it must be because of the hostile and aggressive policies of other rulers.

As important, probably, as the pronouncements of the theologians in determining the international morality of the age was the tradition concerning the honour of princes, pledging themselves in personal undertakings to each other. In the treaties which they signed, each pledged his own personal honour. The signing, as we have seen, was often surrounded by elaborate rituals designed to emphasise the obligations. The treaties were sustained by solemn oaths, sealed under the prince's personal signet, and maintained under the sanction of heavy spiritual penalties. Even these could not, however, always ensure the observance of treaties. The same casuistry which was so often used at this time to secure the annulment of a marriage or the evasion of a contract could be equally devoted to showing that a treaty could be disregarded: as a result, for example, of faulty wording, an inadequate seal or unqualified witnesses. The pope could be asked to grant indulgence for a violated oath (see p.276 above). Or the sanctions could be exorcised by a contrary oath. So Francis I, as we saw earlier, forced into a humiliating treaty after his capture at Pavia, undertook a private oath, in the presence of his own supporters, which justified to his conscience his firm intention of repudiating the treaty as soon as he was released: in this way he avoided keeping the promise he made to submit himself as a prisoner once more if he failed to implement the treaty (as his predecessor John II had voluntarily done when France failed to pay the indemnity demanded by England in 1360).

Some rules even began to be developed about the way in which wars should be conducted. Some of these concerned permissible and impermissible weapons. Crossbows and firearms were both at first denounced as a violation of the knightly code (though some believed this was more because they threatened the pre-eminence of mounted and armoured knights than because of their especially lethal character). Canon law in this period forbade crossbows, siege machines, war on certain holy days and harm to non-combatants; but these rules applied only to wars with Christians and often only to knights, and not to common soldiers.[17] It was generally accepted by theologians that the killing of women and children in war was not permissible. Unnecessary cruelty to civilians was widely condemned (though Vitoria believed that the sacking of a conquered city was justifiable in some circumstances). The enslavement of prisoners was usually forbidden, but only if they were Christians: some held, as did Vitoria, that Saracen prisoners could be killed and their children thrown into slavery. Aquinas condemned lies and the violation of promises, but he permitted the use of "stratagems". There were differing views about the rights enjoyed by the inhabitants of subject territories: Vitoria held that these had the same moral rights as other peoples and on those grounds roundly condemned some of the policies being pursued by Spanish conquistadors in South America.

In certain specialised areas more clear-cut international rules developed. Perhaps the most evolved were those relating to maritime affairs: since this was by its nature an international activity, the need for accepted rules was most apparent here, and in time the *Libre del Consulat de Mar,* which had been first adopted in Barcelona, was accepted as establishing norms that were to be applied all over the world. A few writers, including Vitoria, upheld a rule of freedom of the seas and freedom of commerce (though it was not observed by his own government, nor indeed by most others). A new framework of rules also began to emerge about the conduct of diplomacy. Chivalric doctrine had for long prescribed the treatment to be accorded to heralds and the way in which prisoners and non-combatants should be treated. Already by the fifteenth century it had come to be accepted that ambassadors enjoyed total immunity from arrest and from other interference in the exercise of their duties. There were still some disputes about the precise application of the rules: for example, an ambassador was not always held immune from punishment for crimes of fraud or violence, or for political crimes such as espionage, conspiracy and treason.[18] But generally a code governing the treatment of diplomats began to be fairly widely observed.

So a few conventions began to emerge during this age about the kind of war that was justifiable and the methods of war that were permissible. None of these affected the general assumption among the rulers of the day that from time to time they could legitimately and justly make war against each other: to defend their honour, to assert a right, to promote an interest. War was everywhere regarded as a normal activity in which all the rulers of the age might take part and if possible excel. It was one in which considerable glory (as well as more prosaic rewards) could be won, both by the ruler himself and by his subjects. The church was willing to endorse its use for proper purposes (and not only against infidels); and as we have seen, the pope himself was a constant organiser of wars, both on his own behalf and to reduce the pretensions of any over-powerful state, especially in Italy. The rules that emerged about the types of war that were permissible and the way they should be conducted were few and ambiguous; and they certainly had little influence on the princes' conduct. War was generally seen as an honourable undertaking which, though it had its hardships and its setbacks, was from time to time essential in maintaining the self-respect and dignity of every ruler.

The age of religion (1559-1648)

In the following age, in an international society that cared deeply about religion, it was natural that religious justifications (or explanations) for war were the most widely found. It was generally accepted that war was an evil; but it was an evil God deliberately used to punish sinful men. In the view of Richelieu, war was "a scourge with which it has pleased God to afflict man". Olivares, in writing to Philip IV, held that "the cause of war is the sin in all of us". Whichever explanation was accepted — divine punishment or human sinfulness - the implications were the same: war was an unavoidable evil certain to be encountered in this earthly vale of tears. However undesirable, it was an essentially normal feature of human existence which must be expected to continue. "To speak of peace perpetual in this world of contention", wrote Thomas Digges, "is but as Sir Thomas More's Utopia . . . a matter of mere contemplation, the warre being in this age so deeply rooted that it is impossible to do away with it except with the ruin of the universe".[19]

One reason why war seemed inevitable in such an age was that it was generally seen, by Catholics and protestants alike, as the means by which God's purpose would be achieved, and their own version of his faith established.

The assumption that God used war to work his judgement was gladly accepted by the pope of an age of counter-attacks: Trent, while condemning private duels, was silent on the score of national ones. New military religious orders were founded and military literature suggested, if it did not openly promise, that the soldier who fell in defence of his religion had an especially favourable chance of salvation.[20]

Philip II dedicated his enterprise against England to God's name, and refused to believe that God would not ensure its success.[21] Religious conviction was an equally unanswerable argument for not abandoning a war once begun: when Mateo Vazquez mildly suggested, at a time when Spain was engaged in three major wars in different countries, that foreign commitments should be reduced, Philip replied that this was impossible because "the religious cause takes precedence over all others."[22] Protestant leaders were no less convinced that God must bring them victory. As Gustav Adolph indignantly declared, on being begged by the elector of Saxony to consider peace with his enemies, "he had begun this work with God and with God he would finish it".[23] Fanaticism had the effect that war often became a Christian duty. Frederick, the elector Palatine, in accepting the Bohemian crown, and so making war inevitable, declared himself to be following a divine calling: "My only end is to serve God and his Church".[24] Conversely, his opponent Ferdinand II, in going to war against the Bohemian protestants, declared that he had no choice, since he would "rather lose everything than tolerate the heretics".[25]

Crusades against Moslem heretics had always been seen as justifiable and even glorious; and wars of that general type continued in this age (for example, in the war of the Holy League against the Turks, inaugurated by the pope, in 1570-7). But now crusades against protestant heretics were seen as equally commendable. The Jesuit international lawyer Suarez held that in making war a prince could be the instrument of divine purpose, and this would ensure that his war was a just one. Philip II declared to his ambassador in Rome that he had no choice but to undertake military action against protestants in the Netherlands, since "to negotiate with these people is so pernicious to God's service . . . that I have preferred to expose myself to the hazards of war . . . rather than allow the slightest derogation of the Catholic faith and the authority of the Holy See". Five years later, in 1573, he wrote that "he would rather lose the Low Countries than reign over them if they ceased to be Catholic". This moral compulsion meant that war ceased to be a matter for calculation. The certitude of divine blessing for one's cause made it unnecessary to weigh up the chances of success. As a deputy in the Spanish *cortes* put it in the 1590s (when Spain was up to the hilt in a number of separate engagements), "If we are defending God's cause, as we are, there is no reason to abandon it on grounds of impossibility."[26]

Fanaticism bred a widespread paranoia. Each side feared dark forces believed to be seeking to extend their hold over the entire continent. War was thus seen as an unwelcome necessity, the essential means for defending truth and defeating evil. So the Jesuit adviser of Philip II, Ribadeneyra, wrote of the Spanish attack on England in 1588 that it had the character of a "just and holy war . . . which was . . . defensive, not an offensive war; one in which we are defending our sacred religion and our most Holy Roman Catholic faith".[27] Conversely, Gustav Adolph, equally terrified of Catholic designs, warned in a proclamation of 1616 that the "papacy and its preaching" would use every means to root out the true worship "even though they overthrow governments and destroy kingdoms for that end". Speaking to the Swedish Riksdag in 1617, he denounced the Jesuits and the inquisition who had spared neither "kingly nor low, man nor woman", and the Holy League which planned "through violent and treacherous means . . . to compel all those who have thrown off the black darkness of the papacy to return again to the yoke and thraldom of Rome".[28] And in a further proclamation, in 1623, he asserted, in even more urgent terms, that a "general persecution and open war of religion had been launched . . . whereby whole principalities and lordships which had formerly cast off the yoke of Babylon would be once again brought under it."[29] The forces of darkness were thus seen as a threat not only to the true religion but to the security of the state as well. At the same time as delivering his blood-curdling warning in 1617, Gustav Adolph introduced legislation under which Catholics were given three months to leave the country on pain of being tried for high treason, while anybody who had attended a Catholic university was to be outlawed. In England in Elizabeth's day it became high treason to say mass, high treason to harbour a Catholic priest, high treason to seek to reconcile anyone to the Catholic church, and high treason to bring an *Agnus Dei* into the country. In Bavaria books were censored, protestants forcibly expelled and foreign study prohibited (in case the student became infected with pernicious beliefs). In Spain the Inquisition condemned to death protestants, Jews and Moriscos who practised their own faith. Mutual fear and detestation among rival protestant faiths was almost as great: the Lutheran elector of Brandenburg declared that he would rather burn his only university than allow one Calvinist doctrine to appear in it. It was (as in a later age of ideology) this fear of the evil enemy within the gate which, by raising the intensity of feeling, so often stimulated warlike passions in this age.

War was therefore, at this time, often genuinely seen as defensive rather than offensive: a means of preserving a faith from the dangers that threatened it rather than an instrument for spreading it elsewhere. There were some at least who recognised that war was not well fitted for the purpose of conversion. The French writer de Thou wrote in 1604 that "experience teaches us that the sword and the flame, exile and proscription, are more likely to exacerbate than to cure our ill".[30] Stephen Bathory, king of Poland, himself a Catholic convert, insisted that religion should be propagated "not by violence, fire and the sword, but by instruction and good example." And John Zamoyski, chancellor of Poland during the 1570s, declared that he "would give half my life to bring back to catholicism those who have abandoned it, but I would give my whole life to prevent it being brought back by violence". Even in their own time such people were probably never typical. As the period progressed they became less so. Only the most fanatical believed that military victory alone would save souls: it had to be accompanied by the armies of Jesuit educators, or of impassioned Calvinist preachers, following in its wake. But many were aware that it was the armies, not the preachers, who in the end determined which faith was to be practised. The religious map closely followed the military map. It is thus not surprising that military victory was so widely seen as the best means of spreading the true word. As Loaysa, Charles V's confessor, put it, "force alone suppressed the revolt against the King in Spain; force alone will put an end to Germany's revolt against God".[31]

But war was not only used to promote religious ends. It was widely seen as the means of promoting state interests as well. In an age when rulers were everywhere concerned to impose their authority within their own states — and often to extend it elsewhere too — war obviously had important secular purposes. The belief that war was valuable as a means of distracting a population from domestic grievances persisted. The duke of Rohan, for example, believed it was useful on the grounds that it "occupied ambitious and unquiet spirits, banished luxury, made people warlike, increased a state's reputation among neighbours and reduced the likelihood of civil war". Still more widespread was the view that successful war could add to the prestige of the state and its ruler. By many war was still seen as a glorious undertaking, and essential to preserving the interest of a prince, his dynasty, above all his state. Richelieu, in his Testament Politique, declared that war was not only an "unavoidable evil" but in some circumstances "absolutely necessary". States might need to resort to it, for example, to "recover what belonged to them, to avenge an injury . . . to safeguard allies from oppression, to halt the progress and the pride of a conqueror, to prevent evil which threatens that cannot be prevented by other means", and even to "purge" a state's "bad humours".[32]

These beliefs about the justifiability of war were only marginally affected by the emerging principles of international law. Rulers were still concerned to portray themselves as having justice and right on their side. Philip II consulted a committee of theologians and lawyers about the legitimacy or otherwise of particular wars: such committees endorsed both his invasion of Portugal in 1580 and the "enterprise against England" in 1588. The ministers of Elizabeth I consulted Anglican divines before the decision to intervene in the Netherlands in 1585. Philip III, before embarking on war over the question of the Mantuan succession in 1628, consulted a committee of lawyers and theologians who agreed that war was legitimate for that cause. This does not mean that any objective principles were involved in such decisions. Most rulers were convinced that their own wars were "just" and could usually rely on their advisers to take a similar view (Vitoria, who aroused Charles V's ire by condemning Spanish action in South America, was a rare exception). Thus, though Richelieu told his master that the power of a prince depended on his reputation as much as on armed force and believed that a war ought to be "just", he also declared that in affairs of state "whoever is stronger is often right, and, in the eyes of most of the world, the weak are usually in the wrong".[33] Though Olivares, in recommending war for Montferrat to Philip IV in 1528, declared that "nothing is more important to your majesty over Montferrat than acting with justification", he had no difficulty in concluding that war to "mortify" the French claimant and to promote the Spanish cause would be "extremely justified".[34]

Traditional doctrine in any case provided a wide range of justifications for war. It was generally held that "a lawfully instituted government might go to war in defence of land, faith, goods or liberty; by way of reprisal for acts of piracy; to avenge insults to ambassadors; to defend its friends and allies; when treaties were broken by another party; to stop other nations supplying an enemy with men, munitions or food."[35] The prevailing religious enthusiasm had the effect that "the concept of the just war was broadened to allow military aid to be sent to co-religionaries in another country and to anticipate changes in the balance by a preventive campaign".[36] The Spanish theologians Molina and de Valentia even relaxed the rules to permit a prince to go to war if his cause was "probably, and not demonstrably, just".[37] No wonder that it was recognised that in making war "every man will seem to have his good cause, and do nothing without just cause".[38]

The new writers on international law did not significantly reduce the justifications for war that were available. The writings of Grotius, which were widely known and highly respected (Gustav Adolph — for whom he worked — is said to have carried a copy of his works with him always), allowed war in a wide variety of circumstances. For example, he held that war was legitimate for preventive purposes: to prevent "an injury not yet inflicted which menaces either person or property",[39] or to forestall "an act of violence which is not immediate but is seen to be threatening from a distance".[40] He believed that war was justified if undertaken to preserve the rights or essential interests of a state; to secure "reparation for injury";[41] to secure a guarantee "against a threatened wrong or security against an anticipated injury";[42] for "the recovery of property";[43] to "exact punishment";[44] or to right "wrongs not yet committed or wrongs already done".[45] Even if a ruler was concerned, therefore, to show that his actions were in conformity with international law (which was certainly not always the case), it was not hard to select one from among the many justifications which that law provided.

Developments in political theory also scarcely discouraged war. The widely read writings of Machiavelli, Bodin and Hobbes each in different ways extolled the authority of the state and justified actions undertaken to promote state interest. "A prince", Machiavelli declared, "should have no other aim or thought . . . but war and its organisation and discipline, for that is the only art that is necessary to one who commands . . . ."[46]

The emerging conception of sovereignty these writers developed supported the view of the international lawyers: sovereigns enjoyed the right to make war precisely because of their sovereignty, a right that no non-sovereign body shared. This could be a useful argument for governments seeking, like so many in this day, to defend their power against rebel forces. Ayala, the Spanish international lawyer, regarded rebellion as a heinous crime against God and prince alike, which could not be justified even if the prince was cruel: thus rebels (such as those in the Netherlands) could be treated as brigands and robbers, and if necessary killed or enslaved. Whatever their knowledge of such theorists, most sovereigns certainly shared their distaste for revolution. That is why Elizabeth, for example, was unwilling, despite a clear national interest, to give more help to rebel causes in Scotland, France and the Netherlands; and why rulers of the larger protestant states in Germany were so unwilling to help fellow protestants in Bohemia against their common overlord, the emperor.

The rebels, especially religious rebels, were thus obliged to evolve alternative theories of government, to justify their own use of armed force. These were usually based — as in the Netherlands, in France and in Germany — on the idea of a contract between the ruler and his subjects, under which the ruler held power only on behalf of them and only so long as he abided by certain principles. This view was expressed, for example, by the French Huguenots in the treatise *Vindicae contra Tyrannos,* which set out a justification for revolt; and by the Netherlands rebels in their Act of Abjuration deposing Philip II in 1581, which declared that

> a prince is constituted by God to be ruler of a people: to defend them from oppression and violence, as the shepherd his sheep; and whereas God did not create the people slaves to their prince to obey his commands whether right or wrong, but rather the prince for the sake of his subjects to love and support them as a father his child or a shepherd his flock . . . where he does not behave thus but oppresses them . . . then he is no longer a prince but a tyrant and they may not only disallow his authority but legally proceed to the choice of another prince for their defence.

That opinion was exactly mirrored on the Catholic side by the view of the theology faculty in the Sorbonne (then in revolt against the king) that a king who broke his contract could be resisted, deposed and slain, and that French Catholics at that time were therefore justified in taking up arms against their king.[47] Such theories could be used to justify not only revolution but even assassination (openly endorsed by some Jesuits), and may partly help to explain the very large numbers of assassinations, of both rulers and ministers, that took place in this age.* Not for another 300 years, in another ideological age, would revolution be so widely practised and so eloquently justified.

One effect of the universal commitment to a religious cause was that, except among a small and declining group of politiques, the middle way became unacceptable. Neutrality was no longer seen as an honourable option. As Gustav Adolph put it, in denouncing the elector of Brandenburg's prudent defence of his inaction, "there can be no third way. . . . Neutrality is nothing but rubbish, which the wind raises and carries away"[48] (thus foreshadowing the view of "neutralism" to be held in another ideological society by John Foster Dulles). In an age of religious controversy few leaders and few countries could avoid having to stand up and be counted in the long run. Even the most reluctant to become involved in the Thirty Years War — such as England, Brandenburg and Saxony, each of which twisted and turned to avoid participation — were in the end unable to be totally uninvolved. Religious commitment was generally taken to require, in the long run, military commitment too.

This rejection of the concept of neutrality was reflected in the practice of the age. Neutrals would frequently find their territories crossed by rival armies. Sometimes their land was occupied for many months or even years (as neutral Brandenburg, for example, was occupied by imperial forces in 1627-9). Grotius himself accepted that belligerents had the right to transport troops and supplies across the territory of non-belligerents. The right of neutrals to trade freely was widely denied. They were frequently prevented by one belligerent from trading with its enemy. And many countries maintained the doctrine of "enemy goods, enemy ship", i.e. that any ship carrying the goods of an enemy could be treated as an enemy.[49] Even in Italy, where religious conflicts played only a small part, there was little

---

* Those assassinated included in France two kings, Henry III and Henry IV, the queen of Navarre (probably) and four principal religious leaders (Coligny and three dukes of Guise); in the Netherlands, William of Orange; in Scotland, Cardinal Beaton, Rizzio, Darnley and Moray; in Germany, Wallenstein. Though these were not all killed on religious grounds, the intensity of religious conflict made assassination a more widely accepted expedient in this age than in most other international societies.

willingness to admit neutrality: so, for example, in the early 1600s all the small states of north-western Italy, which had sought to avoid involvement in the major wars of the age, none the less found themselves in turn occupied or coerced by Spain. In a few cases neutrals were able to get their status formally recognised, if only to avoid the inconvenience of invasion by powerful antagonists: thus in the treaty of Mayence in 1632 some Catholic German states persuaded Gustav Adolph to recognise their neutrality to avoid sharing the fate of their less fortunate neighbours. But for the most part, in this age of commitment, the status of neutral secured little recognition. The development of more general rules on neutrality had to await a later day, more tolerant of non-involvement.

Religious conflict also vitiated the efforts which began to be made to humanise the practice of war. The earlier denunciations of the use of guns and gunpowder were now stilled or ineffective. There were now no known cases of weapons, new or improved, being suppressed as a result of moral scruples.[50] When an infernal machine blew up several hundred people at the siege of Antwerp, the reaction was mainly one of "appalled admiration".[51] A few writers advocated minor restraints on the conduct of war. Gentili taught that warfare should spare women, children, priests and vulnerable groups (as classical just-war doctrine had demanded). Grotius suggested that the conquered should be killed only when this was necessary to save victors from death or similar evil, or because of the crimes they had committed; hostages should not be put to death unless they had done wrong themselves; property should not be destroyed except for reasons of military necessity; some religious freedom should be left to conquered peoples.[52] Gustav Adolph issued a standing order that his troops were not to attack hospitals, schools, churches or the civilians connected with them. But there is little evidence that any of these proscriptions had much influence on the way armies behaved. The orders of Gustav Adolph did not prevent Swedish troops (or at least Swedish armies, which were mainly non-Swedish) from engaging in ruthless killing and destruction — for example, in the occupation of Bavaria in 1632-3. The doctrines of Grotius did little to restrain the brutal conduct of the imperial armies after the siege of Magdeburg and of protestant armies on similar occasions. While there may have been, among a very few, a greater concern than before to reduce the horrors of warfare, especially to civilians, it cannot be said that this was reflected in the actual practice of warfare. On the contrary, this reached depths of inhumanity scarcely known in any other age.

The practice of states probably had more influence in affecting the conduct of war than the writings of lawyers. A few new conventions began to emerge. In laying down his terms for a settlement in the Thirty Years War, Gustav Adolph put forward principles that were to remain standard demands for centuries to come. In calling for *satis-factio* (compensation*) for his expenditure in the war, he was not merely dignifying the demand for booty which was so common in this age (p. 246), but also asserting the principle that a victorious power could demand a price from the defeated for the cost of conquering them: a demand to be reproduced in demands for "indemnities", "reparations", "dismantling", and all the other extortions to be put forward by the victors over and over again in future generations. In calling for assecuratio (security) for victors, he established a justification for territorial aggrandisement which was to be used many times in the years to come, even to the most recent times. The principle that a claim to sovereignty required "effective occupation" of the territory concerned, established in the negotiations for the treaty of London between England and Spain in 1604, became an accepted tenet of international law for centuries.

So ideas about war changed in a number of ways. On the one hand, paranoid fears of powers of darkness intent on destroying the true faith encouraged the belief, among minorities within states as well as among governments ruling them, that war was sometimes necessary to defend God's word and God's church against the forces which threatened them. On the other, fanatical faith could create a more positive desire to vindicate that church and spread its word, by war if necessary, to bring about the triumph of good over evil and of right over wrong. War might be a scourge of God but it was sometimes a scourge that could be legitimately used in a righteous cause. This conception of war as having a moral purpose did not displace the more traditional view of war as the time-hallowed means by which secular rulers overcame their enemies and increased their power. It could be the means of strengthening the state, both internally and externally. It could be the means of winning glory for those who undertook it. It could even, some held, be used justifiably against the state, if the ruler betrayed the trust that his subjects had put in him. The teachings of international lawyers and the moralists did little to modify these attitudes. Those teachings were little known; and in any case both still permitted war in a wide variety of circumstances. There was little, therefore, in the intellectual climate of the age, for all its fervour and genuine religious devotion, that could be expected to cause those who exercised responsibility — rulers or ministers, religious leaders or military commanders — to have much compunction in taking up the sword if they thought it necessary for the causes in which they believed.

* This use use of the term for financial recompense differed from that which emerged in the following age, when the word came to be used to refer to a recompense, usually territorial, to match an advantage acquired by some rival power.

The age of sovereignty (1648-1789)

The beliefs that emerged in the following age were those of a different kind of society, with different preoccupations and a different social structure.

The beliefs that were most significant were inevitably those of the sovereigns and chief ministers; for they were the people mainly responsible for the decisions that were reached concerning peace and war. Their beliefs were of course influenced by the opinions held elsewhere: by the nobility, the military leaders, churchmen, members of parliament (where parliaments existed), even to some extent the people as a whole (for example, even an absolute monarch such as Louis XIV, who showed little reluctance to make war when necessary, recognised the danger that his people, "deprived of my relief by the expenses of such a great war, could suspect me of preferring my personal glory to their welfare and tranquillity"[53]). The degree of influence each social group had — and the nature of the beliefs each held — varied somewhat from one state to another; and this could affect the attitudes of the decision-makers in each state. In trading countries, where the merchant community were powerful and vocal, and where the entire fortunes of state could depend on trade, sentiments in favour of peace were sometimes more widely spread and more influential with rulers than in countries where the military, or those who could win glory from military exploits, were prominent. Thus in the United Provinces, where the standard of living of many depended on the maintenance of uninterrupted trade, pressures to avoid war were powerful, especially from 1715 onwards;[54] and as a result she was only engaged twice, briefly, in war from that time on (in 1747-8 and 1780-3), on each occasion when she was herself attacked by others. In England too there were strong pressures in favour of peace when prolonged war interrupted trade: for example, in 1696, 1710 and 1746-8. By contrast, in the absolute monarchies, especially those where the military and the young nobility could expect to win glory only in war, the influences might be quite the other way. Louis XIV frankly recognised in his Memoires how strong were the pressures on him in favour of war from many "fine men . . . enthusiastic for my service who seemed to be constantly urging me to furnish some scope for their valour".[55]

But, in spite of variations from state to state of this sort, there existed among the ruling classes of the entire international community assumptions and understandings about the making of war which were fairly generally shared, and which influenced the thinking of decision-makers in all states. It was no doubt taken for granted, as in most other ages, that, other things being equal, peace was better than war. Rulers would frequently declare their love of peace and their intention to preserve it. Louis XIV, despite his considerable propensity for war, prided himself in 1697, at the end of a nine-year war for which he had the main responsibility, on his sincere desire for "a peace that has always been the single aim . . . of my undertakings"; and proceeded to organise a great celebration on the theme "Louis XIV gives peace to Europe".[56] The Emperor Charles VI in renouncing the throne of Spain for which he had fought so bitterly for a dozen years, said that he did so "because Our natural inclination for peace and Our concern for the common weal are much more powerful motives for Us than any other". In his matching renunciation of the throne of France in 1720, Philip V of Spain declared that he was doing so because he was "a born student of the arts of peace and of the common weal", which were "the strongest of the impulses which motivate us".[57] The fact that Walpole, in telling Queen Caroline in 1734 that, "though 50,000 men had been killed in Europe that year, not one was an Englishman", saw this as a matter of self-congratulation indicates a recognition among some at least of the heavy costs of war and of the blessings of peace. It was a part of the conventional wisdom of the day that rulers, even if they frequently made war, should love peace. And to demonstrate that commitment they pledged themselves in many of the peace treaties of the day to maintain "eternal" or "perpetual" peace with each other.

But generalised undertakings of this kind had little influence on the willingness to make war when necessary. Peter the Great, even though he had firmly decided on war with Sweden two years earlier, in 1700 renewed a treaty of "eternal peace" with her and even sent a personal ambassador a few months before war was declared to assure her of his peaceful intentions. The same Charles VI of Austria who renounced the Spanish throne because of his professed love of peace had only recently fought a long and bitter war in order to acquire it. The same Philip V of Spain who declared his deep concern for "peace and the common weal" had only two years earlier launched an aggressive war against Austria to win Sicily and Sardinia (and was to launch another for similar purposes eight years later). There was not a single leader of the age that did not believe that war was sometimes necessary and right for the prosecution of essential national interests. Only a few years before declaring his deep commitment to peace, Philip V, in declaring war in 1704, had asserted that "war is the ultimate court of appeal for the sovereigns of this world and They may honestly and openly have recourse to it". Frederick the Great, even in preaching his self-righteous denunciation of Machiavelli before he became king, declared that

all wars whose sole design is to guard against usurpation, to maintain unquestionable rights, to guarantee the public liberty and to ward off the oppression and violence of the ambitious, are agreeable to justice. When sovereigns engage in wars of this kind, they have no reason to reproach themselves with bloodshed; they are forced to it by necessity and in such circumstances war is a lesser evil than peace.[58]

This belief that war was necessary and justifiable in certain circumstances was a typical view of the day.

War could be justified on a number of grounds. One of the most widely used was, quite simply, the interest of the state: *raison d'état*. So Frederick the Great wrote that "aggressive wars, though detestable if waged for inadequate reasons, are justified if made necessary by the real interest of the state".[59] And in his *Reflections on the State of Europe* he wrote that "at all times it was the principle of great states to subjugate all whom they could and to extend their power continuously."[60] Similarly, Louis XIV in his *Memoires* made clear that he believed that the state interests of France justified his two wars against Spain and the United Provinces in 1667 and 1672; and he told his son to "have no doubt that I would always . . . have preferred conquering states to acquiring them [by negotiation]".[61] He prided himself that his war against the United Provinces in 1672 had enabled him to "instil fear into my antagonists, to cause astonishment to my neighbours and despair to my enemies".[62] The converse of this was that even peace would sometimes be chosen only for reasons of state: for example, in the same *Memoires* Louis XIV gave as his main reason for agreeing to peace in 1668 a desire to "establish a reputation for moderation and honesty among my weaker neighbours . . . improve my finances, my navy, my contacts and whatever else may be accomplished by a dedicated prince"; and that as a result he "could be more influential throughout Europe and more capable of gaining my ends with each individual state".[63]

War was also widely thought to be justified if undertaken to defend the "honour" of the state. Charles XII of Sweden, rejecting the notion that Sweden should make peace (after 14 years of war) in 1714, wrote that "better times would not come till we get more respect in Europe than we now have. Such respect will not come till we are stronger in the military sense and display our willingness to use the sword in our own defence."[64] George I, in declaring war against Spain in 1718, stated that he "could no longer stand idly by, for Our honour has been impeached, the territories of Our friends and allies unjustly invaded", and he was therefore compelled to make war "in a cause in which the honour of Our Crown, the faithful observance of solemn treaties and pledges, and the safeguarding of our subjects' rights and interests are at stake".[65]

"Glory" was equally often proclaimed as a reason for making war. Frederick the Great, writing to his chamberlain in 1731, said that, if

Prussia could unite her scattered territories by conquering West Prussia, Pomerania, Mecklenburg and other lands, she might "cut a fine figure among the great powers of the world".[66] And later, writing to his foreign minister, Podewils, in 1745, he declared that he had made it "a point of honour to have contributed more than anyone to the aggrandisement of my House" and proclaimed the "obligation I have to fight for the safety of my Fatherland and the glory of my House".[67] Sometimes the glory was to be had by the ruler personally. Louis XIV wrote in his *Memoires* for his son that he "envisaged with pleasure the prospect of these two wars [against England and Spain in 1767-8] as a vast field for me to distinguish myself and to fulfil the great expectation that I had for some time inspired in the public".[68] And later he declared that, "if I sometimes inclined ever so slightly towards war, this was . . . merely because it is undoubtedly the most brilliant way to win glory".[69] Frederick the Great wrote shortly after the invasion of Silesia that he had done this partly from a "desire for glory. . . . The satisfaction of seeing my name in the papers, and later in the history books, seduced me."[70]

War was also sometimes justified on the grounds that it was designed to *anticipate* war by another state. Long before he became king of Prussia, Frederick the Great wrote that

> a prince ought rather to engage in offensive war than wait till desperate times come on. . . . It is a certain maxim that a prince should rather prevent than be prevented: great men have always been successful when they make use of their forces before their enemies take such measures as tie their hands and suppress their power.[71]

In the same work Frederick said that there are "some wars made for the sake of precaution and which princes do well to undertake. They are offensive indeed, but just".[72] This was a doctrine that he himself put into practice in 1740 (when he seized Silesia claiming that he was anticipating similar action against Austria by other powers), and in 1756 (when he invaded Saxony claiming that she was preparing war against him). Because of the widespread acceptance (even by international lawyers) of preventive war, even a patently aggressive war was often declared to be defensive. So Louis XIV, in sending French troops to attack Cologne and the Palatinate in 1688, declared that his action was entirely defensive and had been forced on him by the hostile actions of the emperor, the pope, and the protestant princes, who were in league against him: if they only granted his limited aims, "permanent peace" could be established in Europe.[73]

Another reason often given for war in this age (and another which continued to be used in subsequent periods) was the need to protect the interests of the state's subjects. So Louis XIV, in undertaking his carefully prepared aggression against the United Provinces in 1672, stated that this was undertaken "to protect Our subjects from the aggressions which threaten them" (almost identical to the justification used by Hitler in invading Czechoslovakia and Poland in 1939: see pp. 366-7 below). Frederick the Great in his *Discours sur la Guerre* said that warfare was "the first defence of the oppressed", in which "men risked their lives for their fellow-citizens". George I's declaration of war against Spain in 1718 gave as a principal reason that his subjects had been "attacked and their property raped, their trade interrupted and every conceivable hurt inflicted upon them"; and Britain produced a similar justification for making war against Spain in 1739. In the same way, in many of the colonial wars of the period the justification for declaring war was often that the actions of one European power had caused damage to the subjects of another in some overseas territory.

It was especially the commercial interests of a nation's subjects which it was thought reasonable in this age to protect by war. It was widely believed that trade sometimes needed to be won by war. Colbert made no secret of his desire to win the trade of the Dutch by war.[74] The English statesman Clarendon complained that "the [London] merchants took much delight to discuss the infinite benefit that would accrue from a barefaced war against the Dutch, how easily they might be subdued and the trade carried on by the English".[75] In 1663-4 a petition in the English parliament complained of "the wrongs, dishonours and indignities come to His Majesty by the subjects of the United Provinces, by invading his rights in India, Africa and elsewhere, and the damage, affronts and injuries done by them to our merchants are the greatest obstruction of our foreign trade", and asked the king to "take some speedy and effectual means for the redress thereof and prevention of the like in future": pressure which helped to bring about the second Dutch war in the following year. In the following century an English writer suggested that "our Commerce in general will flourish more under a vigorous and well-managed naval War than under any Peace which should allow an open intercourse with those two Nations [France and Spain]".[76] And the London merchant Beckford declared that "our trade will improve by the total extinction of theirs [France's]".[77] In the eyes of many the main purpose of naval power was to promote and protect trade (on these grounds, Sir Josiah Child had held, "profit and power" were inextricably interlinked).[78] The War of Jenkin's Ear was fought by Britain against Spain almost entirely for that purpose; and, in the eyes of many in England and the United Provinces, one of the main benefits to be expected from the War of the Spanish Succession was the capture of trade from Spain (which was duly achieved by both).

War was thus widely seen as a legitimate instrument for promoting national interests. Rulers themselves were frank in declaring that view. Frederick the Great had no compunction, even in his published writing, in expressing his desire that Prussia should increase her power and status, through war if necessary. So, in his first political testament of 1752 he declared that,

> if the army is maintained in the good discipline it is at present, if the governing authorities save in time of peace to provide the expenses of war, if they can profit wisely and well from the turn of events . . . I do not doubt that the state can continue growing and enlarging, and that in time Prussia will become one of the most considerable states in Europe.[79]

He described precisely the advantages Prussia would gain by acquiring Polish Prussia, Swedish Pomerania and Saxony. He declared openly that, if "we have reason to draw the sword against Austria, we should begin by invading Saxony" and "go on to take Bohemia, which could be exchanged for an Electorate closer to our frontiers". To achieve such aims a ruler must, he believed, be prepared to conceal his true intentions:

> The first concern of a prince must be to sustain his power, the second aggrandisement. This policy demands that he should be flexible and ready for anything. . . . The way of concealing such secret ambitions is to pretend peaceful ambitions until the most favourable moment for revealing one's true intentions. This is the way all great politicians have behaved.[80]

And he accepted that for achieving his ends a ruler might need to break treaties and alliances (though "he ought to do it with as much honour as he can"[81]) — a principle he fulfilled in seizing Silesia in violation of the Pragmatic Sanctions in 1740. The difference between Frederick and other rulers was not that he thought differently on such questions: only that he wrote so prolifically about his views. Louis XIV, one of the few other rulers to commit his thoughts to paper (also in the form of advice to his successor), equally emphasised the benefits of long and secret preparations for war: "plans that are devised long before can be handled so subtly, and hidden under so many pretexts, that in spite of all the warnings and all the suspicions about them they still hardly ever fail to cause surprise".[82] And he too put this into practice not only in so carefully and secretly preparing his war against the Dutch, but also in carrying on negotiations with representatives of Franche Comté about the maintenance of its neutrality at the very moment that he was, as he frankly admitted in his

Mémoires, preparing to invade their territory.[83]

Against these underlying attitudes the new concepts of international law had little, if any, influence. It is likely that in most cases the rulers of the day were quite unaware of them (Charles XII of Sweden who was taught by Pufendorf, one of the most eminent international lawyers of the day, is an exception; but there is no evidence that that supremely combative ruler became as a result much concerned about scrupulous respect for international law). In any case international lawyers did not preach a code of behaviour very different from that proclaimed by the rulers themselves. Most still maintained the traditional belief that a war ought to be "just". But there remained a very wide range of reasons that were held to make war just. Hobbes, a believer in the doctrine, had no difficulty in showing that the Dutch were responsible for the first Dutch war because they had refused to recognise English sovereignty over the North Sea. Vattel, probably the best known international lawyer of his day, believed that war by a state was permissible if it was necessary "for the preservation of its rights".[84] States, he believed, could "use force where necessary" to "anticipate the other's design", or "to prevent a recurrence of . . . attacks". War was widely held to be just if it took the form of a "reprisal" for the purpose of "compelling a state to consent to a satisfactory settlement of a difference created by its own international delinquency". Some believed it to be justified if undertaken to undo any "injustice" committed by another state. Finally, it was widely accepted to be legitimate if undertaken for the "maintenance of the balance of power".[85] Between them these provided an ample range of justifications for would-be aggressors to choose from.

The lawyers thus, as in most other ages, reflected widely shared beliefs rather than created new ones. They provided a legal framework appropriate to the ideology of an age of sovereignty. The right of sovereigns to maintain their authority in their own territory was upheld in the continued proscription of "private war"; but they themselves were in many cases held to be justified in undertaking war to defend their own interests against other rulers. Emphasis on the sanctity of treaties had the effect of stressing the authority to be attributed to the written undertakings of the sovereigns themselves. The new doctrine of "positivism", which emerged at this time, even maintained that international law consisted solely in the undertakings to which the sovereigns had formally assented in treaties and other agreements. The gradual shedding of the old belief in a "law of nature", to which rulers and states were subject, promoted the assumption that the only authority which counted was that of the rulers as expressed in their formal undertakings. But, most important of all, the authority of the rulers was now itself held to be subordinate to that of the state. Some lawyers maintained that the undertakings of a sovereign only held in so far as they did not conflict with the essential interests of the state.[86] It was this concept (together with ancient beliefs in divine right, and the ultimate legitimacy of a ruling family) which led to the view (the source of many conflicts in this age) that even a ruler could not properly renounce inheritance and so deny the rights of his descendants.*

Thus both rulers and international lawyers recognised a wide range of legitimate uses of force. But they also began to define more clearly the rights of those not engaged in war: in other words, the rights of neutrals. This development resulted mainly from the actions of the neutrals themselves, increasingly restive at the affronts they suffered at the hands of belligerent powers, especially Britain.[87] With the growth of international trade and its growing importance for some countries, there was increasing resentment at interference with neutral shipping by states which were at war. Britain frequently made use of her superior sea-power to threaten any shipping which was trading, whether in contraband or not, with her enemies. The anger this practice caused promoted new measures among neutral countries to counter it. The doctrine "free ship, free goods" began to replace the idea of "enemy goods, enemy ship" (p. 343 above): even enemy goods should not be captured at sea if they were carried in neutral ships. This became a burning principle for the United Provinces and other trading countries. In 1759 the Danish government proposed the creation of a maritime union to defend neutral rights. And this culminated in 1780 in the establishment of the so-called Armed Neutrality of Russia, the United Provinces, Sweden and Denmark, subsequently joined by almost every other state in Europe.[88]

There was even some small effort to humanise the practice of war. For the most part this did not derive from agreements among governments: that had to wait till the following period. Individual governments, however, sometimes now issued codes of conduct for armies in the field proscribing certain types of behaviour, particularly towards civilians. It was laid down, for example, that arable fields, meadows and gardens were not to be destroyed (a rule that was sometimes in the interest of occupying armies expecting to live off the country). Improved discipline in armies served to reduce outrages against civilians. Agreements or "cartels" between commanders covered such matters as the ransoming and exchange of prisoners, and the levying of contributions in occupied territories. Agreements were reached relating to protection of the sick and wounded when a besieged city was given up and for the safeguarding of hospitals. In a

---

* This belief was used to cast doubt on the renunciations of inheritance made commonly in this age: for example, by Louis XIV's wife in relation to Spain, by the nieces of Charles VI in relation to the Hapsburg lands and by the elector Palatine in relation to Bavaria in 1777.

few cases poisoned projectiles and missiles of tin or other material were banned.[89] However, all these efforts together had "no direct effects that we can trace".[90] International lawyers tended to maintain that in public and declared war there was no limit on the damage a belligerent could inflict on an enemy.[91] And there was virtually no limit in practice to the terror that invaders could impose. In consequence, though "there was a European community, itself a member of a nebulous and loosely knit world-wide community, . . . it does not appear . . . that there either was, or was believed to be, any important movement towards the humanising of war or towards limiting its political aims".[92]

In this age, therefore, it continued to be held that war was in many circumstances an entirely justifiable activity. Everywhere rulers were expected to proclaim their own love of peace and their desire to avoid the tragedies of war. Yet everywhere war was still seen as a part of the normal behaviour of states. If not actually desirable, it was, those same rulers proclaimed, none the less necessary in certain circumstances, not only in self-defence but also to promote essential state interests: to acquire territories seen, by reason of their geography or strategic value, as legitimate acquisitions; to recover land lost in earlier wars; to humble the overmighty; to anticipate a war planned (or alleged to be planned) by another state; to right a wrong; to protect the interests of subjects; or for other reasons. The writers on international law did not seriously dissent from most of these opinions. They were, anyway, little known and less regarded. In consequence the rulers of the day continued to believe that (if only they had good prospects of prevailing) the making of war could sometimes be the right course: the best way for them to fulfil their principal duty which was to promote the vital interests of the states they ruled.

The age of nationalism (1789-1917)

For all the nationalism of the period that followed a subtle change began to be evident in attitudes to war. It continued to be generally held that war was a normal act of policy in certain situations. But there began to be, almost for the first time, even among statesmen a sense that such acts should not be arbitrary or irrational. Though sometimes necessary, war increasingly required to be justified.

The sense that war was a normal and unavoidable (even sometimes a desirable) feature of human existence was encouraged by much of the general thinking of the era. Martial valour continued to be venerated. Nations still took pride in military prowess. Not only national survival but national honour and national glory could depend on the capacity to win wars. It was sometimes suggested that war fulfilled a higher purpose. The philosophy of Hegel, holding that

all history represented the working out of some divine plan, expounded that war was the way in which sovereign states, through which that plan manifested itself, must resolve their differences, leading to the emergence of superior states (such as the Prussian state), representing the fulfilment of the divine purpose: "God walking on earth".*
The historian Treitschke believed that war "consolidates a people, reveals to each individual his relative unimportance, sweeps away factional hostilities and group selfishness, intensifies patriotism and national idealism. When two nations are at war, each comes more fully to know and respect the other and the exchange of good qualities is made easier." Social Darwinists believed that a law of the survival of the fittest operated, among nations as among species, so that war became the process by which the weaker states were eliminated, and the strong, becoming victorious, were enabled to further human progress. The French writer Ernest Renan believed that "war is one of the conditions of progress, the sting which prevents a country from going to sleep, and compels satisfied mediocrity itself to awaken from its apathy".[93] As the elder von Moltke wrote to Bluntschli, "war is one of the elements of order in the world established by God. The noblest virtues of men are developed therein. Without war the world would degenerate in a morass of materialism." Writers in Britain, France and other countries — Kipling, Jules Ferry, Fabri — believed that the expansion of European power into other parts of the globe, only attainable through the use of armed force, represented a beneficial phase of human history and a boon to mankind as a whole. Finally, racialist doctrines, such as those of Chamberlain and Houston, holding that certain races were intrinsically superior to others, provided, at least by implication, a justification for the attempt of the "superior" races to subdue inferior ones.

The political leaders of the day were probably barely aware of most of these writings, though they may have been indirectly influenced. They were much more affected by the assumptions and traditions that prevailed in political and diplomatic circles. It was still generally believed that war was sometimes necessary to promote essential national interests. War was widely seen as a normal and legitimate instrument of policy: in the famous words of Clausewitz (much quoted at the time), the "continuation of policy [politics] by other means". Though Bismarck was criticised for stating, in his very first speech to the Prussian parliament as chancellor, that it was not by

---

* The younger von Moltke, German chief of general staff at the beginning of the First World War, reflected these ideas when, in the first weeks of that war, he declared that "Germany alone can help mankind develop in the right direction. For this reason Germany will not be vanquished in this war; it is the only nation that can at present take over the leadership of mankind towards higher goals."

speeches and resolutions but by "iron and blood" that the great issues of the day were decided, he was only saying what most other statesmen of the day in their hearts believed. Most national leaders stated, almost equally bluntly, that war might be necessary in certain circumstances to protect national honour or vital national interests. When they signed arbitration agreements promising to submit certain kinds of dispute to pacific settlement, they carefully excluded questions that affected the "vital interests", the "independence" or the "honour" of the state: meaning that these could only be settled in the final resort by war. When Louis Napoleon declared in 1864 that France could only go to war for an issue that directly touched the "dignity and interests" of France ("unless there was a prospect of compensation held out"), he indicated that for those causes at least war was justifiable. Bismarck bluntly prided himself in his memoirs that his three wars had been justified by the interests of Prussia and Germany;[94] he announced openly to Disraeli in 1862, according to his own account, that he intended to "seize the first good pretext to declare war against Austria, and give natural unity to Germany under Prussian leadership";[95] and in July 1882, he justified the war with France by declaring "we could not have set up the German Reich in the middle of Europe without having defeated France. . . . The war with France was a necessary conclusion."

The assumption that war might be necessary and a proper course in certain circumstances was shared by many governments of the time. Palmerston did not conceal his belief that the use of force was necessary in certain circumstances to protect British interests or "rights" (p. 117 above) and he declared that though "diplomats and protocols are very good things", there were "no better peace-keepers than well-appointed three-deckers".[96] Theodore Roosevelt declared that the United States "must play a great part in the world and especially . . . perform those deeds of blood and valour which above everything else bring national renown", for "by war alone can we acquire those virile qualities necessary to win in the stern strife of actual life".[97] The Russian minister of the interior, Plehve, stated that "Russia has been made by bayonets not diplomacy . . . and we must decide the question at issue with China and Japan with bayonets and not with diplomacy", adding, optimistically, that a "little victorious war with Japan" would do much to calm revolutionary agitation in Russia;[98] while Tsar Alexander III, in supporting the Russian alliance with France against Germany, believed that "we must correct the mistakes of the past and crush Germany at the first opportunity". Such views were especially common in the period just before the First World War. The crown prince of Germany wrote a foreword to a book, *Germany in Arms*, declaring that it was essential for the German Reich to maintain its army and navy at the greatest pitch of readiness, because "only in this way, by trusting in our reliable sword, can we attain the place in the sun that is owing to us but which we shall not be given voluntarily."[99] The Kaiser wrote in 1912 of "the struggle for existence which the German people in Europe will eventually have to fight against the Slavs, supported by the Latins". In March 1913 the president of the Russian *duma* told the tsar that "the Straits must become ours: a war will be joyfully welcomed, and will raise the government's prestige".[100] Even Bethmann-Hollweg, the German chancellor, a pronounced dove by the standards of most of his colleagues, said in 1911 that "if necessary [Germany] will draw its sword: only on this basis can there be any foreign policy". In other words, statesmen of this age over and over again were willing to declare their readiness to attain their ends by war if the need arose.

These sentiments of the politicians were continually reinforced and strengthened by the attitudes of the military, including the top officers who advised about military questions. Often these looked forward to the prospect of fighting the right war at the right time. So, in the years before the Franco-Prussian War, the elder von Moltke wrote, "Nothing could be more welcome to us than to have now the war that we must have."[101] The French military, in the same period, were equally impatient to demonstrate their prowess: Louis Napoleon confessed in 1868 that "if anything like a challenge comes from Prussia it will be impossible for him to oppose the feelings of the army and the nation and he must in such a case, for the sake of his own safety, make war".[102] In 1905 Schlieffen, author of the famous plan, wrote that, with Russia then preoccupied in the Far East, "we can settle the account with our bitterest and most dangerous enemy, France, and will be fully justified in doing so".[103] Successive German chiefs of staff, believing that Russian rearmament was altering the balance of power in Europe, called for preventive war against Russia;[104] and in 1913-14 the chiefs of staff of Germany, Austria and Italy all believed in the necessity of such a war.[105] Von Moltke, the German chief of staff, was "disgusted" that Germany did not go to war over Morocco in 1911.[106] And at the end of 1912 he wrote, "I believe a war to be unavoidable, and the sooner the better." He therefore demanded a government programme designed to prepare the German people psychologically for war, and especially to explain the inevitability of a conflict between the Teutons and the Slavs. And in May 1914, well before the Sarajevo assassination, he strongly urged on the German foreign minister that "our policy should be geared to bringing about an early war". The Austrian chief of staff, von Hotzendorff, also favoured the destruction of Serbia even before the Sarajevo crisis.[107]

Retired generals were of course in a particularly strong position to exert pressure: they would still have the authority of expert judge-

ment, yet were free to express themselves publicly. So in Russia
General Skonelov publicly demanded war against Austria-Hungary
at the time of the rising in Bosnia-Herzegovina in 1878-9. Pressure
from this source was powerful in Germany in the period just before
the First World War. In 1912 von Bernhardi, a retired general and
publicist, in his book *Germany and the Next War,* openly declared
that, once rearmament had been achieved, "we shall call upon our
government methodically to bring about war and not wait until we
have been outstripped". And a year or two later, in another book,
the same writer said that Germany must, even at the risk of war,
"consolidate the position of the Reich in Europe" and, whatever the
resistance might be, "the fight was necessary and inevitable: we must
fight it whatever the cost".[108]

In some quarters it was not only resort to war that was advocated
but the utmost ruthlessness. Clausewitz had declared that

> in such dangerous things as war, the errors which proceed from a
> spirit of benevolence are the worst. . . . He who uses force
> unsparingly, without reference to the bloodshed involved, must
> obtain a superiority if the adversary uses less vigour in its applica-
> tion. The former then dictates the law to the latter.

In the same spirit Kaiser Wilhelm II, in addressing the German
contingent sent to put down the Boxers in China, told them, "Give
no quarter. Take no prisoners. Just as a thousand years ago, the Huns
under King Attila created a reputation that still lives in terror through
legend and fable, so may the German name resound through Chinese
history a thousand years from now."

These militaristic attitudes were sometimes spread among a wider
public opinion. They were often reflected in parliaments. Opinion in
the British House of Commons was strongly in favour of war against
Russia in 1854, especially after the destruction of the Turkish fleet
(through Turkey's own folly); and this was one of the pressures
pushing a reluctant Aberdeen to war. In 1870 the nationalist fervour
of the French chamber, who loudly applauded their foreign minister's
foolhardy threats against Prussia, was a major factor in stimulating
Louis Napoleon to war. In Germany before 1914, a large section of
public opinion was equally bellicose: in 1914 Hanz Plehn deplored
the fact that "it is an almost universal belief throughout the country
that we shall only win our freedom to participate in world politics
through a major European war".[109]

But, if public opinion generally was often bellicose, certain sections
of it were even more so. Right-wing groups and individuals frequently goaded their governments into more warlike stances. In France,
Boulanger was the leader of a nationalist pressure group that deman-

ded more forward policies to restore national glory, even at the risk of confrontation. In Germany such groups were even more warlike and even more outspoken. The All-German Union at the end of the nineteenth century did not hesitate to recommend war as the means of promoting German interests. Heinrich Class, its leader, believed that a war against France and Russia was "inevitable and necessary": "France must be crushed" and must be compelled to give up "as much French soil as we need for the purpose of lasting protection".[110] The Army League was another similar pressure group: its leader, Major-General Keim, declared in 1911 that "it is our right and duty to ensure that the German people gains its place in the world": if that can "be achieved only by the use of arms, we must not be deterred".[111] Many individuals expressed similar views. Theodore Schliemann, lecturer at the Prussian War Academy, was for 20 years before 1914 a declared advocate of "preventive war" against Russia and France, believing that Germany "must pursue a determined war policy if we are to restore our moral prestige, the power of the Crown, the security of our political situation and the internal unity of the nation".[112]

Given such widespread nationalist sentiments, it is not surprising that rulers could sometimes feel that a military adventure might be of value in raising their standing among their own peoples. As Bismarck said of Tsar Alexander III, "The emperor is himself well intentioned; his ministers are prudent; but will they have the strength to resist the pressures of popular passion if they are once unchained?" He made a similar point about Louis Napoleon, who continually looked for popular triumphs through military action:

> The adventurer on the throne . . . must always produce an effect. His safety depends on his personal prestige, and, to enhance it, sensations must follow each other in rapid succession. Napoleon III has recently lost more prestige than he can afford: to recover it he will start a dispute with us on some pretence or other. I do not believe he personally wishes war, indeed, I think he wants to avoid it, but his insecurity will drive him on.[113]

And Louis Napoleon himself accepted, after the outbreak of the Franco-Prussian war, that "France has slipped out of my hands, and I cannot rule unless I lead. . . . I have no choice but to advance at the head of public opinion which I can neither stem nor check."[114] In Japan in the early years of this century, large sections of press and public opinion were clamouring for war against Russia and the seizure of Siberia;[115] and in 1904 war followed. In the same way, Japanese nationalist societies and newspapers called for the invasion of Korea for 40 years before that country was finally taken over by

Japan in 1910.

These attitudes often found expression in the press, which intensified the pressure on governments. Lord Aberdeen, prime minister in Britain at the beginning of the Crimean War, seeking to explain the bellicose posture of public opinion in Britain at the time, stated that "it was not the parliament or the public that forced the government to war. The public mind was not at first in an uncontrollable state, but it was made so by the press." In every country there were particular newspapers, and particular writers, who continually stirred up national feelings and hostility to other states, sometimes quite openly recommending war. In Russia in the late nineteenth century the pan-Slav writer Katkov was continually calling, in his newspaper articles, for stronger Russian policy, especially against Austria-Hungary. B. A. Fadeev and N. I. Danislevsky in their writings both demanded the subjection of Constantinople to Slav rule; and Fadeev declared that, to achieve that aim, the destruction of both the Ottoman and Austrian empires would be necessary. In Germany the tone of press comments became continually shriller in the last few years before the First World War. Some papers not only prophesied but demanded war to secure Germany's "place in the sun". On Christmas Eve 1912, the *Berliner neueste Nachrichten* praised war "as part of a divine world order" which ensured the preservation of "all that is good and beautiful, great and noble in nature and in true civilisation". A political review, the *Politische-Anthropologische Revue,* declared that "we Teutons must no longer look upon war as our destroyer. . . . We must see it once more as the saviour, the physician".[116] A month or two later, Otto von Gottberg wrote, in the organ of the Federation of Young Germans, that war was "the noblest and most sacred manifestation of human activity. . . . War is beautiful. Its noble grandeur raises men high above earthly, daily things. . . . Let Germany alone live, flourish and prosper after a war".[117] Even church newspapers in Germany disseminated this view. In November 1913 the *Allgemeine Evangelisch-Lutherische Kirchenzeitung* said that "the will of the people demanded war" because "the European map no longer corresponds to the actual distribution of power".[118] And in the spring of 1914 the German press published a number of officially inspired anti-Russian articles, some of which took it for granted that war must come: one was entitled "The Coming War with Russia".[119]

Yet it was not only Germans who believed that war was sure to come. Many in Britain and France believed that war between the Entente powers and Germany was inevitable: for example, Clemenceau, Churchill, Poincaré, Paléologue and, among the military, Admiral Fisher, Sir Henry Wilson and Lord Roberts. Such people generally believed that the Western powers were superior.

The military in France believed that Britain and France alone (even without Russia) could defeat the central powers; as a result the French general staff (Sir Henry Wilson reported to the Foreign Office in 1913) believed it would be better for France if war was not delayed too long (a belief which Wilson seemed to share). Izvolsky, Russian foreign minister till 1910, and later Russian ambassador in Paris, also believed in the inevitability (and desirability) of war with the Central Powers.

But, for all the feelings that war was normal, acceptable, or even desirable, there emerged in this age a widespread sense that it needed to be justified. It should occur only for a cause that would appear adequate to world opinion. So in 1859 Louis Napoleon, though he unquestionably wanted war, told Cavour that he wanted a *casus belli* that "would be justified in the eyes of diplomacy, and even more in the eyes of public opinion".[120] Bismarck claimed that he would go to war only "when all other means were exhausted", and then only for "a prize worthy of the sacrifice which war demands".[121] Even more important was to show that it was the antagonist, and not one's own country, which was responsible for precipitating war. Governments would go to considerable lengths to provoke their enemies to initiating hostilities. So France and Sardinia, having carefully planned a war against Austria, were determined that Austria should start it and succeeded in getting the latter to issue the ultimatum which precipitated war in 1859. Likewise Bismarck, himself seeking war with Austria and France, in each case put them in a position where they felt obliged to take the first step, on the ground that they could not otherwise avoid national humiliation (thus Clarendon correctly forecast in 1859 that "Prussia does not fear a war if she can show Germany and the world that she is really forced into it"). More than in any previous age leaders now found it necessary to proclaim that war had been "forced" on them. Even in 1914, though many in German ruling circles believed that war was not only inevitable but desirable, there was a concern to show that it was the opponent that was the aggressor. So the younger von Moltke, while convinced in 1913 that "a European war must come in the end" was anxious that "the attack must come from the Slavs",[122] if world opinion was not to be antagonised. The German ambassador in Vienna, von Tschirschky, wrote to the Chancellor that he was trying to persuade the Austrians that, "if they are really convinced of the necessity of a military solution of the Balkan question, they must arrange things so that Russia is in the wrong and that it, or one of its satellites, appears to be the aggressor".[123] The German foreign minister a few weeks later argued that, if Austria found it necessary to go to war, Vienna must be able to claim that there had been "an obviously hostile act by Serbia".[124]

This anxiety to place the blame on opponents is a clear indication that, however much war might be privately desired, it was a desire that statesmen could no longer publicly acknowledge. One of the reasons why ultimata were so popular in this age was that they provided an almost automatic justification for war: if the opponent did not want war he had only to accept the conditions demanded. The ultimatum thus provided a no-lose situation. The opponent, like one challenged to a duel, must either back down and lose face lamentably; or if he rejected the ultimatum, he must take responsibility for initiating a war.*

It could perhaps be argued that there had in this sense been some advance in the attitudes of governments to war. It might only be the homage which vice paid to virtue, but at least some reasonable grounds were needed, it was widely believed, if a declaration of war was to be justified. While in the previous era there had been little attempt by those responsible for aggressions — as by Louis XIV making war against the United Provinces, by Frederick the Great in seizing Silesia, by Maria Theresa in seeking to recover it — to deny responsibility or to plead any very serious excuse, now it was seen as important, if war occurred, to pin the blame on others. A suitable pretext laying the blame on the enemy had to be found: Russia had threatened Turkey (1853), Austria had refused negotiations (1859), Austria would not abandon her claim to dominate Germany (1866), France would not take yes for an answer (1870). Or years had to be spent, as after the First World War, proving that the enemy bore the main responsibility. The pretexts and provocations required were not usually difficult to procure. There were still many situations in which a forcible response seemed to many the only natural, the only honourable, even the only prudent, response. And the beliefs that were current in international society accepted that in such situations — if an ambassador was insulted (1870), a minority people oppressed (1877), an archduke assassinated (1914) — war was a legitimate, an understandable, even (if successful) an admirable, course of action to adopt.

The idea that war was justifiable was encouraged by the widespread belief that it was inevitable. The latter notion was expressed perhaps most forcibly by those who were least dismayed by the prospect. If war was inevitable it could be accepted as normal. Above all it made *preventive* war justifiable: if war was to come anyway, it was reasonable to use the most favourable moment and not wait to have it forced upon you. Before 1870 many in France believed that

* It was Austria above all that specialised in this device, issuing ultimata to Piedmont in 1849 and 1859, to Prussia (in effect) in 1866 and to Serbia in 1914. In every case the gauntlet was taken up; and in every case except the first Austria was defeated.

war with Prussia was certain, and that because at that time she was thought to be better equipped (especially with the *chasse-pot* and the *mitrailleuse*) the sooner it came the more favourable for France: a belief that may well have influenced French actions in 1870. The Japanese chief of staff demanded war against Russia in 1903-4 because he believed that Japan had a strategic advantage that would be lost in a few years.[125] At about the same time, some in the French military staff favoured an early war against Germany for similar reasons. Bismarck believed that preventive war was a perfectly reasonable concept. He wrote in 1893 that "no government, if it regards war as inevitable, even if it does not want it, would be so foolish as to leave to the enemy the choice of time and occasion and to wait for the moment that is most convenient to the enemy". This statement was frequently quoted in Germany in the years before 1914 by those who favoured war against Russia or France or both. The German military staff believed that the most favourable moment for a war against their enemies would be after 1911-12 (since the German people were not at the time psychologically prepared for it) but before 1916-17 (when Russian rearmament would have been completed). Thus Konrad, the Austrian chief of staff, wrote in March 1914, "The programme of France and Russia was clear; they were not yet ready and were waiting to be fully prepared. The Balkan states too are becoming stronger, above all Serbia, Why do we wait?"[126] Von Moltke made the same point forcibly to the German foreign minister in May 1914 when he said, in the latter's words,

> In two to three years Russia would have finished arming. Our enemy's military power would then be so great that he [von Moltke] did not know how he could deal with it. Now we were still more or less a match for it. In his view there was no alternative but to fight a preventive war, so as to beat the enemy while we could still emerge fairly well from the struggle. The Chief of Staff therefore put it to me that our policies should be geared to bringing about an early war.[127]

This idea no doubt remained uppermost in the chief of staff's mind when, less than two months later, he consulted his Austrian counterpart about the response to be made to the assassination of Franz Ferdinand. If war was likely to come anyway sooner or later, would it not be wise to take advantage then of the occasion that had so opportunely emerged?

The doctrines of international law did not significantly counter those widely held views. They continued to reflect the general belief that war was in certain circumstances a justifiable action. War was still held by most writers to be lawful, if, for example, undertaken to maintain the balance of power; to enforce the obligation of a treaty; as an act of "humanitarian intervention" to save lives or prevent injustice in another state; or as a "reprisal" for unlawful action by other states, including non-payment of debts. Even preventive war was regarded by legal tribunals as justifiable (for example in the arbitration on the Caroline case between the United States and Britain in 1837) if there were sufficient grounds for assuming the hostile intentions of the other party. These ideas may have had some influence on politicians. Palmerston had no difficulty in justifying the use of force by the needs of "international right" on occasion: for example, in justifying the use of force against Portugal to secure the repayment of debts and against Greece in the Don Pacifico case. But in the final resort most statesmen did not consider that whether an action was considered "lawful" by international lawyers was the decisive factor: they were more likely to believe that, as Bismarck declared of the Schleswig-Holstein question, "it is not a question of right or wrong but of power and we have it".

There were now some sections of the population, however, who were not so easily aroused in support of a war: certainly not of any war. The kind of justification which satisfied the politicians did not necessarily seem adequate to such groups. A substantial section of the British parliament and public were opposed to the Boer War; while some in Britain had their doubts about the Crimean War, and a much larger number doubts about Palmerston's Don Pacifico intervention (which nearly cost him his job). In France most of the opposition parties were opposed to Jules Ferry's war in Indo-China. In the United States there were some, in congress and elsewhere, who were opposed to the wars against Mexico and Spain. Religious groups in many countries (such as the Quakers), and radicals (such as Cobden in Britain) denounced all wars as the tragic folly of misguided or wicked governments. Such people remained a minority, and a small one, though their influence was probably greater than their numbers. But the belief that war was inevitable, or even glorious, now increasingly had to compete with the conviction that it was futile and immoral. And all were agreed about the need for humanitarian measures to reduce its barbarities: through better treatment of prisoners (as agreed in 1864), through the banning of particular weapons or methods of war (as agreed in 1899 and 1907), and through improved medical care and welfare services for soldiers, as introduced by a number of governments, especially after the highly publicised miseries experienced in the Crimean War. To some at least the horrors of war began to be more visible than its glories.

Ideas about war therefore changed significantly in this age. There were now even a small number who abhorred war and who believed in the importance of securing peace at any price. There were others who preached that the cost of war could never justify the possible gains it could secure. Even the statesmen began to feel that it should only be undertaken to secure major national ends and then had to be shown to be justified. But there remained always some causes — above all, the cause of the nation - which were believed to provide the justification required: attempts to secure national independence, national integrity, national unity, national honour, even to secure a national place in the sun. Few would admit (and they mainly only in one or two countries) that they actively wanted war. But many in all countries believed that war was, anyway, likely to happen, and that their own nation must therefore be prepared to fight it when it did come; even to choose the moment that was most favourable for that conflict. It was this belief in war's inevitability that became one of the most potent factors in increasing its likelihood. For there was also believed to be a huge advantage in striking first. So long as it continued to be so widely held that war must come anyway, it was likely that, once a crisis arose, an attempt would be made to seize the opportunity and to ensure that the initiative was not left to the enemy. And, once it came, nationalist sentiment was still sufficient to ensure that there would be few who would not believe that on behalf of the national cause the conflict must be fought with vigour and enthusiasm.

The age of ideology (1917-   )

The hideous cost of the First World War transformed traditional attitudes to war. For the first time there was, in the following period, an almost universal sense that the deliberate launching of a war could now no longer be justified. The bitter disputes about "war guilt" at least demonstrated that the initiation of war was now seen as a sin. The designation of the previous struggle as a "war to end wars" showed that war was no longer even seen as inevitable. The new League of Nations was seen as the instrument by which war would be banished from the earth. Governments were even willing for the first time to join, almost universally, in a declaration (the Kellogg pact) renouncing war for all time.

The speeches and declarations of statesmen reflected these sentiments. Leaders of the victorious states continually reaffirmed their determination that there should be no more war. The commitment to peace became, as it had never been before, a universal attitude which at first none would explicitly defy. Millions signed "peace pledges" expressing their determination that there should be no more war. Even the dictators who increasingly came to power all over Europe had to pay lip-service to that general desire. So Hitler declared in February 1933 that "nobody wanted peace and tranquillity more than himself and Germany".[128] In September 1938, immediately before the Munich agreement, he declared that, as a former front-line soldier, he knew well the gravity of war and was determined "to tackle problem after problem with the aim of reaching a peaceful solution".[129] On 1 April 1939, immediately after his forces had occupied most of Czechoslovakia and five months before they invaded Poland, he asserted that "Germany had no thoughts of attacking other people".[130] Mussolini, a month after he had issued a secret order to prepare for the total conquest of Ethiopia, firmly assured the British government that "he had absolutely no aggressive intentions" against that country[131] (he was later to write, in May 1939, that Italy's policy should be to "talk of peace and prepare for war"). Japanese leaders, during the years that they were seizing ever more slices of Chinese territory, continually affirmed that, despite these "incidents", they still wished only for peace with China; and after the Marco Polo Bridge incident in July 1937, the Japanese prime minister reaffirmed his country's peaceful intentions at the very moment that he was despatching troops to invade northern China. Even for those that were actively preparing war, therefore, affirmations of peaceful intent now became obligatory.

But this did not mean that, when governments did decide that the use of force was necessary, they could not still find suitable justifications for that course of action. Force might be needed to protect the nationals of the attacking power, said to be under threat. So Japan, in launching its attack on Shanghai in 1932, including the despatch of four divisions and a massive bombardment of the city, claimed that this was made necessary to protect Japanese residents threatened by attack from local Chinese. Hitler, in launching the invasion of Czechoslovakia in 1939, declared it was necessary because of "violent excesses" committed against Germans, and was a response to "appeals for help from the sufferers and the persecuted":[132] a justification that he was to use once more, in almost identical terms, when he invaded Poland later that year. Or force was necessary for "self-defence" against the aggression of others: Mussolini, before launching his invasion of Ethiopia, complained of 91 examples of Ethiopian "aggression" on the border between that country and Italian Somaliland; while Japan, launching her war against China in 1937 (which had been carefully planned for the previous two years) complained of an unprovoked attack on its forces outside Peking. Or force might be necessary to maintain "stability" in neighbouring territories essential to security: so, in the proclamation issued at the time of the German invasion of Bohemia and Moravia in March 1939, Hitler declared that the Reich "could not tolerate permanent disturbances in these territories, which are of such decisive importance for its calm and security as well as for the general welfare and the general peace",[133] while Mussolini said that the Italian invasion of Albania in 1939 was made necessary (after incidents which he himself had deliberately instigated) to "restore law and order" in that country, Or war might be required to respond to "incidents" provoked by others: so Hitler complained to the British ambassador immediately before the invasion of Poland in August 1939, of "21 frontier incidents" for which Poland had been responsible the previous night, a provocation which "had become intolerable"; Mussolini deliberately manufactured incidents on the border between Greece and Italian-occupied Albania to justify the invasion of Greece in October 1940;[134] and Japanese officers arranged the blowing up of a railway line in Manchuria to justify the invasion of that province in 1931. Or force might be necessary to "promote self-determination" in a particular area: as with the armed attacks threatened by Hitler over Austria and the Sudetenland in 1938, and used over Danzig in 1939. Or it might be needed to remedy a long-standing injustice: so Hitler, writing to Daladier on the eve of the Second World War, declared that he and his people might be compelled to "fight for the reparation of an injustice imposed on us".[135] Force might even be justified as necessary to impose peace on others: so Hitler, in the same letter to Daladier, said that war might be necessary because he "could see no way by which I can induce Poland, under the protection of its guarantees, to adopt a peaceful solution" (to Germany's demands for Danzig and the Polish Corridor); while the Japanese emperor, in an imperial rescript, claimed Japan's assault on China in 1937 was designed "to urge grave reflection on China and to establish peace in the east without delay".[136]

The horrors of the Second World War, with a loss of life even greater than 20 years earlier, created more strongly than ever the sentiment among public opinion that war could never be justified. The demonstration of its destructiveness given at Nagasaki and Hiroshima meant that protestations of a desire for peace were now stronger, more sincere and more universal than ever. Between the wars, though all had protested their desire for peace, there had still been some prepared to state, even in public, that they were willing to resort to force if necessary. Mussolini continually glorified war and its ennobling influence. He demanded that Italian women should increase their production of babies to provide more heroes to fight for Italy in the future. He declared that war was to man what motherhood was to women, and nothing but war could demonstrate the fundamental virtues of the Italian race.[137] He said privately (echoing Louis XIV) that he would prefer to win Ethiopia by war than by negotiation since he "wanted war for war's sake, as Fascism needs the glory of a victory",[138] and that Italy would keep healthy only by fighting a war every 25 years.[139] He particularly wished for a war against France, not only to conquer Corsica, Tunis and French Somaliland, but because "the French respect only those who have defeated them".[140] And Italian propaganda continually put out the message that war was heroic and glorious as well as profitable. Hitler too was willing on occasion to boast of the strength of the German army he had created. He maintained that "war is the most natural, the most everyday matter. War is eternal, war is life."[141] Similarly the Japanese was ministry, in a pamphlet published in 1934, stated that

> war is the father of creation and the mother of culture. Rivalry for supremacy does for the State what struggling against adversity does for the individual. It is this impetus . . . which prompts the growth and development of life and cultural creation. . . . To exalt war to such a high level is, in short, the mission of national defence.[142]

After 1945 such declarations became impossible. No statesman would publicly admit the desirability of war. This was no longer just pretence: no statesman could possibly actively desire total war with all the destruction it entailed. In many places a different kind of leader was in power. The bellicose, strutting dictators and militarists of the inter-war period were, at least in developed countries (which had the greatest power to annihilate each other), replaced by cautious, sober-minded politicians who, however fierce their ideological zeal, were fully aware, in East and West alike, of the immense dangers (to themselves as much as their peoples) which major war would now entail. Thus Khrushchev in 1963 warned his people (and those of China) that "only madmen" could hope to destroy capitalism by nuclear war and that "a million workers would be destroyed for every capitalist". Almost simultaneously President Kennedy suggested to his countrymen that they should "not . . . see conflict as inevitable, accommodation as impossible and communication as nothing more than an exchange of threats". It is true that, when crises arose, the statesmen of the age were still quite capable of exchanging precisely such threats as the president had deplored. China warned in 1950 that if UN forces advanced to the Yalu she could not "stand idly by". President Bulganin, at the time of the Suez crisis of 1956, demanding that Britain withdraw, asked her to consider where she would stand "if attacked by a stronger state possessing every kind of modern destructive weapon". President Kennedy, at the time of the Bay of Pigs operation in April 1961, announced that, "if the nations of the hemisphere should fail to meet their commitments against outside communist penetration, then this government will not hesitate to maintain its primary obligation, which is to the security of our nation";[143] and in the following year, at the time of the Cuba missile crisis, he declared that, if Cuba were "to become an offensive military base of significant capacity for the Soviet Union, then this country will do whatever must be done to protect its own security and that of its allies".[144] Though the word "ultimatum" was now no longer respectable, these declarations were almost precisely similar in effect to the ultimata that had so often preceded war in the age before. There was, however, a major difference. In the preceding period they had been threats expressly designed to pave the way for an act of war. Now they were often threats that there was no desire, and sometimes no intention, to carry out.

But this new caution applied only to war at the highest level. Attitudes to more limited use of force were changed far less. If force short of full-scale confrontation was found necessary, the required justifications could still always be found. Many of these were precisely the same as those that had served that purpose for the dictators of the inter-war period. As before, force might be necessary to protect a country's nationals: this was the plea put forward by the British government to justify armed attack against Egypt in 1956; by the US government in justifying its actions in the Dominican Republic in 1965; and by El Salvador in justifying its attack on Honduras in 1969. Force might still be required in "self-defence" against the aggressions of others: this was the plea made by North Korea in invading South Korea in 1950, by Israel in invading Egypt in 1956, by the United States in bombing Cambodia in 1970, and in numerous other cases. Now too it was said (as by Hitler) that war was needed to restore "law and order" in a neighbouring territory essential to security: this was the justification used by China for intervening in Korea in 1950; by the Soviet Union for intervening in Hungary in 1956 and in Afghanistan in 1979; by the United States for intervening in Grenada in 1983; and by Israel for intervening in Lebanon in 1978 and 1982. Now too force might be needed in response to "incidents" caused by others, whatever their cause: the plea used by the United States over the Gulf of Tonkin incident in 1964-5; by Vietnam over incidents caused by Cambodia on her border in 1978; and by South Africa in justifying repeated interventions in neighbouring countries. The need for force to promote "self-determination" has continued to be asserted: as by India over the invasion of Hyderabad and Goa, by Pakistan over the invasion of Kashmir in 1948 and 1965, by Somalia in invading Ethiopia and Kenya, and other cases. The plea that force was needed to "remedy an injustice" was used again: as by Iraq in launching war against Iran in 1980 or by Britain and France in invading Egypt to reverse the nationalisation of the Suez Canal in 1956. Even Hitler's plea that force might be necessary against a country that declined to hand over its territory peacefully was used once more: for example, by Uganda to justify the use of force against Tanzania in 1979, and by

Argentina against Britain in the Falklands in 1982.

Such justifications were not merely empty forms of words, believed neither by those who used them nor by those who heard them. Because public opinion remained essentially partisan, easily convinced of its own country's (or its own alliance's) rights but far less aware of or concerned about the rights of others, the justifications were widely seen as reasonable, even compelling within the states where they were used. Though few now would declare themselves ready to support their country "right or wrong", most were inclined to believe that their own country, or their own ideological alliance, was, in any conflict in which it was engaged, more likely to be right than wrong. Subjective standards habitually distorted judgements. Many were able to convince themselves, for example, that intervention by one super-power to protect its security interests in areas close to its border was justified, while that of the other acting in a precisely similar way, was not; one revolutionary war (in Angola or Nicaragua in the 1980s) was justified, another (in South Vietnam or El Salvador) not. So the establishment of any objective criteria for judging warlike actions was made impossible.

The most fundamental change, therefore, was not so much in the acceptability of war in general as in the reasons for it found acceptable. In the previous age, the cause for which it was easiest to justify warlike action was that of the nation: national unity, national honour and national power (pp.161-2). After 1918 it was harder to find justifications for wars fought in that cause alone. Many, like the students of the Oxford Union, were no longer so ready to fight "for king and country". They sought a wider and higher cause for which they would lay down their lives, one more intellectually convincing and morally compelling. Sometimes this was a principle of international conduct: that aggression should not be allowed to pay (the cause for which only a few years later the young men of Oxford were cheerfully to lay down their lives). But increasingly the causes for which nations and individuals fought were now political principles: in a word, an ideology. Wars were fought for and against fascism; for and against communism; for "progressive" and against "conservative" forces; for "freedom" against "totalitarianism"; for "justice" against "reaction". So Soviet leaders announced in 1956 that they were compelled to intervene in Hungary to safeguard "socialism" and the "socialist commonwealth" against counter-revolutionary forces. So President Johnson declared in 1965 that US forces were intervening in the Dominican Republic because "the American nations cannot and must not and will not permit the establishment of another communist government in the Western hemisphere".

The new morality of war was thus a political one. This was demonstrated most clearly by the fact that most wars were now civil wars.

People were now as willing to fight against their fellow citizens as against those of other nations because they now fought for political causes rather than national ones. It was demonstrated too by the propaganda issued by governments to arouse the fervour of their peoples. The First World War was fought by the Western powers to "make the world safe for democracy". The Second World War was widely seen as a struggle against fascist or totalitarian regimes by democratic or socialist states. The subsequent struggles of the cold war were even more clearly seen as a struggle between the principles of the "free world" and of "communist totalitarianism", between "progressive" and "reactionary" forces, "socialist" and "capitalist" systems. Many of the struggles of the third world, in Indo-China or in Central America for example, were equally seen as conflicts of political belief or principle. War was increasingly regarded as a ghastly, but occasionally necessary course that might be required to defend not a country, still less a king, but a political belief.

Judgements about the justifiability of war were affected not only by political belief but by political situations. Large numbers of people all over the world live in authoritarian states where there was no possibility of political change by peaceful means. To such people, or at least to some groups among them, war — that is, revolutionary war — represented the only available means of altering their situation. It could reasonably be seen by them as the only recourse, forced on the people by the tyrannical character of the ruling regime. It was the sole available means of winning "justice", "progress", "democracy", "power for the people". Under this guise war was seen not as an immoral but as a moral, a righteous activity: the "just war" of medieval times in a new form. And, if such wars themselves were justified, so too must be assistance to them from outside. As in the previous ideological age 300 years earlier, war was sanctified by the cause in which it was fought: now no longer the defence of a religious creed but a more just social and political system.

The majority of the public, because they generally shared the prevailing ideology, could usually be relied on to follow their governments in bellicose policies. But in most countries there was now a part of public opinion — more substantial than before and including some of the most well educated and informed - which was more critical and more independent in judgement. Among this group the policies of governments in resorting to war began to be widely questioned. Even in the First World War there were some prepared to defy the powerful pressures of orthodox opinion and speak out their opposition to that struggle. Later, protests became more powerful. In Britain at the time of the Suez adventure, in France during the Indo-China and Algerian wars, in the United States during the Vietnam war, in Israel during the second invasion of the Lebanon, there were influential sections of opinion expressing outspoken opposition to government action. That view was often strongly represented in certain sections of the press and other media. It remained a minority view, and it was usually, in the final resort, ignored by governments (it was general weariness with the war, rather than the irresistible influence of protestors, which halted US involvement in Vietnam). But the increasing numbers, strength and influence of such opinions certainly had some effect, direct and indirect, on governments. The latter have at the very least been obliged to devote more effort to explaining and justifying acts of war. And the changing climate of opinion may even have marginally modified the attitudes of governments themselves.

These new attitudes were haltingly reflected in the doctrines of international law. The widespread view that large-scale war among nations could no longer be tolerated has been mirrored in a slow hardening of the rules of international law on this question. The creation of the League of Nations after the First World War and some of the provisions of its Covenant implied that international law no longer recognised resort to war as a legitimate act, except in self-defence. The Kellogg pact was believed to have strengthened that prohibition. The Charter of the United Nations, under which all members commit themselves to refrain from the "threat or use of force", extended it still further. The Nuremberg principles, endorsed by the General Assembly of the United Nations, made it an offence to "plan, prepare or initiate" a war of aggression. 25 years later, members of the United Nations agreed, after long years of negotiation, on a definition of "aggression" outlawing a wide range of activities by states that could lead to war (though there remained considerable disagreement about what the definition really meant).

These provisions of international law may have had little practical effect: acts of war have continued to take place, as we have seen, as frequently as ever. But they did reflect a growing consensus that most acts of war, certainly acts of "aggressive" war (whatever they might be), were contrary to the accepted morality of mankind. Legal theory generally (though even now not universally) maintained that the first use of force was no longer admissible. But the effect of this has been substantially weakened by a number of exceptions. Even the UN Charter upholds the right of "self-defence", individual or collective; and views about what is defensive have varied widely. Some lawyers still justify "preventive war": a principle that could be used to defend almost any act of force. Many others justify an act of force undertaken to protect a state's own nationals. International law has been especially ambiguous in its pronouncements on the kinds of conflicts which have now become most common: those between ideologies. Not only are civil conflicts in general excluded, by definition, from the law (since it set out the principles of conduct to be observed among states); but the rules it lays down concerning the duties of other states in relation to civil conflicts elsewhere, and on intervention within them, remain vague and disputed. So there has continued to be controversy whether assistance provided to rebel forces — as in Greece or in Cuba; in Cambodia or in Chad; in El Salvador or in Nicaragua — was justified.* There was still, in other words, no generally accepted code that laid down which kinds of acts of force (if any) could be regarded as legitimate.

The actions of international organisations have scarcely resolved these difficulties. Those organisations too have expressed a general rejection of war between nations. The resolutions of the League and the United Nations continually condemned the use of force, and called for "peaceful settlement" of disputes. The appointment of mediators of commissions of inquiry, the despatch of observers and peace-keeping forces, and similar actions, expressed a determination to prevent, or at least reduce, resort to war. They reflected the generalised desire for "peace" that existed so widely. But, as we have seen so often, a generalised desire for "peace" does not preclude resort to war in particular circumstances. The attitudes taken by such organisations have continually mirrored the divided political views of the age. Ideological differences have affected the response they have made to each conflict (the very word "peace" has become a weapon in ideological warfare, a word each side has sought to appropriate to secure its own political ends). Their membership has been as divided on such issues as the populations of individual states have been. And their judgements have thus frequently been distorted by political divisions. The ideological conflict, in other words, has deprived the institution that should have been the main protector of peace of objectivity; and so robbed it of a large part of its effectiveness.

War was therefore certainly seen in a different way in this age. At a superficial level it was more widely and sincerely condemned than in any earlier time. All joined in condemning "aggression" or the use of force. Yet there have been many qualifications. If its scale could be limited (and above all if the ultimate horror of nuclear war could be avoided), resort to force was still often seen as legitimate. If it was designed to defend the "rule of law" (as was the action taken by Britain and France in 1956), to end colonialism (as was India's

---

* This uncertainty is illustrated by the fact that while Western powers consistently condemned support for revolutionaries (for example in Greece, Lebanon, Vietnam and Latin America) when undertaken by others (even in non-democratic states) as "subversion" and a violation of the international rules, during the 1980s the US herself undertook and justified precisely such external assistance to rebels in other states (such as Nicaragua, Angola, Afghanistan and Cambodia).

invasion of Goa in 1961), to defend democracy (as was US action in Grenada in 1983) or to defend socialism (as was Soviet action against Afghanistan in 1979), it was still held by many in each state to be justified. Of course, such actions were usually not described as war: they were called "police actions", "collective self-defence", "peace-keeping", "socialist solidarity": or whatever euphemism would be most acceptable to opinion, abroad as well as at home. Some sections of public opinion were now more critical, and so less easily roused in favour of warlike action, than in earlier times. But a majority could still nearly always be mobilised in support of whatever action their government claimed was necessary. They would support such action now not because it was needed to defend national honour, national integrity or vital national interests, but because it was, they were told, essential to the defence of "democracy and the free world", or of "socialism and the socialist commonwealth"; to promote "self-determination" or "defeat colonialism". These were, in this age and in this society, the causes for which, it was generally believed, a people should be willing to shed their blood and sacrifice their lives. And for those ends, accordingly, blood has continued to be spilled.

Conclusions

So ideas about war have changed considerably over the years we have surveyed.

In the earliest periods we have looked at, war was seen by many as an honourable course, the source of glory and renown, the legitimate means by which a ruler could seek to acquire territory and title. Though there were some who condemned it as the play-thing of princes and the ruin of their peoples, they were not typical and certainly had little influence on those who reached decisions about such questions. In the following period war could be a duty, the means by which God's word could be defended against evil forces which sought to corrupt it. During the next, war was the prerogative of the sovereigns themselves, who proclaimed the right to use it, if this was necessary, to promote "the real interest of the state" as Frederick the Great put it. In the age of nationalism war was seen above all as the instrument, disagreeable but necessary, for procuring important national goals, especially national independence, national unity or, more simply, national pre-eminence. Finally, in the most recent period, though full-scale war, using all the instruments of destruction available, is universally condemned and generally avoided, there remains a widespread belief that, for certain purposes — to secure independence for a colonised people, to win autonomy for minorities, to maintain the security of major powers, to overthrow a detested government, or to help others overthrow such a government — war on a lesser scale remains legitimate.

In other words, the main change that has come about is not so much in the degree to which war in general has been regarded as legitimate, as in the type of war seen as legitimate in each age; and, in particular, the purposes for which it is believed legitimate. So, in an international society governed by the ideas of dynasts, where the interests of the ruler and his dynasty are seen as paramount, war for dynastic purposes is regarded as normal and acceptable, in a way that wars for nationalist ends — undertaken by linguistic groups to promote national unification or national independence — would not be. When the prevailing ideology is that of sovereignty, wars to protect what are seen as the legitimate interests of the state — to preserve the balance of power, to win trade or colonies abroad, or to acquire territories essential to strategic interests — are widely seen as legitimate; while a war fought by such a state to promote the interest of a particular religious or political creed would not be so regarded. In an age of nationalism a war to secure national independence, or even to assist such a struggle, is believed to be honourable; while a war fought for purely dynastic ends (for example, to settle the dispute between Britain and France over the Spanish marriages or to put a Hohenzollern on the Spanish throne) would no longer be seen as acceptable. Finally, in the age of ideology, war for old-fashioned nationalist ends — to secure territory, trade or colonies — becomes largely taboo; while a war designed to promote the success of a particular ideological faction, or to prevent the victory of another, becomes increasingly acceptable.

Even the rules developed to restrain or regulate the conduct of war have been influenced by the changing character of international society. Instead of being absolute standards, gradually perfected until a wholly peaceful international community is finally established, the rules of each age are relative, carefully adjusted to the needs of that society and its dominant members. So, in the age of dynasties, "private" war may be banned as a threat to the authority of the rulers and the stability of the system; while in the age of ideology it becomes not only the principal, but the most widely accepted form of warfare to be undertaken. In an age of sovereignty the fomenting or encouragement of civil war in the territory of another state is seen as a violation of the rules and traditions of the international community; while in a different society — for example, in an age of religious or ideological warfare — these become the most widely adopted strategies. Rules concerning declarations of war and the issuing of ultimata become firmly established in one society (the age of nationalism) but are totally forgotten in the next. "Just wars" may include wars to preserve the balance of power in one age, preventive wars in the next, and wars to overthrow a tyrannical government in another: each a type that would be rejected altogether in other periods. Rules concerning the precedence to be accorded to different governments, diplomatic intercourse and the treatment of ambassadors, to which huge importance is attached during an age of sovereignty, are increasingly disregarded in an age of conflicting ideologies, so that ambassadors and their staffs are taken hostage with governmental connivance and embassies frequently used for fomenting civil conflict, for the organisation of coups and even the planning of assassinations. The rules concerning the treatment of the ships of neutral states, carefully formulated in one age (the age of nationalism), are almost totally abandoned in another (from 1917 onwards).

One effect is that the rules are often more relevant to past wars than to those to come. In 1899 and 1907 rules were finally formulated concerning the poisoning of wells and the treatment of messengers; but not concerning poison gas and submarine warfare, the most menacing and indiscriminate weapons of the war of 1914-18. Rules about gas and submarine warfare were formulated in the inter-war period; but not about the use of rockets or nuclear weapons, the controversial armaments of the next world war — still less about the use (often against civilians) of napalm or helicopter gunships, the most brutal weapons of the wars after 1945. In the age of nationalism rules were established concerning the treatment of prisoners of war; but not about the bombing of civilian targets in cities, or deforestation and the destruction of crops, as used in the age that followed. In 1907 precise rules were made about the kinds of bullets that could be used, but not about the kind of nuclear warhead. Even in the same age the rules often cover only irrelevant areas. So today rules are made concerning the demilitarisation of the Antarctic and celestial bodies (which nobody has seriously wished to militarise) but not about the military use of satellites or inner space (which they have).

For these reasons it becomes difficult to be convinced (as in the case of procedures) that there is any linear advance in the beliefs held about war over the years. Attitudes towards outright aggression, especially aggression for territorial purposes, may have gradually become more disapproving; it would not be possible for any government in modern times to make the kind of public declarations about the desirability of acquiring the territory of other countries that were made two centuries ago by Frederick the Great, nor about the desirability of war that were made by Mussolini only 50 years ago. Yet this apparent advance may be matched by a decline elsewhere. Some of the restraints which would have been observed by Frederick the Great (concerning, for example, the treatment of non-combatants and the destruction of dwellings and crops) are no longer recognised in the wars fought today, while weapons may be developed in the modern world (and their use seriously contemplated) which would cause far higher casualties than entire wars would have done in Mussolini's days. The destruction of Magdeburg by fire, with many civilian deaths, during the Thirty Years War was generally execrated (though it may well have been an accident[145]), but the number of people killed was a fraction of those deliberately killed by fire in the bombing of Dresden, and possibly less than the number of civilians burned alive by napalm in Vietnam. The widespread bombing of residential areas of cities (as against the traditional protection of "open cities"); the burning or poisoning of forests and crops (as in Vietnam); the use of helicopter gunships to destroy entire villages (as in Afghanistan); the abandonment of the traditional immunity from attack of merchant shipping — and often of the duty to rescue sailors from ships that had been sunk (as in both world wars); indiscriminate bombing by urban guerrillas — all these are examples of the way in which methods of war have become less, rather than more, discriminating in recent times.

In other words, it is not so much an advance in the morality relating to warfare that has occurred, as a change in what kinds of warfare are regarded as morally defensible. In each new age some new purpose arises which overrides traditional conventions and assumptions, and legitimates actions which would otherwise be taboo: the defence of a religion in one age, *raison d'état* in another, the national principle in a third, the victory of a political cause in a fourth. Each of these in turn may be believed to create a morality of its own, under which all things are justified. However unjust the wars of others, therefore, our own are always permissible, because ours are, we claim, for overriding purposes: to remedy an injustice or to defend a principle (whether we call it, in the current age, democracy, socialism or self-determination).

International lawyers are little help in such a situation. In general the law they preach, in this as in other ages, is that which is accepted by states themselves, applying this very morality. There is often little attempt among them to consider what new rules are needed to tame the new types of warfare that mainly occur in their age. Nor do international organisations seriously confront that task. Even if they are concerned at all about international law or morality, therefore, national leaders can still nearly always find, as we have seen (p. 369 above), suitable pretexts to demonstrate that their own use of force falls within the currently accepted rules.

Thus, though they have changed over the years, beliefs about war — whether and how it can be justified — have not necessarily changed in a way that makes war much less acceptable or less probable than in earlier times. Each age has justified the types of war that were appropriate for the purposes it has seen as of supreme importance. Some types, especially the largest and most destructive, have increasingly been effectively outlawed; but this is largely because they now threaten destruction to all, the victorious as much as the vanquished — in other words, largely for self-interested reasons. Wars of lesser kinds, more accurately geared to current national purposes, are still widely seen as permissible. The morality of war has thus not changed beyond all recognition. War continues to be seen by many as a legitimate act, so long as it is appropriately adjusted to the situation it confronts.

9 Conclusions

Does war have a functional value?

In the foregoing pages we have traced the varied pattern of warfare over several centuries.

If war has occurred so commonly in every international society, does this mean that it must have some positive social function? Has it been an eternal feature of human existence precisely because it has been necessary to the welfare, the progress, or the survival of the human race?

There are a number of social functions which, it has been sometimes suggested, war might perform.

First, it has been proposed, war may have a functional value for the individual units which undertake it, rather than for international society as a whole. One theory has suggested that war is necessary as a means of bringing about the social cohesion and political effectiveness of individual states. Just as the struggle for territory, food or mates among individuals can ensure that only the fittest of each species survive and reproduce themselves, endowing the next generation with the qualities which will best equip them to compete, so among nations a similar process of natural selection, it has been held, may ensure that only those states having the best leadership, organisation, martial skills and social cohesion will be in a position to survive. As a result, all nations, whether successful or otherwise, will be compelled to improve their social organisation and military effectiveness in such a way as will make them better able to participate effectively in this struggle for survival.[1]

There are a number of objections that can be made to this thesis. First, it begs the very question that it is supposed to prove. If it were inevitably the case (as may well have been believed by those who have put forward such theories) that all states must participate in an armed struggle with other states for survival, then it is necessarily also the case that this will promote the development of states best equipped for that struggle (though not necessarily the best states in other respects). Once it is admitted, however, that war may not be an inevitable feature of human existence, then the reverse may be the case: a state that devotes itself above all to building up its armed strength may be less capable of providing the flourishing culture, the education, the social services and general amenities which will in

other respects best promote the welfare of its citizens. Secondly, even
if war is a widespread feature of international society, it may serve as
frequently to weaken states as to strengthen them. States that have
devoted themselves to building up their armed strength to participate
in the armed struggle have sometimes in the long run proved less
rather than more capable of survival. Those countries that have been
most heavily engaged in war — Spain in the sixteenth century, France
in the following two centuries, Britain in the nineteenth — have
found themselves eventually weakened and exhausted rather than
strengthened by their efforts. Conversely, countries that are defeated
in war may not be eliminated from the competitive struggle but may
rapidly recover and live to fight again, only to be defeated once more
(like Germany after 1918). In other words, the effect of the balance
of power may be that states that are militarily well organised are none
the less defeated. Given the effect of war in eliminating many of the
most able and courageous elements of the population, there would
seem better reason for suggesting that it tends to reduce a state's
capacities over the long term than that it will increase them. Finally,
even if it were the case that war serves to stimulate civic spirit, social
cohesion, political institutions or technological advance, it does not
follow that it is the only way in which these changes can come about.
Examples could be given of states that have developed in many of
these fields despite the fact that they have engaged very little in war
(for example, Switzerland and Sweden over the past century or two);
and of others that have failed to do so despite frequent military
engagements. Athens could be regarded as having been a superior
state in the period before it embarked on its imperialist wars than it
was after it had done so.

A more sophisticated version of this argument is that, whatever its
costs and burdens, war is necessary as a means of bringing about
political or economic changes which are ultimately of benefit to
mankind and which cannot be secured in any other way. A Marxist
version of this argument would maintain that internal war (revolution) is necessary as the only means of resolving the contradictions
that develop between the relations of production and the forces of
production, and so of moving society to a more advanced level.[2] A
non-Marxist version might maintain that without warfare a society
would stagnate, the sources of invention would dry up, social mobility would cease, new national leaders would not be thrown up and
social evolution would slow down. War provides the incentive for
technological and other advances that would not otherwise occur.[3]

But once again the facts of history do not altogether confirm the
thesis. Technological change and economic progress may sometimes
be furthered by war. But both have probably occurred faster during
the past 40 years, at a time of peace for most developed countries,

than at any earlier time when war was far more frequent. Moreover, even if rapid technical change does occur in wartime, it may not always be of a sort which is of equivalent value in peace. And any advance of this kind that does take place has to be measured against the huge losses, human and social as well as material, which also result from war. So far as the Marxist thesis is concerned, there is no evidence that the transition from capitalism to socialism can occur only as a result of war, whether internal or external. Historically speaking, the most direct effect of war has normally been to introduce more authoritarian types of government, a result that is not what most Marxists claim to desire. And in general there would seem to be grounds for believing that social, economic and political progress is more likely to be advanced in a prolonged period of peace than as a result of the disruptive and destructive processes of war.

Again, war is sometimes said to be a necessary feature of human society in that it can bring about a resolution of fundamental contradictions, both within states and in international society, which cannot be resolved in any other way. It is thus a kind of safety-valve which prevents the entire organism from blowing up.[4]

It is no doubt true (and it is almost tautological to say) that civil war results from contradictions within society which ultimately find expression in armed conflict. But we have no means of determining whether or not it is the only means available for resolving conflicts of this kind. In all countries, whether or not democratic, political life is mainly concerned with the resolution of conflicts and contradictions. Some nations are more successful than others in resolving them peacefully. But there would seem no grounds for saying that in any society war is an especially efficient means of resolving differences, given the costs it entails and the unpredictability of its oucome. Similarly, war between states sometimes occurs when one or other despairs of being able to resolve conflicts by alternative means. But the fact that a particular state reaches that decision is no proof that no alternative means existed, nor that, from the point of view of international society generally, the resolution so attained of the disagreement justified the huge costs involved in war. The fact that some states have lived for centuries without war, and that entire regions of the world have lived for decades without it, seems to suggest that there is no inherent reason why an international society should not be able to exist, and to resolve its internal conflicts effectively, without resort to war.

A more widely used argument is that war is the necessary and essential means by which the power structure of international society can from time to time be adjusted. As time goes by, particular states become more powerful; soon they begin to exploit their power against their neighbours to their own advantage; eventually these neighbours will themselves combine to overcome the dominance of the more powerful state or states. War is thus the means by which the dominance of an individual state can be brought to an end and something like an equilibrium of power brought about among the members of the society.[5]

This is a more persuasive argument than most of those we have examined. For it is the case, as our study has several times demonstrated, that war has often been the means by which the pretensions of a dominant power have been tamed: as Spanish power was in 1648-68, as that of France was, twice, in 1713-14 and 1814-15; and that of Germany was, also twice, in 1918 and 1945. There does seem to be a natural tendency for the weak, or the not so strong, to combine against the strong, so that the mighty are cast down from their seats and a better equilibrium is established.

But that process has been a crude and expensive one, which has often thrown up a new source of domination to replace the old one: France replaced Spain, Britain replaced France, the United States and the Soviet Union replaced Britain and Germany. Nor is war necessarily the only means by which a new equilibrium can be brought about. A combination among states may be able to tame the powerful even without war. Or international society may be organised in such a way that powerful states are anyway unable to impose their will on others. Thus, even though war may have sometimes been the means by which the excessive domination of a particular power has been prevented in the past (and in very many cases it was the powerful state itself which initiated the wars that defeated them), it is not necessarily the only way by which that end can be achieved.

Another argument sometimes used is that war may be the only available means of spreading the true word, or preserving it when it is threatened.[6] When groups believe that they are possessed of absolute truth, religious or political, a truth essential to the progress of mankind or to the welfare of a particular state, circumstances may arise in which war is seen as the only feasible way of preserving it in one place, or spreading it to another. War is thus seen as having the function of ensuring human progress by destroying error and preserving truth.

This view again depends on the presupposition that circumstances can arise in which war is the only available method of preserving a particular doctrine or eliminating a particular falsehood. But it is by no means sure that such circumstances ever exist. Even in the most tyrannical states or the most enclosed empire, it can be argued, there are always some means short of war by which a particular doctrine can be contained and others disseminated. Force is unlikely in any case to be an effective way of convincing opponents or proving a doctrine (as was recognised even during the wars of religion (p. 339

above). Though, therefore, it cannot be said that war can never be believed necessary for this purpose, it seems unlikely that, except in quite exceptional circumstances, it is in fact an appropriate instrument for that end.

But the argument that would perhaps be most widely used today to show that war has sometimes a positive social function is that it can be the essential and indispensable means of eliminating injustice. Situations may arise, both between states or within them, where a gross injustice exists which, it is held, can be remedied by no other means than war. The power that intervenes in the territory of a neighbour (say the United States in Grenada, or Vietnam in Cambodia); the state that invades the territory of another (for example, India in invading Goa, or Somalia in invading Somali-inhabited parts of Ethiopia); still more the guerrilla army in revolt against its government (say, in South Vietnam or Afghanistan) — all of these will claim that these actions have been forced upon them by the necessity to eliminate an injustice which cannot be effectively overcome in any other way.

Once again the validity of the argument depends on the validity of the premises. First, is it the case that the injustice concerned can be remedied only by war? Secondly, even if this is the case (as in some cases it may be), is the cost of war proportionate to the benefits which result from removing the injustice in question? Even if the war is ultimately successful, is it certain that the succeeding situation will be much better than the one before? In the end this is a subjective judgement, depending on the estimate made of the probable length and expense of a war, on the one hand, and on the insupportability of the continued injustice, on the other. It would be difficult to secure universal agreement about the balance of costs and benefits in any such case. The underlying problem is that this is an argument that could be used to defend any act of war for any purpose. Hitler no doubt believed that he was remedying an injustice in invading Poland in September 1939, and had done so in invading Czechoslovakia earlier that year. North Korea no doubt believed she was remedying an injustice in attacking South Korea in 1950; Sukarno that he was doing so in undertaking "confrontation" with Malaysia in 1962; and Iraq that she was doing so in launching war against Iran in 1980. All wars are fought in the name of some great principle; and the fact that governments believe themselves to be fighting to remove an injustice cannot be said to provide an automatic justification. If it were accepted as such, then every war that was claimed to be directed against an "unjust" treaty, an "unjust" frontier or an "unjust" government could be held to be justified. Once again a balance has to be made between likely costs and likely consequences; and whether or not a particular war is justified on these grounds can only depend on the assessment of a reasonable person, not directly involved in the conflict, seeking to assess the balance between ends and means.

None of these arguments, therefore, can show conclusively that war is a necessary or inevitable feature of human society, still less that it has a positive social value. Whatever beneficial consequences — if any — war can be shown to have, either for the individual state or for international society generally, have to be set against the far more obvious negative effects for both. Its destructiveness for the individual state, even if victorious — in lives lost, in material damage, in social disruption, in economic growth forgone and in many other ways — seem likely far to outweigh any benefits it may have in strengthening social cohesion or national self-respect. The damaging consequences for international society are even more apparent. It destroys relationships among its member states. It provokes widespread distrust and insecurity. It discredits attempts to establish recognised principles of international conduct as the basis for social order. It damages and divides international organisations and the world community as a whole. Above all, each war has long-term consequences that go far beyond the individual case: it sets an example for a form of anti-social conduct, which, when repeated by others, will destroy the entire basis of social existence. Because theft in general is undesirable, all thefts, however admirable their motives, are proscribed in domestic societies. In the same way in international societies, if war in general is undesirable, then all wars, however apparently justified in a particular case, must be proscribed also.*

To balance these formidable negative effects, the benefits a war could bring would have to be huge, unmistakable and inevitable. It seems unlikely that the initiation of any war could bring desirable consequences on that scale; still less that war in general, whatever advantage it may bring to a particular victorious power, can ever be found to bring positive, long-term benefits to the society of states as a whole. The contention that warfare has, or can have, a positive social role to play in international society must therefore be regarded as unproven.

The sources of conflict in international society

If war has no social functions, what are its social origins?

There is no society without conflict. In every community there exist

---

* It is the failure to consider this argument — the Kantian categorical imperative — that reduces the force of the justifications for war in particular circumstances put forward in such works as Michael Walzer's *Just and Unjust Wars* (New York, 1977), otherwise an admirable attempt to analyse the morality of warfare in the modern world.

divisions of situation, interest and belief, which may become the cause of friction among its members. What distinguishes different societies, therefore, is not the fact of conflict, but the type of conflict — whether, for example, it results from a competition for status, for power or for wealth; between whom it occurs — whether between clans or classes, economic organisations or religious faiths, ethnic groups or geographical areas, political parties or occupation groups, sexes or generations; above all, whether it is conducted by violent or by peaceful means.

Just as every society contains some conflict, so everywhere most conflict stems from society; results from the social situations the individuals within each experience.

In a sense it can even be said that it is society itself which teaches conflict to its members: tells them when to conflict, with whom and over what issues. The most important single thing society teaches its members is what they should want: whether to value achievement or contentment, wealth or power, social success or artistic attainment, strength of arm or peace of mind. In teaching these wishes society teaches also the subjects of conflict. In a society whose members are taught to value status, conflict will often occur over questions of status; in a society whose members are brought up to value the acquisition of wealth, conflict is likely to occur over the means of acquiring wealth; in a society which values military glory above all, conflict will probably be military; in a society concerned over ideology above everything else, conflict will occur over ideological questions. In practice most societies establish values of a number of kinds; and therefore create various kinds of conflict. Even so, since the mix of values in each society will be peculiar to it, so too will be the sources and subject-matter of conflict.

To some extent society's choice of values also determines the degree of conflict. Values vary in the extent which they can be shared or must be competed for. Some values are by their nature subtractive: in that the more they are enjoyed by one person, the less they are by somebody else. This is true, for example, of such values as relative status, influence, popularity and wealth: these must be competed for, since they can only be gained by one at the expense of somebody else. Other values, however, are additive: in that an addition of the value to one party will often create an addition also for another. This is true, for example, of social intercourse, co-operation, friendship, love and so on. In so far as a society teaches us values that are mainly subtractive, therefore, it builds conflict into its own structure. In so far as it inculcates goals which are mainly additive, it will create a social structure in which conflict will be less obtrusive and more easily appeased.

But society teaches not only the initial values. It teaches also our conceptions about the way they should be secured. For example, even among societies where the acquisition of wealth is seen as the highest value, one society may teach men to seek it by co-operation and another by competition. One will teach that national glory is to be won by military conquest and another by achievement in the arts and sciences. One will teach that conflicts should be settled by force of arms, another by resort to the law-courts. Thus society teaches us not only the values we should cherish, but also the means of attaining them.

There is a final and still more fundamental way in which society teaches its members how much conflict they should engage in. For society teaches not only specific means but also the general type of response to be made to conflict situations. Irrespective of the values concerned and the traditional means of acquiring them, we may be taught a more general disposition to seek our ends by coercive or by concessive means: by compulsion or by compromise. Thus, even where subtractive values are at stake, we may decide to determine their distribution by discussion and negotiation, in an attempt to share the disputed benefits in agreed proportions; or we may demand to determine the question by bluster and force, so that the strongest — whether in physical, social or financial power — can secure their goals in full, while the weakest must sacrifice theirs entirely. Whether a predominantly coercive or concessive policy is adopted by individuals will depend partly on basic personality-traits, deriving from innate and early acquired characteristics; on knowledge of the other party's will or demands, which may serve to induce not only realism, better understanding of the difficulties of securing one's own objectives, but also recognition of the rights and aspirations of others, so that there will be greater readiness to concede; on the image of the other party — that is, whether he is conceived as wholly hostile, so that there is a pre-existing disposition to conflict, or as morally antipathetic, in which case there may be felt a moral as well as personal duty to resist his demands, irrespective of content; finally, on the fields of activity concerned, which may be conceived as by nature competitive or co-operative (so that groups may be ready to adopt a concessive approach in matters connected with social relations, but not in those associated with economic affairs; or to accept international co-operation in the field of trade but to resist it in the field of immigration). But it will depend above all on society: on the culture within which the particular confrontation takes place, whether it is one that encourages a basically competitive or co-operative approach. In most developed societies internal political procedures are such as to encourage a recognition that interest-groups and individuals will rarely attain their original demands unmodified. In the international field, at least until recently, the reverse has been the case: it has been accepted that one state might reasonably impose its will on another to secure its ends. The way in which ends are conceived is the crucial point: whether they are seen as absolute or relative. Sometimes even a total failure to achieve the desired ends will be regarded as preferable to modifying even slightly ends themselves conceived as absolutely "good". It is society itself that will teach which of these is preferred.

International societies vary in these respects in the same way as do domestic societies. Here too different values prevail in different types of society, so creating different types of conflict. Here too some values are additive in effect, so that action to increase them for one state will bring about a corresponding increase for others too: for example, activity designed to increase equilibrium or international trade or peace for one state will automatically produce a similar increment in these for others (at least, some others). Conversely, an attempt by any state to increase its relative status, influence, popularity, or power must, by definition, bring a corresponding reduction in the same value for some or all other states: here the values are subtractive rather than additive, and if states seek them conflict must result. Clearly, nations, like individuals, possess a number of values, some of which fall into either category. It is likely that most will be in some matters co-operative and in some competitive. And the degree to which they are either will depend, for men and for nations alike, on the mix, or hierarchy, of the values established in each society.

In almost all international societies there will be some goals that are subtractive — that is, there will be competition for certain assets that cannot be shared or multiplied indefinitely: territory, power, influence, markets or investment opportunities. There may be disputes about more general questions concerning the way international relationships should be conducted: the treatment that should be accorded to ambassadors, the right to search the ships of neutrals, the right to intervene in the civil wars of other states, and so on. There may be disputes about domestic political questions: what kinds of government ought to exist in individual states: monarchical or republican, authoritarian or constitutional, democratic or socialist. Finally, there may be disputes about the way any of these conflicts should be resolved (through negotiation, legal settlement or war) or about the power which should be accorded to international organisations in settling them. The type of question most in dispute has varied substantially from one international society to another. In international as in domestic societies it is mainly society itself which teaches what are the appropriate subjects of conflict (dynastic competition in one age; religious rights in another; sovereign power, national independence or ideological victory in others) and how such conflicts should be conducted. In one age, as a result, tens of thousands of lives will be sacrificed to win succession to a throne elsewhere, while in another, only 200 or 300 years later, no government anywhere will fight for such a purpose. In one age the great majority of wars will be fought on the question of religious rights to be accorded, while in another, only a century later, virtually no wars will be fought on that question.

What causes these startling differences in the subject-matter and motives for war in different generations? It is clear that over time there may occur radical changes in the pattern of beliefs existing among the same group of states, changes that affect the values that are most widely held and therefore the assets which are thought worth fighting for: differences, in other words, in the fundamental ideology of each society.[7] This ideology colours the thinking of almost all who live within the society, including those who wield power and determine questions of peace and war. While it will vary marginally even in the same age from one state to another, and from one individual to another within the same state, it varies far more from one age to another; and it is sufficiently consistent within each to bring about the dramatic changes in the pattern of warfare from one age to another, and the reasons for which they are fought, which we have traced in this book.

What, then, causes the change in ideology from one age to another? It appears to derive ultimately from the changing class structure in different ages, and above all from the change in the character of the elites who mainly wield power. When power is held by dynasts wielding inherited power within their own states, the entire international society becomes influenced by the ideology of dynasticism, affecting the thinking even of those who are not dynasts (and who may have to pay heavy sacrifices for the sake of the dynasts); and it is this which determines the character of conflicts in that age. When religious teachers and religious publicists become influential, both among rulers and among the public generally, the ideology of religion will govern the society generally and determine the main subject-matter of war. When sovereigns and their chief ministers, dedicated to the building up of state power, are dominant, their concerns become the ideology of the age and determine the main subject of conflicts. When those who care deeply about national rights and national independence become dominant figures (or when dominant figures come to care deeply about those questions) nationalism becomes the ideology of the age and wars are especially concerned with that question. When, as today, those who wield power are people who care deeply about ideological questions, this concern becomes the dominant theme of international politics and the subject of conflict among states. In every age, in other words, the ultimate sources of war are the beliefs of those in power: their idea about what is of most fundamental importance and may therefore ultimately to be worth a war.*

However strong their beliefs on a particular issue, those who wield power will rarely wish for war to determine such questions. As we have seen, war has never been (except, possibly, among some primitive peoples) desired for its own state. It has been seen as an instrument, usually an instrument of last resort, for securing particular ends. Whatever the ideology of the age, however important a particular asset may seem to those in power, those assets have to be measured against the likely cost of procuring them by war. Though, as we saw in Chapter 6, the act of measurement has rarely been systematic, still less scientific, some kind of calculation, if only subconscious, has always been made of the balance between means and ends. The conclusion drawn has depended not only on the valuation placed on the particular ends in question, and not only on the calculation of the probable costs of securing them, but also on beliefs of other kinds, especially beliefs about the acceptability of war as an instrument of policy. Those beliefs have changed, as we saw in Chapter 8, rather less than is often optimistically believed. In all ages, irresponsible and unnecessary wars have been condemned; but in all ages, too, war has in certain circumstances been seen as a reasonable choice of action if all else has failed: whether to win a crown, to defend a faith, to strengthen a state, to promote national independence, or to protect the interests of a particular ideological alliance. There have certainly so far been no international societies in which (whatever may be publicly declared) war has been seen as a totally inadmissible means of securing objectives which are highly valued: that is, a pacifist international society.

Of course, the types of war that have been favoured, or permitted, in particular ages have varied widely. External war — war against another state — is seen as an acceptable course of action where the assets which are valued are dependent on events in other states: in so far, that is, as states are expected to have extra-territorial goals, concerns which extend outside their own state. The ideologies of all recent international societies have presupposed some concerns of that kind. In the age of dynasties rulers were concerned with succession in other countries; in the age of sovereignty with winning trading opportunities, colonies or strategic territories in foreign lands; in the

---

* Of course, beliefs do not change only because of a change in the power structure. To some extent the reverse is also true: certain groups come to wield power because they represent views that are widely held within society — say, belief in the importance of nationalism or a particular ideology. The prevailing pattern of ideas is continually changing as a result of a number of different processes, and this is normally reflected in the type of government which acquires power, and which can then determine what is worth fighting for.

age of nationalism with securing (or preventing) the success of national revolutions elsewhere. But it is in ideological societies — such as the age of religions or the present period — that concern about events in other states has been most intense, for in such ages it is the principles that prevail universally, in all territories, which are in dispute. All these are differences of degree rather than of kind, however. There has not yet existed a society in which governments have been totally indifferent to events elsewhere; and therefore none in which external war has not sometimes occurred.

Of course in all ages there will always be some states that are more outward-turned than others. These states will often include the most powerful. There will be others (often weaker states) who will adopt inward-turned policies that never represent a threat to states elsewhere (Switzerland and Sweden during the nineteenth century; Burma, Malawi and Paraguay today). But there is usually, as we have seen throughout this study, a considerable homogeneity in belief and behaviour among all states within the same society. The prevailing belief will to a considerable extent determine the amount and type of wars they fight against each other. It will not determine every war. Even in the age of religions Spain and France still struggled for dynastic power, just as the Soviet Union and the United States today, in an age of ideology, still fight partly for national power (even if in each case they are sufficiently affected by the prevailing ideology to claim they are fighting for a more intangible cause). Conversely, wars of religion took place (prematurely) in the age of dynasties, and wars of national independence continue sometimes to occur in the age of ideology. In other words, it is the characteristic pattern of warfare which is determined by the prevailing ideology, not every war which occurs.

The prevailing ideology will determine the character and extent of internal, as well as external war. If it is one which is concerned with dynastic power, civil as well as foreign wars will be fought mainly about that question; if it is one concerned with the practice of religion, civil as well as external wars will be fought mainly on that subject; if it is concerned with the strengthening of state power or with national independence or with the victory of an ideology, civil wars as much as external wars may be fought mainly for that objective. And here once again it is the character of the ruling elite which is the ultimately decisive factor. As the class structure changes, as a different type of ruling elite comes to power, so will the nature of their dominant concerns and the type of things which are believed to be worth fighting about, at home as well as abroad.

As the class structure and the political system change, therefore, so does the character of the prevailing ideology, national and international alike. As these change, so do the issues about which war mainly occurs. Different kinds of international society, in other words, give rise to different kinds of social conflict, both within states and within the wider international society, and so to a different type of warfare.

The changing pattern of warfare

What does our survey reveal about the changing pattern of war in recent international societies?

Perhaps the most striking conclusion is the diversity of warfare in the six centuries we have surveyed. Even within the same age there have been wide variations: for example, in the age of dynasties, between the organised campaigns of royal armies against the territory of other rulers, the savage raids of Tartars, Cossacks, and Barbary corsairs on neighbouring peoples, and the bloody insurrections of peasants, cities or religious minorities (such as the Hussites); in the modern era, between sudden mass invasions of overwhelming force (as in Hungary and Grenada), the set-piece tank campaigns of conventional war (as between India and Pakistan, Israel and Egypt, or Iraq and Iran), the desperate guerrilla campaigns of peasant armies (as in Vietnam and Central America), and the sporadic attacks of urban guerrillas (as in Lebanon or Northern Ireland). Between different ages the variations are still greater. Totally different kinds of war have been undertaken for different purposes by different kinds of leaders, using different kinds of strategy and different kinds of armaments. Some have been total wars, involving the entire mass of the population; others professional wars, involving only a relatively small military class and having little impact on the great majority of people. Some have been carefully prepared in advance and organised down to the last detail; others impulsively decided, and improvised or botched in execution. Some have been fought by individual nations or groups; others by large coalitions and alliances. Some have aroused widespread enthusiasm and support; others have been widely unpopular. Some have been entirely between peoples of different states; others fought by rival groups within the same society. There have been equally wide variations in the way war has been seen in different ages: as a noble and glorious venture in one or as a disagreeable but necessary means of defending national honour in another; as the way of preserving the balance of power among states or as the means of defending the true faith; as the undesired but occasionally essential means of countering the delinquencies of other states, or as an essential recourse for remedying an unacceptable injustice; as the continuation of policy by other means, or as a crime and evil to be resorted to only in self-defence if at all. So great has been the diversity of different types of war and the purposes underlying them that to speak of war as an "institution" of international society is a gross oversimplification. It is rather a range of different institutions, which have been used in different ways for different purposes in different international societies.

Almost the only common thread is that in every age organised violence in some form has been undertaken. For all the distaste which has been expressed for it, from the Middle Ages onwards, war has remained an activity that has been tolerated, seen as an essentially *normal* undertaking, at all times until the present. Beliefs about its legitimacy have changed far less than might at first sight appear. Disapproval has certainly increased marginally. The public expression of a positive desire for war (not uncommon only 70 years ago) is now unusual (see p. 368 above). But it remains the case, today as in earlier ages, that war is approved by governments of all kinds for particular purposes at particular times and is nearly always, once decided, endorsed by a majority of their peoples. The capacity to find justification for such decisions is no less today than it has been at all periods in the past (p. 366). The type of war likely to be decided on, and the purposes for which it is likely to be fought, may be different; not the fact that it is seen as a proper course to undertake when other measures have failed.

If the purposes of war are described in sufficiently abstract terms, it can of course be seen as a constant phenomenon that changes little from one age to another: undertaken always to win "power", to defend or promote "national interests", to redress a grievance or remedy an injustice. But to describe the purposes of war in such empty phrases is almost as meaningless as to conclude that crime is undertaken for gain or sport for pleasure. What is significant is the *kind* of interest which states have sought to promote through war in different ages; and the reasons why in one age they have conceived that interest to require particular kinds of demand (territorial, economic, political) from other states and have fought particular kinds of wars to secure them, while in others they have fought different kinds of wars to promote different kinds of interests. In practice, as we have seen, different kinds of assets have been seen as war-worthy in different ages. Just as in domestic societies the kind of conflict which occurs depends on the kinds of wants which society itself instils, among international societies too the different kinds of war that have been fought reflect the different kinds of wants which each such society has established. They reflect in other words the ideology of each age, as established by the elites which wield power at each time.

The effect of changes in ideology is that the same underlying aspirations may take different forms in different ages. The desires for survival, for independence, for security, for satisfying and fruitful economic relationships have been felt to some extent in every age.

But the means of achieving them has varied greatly from one to another; and so too, therefore, has their effect on relationships between groups and states. Survival has been seen in one age as the survival of a ruling dynasty (so the English soldiers at Agincourt fought for King Harry); in another as the survival of a religious group; in others as the survival of the state, or of the nation, or of the ideological alliance. Independence has been perceived in one society as the independence of a self-governing city from emperor or bishop; in another as a state's independence of other states; in others as the independence of an ethnic group within a multinational empire, a satellite country from the domination of a neighbouring super-power. These differences of *perception* have determined the way international relations have been conducted in each age, including what kind of war has been likely to be fought against what kinds of enemies, and the entire role which warfare has played within a particular international society.

The dominant ideology determines the amount and character of war partly by establishing *conventions* concerning the issues about which wars may be fought. These have varied widely from one age to another. In one the convention allows wars to be fought over questions of trading rights (as in the first two of our societies); in another it does not (as today). In one age convention allows one state to intervene to defend the rights of religious groups in another state (as in the age of religion); in another it does not (as in the age of sovereignty). In one age the conception that is held of "honour" will cause war to take place because the ships of one state have not dipped their flags to those of another; in another it will allow powerful states to demand forcible redress for economic damage to their own citizens in the territory of another state; in another it will make small frontier incidents appear a reasonable cause of war. It is equally the effect of convention that some of the issues of greatest importance in their effect on the welfare of a state and citizens are not seen as war-worthy in particular ages; so that today, for example, questions concerning the price and availability of raw materials, debt settlement, tariff barriers and trading rights, the authority to be granted to the Security Council or Secretary-General of the United Nations, or the powers and policies of international organisations such as the International Monetary Fund, though matters of profound importance to the welfare of particular states, are not seen as issues about which war might reasonably be made. Changes in conventions of this kind are affected by changes in the underlying ideology. But they do not simply reflect in a crude way changes in the interests of dominant powers. The most powerful states today have the same interest as their predecessors in the nineteenth century in ensuring the prompt payment of inter-state debts; yet armed action to secure such payments, which was relatively common a century ago, is today unknown. This may be partly because alternative means of pressure are available by which powerful states can seek to ensure that economic obligations are fulfilled. But it is perhaps more because the primary preoccupation with the ideological struggle has pushed economic relationships between states to a lower level of priority.

Thus the type of war fought in different ages has varied widely, with the changing ideology and the varying interests of major groups and powers. How far has this brought changes in the amount of war from one age to another?

In an absolute sense this change is only marginal. The lists in the Appendices reveal only a small decline in the total number of wars per decade in each age (even when allowance is made for differences in the geographical coverage of the lists). It is true that the figures for the number of war-years of each state show a fairly steady decline, especially for Europe and North and South America, but this decline is counterbalanced by the hugely increased destructiveness of war when it does occur. As a result, the total number killed in war in this century is far greater, both absolutely and as a proportion of population, even for European and North American states, than in all earlier times (though the killing has been concentrated into shorter periods). Casualties for the two world wars alone were probably greater for many countries than those suffered in all wars in the previous five centuries. In any case, the decline in the number of wars in those regions is not matched by any similar development elsewhere. In the Middle East, Africa and Asia war has probably been more frequent, and certainly more costly, in the last 40 years than for centuries past. Here too both the scale of war and the level of casualties are much greater on average than in any previous period; and here the number of wars is not significantly less and may even be greater.

War is therefore now overall everywhere more costly, both in blood and treasure. Before 1800 wars causing 250,000 deaths were rare. They occurred perhaps once a century or so: as in the Peasants Revolt in Germany and in the Thirty Years War (which, as we have seen, was in reality several wars). Between 1789 and 1914 there were perhaps four or five such wars (the Napoleonic wars, the Crimean War, the American Civil War, the Taiping rebellion in China, and the Balkan conflict of 1875-8): that is, one every 30 years or so. In the 40 years since 1945 there have already been at least eight wars on that scale (in China, Korea, Indo-China, Colombia, Algeria, Vietnam, Afghanistan and the Gulf): that is one every five years. In addition, civil conflicts in India (1947), in Indonesia (1965) and in Cambodia (1975-8), not sufficiently organised to be characterised here as wars, probably involved a similar number of deaths. These deaths include far more civilian deaths than in earlier times. It is thus probable that in the modern world a larger number of people die each year — and even a larger proportion of world population as a result of war than in any earlier period. Contrary to a widespread impression, therefore, we live today not in a more peaceful international society but in one that is particularly warlike. Nor is this just the result of a small number of very expensive wars. War remains frequent: at the moment of writing (1984) there are at least 20 separate wars occurring in different parts of the world* wars involving a much higher level of military technology and often a higher level of casualties than those of earlier periods.

There have however been spectacular changes in the distribution of war, especially over the most recent period. Over much of the last 200 years war in much of the world, especially in Africa, Asia and Latin America, was restrained, though never suppressed, as a result of the colonial system. During that time the military power available to the rulers was immeasurably superior to that available to potential rebels. During the same period warfare in Europe was at its height; and though it was gradually decreasing in frequency, it was at the same time increasing hugely in destructiveness. Thus the total casualties from war in Europe were probably during much of this time substantially greater than those occurring in all the rest of the world put together.

Over the past 40 years this situation has been suddenly reversed. War has been relatively frequent in Asia, Africa and (to a lesser extent) in Latin America. Europe on the other hand, previously the scene of the most bloody and destructive wars in the world's history, has become almost totally peaceful. In a sense this is only the culmination of a long process. The decline in the amount of warfare in Europe dates back for about 150 years. As we saw in Chapter 2, the number of international wars declined sharply after 1815 and the number of domestic wars also fell, but more slowly. Between 1815 and 1945 the continent enjoyed three periods of 20-40 years in which no major international war occurred: periods of a length unknown in earlier times. The change since 1945, however, has been much more dramatic. Until that date there were still no periods of more than a few years in which no war at all (including civil wars) occurred: the

* In El Salvador, Nicaragua and Guatemala in Central America; in Peru in South America; in Namibia, Angola, Mozambique, Ethiopia (at least two separate wars), Sudan, Chad, Western Sahara in Africa; in Lebanon and the Gulf in the Middle East; in Sri Lanka, Afghanistan, Cambodia, Burma (at least three wars), East Timor, West Irian and the Philippines in Asia. In addition there are sporadic hostilities in a substantial number of other countries, including Colombia, Zimbabwe, Uganda, Thailand, the United Kingdom, and Spain.

longest was between 1885 and 1896. Since then the continent has enjoyed 40 years of almost total peace; and since 1956 a period entirely without war.

This phenomenon is so striking that it is worth seeking the reasons for the change. The most commonly accepted explanation is that peace has been maintained in Europe because of nuclear stalemate, or the "balance of terror". This has probably been a contributory factor. But it seems unlikely to be the whole explanation. There is little evidence in history that the existence of supremely destructive weapons alone is capable of deterring war. If the development of bacteriological weapons, poison gas, nerve gases and other chemical armaments did not deter war before 1939, it is not easy to see why nuclear weapons should do so now. If fear of nuclear war has not deterred wars in other parts of the world, some of them involving nuclear powers, it is not self-evident that if the situation were in other ways similar — that is, strong pressures for war existed — it could do so in Europe. If wars by non-nuclear powers against nuclear powers were not deterred in Vietnam and in the Falklands, there seems no reason why similar wars might not occur in appropriate circumstances in Europe. If governments and groups in those cases have been willing to rely on the assumption that their enemies would avoid nuclear war, even without the possibility of retaliation, potential war-makers might be expected to take similar risks in Europe where the threat was mutual and the use of nuclear weapons therefore more obviously suicidal. Given the modest assumption that their opponent wished to avoid suicide, states desiring to secure limited ends by the use of conventional power alone — as they might have done in Berlin, Austria, Yugoslavia or Turkey, for example — might reasonably have hoped to do so, facing no more risk of a response with nuclear weapons than Hitler risked one with poison gas in 1939.

This leads to a second possible explanation of the peaceful state of Europe in recent years: the fact that in Europe, unlike most other parts of the world, the great majority of the states are tightly enclosed in rival alliances pledged to the defence of any member that might fall victim to aggression from elsewhere.* This again may be a contributory factor, but can hardly be a complete explanation. The existence of such rival alliances, and a reasonable balance of power between them, has not deterred war in the past (for example, in 1756 or in 1914). War can still occur in such a situation, either because an entire alliance makes war against its rival, or because one state is attacked in

---

* In fact the NATO treaty contains no absolute commitment of this kind. Members undertake to regard an attack on one as an attack on all and to consult on the appropriate response in case of attack. But there exists in practice a general expectation of common action.

isolation on the assumption that its allies will not, especially if confronted with a rapid *fait accompli,* undertake the onerous obligation of providing assistance. The existence of alliances may be especially unlikely to deter minor or ambiguous types of military action, forcible pressure or rapid *faits accomplis,* which defence treaties do not unmistakably cover. It clearly could not deter war *within* one or other of the alliances. Still less can it deter internal war, by far the most common type in recent times. Nor can the existence of alliances explain the freedom from war of those European states (Austria, Yugoslavia, Sweden, Switzerland, Ireland and till recently Spain) which are not members of any such alliance. In other words, the existence of alliances can at best only explain the absence of a war of aggression by the member of one such alliance against the territory of a member of the other: the type of war which is, anyway, increasingly rare in the modern world, and is particularly unlikely in contemporary Europe. Conversely, the non-occurrence of the type of war that might easily have been expected in the period since 1945 — a civil conflict in, say, Poland, East Germany, Turkey or Greece, perhaps leading to intervention from outside — cannot reasonably be attributed to the mobilisation of many European states in rival alliances.

A third, and in some ways more plausible, explanation of the peaceful situation of Europe in recent years is that there has been no *reason* for war in that period. War has traditionally been made by dissatisfied powers seeking to redress a grievance and to remove the source of their dissatisfaction. Thus between the wars there were at least three European powers which were, for various reasons, dissatisfied — or "anti-*status quo*" — powers and so a potential source of war: Germany, Italy and Hungary.* In Europe today there are no major dissatisfied powers; and, in so far as any dissatisfaction is felt (over the division of Germany, or over the domination of East European states by the Soviet Union), there is no belief that those grievances could be effectively redressed by war. European frontiers are more firmly established, and more widely accepted, than at any time in history. And, while each alliance might wish ideally to see changes made in the other half of Europe, neither feels strongly enough about this to hazard the unimaginable dangers which even a purely conventional war would entail. This may be an important factor in the peace of Europe in recent times, but it seems unlikely to be the complete explanation of it. It too can only explain the absence of the kind of war that has, anyway, been least likely to occur: a major assault designed to bring about substantial territorial or other

---

* The Soviet Union was equally a dissatisfied power in certain senses, having been deprived of substantial territory by Poland in 1920, yet it was generally believed to be too preoccupied by internal problems to be likely to make war to redress those grievances.

changes in the European scene. It cannot explain the absence of the
kinds of war that have in fact been most probable and have occurred
elsewhere: internal conflicts or revolts leading to intervention from
without.

There are two other explanations that are less often mentioned in
this connection, but which may provide more plausible reasons for
the peaceful condition of Europe in recent years. One is that the
peace of that continent (and of other peaceful areas, such as North
America) results simply from the higher standard of living which is
now enjoyed in those areas. If the peaceful parts of the contemporary
world (Europe, North America, Australasia and Japan) are compared with the non-peaceful parts (Asia, Africa and Latin America),
the most obvious distinction is the fact that the former generally
enjoy a substantially higher standard of living than the latter. Equally, contemporary (and peaceful) Europe enjoys a much higher standard of living than earlier (non-peaceful) Europe. While the correlation could be a chance one, there are two reasons for believing that it
may be significant. First, higher standards of living are associated also
with higher standards of technology and therefore with a higher
capacity to cause unacceptable damage in war. The governments of
Europe are therefore aware (or should be) that any war in Europe,
whether or not it is nuclear, and however limited it may be in its early
stages, could cause casualties that would make both the two previous
world wars appear relatively innocuous. Secondly, and more important (since fear of casualties has not deterred war in the past), the
higher the standard of living that is enjoyed by a people, the less
attractive is the prospect of war. The sacrifices to be made — the loss
of the comforts of peace and of a secure and stable existence —
appear greater to those enjoying higher material comforts and a long
expectation of life than they do, for example, to the starving peasant
or the desperate urban guerrilla, whose fighting life may be more
dangerous, but not materially much harder, than his life in time of
peace. Moreover, where more advanced countries are involved in
war, it is not just the individual citizen but the entire state that may
have to make greater sacrifices than would have to be endured in
poor countries. The cost in cities destroyed, in social and political
disruption, is likely to be much greater in wealthier states than in
poor states, which have a smaller material infrastructure to be destroyed (and whose rulers may even sometimes welcome the diversion
of their citizens' attention from existing hardships to foreign adventure). Finally, it is not impossible that prosperity itself has a civilising
influence which increases attachment to peace and inculcates a more
widespread and deeply held revulsion from war.

There is, however, a final reason which is perhaps of greater
importance than any of these. It may be that the most important

single reason for the peaceful state of Europe over the past 40 years does not lie in external relationships at all. It perhaps results rather from the internal stability of states during that time. It is this above all that distinguishes Europe today from the Europe of earlier times. Even in the nineteenth century, as we have seen (pp. 55-6), a substantial proportion of the wars which occurred arose directly out of internal conflicts, especially those resulting from the disintegration of the Turkish and Austrian empires and the increasing national consciousness of subject peoples. The only two wars in Europe since 1945 — in Greece and Hungary — equally arose from civil conflicts. Today no such internal upheavals occur or seem likely to occur. This greater domestic stability is equally what distinguishes other peaceful areas: Europe, North America, Japan and Australasia are not only better off than the developing continents, where wars still occur, but also much more stable politically (in the developing world, too, where there is greater political stability - in the Caribbean and the Pacific, for example — wars are uncommon). Since a substantial proportion of external wars, in the present age as in former times, have originated in internal conflicts, it is inevitably the case that greater domestic stability must reduce the danger of wars of either kind. The increased stability results partly from the increased military power and mobility available to governments in relation to potential rebel groups: no rebellion in such countries now appears to have any prospect of success (one reason why disaffected groups increasingly turn to terrorism rather than organised war as a means of promoting their cause). Especially in developed countries the power available to states to enforce their authority has increased more rapidly than that available to groups seeking to resist it. But it probably results too from higher standards of living: as these rise there is less incentive to rebellion and domestic instability declines both in democratic and in non-democratic states. The same trend is perhaps now beginning to manifest itself in South America, where, with marginally higher standards of living, a greater degree of political stability is now manifesting itself, civil war has almost ceased, and significant international war has been unknown for several decades. It may be that a reduction of war elsewhere — that is, in Africa and Asia — may be dependent on a similar increase in domestic stability, resulting perhaps, there too, partly from an increase in governmental military power and higher standards of administration, partly from a rise in standards of living generally.

Can war be eliminated?

What are the implications of this survey for the future of war in international society?

We have noted the vast diversity in the types of war that have been
fought in different international societies and the variety of purposes
for which war has been waged. We have seen that the character of the
wars that have been fought in each age has depended on the nature of
the wants that have been generally felt by those in positions of power,
together with their assessment of the possibility of achieving those
wants by war at an acceptable cost. Above all we have noted the
frequency with which war has been adopted as an instrument of
policy in every age. Does this mean that war must continue to be a
feature of international society for the foreseeable future? Or is it, on
the contrary, possible that in future years an international society will
emerge in which it ceases to be seen as a normal means of securing
national or group objectives?

Two methods have been mainly advocated as the means of eliminating war from international society.

The first has been by the elimination of the instruments by which
wars are conducted: in other words by disarmament, total or partial.
For many years negotiations have been undertaken designed to secure agreement among states to abandon some or all of their armed
power. But the history of those negotiations reveals the difficulties
which any such attempt confronts. It is true that a few agreements
have been reached limiting, at least temporarily, the capabilities of
particular states in particular fields or particular areas (for example,
the Washington and London agreements limiting naval strength
among certain powers in 1921 and 1930; agreements between the
United States and the Soviet Union limiting their overall nuclear
capabilities (the SALT agreements); agreements for demilitarising
the Antarctic and banning the placement of weapons of mass destruction on the sea-bed, in outer space and on celestial bodies; and
agreements limiting the testing of nuclear weapons and their proliferation to other states or banning their acquisition in particular
regions). But they have not committed states to abandon, or even to
reduce over the long term, armaments already held. In negotiating
for disarmament each state, and each alliance, has judged its own
security needs subjectively: judgements often based on inflated conceptions of its enemies' capabilities. For this reason the level of arms
each has found it necessary to demand for itself has always been
above the level seen by other states or alliances as necessary for that
purpose. Each state or alliance demands most reductions in the
weapons and fields where it believes its enemy is strongest and the
least where its own advantage is greatest. One or other always
believes itself at a disadvantage in some particular field, and reserves
the right to catch up in that field before any agreement is concluded.
Many states face a range of possible adversaries and thus demand the
right to match all of these combined (so that the Soviet Union today

might demand the right to match the armaments of the United States, Western Europe and China combined, while China might demand the right to match the Soviet Union single-handed; Pakistan may demand the right to match India's level of arms, while India may wish to match those of Pakistan and China combined; and so on). The result is that it has never proved possible to reach agreement on a distribution of arms levels which will miraculously add up, in the eyes of all negotiators simultaneously, to a state of "equilibrium"; still less to agree reductions, in each type of armament and for every state, that will never be seen to represent at any one moment any threat to the security of any of them. Nor will they easily agree on the measures of verification required to confirm that the agreement is being observed; still less on the type of international authority needed to police the agreement (or to police the disarmed world which the agreement aims to establish). At the root of all these difficulties is the fact that arms are seen by most states as a source of security; and they have usually preferred reliance on the defence they provide to the uncertain security of a paper agreement, the implementation of which may be seen as problematical, providing for a world it is difficult to imagine in advance. The flexibility, and range of options, which the absence of agreement affords may seem preferable to the restrictions imposed by a rigid and unchangeable agreed "balance".

Underlying these difficulties is a deeper one. In the eyes of many states the effort to eliminate arms is to treat the symptoms rather than the cause. States hold armaments because they believe they may need them sometime in the future when a war occurs. To believe that war may be eliminated by eliminating arms is, in this view, similar to believing that violent crime could be wiped out by abolishing offensive weapons. So long as the desire to commit crime (or make war) exists, it is widely held, the means of undertaking it will be secured by one means or another. Even if, therefore, all the difficulties just described were overcome, and a disarmament agreement were put into effect, any state which came to feel deep dissatisfaction and resentment, for whatever reason, might resume the manufacture of armaments (for while arms themselves can be destroyed, the capacity to make them cannot be so easily wiped out). The fact that this possibility exists might not only undermine the viability of an agreement once secured, but deter the conclusion of an agreement in the first place. In other words, disarmament is discouraged by the view, which is held by many states, that it is not weapons that make war, but, on the contrary, war that makes weapons: the known possibility of war that creates the demand for weapons to undertake (or deter) it. Thus, the abandonment of armaments, at least on a permanent basis, is only likely to come about, many believe, if war itself can be eliminated from the behaviour pattern of states.

The second means widely advocated as a way of eliminating war is the creation of some international authority powerful enough to deter or prevent individual states from undertaking it; and the substitution, as the means of resolving disputes, of some procedure of legal settlement for the crude arbitrament of armed force. But again it seems doubtful if this is likely to be a feasible means of abolishing war within the foreseeable future. As we saw in Chapter 7, no international authority — whether a political body such as the League or the United Nations or a legal body such as the International Court of Justice — has yet had any significant success in reducing the incidence of war by this means. This is partly because such authorities have lacked the means to enforce their will. States have never been willing to endow them with the armed power which would alone enable them to enforce their authority against individual states. The reluctance to transfer military power in that way is easily understandable. However much individual states dislike war, and the insecurity of an armed world, they may still prefer it to a world in which superior power is vested in the uncertain hands of an all-powerful international authority, however constituted. Even if some states, especially weaker ones, were willing to contemplate that transition (since it would probably make them no more dependent than they are already), it is unlikely that the most powerful, which enjoy the greatest freedom of action in a world of independent states, would be willing to agree to the diminution of their power and influence which such a change would bring about. And without the consent of those powers no such authority is likely to be created in the first place.

In other words, the underlying difficulty here is not unlike that facing disarmament. So long as war remains a normal feature of international life, many states are likely to prefer the security provided by armed defence to that afforded by an uncertain and untried international authority, acting in ways that could not be easily determined in advance. They are only likely to be willing to abandon armed power in return for assurances that the international authority would be so constituted that their own interests would be sure of protection: assurances that could not be provided for all major powers simultaneously. Disputes and disagreements about the powers and constitution of such an authority would therefore almost certainly prevent it from being established in the first place; and would continue to inhibit its effectiveness if it were ever to be set up. Either it would not be accorded sufficient power to resist threats to the peace by the more powerful states; or in exercising such power it would appear as a threat to the independence and sovereignty of every state. It seems likely, therefore, that states would only be willing to accord unchallenged authority to a central authority if it were able to maintain order without resort to force; and that situation can come about only when war has already ceased to be a feature of international existence. Here too, therefore, the elimination of war is the precondition, rather than the consequence, of the institutional change demanded.

But the establishment of a central authority wielding overriding power is not the essential condition of order in any community. Many societies exist in which an orderly existence is maintained even though there exists no such authority able to exercise coercive power. In a large number of primitive societies a viable social order is maintained without an army, a police force or any mechanism for forcible restraint. The ordering of society is maintained through intangible rather than tangible restraints: through custom, consensus, a code of conduct, above all the pressure of opinion, the attitudes and expectations of a majority of society's members. Norms of conduct are established which it is difficult to resist, and which are sufficient to maintain the conformity required for a relatively orderly social existence. Even where coercive power is wielded at the centre, as in most modern states, it is usually not the most important means by which the fabric of society is maintained. The policeman, often unarmed, exercises authority less through force than through the respect in which he is held within society generally.

In all societies, in other words, the ultimate rulers are rules, the publicly accepted conventions by which behaviour is regulated, rather than the force which the state is able in the final resort to mobilise. As David Hume put it many years ago, "As force is always on the side of the governed, the governors have nothing to support them but opinion: it is therefore on opinion alone that government is maintained."[8]

The society of states at present has far more in common with a relatively primitive society of this kind than with highly centralised, tightly integrated modern states, in which obedience can, in the final resort, be enforced through armed power. It is likely therefore that, in the foreseeable future, if order is to be maintained, it will, here too, be through the sanction of opinion: the social pressures which may be mobilised on behalf of the conventions which society has established. Here too the ultimate rulers may be rules to regulate behaviour. And here too war may in time be made to appear a delinquency as unacceptable and outrageous as does crime within the state.

Already, over several centuries, as we saw in Chapter 8, hesitant efforts have been made to develop the outlines of such a code. In the less controversial areas a body of customary law has been established which is now generally observed by states: on the conduct of diplomatic relations, on maritime affairs, on questions of trade, investment and other economic questions, on the rights of neutrals, on the treatment of prisoners of war — to give only a few examples. Already, most of the time on most issues, states do abide by the conventions established in international law and custom. Even on questions close to the vital interests of states, some principles have been fairly widely accepted (if not invariably observed): on the inadmissibility of "aggression", or unprovoked attack by one state on the territory of another; or of the use of war for territorial aggrandisement; or of the use of armed power to coerce or intimidate other states — in other words (as the UN Charter puts it) the "use or threat of force". These represent principles of international behaviour which, even if still occasionally flouted, would now be generally accepted (as they would not have been less than a century ago) by almost all states as established rules of international conduct. They thus represent the embryo of the kind of framework of rules which can alone, in default of a central authority yielding coercive power, provide the basis of peaceful coexistence among states.

Unfortunately that code, as it exists today, remains incoherent and incomplete. Even if it were invariably observed, which is not yet the case, it would not serve to eliminate all wars, since a number of uses of force remain largely outside its provisions, including many of those most commonly employed at the present time. There are thus still gaps in the code, areas where no clear consensus yet exists. As we have seen in our survey, in all ages war has occurred frequently in cases where there is a conflict of expectation between states concerning the justice or reasonableness of a particular situation or demand. We have seen, for example, how in several earlier international societies war frequently occurred where there was a situation of ambiguous sovereignty, so that rival powers could each believe they had reasonable claim to exercise rights there (pp. 90, 96, 112-3). In other cases the conflict of expectations has occurred over the principles to be applied in resolving particular kinds of dispute: for example, whether succession should be based on the rights of inheritance alone or should take account of the balance of power, as in the age of sovereignty; whether priority should be given to the national principle or the claims of traditional sovereignty, as in the nineteenth century. Today, though there exists a reasonable degree of consensus concerning the more obviously illegitimate uses of armed force, there remain substantial areas where no such understanding exists, and where there is therefore such a conflict of expectations. Doubts remain, for example, over the right of intervention by outside powers in civil wars (is this permissible only in support of a recognised government, or in support of any recognised "belligerent" including anti-government forces, or neither?):[9] a frequent source of conflict in recent years. Similarly, disagreements exist over the right of states to protect their own nationals in other states (used to justify war during the Suez conflict and at the time of the US invasion of Grenada in 1983); over the right to use force in support of struggles for self-determination (as in a number of colonial wars); over the legitimacy of boundaries inherited from colonial times (as in the wars of Indonesia against Malaysia, and of Somalia against Ethiopia, for instance); over the right to support a revolution by a minority people (such as that of the Nagas in India, or the Kurds in Iran and Iraq, or the Ibos in Nigeria); or to support a majority of the people against a minority government (as in South Africa).

It is over such questions, where there exist genuine differences of view concerning the rules to be applied, that armed conflict between states has inevitably most frequently occurred. Unless and until more clearly defined principles governing such issues and the means by which they should be resolved, can be established, it is likely that armed force will continue to be used to settle them. Such a consensus is clearly not easy to achieve, since differences of view of that kind often reflect major conflicts of interest, as well as differing value judgements between opposed political philosophies. But only if there is a conscious attempt at least to discuss the disputed issues, and if possible to establish the principles required, is the severity of such conflicts likely to be reduced in the future.*

It is above all over questions of security that such understandings are most required today. We have seen how frequently the use of armed force in the modern world results from the concern of states to protect what they believe to be their own security needs in areas close to their own borders: as in US intervention in Central America and the Caribbean; the Soviet Union's intervention in Afghanistan; China's in Korea and Vietnam; India's in Ladakh, on the north-east frontier and in Bangladesh; Israel's in Sinai, the West Bank and Lebanon; or South Africa's in Angola, Lesotho and Mozambique. With the reduction of distance and increasing strategic mobility, the security needs of states today extend (or are felt to extend) further and further from their own borders. Any code designed to reduce the scope for such interventions must thus take account of the fears that underlie them. A condition of peace is likely to be the avoidance of any steps that will be seen as a threat to the security of major powers in such areas. This may sometimes place limitations on the freedom

---

* An attempt to define principles on some of these questions was made by the United Nations in the drafting of *Principles on Friendly Relations among States* and in *The Definition of Aggression,* each of them arrived at only after prolonged discussions. Unfortunately, both are formulated in such vague terms that they have not gone very far in reducing the differences in viewpoint which exist on such matters. (For a more detailed attempt to define such a code of international conduct, see Luard, Evan, *Conflict and Peace in he Modern International System,* Boston, 1968.)

of action of neighbouring small powers; but that need not be a crippling limitation. The more they can assure adjoining super-powers that their security is not threatened by developments in the area, the greater the freedom of action they will be accorded themselves. Paradoxically, therefore, an increase in the independence of such small powers depends in the long run more on the actions of distant super-powers — in exercising restraint within those regions — than it does on the actions of the neighbouring super-powers which appear to represent the greatest threat. Here, as in other cases, what is fundamentally required is the replacement of a purely national viewpoint on security requirements by a wider concern with the needs of international security generally.

But most wars today are, as we have seen, at least in origin, not international wars but civil wars. Of the 121 wars listed for the period since 1945, a majority have been civil conflicts, even though in a number of cases these have led to intervention by external powers. Principles that relate solely to the conduct of states towards each other are therefore not enough. Equally important are measures that will bring greater stability within states, especially in the large numbers of poorer states where such conflict at present mainly occurs. The measures most likely to have that effect are, arguably, assistance in building stable and viable political systems, help in reducing the more glaring inequalities, the creation of efficient and honest administrations, the promotion of economic development, and similar steps. Such measures, by reducing the likelihood of civil conflict within such states, also indirectly reduce the likelihood of international wars, which so often emerge out of them.

A decline in warfare of this sort will depend above all on the availability of alternative means of securing change. Civil conflicts occur most frequently, as we have seen (p. 68), and as is to be expected, in countries where unrepresentative governments hold power. In such states resort to armed force often appears the only recourse available to bring about change or to remedy injustice. The absence of representative or democratic government may also be seen elsewhere as a reasonable justification for assisting revolutionary war. Conversely, where governments are seen as representative of popular opinion, and especially where they have clearly been democratically elected, not only is major discontent less likely to occur, but intervention designed to overthrow the government will be less easily justified. That is why over recent years civil war has occurred almost entirely in non-democratic systems, where there has been most reason to challenge the representative character of the government. It has been almost unknown among those countries where governments have been democratically elected, not only in Europe and North America, but also in the Pacific, the Caribbean and some parts of Asia. It is thus arguable that the incidence of war in the world today is most likely to be reduced over the long term by the creation of more representative systems of government everywhere. And, for the same reason, in situations where civil conflict has already broken out — where, that is, two political forces are contesting by force the right to rule — democratic elections (if necessary under UN auspices) to establish which of the two sides commands the greatest support among the people as a whole may sometimes represent the best formula for ending the conflict.

A world in which, internationally, governments can agree together on the principles of peaceful coexistence, while domestic political systems everywhere become more stable and more democratic, no doubt appears a utopian dream. At present war remains endemic, as it has in each of the different international societies that we have surveyed. So long as there continue to be groups within states, and states within international society, which demand change sufficiently intensely to believe it worth the cost (a cost which in both cases is continually rising), war in one form or another will continue to take place.

If it is from society itself that conflict ultimately springs, it is only changes in society — national and international — that can reduce its scale. The creation of a more peaceful world depends in part on changes within states, having the effect that disadvantaged and disaffected groups become, for whatever reason, less willing to risk their lives for the sake of change. But it depends equally on changes in the wider international society. Only an international society whose members collectively examine, far more systematically than today, the sources of conflict, and the principles and procedures capable of resolving it, is likely to succeed in reducing significantly the incidence of warfare among its members. In that way a relatively peaceful coexistence may be established, as in many smaller societies, not by imposing the coercive power of a central authority; nor by seeking to secure a voluntary abdication of the means of self-defence; but by creating the essential conditions of social life: that is, by establishing the common traditions, the common institutions and so, ultimately, the common expectations which every genuine society requires.

Notes

Notes to Chapter 1: The Study of War

1. The most important volumes are *The Wages of War, 1815-1965* (New York, 1972) and *Explaining War* (Beverly Hills, 1979).
2. No clear indication is given about the way in which the casualty figures in the Michigan study were arrived at, though it is evident that they derive from secondary sources and not from new research into official records (see, for example, *The Wages of War*, pp. 49-50, 72-3: it is stated (pp. 72-3) that the figures given for "battle-deaths" are based on "estimates from earlier general studies offset by estimates of army sizes, weapons and weapon technology, numbers of "major battles" and a suggested ratio of 3.5.1 for the proportion of wounded to dead). Concentration on "battle-deaths" means that the figures given for war deaths are very much lower than have normally been given in the past. Though earlier estimates may have often been inflated, it is not clear, from the evidence about the way the figures were arrived at, that the new estimates are much more accurate than the old ones; still less that they are accurate enough to justify the conclusions that are based on them. Nor is it self-evident that figures for "battle-deaths" are those that are most relevant: public concern is normally with the destructiveness of war overall — that is, with all deaths caused, whether in battle or not — rather than deaths to servicemen alone. The omission of civilian deaths can have a serious distorting effect, since it reduces the apparent destructiveness of war in the modern world compared with that of older wars, where most deaths occurred to servicemen. This is only one of the reasons for questioning the conclusions reached in the Michigan study about the declining scale of war in recent times; another is the computing of the number of wars in relation to the number of states in existence (so reducing the apparent prevalence of war in the post-1945 period, when many more states exist) and the omission of civil wars, which represent the great majority of wars today. (For a different conclusion about the warlikeness of the modern world, see pp. 394-5.)
3. For example, it has been concluded, sometimes from "scientific" studies using the same data-bank, that the adoption by states of strong military capabilities promotes peace (R. Naroll, V. L. Bullough and F. Naroll, Military *Deterrence in History* (New York, 1974)); and that it promotes war (W. Ferris, *The Power Capabilities of States* (Lexington, Mass., 1973)); that war is more likely to occur when the power disparity between states is small (R. Garnham and J. Weede, "Power Parity and Lethal International Violence", *Journal of Conflict Resolution,* September 1976, pp. 379-94); or where it is large (Ferris, *Power Capabilities*); that multipolar systems are more stable than bipolar (J. D. Singer and M. Small, "Alliance Aggregation at the Outset of War", in *Quantitative International Politics,* New York, 1968, pp. 274-86) and vice versa (K. Waltz, "The Stability of a Bipolar World, *Daedalus,* Summer 1964, pp. 881-909). These are only random examples: many other contradictory findings can be quoted from the literature.
4. All of these are factors considered in the "Correlates of War" study.
5. For a classic study of this kind, see Ruth Benedict, *Patterns of Culture* (London, 1935).

6. For analysis of the way these different factors vary in differing international societies, see E. Luard, *Types of International Society* (New York, 1976).
7. For a more detailed analysis of the differences between these different periods, and the reason for the dividing-lines chosen, see Luard, *Types of International Society,* especially Chapter 5.

Notes to Chapter 2: The Conflicts

1. For a discussion, see Q. C. Wright, *Study of War* (Chicago, 1942), pp. 227-32. Wright concluded (writing before the Second World War) that there is a "tendency . . . for concentrations of warfare to occur in approximately fifty-year oscillations". Singer and Small (after stating that "periodicity is one of the most important forms of regularity associated with the incidence of international violence and one whose presence has important implications for its understanding and ultimate elimination") conclude that there is no regularity in the intervals between the beginnings of wars, but that there is a "modest periodicity" in the amount of war in progress at any one time "with the dominant peaks about 20 years apart" (Singer and Small, *The Wages of War,* p. 215).
2. See Charles Wilson, *Queen Elizabeth and the Revolt of the Netherlands* (London, 1970), especially pp. 127-9.
3. All estimates of casualties in this period are highly speculative since there were usually no official records: see G. Bodart, *Losses of Life in Modern Wars* (Oxford, 1916), pp. 13, 82-3.
4. For an examination of the motives for the penetration of European powers into Africa, see D. K. Fieldhouse, *Economics of Empire, 1830-1914* (London, 1973). For a more general consideration of economic motives, see Evan Luard, *Economic Relationships among States* (London, 1984), pp. 30-5, 84-95, 136-46.

Notes to Chapter 3: Issues

1. Quoted in A. F. Pollard, *Henry VIII* (London, 1902), pp. 118-19.
2. See C. M. Kortepeter, *Ottoman Imperialism during the Reformation* (New York, 1972), pp. 52, 214.
3. See P. Earle, *Corsairs of Malta and Barbary* (London, 1970), pp. 109, 115.
4. See Kortepeter, *Ottoman Imperialism,* pp. 213-14.
5. Frederick the Great, Anti-Machiavel (London, 1741), p. 322.
6. See C. W. Cole, *Colbert and a Century of French Mercantilism* (New York, 1939), i, 345.
7. See R. C. Anderson, *Naval Wars in the Levant, 1559-1853* (Liverpool, 1952), pp. 163-7, 175-6.
8. See F. C. Langdon, "Expansion in the Pacific and the Scramble for China", in *The New Cambridge Modern History,* xi (Cambridge, 1962), p. 646.
9. Cf. R. E. Robinson and J. Gallagher, "The Partition of Africa", in *ibid.,* xi, pp. 593-640.

Notes to Chapter 4: Motives

1. For a more detailed examination of the motives of states see E. Luard, *Conflict and Peace in the Modern International System* (Boston, Mass., 1968), ch. 2.
2. Niccolo Machiavelli, *The Prince* (Oxford, 1935), p. 13.
3. *Ibid.*, pp. 43-5.
4. G. Mattingly, *Renaissance Diplomacy* (London, 1955), p. 119.
5. K. Brandi, *The Emperor Charles V* (London, 1939), p. 498.
6. Quoted from *The Tree of Battles*, ed. G. W. Coopland (Cambridge, Mass., 1949), p. 120.
7. Machiavelli, *The Prince*, p. 99.
8. Quoted in Brandi, The Emperor Charles V, p. 207.
9. William Allen, *A True, Sincere and Modest Defence of English Catholiques* (London, 1583), p. 103.
10. William Gouge, *God's Three Arrowes* (London, 1631), pp. 215 and 217.
11. Brandi, *The Emperor Charles V*, pp. 547-8.
12. Cf. J. R. Hale., *Renaissance Europe 1480-1520* (London, 1971), p. 98.
13. For the importance of these motives for each ruler, see Pollard, *Henry VIII*, pp. 110 and 247-8; and Brandi, *The Emperor Charles V*, pp. 49, 278-9, 347, 481.
14. See C. V. Wedgwood, *The Thirty Years War* (London, 1930), pp. 115-16.
15. Quoted in J. H. Elliot, *Europe Divided 1559-1598* (London, 1968), pp. 93-4.
16. Louis XIV, *Mémoires for the Instruction of the Dauphin*, ed. Paul Sonnino (New York, 1970), pp. 224-5.
17. Letter to Louis XIV, 29 June 1658.
18. Frederick the Great, *Die Politischen Testamente* (Berlin, 1920), p. 49 (author's translation). (First published in 1752.)
19. Memorandum to Louis XIV, 1664.
20. Samuel Pepys, *Diary*, 2 Feb 1664.
21. See Luard, *Economic Relationships among States*, pp. 174-5, 219-20.
22. Addressed to the Council of the People's International League (1847).
23. Cf. R. Storry, *The Double Patriots: A Study of Japanese Nationalism* (London, 1957): "At least from the time of the Sino-Japanese war of 1894-5 there was a generally accepted belief [in Japan] that Japan was bound to follow the path of expansion abroad" (p. 3); "It became clear that war paid dividends and was the road to international recognition as a potential equal in the family of civilised states" (p. 14).

Notes to Chapter 5: Decisions

1. See Pollard, *Henry VIII*, pp. 128, 130-1.
2. Quoted *ibid.*, p. 53.
3. Quoted *ibid.*, p. 104.
4. *Ibid.*, p. 179.

5. Brandi, *The Emperor Charles V*, p. 537.
6. See J. R. Hale, "International Relations in the West: Diplomacy and War", in *The New Cambridge Modern History*, ɪ(Cambridge, 1957), 260.
7. See Elliot, *Europe Divided 1559-1598*, pp. 163-72.
8. See Pollard, *Henry VIII*, p. 128.
9. Hale, *Renaissance Europe 1480-1520*, p. 96.
10. Hale, "International Relations in the West: Diplomacy and War", in *The New Cambridge Modern History*, ɪ, 261.
11. Quoted in Brandi, *The Emperor Charles V*, p. 415.
12. *Ibid.*, pp. 546-9.
13. See J. P. Cooper, "The Fall of the Stuart Monarchy", in The New Cambridge Modern History, ɪv (Cambridge, 1970), 550: "Elizabeth had denied her parliament's right to discuss foreign policy uninvited"; and James "did not wish the Commons to debate foreign policy".
11. See Wedgwood, *The Thirty Years War*, pp. 97-8.
15. See Sir C. Petrie, *Philip II of Spain* (London, 1963), p. 132.
16. See C. Wilson, *The Transformation of Europe, 1558-1648*, (London, 1976), p. 145.
17. See Wedgwood, *The Thirty Years War*, pp. 166, 240.
18. Cardinal Richelieu, *Testament Politique*, ed. L. André (Paris, 1947), p. 323 (author's translation).
19. Quoted in G. Parker, *Europe in Crisis 1598-1648* (London, 1979), pp. 163-4.
20. Quoted in Elliot, *Europe Divided 1559-1598*, pp. 31-2.
21. See J. H. Elliot, "The Statecraft of Olivares", in *The Diversity of History*, ed. J. H. Elliot and H. G. Koenigsberger (London, 1970), p. 140.
22. See Wedgwood, *The Thirty Years War*, pp. 58, 166.
23. See H. R. Trevor-Roper, "Spain and Europe 1598-1621", in *The New Cambridge Modern History*, ɪv, 278-82.
24. Parker, *Europe in Crisis 1598-1648*, p. 148.
25. See J. H. Elliot, *Imperial Spain 1469-1716* (London, 1963), p. 321; and Parker, *Europe in Crisis 1598-1648*, pp. 170-1.
26. Kortepeter, *Ottoman Imperialism*, pp. 214-18.
27. *Ibid.*, pp. 45-6.
28. Wilson, *The Transformation of Europe, 1558-1648*, p. 259.
29. H.G. Koenigsberger, "Western Europe and the Power of Spain", in *The New Cambridge Modern History*, ɪɪɪ (Cambridge, 1968), 242.
30. J. C. Rule, "Louis XIV and Colbert de Torcy", in *William III and Louis XIV*, ed. R. M. Hatton (Liverpool, 1958), p. 215.
31. "Louis himself laid down his foreign policy after pre-discussion in the Conseil d'en Haut. . . . The Foreign Secretary then worked out the details in daily consultation with the king, who frequently altered his drafts" (A. Lossky, "International Relations in Europe", in *New Cambridge Modern History*, vɪ, (Cambridge, 1970), 177.
32. S. B. Baxter, *William III* (London, 1966), p. 274.
33. *Ibid.*, p. 274: William "kept policy in his own head and used the heads of department as if they were clerks" (*ibid.*, p. 274).
34. W. H. Bruford, "The Organisation and Rise of Prussia", in *The New Cambridge Modern History*, vɪɪ (London, 1970), 310.

35. R. M. Hatton, *Charles XII of Sweden* (London, 1968), p. 107.
36. See J. C. Rule, "Colbert de Torcy and the Formulation of French Foreign Policy", in *Louis XIV and Europe,* ed. R. M. Hatton (London, 1976), pp. 280-1.
37. G. Zeller, "French Diplomacy and Foreign Policy in their European Setting", in *The New Cambridge Modern History,* v (Cambridge, 1961), 119.
38. See H. Kamen, *Spain in the late 17th Century* (London, 1980), p. 25.
39. Hatton, *Charles XII of Sweden,* p. 99.
40. R. M. Hatton, "Charles XII and the Great Northern War", in *The New Cambridge Modern History,* vi, 674.
41. Quoted in J. B. Wolf, *Louis XIV* (London, 1968), p. 216.
42. See Hatton, *Charles XII of Sweden,* p. 106.
43. See D. McKay, and H. N. Scott, *The Rise of the Great Powers 1648-1815* (London, 1983), p. 103.
44. J. O. Lindsay, "International Relations", in *The New Cambridge Modern History,* vi, 196-7.
45. See McKay and Scott, *The Rise of the Great Powers 1648-1815,* p. 154.
46. Quoted in G. P. Gooch, *Frederick the Great* (London, 1947), p. 51.
47. See G. Symcox, "Louis XIV and the Outbreak of the Nine Years' War", in *Louis XIV and Europe,* ed. Hatton, pp. 178-212.
48. See McKay and Scott, *The Rise of the Great Powers 1648-1815,* p. 164.
49. Quoted in G. P. Gooch, *Maria Theresa and Other Studies* (London, 1951), p. 85.
50. *Il Carteggio Cavour-Migra* (Bologna, 1926) i, 103.
51. See A. J. P. Taylor, *The Struggle for Mastery in Europe, 1848-1918* (London, 1944), p. 138, in relation to the war of 1866: "Even the Austrian decision was made from political motives, not after military calculation. In fact it is extraordinary how little each side (and indeed anyone else) weighed the military chances."
52. Even if there was a serious attempt to assess the balance, it was likely to be distorted by the over-confidence of military advisers. In 1914, for example, it has been suggested that

    the General Staffs, afraid of losing prestige, or completely enslaved to the mechanical preparations for mobilisation, would not confess to any qualms. The absence of such objections indicates that the World War started at a moment of competition when all parties were running abreast in the arena and felt tempted to spurt ahead. . . . . The balance of power was so even that each side could believe itself ready and the other about to attack   (A. Vagto, *A History of Militarism* (New York, 1937), Ch. 10).

53. See B. Croce, *A History of Italy 1871-1915* (Oxford, 1929), pp. 259-63.

Notes to Chapter 6: Profitability

1. Brandi, *The Emperor Charles V*, pp. 278-9, 414-15.
2. Quoted *ibid.*, p. 414.
3. *Nef des Princes et des Batailles*, quoted in Hale, "International Relations in the West", in *The Cambridge Modern History* I, 276.
4. *Ibid.*, p. 274.
5. Brandi, *The Emperor Charles V*, pp. 220-1.
6. See Pollard, *Henry VIII*, pp. 132, 331.
7. Wedgwood, *The Thirty Years War*, p. 109.
8. *Ibid.*, p. 133.
9. *Ibid.*, p. 444.
10. Parker, *Europe in Crisis 1598-1648*, p. 241.
11. See G. Parker, *Philip II* (London, 1979), pp. 125-6.
12. Quoted in Kortepeter, *Ottoman Imperialism*, pp. 45-6.
13. See G. Parker, *Spain and the Netherlands 1559-1659* (London, 1979), p. 96.
14. Cardinal Richelieu, *Testament Politique*, pp. 427-9.
15. See Parker, *Europe in Crisis 1598-1648*, p. 71.
16. Quoted in G. P. Gooch, *Frederick the Great* (London, 1947), p. 318.
17. Whig administrations in Britain in 1746-8 and in 1756-60 were mainly concerned about commercial or colonial gains. See W. L. Dorn, *Competition for Empire 1740-1763* (New York, 1940), p. 8: "There was not difference between Whigs and Tories in this respect for both directed foreign policy to support and enlarge their trading interests."
18. M. S. Anderson, *Europe in the Eighteenth Century 1713-83* (London, 1961), p. 131.
19. See *War, Diplomacy and Imperialism, 1618-1763*, ed. G. Symcox (London, 1974), pp. 22-4.
20. See P. G. M. Dickson, "War Finance 1689-1714", in *The New Cambridge Modern History*, VI, 284-315.

Notes to Chapter 7: Procedures

1. Quoted in G. Mattingly, *Medieval Diplomacy* (London, 1955), p. 103.
2. *Ibid.*, pp. 74-5.
3. *Ibid.*, p. 103.
4. Brandi, *The Emperor Charles V*, p. 585.
5. Hale, *Renaissance Europe 1480-1520*, p. 92.
6. Brandi, *The Emperor Charles V*, p. 159.
7. For further discussion, see F. H. Hinsley, *Power and the Pursuit of Peace* (Cambridge, 1967), pp. 15-16, 24-9.
8. For a fuller description see G. Mattingly, "An Early Non-Agression Pact", *Journal of Modern History*, x (1938), 1-30.
9. Quoted in E. F. Rice, *The Foundation of Modern Europe*, 1460-1559 (London, 1970), p. 116.
10. G. Mattingly, "International Diplomacy and International Law", in *The New Cambridge Modern History*, III (Cambridge, 1958), p. 154.
11. *Ibid.*, pp. 156-7.

12. See Mattingly, *ibid.*, pp. 157-61, and *Medieval Diplomacy*, p. 186.
13. See Earle, *Corsairs of Malta and Barbary*, p. 70.
14. Quoted in Petrie, *Philip II of Spain*, p. 302.
15. For a description of the development of diplomacy in this age, see Anderson, *Europe in the Eighteenth Century, 1713-1783*, pp. 152-63.
16. Gooch, *Marie Theresa and Other Studies*, pp. 199-202.
17. E. E. Rich, "Europe and North America", in *The New Cambridge Modern History*, v, 365.
18. See R. Pick, *The Empress Maria Theresa* (London, 1966), pp.108-110, 128.
19. Frederick the Great, *Anti-Machiavel*, p. 107.
20. See Gooch, *Marie Theresa and Other Studies*, p. 200, and *Frederick the Great*, p. 91.
21. Cf. V.-L. Tapie, "Louis XIV's Methods in Foreign Policy", in *Louis XIV and Europe*, ed. Hatton, p. 5.
22. Gooch, *Marie Theresa and Other Studies*, pp. 111-13.
23. Quoted in Sir Charles Webster, *The Foreign Policy of Palmerston, 1830-1841* (London, 1951), p. 594.
24. Quoted in C. J. Bartlett, *Castlereagh* (London, 1966), p. 202.
25. Taylor, *The Struggle for Mastery in Europe, 1848-1918*, p. xxiii.

Notes to Chapter 8: Beliefs

1. See Brandi, *The Emperor Charles V*, p. 155: "He had no choice but to assume that Charles' representations were meant as a challenge. He would act accordingly."
2. *Ibid.*, p. 265: "He told the French ambassador that his king had acted the part of a coward and a varlet and had broken his word. In support of this accusation, he continued, he would be ready to risk life in hand-to-hand conflict."
3. In his reply, sent by the French herald, Francis declared that "if Charles wished to fight, he had only to name a place and time for the meeting" (*ibid.*, p. 266).
4. *Ibid.*, p. 378.
5. Mattingly, "International Diplomacy and International Law", in *The New Cambridge Modern History*, iii, 150.
6. Hale, "International Relations in the West: Diplomacy and War", in *The New Cambridge Modern History*, i, 259.
7. *Ibid.*, pp. 259-60.
8. Brandi, *The Emperor Charles V*, p. 158.
9. Quoted in Hinsley, *Power and the Pursuit of Peace*, p. 17.
10. Quoted in J. R. Hale, *Europe 1480-1520* (London, 1971), p. 95.
11. *Ibid.*, pp. 91-2.
12. For further discussion, see J. T. Johnson, *The Just War Tradition and the Restraint of War* (Princeton, 1981), pp. 151-4.
13. Brandi, *The Emperor Charles V*, pp. 410, 419.
14. *Ibid.*, p. 318.

15. See A. Nussbaum, *A Concise History of the Law of Nations* (New York, 1947), p. 310, n. 13.
16. Brandi, *The Emperor Charles V*, p. 361.
17. See J. T. Johnson, *The Just War Tradition*, pp. 124-41.
18. See Mattingly, *Renaissance Diplomacy*, pp. 42-4.
19. Thomas Digges, *Foure Paradoxes* (London, 1604), p. 109; quoted in J. R. Hale, "Armies, Navies and the Art of War", in the *New Cambridge Modern History*, III, p. 171.
20. Hale, *ibid.*
21. See Parker, *Philip II*, p. 154.
22. *Ibid.*, p. 102.
23. Wedgwood, *The Thirty Years War*, p. 311.
24. *Ibid.*, p. 98.
25. *Ibid.*, p. 56.
26. Quoted in Elliot, *Europe Divided 1559-1598*, p. 347.
27. Quoted in J. H. Elliot, *Imperial Spain* (London, 1963), p. 282.
28. N. Ahnlund, *Gustav Adolph the Great* (Princeton, NJ, 1940), pp. 262-3.
29. *Ibid.*, p. 276.
30. Quoted in Elliot, *Europe Divided 1559-1598*, p. 394.
31. Quoted in Brandi, *The Emperor Charles V*, p. 305.
32. Cardinal Richelieu, *Testament Politique*, pp. 381-2 (author's translation).
33. *Ibid.*, pp. 372-82.
34. Elliot, "The Statecraft of Olivares", in *The Diversity of History*, ed. Elliot and Koenigsberger, p. 140.
35. Hale, "Armies, Navies and the Art of War", in *The New Cambridge Modern History*, III, 173.
36. *Ibid.*
37. *Ibid.*
38. Matthew Sutcliffe, *The Practice, Proceedings and Lawes of Armes* (London, 1593), quoted *ibid.*, p. 173.
39. Grotius, *De Jure Belli ac Pacis*, II, 1. ii.
40. *Ibid.*, II. 1. xvi.
41. *Ibid.*, II. 1. iii.
42. *Ibid.*, II. 1. iii.
43. *Ibid.*, II. 1. ii.
44. *Ibid.*, II. 1. xvi.
45. *Ibid.*, II. 1. xvi.
46. Machiavelli, *The Prince*, ch. 14.
47. See Elliot, *Europe Divided 1559-1598*, pp. 293, 336.
48. Quoted in E. A. Beller, "The Thirty Years War", in *The New Cambridge Modern History*, IV (Cambridge, 1970), 330.
49. See Nussbaum, *A Concise History of the Law of Nations*, p. 91.
50. Hale, "Armies, Navies and the Art of War", in *The New Cambridge Modern History*, III, 174.
51. *Ibid.*
52. Nussbaum, *A Concise History of the Law of Nations*, pp. 106-7.
53. Louis XIV, *Mémoires for the Instruction of the Dauphin*, p. 260.
54. See Dorn, *Competition for Empire, 1740-1763*, pp. 162-3.

55. Louis XIV, *Mémoires for the Instruction of the Dauphin*, pp. 258-60.
56. Quoted in J. B. Wolf, *Louis XIV* (London, 1968), p. 487.
57. The full text is in *Spain under the Bourbons 1700-1833*, ed. W. H. Hargreaves-Mawdsley (London, 1973), p. 75.
58. Frederick the Great, *Anti-Machiavel*, p. 327.
59. Quoted in Gooch, *Frederick the Great*, pp. 3-4.
60. Quoted in G. Ritter, *Frederick the Great* (Heidelberg, 1954), p. 66.
61. Louis XIV, *Mémoires for the Instruction of the Dauphin*, pp. 95-6.
62. Quoted by P. Sonnino, in "Louis XIV and the Dutch War", in *Louis XIV and Europe*, ed. Hatton, p. 158.
63. Louis XIV, *Mémoires for the Instruction of the Dauphin*, pp. 261-2.
64. Quoted in Hatton, *Charles XII of Sweden*, p. 375.
65. Quoted in *Spain under the Bourbons*, ed. Hargreaves-Mawdsley, p. 67.
66. Quoted in Ritter, *Frederick the Great*, p. 37.
67. Quoted in Gooch, *Frederick the Great*, pp. 24-5.
68. Louis XIV, *Mémoires for the Instruction of the Dauphin*, p. 123.
69. *Ibid.*, p. 242.
70. Quoted in Gooch, *Frederick the Great*, p. 39.
71. Frederick the Great, *Anti-Machiavel*, p. 326.
72. *Ibid.*, p. 325.
73. Louis XIV's Manifesto of 24 September 1688.
74. See Cole, *Colbert and a Century of French Mercantilism*, I, 345.
75. Quoted in C. H. Wilson, *Profit and Power* (London, 1957), p. 106.
76. Quoted by C. H. Wilson, "The Growth of Overseas Commerce and European Manufacture", in *The New Cambridge Modern History*, VII, 36.
77. Quoted in Dorn, *Competition for Empire 1740-1763*, p. 9.
78. Sir Josiah Child, *New Discourses on Trade* (London, 1693), ch. 4.
79. Frederick the Great, *Die politischen Testamente*, p. 67 (author's translation).
80. *Ibid.*, p. 212.
81. Frederick the Great, *Anti-Machiavel*, p. 20.
82. Louis XIV, *Mémoires for the Instruction of the Dauphin*, p. 183.
83. *Ibid.*, pp. 250-1. Louis explained that he "believed that this negotiation would be good for keeping them occupied while I made my preparations for the invasion".
84. E. de Vattel, *Le Droit des Gens (Paris, 1758)* III. 1.
85. *Ibid.*, III. iv.; III. i.
86. See Lossky, "International Relations in Europe", in *The New Cambridge Modern History*, VI, 173.
87. See Anderson, *Europe in the Eighteenth Century, 1713-83*, p. 165.
88. For the development of recognition of neutrality in the era, see Lossky, "International Relations in Europe", in *The New Cambridge Modern History*, VI, 174-6.
89. See Sir G. Clark, *War and Society in the Seventeenth Century* (Cambridge, 1958), p. 86.
90. *Ibid.*, p. 87.
91. Nussbaum, *A Concise History of the Law of Nations*, p. 124.
92. Clark, *War and Society in the Seventeenth Century*, p. 89.
93. Ernest Renan, *La Reforme Intellectuelle et Morale* (Paris, 1871), p. 111.

94. O. von Bismarck, *Memoirs,* English trans. (New York, 1966), pp. 293-4.
95. A. J. P. Taylor, *Bismarck* (London, 1955), p. 49.
96. Quoted in D. Southgate, *The Most English Minister* (New York, 1966), p. 137.
97. Quoted in N. Angell, *The Great Illusion* (London, 1912), p. 169.
98. Quoted in J. L. H. Keep, "Russia", in *The New Cambridge Modern History,* xi (Cambridge, 1962), 374.
99. Quoted in F. Fischer, *War of Illusions: German Policies from 1911 to 1914* (London, 1975), p. 254.
100. Quoted in P. C. B. Lieven, *Russia and the Origins of the First World War* (London, 1983), p. 129.
101. Quoted in Taylor, *Bismarck,* p. 105.
102. Thompson, *Louis Napoleon and the Second Empire,* p. 288.
103. Quoted in Fischer, *War of Illusions,* p. 75.
104. *Ibid.,* pp. 45, 55.
105. *Ibid.,* p. 399.
106. *Ibid.,* p. 88.
107. *Ibid.,* p. 405.
108. *Ibid.,* p. 24.
109. L. Dehio, *Germany and World Politics in the Twentieth Century* (London, 1929), p. 16.
110. Quoted in Fischer, *War of Illusions,* p. 46.
111. *Ibid.,* p. 106.
112. *Ibid.,* p. 41.
113. Quoted in Taylor, *Bismarck,* pp. 103-4.
114. Quoted in Michael Foot, "The Origins of the Franco-Prussian War", in *The New Cambridge Modern History,* x (Cambridge, 1960), 598. Bismarck recalled a conversation with Louis Napoleon in 1867 in which the emperor had accepted that he must either grant more internal liberty or go to war; "and the Emperor had told him very clearly that if the one failed there would be no alternative [to war]" (Thompson, *Louis Napoleon and the Second Empire,* p. 289).
115. Storry, *The Double Patriots,* pp. 3ff.

    Public opinion was almost unanimous in pressing for war against Russia. The newspapers, with [one] exception ... were extremely bellicose. . . . Leading professors of the law department of Tokyo Imperial University demanded war in the press and at public gatherings. Many Japanese, including the most important nationalist society, demanded that Siberia should be taken from Russia as part of the settlement in any such war. Another such society, the Society of the Amur River, openly demanded war with Russia.
116. Quoted in Fischer, *War of Illusions,* p. 194.
117. *Ibid.,* pp. 192-3.
118. *Ibid.,* p. 249.
119. *Ibid.,* p. 402.
120. *Ibid.,* p. 402.
121. Quoted in Taylor, *Bismarck,* p. 79.
122. Quoted in Fischer, *War of Illusions,* p. 191.

123. *Ibid.*, p. 210.
124. *Ibid.*, p. 212.
125. See Storry, *The Double Patriots*, p. 17.
126. Quoted in Fischer, *War of Illusions*, p. 398.
127. *Ibid.*, p. 402.
128. Interview with British and American journalists, February 1933, quoted in *The Speeches of Adolf Hitler, 1922-1939* (New York, 1969), ii, 1003.
129. *Ibid.*, p. 1513.
130. *Ibid.*, p. 1598.
131. D. Mack Smith, *Mussolini* (London, 1981), pp. 191-2.
132. *The Speeches of Adolf Hitler, 1922-1939*, ii, 1585.
133. *Ibid.*, p. 1586.
134. D. Mack Smith, *Mussolini*, pp. 258-9.
135. *The Speeches of Adolf Hitler, 1922-1939*, ii, 1697.
136. Quoted in D. Bergamini, *Japan's Imperial Conspiracy* (New York, 1971), p. 14.
137. Mack Smith, *Mussolini*, p. 184.
138. *Ibid.*, p. 195.
139. *Ibid.*, p. 191.
140. *Ibid.*, p. 227.
141. Quoted in Sir Robert Vansittart, *Black Record* (London, 1941), p. 49.
142. Quoted in K. W. Colegrove, *Militarism in Japan* (Boston, Mass., 1936), pp. 52-3.
143. Speech to the American Society of Newspaper Editors, quoted in A. Schlesinger, *One Thousand Days* (London, 1965), p. 261.
144. *Ibid.*, p. 267.
145. Wedgwood, *The Thirty Years War*, pp. 288-91.

Notes to the Conclusions

1. See, for example, Herbert Spencer, *The Study of Sociology* (London, 1973), esp. pp. 192-9.
2. The classic statement of this view is in the Preface to Marx's *Critique of Political Economy* (1859).
3. This view was put forward by a number of nineteenth-century writers: see, for example, Spencer, *The Study of Sociology*, pp. 195-6.
4. A theory on these lines was put forward, for example, by Hegel, in *The Philosophy of Right* (1821), paras 331-7.
5. This is the view of classical balance of power theories, from the time of Gucciardini to David Hume and Friedrich von Getz.
6. For examples of this view, see pp. 145-6, 337-9 above.
7. For a fuller discussion of the changing ideology of different international societies, see Luard, *Types of International Society*, ch. 5.
8. David Hume, *Essays*, i. vii.
9. For further discussion of this question, see I. L. Brownlie, *International Law and the Use of Force by States* (Oxford, 1963), pp. 321-7; H. Wehberg, *Civil War and International Law* (London, 1938); R. A. Falk, "The International Law of Internal War", in *International Aspects of Civil Strife*, ed. J. N. Rosenau (Princeton, NJ, 1964); and Luard, *Conflict and Peace in the Modern International System*, pp. 154-69.

Appendixes

APPENDIX 1   PRINCIPAL WARS 1400–1559

In this and subsequent lists the dates given for each war are those in which the main hostilities took place (not necessarily those in which war was declared or peace treaties signed). Some wars, especially civil wars, began only slowly, often without declaration of war, while others died away gradually without formal peace agreement: in both cases the main years of fighting are given. Where truces were long, these are indicated as years of peace; short truces are ignored. Where there were many participants, only the most important are given. Separate dates for different participants are given only where there were significant differences. In general, the country or countries thought to have greater responsibility for starting a war are placed first.

International Wars in Europe[ab]	Civil Wars in Europe[bc]	International Wars outside Europe[d]
[1399]–1401 Turkey – Byzantium		
1400–2 England – Scotland	1400–9 England (Wales, with	1400–2 Mongols – Syria, Iraq,
1401–2 "Emperor" (Rupert) –	intervention by France)	Turkey
Milan	1401 Hungary	
1402–3 Naples – Hungary	1402–12 Milan (succession, with	
1404–5 Padua – Verona, Vicenza,	intervention by Venice)	
Venice		
1404–8 Swiss Confederation –	1404–8 England (earl of	
Austria	Northumberland's rebellion)	
1404–35 Denmark – Holstein,	1405–13 Turkey (succession)	
Hanse towns (from 1426)		
1405–12 Naples – pope, Anjou,		1405–28 China – Annam
Florence, Siena, emperor		
(Sigismund)		
1406–8 Muscovy – Poland,		1406–8 Muscovy – Volga, Tartars
Lithuania		
1406 Florence – Pisa		
	1407–12 Naples (succession)	
	1409 France (Genoa)	
1409–11 Poland–Lithuania –	1409–13 Aragon (Catalonia)	
Teutonic Order	1410–12 Sicily (succession)	1410 Mongols – China
1411–21 Emperor (Sigismund) –	1411–18 France (Burgundians,	
Venice	with intervention by England)	
1412–20 Milan – Lombard cities,	1412–25 Brandenburg	
Genoa		
1413–14 Naples – Pope		
1413–21 Turkey – Wallachia,		
Bosnia, Hungary, Venice,		
Serbia (from 1419)		
1413–22 Poland–Lithuania –		
Teutonic Order		
1414–26 Swiss Confederation –		
Savoy, Milan		
1415–44, 1449–53 England,		1415 Portugal – Ceuta
Burgundy (till 1435) – France		
1420–6 Pope – Papal States	1420–4 Naples (succession, Anjou	
	and Aragon)	
	1420–34 Bohemia (Hussites, with	
	intervention by German and	
	other states)	
	1421 Turkey (succession)	

International Wars in Europe[ab]	Civil Wars in Europe[bc]	International Wars outside Europe[d]
1422 Turkey – Byzantium		
1423–8 Milan – Florence, Venice (from 1425)		
	1425–40 Muscovy (succession)	
1426 Egypt – Cyprus		
1429–40 Turkey – Serbia, Greece, Venice, Hungary		
	1430 Liège (with intervention by Burgundy)	
1431–3 Florence, Venice – Lucca, Milan		
1434–41 Milan, emperor – Florence, Venice, pope		
1434–5 Teutonic Order – Poland– Lithuania	1434–5 Denmark (peasants in Sweden and Norway)	
1435– Genoa – Aragon	1435–42 Naples (succession, Anjou and Aragon, with intervention by Genoa and pope)	
	1436–40 Burgundy (Ghent and Bruges)	
	1436–50 Swiss Confederation (Zurich)	
	1437 Hungary (peasants)	
	1438–9 Bohemia (succession)	
	1440 France (nobles)	
	1440–2 Hungary (succession)	
	1441–50 Castile (nobles)	
1442–7 Sforza, Venice, Florence – pope, Naples, Milan		
1442–8 Hungary, Poland– Lithuania, pope – Turkey		
1442–50 Emperor – Swiss Confederation		
1443–61 Albanians – Turkey	1443–51 Saxony (Wettin family dispute)	
1446–8 Cologne – Westphalian towns	1446–54 Muscovy (succession)	
	1447–50 Milan (succession, with intervention by Venice and Naples)	
	1448–51 Bohemia (religious)	
	1448–53 Burgundy (Ghent)	
1449–50 Brandenburg – Franconian towns	1449–52 Navarre (succession)	1449–52 Mongols – China
	1450 England (Cade's rebellion)	
1452–3 Turkey – Byzantium		
1452–4 Milan, Genoa, Florence, Bologna, Mantua – Venice, Naples, Siena		
1454–66 Prussian League, Poland– Lithuania – Teutonic Order		1454–60 Uzbeks – Persia
1455–6 Muscovy – Novgorod	1455, 1459–65, 1470–1 England (dynastic, nobles)	
1455–7 Castile – Granada		
1455–64 Turkey – Serbia, Hungary, Bosnia, Wallachia, Athens, Morea, Greek islands		
	1456–7 Hungary	
	1460–4 Naples (succession, Anjou and Aragon)	

International Wars in Europe[ab]	*Civil Wars in Europe*[bc]	*International Wars outside Europe*[d]
61–3 Scotland – England		
61–2 Emperor – Hungary		
61 Turkey – Trebizond	1461 France (Genoa)	
	1462–72 Aragon (Catalonia)	
63–79 Venice, Albania – Turkey		1463–70 Persia – Turkey
	1464 Denmark (Sweden, peasants)	
	1465–6 France (nobles, with intervention by Burgundy, Brittany)	
	1465–8 Liège (with intervention by Burgundy)	
65–72 Brandenburg – Pomerania	1465–7 Bohemia (religion, with intervention by Hungary)	1465–6, 1470, 1474 Turkey – Karaman
67–8 Swiss Confederation – Tyrol	1467 Burgundy (Ghent)	1467–9 Muscovy – Kazan Tartars
68 France – Brittany	1467 Denmark (Sweden)	
68–74 England – Hanseatic League	1467–8 Florence (with intervention by Venice)	
68–79 Hungary – Bohemia, emperor, Poland–Lithuania	1467–74 Castile (succession)	
	1470–1 Denmark (Sweden)	
71–2 France – Burgundy	1470–4 Turkey (Anatolia)	
71–5 Teutonic Order – Poland–Lithuania		
71–8 Muscovy – Novgorod		
72–3 Burgundy – Gelderland	1472–5 France (Cerdagne and Roussillon)	1472 Kazan Tartars – Muscovy
74 Burgundy – Cologne	1475–9 Castile (succession, with intervention by Portugal)	
75 England – France		
75–6 Turkey – Moldavia, Crimea		
75–7 Burgundy, Savoy – Swiss Confederation, Tyrol, Lorraine		
	1476–9 Milan (Genoa)	
77–82 France – Burgundy, Austria	1477 Swiss Confederation (Zurich, Lucerne and Berne)	
78–9 Turkey – Albania, Ionian islands	1478 Austria (Carinthian peasants)	
78–9 Pope, Naples, Siena – Florence (aided by Milan and Venice)		1478–9 Kazan Tartars – Crimean Tartars
80 Turkey – Naples (Otranto)		
81–9 Muscovy – Teutonic Order		1481 Siberian Tartars – Kazan Tartars
81–3 Turkey – Hungary	1481 Naples	
82–3 England – Scotland		1482 Crimean Tartars – Poland–Lithuania
82–92 Spain – Granada		
82–4 Venice, pope (till 1483) – Ferrara (aided by Milan, Naples and Florence, after 1483)		
	1483–5 Burgundy (Utrecht, Ghent)	
85–9 Turkey, Tartars – Moldavia, Poland–Lithuania	1485 France (nobles)	1485 Muscovy – Tver
		1485–90 Turkey – Egypt (Cilicia)

International Wars in Europe[ab]	Civil Wars in Europe[bc]	International Wars outside Europe[d]
	1485 Naples (nobles, with intervention by pope and Venice)	
	1485–7 England (dynastic, Ireland)	
1487–8 France – Brittany		
	1488 Scotland	
1489–92 England – France	1489–93 Burgundy (Ghent, Bruges, Cleves, aided by France)	1489 Muscovy – Vyatka
1489–90 Muscovy – Poland–Lithuania		
1491 France – Brittany		1491–1502 Crimean Tartars – Kazan Tartars
1492–4 Muscovy – Lithuania	1492 France (Brittany)	
1492–5 Turkey – Bohemia–Hungary		
	1493–6 England (Ireland)	
1494–5 France – Naples	1494 Burgundy (Gelderland)	1494–7 Spain – Fez, Mellilla
1495–6 Pope, Spain, emperor, Venice, Milan – France		
1495–6 Muscovy – Sweden		
1495–1509 Florence – Pisa		
	1496–7 Denmark (Sweden)	
1497–9 Poland–Lithuania – Moldavia, Turks, Tartars	1497 England (Cornwall)	1498 Portugal – Calicut
1499 Swiss Confederation, Grisons – Tyrol, Swabian League, emperor	1499–1500 Spain (Moors)	
1499–1501 France, Venice – Milan, emperor		
1499–1503 Turkey – Venice, Hungary, pope		
1500–3 Muscovy, Tartars – Poland–Lithuania, Livonian Order		
1501–8 Popes – Tuscany, Romagna		
1501–2 France, Spain – Naples		
1502–4 Spain – France (Naples)		1502 Crimean Tartars – Kazan Tartars
1503–4 Palatinate – Bavaria, Swabian League, emperor		1502 Portugal – Kilwa, Mombas
	1505 Burgundy–Castile (Gelderland)	1505–11 Spain – Mers-el-Kebir, Oran, Tripoli, etc.
1506–7 Emperor – Bohemia–Hungary	1506–9, 1510–12 Denmark (Sweden)	1506–7 Muscovy – Kazan
1507–8 Poland–Lithuania, Tartars–Moldavia, Muscovy	1507 France (Genoa)	
1508–10 Pope, Spain, France, emperor, Mantua – Venice		
1509 Turkey, Egypt – Knights of Malta	1509–11 Spain (Moors)	1509 Portugal – Egypt (Red Sea)
		1510 Muscovy – Pskov
		1510 Portugal – Goa
		1510–12 Uzbeks – Persia
1511–13 Pope, Spain, Venice, Swiss Confederation, emp., England (till 1514) – France, Scotland, Florence	1511–12 Turkey (succession)	1511–6 Algiers – Spain (Tunis, Bona, Tlemcen)
		1511 Portugal – Malacca

International Wars in Europe[ab]	Civil Wars in Europe[bc]	International Wars outside Europe[d]
1512–14 Muscovy, Teutonic Order – Poland–Lithuania, Tartars, Cossacks		
1512 Spain (aided by England) – Navarre		
	1514 Hungary (peasants)	1514–16 Turkey – Persia
1515–16 France, Venice – Milan, Swiss Confederation, emperor, pope	1515 Austria (Styrian peasants)	1515 Portugal – Kurdistan
	1515–17 Burgundy (Gelderland)	
1516 Navarre – Spain	1516–17 Spain (Sicily)	1516 Algiers – Spain (Tunis)
		1516–17 Turkey – Syria, Egypt
	1517–18, 1520–3 Denmark (Sweden)	
	1518 Turkey (Shias)	
1519 Swabian League – Württemberg		1519–21 Spain – Mexico
1519–22 Poland–Lithuania – Teutonic Order, Muscovy, Tartars	1519–21 Spain (Valencia)	
	1520–2 Spain (*comuneros,* Castile and Valencia)	
	1520–1 Turkey (Syria)	
1521–3 Turkey – Hungary, Venice, Knights of St John (Rhodes)		
1521–5 France, Navarre – emperor, England, Italian states (from 1523), pope (1523)		1521–4 Crimean and Kazan Tartars, Cossacks – Muscovy
1522–3 England – Scotland	1522–3 Trier, Hesse, Palatinate (imperial knights)	
1522–4 Denmark – Holstein, Lübeck	1522–4 Netherlands (Friesland)	
	1523–4 Turkey (Egypt)	
	1524–5 German states (peasants)	
	1525 Tyrol (peasants)	1525 Turkey – Yemen
1526–8 Pope, Venice, Florence – emperor	1526 Papal States (Colonna revolt)	
1526–33 Turkey – Hungary– Bohemia, emperor	1527–3 Hungary (succession)	
1527–31 Poland – Moldavia	1527–8 Turkey (Cilicia)	
1528–9 France, Venice, England, Genoa (till June 1528) – emperor, Genoa (after June 1528)	1528 Spain (Brussels, Gelderland)	1528–39 Turkey – Persia
		1529 Algiers – Penon de Vela
	1531 Switzerland (religious)	1531–2 Spain – Peru
	1531–2 Denmark (succession, with intervention by Lübeck and Netherlands)	
1532 Lübeck – Sweden, Denmark	1532 Spain (Brussels)	
1532–3 Emperor – Poland– Lithuania, Moldavia		
1534 Hesse, protestant German states – Württemberg	1534–6 England (Ireland)	1534 Algiers – Spain (Tunis)
	1534–6 Denmark (succession, with intervention by Lübeck)	

International Wars in Europe[a][b]	Civil Wars in Europe[b][c]	International Wars outside Europe[d]
1534–7 Muscovy – Poland– Lithuania, Tartars		
1535–6 Savoy – Geneva, Berne		1535 Emperor – Algiers (Tunis)
1536–8 France — Savoy, emperor	1536–7 England (religious)	
1537–40 Turkey, Algiers – Venice, emperor		1537–41 Spain – Peru
1538 Turkey – Moldavia	1538–40 Spain (Ghent)	1538 Turkey – Aden
1540–5 Pope – Papal States, Camerino		
1541–7 Transylvania, Turkey – emperor (Ferdinand)		1541 Emperor – Algiers
1542–4 France, Cleves (till 1543), Denmark, Sweden, Turkey – emperor, England (1544–6)	1542–3 Sweden (religious, peasants, with intervention by France)	
1542 Saxony, Hesse – Brunswick		
1542 England – Scotland		
		1543 Emperor – Tlemcen
1544–7 England – Scotland		
1546–7 Emperor, German allies, pope – Protestant German states		
		1547–52 Muscovy – Kazan
		1548–54 Turkey – Persia
1549–50 France, Scotland – England	1549–50 England (Cornwall and East Anglia)	
1551–[62] Turkey, Transylvania – emperor		1551–2 Turkey – Knights of Malta (Tripoli)
1551 Pope – Parma		
1552–5 France, Protestant German states – emperor		1552 Muscovy – Kazan Tartars
1553–5 Florence – Siena		1552–4 Spain – Peru
1554–7 Muscovy – Sweden	1554 England (Wyatt's rebellion)	1552–5 Turkey – Persia
		1555 France – Portugal (Brazil)
1556–9 Pope (till 1557), France – emperor, Savoy, England (from 1557)		1556 Muscovy – Astrakhan
1557–8 Muscovy – Teutonic Order, Knights of Livonia		
1558–[81] Muscovy – Sweden		

[a] The eastern and western Hapsburg territories are treated as one entity till 1556.

[b] Brittany is considered an independent country until 1491. Gelderland is considered as part of Burgundy from 1473 (though in practice largely independent till 1543). Sweden is considered independent from 1523 (though independent at intervals from 1448).

[c] Turkish domestic wars are included here, even if occurring outside Europe, since Turkey was in considerable part a European state. Only major wars (and not all the struggles for succession, which occurred almost every time a sultan died) are included.

[d] This list is confined to major wars involving at least one recognised state.

APPENDIX 2   PRINCIPAL WARS 1559–1648

International Wars in Europe	Civil Wars in Europe	International Wars outside Europe[a]
1551]–62 Turkey – emperor		
1558]–81 Muscovy – Sweden		
1559–64 Spain, Venice – Turkey, Tripoli	1559–60 Scotland (with intervention by France and England)	
	1559–67 Ireland (succession to the earldom of Tyrone)	
	1560–1 Savoy (Vaudois)	1560 Spain, Knights of St John – Tripoli
	1562–3 France (Huguenots, with intervention by England)	
	1562–3 Sweden	
1563–82 Muscovy – Poland–Lithuania		
1563–70 Denmark, Poland, Lübeck – Sweden		
1564–6 Emperor – Transylvania	1564–8 Genoa (Corsica)	1564–7 Spain – Filipinos
		1564–9 Moluccas – Portugal (aided by Spain)
1565 Turkey – Malta, Spain	1565–7 Scotland (religious)	1565 Spain – France (Florida)
1566–8 Turkey – emperor	1566–8, 1572–1609 Spain – Netherlands (with intervention from Germany, France and England)	1566–7 Portugal – France (Brazil)
	1567 Scotland	
	1567–8 France (Huguenots)	
	1568–70 Spain (Moriscos)	
	1568–70 France (Huguenots)	1568 England – Spain (Caribbean)
	1569 England (Catholic lords of the north)	1569 Turkey – Russia (Astrakhan)
		1569–70 Algiers – Tunis
1570 Muscovy – Novgorod	1570–3 Austria (Croatia, Hapsburg Hungary)	1570–1 American Indians – Portugal
1570–8 Turkey, Barbary states – Venice (till 1573), pope, Spain		
		1571–2 Crimean Tartars – Muscovy
	1572–3 France (Huguenots)	
	1572–4 Turkey (Moldavia)	
		1573–4 Spain – Algiers, Turkey (Tunis)
	1575 Transylvania	
	1575 France (Huguenots)	1575–85 Portugal – Malabar
	1576–7 France (Huguenots)	1576 Turkey – Hejaz
	1577 Poland (Danzig)	
		1578 Portugal – Morocco
		1578–84 Muscovy – Siberian Tartars
		1578–90 Turkey – Persia
	1579–80 England (Ireland, with intervention by pope, Spain)	
1580 Spain – Portugal	1580 France (Huguenots)	
		1582–3 France – Spain (Azores)
	1583–9 Cologne (with intervention by Spain, Palatinate and others)	
1585–1604 England – Spain	1585–94 France (Huguenots, with intervention by Spain and England)	1585–7 England – Spain (Caribbean)

International Wars in Europe	*Civil Wars in Europe*	*International Wars outside Europe*[a]
		1585–90 East Africans – Portugal (Kilwa and Mombasa) 1586–7 Muscovy – Tartars (Siberia)
1588 Emperor – Poland 1588, 1590–8 Savoy – France 1588–9 Savoy – Geneva 1590–5 succession – Sweden 1591–8 Crimean Tartars – Muscovy	1591–3 Poland (Cossacks) 1591 Spain (Aragon)	
		1592–8 Japan – Korea, China
1593–1606 Turkey, Tartars – emperor, pope 1594–8 France – Spain	1595 Scotland (Catholic lords) 1594–8 Turkey (Wallachia and Moldavia, with intervention by Transylvania) 1594–5 France (peasants) 1594–1603 England (Ireland, with intervention by Spain) 1594–7 Austria (Austrian peasants) 1597–9 Poland (Cossacks) 1596–7 Sweden (Finland) 1598–9 Poland (Sweden)	
1599–1600 Wallachia – Transylvania, Moldavia 1600 Poland – Moldavia, Wallachia 1600–14, 1617–18, 1621–2, 1625–9 Poland – Sweden 1600–1 France – Savoy 1601–4 Emperor – Transylvania 1602–3 Savoy – Geneva		1601–3 Portugal[b] – Ceylon 1603–12 Persia – Turkey
1604 Transylvania – emperor	1604–13 Muscovy (with intervention by Poland, Sweden)	
		1605–6 Crimean Tartars – Muscovy 1605–6 United Provinces – Portugal (Malacca)
1607 Bavaria – Donauwörth 1609–10 Emperor – Jülich (aided by France, Brandenburg) 1611–13 Emperor – Transylvania 1611–13 Denmark – Sweden 1611–18 Poland – Russia 1613–17 Sweden – Russia 1613–16 Savoy – Mantua, Spain	1606–8 Poland (gentry) 1607–8 Transylvania (Haiduks)	1609 Spain, France – Tunis 1611–28 United Provinces – Ceylon (Portugal)
1615–18 Venice (aided by United Provinces) – Uskoks, Austria (Styria) 1616–17 Poland – Turkey	1614–15 France (Brittany)	1615–18 Turkey – Persia 1616–19 United Provinces – Macassar

International Wars in Europe	Civil Wars in Europe	International Wars outside Europe[a]
	1617, 1619–20 France (nobles)	
1618–22 Emperor, Bavaria, Spain, Saxony – Bohemia, Silesia, Moravia etc., Palatinate, Transylvania		1618–44 Manchus – Korea, China
		1619 France – Algiers
		1619 United Provinces – Djakarta
1620–1 Poland, emperor – Transylvania, Turkey, Tartars	1620 Spain (Naples)	
	1620–3 Switzerland (Valtellina, with Spanish intervention)	
1621–48 Spain – United Provinces	1621–2, 1625, 1627–30 France (Huguenots, with English intervention from 1627)	1621 England – Algiers
1622–53 Palatinate, Brunswick, Baden, Saxe-Weimar, Transylvania – emperor, Spain, Bavaria, etc.		1622 United Provinces – Portugal (Macao)
		1623–31 Persia – Turkey
		1624–5 England – Morocco
		1624–30, 1645–6, 1651–4 United Provinces – Portugal (Brazil)
1624–6 France, Savoy, Venice – Spain, emperor, Genoa (Valtellina)		1624–5 England – Morocco
1624–30 England – Spain		
1625–9 Denmark, Brunswick (till 1626), Saxe-Weimar, Mecklenburg (till 1628), emperor, Spain, Bavaria, etc.		
1625–7, 1631–4 Turkey, Tartars – Poland, Hungary		
	1626 Austria (Upper Austria)	
1628–31 Savoy, Spain, emperor – Mantua, France		1628–9 Mataram – United Provinces (Java)
	1629–30 France (tax revolts)	1629 France – Morocco
1630–48 Sweden, Saxe-Weimar, Hesse – Cassel, Brunswick, Saxony, emperor, Spain	1630 Poland (Cossacks)	
1631–5 Brandenburg – emperor, Spain, Bavaria, etc.		
1632–5 Russia – Poland	1632–3 Austria (Upper Austria, peasants)	1632–41 Crimean Tartars – Russia
	1633–4 Bavaria (peasants)	
1635–48 France, Savoy, Parma – Spain, emperor, Bavaria, Brandenburg (till 1641), Saxony (till 1645)	1635–6 France (tax revolts)	1635 Turkey – Yemen
		1635–7 England – Morocco
	1637–8 Poland (Cossacks)	1637–8 Cossacks – Tartars (Azov)
	1637–9 Savoy	
1638 Denmark – Poland	1638–40 England (Scotland)	1638–40 United Provinces – Portugal[b] (Ceylon and Goa)
	1639 France (Normandy)	1638 Venice – Barbary states
	1640–[52] Spain (Catalonia)	
	1640–[68] Spain (Portugal)	1640–1 United Provinces – Portugal (Malacca)

International Wars in Europe	Civil Wars in Europe	International Wars outside Europe[a]
	1641–3 England (Ireland)	1641 United Provinces – Portug (Angola)
1642–4 Pope – Parma, Venice, Tuscany	1642–[9] England	
1643–5 Sweden – Denmark	1643–4 France (south-west)	
1644–5 Transylvania – empire		
1644–[69] Turkey – Venice		
	1647 Spain (Sicily)	1646 Moluccas – United Provinc
	1647–8 Spain (Naples, with intervention by France)	
		1648 Portugal – United Province (Angola)

[a] This column only includes wars involving at least one widely recognised state.

[b] Though Portugal was united with Spain during this period, these wars mainly concerned Portugal alone.

[c] These wars are often considered as parts of a single Thirty Years War.

APPENDIX 3 PRINCIPAL WARS 1648–1789

International Wars in Europe	Civil Wars in Europe	Wars elsewhere[a]
		[1625]–63 United Provinces – Portugal (East Indies, Ceylon, India, Angola, Brazil, Malabar, etc.
635–59 France, England (from 1657) – Spain		
	[1640]–68 Spain (Portuguese rebellion)	
	[1640]–52 Spain (Catalonia)	
644]–69 Venice (assisted by France, German states – Turkey		[1644]–81 Manchus – China
	[1647]–9 Spain (revolts in Sicily and Naples)	
	1648–9 Turkey (Anatolia)	
	1648–52 England (Scotland and Ireland)	
	1648–52 France (the Fronde)	
	1648–54 Poland (Cossacks, aided by Tartars till 1651)	
650–4 Portugal – England	1650 Russia (Novgorod and Pskov)	1650–6 United Provinces – Amboyna
		1651 United Provinces – Ceram
52 Sweden – Bremen	1652–3 Switzerland (peasants)	
652–4 United Provinces – England		
54–6, 1658–68 Russia, Cossacks – Poland		1654–70 United Provinces – Sumatra
655–60 Sweden, Brandenburg (until 1657) – Poland, Russia, Denmark, Austria (from 1657), Tartars, United Provinces, Brandenburg (after 1658)		1655–7 England – Spain (West Indies)
		1655 England – Tunis
	1656 Switzerland	
57–61 United Provinces – Portugal		
658–61 Transylvania – Poland, Tartars, Turkey		
		1661–2 Chinese – United Provinces (Taiwan)
		1661–7 Spain – Algiers, Tunis
		1662 United Provinces – Algiers
663–4 Turkey – Austria (assisted by France, Spain and German states)		1663–5 England – United Provinces (West Africa, North America)
	1664–6 Poland (Lubomirski revolt)	
65–7 England, Münster – United Provinces, Denmark, France		
66 Sweden – Bremen		1666 France – Tunis

International Wars in Europe	*Civil Wars in Europe*	*Wars elsewhere*[a]
1667–8 France – Spain	1667–71 Russia (Stenka Razin revolt)	
	1668–8 Poland (Cossacks, aided by Tartars)	
		1669–81 United Provinces – Java (intervention in local conflic
	1670, 1672–5, 1678–82 Austria (Hungarian rebellion)	1670– 1 England – Algiers
		1670–2 France – Tunis
	1670 Austria (Bohemian peasants)	1672–3 Spain – Algiers
1672–4 Savoy – Genoa		
1672–9 France, Cologne, England (till 1674) Sweden – United Provinces, Brandenburg, Spain, Austria, German states, Denmark		
1672–6 Turkey, Tartars, Cossacks – Poland		
	1674 Spain (Sicily)	
	1674–81 Russia (Bashkirs)	
1675–9 Denmark – Sweden		1675–6 England – Tripoli
1677–81 Turkey, Cossacks – Russia		
	1678–9 England (Scottish Covenanters)	
		1679–80 United Provinces – Algiers
		1681–2 England – Algiers
		1682–3, 1688–9 France – Algiers
1682–99 Turkey – Austria, German states, Poland, Venice, Russia (from 1685)		1682–92 Tunis – Venice
1682 Denmark – Holstein		
1683–4 Spain – France		1683, 1687–9 France – Iroquois Indians
1684–5 France – Genoa		
1686–7 Denmark – Hamburg	1685 England (Monmouth and Argyll rebellions)	
		1687–9 Russia – Crimean Tarta
1688–97 France, Savoy (from 1696) – Cologne, Austria, Prussia, German states, England, United Provinces, Spain, Savoy (1690–6)		
	1689–90 England (Scotland)	1689 Russia – China (Amur)
	1689–91 England (Ireland with intervention by France)	1689–94 Spain – Algiers
		1689–1702 Algiers, Tripoli – Morocco, Tunis
		1696–1720 China – Mongols
	1699 Poland (Lithuanian peasants)	
1700–19/21 Denmark, Saxony – Poland, Russia, Prussia (from 1715), Hanover (form 1715), Britain (from 1717) – Sweden		

International Wars in Europe	Civil Wars in Europe	Wars elsewhere[a]
1/2–1713/14 Austria, Britain, United Provinces, Prussia, German states, Portugal, Savoy (after 1703) – France, Spain, Bavaria, Savoy (till 1703)		
	1702–6 France (Cevennes, Languedoc)	
	1703–11 Austria (Hungarian rebellion)	1703–5 United Provinces – Mataram (Java)
	1705–11 Russia (Bashkirs)	
		1708 Algiers – Spain (Oran and Mers-el-Kebir)
		1709–16 Afghanistan – Persia
0–13 Turkey–Russia		1710–11 France – Portugal (Brazil)
	1712 Switzerland	
4–18 Venice, Austria (from 1716) – Turkey	1714–16 Poland	
	1715–16 Britain (Scotland)	1715–26 Algiers – United Provinces
		1716–17 Russia – Khiva
8–20 Spain – Austria, Britain, France, United Provinces		
		1720–2 Afghanistan – Persia
		1722–4 Russia – Persia
		1722–4 Turkey – Persia
		1725–6, 1729–30 Afghanistan – Turkey
7–8 Spain – Britain		1727–50 Morocco
		1728–9 France – Tripoli
	1729–45 Genoa (Corsica)	1729–36 Persia – Turkey
	1730–1 Turkey	
		1732 Spain – Algiers (Oran and Mers-el-Kebir)
3–5 France, Spain, Sardinia – Austria, Russia, Saxony, Prussia		1738–9 Persia – Afghanistan, India
4–9 Russia, Austria (from 1737) – Turkey	1734 Poland (Cossacks)	
	1735 Russia (Bashkirs)	
9/40–48 Britain, Austria, United Provinces – Spain, Prussia (1740–2, 1744–5), France, Bavaria		
1–3 Sweden – Russia		1741 France – Tunis
	1744–6 Britain (Scotland)	
	1747 United Provinces (Orange revolt)	1747–69 Afghanistan – India
	1751–3 Russia (peasants)	
	1754–5 Russia (Bashkirs)	1754–6 Britain – France (North America)
		1754–6 Algiers – Tunis
	1755–68 Genoa (Corsican revolt)	

International Wars in Europe	Civil Wars in Europe	Wars elsewhere[a]
1756–63 Prussia, Britain, Portugal (from 1762) – France, Austria, Russia (till 1762), Sweden, Savoy, Spain (from 1762)		
		1761 Mahrattas – Afghanistan
		1763–5 Britain – Bengalis
		1765 France – Morocco
1768–74 Turkey – Russia	1768–9 Poland (Ukraine)	1769 Morocco – Portugal
	1768–9 France (Corsica)	
	1768–71 Poland (with Russian, French and Austrian intervention)	
	1770 Turkey (Greece)	
	1773–4 Russia (Pugachev revolt)	
	1774–5 Austria (peasants' revolt in Bohemia)	1774 China (Shantung rebellion
		1774 Morocco – Spain (Mellilla
		1776–83 American colonies – Britain
		1776–83 Mahrattas – Britain
		1776–7 Spain – Portugal (South America)
1778–83 France, Spain (from 1779), United Provinces (from 1780) – Britain		
1778–9 Prussia – Austria		
1781–2 Russia – Crimea		1781–4 Mysore – Britain
		1782–92 Tunis – Venice
	1784–5 Austria (Transylvania)	1784 Spain, Portugal, Knights o Malta – Algiers
1787–[92] Turkey – Russia, Austria	1787 United Provinces (with intervention by Prussia)	
1788–[90] Sweden – Russia, Denmark		
	1789–90 Austrian Netherlands (Brabant)	

[a] This column includes only wars, whether international or civil, involving at least one recognised sovereign state.

APPENDIX 4 PRINCIPAL WARS 1789–1917

Wars in Europe

International Wars	Wars of National Independence	Other Civil Wars
2–1802 French revolutionary wars (3)[a]		
2–3 Russia, Prussia – Poland		
		1793–4 France (Vendée revolt)
	1794–5 Poland – Russia, Austria, Prussia	
	1798 Ireland – Britain	
3–15 Napoleonic wars (7)[b]		
	1804–12, 1815 Serbia – Turkey	
6–12 Russia – Turkey		
8–9 Russia – Sweden		
		1808–9 Spain
		1820–1 Naples[d] (revolution suppressed with help of Austria)
		1820–2 Albania
		1820–3 Spain[d] (revolution suppressed with help of France)
	1821–4 Moldavia, Wallachia – Turkey (aided by Russia)	1821 Sardinia[d] (revolution suppressed with help of Austria)
	1821–5 Crete – Turkey	
	1821–9 Greece (aided by France, Britain, Russia) – Turkey	
3–9 Russia – Turkey		1828–34 Portugal (with intervention by Britain and Spain)
	1830–1 Albania – Turkey	
	1830–3 Belgium (aided by France, Britain) – Holland	
	1830–1 Poland – Russia	
	1831–6 Bosnia – Turkey	1831 Italian cities[d] (revolutions suppressed by Austria)
		1833–40 Spain (with intervention by Britain)
	1846 Poland – Austria	1846–50 Portugal (with intervention by Spain and Britain)
		1847 Switzerland
, 1849 Sardinia – Austria[c] Prussia – Denmark (Schleswig-Holstein)	1848 Moldavia, Wallachia – Russia, Turkey	1848 Revolutionary conflicts in France
	1848–9 Hungary – Austria	1848–9 Revolution in Austria
	1848–9 Italian cities, Naples – Austria, France, pope	1848 Sicily, Naples, Rome[d]
		1849 Germany (risings in German states suppressed by Prussia)
	1852–3, 1858–9 Montenegro – Turkey	
/4–6 Turkey, Britain, France, Sardinia – Russia, Greece (1854)		
Sardinia, France – Austria		

International Wars	Wars of National Independence	Other Civil Wars
	1860–1 Italy (successful revolution in south and centre) 1862 Bosnia – Turkey 1862 Serbia – Turkey 1863–4 Poland – Russia (aided by Prussia)	
1864 Prussia, Austria – Denmark 1866 Prussia, German states, Italy – Austria, German states	1866 Crete – Turkey 1867 Italians – Papal States, France	
		1868–9 Spain
1870–1 Prussia, German states – France		
		1871 France (Commune) 1872–6 Spain (Carlists)
	1875–8 Bosnia, Bulgaria (aided by Montenegro, Serbia, Russia) – Turkey	
1877–8 Russia – Turkey	1878 Bosnia, Herzegovina – Austria-Hungary 1878 Crete (aided by Greece) – Turkey	
1885 Serbia – Bulgaria	1896–8 Crete (aided by Greece) – Turkey	
1898 Greece – Turkey		
	1903 Macedonia – Turkey 1905 Crete – international force	
		1909 Romania (peasants)
1911–12 Italy – Turkey 1912–13 Montenegro, Bulgaria, Greece, Serbia – Turkey 1913 Bulgaria – Serbia, Greece, Romania, Turkey 1914–[18] First World War	1912 Albania – Turkey	
[TOTAL 28]	[TOTAL 28]	[TOTAL 19]

[a] The principal wars were the War of the First Coalition, the Egyptian expedition and the War of the Second Coalition. The antagonists varied in each war: only Britain remained at war with France throughout this period (Portugal being defeated by France and Spain in 1801).

[b] The principal wars were the War of the Third Coalition, the Franco-Prussian War, the Peninsular War, the fourth Franco-Austrian war, the Russian expedition, the War of Liberation and the Hundred Days. The antagonists varied: only Britain remained at war with France throughout this period.

[c] These international wars are listed separately from the wars of independence with which they are associated because they had, or acquired, objectives separate from those struggles.

[d] These are listed as civil wars rather than as international wars, or wars of national independence, because they were fought in the first place against local rulers and on domestic political issues.

) *Principal wars outside Europe*

Wars of Colonisation[a]	Wars of Decolonisation[b]	Wars in the Americas	Other Wars[c]
	1789–92, 1798–9 Mysore – Britain		
			1793–1803 Afghanistan with intervention by Persia
96–7 Russia – Persia			
			1797 Denmark – Tripoli 1798–1800 USA – France 1801–5 USA – Tripoli
	1802–4 Mahrattas – Britain		
05–13 Russia – Persia			
	1809–24 Latin American wars of independence(6)[d]		
			1811–18 Egypt – Arabia 1812–15 USA – Britain
14–16 Britain – Gurkhas			1815 USA – Algiers 1816 Britain, Holland – Algiers
17–18 Britain – Mahrattas			
19–21 Holland – Sumatra		1819–20 Argentina	
20–1 Egypt – Sudan			
	1822–3 Nicaragua, El Salvador – Mexico	1822 Haiti – Santo Domingo	
23–6 Britain – Burma	1824–6 Ashantis – Britain		
25–6 Britain – Burma 25–30 Britain – Tasmanians	1825–30 Java – Holland	1825–8 Argentina, Uruguay – Brazil	1825 Sardinia – Tripoli
25 Holland – Celebes 27–9 Russia – Georgia		1827 Peru – Bolivia, Colombia 1828 Argentina	1827–8 Persia – Russia
29 Spain – Mexico 30, 1839–47 France – Algeria (aided by Morocco)		1829–30 Central American Republic	
32–39 Russia – Circassians	1831–32 Egypt – Turkey (Syria)	1831–40 Brazil 1832–4 Mexico	
33–4 Argentina – Indians 33–9 France – Annamese			
	1835–6 Texas – Mexico	1835 Bolivia – Peru 1836–9 Chile, Argentina – Bolivia, Peru	1836–7 Afghanistan – Sind 1837–8 Persia – Afghanistan

Wars of Colonisation[a]	*Wars of Decolonisation*[b]	*Wars in the Americas*	*Other Wars*[c]
1838–9 Boers – Zulus		1838–9 France – Mexico	
1838–42 Britain – Afghanistan			
1839–40 Russia – Khiva	1839–40 Egypt – Turkey (assisted by Britain and Austria)	1839–52 Argentina – Uruguay (assisted by France, Britain, Brazil)	
1839–42 Britain – China		1840–2 Colombia (with intervention by Ecuador)	
		1841 Peru – Bolivia	
1842–52 Muscat – East African coast			
1843 Britain – Sind			
1844 France – Morocco			
1845–6, 1848–9 Britain – Sikhs			
1845–7 Britain – Maoris			
1846–9 Holland – Bali		1846–8 Mexico – USA	
1847–53 Russia – Kazakhs			
	1848–50 Filipinos (Moslems) – Spain		
1851–2 Britain – Basutos	1851 Sumatrans – Holland	1851 Chile	1851–64 China (Taip rebellion)
1852–3 Britain – Burma			
		1854, 1857–8 Peru	
		1854 Colombia	
		1855–6 Haiti – Santo Domingo	
		1855–7 Costa Rica, Honduras, El Salvador –	
1855–9 Russia – Circassians		Nicaragua	
1856–7 Britain – Persia			
1856–60 Britain, France – China			1856–7 Britain – Pers
1857–61 France – Senegal			
1857–8, 1864 Russia – Georgia	1857–9 Indians – Britain (Indian Mutiny)		
		1858–61 Mexico	
		1858–63 Venezuela	
1859–60 Spain – Morocco		1859 Peru – Ecuador	
		1859–61 Argentina	
1859–61 Holland – Celebes			
		1860–2 Colombia	1860 Syria (with intervention by France)
			1861–5 USA
			1861–78 China (Mos rebellion)
1862–7 USA – American Indians		1862–5 Dominican Republic – Spain	1862–3 Siam – Cambodia
1862–7 France – Mexico			

Wars of Colonisation[a]	Wars of Decolonisation[b]	Wars in the Americas	Other Wars[c]
4–5 Britain – Bhutan 4–9 Britain – Maoris		1863 Colombia – Ecuador 1864–70 Paraguay – Brazil, Uruguay, Argentina	1863–8 Afghanistan 1864–8 Japan
5–8 Russia – Bokhara 5–9, 1873–6 Russia – Khokand	1865 Ashantis – Britain	1865–6 Chile (supported by Peru, Bolivia, Ecuador) – Spain 1865–7 Guatemala, Nicaragua – El Salvador, Honduras	
–78 Egypt – Eritrea –6 Egypt – Sudan, Somalia, Ethiopia	1868–78 Cubans – Spain	1868–71 Venezuela	1867–8 Britain – Ethiopia
Russia – Khiva –4 France – Tonkin –1902 Holland – Achin	1873–4 Ashantis – Britain		
	1876–7, 1890 Sioux – USA	1876 Colombia	
–81 Russia – Turcomans –81 Britain – Afghanistan –83 Argentina – American Indians –80 Britain – Zulus			1877 Japan
	1879–81 Transvaal – Britain 1880–3 Basutos – Britain	1879–83 Chile – Peru, Bolivia 1880 Argentina (Buenos Aires)	
5 France – Senegal 2 France – Tunisia Britain – Egypt 5 France – Tonkin, China (from 1884) 5 Britain, Egypt – udan 5 France – Madagascar			
		1884–5 Colombia	
7 Italy – Eritrea 5 Britain – Burma		1885 Guatemala – El Salvador	
9 Italy – Somalis	1888 Tanganyikans – Germany		
2 France – Senegal 4 France – Soudan 4 Holland – Bali 4 France – ahomey		1891 Chile	

Wars of Colonisation[a]	Wars of Decolonisation[b]	Wars in the Americas	Other Wars[c]
1892–4 Belgium – eastern Congo			
1893 France – Siam		1893–4 Brazil	
1893–5 France – Tuaregs			
1893–4, 1896–9 Britain – Matabele, Shonas			
1894 Britain – Bunyoro			1894–5 Japan – Chin[a]
1894–5 France – Madagascar			
1894–6 Italy – Ethiopia			
	1895–8 Cubans (assisted by USA) – Spain	1895 Peru	
1896–1900 Britain – Ashantis	1896–8 Filipinos – Spain		
1896–70 France – Upper Volta, Niger			
1897 Britain – western Nigeria	1897–9 Ugandans, Sudanese – Britain, Egypt	1897 Nicaragua – Costa Rica	
			1898 USA – Spain
1899–1902 Britain – Boers	1899–1902 Filipinos – USA	1899–1902 Colombia	
	1899–1904 Somalis – Britain		
1900–1 France – Chad			1900–1 China (Boxe[r] rebellion with intervention by European powe[rs])
1900–4 Britain – Somalis (Dervishes)			
1900–11 France – Central Africa			
		1902 Brazil – Bolivia	
1903 Britain – northern Nigeria	1903–8 South-west Africans – Germany		
1904 Britain – Tibet			1904–5 Japan – Rus[sia]
	1905–6 Tanganyikans – Germany		
	1906 Zulus – Britain	1906 Guatemala – Honduras, El Salvador	
		1907 Nicaragua – Honduras, El Salvador	
1907–11 France – Morocco			1908–9 Morocco
1909–10 Spain – Morocco		1909–10, 1912 Nicaragua (with intervention by USA)	1909–10 Persia (wit[h] intervention by Russia)
		1910–20 Mexico (with intervention by USA)	
		1910–11 Honduras (with intervention by USA)	1911, 1913–[20] Ch[ina]
	1912–17 Moroccans – France		
	1912–17 Libyans – Italy		
1913–20 Britain – Somalis (Dervishes)			
	1916 Kirghiz – Russia		
	1916–20 Haitians – USA		
[TOTAL 83]	[TOTAL 36]	[TOTAL 47]	[TOTAL 29]

* This category includes wars leading to a state of dependence short of full-scale colonisation (for example, the wars against China, Persia, Afghanistan and Egypt) but omits armed actions by the United States in Central America, which had similar aims but were largely unresisted (as in Honduras and Nicaragua in 1911–12 and the Dominican Republic in 1915–16).

* This category includes wars of resistance to colonial powers, even if not aiming at full independence.

Only the more important civil wars are included in this list.

* The most important wars in this group were the expedition from Buenos Aires to upper Peru in 1810–14, the successful war to liberate the Banda Oriental (Uruguay) at the same time, Bolívar's unsuccessful campaign in the north in 1813–15, his successful war in the north in 1817–23, San Martín's expedition to Chile and Peru in 1817–20, and the long war in Mexico, as much a civil war as a war of liberation, in 1810–20.

APPENDIX 5 PRINCIPAL WARS 1917–84

Wars in Europe	Wars in the Middle East	Wars in Africa	Wars in Asia	Wars in Latin America
1917–21 Soviet Union (with intervention by Britain, France, USA, Japan, Czecho-slovakia, etc.)				1917–18 Dominican Republic – USA
1918 Finland – Soviet Union				
1918–19 Poland – White Russia, Ukraine, Soviet Union				
1918–19 Serbia – Montenegro				
1919 Latvia, Estonia – Germany, Russia	1919–26 Morrocans (Rifs) – France	1919 Afghanistan – Britain		
1919–22 Irish – Britain				
1919–20 Poland (assisted by France) – Soviet Union				
1919 Lithuania – Poland				
1920–2 Turkey – Greece (aided by France, Britain)	1920 France – Syrians			
		1920–30 Libyans (Senussi) – Italy		
		1921–6 Moroccans (Rifs) – Spain	1921–2 Indians (Moplahs) – Britain	
			1921–36 China (Nationalists, warlords, Peking government, Communists)	
	1924–5 Hejaz (Wahhabi revolt)			1924 Honduras (with intervention by USA)
	1925–6 Syrians (Druzes) – France			
			1926–9 Afghanistan	1926–30 Mexico
			1926–7 Javanese – Netherlands	1927–33 Nicaragua (with intervention by USA)

ars in Europe	*Wars in the Middle East*	*Wars in Africa*	*Wars in Asia*	*Wars in Latin America*
			1930–1 Vietnamese – France	
			1931–2 Japan – China (Manchuria)	
				1932 Ecuador
				1932 Peru – Colombia
				1932–5 Bolivia – Paraguay
		1935–6 Italy – Ethiopia	1933 Japan – China (Jehol)	
			1935 Japan – China (Inner Mongolia)	
5–9 Spain (with intervention by Germany, Italy)				
			1937–45 Japan – China	
			1938, 39 Japan – Soviet Union	
3–45 Germany, Italy, Hungary – Poland, Britain, France, Norway, Belgium, Netherlands, Greece, Soviet Union, USA, etc.				
●–40 Soviet Union – Finland				
			1940–1 Thailand – France	
			1941 Japan – USA, Britain, Australia, etc.	1941–2 Peru – Ecuador
4–5, 1946–9 Greece (with intervention from Yugo-slavia, Bulgaria, Albania)				
	1945 France – Syria			
			1945–9 Netherlands – Indonesia	
			1945–54 Philippines (Huks)	
			1946 Iran (southern tribesmen)	
			1946–54 Indochinese – France	1946 Bolivia

Wars in Europe	Wars in the Middle East	Wars in Africa	Wars in Asia	Wars in Latin America
			1946–50 China	
			1947 China (Taiwan)	
			1947–8 India, Pakistan (inter-communal)	
			1947–9 Pakistan – India (Kashmir)	
		1947 France – Malagasys	1947–56 Malayans – Britain	1947–8 Paraguay
	1948–9 Transjordan, Egypt, Syria, Iraq, Lebanon – Israel		1948– Burma (minorities, communist factions)	1948 Costa Rica 1948–58 Colombia
			1948 India – Hyderabad	
			1950–3 North Korea (aided by Chinese) – South Korea (aided by UN forces)	
			1950–4 Nationalists Chinese – Burma	
			1950 Indonesia (South Moluccas)	
		1952–4 Kenyans (Mau-Mau) – Britain		
		1952–4 Tunisians – France		
		1953–6 Moroccans – France		
	1954–8 Yemen – Aden	1954–62 Algerians – France	1954–8 China (offshore islands)	1954 Guatemala (with intervention from Honduras and Nicaragua)
1956 Soviet Union – Hungary			1955–69 India – Nagas	1955 Costa Rica (with intervention from Nicaragua)
	1955–9 Cypriots – Britain	1955–72 Sudan (south – north)		
		1955–60 Camerounians – France		
	1956 Israel, Britain, France – Egypt			1956–9 Cuba
	1957 Oman (imam of Oman)		1957–8 Western Saharans – Spain, France	1957 Nicaragua – Honduras
			1957–61 Indonesia (north Celebes, Sumatra)	

...rs in Europe	Wars in the Middle East	Wars in Africa	Wars in Asia	Wars in Latin America
	1958 Lebanon (with intervention by Syria, USA)			
		1959 Ruanda (Tutsis)	1959 China (Tibet) 1959–62 Laos 1959–75 South Vietnam (with intervention by North Vietnam, USA and others)	
	1961–75 Iraq (Kurds)	1960–5 Congo (with intervention by the United Nations)	1960–2 Indonesia (western Java)	1960–79 Nicaragua
		1961– Ethiopians (Eritrea) 1961–7 Angolans – Portugal	1961 India – Portugal (Goa) 1961–2 Nepal	1961 Cuba (with intervention from USA)
	1962–7 Yemen (with intervention by Egypt, Saudi Arabia)	1962– Chad (with intervention by Libya and France) 1962 Algeria – Morocco	1962 Brunei 1962 Indonesia – Netherlands (West Irian) 1962 India – China	1962 Guatemala
	1963–4 Cyprus (with intervention by Britain and UN forces) 1963–7 South Arabians – Britain	1963–4 Ruanda (with intervention from Burundi) 1963–4 Somalia – Ethiopia 1963–7 Somalia – Kenya 1963–74 Bissau Guineans – Portugal	1963–74 Laos 1963–6 Indonesia – Malaysia (assisted by Britain, Australia, New Zealand)	
		1965–74 Mozambique – Portugal	1965 Pakistan – India 1965– Indonesia (West Irian)	1965 Dominican Republic (with intervention by USA) 1965– Colombia (various left-wing groups)
	1967 Israel – Egypt, Jordan, Syria 1968–76 Oman (with intervention by South Yemen)	1966– Namibians – South Africa 1967–70 Nigeria	1966–8 India (Mizos)	
			1969–78 Philippines (Moslems of the south)	1969 El Salvador – Honduras

Wars in Europe	Wars in the Middle East	Wars in Africa	Wars in Asia	Wars in Latin Americ
	1970 Jordan		1970– Philippines (communists) 1970–5 Cambodia (with intervention by USA and North Vietnam) 1971 Pakistan (East Bengal with intervention by India)	
	1972 South Yemen – Yemen 1973 Egypt, Syria, Jordan, Saudi Arabia, Iraq, Morocco – Israel	1972 Burundi (Hutus) 1973–80 Rhodesia		
	1974 Turkey – Cyprus	1974–5 Angola (with intervention by South Africa and Cuba)		
	1975– Lebanon with intervention by Syria)	1975– Morocco, Mauretania (till 1979) – Western Saharans (aided by Algeria) 1975– Ethiopia (Tigre) 1976– Angola (with intervention by South Africa) 1977–8 Somalia – Ethiopia	1975– Indonesia – East Timor 1975– Vietnam (*montagnards*)	1975–9 Argentin 1976– Guatemala
	1978–9 Yemen (with intervention by South Yemen) 1979–80 Iran (Kurds and other groups) 1979– Iraq (Kurds) 1980– Iraq – Iran	1978–9 Uganda – Tanzanians 1981– Uganda	1978–9 Afghanistan 1978–9 Afghanistan 1978–9 Vietnam – Cambodia 1979 China – Vietnam 1979– Soviet Union – Afghanistan 1980– Cambodia (with intervention by	1979 El Salvador 1980 Peru 1981 Ecuador–Pe
	1982 Syria (Hama) 1982 Israel – Lebanon	1982– Somalia 1982– Sudan (south)	Vietnam and from Thailand)	1982 Argentina – Britain 1982– Nicaragua (with intervention from Honduras)
			1983 Sri Lanka (Tamils)	1983 USA – Grenada

[a] Sporadic engagements not involving sustained offensive action are not included (on these grounds actions on the north-western frontier of India in the 1930s, for example, or between Egypt and Israel between 1950 and 1956 and 1968–72 are not listed). Similarly terrorist actions, even over a long period, as by the IRA and other groups in Northern Ireland or be ETA in Spain, or the activities of urban terrorists in Western Europe, Latin America or Turkey are not included. Nor are massacres and large-scale killings that were unorganised (as in Indonesia in 1965–6).

[b] The naming of a single country denotes a civil war. "Intervention by" a state implies action by the armed forces of the intervening country, whether on behalf of rebels or on behalf of the government.

[c] Where action has been undertaken by unofficial groups rather than regular forces, as in most colonial conflicts, a people rather than a state is named.

Index

While it is accepted that not all wars in a particular period were of the same nature, for clarity they are grouped under headings in this index corresponding to the period divisions used in the text:

Dynastic wars (1400–1559)
Religious wars (1559–1648)
Sovereignty, wars of (1648–1789)
Nationalist wars (1789–1917)
Ideological wars (1917 onwards)

Where a page reference covers several consecutive pages, it should be assumed that the concept indexed appears *passim,* and is not the subject of a continuous passage. Under the names of countries, page references are given for internal matters or multilateral involvement. This is followed by the names of countries with whom they have interacted bilaterally, with the appropriate page references.